T0235419

Lecture Notes of the Institute for Computer Sciences, Social Informatics and Telecommunications Engineering 308

More information about this series at http://www.springer.com/series/8197

Nigus Gabbiye Habtu · Delele Worku Ayele ·
Solomon Workneh Fanta ·
Bimrew Tamrat Admasu ·
Mekuanint Agegnehu Bitew (Eds.)

Advances of Science and Technology

7th EAI International Conference, ICAST 2019
Bahir Dar, Ethiopia, August 2–4, 2019
Proceedings

 Springer

Editors
Nigus Gabbiye Habtu ⓘ
Bahir Dar University
Bahir Dar, Ethiopia

Solomon Workneh Fanta ⓘ
Bahir Dar University
Bahir Dar, Ethiopia

Mekuanint Agegnehu Bitew ⓘ
Bahir Dar University
Bahir Dar, Ethiopia

Delele Worku Ayele
Bahir Dar University
Bahir Dar, Ethiopia

Bimrew Tamrat Admasu
Bahir Dar University
Bahir Dar, Ethiopia

ISSN 1867-8211   ISSN 1867-822X (electronic)
Lecture Notes of the Institute for Computer Sciences, Social Informatics
and Telecommunications Engineering
ISBN 978-3-030-43689-6   ISBN 978-3-030-43690-2 (eBook)
https://doi.org/10.1007/978-3-030-43690-2

This Springer imprint is published by the registered company Springer Nature Switzerland AG
The registered company address is: Gewerbestrasse 11, 6330 Cham, Switzerland

Nigus Gabbiye Habtu · Delele Worku Ayele ·
Solomon Workneh Fanta ·
Bimrew Tamrat Admasu ·
Mekuanint Agegnehu Bitew (Eds.)

Advances of Science and Technology

7th EAI International Conference, ICAST 2019
Bahir Dar, Ethiopia, August 2–4, 2019
Proceedings

 Springer

Editors
Nigus Gabbiye Habtu (ID)
Bahir Dar University
Bahir Dar, Ethiopia

Solomon Workneh Fanta (ID)
Bahir Dar University
Bahir Dar, Ethiopia

Mekuanint Agegnehu Bitew (ID)
Bahir Dar University
Bahir Dar, Ethiopia

Delele Worku Ayele
Bahir Dar University
Bahir Dar, Ethiopia

Bimrew Tamrat Admasu
Bahir Dar University
Bahir Dar, Ethiopia

ISSN 1867-8211 ISSN 1867-822X (electronic)
Lecture Notes of the Institute for Computer Sciences, Social Informatics
and Telecommunications Engineering
ISBN 978-3-030-43689-6 ISBN 978-3-030-43690-2 (eBook)
https://doi.org/10.1007/978-3-030-43690-2

This Springer imprint is published by the registered company Springer Nature Switzerland AG
The registered company address is: Gewerbestrasse 11, 6330 Cham, Switzerland

Preface

On behalf of the organizing team, it is our pleasure to introduce the 7th EAI International Conference on Advancement of Science and Technology (ICAST 2019). The conference is an annual platform for researchers, scholars, scientists in the academia, and practitioners in various industries to share know-hows, experiences, challenges, and recent advancements in science and technology. In addition, the conference has continued to show promise and applications of research findings and innovations in all areas of science and technology. ICAST 2019 attracted more than 150 submissions of which 105 of them were sent out for peer reviews where each paper was evaluated by, on average, three experts in the area. The technical program of ICAST 2019 consisted of 76 full papers in the oral presentation sessions during the main conference tracks. The conference was organized into five tracks: Track 1: Agro-processing industries for sustainable development; Track 2: Water Resources and environmental engineering; Track 3: Recent advances in electrical, electronics, and computing technologies; Track 4: Product design, manufacturing, and systems optimization; and Track 5: Material science and engineering. In addition to the high-quality technical paper presentations, the technical program also featured three opening keynote and seven session keynote speeches. The three keynote speakers were Prof. Kiflai Gebremedh from the School of Civil and Environmental Engineering, Cornell University, USA; Prof. Samuel Lakeou, Professor Emeritus, District of Columbia, USA; and Dr. Michael M. Moges, Commissioner of Irrigation Development Commission and Associate Professor at Bahir Dar Institute of Technology in the Faculty of Civil and Water Resource Engineering, Ethiopia. The seven session keynote speakers were Prof. Eduardo Ojito (Addis Ababa University, Ethiopia), Dr. Mulugeta Admassu (KU Leuven, Belgium, and Bahir Dar University, Ethiopia), Dr. Adanech Yared (FDRE Basins Development Authority Director General, Ethiopia), Dr. Tena Alamirew (Addis Ababa University, Ethiopia), Dr. Dereje Yohannes (Addis Ababa Science and Technology University, Ethiopia), Dr. Eshetie Berhan (Addis Ababa University, Ethiopia), and Prof. Teketel Yohannes (Addis Ababa Science and Technology University, Ethiopia). The five tracks were conducted as parallel sessions in five halls. Coordination with the Steering Committee chair, Prof. Imrich Chlamtac, the Organizing Committee chair, Prof. Kibret Mequanint (The University of Western Ontario, Canada), the co-chairs, Dr. Atikilt Abebe and Dr. Bereket Haile, and the Technical Program Committee chair, Dr. Nigus Gabbiye Habtu, was essential for the success of the conference. We sincerely appreciate their constant support and guidance. It was also a great pleasure to team up with such an excellent Organizing Committee who worked hard in organizing and supporting the conference. In particular, the Technical Program Committee, led by Dr. Nigus Gabbiye Habtu, and the co-chairs, Dr. Bimrew Tamrat, Dr. Solomon Workneh, Dr. Mamaru Moges, Prof. A. Pushparaghavan, Dr. Fikreselam Gared, Dr. Mekuanint Agegnehu, and Dr. Delele Worku, were instrumental in organizing the peer-review process of the technical papers, which led to a high-quality technical program. We are also grateful to the conference manager, Radka Pincakova, for her support, and to all the authors who submitted their papers to the ICAST 2019 conference. This volume contains the papers presented at the 7th edition of the conference series, which was held during August 2–4, 2019, at Bahir Dar Institute of Technology, Bahir Dar University, Ethiopia. All submissions were strictly peer reviewed by experts in the areas and the Technical Program Committee of which only the papers accepted with excellent quality were presented. We strongly believe that ICAST 2019 provided a good forum for all researchers, developers, and practitioners to discuss all science and technology aspects that are relevant to advancements in this subject. We also expect that future ICAST conferences will be as successful and stimulating as indicated by the contributions presented in this volume.

November 2019   Kibret Mequanint
Bereket Haile
Nigus Gabbiye Habtu

Organization

Steering Committee

Chair

Imrich Chlamtac   University of Trento, Italy

Members

Seifu Tilahun   Bahir Dar University, Ethiopia
Kibret Mequanint   The University of Western Ontario, Canada
Tammos S. Steenhuise   Cornell University, USA

Organizing Committee

General Chairs

Kibret Mequanint   The University of Western Ontario, Canada
Atikilt Ketema   Bahir Dar University, Ethiopia
Bereket Haile   Bahir Dar University, Ethiopia

Program Chairs

Nigus Gabbiye Habtu   Bahir Dar University, Ethiopia
Bimrew Tamirat   Bahir Dar University, Ethiopia
Delele Worku   Bahir Dar University, Ethiopia
Solomon Workneh   Bahir Dar University, Ethiopia
Pushparaghavan Annamalai   Bahir Dar University, Ethiopia
Mekuanint Agegnehu   Bahir Dar University, Ethiopia
Fikreselam Gared   Bahir Dar University, Ethiopia
Mamaru Moges   Bahir Dar University, Ethiopia
Abebech Abera   Bahir Dar University, Ethiopia

Publicity and Social Media Chairs

Abaynesh Yehedgo   King Abdullah University of Science and Technology,
                                  Saudi Arabia
Fikreselam Gared   Bahir Dar University, Ethiopia
Tadele Assefa   Bahir Dar University, Ethiopia

Workshops Chairs

Seifu Admasu   Bahir Dar University, Ethiopia
Sisay Geremew   Bahir Dar University, Ethiopia

Sponsorship and Exhibits Chairs

Tadele Andargie   Bahir Dar University, Ethiopia
Fasikaw Atanaw   Bahir Dar University, Ethiopia

Publications Chair

Nigus Gabbiye Habtu   Bahir Dar University, Ethiopia

Panels Chair

Moges Ashagre   Katholieke Universiteit Leuven, Belgium

Tutorials Chair

Yeneneh Tamirat   Asia University, Taiwan

Demos Chair

Addise Aschenik   Bahir Dar University, Ethiopia

Posters and PhD Track Chair

Solomon Workeneh   Bahir Dar University, Ethiopia

Web Chair

Tewodros Worku   Bahir Dar University, Ethiopia

Local Chair

Bimrew Tamrat   Bahir Dar University, Ethiopia

Conference Manager

Radka Pincakova   EAI, Slovakia

Contents

Agro-Processing Industries for Sustainable Development

Organic Biofertilizer from Brewery Wastewater Sludges via Aerobic
Composting Process   3
  Mequanint Demeke and Nigus Gabbiye

Endosulfan Pesticide Dissipation and Residue Levels in Khat
and Onion in a Sub-humid Region of Ethiopia   16
  Feleke K. Sishu, Elsabeth K. Thegaye, Petra Schmitter, Nigus G. Habtu,
  Seifu A. Tilahun, and Tammo S. Steenhuis

Assessment of Ergonomics of Farming Activities for Backyard Vegetable
Production in the North Western Ethiopia: Case of Dangishta Community . . .   29
  Getnet K. Awoke, Seifu A. Tilahun, and Manuel R. Rayes

An Integrated Approach to Solve Small Farm Holder's Mechanization
Barriers in Ethiopia   42
  Dessie Tarekegn Bantelay, Tsehaye Dedimas, and Nigist Kelemu

Production and Characterization of Glue from Tannery Hide
Trimming Waste   59
  Tadele Negash G., Ayalew Emiru, Dessie Amare, and Mahlet Reda

Kinetic Modeling of Quality Change in Ethiopian Kent Mango Stored
Under Different Temperature   71
  Mekdim K. Assefa, Berhanu A. Demessie, E. A. Shimelis,
  Pieter Verboven, Maarten Hertoga, and Bart Nicolai

Modeling of Gasification of Refuse Derived Fuel:
Optimizations and Experimental Investigations   82
  Dawit Musse, Wondwossen Bogale, and Berhanu Assefa

On-Farm Performance and Assessment of Farmers' Perceptions
of Hermetic Bags for Farm-Stored Wheat and Maize
in Northwestern Ethiopia   98
  Karta Kaske Kalsa, Bhadriraju Subramanyam, Girma Demisse,
  Admasu Worku, Solomon Workneh, and Nigus Gabbiye

Water Resource and Environmental Engineering

Developing Domestic Water Security Index in Urban Cities,
Bahir Dar City, Ethiopia 113
  Marshet B. Jumber, Eshetu Assefa, Seifu A. Tilahun,
  and Mukand S. Babel

Performance Evaluation and Assessment of Quashni Small Scale Irrigation
Scheme, in Amhara Region 126
  Muluedel Aseres, Mamaru A. Moges, Seifu Tilahun, Berhanu Geremew,
  Daniel Geletaw, and Enguday Bekele

Evaluation of Shallow Ground Water Recharge and Its Potential for Dry
Season Irrigation at Brante Watershed, Dangila, Ethiopia 148
  Daniel G. Eshete, Seifu A. Tilahun, Mamaru A. Moges, Schmitter Petra,
  Zoi Dokou, Berhanu G. Sinshaw, Enguday B. Atalay,
  Muluedel A. Moges, Dagne Y. Takele, and Wondale A. Getie

Evaluating the Impacts of Climate Change on the Stream Flow
Events in Range of Scale of Watersheds, in the Upper Blue Nile Basin 169
  Gerawork F. Mulu, Mamaru A. Moges, and Bayu G. Bihonegn

Soil Water Dynamics on Irrigated Garlic and Pepper Crops Using
Hydrus–1D Model in the Lake Tana-Basin, Northwestern Ethiopia 193
  Enguday Bekele, Seifu Tilahun, Abebech Beyene, Sisay Asres,
  Berhanu Geremew, and Haimanot Atinkut

Evaluation of Stream Flow Prediction Capability of Hydrological Models
in the Upper Blue Nile Basin, Ethiopia 210
  Bayu G. Bihonegn, Mamaru A. Moges, Gerawork F. Mulu,
  and Berhanu G. Sinshaw

Dynamics of Eutrophication and Its Linkage to Water Hyacinth
on Lake Tana, Upper Blue Nile, Ethiopia: Understanding Land-Lake
Interaction and Process 228
  Minychl G. Dersseh, Aron Ateka, Fasikaw A. Zimale,
  Abeyou W. Worqlul, Mamaru A. Moges, Dessalegn C. Dagnew,
  Seifu A. Tilahun, and Assefa M. Melesse

Multi-purpose Reservoir Operation Analysis in the Blue
Nile Basin, Ethiopia 242
  Dereje M. Ayenew, Mamaru A. Moges, Fasikaw A. Zimale,
  and Asegdew G. Mulat

Evaluation of Co-composting Methods Using Effective Microorganisms 258
  Tilik Tena, Atikilt Abebe, Endawoke Mulu, and Kefale Wagaw

Impact of Land Use and Landscape on Runoff and Sediment
in the Sub-humid Ethiopian Highlands: The Ene-Chilala Watershed   268
   Nigus H. Tegegne, Temesgen Enku, Seifu A. Tilahun,
   Meseret B. Addisea, and Tammo S. Steenhuis

Urban Growth and Land Use Simulation Using SLEUTH Model
for Adama City, Ethiopia   279
   Yanit Mekonnen and S. K. Ghosh

Integration of SWAT and Remote Sensing Techniques to Simulate
Soil Moisture in Data Scarce Micro-watersheds: A Case of Awramba
Micro-watershed in the Upper Blue Nile Basin, Ethiopia   294
   Berhanu G. Sinshaw, Mamaru A. Moges, Seifu A. Tilahun, Zoi Dokou,
   Semu Moges, Emmanouil Anagnostou, Daniel G. Eshete,
   Agumase T. Kindie, Engudye Bekele, Muludel Asese,
   and Wondale A. Getie

Pilot-Scale Horizontal Subsurface Flow Constructed Wetland for Removal
of Chromium from Tannery Waste Water with Suitable Local
Substrate Material   315
   Gemechu Kassaye, Agegnehu Alemu, and Nigus Gabbiye

Assessment of Industrial Effluent Pollution on Borkena River,
Kombolcha, Ethiopia   325
   Alemayehu Ali Damtew, Atikilt Abebe Ketema,
   and Beshah Mogesse Behailu

Electrical, Electronics and Computing

Planning, Designing and Performance Evaluation of Micro Wave Link Case
Study from Wegeda to NefasMewucha   337
   Gashaw Mihretu, Pushparaghavan Annamalai, and N. Malmurugan

Enhancement of Power Flow with Reduction of Power Loss Through
Proper Placement of FACTS Devices Based on Voltage Stability Index   355
   Yeshitela Shiferaw and K. Padma

Designing and Modeling of a Synchronous Generator Using AGC, PSS,
and AVR Case Study on Tis Abay II Hydroelectric Power System   366
   Abdulkerim Ali and B. Belachew

Generator Excitation Loss Detection on Various Excitation Systems
and Excitation System Failures   382
   Alganesh Ygzaw, Belachew Banteyirga, and Marsilas Darsema

Performance Enhancement of Distribution Power System by Optimal
Sizing and Sitting of Distribution Statcom   395
   Nebiyu Yisaye, Elias Mandefro, and Belachew Bantyirga

Power Distribution System Reliability Assessment and Improvement Case
of Jimma Town, Ethiopia.   415
   Eyasu Berhanu Abrha, Getachew Biru Worku, and Tadele Abera Abose

Joint Evaluation of Spectral Efficiency, Energy Efficiency
and Transmission Reliability in Massive MIMO Systems   424
   *Tewelgn Kebede, Amare Kassaw, Yihenew Wondie,
   and Johannes Stenibrunn*

Optimal Allocation of Distributed Generation for Performance
Enhancement of Distribution System Using Particle Swarm Optimization. . . .   436
   Elias Mandefro and Belachew Bantiyrga

Mobility Prediction in Wireless Networks Using Deep
Learning Algorithm.   454
   *Abebe Belay Adege, Hsin-Piao Lin, Getaneh Berie Tarekegn,
   and Yirga Yayeh*

Basic Facial Expressions Analysis on a 3D Model: Based on Action Units
and the Nose Tip   462
   Meareg A. Hailemariam

Pareto Optimal Solution for Multi-objective Optimization
in Wireless Sensor Networks   472
   *Haimanot Bitew Alemayehu, Mekuanint Agegnehu Bitew,
   and Birhanu Gardie Shiret*

E-Learning Readiness of Technology Institutes in Ethiopian Public
Universities: From the Teachers' Perspective   480
   Abinew Ali Ayele and Worku Kelemework Birhanie

Reconfigurable Integrated Cryptosystem for Secure Data Exchanges
Between Fog Computing and Cloud Computing Platforms   492
   *Abiy Tadesse Abebe, Yalemzewd Negash Shiferaw,
   and P. G. V. Suresh Kumar*

Ethiopic Natural Scene Text Recognition Using Deep
Learning Approaches.   502
   Direselign Addis, Chuan-Ming Liu, and Van-Dai Ta

Automatic Amharic Part of Speech Tagging (AAPOST): A Comparative
Approach Using Bidirectional LSTM and Conditional Random
Fields (CRF) Methods   512
   Worku Kelemework Birhanie and Miriam Butt

Product Design, Manufacturing, and Systems Optimization

Effects of Shielded Metal Arc Welding Process Parameters on Mechanical
Properties of S355JR Mild Steel 525
   Kishor Purushottamrao Kolhe, Fetene Teshome, and Aragaw Mulu

Development and Testing of Improved Double Skirt Rocket Stove
for Reducing the Emission Level of Carbon Monoxide 537
   Fetene Teshome, Eyob Messele, and Kishor Purushottam Kolhe

Shell and Tube Heat Exchanger, Empirical Modeling Using
System Identification 548
   *Firew Dereje Olana, Beza Nekatibeb Retta, Tadele Abera Abose,
and Samson Mekibib Atnaw*

A Review on Design and Performance of Improved Biomass Cook Stoves. . . 557
   Atsede Tariku Woldesemayate and Samson Mekbib Atnaw

Experimental Investigation of Augmented Horizontal Axis Wind Turbine . . . 566
   Abiyu Mersha Tefera, Abdulkadir Aman, and Muluken Temesgen Tigabu

Design and Simulation of Waste Heat Recovery System for Heavy Oil
Preheating in Dashen Brewery Company 576
   Addisu Yenesew Kebede and Abdulkadir Aman Hassen

Performance Evaluation of Motorized Maize Sheller 587
   Solomon Tekeste and Yonas Mitiku Degu

Computational Fluid Dynamic Modeling and Simulation of Red Chili Solar
Cabinet Dryer 597
   *Eshetu Getahun, Maarten Vanierschot, Nigus Gabbiye,
Mulugeta A. Delele, Solomon Workneh, and Mekonnen Gebreslasie*

Development and Performance Evaluation of a Solar Baking Oven 610
   Bisrat Yilma Mekonnen and Addisu Yenesew Kebede

Design and Optimization of Continuous Type Rice Husk Gas Stove 623
   Bimrew Tamrat, Bisrat Yilma, and Million Asfaw

Material Science and Engineering (MSE)

Assessment of Quality of Sand Sources and the Effect on the Properties
of Concrete (The Case of Bahir Dar and Its Vicinities) 637
   Abel Fantahun and Kassahun Admassu

Fabrication and Characterization of Metakaolin Based Flat Sheet
Membrane for Membrane Distillation   651
   Tsegahun Mekonnen Zewdie, Nigus Gabbiye Habtu, Abhishek Dutta,
   and Bart Van der Bruggen

The Effect of Mechanical Treatment and Calcination Temperature
of Ethiopian Kaolin on Amorphous Metakaolin Product.   662
   Tadele Assefa Aragaw

Analysis of Bending and Tensile Strength of Sisal/Bamboo/Polyester
Hybrid Composite.   672
   Yesheneh Jejaw Mamo

Dynamic Mechanical Properties of Kenaf, Thespesia Lampas
and Okra Fiber Polyester Composites   684
   Melak Misganew, D. K. Nageswara Rao, K. Raja Narender Reddy,
   and Muralidhar Avvari

Synthesis and Characterization of β–Wollastonite from Limestone
and Rice Husk as Reinforcement Filler for Clay Based Ceramic Tiles   695
   Chirotaw Getem and Nigus Gabbiye

Experimental Investigation of Bending Strength of Oxytenanthera
Abyssinica and Yushania Alpina Bamboos.   707
   Fentahun Ayu Muche and Yonas Mitiku Degu

Plasma Polymer Deposition of Neutral Agent Carvacrol on a Metallic
Surface by Using Dielectric Barrier Discharge Plasma in Ambient Air.   716
   Tsegaye Gashaw Getnet, Nilson Cristino da Cruz, Milton Eiji Kayama,
   and Elidiane Cipriano Rangel

Correction to: Dynamics of Eutrophication and Its Linkage
to Water Hyacinth on Lake Tana, Upper Blue Nile, Ethiopia:
Understanding Land-Lake Interaction and Process.   C1
   Minychl G. Dersseh, Aron Ateka, Fasikaw A. Zimale,
   Abeyou W. Worqlul, Mamaru A. Moges, Dessalegn C. Dagnew,
   Seifu A. Tilahun, and Assefa M. Melesse

Author Index   727

Agro-Processing Industries for Sustainable Development

Organic Biofertilizer from Brewery Wastewater Sludges via Aerobic Composting Process

Mequanint Demeke$^{(\boxtimes)}$ and Nigus Gabbiye

Faculty of Chemical and Food Engineering, Bahir Dar Institute of Technology,
Bahir Dar University, P.O. Box 26, Bahir Dar, Ethiopia
mequanintdemeke@gmail.com, nigus_g@yahoo.com

Abstract. The main purpose of this research was investigating the potential of aerobic composting process for Preparation of biofertilizer from brewery wastewater sludge (BWS) and spent brewery diatomaceous sludges (BSDS). In this study, BWS was mixed with BSDS sludges and, yielding three different mixtures to be composted. The composting process was assessed through measurements of temperature, moisture, pH, electrical conductivity, organic carbon, organic nitrogen, and total organic phosphorus contents. Moreover, the total concentration of heavy metals (Cr, Cu, Cd, Hg, and Pb) and the plant nutrients (Na, K, Mg, Ca, and Fe) were determined. Additionally, the degradation degree was evaluated through the detection and quantification of E. coli, Salmonella, and Fecal Coliform. It was found that the ratio of C/N was 9:1 and phosphorus fluctuated around 8.5%. Cr, Cu, Cd, Hg, and Pb were found 1.95 ± 0.045, 5.36 ± 0.03, 0.475 ± 0.004, 0.165 ± 0.004 and 0.273 ± 0.005 mg/kg respectively. Plant Nutrients Na, K, Mg, Ca and Fe were found at a concentration level of 100.16 g/kg, 122.95, 869.92, 4084.08 and 26.86 mg/kg respectively. Generally, aerobic compost of BWS and BSDS yielded acceptable quality of biofertilizer in line with EPA standard value limits. The higher pathogen (E. coli and Fecal Coliform) contents of raw sludges are stabilized in composting to the required standards and found far below upper EPA standard limits for unrestricted agricultural application.

Keywords: Aerobic composting · Fertilizer · Kieselguhr sludges · Brewery wastewater sludges · Metal contents

1 Introduction

The brewing industry is one of the largest water users industries and approximately 3–10 L of waste effluent is generated per litre of beer [1]. Breweries in Ethiopia have the potential to produce more than 12 million hectoliters of beer per year [2]. The high organic content of brewery effluent classifies it as a very high strength waste 1000–4000 mg/L COD and 1000–1500 mg/L BOD [3, 4]. Due to increasing environmental concerns and regulations, attempts are to utilize this brewery byproduct in an environmentally friendly manner [3, 5]. In developing countries, non-utilization of byproducts is a drag on economic growth in addition to their environmental burden [5].

© ICST Institute for Computer Sciences, Social Informatics and Telecommunications Engineering 2020
Published by Springer Nature Switzerland AG 2020. All Rights Reserved
N. G. Habtu et al. (Eds.): ICAST 2019, LNICST 308, pp. 3–15, 2020.
https://doi.org/10.1007/978-3-030-43690-2_1

Since all Ethiopian breweries use diatomite for clarification, the total amount of brewery spent diatomite sludge (BSDS) produced, each year is estimated to be about 69,000 metric tons [6]. Diatomite waste is a major challenge for all breweries due to its economic and environmental consequences [5]. Consequently, BSDS is often dumped in landfills that releases leachate to ground water and carbon monoxide as well as carbon dioxide to the atmosphere. This contributes to global climate change and promotes growth of microbes [7]. Moreover, the high moisture content of BSDS (approximately 70%) and its chemical composition lead to rapid degradation, so that the open dumping produces unpleasant odors [8]. Although chemical analysis of spent diatomaceous earth has high nutrient content, particularly of organic nitrogen [9], the environmental risks associated with its application are not well known. Moreover, nitrate production from BSDS is released slowly; hence, it has a lower leaching risk and advantages for crop production [10]. Waste Management and disposal by composting is one of the most promising technologies for treating biosolids allowing their recycling. Brewery sludge originates from the food industry is rich in nutrients and organic matter, so it can be used to produce a high-quality organic compost. This reduces environmental impact and increases crop productivity [11]. Waste sludges generated from Dashen Brewery Share Company was given to farmers for crop production. However, due to its bad odors and other problems, the farmers stopped using sludges and nowadays it is discharged as landfill. Thus, this paper investigates the suitability of brewery wastewater sludge through an aerobic composting as organic fertilizer for agriculture application.

2 Materials and Methods

2.1 Reagents and Chemicals

Analytical grade Ammonium Molybdate, Ammonium Meta Vanadate, Orthophosphate (KH_2PO_4), Hydrochloric acid (HCl 36%) were purchased from Addis Ababa. Concentrated Sulfuric acid (H_2SO_4 98%), Hydrochloric acid (HCl 37%), Potassium sulphate (K_2SO_4 99%), Copper sulphate ($CuSO_4.10H_2O$), Boric acid (H_3BO_3 99.5%), Sodium hydroxide (NaOH 98%), Bromcresol green and Methyl red indicator were used in nitrogen determination. In plant nutrients determination, Acetic acid (36%) and Ammonium hydroxide (NH_4OH 30%) were used. Distilled and deionized water were used to prepare the mother solution.

2.2 Experimental Setup and Description

The aerobic composting reactors (Fig. 1) are connected to cold-water tank and air pipe (perforated part in composters). The composting materials such as brewery wastewater sludges (BSW), brewery spent diatomaceous sludges (BSDS), cow dung and tap water were fed to the aerobic batch composter. It was well mixed and aerated.

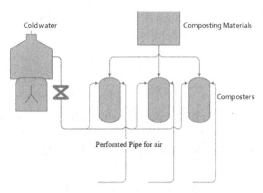

Fig. 1. Experimental setup

2.3 Raw Sludges Preparation and Composting

Dry Brewery wastewater sludges (BWS) and brewery spent diatomaceous sludge (BSDS) were collected from Dashen brewery Share Company and ground by Roller Mill (D-55743 Idar-Oberstein) and sieved through a 1.8 mm sieve. Samples were weighed by digital balance (CAS-164) and slurry was prepared using tap water for composting. The composting experiment is designed using full factorial design i.e. two factors (brewery sludges ratio and moisture content) and three levels with replicate. In composting when the BWS to BSDS ratio is lower than 0.50 the microbial activity is hindered due to lack of enough food. As a result, in order to breakdown the waste, the ratio was maintained between 0.50 and 0.95. The composting sludge substrate contains moisture content of 60–80% [12]. If moisture falls below 40%, microbial activity will slow down. If the moisture exceeds 80%, aeration is hindered, and anaerobic decomposition appeared [12]. Experiments were conducted using mixtures of milled BWS and BSDS in a batch plastic composters (1.5 kg) at different ratios and moisture contents over 30 days. The composting material was manually stirred three times each week to ensure proper mixing and aeration. Compost samples were collected from composters to analyze the physicochemical parameters.

2.4 Characterization and Analysis

2.4.1 Determining Organic Matter and Water Holding Capacity (WHC)

Volatile solids were determined by the loss-on-ignition (LOI) method. The 25 g sample was put in a weighed crucible and was dried in oven dryer (DHG-9140) for 24 h at 105 °C. It was cooled in desiccators and it was reweighed and then ignited in the furnace (AF-11/16) at 500 °C for 30 min. Percentage of organic matter (OM) was calculated using the following equations.

$$\text{Organic Matter } (\%) = \frac{wd - wa}{wd} \times 100\% \tag{1}$$

Where Wd = dry weight sample and Wa = ash weight after combustion.

The organic carbon was determined using empirical equation developed by Pribyl [13]. The percentage of carbon was estimated satisfactorily from the percentage of organic matter by the Eq. (2)

$$\text{Organic Carbon } (\%) = \frac{Organic\ matter\,(\%)}{1.8} \tag{2}$$

In water holding capacity (WHC) determination, a dried 100 g sample was added in funnel covered with filter paper and 100 mL tap water was poured. Amount of water added and drained was recorded. Then the quantity of water retained in 100 g sample was calculated.

$$\text{WHC } (\%) = \frac{\text{Water Added (mL)} - \text{Water Drained (mL)}}{\text{Water Added (mL)}} * 100\% \tag{3}$$

2.4.2 Determination of Organic Phosphorous and Total Organic Nitrogen

The amount of organic Phosphorous in the sample was determined by UV-Vis spectrophotometer (Cary 60) at a wavelength (λ) of 410 nm according to the method described in APHA (1999).

Nitrogen was determined by Kjeldahl method. A 1 g sample was placed in Kjeldahl flask digester (DK-20) and 15 mL concentrated sulfuric acid was added. A 1 g catalyst (mixture of copper sulphate and potassium sulphate) was added to the flask and it was heated. The solution then was distilled in distiller (UDK-169) with 40% NaOH solution that can convert the ammonium salt to ammonia. The amount of ammonia present in the sample was determined by titrating it with 0.1 N HCl in boric acid. The boric acid captures the ammonia gas. Finally, the amount of nitrogen in a sample can be calculated from the quantified amount of ammonia ions in the receiving boric acid solution (APHA, 1999).

2.4.3 Metal Analyses Using Di-Acid and Ammonium Acetate Method

A Di-Acid (HNO_3-$HClO_4$) method was used to determine metal contents. A 1 g air-dry sample (0.15 mm) was added into 300 mL calibrated tube. Then 3 mL concentrated HNO_3 was added and swirled carefully. The temperature setting was slowly increased to 145 °C for 1 h. Then, 4 mL of concentrated $HClO_4$ was added and heated it to 240 °C for further 1 h. Then the tubes were cooled to room temperature, and filtered through Whatman No. 42 filter paper, and brought to 50 mL volume. Each batch has one reagent blank (without samples). Finally, the metals were determined through Atomic Absorption Spectrophotometer (NOV400P).

In Ammonium Acetate Solution preparation, 700 mL of distilled water, 57 mL acetic acid and 68 mL ammonium hydroxide were added and mixed together. The solution was stirred using magnetic stirrer (MS7-H550-Pro) and its pH was adjusted to pH 7 using droplet acetic acid or ammonium hydroxide. The solution was then transferred to a 1.0 L volumetric flask and top up to the mark with distilled water. 4 g air-dried and milled sample was put in a plastic centrifuge tube. 33 mL of ammonium acetate solution was added and was shaken in a mechanical shaker (@Heidolph Unimax 2010) for 1 h. Then, the tube was centrifuged and clear supernatant was decanted into 100 mL volumetric flask and top-up to the mark with distilled water. Finally, metals were determined through Photometer (7100 Palintest).

2.4.4 Microbiological Analysis

Using Eosin Methylene blue agar (modified) Levine: This versatile medium, modified by Levine (Levine M., 1921) was used for the differentiation of Escherichia coli and Enterobacteria aerogenes. Medium was prepared to the formula specified by the APHA for detection and differentiation of coliform group of organisms (10 g peptone, 10 g lactose, 2 g Dipotassium hydrogen phosphate, 0.4 g Eosin Y, 0.065 Methylene blue, 15 g agar at pH 6.8). The sum of these medium types 37.5 g was dissolved in 1 L of distilled water. It was brought to the boil to dissolve completely and which was sterilized by autoclaving at 121 °C for 15 min. Then it was cooled to 60 °C and the medium was shaken in order to oxidize the methylene blue and to suspend the precipitate, which is an essential part of the medium. Using Brilliant green bile (2%) broth: the medium is recommended for the 44 °C confirmatory test for Escherichia coli. Sum (10 g peptone, 10 g lactose, 20 g ox bile (purified), 0.0133 g brilliant green, 0.065 Methylene blue, 15 g agar at pH 7.4) weight of 40.0783 g was dissolved in 1 L of distilled water. It was mixed well and it was distributed into containers fitted with tubes and sterilized by autoclaving at 121 °C for 15 min. To indicate the presence of Escherichia coli, Brilliant Green Bile Broth is incubated at 44 ± 1 °C for 48 h. Standard plate count (SPC) method: 23.5 g Plate Count Agar was diluted in 1 L distilled water. Serial dilution: A solution was prepared from 9.5 g Maximum recovery diluents and 1 L distilled water, which was used to dissolve the sample.

2.4.5 Statistical Analysis

IBMS Statistics 20 statistical software was used in this study for all statistical analysis. Two Way ANOVA was used for testing whether there was any significant difference in compost quality among compost profiles for two factors (moisture content and brewery sludge ratio) and three levels of factors at 5% level of probability.

3   Results and Discussion

3.1 Organic Nutrients Analysis of Raw Sludges

The analysis of selected nutrients in brewery wastewater sludge (BWS) and brewery spent diatomaceous sludge (BSDS) is shown in Table 1. These results revealed that the sludge is rich in organic nitrogen, phosphorous, organic matter, organic carbon, high water holding capacity (WHC) and high conductivity. These sludges have high total dissolved solid (TDS) content, but it contained very low salinity.

With respect to pH, the sludges contained pH of 8.13 ± 0.07 BWS and 7.71 ± 0.06 BSDS indicating slightly basic properties and previous studied show 6.5–11.5 pH of brewery sludges [14]. These results indicated that the two sludges could be used as organic fertilizer with proper treatments.

Table 1. Raw brewery and Kieselguhr sludges physicochemical characteristics

Parameters	BWS	BSDS
	Value	Value
Organic nitrogen %	4.79 ± 0.05	2.74 ± 0.04
Organic phosphorous %	8.29 ± 0.26	4.03 ± 0.04
Organic matter %	53.25 ± 0.43	28.28 ± 0.23
Organic carbon %	33.28 ± 0.27	17.68 ± 0.14
WHC (%)	66.66 ± 0.54	40.4 ± 0.33
Conductivity (μS/cm)	803.96 ± 6.5	424.91 ± 3.43
TDS (mg/L)	286.89 ± 2.32	279.67 ± 2.26
Salinity	0.293 ± 0.002	0.293 ± 0.003
pH	8.13 ± 0.07	7.71 ± 0.06

3.2 Metal Analysis and Pathogen Determination of Raw Sludges

As it can be seen in Table 2, characterization results revealed that primary nutrients (N, P, K) and secondary nutrients with high organic matter content and high water holding capacity indicate that brewery sludges is a potential source of organic fertilizer. As it can be seen in Table 2, the heavy metal concentrations in BWS are higher than threshold limit [16]. The sources of heavy metals in BWS is disinfection agents, cleaning detergents, antifungal paste solution, residual furnace oil, chemicals in beer quality analysis laboratory, residual printer inks (Fe), paper ash (Cd and Pb) [17] and toilet sludges (feces and urine). But, heavy metal content in BSDS is below the threshold limit and it has a high silicon dioxide content exceeding 33.51 ± 0.065% that can scavenge [18] heavy metals ions and reduce heavy metal contents in composting process since they are non-biodegradable and toxicity nature once they are present [18, 19].

The concentrations of total fecal coliforms (TFC) and Escherichia coli (E.coli) as dry weight in BWS and BSDS were determined. In BWS it was found 2031 CFU/g TFC and 160 CFU/g E.coli, which are higher than the EPA value 100 CFU/g. Similarly, total fecal coliforms (TFC) and E.coli as dry weight in the BSDS samples were 65 CFU/g and 55 CFU/g respectively, which were lower than the EPA 100 CFU/g. However, the pathogen content in BWS was high which needs further treatment.

Table 2. Composition of Raw BWS and BSDS sludges

Metals	BWS	BSDS	Limit [28, 29]
Copper, Cu (mg/kg)	6.28 ± 0.04	0.97 ± 0.01	70
Iron, Fe (mg/kg)	25.56 ± 3.52	26.03 ± 3.25	266
Sodium, Na (mg/kg)	112.2 ± 0.91	58.83 ± 1.84	214
Magnesium, Mg (mg/kg)	1126.93 ± 2.59	838 ± 34.29	1478
Calcium, Ca (mg/kg)	3433.79 ± 15.45	3118.5 ± 5.31	5789
Potassium, K (mg/kg)	116.95 ± 0.48	119.2 ± 2.29	6108
Lead, Pb (mg/kg)	10.627 ± 0.65	0.205 ± 0.012	45
Cadmium, Cd (mg/kg)	1.633 ± 0.025	0.305 ± 0.02	0.70
Mercury, Hg (mg/kg)	0.82 ± 0.21	0.215 ± 0.004	0.70
Chromium, Cr (mg/kg)	31.5 ± 0.24	0.89 ± 0.041	25
Silicon oxide (SiO2) (%)		33.51 ± 0.065	

3.3 Compost Product Characterization

The pH of final compost was measured by pH (BANTE 90-UK) meter and was found between 7.5–7.63 that indicates alkaline properties and similar results were observed in previous studies [3]. The electrical conductivity (EC) values of compost samples were measured (YSI Pro 30) and found to be 900–1650 μS/cm that is far below the permissible limit (4000 μS/cm). The extraction of total dissolved solid (TDS) is influenced by moisture content of composting substrates and found 500–1100 mg/L which is far above the control soil (3.33 mg/L). Organic matter was fluctuated in all treatments. It ranges between 41–48% of organic matter and 28–30% organic carbon. This fluctuation points out the mineralization and degradation of organic matter [20].

3.4 Organic Nitrogen

The nitrogen content of compost samples from 50%, 60%, 70% and 80% moisture content show different trends as the BWS ratio was increased as it is illustrated in Fig. 2. In 70% moisture content, the results revealed that organic nitrogen was increased as the BWS ratio is became high and then it was decreased due to volatilization of ammonia [22]. When the moisture content is increased to 80% the organic nitrogen is decreased due to the creation of anaerobic conditions for microorganisms that they cannot completely decompose biodegradable content of composting materials. Since aeration is hindered, nutrients are leached out and decomposition slows down. Organic nitrogen content of 50% moisture content is lower than the 60%, 70% moisture contents experiments because microbial growth and activity was hindered by lower moisture content. Nitrogen content is significantly different at various moisture content and brewery wastewater sludges (BWS) ratio (P < 0.05) because the brewery sludge is abundant in organic nitrate came from residue barley malts, hot trub and others [17].

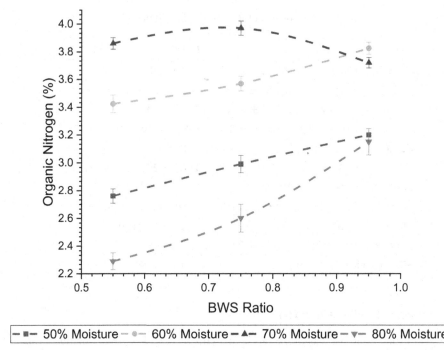

Fig. 2. Organic nitrogen percentage of final compost as function of BWS ratio

3.5 Total Organic Phosphorus

In compost samples, the maximum concentration of total phosphorus (9.5%) was found at 0.95 BWS ratio and 70% moisture content in the compost samples, while the minimum phosphorus was found between 0.55 and 0.95 BSW ratio and 80% moisture content, as illustrated in Fig. 3. As shown in Fig. 3, phosphorus percentage of the compost increases as BWS increases since the BWS and BSDS sludge are naturally rich in phosphate compounds [17]. During composting process, phosphorus does not experience volatilization as nitrogen. Phosphorus settles in bacterial cells and mixed with composts, phosphorus is the sum of dissolved and insoluble forms [24]. As a result, phosphorous content of compost is increased with increasing BWS ratio. In previous studies, similar findings were found in the final composts [23]. Phosphorus content was significantly different at various moisture and BWS ratios (P < 0.05).

3.6 Water Holding Capacity (WHC)

This shows that all the substrates presented high water holding capacity values irrespective of the formulation employed (Fig. 4). The water holding capacity of compost samples of 60%, 70% and 80% was found to be high at 0.55 BWS ratio where high BSDS that has large porosity [6] to retain water. However, the 70% moisture content experiment contained higher WHC than other compost samples. In the 50% moisture content experiment, the microbial activity of degrading of organic compounds were slow

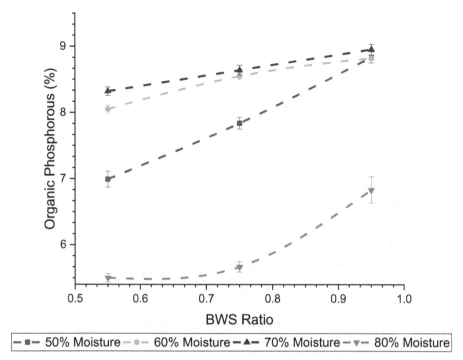

Fig. 3. Organic phosphorus percentage of final compost as function of BWS ratio

due to the lower moisture content. The results revealed that the water holding capacity of all compost samples (57–62%WHC) are greater than the control soil (22%WHC).

Organic matter of compost adds to the water retention capacity of a soil because humus particles absorb water and increase the ability of a soil to retain moisture against drainage due to the force of gravity [25].

3.7 Metal Analysis of Compost

The nutrient contents of compost samples were characterized and were found containing essential plant nutrients as seen in Table 4 and their value is lower than the maximum permissible limit. As it can be seen in Table 3, the heavy metal concentration in the final compost is found far below permissible limit. The brewery spent diatomaceous slugdes (BSDS) that was used in the compost samples was scavanging heavy metal ions and there was reduction of heavy metals as compared to raw sludges because BSDS contained high silicon dioxide content shows scavanging effect for metal ions [18]. The compost samples can be used as organic fertilizer [15].

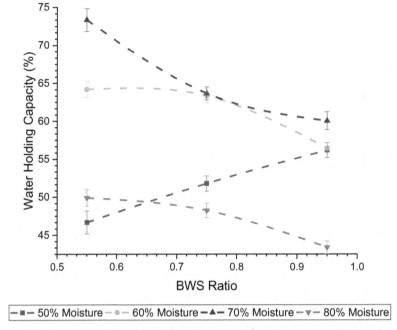

Fig. 4. Water holding capacity (%) of final compost as function of BWS ratio

Table 3. Metal composition of the final compost

Metals	Value	Limit [28, 29]
Copper, Cu (mg/kg)	5.36 ± 0.03	70
Sodium, Na (g/kg)	111.29 ± 0.91	214
Potassium, K (mg/kg)	123.67 ± 1.39	1608
Magnesium, Mg (mg/kg)	846 ± 82.58	1478
Calcium, Ca (mg/kg)	4004 ± 408.3	5789
Iron, Fe (mg/kg)	26.34 ± 0.48	266
Lead, Pb (mg/kg)	0.273 ± 0.005	45
Cadmium, Cd (mg/kg)	0.475 ± 0.004	0.7
Mercury, Hg (mg/kg)	0.165 ± 0.004	0.7

3.8 Microbiological Analysis of Composts

In present study, composting temperature was found higher than 55 °C [26]. The microbiological analyses results of the final composts are presented in Table 3. Compost samples were analysed for coliforms, salmonella and Escherichia coli (E. coli). The results indicate that composting practices is effective for pathogen reduction of brewery sludges composting. As it can be seen in the table, Salmonella, which is considered a

Table 4. Microbiological groups in composts and legislation

	Concentration	EPA standard
E.coli (CFU/g)	4.24 ± 0.11	<100 MPN/g
Salmonella (CFU/25 g)	Not detected	<1/25 g
Fecal coliform (CFU/g)	2.87 ± 0.4	<100 MPN/g

*MPN = Most Probable Number

good index for the hygienic status of the composts [27] was not detected in the composts. The compost samples contained total fecal coliforms (TFC) and E. coli lower than the permissible EPA standard value, which indicates that composting practice reduces the pathogen concentrations and hygienic status of the compost samples.

4 Conclusion

Brewery is among the industries known for production of byproducts (spent grains, spent yeast) and sludge (BWS and BSDS) from the brewery wastewater treatment plant at different stages of manufacturing process. Aerobic composting experiment was conducted for a wide range of sludge moisture and sludge ratio. Based on the findings of this study, it was found that the compost material obtained by aerobic degradation of the raw sludge is within the standard organic fertilizer requirement. This research revealed that brewery sludge compost is a rich source of nitrogen, phosphorous and potassium with other plant nutrients. Besides, analysis of selected heavy metals in brewery sludge composts suggested that Lead, Mercury and Cadmium were found below the threshold levels and the compost can be safely used. Water holding capacity of the compost products were found between 57 and 62% WHC, which is much higher than the soil (22% WHC). This suggested that, which is linked to high organic matter, high cation exchange capacity and other nutrients that can improve water holding capacity of soils. It can be used for sustainable agricultural land reuse. The future work is to study compost samples to soil ratio and effect of compost fertilizer on composition of vegetable.

Acknowledgements. The authors would like to thank Bahir Dar University, Bahir Dar Institute of Technology for financial supports. The authors honestly acknowledge laboratory technicians for their patience, friendly approach and collaboration for accomplishment of this work.

References

1. Dorman, L.I.: Variations of Galactic Cosmic Rays, p. 103. Moscow State University Press, Moscow (1975)
2. International beverage news (2017)
3. Kanagachandran, K.: Biogas generation from brewery wastes demonstration at a laboratory scale. Tech. Q. Master Brew. Assoc. Am. **41**(4), 394–397 (2004)
4. Kanagachandran, K.: Optimisation of spent grain slurry for energy generation. Tech. Q. Master Brew. Assoc. Am. **42**(4), 324–328 (2005)

5. Kanagachandran, K., Jayaratne, R.: Utilization potential of brewery wastewater sludge as an organic fertilizer. J. Inst. Brew. **112**(2), 92–96 (2006)

6. Gashaw, D., Abebe, B., Amsalu, N., Morgan, L.: Use of industrial diatomite wastes from beer production to improve soil fertility and cereal yields. J. Cleaner Prod. **157**(1), 22–29 (2017)

7. Iliescu, M., Faraco, M., Popa, M., Cristea, M.: Reuse of residual kieselguhr from beer filtration. J. Environ. Prot. Ecol. **10**, 156–162 (2009)

8. Mathias, T., Mello, P., Servulo, E.: Solid waste in brewing process: a review. J. Brew. Distill. **5**, 1–9 (2014)

9. Johnson, M.: Management of spent diatomaceous earth from the brewing industry. Thesis, the University of Western Australia (1997)

10. Snyman, H.G., Van der Waals, J.: Laboratory and Field Scale Evaluation of Agricultural Use of Sewage Sludge. Report to the Water Research Commission on the Project Laboratory and field scale evaluation of agricultural use of sewage sludge, March 2004

11. Cáceres, R., Coromina, N., Malińska, K., Marfà, O.: Evolution of process control parameters during extended co-composting of green waste and solid fraction of cattle slurry to obtain growing media. Bioresource Technol. **179**, 398–406 (2015)

12. Gautam, S., Bundela, P., et al.: Composting of municipal solid waste of Jabalpur city. Glob. J. Environ. Res. **4**(1), 43–46 (2010)

13. Pribyl, D.W.: A critical review of the conventional SOC to SOM conversion factor. Geoderma **156**, 75–83 (2010)

14. Selnur, U., Ufuk, A.: Composting of wastewater treatment sludge with different bulking agents. J. Air Waste Manag. Assoc. **66**(3), 288–295 (2016)

15. Barker, A., Pilbeam, D.: Handbook of Plant Nutrition. CRC Press, Boca Raton (2015)

16. Brinton, F.W.: Compost quality standards & guidelines: an international view. Final report, Woods End Research Laboratory, Inc. (2000)

17. Kunze, W.: Technology Brewing and Malting, 3rd International edn. VLB Berlin, Berlin (2004). (Translated by Pratt, S.)

18. Khraisheh, M.A.M., Al-Ghouti, M.A., Allen, S.J., Ahmad, M.N.M.: The effect of pH, temperature and molecular size on removal of dyes from textile effluent using manganese oxides modified diatomite. Water Environ. Res. **76**, 2655–2663 (2004)

19. Nicholson, F.A., Chambers, B.J.: Sources and impacts of past, current and future (SP0547). Appendix 1: heavy metals, 2008 February

20. Mena, E., Garrido, A., Hernández, T., García, C.: Bioremediation of sewage sludge by composting. Commun. Soil Sci. Plan **34**(7–8), 957–971 (2003)

21. Tiquia, S.M.: Microbiological parameters as indicators of compost maturity. J. Appl. Microbiol. **99**, 816–828 (2005)

22. Awasthi, M., et al.: Co-composting of organic fraction of municipal solid waste mixed with different bulking waste: characterization of physicochemical parameters and microbial enzymatic dynamic. Bioresource Technol. **182**, 200–207 (2015)

23. Eggleston, H., et al.: Guidelines for National Greenhouse Gas Inventories. A primer, Prepared by the National Greenhouse Gas Inventories Programme (2006)

24. Ratnawati, R., et al.: Composting process of slaughterhouse solid waste using aerobic system. In: Green Technology towards Sustainable Environment (2015)

25. Paradelo, R., Basanta, R., Barral, M.T.: Water-holding capacity and plant growth in compost-based substrates modified with polyacrylamide, guar gum or bentonite. Sci. Hortic. **243**, 344–349 (2019)

26. Banegas, V., Moreno, J., Moreno, J., García, C., León, G., Hernandez, T.: Composting anaerobic and aerobic sewage sludges using two proportions of sawdust. Waste Manag. **27**(10), 1317–1327 (2007)

27. Kalatzi, E., Sazakli, E., Karapanagioti, H.K., Leotsinidis, M.: Composting of brewery sludge mixed with different bulking agents. Lab of Public Health, School of Medicine, University of Patras, Patras, GR-26504, Greece (2006)
28. ANNEX 2: Heavy metals and organic compounds from wastes used as organic fertilizers, legislation and standards (2004)
29. McLachlin, I.: Compost report. A & L Canada Laboratories Inc. (2017)

Endosulfan Pesticide Dissipation and Residue Levels in Khat and Onion in a Sub-humid Region of Ethiopia

Feleke K. Sishu[1(✉)], Elsabeth K. Thegaye[2], Petra Schmitter[3], Nigus G. Habtu[2], Seifu A. Tilahun[1], and Tammo S. Steenhuis[4]

[1] Faculty of Civil and Water Resources Engineering,
Bahir Dar Institute of Technology, Bahir Dar University, Bahir Dar, Ethiopia
felek2004@gmail.com
[2] Faculty of Chemical and Food Engineering,
Bahir Dar Institute of Technology, Bahir Dar University, Bahir Dar, Ethiopia
[3] International Water Management Institute, Yangon, Myanmar
[4] Departments of Biological and Environmental Engineering, Cornell University,
206 Riley Robb Hall, Ithaca, NY 14853, USA

Abstract. Endosulfan, a mixture of α- and β-isomers, is used by farmers in the wet and dry season for khat and onion production. Khat leaf samples were collected in farmer fields at intervals of 1 h; 1, 5, 9 and 14 d after application. The dissipation rate of α- and β-isomers and residue level in khat were compared with residue levels in onion. The extraction was done by using Quick Easy Cheap Effective Rugged and Safe (QuEChERS) method and analyzed by Gas Chromatography – Electron Capture Detector (GC-ECD). Greater residue α- and β-isomer endosulfan levels were found in khat compared to onion as khat leaves are sprayed repeatedly in two week. Residue levels of khat exceeded the tolerable EU limit of 0.05 mg.kg^{-1} for leafy vegetables and herbs. For both raw and processed onion sample α- and β-endosulfan residues level were below the tolerable of limit EU regulation for bulb vegetables (i.e. 0.1 mg.kg^{-1}). The mean half-life for the α-isomer of endosulfan was 3.4 d in the wet season and 3.6 d in the dry season whilst that for the β-isomer was 5.0 d and 5.4 d respectively. Both isomers dissipated fastest in the wet season under conditions of high humidity and precipitation. The β-isomer persisted longer and had a lower dissipation rate from plants surface compared to the α-isomer.

Keywords: Pesticide · Endosulfan · Dissipation · Residue · Khat · Onion · Ethiopia · East Africa · Sub-humid tropical

1 Introduction

Endosulfan α- and β is a widely used pesticide all over the world since 1960 [1]. It used to protect crops like cotton, soya bean, coffee tea and vegetables. But the residue in plant tissue and water causes both acute and chronic health risks for aquatic and terrestrials organisms including humans [2–4]. Hence, use of endosulfan in agriculture was banned

© ICST Institute for Computer Sciences, Social Informatics and Telecommunications Engineering 2020
Published by Springer Nature Switzerland AG 2020. All Rights Reserved
N. G. Habtu et al. (Eds.): ICAST 2019, LNICST 308, pp. 16–28, 2020.
https://doi.org/10.1007/978-3-030-43690-2_2

by the EU in 2007, UNEPA since 2012, and USEPA in 2016. Endosulfan is still used in countries like Ethiopia for irrigated vegetable production (i.e. onion, tomato, pepper) and khat [5, 6]. Khat (*Catha edulis Forsk, Celastraceae*) is a perennial cash crop where fresh leaves are harvested and consumed in the Horn of Africa and some Arabian countries as a mild narcotic stimulant [7–11].

The endosulfan belongs to the organochloride pesticide family and it is persistence in the environment. However, its persistence is influenced by environmental factors including temperature, humidity, precipitation and microbial activity [12–15]. Therefore, the half-life of residue levels in crops, soil and water vary with weather conditions. For instance, in cold sub-tropical and temperate regions, the half-life of endosulfan in soils was estimated between 39 and 42 d and took 238 d for 99% dissipation [16] and between 9.5 and 14 d in plant tissue [17]. However, half-life decreases in tropical hot humid climates to 3.3 to 21 d in soil [14, 18] and, between 3.3 and 3.6 d in plant tissue [18, 19]. Therefore, understanding the dissipation of pesticides under local weather conditions could help to determine appropriate consumption time after harvest to reduce potential human health risks associated with high dose intake.

Despite intensive applications of endosulfan on khat and vegetables in Ethiopia, data on dissipation and residue levels on plant surfaces under the sub-humid climatic condition are very limited. For that reason, we investigated the rate of dissipation for endosulfan pesticide used by farmers under repeated application on khat and compared residue levels in khat with onion. To address this we assessed: (1) the effect of seasonal variation on dissipation rate of pesticide (endosulfan α and β) from plant leaf; (2) the influence of repeated application of pesticide on residue levels, and (3) the residue level in khat compared to onion that only once treated by pesticide and consumed after processing such as peeling and cooking.

2   Materials and Methods

2.1   Description of Study Area

The study was conducted in Robit Bata watershed located in Northwest Ethiopian highlands, Lake Tana basin (3322523 N, 1291087 E) and an elevation of 1847 m (Fig. 1). Main rainfall season occurs from May to September. The average annual rainfall from 2014 to 2018 was 1420 mm a^{-1} at the Bahir Dar Zuriya weather station. According to [20], 82% of Robit Bata watershed is cultivated in the wet phase and 10% of the area is irrigated from wells in the dry season of which half is in khat (*Catha edulis Forsk, Celastraceae*), one fifth in hop and the remaining are vegetables.

The agricultural system is predominantly a mixed crop-livestock system with maize, millet and teff primarily cultivated during the rainy season [21]. Khat and vegetables, such as tomato, are irrigated through shallow groundwater pumping and surface water river diversion.

Pesticide Survey. Prior to field selection, a survey was conducted to determine the type of pesticides applied and their application rate. In total 5 farmers, 2 local pesticide sellers and 3 pesticides applicators were surveyed. Dimethoate, endosulfan with alpha and beta isomers, 2,4-D, chlorpyrifos and profenofos were used at different growth stages

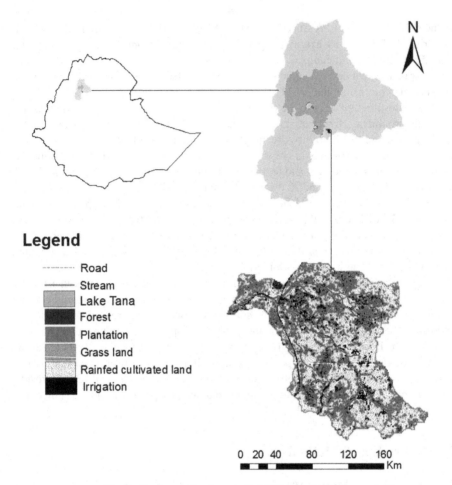

Fig. 1. Study area land use in Robit Bata watershed.

depending on the crop (Table 1). Due to its wide application in dry and wet seasons, endosulfan (containing a technical grade mixture of alpha 70% and 30% beta isomers) was selected for this study. Commercially, the formulation of endosulfan contains abundant the α-isomer and the less abundant but more volatile and less degradable metabolite than β [22, 23].

Experimental Design and Sample Collection. Three experimental plots 8 m × 10 m were selected within a 25 m × 35 m farmer-cultivated khat plot. The plant spacing of khat was 50 cm by 50 cm. The farmer used an endosulfan mixture as described in Table 1 and applied the pesticide using a backpack sprayer on a biweekly basis.

Experimental investigation of the degradation rate was carried out during two consecutive application cycles in the dry period (May–June) and wet season (July–August). In each cycle, a plant sample was taken before application (background sample) followed by samples at 1 h and 1, 5, 9 and 14 d after application. From each experimental plot

Table 1. Trend in pesticide applications and formulation by local farmers in study area for maize, khat, and onion

Crop types	Dose (ha^{-1} in 40 L H$_2$O)	Frequency of pesticide application	Active ingredient formulation (mix)	Cropping season
Maize	256 ml	1 per cropping season	Profenofos	Wet season
Khat	1536 ml	2 to 3 times per month	Dimethoate (16 ml) + endosulfan(16 ml) + profenofos (16 ml)	Irrigated dry season
	1536 ml	2 to 3 times per month	Dimethoate (16 ml) + chlorpyrifos (32 ml) or endosulfan (32 ml)	Wet season
Onion	256 ml	1 per cropping season	Dimethoate (16 ml) + endosulfan (16 ml) + profenofos (16 ml)	Irrigated dry season

500 g of young leaves was collected at each sampling event. A total of 60 samples were taken to investigate the degradation rate.

During the dry season, six harvested onion samples were collected from two onion irrigated fields in the study area. The samples were put in polyethylene plastic bags, chilled and transported to the laboratory within 24 h for analysis. The endosulfan compound was analyzed in raw and boiled onion samples to evaluate the impact of processing such as cooking, peeling and washing before consumption in the reduction of pesticides.

The climate data, including daily temperature, rainfall amount between first day after application to up to date of sampling and humidity were collected (Table 2). A manual rainfall collector with a container of 2.5 L was installed to measure daily precipitation.

Sample Preparation and Pesticide Analysis. Pesticide (endosulfan) was extracted from khat leaves and onion peels using the AOAC Quick Easy Cheap Effective Rugged and Safe (QuEChERS) method [24]. The khat and onion samples were grounded to obtain homogenous mixture. Fifteen mL of acetonitrile containing 1% of acetic acid was added to 15 g of the homogenized sample and followed by shaking using vortex shaker for 30 s. After shaking, 1.5 g sodium acetate and 6 g of anhydride magnesium sulphate were added and centrifuged for 1 min at 4000 rpm for 5 min. Afterwards; 8 mL of the supernatant acetonitrile phase was transferred into 15 ml centrifuge tube. Given the high pigment concentration of khat, the sample was extracted using 125 mg mL^{-1} Primary and Secondary Amine (PSA) (Agilent Technologies group) and 125 mg mL^{-1} US

Table 2. Weather conditions during the field experimental period and pesticides application cycles in dry and wet seasons in 2018 in the Robit Bata watershed

Sampling season	Application cycles	Sampling date (2018)	Days after treatment	Weather conditions		
				Temp. (°C)	Humidity (%)	Cumulative rainfall (mm)
Dry	1	8 May	0	29	38	0
		8 May	1 h	32	30	0
		9 May	1 d	29	35	0
		12 May	5 d	26	54	0
		16 May	9 d	25	50	0
		21 May	14 d	29	47	0
	2	2 May	0	24	54	0
		22 May	1 h	31	39	0
		23 May	1 d	29	37	0
		26 May	5 d	21	49	0
		30 May	9 d	23	52	0
		4 Jun	14 d	23	66	0
Wet	1	25 Jul	0	22	85	0
		25 Jul	1 h	25	75	0
		26 Jul	1 d	18	74	31
		29 Jul	5 d	20	71	71
		2 Aug	9 d	16	92	84
		7 Aug	14 d	22	82	91
	2	10 Aug	0	18	74	0
		10 Aug	1 h	18	75	0
		11 Aug	1 d	24	72	3
		14 Aug	5 d	21	80	54
		18 Aug	9 d	23	76	112
		23 Aug	14 d	25	64	148

and Graphitized Carbon Black (GCB) (Waters, Ireland) and 150 mg $MgSO_4$. However, for raw and boiled onion samples, in the extraction and clean-up, the AOAC QuEChERS values described in [24] were taken.

The solution was centrifuged 5 min at 4000 rpm and 2 mL of the final extract containing the solvent and pesticide compound was taken and transferred to a GC vial. The 2 mL solution was evaporated to dryness under a stream of gentle flow of nitrogen in water bathe at 40 °C to make more concentrated and ready for GC injection. The dried extract was reconstituted in 200 μL of acetonitrile and the vials were kept at −18 °C until analysis.

GC-ECD GC-ECD Operating Conditions. A 2 μL sample was injected into the gas chromatograph-electron capture detector GC-μECD and analyzed according the stated GC parameters. The capillary column HP-5 length 30 m, 0.25 mm i.d., and 0.25 μm film was used. Detector temperature was 300 °C. The temperature program was: initial temperature 70 °C hold for 1 min, 10 min to bring the temperature to 160 °C then hold for 5 min, finally, by 24 °C min^{-1} to 280 °C hold for 9.5 min. The total analysis time was 30 min and the equilibration time 0.5 min. Nitrogen was used as a makeup and carrier gas at a constant flow of 50 ml min^{-1}.

Method of Validation and Quality Control. The linearity of the methods for targeted pesticides was evaluated by analyzing a reference standard and spiked samples. Endosulfan-α and-β, standards (Sigma Aldrich) were prepared in series 30, 60, 90, 120 and 150 μg L^{-1} and analyzed for six-points of calibration. The recovery and precision (repeatability) of the method was evaluated before the samples were analyzed. Five replication of blank samples for method blanks and (MB) and five spiked samples were analyzed for laboratory control sample (LCS). Control samples were prepared spiking 15 g of khat with a known amount of a standard mixture of 1 ml target pesticides at concentration of 90 μg L^{-1}. The GC with ECD chromatograms of standard sample peaks for α- and β- isomers are shown in (Fig. 2). The mean percent recovery for endosulfan-α was 84–88% and for endosulfan-β was 81–85%. The relative standard deviation for repeatability (RSD) endosulfan-α was 7 μg kg^{-1} Endosulfan-β was with 11 μg kg^{-1} which is less than 20% according to USEPA method 508 [25]. The limit of detection (LOD), a signal-to-noise of 3 [26] for endosulfan-α and β were 0.22 and 0.8 μg g^{-1}, respectively.

Determination of the Pesticide Half-Life in Plant Samples. Pesticides dissipation rate from plant surface, soil and sediment undergoes first order kinetics [5, 12, 17, 22, 27]. The dynamic was calculated using first order kinetics for both endosulfan α and β for each of cycles and seasons.

$$C(t) = C_o e^{-kt} \tag{1}$$

Where $C(t)$ is the concentration of pesticides on the khat leaf at time t, C_o is the concentration of pesticides at time $t = 0$, and k is the dissipation rate constant. Using natural log fit of concentration ratio versus t of Eq. 1, the k values were calculated from the slope of linear graph for each cycle. Finally, solving Eq. 1 for the field half-life ($t_{1/2}$) yields.

$$t_{1/2} = \frac{0.69}{k} \tag{2}$$

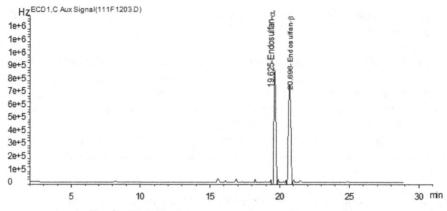

Fig. 2. GC-ECD chromatogram of pure reference sample.

3   Results and Discussion

3.1   Temporal Variability of Residue Level of Endosulfan α and β Isomers

The results of residue levels in khat, conducted for two spraying cycles in the dry and wet seasons are shown in (Table 3). One hour after spraying, the α-endosulfan was more abundant than β isomer endosulfan in all cycles of the experiment. In every cycle the residues of α-endosulfan were greater than 50 μg.kg^{-1} during one hour interval sampling whilst maximum levels for β-endosulfan were recorded at 41.8 μg kg^{-1}.

Slight differences in residues levels were observed in the dry and rain monsoon seasons for samples collected at the same sampling time after application between the two cycles. For instance, residue concentrations found in the dry season one hour after spraying in cycle one for β-isomer was 38.8 μg.kg^{-1} and increased to 41.8 μg.kg^{-1} in cycle two. Similar trend was observed for α-endosulfan dry period cycle one spray residue was 63.8 μg.kg^{-1} but in cycle two it increased to 65.1 μg.kg^{-1}. This was probably due to the residue left in first cycle on the biomass increase residue level in samples of the second cycle. A previous study found that photolysis did not significantly affect endosulfan degradation in duplicate experiments in the dark and direct sun light [28]. Temperature, which increases degradation rate, was slightly greater in the dry than in rain season (Table 2). Despite this endosulfan concentration was less in the wet season indicating that the greater humidity that increase moisture in the wet season had the greatest effect on increasing the degradation rate and precipitation wash off the pesticides from plant surface reduce the residues level.

Based on results in Table 3, the amount dissipated from plant surface was smaller in the dry season than in the wet season and faster for the α-isomer than the β-isomer (Fig. 2). For example in the first 24 h after spraying during a 80% of the sprayed α isomer dissipated from plant surface in the wet season while only 50% was degraded in the same time span during the dry season (see Fig. 3). Similarly, for the β-isomer 68% degraded within one day after spaying in the wet season whilst only 35% degraded within the first 24 h in the dry season. Pesticide dissipation was favored by an increase in humidity (wet season range 71–92%; dry season range: 30–54%) and the occurrence of

Table 3. Residue levels of α- and β-endosulfan isomers (μg.kg^{-1}) in khat leaf samples collected at 1 h to 14 d after spraying for two spraying cycles in wet and dry season.

Sampling season	Application cycle	Sampling date (2018)	Days after treatment	α-isomer Mean ± SD	β-isomer Mean ± SD	α + β-isomers
Dry	1	8 May	1 h	63.8 ± 1.5	38.8 ± 1.02	102.6
		9 May	1 d	32.4 ± 0.96	25.2 ± 0.71	57.7
		12 May	5 d	20.8 ± 0.56	11.2 ± 0.70	32.1
		16 May	9 d	9.3 ± 0.15	9.4 ± 0.42	18.7
		21 May	14 d	3.5 ± 0.53	5.4 ± 0.49	8.8
	2	22 May	1 h	65.1 ± 0.63	41.8 ± 0.84	106.9
		23 May	1 d	36.8 ± 0.60	28.5 ± 1.52	65.3
		26 May	5 d	24.5 ± 0.70	14.9 ± 0.97	39.5
		30 May	9 d	12.3 ± 0.80	10.4 ± 1.58	22.7
		4 Jun	14 d	3.6 ± 0.43	6.4 ± 0.74	10.0
Wet	1	25 Jul	1 h	50.3 ± 0.73	34.0 ± 1.30	84.3
		26 Jul	1 d	22.7 ± 0.52	14.1 ± 2.12	36.8
		29 Jul	5 d	12.6 ± 0.45	9.82 ± 0.72	22.5
		2 Aug	9 d	5.7 ± 0.45	5.26 ± 0.81	11.0
		7 Aug	14 d	2.5 ± 0.24	3.2 ± 1.36	5.7
	2	10 Aug	1 h	50.8 ± 0.40	34.1 ± 1.29	84.9
		11 Aug	1 d	14.3 ± 0.74	15.9 ± 1.72	30.2
		14 Aug	5 d	9.9 ± 0.56	7.7 ± 1.74	17.6
		18 Aug	9 d	5.2 ± 1.02	5.7 ± 0.75	10.96
		23 Aug	14 d	1.7 ± 0.79	4.5 ± 0.67	6.1

rainfall. Microbial degradation of pesticides could increase with an increasing humidity and temperature. The moisture creates a conducive environment for microbial activities [29, 30]. Studies have found that endosulfan degraded to its major metabolite due to microbial degradation of the two isomers [31, 32]. Furthermore, precipitation washes the pesticide from plant surface more easily as their affinity to the plant surface is lower compared to the soil [19, 33].

Total residue (α + β) after one day of application in the wet period was below the tolerable limit (50 μg.kg^{-1} or 0.05 mg.kg^{-1}) of the EU commission regulation for leaf vegetables and herbs [27]. However, in the dry period a longer timespan was needed for the residue levels to fall below the threshold.

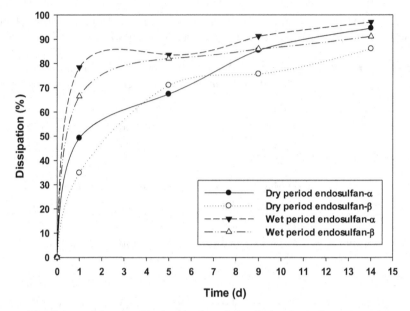

Fig. 3. α- and β-endosulfan isomer degradation during dry and wet seasons.

3.2 Kinetics and Half-Life of α- and β-Isomers

The dissipation rate and half-life of pesticide were related to season of application and the isomer type (see Table 4). For α isomer, the half-lives were shorter during the wet season with an average of 3.4 d compared to 3.6 in the dry period whilst for β- isomer the average value in the wet season was 5.0 compared to the 5.4 d in the dry season. This suggests that α-isomer is dissipated faster compared to the β- isomer in both the dry and wet season. These results correspond with others findings [16, 34]. The estimated half-life for α-isomer in Ethiopian sub-humid tropic in both the dry and wet season was similar to the 3.6 d half-life observed in Benin, West Africa tropical climate [19].

3.3 Comparison of Dry Period Residue Levels in Onion and Khat

The residue levels were higher in khat than raw and boiled onion (Fig. 4). This difference can be explained by the fact that for onion the pesticide is mixed with irrigation water and only applied once, hence dependent on pesticide uptake from the roots and the allocation within the onion bulb. For khat, on the other hand, pesticides are repeated applied in 14 d cycles directly on the leaf tissue. Farmers sprayed pesticides on khat at levels six times more than commercial recommendations for maize (Table 1). Pesticides are repeatedly applied on khat, a cash crop which is harvested frequently. To retain the shine on chewable fresh leaves, the farmers harvest khat within 3 d of the last spraying application. However, according to the findings in the study at least 3.3 d are required for the α-isomer to reach its half-life. But, a pre-harvest interval at least 2 week are suggested for persistence pesticides given a commercial dose of application [35]. On the other hand, onion was below the EU pesticide regulation for α- and β- endosulfan

Table 4. α- and β-endosulfan isomers dissipation kinetics on khat leaf surfaces and the half-life during different application cycles in dry and wet seasons

Sampling seasons	Cycles in season	α-isomer			β-isomer		
		Kinetics	Half-life (d)	R^2	Kinetics	Half-life (d)	R^2
Dry	1	$C(t) = 64e^{-0.193t}$	3.6	0.98	$C(t) = 39e^{-0.131t}$	5.2	0.93
	2	$C(t) = 65e^{-0.189t}$	3.7	0.97	$C(t) = 42e^{-0.128t}$	5.4	0.96
	Mean	$C(t) = 64e^{-0.190t}$	3.6	0.98	$C(t) = 40e^{-0.129t}$	5.4	0.95
Wet	1	$C(t) = 50e^{-0.214t}$	3.5	0.96	$C(t) = 34e^{-0.13t}$	4.6	0.91
	2	$C(t) = 51e^{-0.182t}$	3.3	0.91	$C(t) = 34e^{-0.127t}$	5.3	0.83
	Mean	$C(t) = 51e^{-0.202t}$	3.4	0.94	$C(t) = 34e^{-0.139t}$	5.0	0.87

residue in bulbs and vegetables at the time of harvest. The EU pesticides regulation for α- and β-endosulfan residue in bulbs and vegetables recommended a tolerance level of 100 µg.kg^{-1} [27].

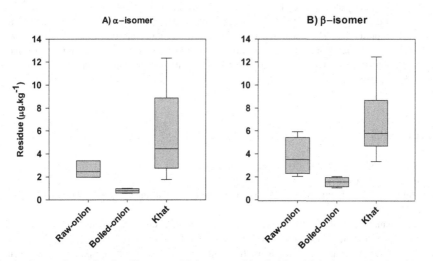

Fig. 4. Comparison of endosulfan α- and β-isomer residue in khat 14 d after application for raw and processed onion

The raw onion contained higher residue levels than boiled onion. Fruit and vegetable processing, such as peeling, boiling, and washing before consumption significantly reduces pesticides residue levels [36, 37]. Both raw and processed onion sample α- and β- endosulfan residues levels were below tolerable limit of EU guidelines for α- and β- endosulfan of bulbs and vegetables.

4 Conclusion

The dissipation rate of endosulfan isomer applied by farmers under sub-humid tropical conditions was investigated during dry and wet season. A shorter half-life was noted in the wet season compared to the dry because of increased humidity and precipitation, which likely increased hydrolysis, microbial degradation and pesticide loss during precipitation from plant surfaces. The α-isomer was less persistent compared to the β-isomer. Fourteen day after application, residue levels of β-isomer on khat were higher compared to the α-isomer in the wet and dry seasons. The residue level in khat 14 day after spraying was compared with onion grown locally under endosulfan application. We observed that the residue levels of the two isomers on khat were higher than the residue on onion. Whereas, the residue for onion was lower than EU endosulfan MRL in bulb fruits at harvest those of khat were well above. Therefore, with the current farmers' pesticide formulation and repetition of spraying, the residue levels in khat are a risk to the consumer. The risk for onion consumption both in raw and boiled form is less but not insignificant.

Acknowledgement. The study was made possible through the support of the Feed the Future Evaluation of the Relationship between Sustainably Intensified Production Systems and Farm Family Nutrition (SIPS-IN) project (AID-OAA-L-14-00006), a cooperative research project implemented through the United States Agency for International Development (USAID) in support of the Feed the Future (FtF) program. The study did not apply pesticides, but monitored the fate of pesticides from farmer application. The research was implemented under a collaborative partnership between the International Water Management Institute and Bahir Dar University. The contents of the paper are the responsibility of the authors and do not necessarily reflect the views of USAID or the United States government.

References

1. Sparks, T.C.: Insecticide discovery: an evaluation and analysis. Pestic. Biochem. Physiol. **107**(1), 8–17 (2013)
2. Mahapatro, G., Panigrahi, M.: The case for banning endosulfan. Curr. Sci. **104**(11), 1476–1479 (2013)
3. Hapeman, C.J., et al.: Endosulfan in the atmosphere of South Florida: transport to Everglades and Biscayne National Parks. Atmos. Environ. **66**, 131–140 (2013)
4. Rajakumar, A., et al.: Endosulfan and flutamide impair testicular development in the juvenile Asian catfish, Clarias batrachus. Aquat. Toxicol. **110**, 123–132 (2012)
5. Mengistie, B.T., Mol, A.P., Oosterveer, P.: Pesticide use practices among smallholder vegetable farmers in Ethiopian Central Rift Valley. Environ. Dev. Sustain. **19**(1), 301–324 (2017). https://doi.org/10.1007/s10668-015-9728-9

6. Mekonen, S., Ambelu, A., Spanoghe, P.: Pesticide residue evaluation in major staple food items of Ethiopia using the QuEChERS method: a case study from the Jimma Zone. Environ. Toxicol. Chem. **33**(6), 1294–1302 (2014)
7. Odenwald, M., et al.: The stimulant khat—another door in the wall? A call for overcoming the barriers. J. Ethnopharmacol. **132**(3), 615–619 (2010)
8. Alsanosy, R.M., Mahfouz, M.S., Gaffar, A.M.: Khat chewing habit among school students of Jazan region, Saudi Arabia. PLoS ONE **8**(6), e65504 (2013)
9. Haile, D., Lakew, Y.: Khat chewing practice and associated factors among adults in Ethiopia: further analysis using the 2011 demographic and health survey. PLoS ONE **10**(6), e0130460 (2015)
10. Dessie, G.: Is Khat a Social Ill? Ethical Argument About a Stimulant Among the Learned Ethiopians. African Studies Centre, Leiden (2013)
11. Gebissa, E.: Khat in the Horn of Africa: historical perspectives and current trends. J. Ethnopharmacol. **132**(3), 607–614 (2010)
12. Daam, M.A., Van den Brink, P.J.: Implications of differences between temperate and tropical freshwater ecosystems for the ecological risk assessment of pesticides. Ecotoxicology **19**(1), 24–37 (2010). https://doi.org/10.1007/s10646-009-0402-6
13. El Sebaï, T., et al.: Diuron mineralisation in a Mediterranean vineyard soil: impact of moisture content and temperature. Pest Manag. Sci. **66**(9), 988–995 (2010)
14. Dores, E.F., et al.: Environmental behavior of chlorpyrifos and endosulfan in a tropical soil in central Brazil. J. Agric. Food Chem. **64**(20), 3942–3948 (2015)
15. Rice, C.P., Nochetto, C.B., Zara, P.: Volatilization of trifluralin, atrazine, metolachlor, chlorpyrifos, α-endosulfan, and β-endosulfan from freshly tilled soil. J. Agric. Food Chem. **50**(14), 4009–4017 (2002)
16. Kathpal, T.S., et al.: Fate of endosulfan in cotton soil under sub-tropical conditions of Northern India. Pestic. Sci. **50**(1), 21–27 (1997)
17. Antonious, G.F., Byers, M.E., Snyder, J.C.: Residues and fate of endosulfan on field-grown pepper and tomato. Pestic. Sci. **54**(1), 61–67 (1998)
18. Ntow, W.J., et al.: Dissipation of endosulfan in field-grown tomato (Lycopersicon esculentum) and cropped soil at Akumadan, Ghana. J. Agric. Food Chem. **55**(26), 10864–10871 (2007)
19. Rosendahl, I., et al.: Insecticide dissipation from soil and plant surfaces in tropical horticulture of southern Benin, West Africa. J. Environ. Monit. **11**(6), 1157–1164 (2009)
20. Takele, S.A.T., Schmitter, P., Atanaw, F.: Evaluation of shallow ground water recharge and irrigation practices at Robit watershed. Department of Hydraulic and Water Resources Engineering, Faculty of Technology, School Of Graduate Studies, Bahir Dar University, Bahir Dar (2019)
21. Getahun, A.: Agricultural systems in Ethiopia. Agric. Syst. **3**(4), 281–293 (1978)
22. Sutherland, T.D., Horne, I., Weir, K.M., Russell, R.J., Oakeshott, J.G.: Toxicity and residues of endosulfan isomers. In: Ware, G.W. (ed.) Reviews of Environmental Contamination and Toxicology. Reviews of Environmental Contamination and Toxicology, vol. 183, pp. 99–113. Springer, New York (2004). https://doi.org/10.1007/978-1-4419-9100-3_4
23. Ciglasch, H., et al.: Insecticide dissipation after repeated field application to a Northern Thailand Ultisol. J. Agric. Food Chem. **54**(22), 8551–8559 (2006)
24. Lehotay, S.: AOAC official method 2007.01 pesticide residues in foods by acetonitrile extraction and partitioning with Magnesium Sulfate. J. AOAC Int. **90**(2), 485–520 (2007)
25. USEPA: Method 508 Determination of Chlorinated Pesticides in Water by Gas Chromatography with an Electron Capture Detector, USEPA, Editor (1995)
26. Currie, L.A.: Nomenclature in evaluation of analytical methods including detection and quantification capabilities (IUPAC Recommendations 1995). Pure Appl. Chem. **67**(10), 1699–1723 (1995)

27. EU, Commission Regulation: European Parliament and of the Council as regards maximum residue levels for aldicarb, bromopropylate, chlorfenvinphos, endosulfan, EPTC, ethion, fenthion, fomesafen, methabenzthiazuron, methidathion, simazine, tetradifon and triforine in or on certain products Text with EEA (2011)

28. Barcelo-Quintal, M.H., et al.: Kinetic studies of endosulfan photochemical degradations by ultraviolet light irradiation in aqueous medium. J. Environ. Sci. Health Part B **43**(2), 120–126 (2008)

29. Edwards, C.: Factors that affect the persistence of pesticides in plants and soils. In: Pesticide Chemistry–3, pp. 39–56. Elsevier (1975)

30. Rüdel, H.: Volatilisation of pesticides from soil and plant surfaces. Chemosphere **35**(1–2), 143–152 (1997)

31. Ghadiri, H.: Degradation of endosulfan in a clay soil from cotton farms of western Queensland. J. Environ. Manag. **62**(2), 155–169 (2001)

32. Guerin, T.F.: The anaerobic degradation of endosulfan by indigenous microorganisms from low-oxygen soils and sediments. Environ. Pollut. **106**(1), 13–21 (1999)

33. Boehncke, A., Siebers, J., Nolting, H.-G.: Investigations of the evaporation of selected pesticides from natural and model surfaces in field and laboratory. Chemosphere **21**(9), 1109–1124 (1990)

34. Jayashree, R., Vasudevan, N.: Persistence and distribution of endosulfan under field condition. Environ. Monit. Assess. **131**(1–3), 475–487 (2007). https://doi.org/10.1007/s10661-006-9493-1

35. Gerald, E., Brust, K.L.E., Marine, S.: Commercial Vegetable Production Recommendations, U.o.M. EXTENSION, Editor (2015)

36. Abou-Arab, A.: Behavior of pesticides in tomatoes during commercial and home preparation. Food Chem. **65**(4), 509–514 (1999)

37. Inonda, R., et al.: Determination of pesticide residues in locally consumed vegetables in Kenya. Afr. J. Pharmacol. Ther. **4**(1), 1–6 (2015)

Assessment of Ergonomics of Farming Activities for Backyard Vegetable Production in the North Western Ethiopia: Case of Dangishta Community

Getnet K. Awoke[1](✉), Seifu A. Tilahun[2], and Manuel R. Rayes[3]

[1] Faculty of Mechanical and Industrial Engineering,
University Bahir Dar, 76, Bhair Dar, Ethiopia
getied1980@gmail.com
[2] Faculty of Civil and Water Resources Engineering,
University Bahir Dar, 76, Bhair Dar, Ethiopia
[3] Sustainable Intensification Innovation Lab, SIIL Coordinator Center of Excellence on
Sustainable Agricultural Intensification and Nutrition in Cambodia, Phnom Penh, Cambodia

Abstract. A problem of improving crop productivity is usually related to poor agronomic practices and scarce water resources but the poor gap in use of appropriate technologies within the farming system has also a role. In order to modify and design ergonomically safe, affordable, efficient and friendly tools that improving the farming system, task analysis is needed which is not done usually in within the agricultural system of Ethiopia. This paper presented analysis of farming tasks for vegetable production using local tools in Ethiopian during dry period garlic production in Dangishita Kebele. The study was performed by interviewing 32 women farmers. In addition, three women farmers were used to do task breakdown, postural ergonomic risk assessment. Farming tasks such as soil preparation, seedling, irrigation and harvesting were complained by farmers for causing pains on different body parts. The most affected body parts during dry period irrigation farming practices were lower back, elbow, shoulder, wrist, neck and knee. Farm task analysis showed that the risk severity from soil preparation and irrigation tasks were serious and needed alternative intervention to reduce the risk. Possible solutions include conservation agriculture, adopting ergonomic tools for soil preparation, and adopting of drip irrigation system. As a result, these will affect the productivity and quality of farm production besides affecting safety and health condition of farmers.

Keywords: Ergonomics · Postural ergonomic risk assessment · Task analysis · Body parts discomfort rate

1 Introduction

As stated by Mekuria (2018), Ethiopia is one of the least developed countries in Sub-Saharan Africa with nearly 100 million people, of which 80.5% of the rural population

N. G. Habtu et al. (Eds.): ICAST 2019, LNICST 308, pp. 29–41, 2020.
https://doi.org/10.1007/978-3-030-43690-2_3

is relied on agriculture for their livelihoods. However, there are still major gaps between farmers' yield and exploitable yield due to limited use of technological packages and inputs. As identified by Birara et al. (2015), population pressure, poor soil fertility, land shortage, high labor wastage, poor farming technologies, pre and post-harvest crop loss, poor social and infrastructural situation and other factors have caused the problem of food insecurity in Ethiopia.

Dagninet et al. (2016) have discussed the current status of Ethiopian farming system which is characterized as low and subsistence production, animals and human powered farm, use of less productive farm tools, high drudgery and work burden, high post-harvest loss, single employment field, low market orientation and less commercialization. According to FAO (2013), the production of food in developing countries is generally very labor intensive particularly in smallholder agriculture. Especially, women are the most affected group in Africa as the average female labor share in crop production during agricultural activities such as land preparation, planting, weeding and harvesting reaches to 40% in Sub-Saharan African countries (Palacios-lopez et al. 2017). The technological interventions in agriculture has not made much progress at all so that the problem of the agricultural activities being labor intensive is inevitable (FAO 2013). Many sub-Saharan African countries including Ethiopia are therefore looking for the application of scientific and technical methods of farming that can be adapted to their conditions.

From the literatures it was evidenced that the current statutes of technology adoption and utilization within Ethiopian farming system is much less and limited as compared to the developed countries. Mekuria (2018) suggested that the crops productivity levels of Ethiopian farming system can be increased significantly by improving the traditional farming practices and adoption of technologies. Similarly, FAO (2013) revealed in its report that there exist a large potential for improvement in agricultural productivity within Sub African countries including Ethiopia. Palacios-lopez et al. (2017) viewed that introduction of medium or low level mechanization implements and technologies enables lighten burden of women who contribute most of the labor for agricultural production in Ethiopia.

Therefore, it is highly recommended that Ethiopia need to adopt, modify and use appropriate scaled technologies or mechanized methods for improving labor productivity as well as human drudgery besides guarantying food security. Having recognized that introducing modern farming technologies for increasing productivity and solving food security problem, ergonomic evaluation is essential for its successful modification, effective application and efficient utilization by farmers. Ergonomics contributes to design and evaluation of farming tasks and farm tools in order to make them compatible with the needs, abilities and limitations of farm works.

Many researchers have attempt to show in their study how agricultural tasks can expose to ergonomic hazards and reduce productivity of farmers due lack of consideration of ergonomics in agriculture. For instance, Bernard et al. (1993) and Murphy (1992) explained that agricultural work involves risk factors associated with musculoskeletal disorders because field jobs (harvesting, weeding, irrigating, cultural practices, etc.) remain demanding physical tasks, involving stooped postures, lifting and carrying, and repetitive hand work. Meyers et al. (1998) mentioned three general risk factors as both endemic and of highest priority throughout the agricultural industry. They are: lifting and carrying heavy loads, sustained or repeated full body bending (stoop) and very highly repetitive hand work (clipping, cutting). According to world health organization (1980) most musculoskeletal problem occurs in agriculture working cases due to excessive physical effort on the body, awkward postures, prolonged standing and kneeling, stooping, bending, and repetitive muscle activities. Chavalitsakulchai and Shahnavaz (1990), and Praveena et al. (2005) pointed out that women are the backbone of agricultural who does the most tedious and back-breaking tasks in agriculture but the problems of labor and hardship faced by women are less addressed in Africa.

According to Stanton et al. (2006), ergonomic task analysis procedure should consist five phases: recognition, video recording, subtasks separation, video analysis, and frame classification. Chander and Cavatorta (2017) explained that methods such as Ovako Working Posture Analysis System – OWAS, Rapid Upper Limb Assessment- RULA, Strain Index (SI), Rapid Entire Body Assessment – REBA, Quick Exposure Check – QEC and postural ergonomic risk assessment (PERA can be used to evaluate the degree of discomfort and overload of the musculoskeletal system caused by various postures of the human body during the work. André and et al. (2017) commented that postural ergonomic risk assessment (PERA) is better since the criteria developed for classification of demands of posture, duration and force clear and easy for applying.

Thus, the aim of this paper is to present research report done on ergonomic analysis using the approach of postural ergonomic risk assessment of agricultural tasks during dry home garden garlic production in Ethiopia, Amhara Region at Dangishita Kebele. Particularly, the result of such analysis is worth enough to help government of Ethiopia during making decision regarding to prioritization of introducing and adopting of agricultural technologies or mechanized methods for reducing human drudgery or ergonomic risk factors along with ensuring food security of the nation by improving agricultural productivity.

2 Methodology

The farming activities for garlic production in Dangishta community, West Gojam, Amhara regional state of Ethiopia have been analyzed starting from October 2017 till April 2018 for three consecutive months. The targets were women who were organized by the innovational lab for sustainable intensification project to produce garlic in their home garden using hand dug shallow ground water wells (Fig. 1).

The study was basically performed by using field survey through structured interview and video recording technique. Thirty-two women farmers having an age between 24–55 years were interviewed using a modified Nordic musculoskeletal disorder questionnaire for assessing body parts discomfort or pain feeling during farming tasks and identifying tasks that were most complained by farmers.

The study used three selected women farmers for intensive video recordings while they were in real situation of performing their farming tasks to break down in to key activities. The video used in this data collection was Fujifilm X100F Digital Camera – Silver. Moreover, videotaping of farming tasks is necessitated for understanding the working posture, physical force exertion or nature of motions and task time. Estimated average time for each key activities of farming tasks and total task time taken were

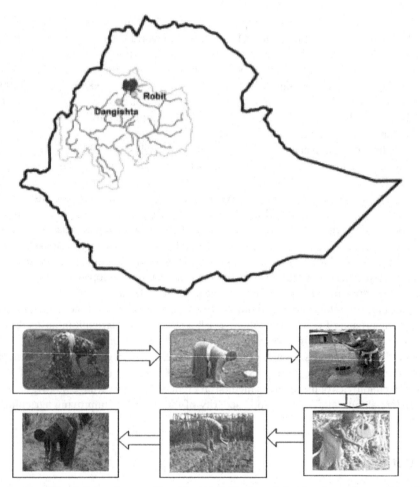

Fig. 1. Location of the study area Dangishta in Ethiopia and the farming tasks considered in the study (soil preparation, seed planting, ground water lifting, manual irrigation, weeding and harvesting)

obtained from slow motion playing of recorded videos during performing the tasks. Here, 10 trials for each estimation were considered.

Ergonomic risk level estimation for farming tasks were conducted by using postural ergonomic risk assessment (PERA) method. The risk scores for each activity were estimated based on the risks level classification criterion for activity duration developed by Chander and Cavatorta (2017) and supported with postural ergonomic risk assessment (PERA) method. According to PERA method overall ergonomic risk score for work task was obtained as the product of risk of physical effort, risk of task duration (time percentage) and risk of working posture. The risk from exertion of physical effort was estimated by observing the nature of the workers' motions. Positions of workers' trunk, hand, neck and shoulder were considered to estimate the ergonomic risk level due to working postures. The risks level related to duration was judged by considering the time percentage of total time taken for task.

3 Results and Discussion

It was observed that women were accomplishing all agricultural tasks beginning from soil preparation up to transporting the farm yield to home and market place. The women workers attained various working postures, exert forces and work continuously until they accomplished the agricultural tasks.

3.1 Body Parts Discomfort Feeling Assessment

Body discomfort assessment during five months based on women farmers' response rate was considered in Table 1. It was reported that highest number (100%) of the respondents perceived discomfort or pain to lower back of their body part and least number (38%) of respondents perceived pain related to hip body parts.

Table 1. Body parts discomfort assessment during farming tasks

Sr. No.	Body parts affected	No. of women's responses	% of women's responses
1	Neck	26	81%
2	Shoulder	26	81%
3	Elbow	30	94%
4	Wrist/hands	26	81%
5	Upper back	14	44%
6	Lower back	32	100%
7	Hips	12	38%
8	Knees	24	75%
9	Ankles/feet	18	56%

Using women farmers' response rate, pareto analysis for identifying body parts of farmers that were most affected during farming activities was conducted. The result showed that almost 80% of the body discomfort or pain was caused due to stress on lower back, elbow, shoulder, hand, neck and knee are most affected body parts respectively (Fig. 2).

It was also reported that women farmers complained about the various agricultural activities they performed and the possible pains or body parts discomforts associated with the tasks. Accordingly, 47% of respondents told that they experienced lower back pain or discomfort during soil preparation task, while 41% of respondents feel lower back pain or discomfort associated with seedling task. Nearly 47% of women farmers complained shoulder pain or discomfort during irrigation of the farm area. 34%

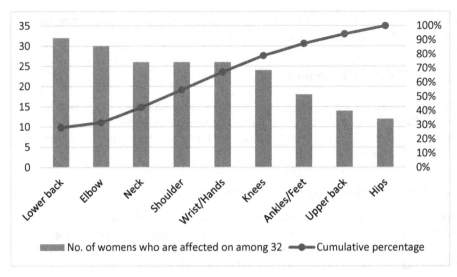

Fig. 2. Body discomfort assessment during farming activity

of respondents experienced Wrist/hands pain or body parts discomfort associated with weeding activities. Another 22% of respondents informed that they complained harvesting and post harvesting tasks for causing neck, wrist/hands and lower back pain or body parts discomfort feeling.

Based on women farmers' response rate, body parts discomfort rate was assessed and prioritized during each farming activities. Thus, as shown in Fig. 3 it was found that farming tasks of soil preparation, overhead irrigation and weeding tasks have more ergonomic hazard.

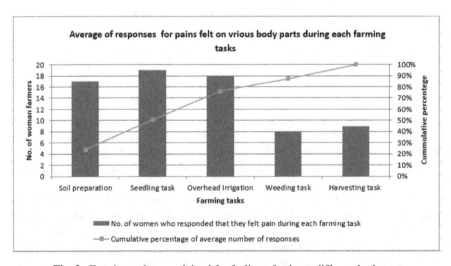

Fig. 3. Farming tasks complained for feeling of pain on different body part

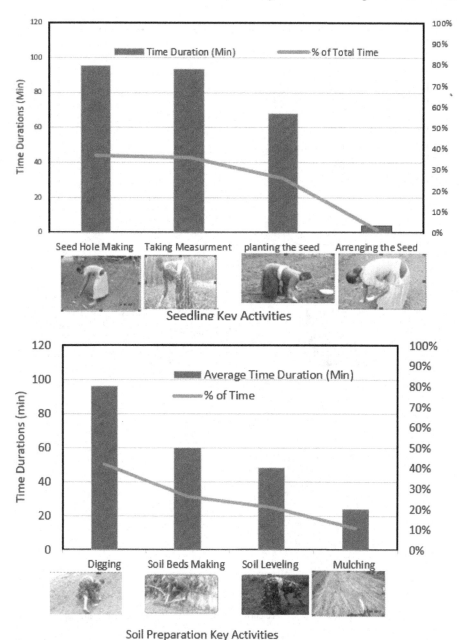

Fig. 4. Time percentage and risk estimation for soil preparation, seedling, weeding, and irrigation tasks

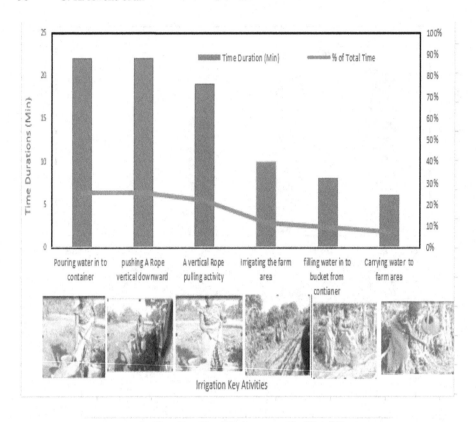

Irrigation Key Ativities

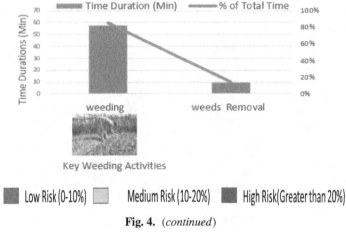

Key Weeding Activities

■ Low Risk (0-10%)   ▢ Medium Risk (10-20%)   ■ High Risk(Greater than 20%)

Fig. 4. (*continued*)

3.2 Ergonomic Analysis of Working Postures, Physical Effort and Time Percentage of Farming Tasks Using Videotapes

Ergonomic analysis of task considers time duration, working posture and required physical effort. Thus, in this study the ergonomic risk levels associated with dry season home garden vegetable production process caused by these factors have been estimated using the analysis of recorded videotape of farming tasks.

Figure 4 shows the time duration, time percentages of activities and the ergonomic risk level of each farming activities from task repetitiveness point of view. The risk classification levels and their time percentages are shown below Fig. 4 as keys of the chart.

The results obtained from ergonomic analysis of working posture of women farmers, body parts such as elbow, head, neck and lower back were severe and painful work posture during performing their farming tasks as compared the standards for women work position. The farming tasks which were considered in the analysis of the work posture position included digging & soil leveling, shoveling, seedling, overhead irrigating, weeding and harvesting activities. However, the reaching work position that women farmers use during performing all farming tasks is optimal.

Recorded Videotapes of tasks were allowed to play slowly and analysis were made to identify and understand nature of activity motions. Therefore, activities motion was characterized subjectively as not visible, visible and clearly visible. The result showed that activities like digging, shoveling, water lifting, transporting, filing the bucket and irrigating demanded high physical effort and led to high ergonomic risks (Table 2).

Table 2. Ergonomic analysis of physical effort required for agricultural tasks

Tasks	Nature of the motion during performing the activity				
Soil preparation	Detail activities	Not visible	Visible	Clearly visible	Risk level
	Digging	–	–	***	High
	Moving shoveling	–	–	***	High
	Leveling	–	**	–	Medium
	Mulching	*	–	–	Low
Seedling	Measure	*	–	–	Low
	Arrange seed	*	–	–	Low
	Scratching the farm for seed hole	*	–	–	Low
	Inserting the seed	–	**	–	Medium
Irrigation	Vertical rope pulling	–	–	***	High
	Pouring water in to container	–	–	***	High
	Vertical rope pushing	–	**	–	Medium
	Water carrying to farm area	–	–	***	High

(*continued*)

Table 2. (*continued*)

Tasks	Nature of the motion during performing the activity				
	Filling water in to bucket	–	–	***	High
	Irrigating the farm	–	–	***	High
Weeding	Weeding	–	**	–	Medium
	Weeding removal	*	–	–	Low
Harvesting	Loosening the soil	*	–	–	low
	Pull garlic bulb from the soil	–	**	–	Medium
	Brushing the soil	*	–	–	Low

Note:
1. (*) Low risk level: - not visible or manipulation of light objects
2. (**) medium risk level: - visible or smooth and controlled motions; use of both hands when the task does not seem very heavy
3. (***) high risk level: - clearly visible, low control over motion, bulging muscles, facial expression, gestures, and vibration from powered hand tools

3.3   Overall Risk Level Estimation for Tasks of Home Garden Garlic Farming

Based on the risk score analysis, all farming tasks are potential to cause body part discomfort or pain. However, the severity level of the risk associated with farming activities in soil preparation and irrigation tasks were most important which demands serious measurements to be taken rapidly. One reason for the risks during performing these farming practices is due to absence of farming technologies or equipment that can support farmers to dig, seed, irrigate and harvest (Fig. 5 and Table 3).

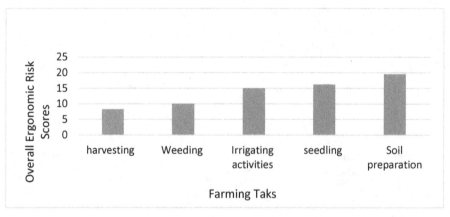

Fig. 5. Overall risk scores calculated using postural ergonomic risk assessment method

Table 3. Overall risk level estimation for each farming tasks

Task	Key activities	Force score (F)	Posture score (P)	Duration score (D)	Activity score	Overall risk score
Soil preparation	Digging	H(3)	H(3)	H(3)	27	(27 + 27 + 18 + 6)/4 = 16.25
	Shoveling	H(3)	M(2)	H(3)	18	
	Leveling	M(2)	H (3)	H(3)	18	
	Mulching	L(1)	M(2)	L(1)	2	
Seedling	Measuring	L(1)	H(3)	H(3)	9	(9 + 6+9 + 9)/4 = 8.25
	Arranging the seed	L(1)	H(3)	M(2)	6	
	Seed hole making	L(1)	H(3)	H(3)	9	
	Inserting the seed	L(1)	H(3)	H(3)	9	
Irrigation	Vertical rope pulling	H(3)	H(3)	H(3)	27	(27 + 27 + 27 + 9+27 + 18)/6 = 19.5
	Powering water in to container	H(3)	H(3)	H(3)	27	
	Vertical rope pushing	H(3)	H(3)	H(3)	27	
	Carrying water to farm area	H(3)	H(3)	L(1)	9	
	Filling water in to bucket	H(3)	H(3)	H(3)	27	
	Irrigating	H(3)	H(3)	M(2)	18	
Weeding	Weeding	M(2)	H(3)	H(3)	18	(18 + 2)/2 = 10
	Weeds removing	L(1)	L (1)	M(2)	2	
Harvesting	Loosening the soil	L(1)	L(1)	H(3)	9	(9 + 12 + 9)/3 = 15
	Pulling up garlic bulb	M(2)	H(3)	M(2)	12	
	Brushing the soil	L(1)	H(3)	L(1)	9	

4 Conclusion

Production of vegetable such as garlic at home garden during dry period included various agricultural tasks such as preparing the land or soil, seedling or planting of the seed, periodical irrigating of the farm, weeding activities, harvesting activities and transporting the farm yields to home and then market. Based on the survey of women farmers, lower back, elbow, shoulder, wrist or hand, neck and knee are most affected body parts of the women during the dry period vegetable production. The case showed that highest number (100%) of the respondents informed they perceived discomfort or pain at the lower back of their body part and minimum number (38%) of respondents informed they perceived pain at their hips. From the study of ergonomic analysis, we concluded that the severity level of the risk associated with farming activities were sever in soil preparation and irrigation tasks. The possible intervention to reduce these sever risk are adoption of conservation agriculture i.e., no till, mulching and crop rotation, adopting and use of ergonomic tools and equipment that can support soil preparation, adopt and use of water lifting technologies with drip irrigation system and redesigning of farming hand tools.

Acknowledgment. This research is made possible by the generous support of the American people through support by the United States Agency for International Development (USAID) Feed the Future Innovation Lab for Collaborative Research on Sustainable Intensification (Cooperative Agreement No. AID-OAA-L-14-00006, Kansas State University) through Texas A&M University's Sustainably Intensified Production Systems and Nutritional Outcomes, and University of Illinois Urbana-Champaign's Appropriate Scale Mechanization Consortium projects. The contents are the sole responsibility of the authors and do not necessarily reflect the views of USAID.

References

U.S. Department of Labor Occupational Safety and Health Administration: Ergonomics: the study of work, OSHA 3125 revised (2000)

Divyaksh, S., Maria, P.: An observational method for postural ergonomic risk assessment (PERA). Int. J. Ergon. **57**, 32–41 (2017)

Kai, W.: Ergonomic design and evaluation of wire-tying hand tools. Int. J. Ind. Ergon. **30**, 149–161 (2002)

Putz, A.: Cumulative Trauma Disorders: A Manual for Musculoskeletal Diseases of the Upper Limbs. Taylor & Francis, London (1988)

Karla, G., Juan, L., Gabriel, I.: A proposed methodology for task analysis in ergonomic evaluations. Procedia Manuf. **3**, 4756–4760 (2015). 6th International Conference on Applied Human Factors and Ergonomics (AHFE 2015) and the Affiliated Conferences, AHFE 2015

Lane, R., Stanton, A., Harrison, D.: Applying hierarchical task analysis to medication administration errors. Appl. Ergon. **37**, 669–769 (2006)

Robertoes, K., Wibowoa, P.: Farmers' Injuries, discomfort and its use in design of agricultural hand tools: a case study from East Java. Indonesia. Agric. Agric. Sci. Procedia **9**, 323–327 (2016). International Conference on Food, Agriculture and Natural Resources, IC-FANRes 2015. Elsevier B.V

Tahseen, J., David, H.: The application of ergonomics in rural development: a review. Appl. Ergon. **31**(3), 263–268 (2000)

Holmer, I., Takala, J., Chavalitnitikul, C.: Implementation of ergonomics in Thailand. In: Ergonomics in Developing Countries. An International Symposium. International Labor Organization (ILO), Occupational Health and Safety Series, ILO, Geneva, no. 58, p. 502 (1985)

Barenklau, K.: Agricultural Safety. CRC Press, Boca Raton (2001)

André, L., Gilberto, J., Airton, D., Aimê, R.: Ergonomics applied to aquaculture: a case study of postural risk analysis in the manual harvesting of cultivated mussels. Aquac. Eng. **77**, 112–124 (2017)

Steven, M., Arun, G.: The strain index: a proposed method to analyze jobs for risk of distal upper extremity disorders. Am. Ind. Hyg. Assoc. J. **56**, 443–458 (1995)

Liu, C., Zhang, X., Zhang, Y.: Determination of daily evaporation and evapotranspiration of winter wheat and maize by large-scale weighing lysimeter and microlysimeter. Agric. Forest Meteorol. **111**, 109–120 (2002)

Monks, D., Monks, D., Basden, T., Selders, A., Poland, S., Rayburn, E.: Soil temperature, soil moisture, weed control, and tomato (Lycopersicon esculentum) response to mulching. Weed Technol. **11**, 561–566 (1997)

Surabhi, S., Renu, A.: Ergonomic intervention for preventing musculoskeletal disorders among farm women. J. Agric. Sci. **1**, 61–71 (2017)

Hassan, S., Karmegam, K., Shamsul, B., Koustuv, D.: Ergonomics in agriculture: an approach in prevention of work-related musculoskeletal disorders (WMSDs). J. Agric. Environ. Sci. **2**(3), 33–51 (2014)

Villarejo, D., Baron, S.: The occupational health status of hired farm workers. Occup. Med. State Art Rev. **114**(3), 613–635 (1999)

Praveena, P., Achuta, R., Venkata, R.: Decision making pattern of rural women in farm related activities. Agric. Extn. Rev. **3**, 3–7 (2005)

Meyers, J., et al.: Ergonomics risk factors for musculoskeletal disorder in wine grape vineyard work. Paper presented at the National Institute for Farm Safety, Winnepeg, Canada (1998)

Engberg, L.: Women and agricultural work. Occup. Med. **8**, 869–883 (1993)

Falkel, J., Sawka, N., Levine, L., Pimental, N., Pandolf, K.: Upper-body exercise performance: comparison between women and men. Ergonomics **29**, 145–154 (1986)

Mackay, D., Bishop, C.: Occupational health of women at work: Some human factors considerations. Ergonomics **27**, 489–498 (1984)

FAO: Agricultural Mechanization in Sub-Saharan Africa Guidelines for preparing a strategy, vol. 22. Rome (2013)

Mekuria, W.: The link between agricultural production and population dynamics in Ethiopia: a review. Adv. Plants Agric. Res. **8**(2), 348–353 (2018). https://doi.org/10.15406/apar.2018.08. 00336

Palacios-lopez, A., Christiaensen, L., Kilic, T.: How much of the labor in African agriculture is provided by women? Food Policy **67**, 52–63 (2017). https://doi.org/10.1016/j.foodpol.2016. 09.017

Endalew, B., Muche, M., Tadesse, S.: Assessment of food security situation in Ethiopia: a review. Asian J. Agric. Res. **9**, 55–68 (2015)

Amare, D., Endalew, W.: Agricultural mechanization: assessment of mechanization impact experiences on the rural population and the implications for Ethiopian smallholders. Eng. Appl. Sci. **1**(2), 39–48 (2016). https://doi.org/10.11648/j.eas.20160102.15

An Integrated Approach to Solve Small Farm Holder's Mechanization Barriers in Ethiopia

Dessie Tarekegn Bantelay[1]($\boxtimes$), Tsehaye Dedimas[1], and Nigist Kelemu[2]

[1] Faculty of Mechanical and Industrial Engineering, Bahir Dar Institute of Technology, Bahir Dar University, 26, Bahir Dar, Ethiopia
dessie2000ec@gmail.com, tsehayezechu@gmail.com
[2] Department of Marketing Management, College of Business and Economics, Bahir Dar University, 26, Bahir Dar, Ethiopia
nigistkelemu92@gmail.com

Abstract. Ethiopia has a long history of agricultural practices. But the deployment of agricultural mechanization is still minimal. Farm power is largely dependent on human muscle and oxen driven traditional farm techniques. Even though the effort and interest of agricultural mechanization grew from time to time yet it is not effective due to poor deployment strategy. The main objective of this study was to review and assess the effectiveness of the existing agro-machinery manufacturing, distribution and use in Amhara region of Ethiopia; identify the barriers of agro-machinery deployment actions and design an effective deployment model. The study carried out through collecting and analysis of secondary data related to past attempts followed by. Then primary data gathered and analyzed from the target audience using survey questionnaire, focused group discussion and interview. The study result reveals that poor agricultural mechanization in the region basically associated with inadequate infrastructure, lack of financing institute, fragmented lands, working culture and related ones. In addition there is no clear, adequate and comprehensive agricultural mechanization deployment model. The level of these problems were analyzed quantitatively. Then agricultural mechanization deployment model has been designed. The model offers particular responsibilities for each deployment tasks and protect overlap of responsibilities, remove task redundancy and trace out failure easily.

Keywords: Agricultural mechanization · Mechanization barriers · Mechanization deployment model

1 Introduction

The agricultural sector in Ethiopia provides employment to 85% of the population (of which women constitute 49.5% according to the 2007 census data), contributes 44% to the country's Gross domestic product (GDP) and 85% of the country's export earnings [1]. Agricultural mechanization implies the use of various power sources and improved farm tools and equipment, with a view to reduce the drudgery of the human beings and

© ICST Institute for Computer Sciences, Social Informatics and Telecommunications Engineering 2020
Published by Springer Nature Switzerland AG 2020. All Rights Reserved
N. G. Habtu et al. (Eds.): ICAST 2019, LNICST 308, pp. 42–58, 2020.
https://doi.org/10.1007/978-3-030-43690-2_4

draught animals, enhance the cropping intensity, precision and timelines of efficiency of utilization of various crop inputs and reduce the losses at different stages of crop production. The end objective of farm mechanization is to enhance the overall productivity and production with the lowest cost of production. In many developing countries up to 80% of farm power is provided by human beings [2]. In most developed countries human beings are used less and less as a source of power and more for machine operation and control. The level, appropriate choice and subsequent proper use of mechanized inputs into agriculture has a direct and significant effect on achievable levels of land productivity, labor productivity, the profitability of farming, the environment and, last but not least, on the quality of life of people engaged in agriculture [3]. In developing countries human power and animal power used as farm power for small farm holder agricultural activities. In this countries it is extremely difficult to access mechanized farm tools [4].

Although there is a clear trend for animals to be replaced by engine power, this will take long time to achieve, even in rapidly developing countries such as India and China [5]. In some developing country animal power contribution declined practically from time to time. In these country the contribution of animal driven power is not more than 25% in small farm holders in today's agriculture activities. On the other hand similar to other sub-Saharan Africa countries, animal power and human muscles are still a central source of farm power in Ethiopia. Animal power contribute up to 25% and human power accounts 65% of farm power still now. As a result the contribution of mechanized tools is not beyond 10%. This hinder land and labor productivity in the region. Even though the African Union has proclaimed that the hand-hoe should be "consigned to the museum" by 2035, the current trend doesn't show significant improvements [7]. A study conducted in Kenya and Ethiopia revealed that, women usually contribute up to 80% of the labor needed for food preparation in sub-Saharan Africa [8].

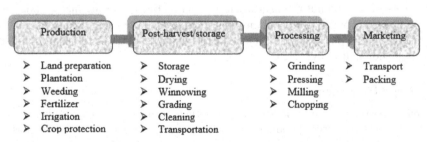

Fig. 1. The potential contribution of mechanization in agriculture sector. (Source: Breuer et al. 2015)

Similar to indoor activities they are extremely engaged in farm activities starting from land preparation to postharvest activities [4]. This implies that unless mechanization implements address properly in the region it is difficult to reduce the work burden and improve the life of women. Agricultural machineries has a key role to improve labor productivities as shown in Fig. 1.

Inadequacy of farm power and machinery with the farmers continue as one of the major constraint for increasing agricultural productivity [9]. Ethiopian economy largely depend on agriculture. The overall economic growth in the country depends on the performance of the sector. The government with development allies put great effort to improve the productivity of the sector. However, small farm holder agricultural mechanization hasn't got equal attention to other yield improving inputs like improved seeds and fertilizers [10]. In the past, ambitious politically motivated and fragmented mechanization schemes and misunderstood concepts and inappropriate selection and use of certain mechanization inputs have led to heavy financial losses, limit agricultural productivity and create negative interest on mechanization in the farming community rather than being a productive input [11]. Therefore, it is important to review and assess the current detached practice made by different stalk holders, identify and quantify the barriers then design an effective deployment model specific to the selected agro-climatic zone.

2 Research Methodology

2.1 Research Approach

Team of experts comprises of industrial engineering have experience in technology transfer, manufacturing engineering have experience in agro-mechanization and marketing management have experience on marketing strategy in collaboration with crop science and agriculture extension experts conducted the study. The study carried out through collecting and analysis of the necessary secondary data related to past attempts in transferring agro-equipments, followed by preliminary discussion with stock holders to guide and strength the primary data collection and analysis.

2.2 Research Design

The purpose of this survey is to identifying potential entrepreneurs and promoting the technology of agricultural mechanization in Amhara Region. In the mean while this study followed a positivism paradigm with a survey type research design. A survey scheme provides a quantitative or numeric explanation of attitudes, trends or opinions of a population in the target area.

2.3 Target Population

The purpose of this survey is focused at promoting mechanized agriculture in selected woredas. Therefore target population of this project were five potential woredas in Amhara region including selected by base line survey; Bahir Dar Zuria, Merawi, Dangila, Bure and Jabi-Tehnan as shown in Fig. 2.

2.4 Sampling Design and Sample Size Determination

This research is a purposive research conducted to examine the level and barriers of mechanization practice in selected areas by base line study. As a result this study follow a purposive/judgmental sampling to determine the sample size of the research. Researchers prefer this sample design to include all potential stalk holders (enterprises, government's technology transfer offices, agriculture extension workers, farmer cooperatives and unions, non-governmental organizations (NGOs) and financial institutes) in the study areas as respondents.

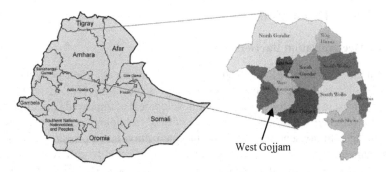

Fig. 2. Study area (Ethiopia; Amhara region, west Gojjam)

2.5 Data Sources and Data Collection Instruments

The researchers gathered both secondary and primary data regarding agro-mechanization practice. Initially secondary data were gathered from current records of enterprises, government's technology transfer offices, agriculture extension workers, farmer cooperatives and unions, NGOS & financial institutes. These documents reviewed in office were mainly strategic plans, reports, manuals and regulations. Then primary data collected from stock holders, enterprises, technology transfer experts, agriculture extension workers, cooperative unions and financial institutes using survey questionnaire focused group discussion and interview. Researchers also conduct interview for the key informants from Amhara national regional state (ANRS) agriculture and technical and vocational education and training (TVET) bureau representatives, NGO representatives, enterprises owners, technology transfer experts, agriculture extension workers, cooperative unions and financial institute's representatives. Focused group discussions were conducted for managers and leaders of the union/entrepreneurs collect qualitative data.

2.6 Reliability and Validity Test

The study conducted a pilot study across five unions to pre-test the questionnaire prior to the main data collection exercise with a view to check for errors and test the tools for reliability. Cronbach alpha via SPSS software, which is a measure of internal consistency, used to test the internal reliability of the tools.

2.7 Data Analysis

In this study a mixed approach used. Both quantitative and qualitative data analysis techniques were employed. Linear regression analysis used to measure the relationship between the dependent variables (mechanization) and independent variables (mechanization barriers).

3 Result and Discussion

3.1 Agro-Mechanization Barriers

In Ethiopia the "agricultural led industrialization development" framework encourages deployment of agriculture mechanization in large scale farms [12]. Even though it promises to invest in the sector and encourage development of improved farm implements and help to strengthen the production capacity of rural technology centers in implement manufacturing, still household agricultural mechanization is not properly addressed in policy documents. Small farm holder mechanization affected by different constraints. Identifying constraints and addressing policy issue is mandatory. In Ethiopia, most of the cultivated lads owned by small farm holders. As a result it is important to give proper attention for small farm holders than large scale mechanization.

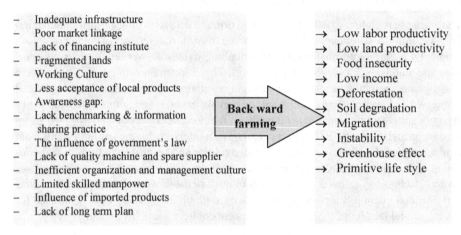

Fig. 3. Root cause analysis of back ward farming practice in Ethiopia, west Gojjam

A survey was conducted to identify the basic constraints which hinder agriculture mechanization in the region. In this study all technical, economical social data relating mechanization influencing factors were studied by collecting data from manufacturer, facilitators and users as shown in Fig. 3. The survey result in Table 1 shows the basic factors influencing transfer farm equipment in stallholder farms (typically less than 2 ha). Some of the potential challenges are discussed below.

1. **Inadequate Infrastructure:** According to the survey result 72% of the respondent believe that infrastructure including electricity, road and water have significant impact on farm mechanization. The availability of infrastructure facilities and services as well as the efficiency of such services to a large extent determine the success of all other production endeavors. Investments in infrastructures such as energy, water, transportation and communication technologies promote economic growth and help to alleviate poverty and improve living conditions in the country [13]. Similar research's shows that productivity increase in agriculture, which is an

Table 1. Analysis of agricultural mechanization barriers data collected from manufacturer, facilitators and users. (Source: survey on March 2018)

SN	Independent variable (mechanization barriers)	Percentage share					Influence 100%
		Strongly disagree	Disagree	Not decided	Agree	Strongly agree	
1	Inadequate infrastructure	0.00	1.23	6.67	24.00	68.10	**92.10**
2	Poor market linkage	0.00	2.57	6.33	23.50	67.60	**91.10**
3	Lack of financing institute	0.80	4.43	5.67	22.50	66.60	**89.10**
4	Fragmented lands	1.30	5.27	5.33	22.00	66.10	**88.10**
5	Working culture	1.80	6.10	5.00	21.50	65.60	**87.10**
6	Less acceptance of local products	2.80	7.77	4.33	20.50	64.60	**85.10**
7	Awareness gap on farm equipments	3.30	8.60	4.00	20.00	64.10	**84.10**
8	Lack benchmarking & information sharing practice	4.30	10.27	3.33	19.00	63.10	**82.10**
9	Influence of government's law, policy, rules & regulations	7.10	7.67	4.13	41.70	39.40	**81.10**
10	Lack of quality machinery and spare suppliers	7.10	7.67	4.13	41.70	39.40	**81.10**
11	Inefficient organization and management culture	7.60	7.33	4.97	41.20	38.90	**80.10**
12	Limited skilled manpower	8.10	7.00	5.80	40.70	38.40	**79.10**
13	Influence of imported products	8.60	6.67	6.63	40.20	37.90	**78.10**
14	Lack of long term plan	8.60	6.67	6.63	40.20	37.90	**78.10**

effective driver of economic growth and poverty reduction, depends on good rural infrastructure and access to appropriate technology [14].

2. **Poor Market Linkage:** Similar to other developing countries, the majority of the rural households engaged in smallholder agriculture characterized by low productivity, low information sharing mechanism, and limited market linkage. Many of these small farm holder farmers sold their product in the village markets where there is no potential consumers. Due to this most of them sold through intermediaries, due to the small scale of their production, the high transaction costs involved in reaching more distant markets, and their inability to comply with the stringent requirements relating to volume, quality, and timely delivery demanded by modern agricultural value chains. As a result the farmers are not properly from their products. They are benefiting intermediaries involved in the sector.

3. **Lack of Financing Institute:** Majority of the farmers are not capable to buy their own farm machinery. It is difficulty to possess their own machinery either individually or in group. On the other hand few rich farmers having own agricultural machines such as; maize thrasher, tractors and surface water pumps benefited from rental service in addition to their own agricultural productivity improvement. They use their machines in their own lands principally in the farming season and also operate them on hiring basis in others' lands after they complete their own farm activity and earn a substantial return. But, the number of such farmers is very limited. Till now there is no well-organized financing institutes in the community who can offer low interest farm machinery lease financing. Unless this issue addressed soon the problem well continue as it is.

4. **Fragmented Lands:** In Ethiopia, the average farm holding land size ranges from 0.25 ha–2 ha. In addition the total holding of land is not located in one place, rather, it is found in different places. This limits farm machines to perform at optimal efficiency. Even mini tractors, maize thrasher and surface water pumps face serious problems from frequent turnings in such fragmented lands. Even though there are few areas rental service offer in few farm machinery, it has been observed that many farmers cultivate their own land by traditional method.

5. **Working Culture:** Similar to farm machinery rental services barriers exist in other developing countries, there are various limiting factors in Ethiopia. Out of these inadequate infrastructure, poor market linkage, lack of financing institute, fragmented lands, low acceptance of local products, awareness gap, lack of quality machine and spare supplier are common ones [15]. But in the study area we have observed that there are cultural and spiritual norms which restrict the number of working days. They can't work consecutive days. One working day may be followed by a number of off-days. This reduce equipments utilization and increase depreciation cost. This makes the hire services infeasible in the region. Similar studies proved the existence of cultural barriers on using improved farm machineries and tools [16].

6. **Less Acceptance of Local Products:** Due to objective less deployment practice a lot of machinery have been produced and distributed to the community were not meet their objective. Proper attention was not given to farm mechanization until this day. Only a few manufacturers trying to fabricate simple manually operated and semi-automated farm machineries. To satisfy the ever growing population and subsequent food need, Ethiopia agriculture will have to improve its productivity through adopting modern mechanized implements. This includes promoting agricultural manufacturing workshops in the country.

Today, there are a lot of small and medium sized local metal workshops trying to manufacture agricultural machinery throughout the region as shown in Fig. 4. Many of them are manufacturing under standard machinery creating negative interest among the farmers. These small workshop owners, in general, do not have enough technical skill, use jigs and fixtures to produce any type of machineries. They get the prototype from the market and duplicate them without understanding their design and manufacturing requirements. While trying to copying these machines, they do not use exact quality materials and specifications as a result they are producing low quality machines. Due to this and similar factors locally produced machinery perceived as low quality and high in price [17].

Fig. 4. Sample maize thresher manufactured locally at higher cost than imported ones having low productivity and heavy to transport. (Source: survey result)

7. **Awareness Gap:** Similar to other developing countries in African small holder farmers have a huge traditional knowledge derived from experience over generations. But they have relatively limited access to new skill and knowledge. Farmers lack the knowledge and skills to select, operate and fix minor failures as a result misuse and mismanagement of farm machinery observed as a common challenge. Even though there is attempts through farmers trading center, it has been observed that the level of farmer training is relatively low and opportunities for further training are limited. In addition farmers trading center do not easily reach rural and remote communities. Since there is huge awareness gap on far tools the demand for related training is low. As a result it is not economical for private sectors. This enforce the government to take the burden to minimize awareness gap and work day and night. If not its influence agricultural productivity will continue [18].

8. **Lack Benchmarking & Information Sharing Practice:** Even though there are a lot of farmers training centers in the area built to for information and experience sharing goal they are not working effectively. As a result farmers restricted from benchmarking best method and technology.

9. **The Influence of Government's Law:** The whole stalk holders participating on farm machinery manufacturing, importing, distribution, retailing and rental services, faces organization and management constraints that prohibit its development. Most management constraints are common to private sector arise from Government's law, policy, rules and regulations. These includes lack of incentive mechanism, beurocratic licensing procedure, lack of enabling laws to facilitate business start-ups and enterprise operations, punitive import regulations. Private sector agricultural machinery manufacturing and distribution is at a premature stage in the country. It is vulnerable by international competition and imports, and held back by less developed distribution networks. Markets for mechanization rental services are also in their early stage.

10. **Lack of Quality Machine and Spare Supplier:** Farm equipments such as two wheel tractor, weedier, thresher and water pump introduced to the community by donors, government and private owner. Unfortunately, most of these equipments fail to produce the desired results as shown in Fig. 5. Even though there are a few factors attributed for these failure, lack of compatibility between equipments manufactured in donor countries and spare parts available in the market. Once the first breakdowns occur, the machines cannot be repaired and machinery garbage exist. Further, the high price of spare parts has discourage the imports to supply spare parts in the local market.

Fig. 5. Machinery "graveyards" due to quality inferiority and spare limitation. (Source: survey result)

11. **Inefficient Organization and Management Culture:** It refers to systemic application of scientific knowledge on planning, organizing, staffing and directing of resource to achieve the predefined goal of the firm. It is the core activity for any organization achievement. So proper organization structure staffed by the right professional and managed in the right way can achieve its objective with in short time and limited resource [19] (Fig. 6).

Fig. 6. Inefficient organization management and utilization practice. (Source: survey result)

12. **Limited Skilled Manpower:** The manufacturers, artisans, machine users and traders are mostly illiterate and don't have substantial knowledge and skill about machine selection, operation and maintenance. The manufacturers do not provide after sale technical service to the users. From the survey it has been found that machines are damped for minor and easily repairable faults. On the other hand in limited areas around towns mechanics provide repair and maintenance service at the expense of high charges. But in other cases, where mechanics are not readily available, they leave the machine without operation for long time till they got transportation. Most artisans responsible for technical support are rarely trained and lack adequate knowledge and skill about machines [20] (Fig. 7).

Fig. 7. Artisans trying to train themselves two wheel tractor operation (left) and tractors dismantled for spare part consumption to solve spare scarcity. (Source: survey result)

13. **Influence of Imported Products:** In Ethiopia, low cost imported farm machines and high cost of spare parts and materials have downcast the local manufacturers engaged in farm machinery production and distribution. In addition there is no strong quality control system on imported machinery. In Ethiopia similar to production machineries farm machineries are imported and distributed directly by the local importers to end users are low quality. This made the farmers unwilling to use them. Once these farmers decide not to use the machines, it becomes hard to convince them for a new machine.

14. **Lack of Long Term Plan**: The manufacturer and rental service providers focus on short term benefit. Agricultural mechanization takes place in a specific process with continual improvement. The process needs a long term goal that can be achieved through long term, well organized missions. Unless long-term establishment made it is difficult to penetrate the current technical, economical, political and social barriers in the sector. Therefore, provision of demand driven support to operational systems and processes, facilitating innovative solutions for institutional capacity development, long base establishment needed.

3.2 Agro-Mechanization Deployment Model

In Ethiopia, there was no clear, adequate and comprehensive agricultural mechanization deployment model that can alleviate the upper mentioned barriers. The country mechanization strategy is in compass different agricultural mechanization alternatives for different farm sizes. The document focuses on value chain's perspective starting from machinery design to distribution for end users. But it lacks integration of activities and stalk holders. In addition the strategy doesn't offer particular responsibilities for each deployment tasks. The country's strategy needs specific deployment model for each agro-ecological zone. The need of designing and implementing agricultural mechanization deployment model for effective and efficient strategy is mandatory. For the purpose of developing agribusinesses contributing to poverty reduction, and increasing farm income through production, processing, and sales, a comprehensive model has been developed for effective deployment of agricultural machinery, through introduction of agricultural machinery mainly driven by motive power. Based on the study results following business model is developed as shown in Fig. 8 below:

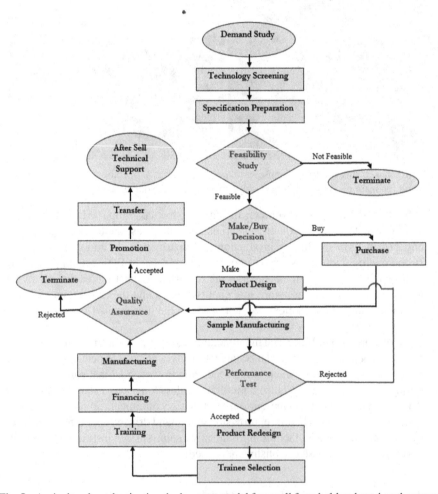

Fig. 8. Agricultural mechanization deployment model for small farm holders based on the survey result.

3.3 Process Description

The use of quality farm equipments at lowest possible cost is a request for Ethiopia agriculture productivity improvement. Similarly development of competitive Agricultural or farm equipment is a prerequisite for any micro- enterprise involved on farm equipment production success. Product development does not certainly mean discovering revolutionary new inventions, nor does it just involve retrieving on an old solutions. A successful product development strategy commonly results from structural thinking along with new approach, free from old approaches and none scientific designs procedure and materials selection. The designed deployment model categorized in to 18 distinct tasks having a particular responsibility and approaches as presented herein:

1. **Demand Study:** Out of all the steps in product deployment process, definition of need is the most important step. A complete and systematic understanding of the need is a fundamental requirement in achieving the desired solution. The final goal of product deployment is how well it sells or accepted by the customer (Farmers/Unions/Government). This can be achieved through well understanding of customer's requirement and providing what a customer wants in the product. This implies well defining the product requirements precisely before any design or manufacturing task carried out is far the most important task. It is important to understand customers drive the development of a better products. It is thus important to gather the need of farmers when starting farm equipment design. The needs of the farmers can be gathered either of any surveying techniques; either using interview, conducting focus group discussion, conducting customer survey and collecting customer complaints. Then customer requirements must be characterized on the basis of performance, time, cost and quality.

2. **Technology Screening:** It is the process of selecting the best machinery from available alternatives using technical, economic, social factors. Every technology wants a formal and organized evaluation process that must suitable with facility and labor skills, contribution margin, size of market, break-even analysis and return on sales. Machinery screening criteria should include at least product quality, product cost, safety level, size (weight and dimension), mode of operation (manual or automatic), energy source (electric/fuel/solar), running cost, manufacturability by local material, machine and man power, ease of operation and maintenance, availability of spare and simplicity of transportation.

3. **Specification Preparation:** Specification preparation reference to preparing a comprehensive picture of the product requirements. The specification should have to include the capacity of the machine, reliability, skilled man power required for operation and maintenance, power in put, mode of operation is either manual or automatic, transportation mechanism, and related technical terms. Basically the productivity and safe operation of any farm machinery and equipments depends on specification preparation before design or purchase. The equipment specification should be predefined before any financial analysis made for selection. The product specification is important to control the quality of the product deployment exercise. It should define all design and manufacturing process of any specific part or

product. The quality function deployment tool provides the most crucial inputs in writing the product design/purchase specifications.

4. **Feasibility Study:** Agricultural mechanization practice should be technically capable, economically feasible, environmentally friendly and socially acceptable. A feasibility study should be conducted to examine the feasibility of a proposed equipment. It is used to determine the proposed farm machines are viable. A complete feasibility study states whether the product is worth investment or not. A well-designed study should be free of political motivation and special group interest. But it should offer a historical background of the business/service provision, such as a description of the product capacity and capabilities, financial statements, marketing researches, details of operations and management tasks, policy issues, legal requirements and tax obligations. Then after feasibility assessment technical implementation and project operation modality will come up. Agro-machinery deployment project feasibility study needs detail investigation of technical, economic, legal, operational and scheduling feasibility.

5. **Manufacture or Buy Decision:** Any production businesses always have to consider low cos alternatives on a daily business activities. One of these decisions is whether the component/product shall be manufactured inside or Buy/outsource decision. It is the action of deciding between manufacturing an item internally (or in-house) or buying it from an external supplier (also known as outsourcing). Some companies perform all activities starting from manufacturing of raw materials to the final distribution of the product and delivery of after sales technical services. Contrary other companies may interested on buying a lot of the parts and materials that are required for their finished products assembly. The second alternative considered when cause better quality and lower expenses than would be possible if the business were to attempt to manufacture the whole/parts of the product or provide a service by itself. On the other hand it is important to take control over those outsourced services or parts/products for maintaining its competitive position. To come up for good make or buy decision, it is indispensable to thoroughly examine all of the expenses associated with product manufacturing and costs associated with buying the goods/service. Generally the evaluation process has to consider strategic impact, expertise, quality considerations, available capacity and speed of production and cost components.

6. **Purchasing**: The purchase process shall be done according to Amhara regional state purchasing regulation.

7. **Product Design:** It is the process of determining the product's characteristics including its appearance, dimensions, tolerances, materials and performance standards. Product design must support product manufacturability (the ease with which a product can be made). Product design task is a continuity of specification preparation. The design work should solves potential problems, reduces costs & shortens time to market. All the design work starting from conceptual design to the final embodiment design and detail design needs due attentions and done by the right professionals.

8. **Sample Manufacturing:** Based on the design document single product will be manufactured. The manufacturing process should be asper the designed process plan and consistent to the actual manufacturing equipments. In past practice we have

observed that the sample products manufactured in highly automated industries like Ethiopian metal and engineering corporation (METEC) at higher precision. But the products produced at small enterprises having less experience, medium skill and simple hand tools. As a result there is great deviation between actual products and sample ones.

9. **Performance Test:** The development of a new customized technology at early stage commonly the evolution is limited by the lack of ideas. A single good idea can solve several constraints and foster the products development exponentially. Gradually the growth becomes linear when the fundamental ideas are in place and the progress is focused on filling the minor gaps between the fundamental ideas. During this phase the marketing task will come to stage. But through time the product technological competency will begins to decline and improvements come with greater difficulty. Finally matured products improved slowly and approaches to its death. The success of a technology based company lies on its research & development (R&D) program, transfer to another technology growth curve offers greater possibilities. In addition to conformance of the product to the designed purpose product performance test criteria might include reliability, throughput time, process velocity, productivity improvement, utilization of capacity and efficiency.

10. **Product Redesign:** Based on performance test the geometric dimension, feature, material and other design parameters of the machine should be modified. Revised calculations are carried out for better operating capacity, improved safety, optimizing cross sections and resultant stress, considering the effect of stress concentration. When this values differ from desired values, the dimensions of the component are modified. The process will continued up to the desired values of operating capacity, better factor of safety and stress at grave cross section are obtained. The modification may include optimization of product size and shape, material type and production process.

11. **Trainee Selection:** The other most important issue is trainee selection. In past practice it is observed that the selection process is unfair and corrupted. As a result of this it is not possible to create a significant amount of enterprises in the area nevertheless of the huge effort made. The selection criteria should be objective oriented and must be made based on real interest, working culture and ethics, professional back ground, financial capability and existing practice in similar activities.

12. **Training:** Specific theoretical and practical training should be given for both manufacturer, operator and maintenance experts. Manufacturer trainings are should be designed for new or experienced manufacturers. The training has to insure the selected manufacturers can manufacture the product at predefined quality and productivity level. Similarly proper training should be given for operators and maintenance craft. The training should be able to operate the machine at optimal performance; imperative to know and understand the machine they are going to operating in order to ensure safety and minimize accident or injury risk on the job site; be able protecting the investment and the durability of the machine and optimizing utilization of the machine.

13. **Financing**: Even though pilot-scale farm equipments have been developed with better performance characteristics, use of such equipments remains limited due

financial limitations. Currently Amhara credit and saving institute (ACSI), Walya capital financing and Development bank of Ethiopia has started lease financing for micro and medium manufacturing industries. But it is a short term financing and doesn't include operational costs adequately. Manufacturers perceive high risks in financing farm equipment, primarily due to technological uncertainties and low affluence of users. In the absence of appropriate micro-financing arrangements, manufacturers are often unwilling to be involved in the sector. So there must be special financial arrangement to deploy farm equipments. This includes integration of donor, long term low interest loan for both manufacturers and users, subsidizer farm equipment supply and subsidizer farm equipment rental service.

14. **Manufacturing:** Manufacturing, which is an extremely important issue. Some of the problem in manufacturing process are fabrication without design, scarcity of skilled man power, materials and production machinery. The production of farm equipments involve various manufacturing processes such as casting and molding, machining, joining, and shearing and forming. But some components must be purchased or out sourced to other manufacturers.

15. **Quality Assurance:** The quality of most farm machinery manufactured by small scale industries in the country observed they are not meet the required service. Farmers are suffering from non-standard low quality products. The machines encountered longer down time, low output and high operational cost. The quality of equipment has to be improved. So it is important to inspections at various stages till they are finally assembled & packed as per their quality standards through well designed quality assurance procedures.

16. **Promotion:** Technological product passes through a cyclic process starting from birth, followed by an initial growth phase, then a relatively stable matured phase and finally into a decreasing phase that eventually ends in the death of the product. In early phase the product is new to the market and the customer acceptance is minimum and its market share is minimum. As a result the product needs to promote effectively. In this regard using sample product demonstrating its benefit practically in site required. Mouth promotion will not work longer. The farmers has lost their trust by old practices. So it is important to allocate enough budget and demonstrate the products productivity, ease of operation and maintenance, consistent with their culture and working habits is mandatory. But during the growth phase information of the product and its acceptance reaches to a wider customers. Needs less promotional effort. Rather it is better to focus on technical and managerial support. Through the maturity phase the product is broadly acceptable and market share are now stable, and it grows as parallel to the growing rate of the sector economy. Needs only strong technical support. This includes on job training, maintenance service, supply of spare etc.

17. **Transfer (sell/rent):** To transfer the product to the community there is two alternatives, sell or rental. To sell the product for the community the product has to be affordable and needy for individual applications. Such products have low capacity and small in size. This includes manual tools, semi mechanized equipments and to some extent small capacity mechanized equipments. Contrary devices having large capacity and high initial cost shall be considered for rental. This devices include fully mechanized devices such as high capacity tractor, combiner and thrashers.

So before any promotion activity performed the technical team has to decide the way of transfer. Farmers' cooperatives and unions and privet business sectors has to promote, financially and technically support to invest on farm machinery rentals. In this regard the government structure (bureau of Agriculture) and NGOs involved in the sector has to do more.

18. **After Sell Technical Support:** After sales technical and managerial support after distribution of farm machinery is another hot concern in Ethiopia. There is huge knowledge and skill gap among the majority of farmers. Even though there are farmer training centers among the community they are not operational and provide the required service. There must be well organized regular on job operation and maintenance training before hand over and on job practice. In addition to training it is important to create product and spare supply channels. This is a particularly important issue. In this regard Ethiopian agricultural transformation agency (ATA) with Bahir Dar Institute of Technology (BiT) has started to create qualified technical entrepreneurs who can give maintenance service, rental service, supply spares. This effort should be strengthen. One of the factors that can ensure availability of agricultural equipments is an effective and efficient maintenance engineering system. Gone were the days when maintenance was not given adequate attention. For any farm machinery, more attention is now given to maintenance function. Therefore, considering the need for maintenance with technological advancement in production facilities, technical and vocational colleges, universities, manufacturers and suppliers have the responsibility for knowledge transfer. Similarly effectiveness of preventive maintenance relay on availability of quality spare at reasonable price. Any responsible governmental agencies, manufacturer and suppliers. Users have to provide important selection criteria before purchase. Spare parts requirement and its purchase must be planned and managed systematic way by the right professional.

4 Conclusion and Recommendation

The need for agricultural mechanization in Amhara Region of Ethiopia has become more acute in recent years due to rapid population growth and high labor wage. The production and productivity in Ethiopia agriculture cannot be enhanced by primitive and traditional practices of farming. There is a strong need for farm machinery rental service among small farm holders. Similarity quality manufacturing and after sales support provision for farm machinery are also needed to assure reliability of farm machinery deployment. The survey results outlined the most important factors inhibiting introduction of mechanization on small-scale farms in the region. To alleviate these challenges an agricultural mechanization deployment model has been designed. The model will create clear Responsibility, integration between activities and stalk holders to foster manufacturing, distribution and utilization of farm equipments. So the government has to take the lead to bring the fragmented mechanization practice performed by manufacturers, TVET colleges, unions/farmers, GOs, NGOs by implement the model.

Acknowledgments. This survey was performed by the support of ASMIC BiT. The authors would like to thank all participants included in the survey for their kind cooperation and comments. The authors furthermore wish to acknowledge Dr. Sisay Geremew, ASMIC BiT coordinator, for his particular contribution in the survey.

References

1. UNDP strengthening national capacity through sustainable increases in agricultural production and productivity, March 2011–June 2016
2. Cervantes-Godoy, D., Dewbre, J.: Economic importance of agriculture for poverty reduction. OECD Food, Agriculture and Fisheries Working Papers, No. 23, OECD Publishing (2010)
3. Josef, K., John, E., Brian, G.: Mechanization for rural development: a review of patterns and progress from around the world. Integrated Crop Management, vol. 20 (2013)
4. Brian, S., Martin, H., Josef, K.: Agricultural mechanization a key input for sub-Saharan African smallholders. Integrated Crop Management, vol. 23 (2016)
5. Singh, G., Zhao, B.: Agricultural mechanization situation in Asia and the Pacific region. Agric. Mech. Asia Afr. Latin Am. **47**, 15–25 (2016)
6. FAO: Farm power and mechanization for small farms in Sub-Saharan Africa. Food and Agriculture Organization of the United Nations, Agricultural and Food Engineering Services Technical Report 3, Rome, Italy, p. 65 (2006)
7. Mrema, G.: The process of developing a draft framework for SAMS for the transformation of agriculture in Africa: sending the hand-hoe to the museum. In: Proceedings of the Consultative Meeting on Mechanization Strategy: New Models for Sustainable Agricultural Mechanization in Sub Saharan Africa, Nairobi, Kenya, 1–3 December 2016 (2016)
8. Van Eerdewijk, A., Danielsen, K.: Gender matters in farm power. KIT, CIMMYT, CGIAR (2015). https://www.researchgate.net/publication/282976045. Gender Matters in Farm Power
9. Mehta, C.R., Chande, N.S., Senthilkumar, T.: Status, challenges and strategies for farm mechanization in India. Ama Agric. Mech. Asia Afr. Latin Am. **45**(4), 43–50 (2014)
10. Fatunbi, A.O., Odogola, R.W.: Status of smallholders agricultural mechanization in Sub-Saharan Africa. FARA Res. Rep. **2**(10), 27 (2018)
11. Dagnaw, Y.T.: Critical factors hampering agricultural productivity in ethiopia: the case of northern ethiopian farmers. In: International Conference on African Development Archives, Paper 123 (2007)
12. GoE: The Agricultural Development Led Industrialization (ADLI) strategy of Ethiopia. Government of Ethiopia (2007)
13. Hassan, O., Abdulle, A.: Lack of infrastructure: the impact on economic development as a case of Benadir region and Hir-shabelle, Somalia. Dev. Country Stud. **7**(1) (2017). 2225-0565
14. Andersen, P., Shimokowa, S.: Rural infrastructure and agricultural development. Paper Presented at the Annual Bank Conference on Development Economics, Tokyo, Japan, 29–30 May (2007)
15. Hilmi, M.: Hire services as a business. Agric. Dev. **19**, 21–25 (2013)
16. Sims, B., Thierfelder, C., Kienzle, J., Friedrich, T., Kassam, A.: Development of the conservation agricultural equipment industry in sub-Saharan Africa. FAO (2006)
17. Sims, B., Kienzle, J., FAO: Farm equipment supply chains. Guidelines for policy-makers and service providers: experiences from Kenya, Pakistan and Brazil. Agricultural and Food Engineering Technical Report 7, Rome, Italy (2009). 48 pp
18. Ashburner, J.E., Kienzle, J. (eds.), FAO: Investment in agricultural mechanization in Africa: conclusions and recommendations of a round table meeting of experts. Agricultural and Food Engineering Technical Report 8, Rome, Italy (2011). 76 pp
19. Moon, M.: Organizational commitment revisited in new public management: motivation, organizational culture, sector and managerial level. Public Perform. Manage. Rev. **24**(2), 177–194 (2000)
20. Houmy, K., Clarke, L.J., Ashburner, J.E., Kienzle, J., FAO: Agricultural mechanization in sub-Saharan Africa: guidelines for preparing a strategy. Integrated crop management, Rome, Italy, vol. 22, pp. 1–92 (2013)
21. Sims, B., Kienzle, J.: Making mechanization accessible to smallholder farmers in sub-Saharan Africa. Environments **3**, 11 (2016)

Production and Characterization of Glue from Tannery Hide Trimming Waste

Tadele Negash G.$^{(\boxtimes)}$, Ayalew Emiru, Dessie Amare, and Mahlet Reda

Faculty of Chemical and Food Engineering, Bahir Dar Institute of Technology,
Bahir Dar University, P.O. Box 26, Bahir Dar, Ethiopia
tadelenegash@gmail.com

Abstract. Animal glue is the most important protein adhesive obtained from animal hides, skins, and bones through hydrolysis of the collagen. The main raw material used for the study is hide trimming waste from Bahir Dar tannery plc. In this research parameter that were studied are pretreatment and conditioning techniques during animal glue production. The hide trimming waste after pretreatment were soaked for 4 h in lime solution and washed with water and followed by neutralized by hydrochloric acid. The extraction processes were taken place at temperature of 60, 65 & 70 °C and the time of 2.5, 3 & 3.5 h in water bath. After extraction the solution was filtered with nylon cloth to separate the non collageneous materials. The filtered glue solution was concentrated in rotary vacuum evaporator. Then the glue was cooled and characterized and best results were obtained at a temperature of 6 °C and at time of 3 h. The best results or quality indicators at the optimum temperature (6 °C) and time (3 h) were viscosity (90 cp), moisture content (14.6%), ash content (2.23%), density (1259 kg/m^3), yield (32 g glue/100 g of hide), PH (5.98), water solubility by color (black), and shear strength (260 MN).

Keywords: Hide · Soaking · Collagen · Hydrolysis · And glue

1 Introduction

The leather industry generally uses hides and skins as raw materials, which are the by-products of meat and meat products industry. A recent report revealed that leather and leather products are one of the major external trade sectors which contribute up to 1.39% share of the total export earnings. However, these industries are discharging and dumping their wastes and effluents without treatment into nearby water bodies. Out of 1000 kg of rawhide, nearly 850 kg is generated as solid wastes in leather processing. Only 150 kg of the raw material is converted into leather. Tannery generates a huge amount of solid waste as follows: fleshing, 50–60; chrome shaving, chrome splits and buffing dust 35–40%; skin trimmings, 5–7; and hair, 2–5%. Solid wastes in leather processing constitute beam house, 80; tanning, 19; finishing, 1% [1].

An adhesive is a material that is applied to the surfaces of articles to join them permanently by an adhesive bonding process. Adhesives, also known as glue, cement,

© ICST Institute for Computer Sciences, Social Informatics and Telecommunications Engineering 2020
Published by Springer Nature Switzerland AG 2020. All Rights Reserved
N. G. Habtu et al. (Eds.): ICAST 2019, LNICST 308, pp. 59–70, 2020.
https://doi.org/10.1007/978-3-030-43690-2_5

mucilage, or paste, is any substance applied to one surface, or both surfaces, of two separate items that binds them together and resists their separation [2]. The use of adhesives offers many advantages over binding techniques such as sewing, mechanical fastening, thermal bonding, etc. These include the ability to bind different materials together, to distribute stress more efficiently across the joint, the cost-effective of an easily mechanized process, an improvement in aesthetic design, and increased design flexibility [3]. One of Natural adhesives (glues) is Hide glue which is used in woodworking. It may be supplied as granules, flakes, or flat sheets, which have an indefinite shelf life if kept dry. Hide glue is a protein derived from the simple hydrolysis of collagen which is a principal protein constituent of animal hides. Collagen, hide glue and gelatin are very closely related with respect to protein and chemical composition. An approximate chemical composition is Carbon (51–52%), Hydrogen (6–7%), Oxygen (24–25%) and Nitrogen (18–19%) [4].

The first stage in glue or gelatin production is the pretreatment and curing process. Pretreatment is the process by which tissue is soaked in either acid or alkali in order to increase the availability of collagen to the hydrolytic environment. The pretreatment procedure used depends upon the facilities and the nature of the stock. In its natural state, collagen is water-insoluble and must be conditioned to solubilize the protein. Collagen molecules are triple helices of amino acid sequence and contain both non-polar and charged acidic and basic side chains. The conversion of collagen to soluble protein of animal glue involves the breaking of the intra- and intermolecular polypeptide bonds through the use of acid or alkali pretreatment before the extraction takes place. There are acidic, alkaline and enzymatic pretreatment methods.

Ethiopia has more than forty tannery industries that process leather for production of bags, gloves, shoes, clothes, etc. in the country. In addition to this, the country is exporting leather to abroad countries to support its economy. Even though the country has many numbers of tanneries and the tanneries support the country's economy, the wastes generated by those industries are harmful to the environment. The waste types generated in these tannery industries are hide trimming, fleshing, chrome shaving dust, glue blue, etc., In Bahir Dar tannery plc, these waste are discharged around Abbay River and some of them are simply landfilled. Hide trimming waste and other tannery wastes are dangerous for humans, animals as a whole to the environment.

Now a day's Ethiopia is importing glue from abroad countries with high currency for different purposes [5]. But many researches indicate that glue can be produced from hide trimming waste. During production, there is a step that yields a glue called an extraction. So, in the extraction process the treated/conditioned collagen is transferred to extraction kettles or tanks, where it is heated with water to convert the collagen and extract the glue. Several hot water extractions at progressively higher temperatures are made under carefully controlled conditions. Separate, successive dilute glue solutions are removed from the stock until the glue is completely extracted, usually in four extractions. Cooking at the correct temperature and for the right length of time breaks down the collagen and converts it into glue. If the temperature or timing is off, the quality of the glue will be poor and/or ruined. Therefore, the temperature and timing of extraction need to be studied carefully. So, this research focuses on the production and characterization of glue from hide trimming waste to protect environmental pollution and to save foreign currency and to determine the effect of temperature and time on the yield of glue during the extraction process.

2 Methodology

The extraction of hide glue carried out by alkaline and thermal method. The Alkaline method used for soaking in order to weaken the peptide bond which holds protein molecule together and the thermal method was used to break down the peptide bond completely.

2.1 Glue Production

Raw Material Preparation: 10 kg of samples were brought from Bahir Dar Tannery plc. The sample was cleaned with tap water. Large size of hide was cut with uniform size (2 cm × 2 cm) by using sharp knife. 1% sodium hydroxide solution was prepared (8 g of sodium hydroxide pellet was dissolved in 200 ml of water). 100 g of cutted hide trimming waste sample was weighed by beam balance and dropped in to the plastic jar which contains the NaOH solution. The plastic jar which contains the sample was shaken for 4 h at 120 rpm.

Glue Extraction: The collagen solution which was obtained from the soaked hide was transferred to the extraction vessel by water bath. The extraction was taken place at various time (2.5, 3 & 3.5 h), and temperatures (60, 65 and 70 °C). After extraction process completed, none collagen part from the extraction vessel was separated from the liquor solution. The liquor solution was filtered by using nylon cloth and concentrated using vacuum evaporator. The concentrated glue was cut by knife in to flake forms. The flake glue was characterized and finally packed.

2.2 Physicochemical Analysis

Moisture Content: The ash and moisture content of glue was determined by using Association of Official Analytical Chemists (AOAC International) method [6]. The 10 g sample was measured and transfer to Petri-dish with a temperature of 103–105 °C for 1 h. After 1 h, the moisture content was determined by the equation of above literature. 2 g mass of sample was weighed before drying (m_1) and Mass of sample was weighed after drying (m_2). The moisture of the sample was obtained by subtracting m_2 from m_1. Then the moisture content of the sample was determined by the following formula.

$$\text{Moisture content} (\%) = \frac{\text{Weight of moisture in glue} \times 100\%}{\text{Weight of glue before drying}} = \frac{(m1 - m2)}{m1} \times 100\%$$

(1)

Ash Content: The ash content of glue was determined by taking 2 g of sample in the furnace at 950 °C for 12 h. 2 g mass of sample was weighed before burn (m_1) and Mass of sample was weighed after burn (m_2). Ash content of the glue was determined by the following formula:

$$\text{Ash content } (\%) = \frac{\text{Mass of dry glue sample} \times 100\%}{\text{Mass of original glue sample}} = \frac{m2}{m1} \times 100\% \qquad (2)$$

Viscosity Determination: The Viscosity profile of the glue was obtained using a viscometer (LvDv I+, Brookfield, USA) with the spindle set at 200 rpm and at a temperature of 60 °C following the technique proposed by Association of Official Analytical Chemists (AOAC International) [3].

Water Solubility of Adhesive Resin: Water solubility of the cured resin was tested depends on the conations of water (hot or cold). One gram of cured resin was finely grounded and soaked in 5 ml of water for five days. The water solubility was soak solution. Any discoloration in the soak solution is an indication that the resin has not been fully cured and the adhesive is dissolving in water the darker the color of the soak solution, the greater the solubility of the resin [3].

Determination of Density: The densities of the glue were determined by taking the weight of a known volume of the glue in a density bottle (pycnometer) using an analytical balance.

$$\text{Density of glue} = \frac{\text{Mass of glue obtained}}{\text{Volume of solution taken}} \qquad (3)$$

Shear Strength: The test consists essentially of two rectangular sections, typically 25 mm wide, 100 mm long and 1.6 mm thick, bonded together, with an overlap length of 25 mm ASTM (American Society for Testing of Materials). The single-lap specimen is easy to prepare and test. A fixture is used to ensure correct overlap and accurate alignment of the adherend. This may include control of the fillet. Testing can be conducted using standard tension/compression mechanical test equipment. The lap-shear strength (t) is given by: [7].

$$t \text{ (shear strength)} = \frac{\text{pressure}}{\text{area}} = \frac{P}{bL} \qquad (4)$$

3   Results and Discussion

The laboratory test results of some quality indicators performed on the produced glue are shown in Table 1.

Table 1. Laboratory test result of quality indicator for produced glue at optimum conditions.

Parameter	Produced glue	Standard glue	Deviation
PH	5.89	6.06	0.17
Density (g/cm^3)	1.259	1.270	0.11
Viscosity (cp)	90	80.0	10
Moisture content (%)	14.6	15.0	0.4
Ash content (%)	2.23	2.00	0.23
Solubility (color)	Black	Black	0
shear strength (MN)	260	>200	60

Table 1 shows that the quality indicator ash content had the maximum deviation while PH had the minimum deviation density between the values of the quality indicators for standard glue compared with values obtained for the produced glue.

The hide extracted glue was solubilized completely in hot water 50–55 °C, but the solubility was decreased in cold water. The colors of all the dissolved glue are black shows that the glue is best soluble in water.

Density is the mass per unit volume of a substance; increase in water quantity in produced glue increases the volume of the glue thus reduces its density. Increase in water content of the glue makes the glue less dense, hence reduces its ash content.

PH is a measure of acidity or basicity of glue. The standard PH value of glue is 6.06. The most equivalent PH value of the produced to the standard glue (6.06) is 5.89 with deviation of 0.17.

The viscosity of the produced glue was higher when compared with standard glue, this might be due to the temperature of glue was lower.

The moisture content of the glue was small to compare with standard glue this due to the length of time was higher in the vacuum evaporator. So that most of water removed.

The higher ash content shows that the glue contains inorganic substance. This is because of salt and other substance which retards the rate of burning.

The shear strength of the produced glue was higher than the standard glue. This might be the extraction process was takes place at optimum parameter.

3.1 Effect of Temperature on Physiochemical Property of Glue

Effect of Temperature on Yield: Temperature is one of the basic important factors for the production of hide glue, because hide glue is protein in nature and proteins denature at high temperature. So, determining the optimum temperature is one of the major tasks during glue production. As shown in Fig. 1 below the yield is highest (32 g glue/100 g hide) at 65 °C. But above and below 65 °C the yield is lower. This due to denaturation of the glue (above 65 °C) and there is still some unextracted glue with the hide (below 65 °C).

It is also because elevated temperature (i.e., 65 °C) breaks high amount of collagen in the pelt, which in turn facilitates the conversion of collagen in to glue than low temperature [8].

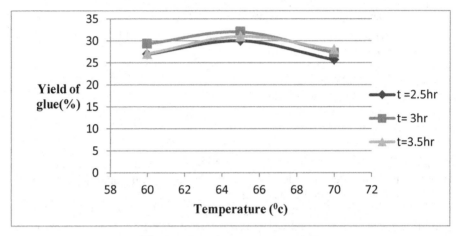

Fig. 1. Effect of temperature on yield

Effect of Temperature on Viscosity: Viscosity is the resistance to flow. The more water added to the glue, the lighter and less sticky it becomes, it flows faster (its resistance to flow reduces). Hence, the viscosity reduces. As shown in Fig. 2, the maximum viscosity is occurred at a temperature of 65 °C. But after this temperature the viscosity is gradually decreased. Therefore, the best temperature that gives the maximum viscosity (90 cp) is 65 °C. The viscosity increment at this temperature, i.e. 65 °C, is probably due to linking of glue molecule to form aggregate. In other word, at high temperature the protein molecule may denature [9].

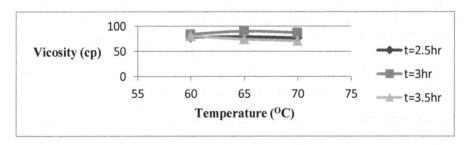

Fig. 2. Effect of temperature on viscosity

Effect of Temperature on Moisture Content: At temperatures of 60, 65 and 70 °C, the corresponding minimum moisture contents are 15.04, 14.6 and 15% respectively. Generally, the moisture content of the glue increases, as the temperature increases except for the time of three hours (Fig. 3). The lower the moisture content is the better the glue.

So, the optimum temperature is 65 °C which gives 14.6% moisture content that is less than the standard value (which is 8%–16%). Moisture content is the amount of water in the glue. The high amount of water in the glue makes the glue easily putrefied. The glue will be brittle in little amount of moisture. The standard value for moisture content of the glue is 8%–16% [10].

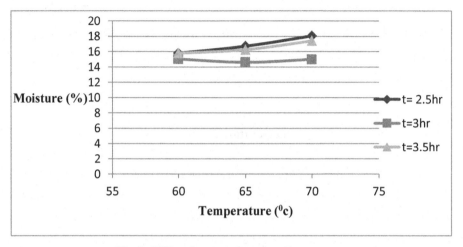

Fig. 3. Effect of temperature on moisture content

Effect of Temperature on Ash Content: Ash content is the amount of residue obtained when a sample is burnt under controlled condition so that all ignitable mass is removed. The denser the glue, the more the ash obtained [11]. Increase in water content of the glue increases the volume of the glue and reduces its density. Therefore, increase in water content of the glue makes the glue less dense, hence reduces its ash content. The lower the ash content is the better the glue. As shown from Fig. 4, the minimum ash content (2.33%) is occurred at a temperature of 60 °C. The ash content also increased with temperature. So, the optimum temperature for the case of ash content is 60 °C. The ash content of the glue is affected by the curing method used. The standard value for ash content is 2%–5% [10, 12].

Effect of Temperature on Shear Strength: The higher the shear strength is the better the glue. From Fig. 5 shown below the maximum shear strength (260 MN) occurs at 65 °C. So, the optimum temperature that gives the maximum shear strength of the glue is 65 °C. This is the most important of all the test factors and, unless considered in conjunction with this, the others are of only limited value. The stronger a glue, the greater the resistance offered by its jelly to outside pressure [12].

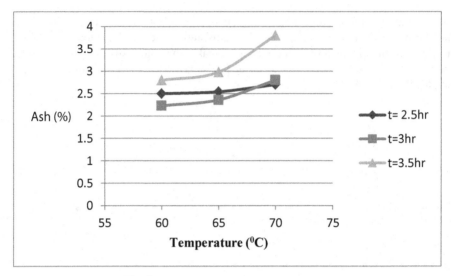

Fig. 4. Effect of temperature on ash content

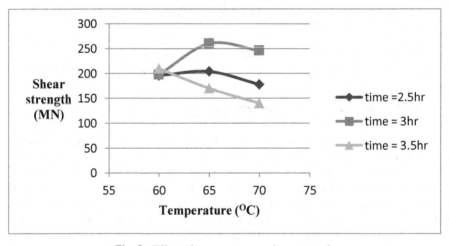

Fig. 5. Effect of temperature on shear strength

3.2 Effect of Time on Physio-Chemical Property of Glue

Effect of Time on Yield: Not only temperature affects the yield of glue, but time also affects its amount in the extraction process. So, determining the optimum time requirement is important for glue production. From Fig. 6 below the highest yield is obtained at 3 h. But before and after 3 h duration of extraction time the yield is lower. This is due to before 3 h there is still some unextracted glue with the hide and after 3 h there is some denaturation of the glue. Generally, the yield is maximum at 65 °C and 3 h [8].

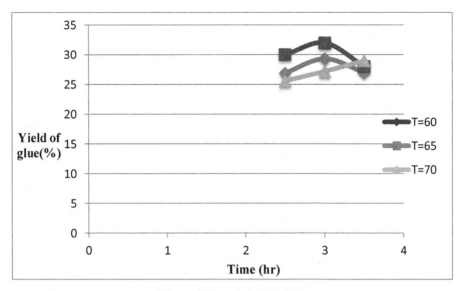

Fig. 6. Effect of time on yield

Effect of Time on Viscosity: As shown in Fig. 7 for the case of time effect, the maximum viscosity is occurred at a time of 3 h. So as shown from Figs. 2 and 7, the maximum viscosity is obtained at a temperature of 65 °C and a time of three hours, this is probably due to the time needed for linking of glue molecule to form aggregate [9]. Therefore, the optimum time and temperature are 3 h and 65 °C.

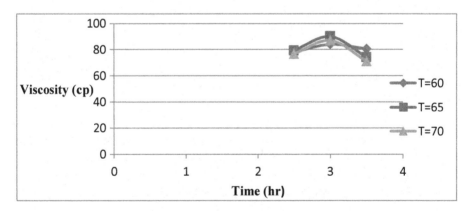

Fig. 7. Effect of time on viscosity

Effect of Time on Moisture Content: Time has an equivalent effect on the moisture content of the glue as temperature. As shown from Fig. 8, the minimum moisture content is 14.6% at a time of 3 h. So, the optimum time that gives the minimum moisture content (14.6%) is 3 h. Generally, as shown from Figs. 3 and 8 the optimum time and temperature are 3 h and 65 °C respectively [10].

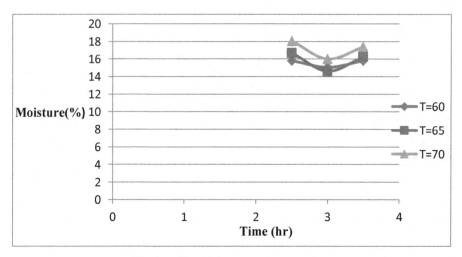

Fig. 8. Effect of time on moisture content

Effect of Time on Ash Content: As shown from Fig. 9, the ash content is minimum at a time of 3 h. So, the optimum time and temperature that gives the minimum ash content (2.23%) are 3 h and 60 °C. This value (2.23%) is almost equivalent to the standard value (2.0%) [10, 12].

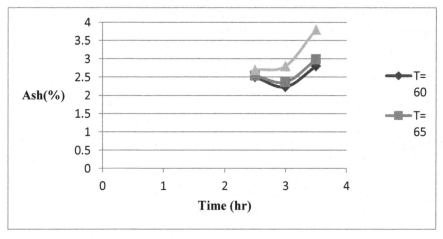

Fig. 9. Effect of time on ash content

Effect of Time on Shear Strength: The maximum shear strength (260 MN) occurs at a time of 3 h. Above three hours of extraction time the shear strength of the produced glue declines very quickly as shown in Fig. 10 which is due to the presence of non-collagen materials in the glue and resulted in denaturation of glue. Generally, the optimum time and temperature that gives the maximum shear strength are 3 h and 65 °C respectively [12].

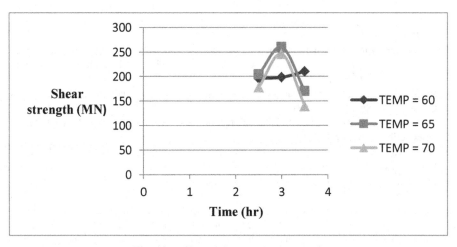

Fig. 10. Effect of time on shear strength

4 Conclusion

One of the well-known types of glue is animal glue. Animal glue could be bone glue, hide glue, fish glue, flesh glue, etc. Hide glue is the most important type of animal glue. It can be produced by the methods that were developed by the above work. The ph, density, viscosity, moisture content, ash content, solubility (color) and shear strength with the value of 5.89, 1.259 g/cm^3, 90 cp, 14.6%, 2.23%, black color and 260 MN were obtained are within the standard range. The effect of temperature and time during extraction of glue also investigated and showed that the optimum value were 65 °C and 3 h for temperature and time respectively. So producing hide glue by the method that was formulated in the above is acceptable.

Even though Ethiopia has plenty of raw materials from its tannery industries for the production of animal glue; it is still importing glue from abroad countries with high currency. Therefore, producing glue by studying its feasibility to replace the imported glue and saves foreign currency is not questionable.

References

1. Aftab, Md., et al.: Resource addition to leather industry: adhesive from chrome shaving dust. J. Sci. Innov. Res. **6**(4), 138–141 (2017)
2. Adhesive – Wikipedia. https://en.wikipedia.org/wiki/Adhesive. Accessed 24 Mar 2019
3. ASTM D2559-04: Standard Specification for Adhesives for Structural Laminated Wood Products for Use Under Exterior (Wet Use) Exposure Conditions, ASTM International, West Conshohocken, PA (2004)
4. Hide Glue Info | Bjorn Hide Glue. https://bjornhideglue.com/hide-glue-info/. Accessed 24 Mar 2019
5. The data source for import statistics i.e. Ethiopian Revenue and Customs Authority and Central Statistic Agency of Ethiopia. http://www.csa.gov.et

6. Horwitz, W. (ed.): Official Methods of Analysis AOAC International, 17th edn. Association of Official Analytical Chemists, Gaithersburg (2000)
7. Broughton, W.R., Mera, R.D.: Review of durability test methods and standards for assessing long term performance of adhesive joints. National Physical Laboratory Teddington, Middlesex, UK (1997). ISSN 1361-4061
8. Pizzi, A., Mittal, K.L. (eds.): Handbook of Adhesive Technology, 2nd edn. Taylor & Francis Group, LLC, New York (2003)
9. Thomas, R.K.: Encyclopedia of Chemical Technology, vol. 12, pp. 436–440. Wiley. http://www.scribd.com/doc/30116669
10. Hand World lingo, Animal glue. http://www.worldingo.com/ma/enwiki/en/animalglueanf.htm. Accessed 27 Nov 2010
11. Milligan, M., Higgins, B.: Hide Glues. Bone Glues and Industrial Gelatins, Johnstown, New York, USA (2009)
12. Testing of glue. http://www.oldandsold.com/articles30/glue-2,shtml. Accessed 27 Apr 2018
13. Taylor, M.M., et al.: Chemical modification of protein products isolated from chromium-containing solid tannery waste and resultant influence on physical and functional properties. JALCA **94**, 171–181 (1999)
14. Khatoon, M., Kashif, S., Saad, S., Umer, Z., Rasheed, A.: Extracton of amino acids and proteins from chrome leather waste. J Waste Recycl. **2**(2), 6 (2017)
15. Islam, R.M.S.: Physical, chemical and environmental parameter of glue manufacture in Bangladesh. IOSR J. Appl. Chem. (IOSR-JAC) **11**(2), 1–7 (2018)
16. Hadush, A., Hagos, Z., Gebrehawaria, G., Brhane, Y., Gopalakrishnan, V.K., Krishna Chaithanya, K.: Production and characterization of animal glue from solid skin waste of Axum town, Ethiopia. J. Pharm. Res. **12**(2), 174–177 (2018)
17. Gunorubon, A.J., Misel, U.: Production of glues from animal bones. ARPN J. Eng. Appl. Sci. **9**(9), 1592–1597 (2014)
18. Milligan, M., Higgins, B.: Hide Glues. Bone Glues and Industrial Gelatins. Johnstown, New York (2009)
19. Animal glues: a review of their key properties relevant to conservation. https://www.researchgate.net/publication/272311539
20. Omm-e-Hany, Syed, S.S., Beena, Z., Aamir, A., Asia, N.: Wood adhesives derivation from tannery waste protein: a comparison with some commercial wood adhesives. Bull. Env. Pharmacol. Life Sci. **4**(7), 172–178 (2015)
21. Sunder, V.J., Gnanamani, A., Muralidharan, C., Chandrbabu, N.K., Mandal, A.B.: Recovery and utilization of proteinous wastes of leather making: a review. Rev. Environ. Sci. Biotechnol. **10**, 151–163 (2011)
22. Frihart, C.R., Hunt, C.G.: Adhesives with wood materials, bond formation and performance, chapt. 10, pp. 10–24 (2010)
23. da Silva, L.F.M., Öchsner, A., Adams, R.D. (eds.): Handbook of Adhesion Technology. Springer, Heidelberg (2011). https://doi.org/10.1007/978-3-642-01169-6

Kinetic Modeling of Quality Change in Ethiopian Kent Mango Stored Under Different Temperature

Mekdim K. Assefa[1,3]([✉]), Berhanu A. Demessie[3], E. A. Shimelis[3], Pieter Verboven[1], Maarten Hertoga[1], and Bart Nicolai[1,2]

[1] Postharvest Group, BIOSYST-MeBioS, KU Leuven, 3001 Leuven, Belgium
mekdim.a@gmail.com
[2] Flanders Centre of Postharvest Technology, 3001 Leuven, Belgium
[3] School of Chemical and Bio-Engineering, Addis Ababa University,
P.O. Box 385, Addis Ababa, Ethiopia

Abstract. Model simulations permit to identify and predict the levels of loss arising under different storage temperature and maturity conditions in the supply chain. In this research kinetic model was developed for predicting relationship between storage temperature and mango quality attributes. Three quality attributes of mango (color, firmness and total soluble solids (TSS)) were measured and used for the kinetic modeling by estimating the parameters of the model. Mangoes were stored at 7, 13 °C and room temperature. The measurements were carried out with eight repetitions at one week intervals. From the tested equations exponential model for color and TSS found to be the best fit and logistic model for firmness. The model parameters were estimated by the simulation and also validated with a separate experiment with acceptable standard errors and minimum confidence interval of 87.58% which means that the variation in the measured data could be explained by the model. After developing the model a ripening stage were assigned from 1 to 5 with the corresponding quality values; where 1 is the mature green and 5 is the over ripe stage. The result shows that softening was the limiting quality factor for mangoes stored at 7 °C and color was the limiting quality factor for mangoes stored at 13 °C and room temperature. Equations used in this research could be used to estimate quality loss at different conditions of mango fruit in the supply chain.

Keywords: Mango · Quality · Kinetic modeling · Firmness · Color · Total soluble solids · Temperature

1 Introduction

Consumers and retailers prefer good quality fresh fruits in the market and through the supply chain. Quality changes, including physiological, microbiological, and physical and biochemical happen during postharvest cold storage [1]. These changes are mainly

N. G. Habtu et al. (Eds.): ICAST 2019, LNICST 308, pp. 71–81, 2020.
https://doi.org/10.1007/978-3-030-43690-2_6

depending on temperature because temperature of the fruit affects respiration rate, shelf-life and quality deterioration during storage period [9]. Therefore, it is important to have tools to control, and to predict the quality of fruit stored under different temperatures [7]. Mathematical modeling can help to gain insight in the mechanisms underlying postharvest losses and quality changes by screening hypothetical conceptual models on their fitness to explain the data. Model simulations permit to identify and predict the risk and levels of quality change [1] and waste arising under different ambient variables, processing conditions and logistic scenarios.

To understand the postharvest physiological behavior of fresh produce knowledge of the physiological, biochemical processes, and their relations are critical [8]. Physical, chemical, and biochemical factors are internal factors, however external factors like temperature in the fruit supply chain also affect fruit quality and can be modeled [11]. The focus of this study was to develop models describing the evolution of specific quality attributes (firmness, color and (TTS) total soluble solids) as a function of temperature. Firmness and color are the most important quality parameters used by consumers and retailers to determine the quality of mango and TTS is usually used in research and commercial farms [12]. These phenomena were modeled with mechanistic models that are based on physiological phenomena taking place in the fruit. These equations are solved numerically. The model parameters were estimated and validated based on experiments with Ethiopian Kent mango fruit stored under different temperature conditions in the refrigerated units.

2 Materials and Methods

2.1 Experimental Study

Mango fruits were obtained from a Horizon commercial farm through Etfruit (Ethiopian Fruit marketing agency). Normally the export standard mangos in Ethiopia are from Tommy Atkins, Keitt and Kent cultivars which are being cultivated by the commercial farms. One of the main reasons for the drop in mango exports from Ethiopia has been the variable and low quality of mango on arrival in overseas countries [9]. The experimental work was conducted with the cultivar Kent because of its longer shelf life and importance for the export market. Kent is quite similar looking cultivar with Keitt but Kent matures earlier March in Ethiopia [10]. Harvesting was carried out manually at commercial maturity. Plastic containers were used for transporting the fruits to the storage facility at the chemical and bio engineering, analytical laboratory of Addis Ababa institute of technology, immediately after harvest. Fruits were selected for weight in the range of 200–300 g. The mangoes were washed with tap water to remove field heat, soil particles, and to reduce microbial populations on the surface.

Mangoes were stored at 7, and 13 °C and at room temperature (25 °C) for experiment periods up to 21 days. 7 °C was selected to check the occurrence of chilling and quality change with other temperatures because some mango cultivars can safely be stored at 7–8 °C for up to 25 days [13]. Analyses were done for firmness, color, total soluble solid (TTS) content, total titratable acidity and weight loss but only three parameters were discussed in this study. Firmness was measured using a hand held FT-10 fruit tester penetrometer with a reading range of 5 kgf to 50 kgf with accuracy of ±0.5 and a cylindrical plunger with surface area of 1 cm² at the tip. First the outer skin from both cheeks was peeled from each fruit to reduce the effect of the hard skin and then the force applied per area of the inner fruit flesh is measured to a depth of 8 mm. Two measurements were taken on the equator for each mango fruit flesh after peeling the skin and the average was taken as the firmness.

Color change of mango fruit was measured by using a standard color chart used for Kent cultivar. For this cultivar due to pigment accumulation, flesh color change from 1-deep green, 2-light yellow-green, 3-yellow-light green, 4-yellow-orange and 5-golden orange during the ripening period [8]. The color was measured at the cheeks of the fruit near the two equators and the average was calculated for each fruit. TTS was measured by using a bench-top 60/70 ABBE refractometer, with a reading range of 0–32° Brix with accuracy of ±1. The mango peal was cut off and a few drops of juice squeezed by hand directly onto the sensor of a digital refractometer and read the °brix from the measuring device and the average value is taken from two measurement of a mango fruit around the cheeks.

2.2 Modeling and Simulations

Kinetic model was developed for predicting relationship between storage and shelf life conditions and mango quality attributes. Three quality attributes of mango (colour, firmness and total soluble solids) were selected for the kinetic modelling from the measured parameters. These selected parameters are the most important quality parameters used by consumers and retailers to determine the quality of mango. Moreover, they are traditionally used for grading and fixing the price of mango fruits in the Ethiopian supply chain [2]. The quality model was then simulated using OpitiPa software which is used to model and validate ordinary differential equations based simulation models in the area of food and postharvest [6].

Firmness Change Modeling. Fruit softening is correlated to the amount of pectin being cleaved [7] and converted to Galacturonic acid and demethylated pectin by pectic enzymes [5]. Simplified equation of the reaction is

$$P + E_{pect} \xrightarrow{k_{pect}} G + E_{pect} \tag{1}$$

where P is the amount of pectin; E_{pect} is the amount of the pectic enzyme; and k_{pect} is the rate of conversion of pectin to Galacturonic acid (G).

The amounts of pectic enzymes in fruit are generally governed by two reactions, one for formation and the other for denaturation [1]. The model was developed describing the activity of pectin enzyme during storage [5]. It was assumed that an inactive precursor (E_{pre}) that is activated into the active form of pectin enzyme (E_{pect}) that subsequently can be denatured again (E_{den}) [1].

$$E_{pre} + E_{pect} \xrightarrow{k_e} 2E_{pect} \tag{2}$$

$$E_{pect} \xrightarrow{k_{E_{den}}} E_{den} \tag{3}$$

where E_{pre} is the precursor of the pectic enzyme; k_e is the rate of formation of pectic enzyme; k_{Eden} is the rate of denaturation of pectic enzyme; E_{den} is the denatured enzyme and E_{pect} is the pectic enzyme.

The following equations of chemical kinetics assuming first order reactions can be derived:

$$\frac{d[P]}{dt} = -k_{pect}[P][E_{pect}] \tag{4}$$

$$\frac{d[E_{pect}]}{dt} = 2 * k_e[E_{pre}][E_{pect}] - k_{Eden}[E_{pect}] \tag{5}$$

$$\frac{d[E_{pre}]}{dt} = -k_e[E_{pre}][E_{pect}] \tag{6}$$

For modeling the firmness change of mango during storage period autocatalytic enzyme reaction, Michaelis-Menten enzyme kinetics and exponential models were tested for their accuracy in determining the change of firmness at 7, 13 °C and room temperature. From the tested equations exponential model shows the best fit and also happen to be less complex than autocatalytic enzyme reaction and Michaelis-Menten enzyme kinetics equations.

Color of Mango Fruit. Color changes in mango fruit are due to the disappearance of chlorophyll and appearance of other pigments [6]. Chloroplasts are transformed to chromoplasts containing yellow or red pigments [9]. These are two parallel pathways, the net reaction is assumed to be autocatalytic in a sense that the process is catalyzed by an enzyme that itself is being promoted as a result of the underlying ripening process. For this study, the whole process was simplified into one simple reaction:

$$P_1 + E_C \xrightarrow{k_C} P_2 + 2E_C \tag{7}$$

where P_1 refers to one pigment complex (chlorophyll) that is being converted into another pigment complex P_2 (lycopene) while E_C is doubled.

Three different reaction rate kinetic models (zero-order, first order and logistic model) were tested in this study and first order exponential model was selected for the simulation by considering the model complexity and model applicability, while respecting literature knowledge on color change as explained above. The ordinary differential equation used is;

$$\frac{dC_C}{dt} = k_C C \tag{8}$$

Where C is the color of mango fruit; and k_C is the rate constant and depend on temperature through an Arrhenius relationship.

Total Soluble Solid Change Modeling. During storage starch is hydrolyzed and break down to hexose sugar by amylase enzyme and hexose units are converted to carbon dioxide and water [9]. As fermentation during commercial storage is avoided and only aerobic respiration is considered.

$$S + E_{amy} \xrightarrow{k_{star}} Hexose\ Sugar + 2E_{Amy} \qquad (9)$$

$$Hexose\ Sugar + 6O_2 \xrightarrow{k_{resp}} 6CO_2 + 6H_2O \qquad (10)$$

where S is the amount of starch; E_{amy} is the amount of the amylase enzyme; and k_{star} is the rate of conversion of starch to hexose sugar. It is assumed that percentage of brix measured is related to the hexose sugar concentration according to the following equation

$$Brix = Hexo \qquad (11)$$

$$\frac{d[Brix]}{dt} = \frac{d[Hexo]}{dt} = k_{star}[E_{amy}] - k_{resp}[Hexo] \qquad (12)$$

$$\frac{d[E_{amy}]}{dt} = k_{star}[E_{amy}] \qquad (13)$$

Rate dependency on temperature. Arrhenius model was used to model the dependency of the different rate constants for all the three qualities with temperature [1].

$$k_i = k_{i,ref} exp\left(\frac{E_{a,i}}{R}\left(\frac{1}{T_{ref}} - \frac{1}{T}\right)\right) \qquad (14)$$

Where k_i is the rate constant of the reaction; $k_{i,ref}$ is the rate constant at the reference temperature; $E_{a,i}$ is the activation energy for the reaction; R is the universal gas constant and T is the temperature.

3 Results and Discussion

The measured firmness data are plotted in the figure below together with the corresponding simulated model results. Four model parameters were estimated by the simulation with acceptable standard errors and confidence interval of 87.58% which means that the variation in the measured data of the firmness could be explained by the model. The firmness of mango fruit at all conditions decreases significantly during the storage period but the extent is higher at higher temperature. Slow firmness drop was observed at 7 °C but due to the occurrence of chilling injury mango cannot stored at this temperature for a long period of time. Due to this 13 °C is the optimum temperature to store Ethiopian Kent mango fruits which is also observed in other mango cultivars [3]. The result in Fig. 1 also shows high rate of firmness loss at the beginning of the storage period and slows down after one week period which may be related to an increase in ethylene formation. Fast firmness drop and lower shelf was obtained at room temperature but this loss relatively decreased at 13 and 7 °C.

As it can be easily inferred from the figure the firmness change as a function of temperature can be used to determine the optimum time-temperature storage conditions

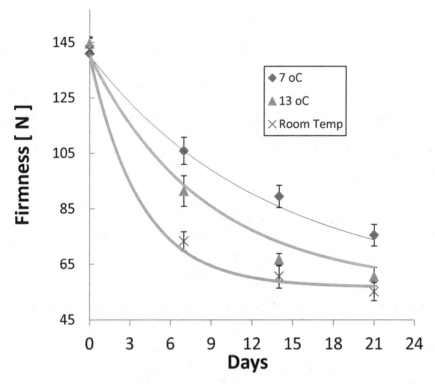

Fig. 1. Firmness of mango fruit during storage at 7, 13 °C and room temperature for storage durations of 21 days. The lines represent the model, and the points are the mean of the measured values.

to handle mango fruit. The evaluation of quality and prediction of postharvest life of mango fruit is a significant means in the handling of the fruit throughout the supply chain [3]. Overall, the fruit used in the present study stored at 7 °C had a longer shelf life compared with those stored at higher temperatures had a shorter shelf life.

After harvest, mango and other fresh fruit undergo continuous changes in color as part of the normal ripening and senescence. Ripening may be desirable in that it makes the fruit palatable, but it limits the storage life of the fruit. The measured color data are plotted in the Fig. 2 together with the corresponding simulated model results. Model parameters were estimated by the simulation with acceptable standard errors and confidence interval of 91.62% which means that the variation in the measured data of the color could be explained by the model. As observed in the figure color change increase from stage 1 to stage 5 at higher rate at high temperature and lower rate at low temperature. This may be due to chlorophyll breakdown, the rate of which was dependent on temperature and ethylene concentration. The change of flesh color is relatively rapid at the start of the experiment but slows down later.

The measured TSS data are plotted in the Fig. 3. together with the corresponding simulated model results. Model parameters were estimated by the simulation with acceptable standard errors and confidence interval of 88.63%. TSS was high in fruits

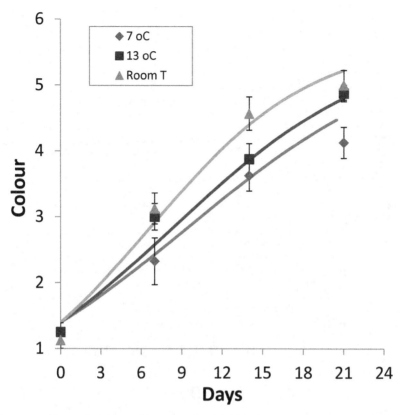

Fig. 2. Color change of mango fruit during storage at 7, 13 °C and room temperature for storage durations of 21 days. The lines represent the model, and the points are the mean of the measured values (Color figure online).

stored with ambient temperature, next fruits stored at 13° C and minimum TSS was observed fruits sored at 7 °C during three weeks of storage. After developing the model for predicting firmness, colour and total soluble solids a ripening stage are assigned from 1 to 5 as shown in the Table 1. with the corresponding quality values; where 1 is the mature green and 5 is the over ripe stage. For each temperature, a limiting quality factor [3] was established considering the rating value of 3 as the maximum acceptable quality before the fruit becomes unmarketable [4]. More specifically, for each temperature, the factor that limited the product marketability was identified from the quality curves.

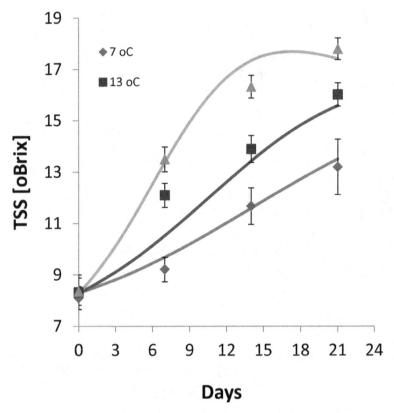

Fig. 3. Total soluble solids of mango fruit during storage at 7, 13 °C and room temperature for storage durations of 21 days. The lines represent the model, and the points are the mean of the measured values (Color figure online).

From these curves it was observed that a single quality factor cannot be used to express the loss of quality of mangoes over the storage period. As it can be easily inferred from the graph softening was the limiting quality factor for mango stored at

Table 1. Average seven-eighths cooling time for mangoes inside different packages.

Ripeness stage	Stage	Flesh color	Firmness (kg/mm2)	TSS
Mature green	1	Very light yellow	>14	>17
Partially ripe	2	Light yellow	10–14	15–17
Full ripe	3	Yellow-light	6–10	12–15
Soft ripe	4	Yellow-orange	2–6	9–12
Over ripe	5	Golden orange	<2	<9

7 °C and color was the limiting quality factor for mango stored at 13 °C and room temperature (Fig. 4).

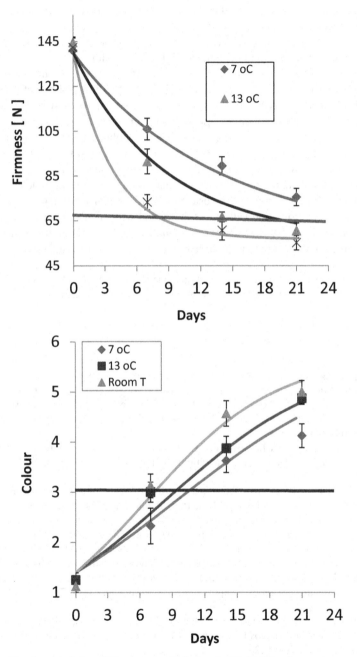

Fig. 4. Quality characteristics of Kent mango fruit stored at 7, 13 °C and room temperature. The red horizontal line represents the maximum acceptable quality (rating ~ 3).

4   Conclusion

Kinetic model was developed for predicting relationship between storage and shelf life conditions and mango quality attributes. Significant quality changes were observed under the three temperature storage conditions which show the effect of temperature on quality parameters. The firmness of mango fruit at all conditions decreases significantly during the storage period but the extent is higher at higher temperature. Slow firmness drop was observed at 7 °C but duse to the occurrence of chilling injury mango cannot stored at this temperature for a long period of time. Softening was the limiting quality factor for mango stored at 7 °C but color was the limiting quality factor for mango stored at 13 °C and room temperature. The Ethiopian mango supply chain from harvest to consumer is expected to take between 15–19 days. So using a cold chain throughout the chain is a must to keep the quality of mango fruit to the standard and in order to avoid the variable quality of mango on arrival in overseas countries. As a result single quality factor cannot be used to express the loss of quality of mangoes over the storage period at variable temperature. Further analysis is recommended to use the quality model for dynamic temperature which needs to determine the validity of the model with such storage conditions. It is also possible to improve the accuracy of the quality model by doing the measurements at shorter time interval and including other cultivars and maturity stages.

Acknowledgements. The financial contribution of the VLIR-UOS TEAM project 'Technologies to reduce postharvest losses of Ethiopian fresh fruit' is greatly acknowledged.

References

1. Gwanpua, S.G., et al.: Kinetic modeling of firmness breakdown in 'Braeburn' apples stored under different controlled atmosphere conditions. Postharvest Biol. Technol. **67**, 68–74 (2012)
2. Tefera, T., Seyoum, T., Woldetsadik, K.: Effect of disinfection, packaging, and storage environment on the shelf life of mango. J. Biosyst. Eng. **96**(2), 201–212 (2007). https://doi.org/10.1016/j.biosystemseng
3. Nunes, M.C.N., Emond, J.P., Brecht, J.K., Proulx, E.: Quality curves for mango fruit (cv. Tommy Atkins and Palmer) stored at chilling and non-chilling temperatures. J. Food Qual. **30**, 104–120 (2006)
4. Mitchell in Kader: Postharvest Technology of Horticultural Crops. University of California, Division of Agriculture and Natural Resources, Publication 3311, pp. 290–296 (1992)
5. Gwanpua, S., et al.: Pectin modifications and the role of pectin-degrading enzymes during postharvest softening of Jonagold apples. Food Chem. **158**, 283–291 (2014)
6. Hertog, M.L.A.T.M., Verlinden, B.E., Lammertyn, J., Nicolaï, B.M.: OptiPa, an essential primer to develop models in the postharvest area. Comput. Electron. Agric. **57**, 99–106 (2007)
7. Johnston, J.W., Hewett, E.W., Hertog, M.L.A.T.M., Harker, F.R.: Temperature induces differential softening responses in apple cultivars. Postharvest Biol. Technol. **23**, 185–196 (2001)
8. Talcott, S.T., Moore, J.P., Lounds-Singleton, A.J., Percival, S.S.: Ripening associated phytochemical changes in mangos following thermal quarantine and low temperature storage. J. Food Sci. **70**(5), 337–341 (2005)
9. Singh, Z., Singh, R.K., Sane, V.A., Nath, P.: Mango - postharvest biology and biotechnology. Crit. Rev. Plant Sci. **32**(4), 217–236 (2013)

10. ILRI: Fruits - A Synthesis of IPMS Value-Chain Development Experiences, pp. 116–132. ILRI, Nairobi (2011)
11. Gomer-Lim, M.A.: Post harvest physiology. In: Litz, R.E. (ed.) The Mango: Botany, Production and Uses, pp. 425–446. CAB International, New York (1997)
12. Kittur, F.S., Saroja, N., Habibunnisa, Tharanathan, R.N.: Polysaccharide-based composite coating formulations for shelf-life extension of fresh banana and mango. Eur. Food Res. Technol. **213**, 306–311 (2001)
13. Mann, S.S., Singh, R.N.: The cold storage life of Dashehari mango. Sci. Horticultureae **5**, 249–254 (1976)

Modeling of Gasification of Refuse Derived Fuel: Optimizations and Experimental Investigations

Dawit Musse[1(✉)], Wondwossen Bogale[1], and Berhanu Assefa[2]

[1] School of Mechanical and Industrial Engineering, Addis Ababa Institute of Technology,
Addis Ababa University, Addis Ababa, Ethiopia
dwtmus@gmail.com
[2] School of Chemical and Bio Engineering, Addis Ababa Institute of Technology,
Addis Ababa University, Addis Ababa, Ethiopia

Abstract. Nowadays, renewable energy technologies for decentralized electrification are promising in addressing electrification issues. In this study, gasification of Refuse Derived Fuel is investigated for its potential to generate good quality producer gas for use in internal combustion engines for electricity generation. Representative Municipal Solid Waste is separated, screened, prepared and characterized. Lower heating value of the RDF is 16.63 MJ/kg which is an acceptable yield. The gasification was modeled using non-stoichiometric thermodynamic equilibrium model and implemented on MATLAB for optimization. Optimal values of temperature and equivalent ratios were determined to be 850 °C and 0.2, respectively, at a moisture content of 6%. A downdraft gasifier with the gas cleaning and conditioning system has been designed, manufactured and tested experimentally to validate the model. Based on the result, the producer gas heating value was 8.164 MJ/m^3, which is acceptable for utilization in ICEs. The capacity of the gasifier is 147 kW at feed rate of 46 kg/h and product gas flow rate of 65.14 m^3/h to meet engine requirements. The cold gas efficiency of the gasifier is 70%. In conclusion, a good agreement was observed between experimental and simulation results for gas characterization. Catalytic gasification gives promising results for future investigations on the use of Dolomite as a primary cleaning along with advanced secondary gas cleaning system.

Keywords: Gasification · Modeling · Refuse Derived Fuel · Equivalence ratio (E.R) · Gas cleaning

1 Introduction

Solid Waste Management is becoming a very challenging issue in developing countries due to lack of regulation on solid waste collection, recycling and disposal [1–3]. In Ethiopia, the first waste to energy plant with a capacity of 25 MW$_{el}$ is under construction in its capital city, Addis Ababa. However, Ethiopia is a country with a population of 100 Million people and 80% of the populations live in rural areas [4]. In addition to the waste management problem, 75% of the population is living without access to electricity

© ICST Institute for Computer Sciences, Social Informatics and Telecommunications Engineering 2020
Published by Springer Nature Switzerland AG 2020. All Rights Reserved
N. G. Habtu et al. (Eds.): ICAST 2019, LNICST 308, pp. 82–97, 2020.
https://doi.org/10.1007/978-3-030-43690-2_7

[5]. Considering a waste generation rate of 0.25 kg/day/person and the considering the current population of Ethiopia, i.e., 102 Million, potentially 25.5 Million kg of waste is generated daily [4]. Although several waste-to-energy plants exit in most of the developed countries, it is still at its infancy stage in Africa and Ethiopia, in particular.

Municipal Solid waste (MSW) is a good source of energy [10, 11]. The specific energy content of MSW can be enhanced by further processing it into Refuse Derived Fuel (RDF). RDF refers to a separate high calorific fraction of municipal solid waste, solid and dry commercial and/or industrial process wastes [7]. Other terms are also used for MSW derived fuels, such as: Refused Fuel (RF), Packaging Derived Fuels (PDF), and Process Engineered Fuels (PEF) [7]. RDF from MSW can be a good alternative source of energy that can replace fossil fuels [6, 7].

Thermo-chemical conversion of waste is a high temperature process causing modifications on the chemical nature/structure of the feed material. Combustion, gasification and pyrolysis are the three main technological options for thermo–chemical processes [8, 9, 14].Gasification provides good thermo-chemical conversion efficiency by offering high flexibility in terms of various materials as feedstock and due to this, it has an interesting advantage over direct combustion and pyrolysis in some technological applications such as prior gasification of biomass and waste and subsequent utilization of producer gas in ICEs, which is a rational way to use in small scale energy producing units [9, 14, 15]. In gasification, the four important processes that occur inside the reactor are: drying, pyrolysis, oxidation and reduction. Each process inside the gasifier is associated with its certain physical and chemical features in the respective zones. Modeling implies the representation of a chemical or a physical system by a set of equations so that it can represent the system under study [12]. When considering a downdraft gasifier, the modeling of chemical reactions taking place in each zone can be carried out separately as shown in Fig. 1.

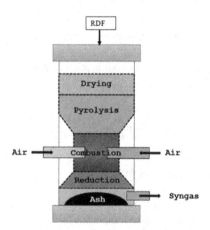

Fig. 1. Schematics of key process zones of downdraft gasifier [16]

Gasifier simulation models are classified into thermodynamic equilibrium model, kinetic model, CFD model and artificial neural network [12, 17]. In thermodynamic equilibrium models, either stoichiometric or non-stoichiometric approaches can be employed. Stoichiometric equilibrium approach includes thermodynamics along with the chemical equilibrium of chemical reactions. This method can be designed in two ways. It can be used for the global gasification reaction or can be used for each zone of drying, pyrolysis, oxidation and reduction [13]. The non-stoichiometric equilibrium approach is basically designed by minimizing Gibbs free energy of the system [17]. However, elemental composition and moisture content of the fuel is needed. These values can be obtained from ultimate and proximate analysis data of the feed. This approach is typically preferable for feedstocks, like biomass and RDF, as the chemical formula of these feedstocks is not exactly known [18]. Kinetic model is suitable for prediction of product gas composition and gas yield after finite residence time, in a finite volume of reactor at a gasification temperature [17]. Even though kinetic model is computationally intensive, it provides multi-dimensions to investigate the behavior of gasification and gasifier via simulation and it is considered to be the most accurate model [19].

For a product gas to be used in heating/burner applications, with no cleanup, an updraft gasifier can be used. However, if the product fuel gas is to be used in ICEs for an application as that of electricity generation, then a downdraft gasifier is commonly used for its relatively high tar cracking ability among the other gasifier types. In addition, the gas must be cleaned and conditioned before it is fed to the engine [14, 15]. The producer gas exiting the downdraft gasifier is hot and laden with dust, containing up to 1% tars and particulates [27]. If these contaminants are not removed properly, maintenance and reliability problems will occur on engine, heat exchangers and other parts of the system making it more costly and troublesome. In fact, failure of many gasifier-engine systems have been attributed due to the problem of improper cleanup systems alone [20]. The gas cleaning and conditioning system also plays important role in controlling hazardous emissions. In order to design effective gas clean up systems, nature of contaminants with the magnitude of potential problem has to be determined.

Well-carried out design of an economical gas cleaning and conditioning system was performed to achieve conditions demanded by the internal combustion engines (Table 1).

Table 1. Gas quality requirements for power generation applications in ICEs [27]

Major contaminants	Level of purification demanded by IC engine
Particle concentration	<50 mg/Nm^3
Particle size	<10 μm
Tar	<100 mg/Nm^3

The recommended procedure is as follows [28]:

1. Particulates are first removed at temperature below dew point of tar ($\approx300\,°C$)
2. Next, tar is removed at intermediate temperatures ($\approx100\,°C$)
3. Finally, water is removed at 30 °C to 60 °C, and each separate contaminant will be handled more easily.

The cleaning subsystem is designed with properly-sized components of the following selected methods (Table 2).

Table 2. Gas contaminants cleaning methods selection

	Contaminants	Available cleaning/filtering methods [25, 29–31]	Methods employed on this study
1	Particulates	• Cyclone separator • Barrier filter • Electrostatic precipitator • Wet scrubber	• Cyclone separator (**Justification**: easy design and uses gravity for settling of particles out of gas line. A cyclone of high efficiency can be fabricated a low effort and cost)
2	Alkali Compounds	• Cooling below 600 °C + electrostatic precipitator • Cooling below 600 °C + fabric filter • Cooling below 600 °C + bag filter	• Cooling below 600 °C + fabric filter (**Justification**: has good efficiency, ease of manufacturing and cost-effective)
3	Nitrogen Compounds	• Standard Catalytic Methods	• Catalytic distraction
4	Sulfur and Chlorine	• Wet scrubbing • Additives	• Additives (**Justification**: Abundant availability of Dolomite catalyst in Ethiopia for a primary cleaning (cleaning performed inside the gasifier) than wet scrubber)
6	Tar	• Thermal destruction • Catalytic destruction • Barrier filters • Wet scrubbers	• Catalytic destruction + Barrier filters (**Justification**: use of barrier filters of high efficiency and the inexpensive dolomite catalyst that will affect heating value of the gas positively along with the primary cleaning advantage)

The schematic of the pilot setup is shown below (Fig. 2).

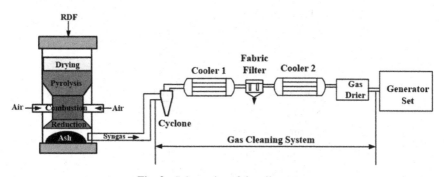

Fig. 2. Schematics of the pilot setup

This study aims to build a realistic model for gasification of RDF in a fixed bed downdraft gasifier, to estimate species concentration in the producer gas and the heating value for wide range of gasification temperatures. The optimal equivalence ratio and operating temperature will be computationally estimated at a moisture content of 6%. Equivalence ratio (E.R) is the ratio of actual air fuel ratio to stoichiometric air fuel ratio and provides the basis for evaluating the amount of air supplied for gasification with respect to the amount of air required for complete combustion or stoichiometric oxidation of the feedstock. It also involves performing process design of the gasifier and a gas cleaning and conditioning system with proper sizing, and fabrication of the pilot set up that can produce a producer gas that meets the minimum requirements of ICEs. Further, experimental investigations on the pilot setup will be carried out to draw valid conclusions on the characterization of the product gas by validating with model outputs and a preliminary investigation on catalytic gasification will be done by the use of Dolomite mineral for primary gas cleaning.

2 Methodology

2.1 Characterization of RDF Sample

The ultimate and proximate analysis results for the RDF sample are depicted as shown in Table 3. The moisture content, ash content, volatile matter and fixed carbon were determined by standard procedures [21]. The moisture content is determined by the loss in weight that occurs when a sample is dried in a laboratory oven at 105 °C for 1 h. The volatile matter is determined by measurement of weight loss following combustion of about 1 g RDF sample in a furnace at 950 °C for 6 min. To determine the ash content, the samples were heated in a laboratory ash furnace at 750 °C for at least 3 h. The ultimate analysis of the sample was determined using ultimate analyzer. Thus, based on the elemental analysis, the chemical formula of the RDF sample is determined and normalized with respect to Carbon. The chemical formula of the RDF sample is $CH_{1.7155}O_{0.6510}N_{0.01172}$.

Table 3. Characterization of the RDF

Ultimate analysis (w/w %)	
Carbon	41.7241
Hydrogen	5.9648
Oxygen	36.2183
Nitrogen	0.5703
Sulfur	0
Proximate analysis (w/w %)	
Moisture content	6.56
Volatile matter	7.12
Fixed carbon	11.36
Ash content	8.96
LHV [MJ/kg]	16.63

2.2 Mathematical Model

The non-stoichiometric equilibrium model for gasification of the RDF was formulated by developing empirical relations for predicting the individual fraction of major combustible constituents of the producer gas. These relations can be used for any gasifier and are more accurate and realistic for downdraft gasifier due to its relatively higher tar cracking ability. In this work, the following assumptions were made [22–24]: The species considered to appear in the producer gas are: CO, CO_2, H_2, CH_4, N_2 and water; 100% carbon conversion efficiency; the residence time is high enough to achieve thermodynamic equilibrium; ash in feedstock is inert in all gasification reactions (although this hold true only for reaction temperatures below 700 °C); the pressure drop inside gasifier is negligible and all gaseous products behave as ideal gases, the process is adiabatic, Sulfur and Chlorine content in RDF is negligible (they have a very small share (<0.6%) in the total feedstock).

The chemical composition of RDF is taken to be in the form $CH_X O_Y N_Z$ and the global gasification reaction can be written as:

$$CH_X O_Y N_Z + m_w H_2O + X_{air}(O_2 + 3.76N_2)$$
$$\rightarrow n_1 CO + n_2 H_2 + n_3 CO_2 + n_4 H_2O + n_5 CH_5 + n_6 N_2$$

m_w is calculated from:

$$M_{RDF} \times m = m_w[18(1 - m)] \rightarrow m_w = \frac{M_{RDF} \times m}{[18(1 - m)]}$$

Mass Balance

$$\text{Carbon Balance: } n_1 + n_3 + n_5 = 1 \tag{1}$$

$$\text{Hydrogen Balance: } x + 2m_w = 2n_2 + 2n_4 + 4n_5 \tag{2}$$

$$\text{Oxygen Balance: } y + m_w + 2X_{air} = n_1 + 2n_3 + n_4 \tag{3}$$

$$\text{Nitrogen Balance: } n_6 = 0.5Z + 3.76X_{air} \tag{4}$$

Basic Chemical Equilibrium Reactions and Equilibrium Constants
The major reactions that occur inside downdraft gasifier are [14]:

$$C + CO_2 \rightarrow 2CO \tag{5}$$

$$C + H_2O \rightarrow H_2 + CO \tag{6}$$

The two reactions shown above can be combined into one single reaction known as water-gas shift reaction.

$$CO + H_2O \leftrightarrow CO_2 + H_2 \tag{7}$$

The other reaction that is important in the gasification process is the methane formation reaction.

$$C + 2H_2 \leftrightarrow CH_4 \tag{8}$$

Now, Eqs. 7 and 8 are the two major reactions in the gasification process. The equilibrium constants for the above two major reactions as a function of their molar composition are as follows:

$$K_1 = \frac{n_{CO_2} * n_{H_2}}{n_{CO} * n_{H_2O}} = \frac{n_3\, n_2}{n_1\, n_4} \tag{9}$$

$$K_2 = \frac{n_{CH_4} * n_{tot}}{\left(n_{H_2}\right)^2} = \frac{n_5\, n_{tot}}{n_2\, n_2} \tag{10}$$

Gibbs free energy is used in determining the values of K_1 and K_2. For the given ideal gases, the Gibbs free energy is a strong function of temperature.

$$\ln K(T) = \frac{-G(T)}{RT} \tag{11}$$

$$\Delta G\,(T) = \sum_i n_i \Delta g_{f,i}^o(T) \tag{12}$$

The change in Gibbs free energy for each individual gas is empirically given by (Table 4):

$$\Delta g_{f,i}^o(T) = H_{f,i}^o + aT\ln T - bT^2 - 0.5cT^3 - (d/3)T^4 + (e/2T) + f \tag{13}$$

Table 4. Enthalpy of formation and constants for Eq. 13 [14]

Species	$\tilde{H}_{f,298}^o$	$a \times 10^2$	$b \times 10^5$	$c \times 10^8$	$d \times 10^{12}$	$e \times 10^{-2}$	f	g
CH_4	−74.8	−4.62	1.13	1.32	−6.65	−4.89	14.1	−0.223
CO	−110.5	0.562	−1.19	0.638	−1.85	−4.89	0.868	−0.0613
CO_2	−393.5	−1.95	3.12	−2.45	6.95	−4.89	5.27	−0.121
H_2O	−241.8	−0.895	−0.367	0.521	−1.48	0	2.87	−0.0172

Energy Balance inside the Gasifier

The total energy content in any chemical species is the sum of its chemical enthalpy and sensible enthalpy, which can be written as:

$$H_{f,RDF}^o + m_w \left(H_{f,H_2O(l)}^o + H_{vap}\right) + X_{air}\left(H_{f,O_2}^o + 3.76 H_{f,N_2}^o\right)$$

$$= n_1\left[H_{f,CO}^o + \int_{298\,K}^{T_g}(C_{p,CO}dT)\right] + n_2\left[H_{f,H_2}^o + \int_{298\,K}^{T_g}(C_{p,H_2}dT)\right]$$

$$+ n_3 \left[H^O_{f,CO_2} + \int\limits_{298\,K}^{T_g} (C_{p,CO_2}dT) \right] + n_4 \left[H^O_{f,H_2O} + \int\limits_{298\,K}^{T_g} (C_{p,H_2O}dT) \right]$$

$$+ n_5 \left[H^O_{f,CH_4} + \int\limits_{298\,K}^{T_g} (C_{p,CH_4}dT) \right] + (0.5z + 3.76X_{air}) \int\limits_{298\,K}^{T_g} (C_{p,N_2}dT) \tag{14}$$

Since heat of formation of all diatomic molecules (H^O_{f,N_2}, H^O_{f,O_2}, H^O_{f,H_2}) is zero at reference temperature and pressure of 298 K and 1 atm, Eq. 13 reduces to:

$$H^O_{f,RDF} + m_w \left(H^O_{f,H_2O(l)} + H_{vap} \right) = n_1 \left[H^O_{f,CO} + \int\limits_{298\,K}^{T_g} (C_{p,CO}dT) \right]$$

$$+ n_2 \left[H^O_{f,H_2} + \int\limits_{298\,K}^{T_g} (C_{p,H_2}dT) \right] + n_3 \left[H^O_{f,CO_2} + \int\limits_{298\,K}^{T_g} (C_{p,CO_2}dT) \right]$$

$$+ n_4 \left[H^O_{f,H_2O} + \int\limits_{298\,K}^{T_g} (C_{p,H_2O}dT) \right] + n_5 \left[H^O_{f,CH_4} + \int\limits_{298\,K}^{T_g} (C_{p,CH_4}dT) \right]$$

$$+ (0.5z + 3.76X_{air}) \int\limits_{298\,K}^{T_g} (C_{p,N_2}dT) \tag{15}$$

C_p can be determined from an empirical correlation given by [14] (Table 5):

$$C_p(T) = C_1 + C_2T + C_3T^2 + C_4T^4 \tag{16}$$

Table 5. Coefficients of specific heat capacity for various gases [14]

Species	C_1	C_2	C_3	C_4
N_2	31.2	$-1.36\,(10)^{-2}$	$2.68\,(10)^{-5}$	$-1.17\,(10)^{-8}$
CO_2	19.8	$7.34\,(10)^{-2}$	$-5.60(10)^{-5}$	$1.72\,(10)^{-8}$
H_2	29.1	$-1.92\,(10)^{-2}$	$4.00\,(10)^{-6}$	$-8.70\,(10)^{-10}$
CO	30.9	$-1.29\,(10)^{-2}$	$2.79\,(10)^{-5}$	$-1.23\,(10)^{-8}$
CH_4	19.3	$5.21\,(10)^{-2}$	$1.20\,(10)^{-5}$	$-1.13\,(10)^{-8}$
H_2O (g)	32.2	$1.92\,(10)^{-2}$	$1.06\,(10)^{-5}$	$-3.60\,(10)^{-9}$

Model Implementation

The equilibrium constants of gasification reactions (Eqs. 9 and 10) and the elemental composition of the fuel (RDF) from ultimate analysis data are input to the model to obtain producer gas composition. It involves solving the system of equations in MATLAB using Newton–Jacob Iteration. Once the producer gas composition is determined from the feedstock, a linear equation is developed to calculate the concentration of each gas species in the producer gas.

Experimental Setup

The pilot set up used for experiment is shown in Fig. 3 with gasifier dimensions in Table 6.

Table 6. Design parameters of the gasifier

Gasifier design parameter	Value
The throat diameter, d_t	10 cm
The superficial velocity of the gas, v_g,	2.5 m/s
Throat Inclination, θ	45°
Height of Nozzle Plane above the Throat, h	9.79 cm
Height of Oxidation Zone, h_{oxd}	19.58 cm
The nozzle inner diameter, d_m	1.043 cm
Number of nozzles, N	5
Top Nozzle Ring Diameter, d_n	22.08 cm
Height of the Reduction Zone, h_r	18.72 cm
Height of the Pyrolysis Zone, h_p	130 cm
Total Height of the Reactor, H	180 cm

Fig. 3. The fabricated experimental setup

3   Result and Discussion

Molar fractions of compositions of the producer gas for gasification temperatures ranging from 573.15 K to 1523.15 K (300 °C to 1250 °C) and for equivalence ratios ranging from 0.2 to 0.35 are simulated. Model results are shown in Figs. 4, 5, 6, 7 and 8. The variation of LHV at different temperatures and equivalence ratios at a moisture content of 6%, are estimated using the following formula and is shown in Fig. 8. LHV of the producer gas (LHV_g) is calculated from the gas analysis data of the producer gas. Lower heating value of different constituent of the producer gas at STP (20 °C and 1 atm) is used in the calculation. The following expression is used for calculation of lower heating value of the producer gas.

$$LHV_g = \sum X_i H_i$$

Where, X_i = Volume fraction of producer gas constituent and H_i = Heating value of constituent gases. Heating values of constituent gases are referred from Table C.2 of [14]. E.R is the most influential parameter in any gasification process and often has significant impact on product gas composition. The theoretical gasification occurs between E.R values of 0.19–0.43 and the optimum point is near to 0.25 [14].

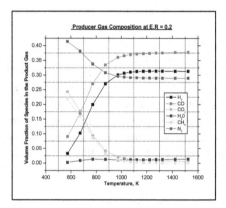
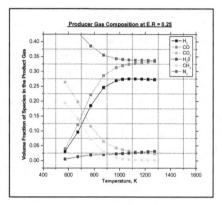

Fig. 4. Producer gas composition at E.R = 0.2 **Fig. 5.** Producer gas composition at E.R = 0.25

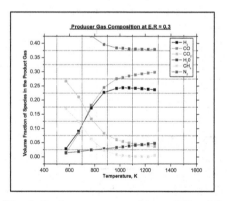
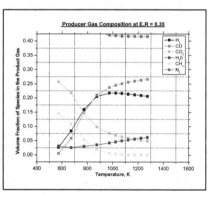

Fig. 6. Producer gas composition at E.R = 0.3 **Fig. 7.** Producer gas composition at E.R = 0.35

From the above results, it can be seen that concentrations of H_2 and CO increase in a similar trend towards higher temperature values. This is attributed to the fact that the water-gas shift reaction (Eq. 7) and the methane formation reaction (Eq. 8) favor backward reactions at higher temperatures (800 °C and 700 °C, respectively) to give more CO and H_2 at the expense of CO_2 and CH_4, respectively. This agrees with the points discussed in [14]. Additionally, it can be observed that molar concentrations of H_2 and CO decrease at higher E.R values. This results in decreased heating value of the product gas at higher E.Rs. The concentrations of H_2 and CO increase for temperatures above 800 °C and slightly decrease as E.R increases. This is because, as E.R increases, more air/oxygen is supplied to the process. Oxidation will dominate the reduction reaction and, thus, reducing the heating value by providing less room for the most important process of reduction where chemical energy is bonded in the constituents of the producer gas. If E.R is kept on increasing, finally, when E.R = 1, the gas will be of no heating value and, hence, a flue gas. It can also be observed from Fig. 8 that, heating value of the gas will decrease at higher temperatures for a given equivalence ratio. This is due to a decrease in the concentration of CH_4 at higher temperatures of thermo-chemical conversion. As seen from the results, as the methane formation reaction tends to a backward reaction at higher temperatures to give more H_2 than CH_4. Methane has the highest LHV among all the other gases according to Table C.2 of [14] and, thus, decline of its concentration will significantly affect the total LHV value of the gas. Another option to maximize the LHV of the gas is to maximize production of species with relatively higher LHV next to CH_4 (CO and H_2) at higher temperatures. However, the LHV value at higher temperatures will be lesser than that of the LHV at lower temperatures. This shows that the LHV of Methane significantly affects the LHV of the producer gas. In fact, this is one of the rationales behind the need for optimization.

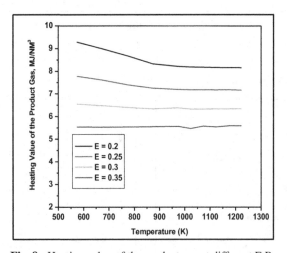

Fig. 8. Heating value of the product gas at different E.Rs

The computation results indicate that in each cases carbon monoxide is the most dominant component in the product gas, followed by hydrogen and carbon dioxide, at higher temperatures. This is due to the water-gas reduction and partial combustion of carbonaceous char materials at the bed. Hydrogen is formed in the bed due to gasification reactions involving water with further release of carbon monoxide and carbon dioxide.

Methane formation is favored at temperatures less than 700 °C as postulated from its reaction thermodynamics and at temperatures above 900 °C, production of methane is almost negligible (Figs. 4, 5, 6 and 7).

Fig. 9. The produced producer gas   **Fig. 10.** Experimental apparatus

Molar concentrations of carbon monoxide and hydrogen reach peaks at temperatures above 800 °C with no or slight variation after the peak value. This makes LHV of the producer gas to be constant after 800 °C for each equivalence ratio. The LHV of species concentration gives the maximum value of 8.164 MJ/m^3, which is a well-accepted yield as recommended by [26, 27]. The optimal parameters for this maximum LHV value are a gasification temperature of 850 °C and an equivalence ratio of 0.2. This temperature is a point at which more carbon monoxide and hydrogen gas discovered in the product gas at equivalence ratio of 0.2, with a remarkable contribution to the maximization of the gas heating value. At these optimal operating conditions, the gasifier power will be 147 kW at cold gas efficiency of 70% and at feed rate of 46 kg/h to produce gas flow rate of 65.14 m^3/h, which is fit for engine operational requirements.

The results obtained with the model implementation in this work have been validated with experimental results from the test runs conducted on the pilot setup (Figs. 9 and 10). During the first test, experimental characterization of the producer gas was performed and results were compared with model output at optimal operating conditions for validation, shown on Fig. 11. Very similar results are achieved for CO and CH_4 concentrations in the product gas. Both approaches estimate very small production of CH_4 and relatively higher CO. The very small concentration of methane in the product gas confirms the fact that no chemical equilibrium can be achieved in reality, especially below 800 °C. The methane formation reaction favors backward reaction and production of carbon and hydrogen gas is facilitated at higher temperatures, which is expected to have major share in other gases (collective gases remained in ppm). As a result, insignificant amount of methane is predicted and obtained in both cases. Therefore, carbon is the most dominant in the product gas in the form of CO, CO_2 and CH_4. The experimental and modeling results show a very good agreement on the contents of CO, CH_4 and other collective gases with unexpected deviation on CO_2 content as shown on Fig. 11. The CO_2 content, which is estimated to have fewer shares in the product gas in both approaches, has shown significant deviation one from the other, experimental result has overestimated the CO_2 content as the following gaps were identified on the experiment to attribute to the deviation.

- The control of the gasification temperature exactly at 850 °C is difficult. The experiments were conducted at various temperature ranges and sampling was taken only at temperatures near to the optimal value. With slight difference on the gasification temperature, exaggerated deviation on CO_2 yield is observed. The water gas shift reaction is a reversible reaction more active at temperatures above 800 °C. The reaction is forward reaction in the instantaneous temperatures of sampling and is characterized by increased mole fractions of CO_2.
- The air flow rate was measured well to meet the condition (E.R = 0.2), but to make continued tests, two air compressors was used interchangeably with repeated calibrations in the middle of the test each time air lines are changed. There is a possibility for the combustion zone to be air-rich contributing for the increase in CO_2 content.

On the second test, catalytic gas purification was evaluated by comparing the results with that of the gasification without catalyst from test 1 as shown in Fig. 12. Using the above measured species, the tar cracking performance of the catalyst was preliminarily examined. The catalytic gasification is observed to yield more CO and reduce CO_2 content. This effective reduction process has come to effect by tar cracking action imposed by the Dolomite catalyst. Experiment reveals slightly overestimated values for the other gases and the best analysis referred to this case is increase of contents from broken compounds like NO_X to which the catalyst is sensitive to. The experiment gives well agreed results for CO, CO_2 and CH_4 expected variations before and after the cleaning process. This can be clearly seen that these species are more of sensitive to the methane formation and water gas shift reduction process in the bed of the gasifier than other thermal and filtration processes outside the gasifier. The oxygen content in both samples (before and after) is quiet low and yet much underestimated result was obtained from the sample after the clean-up. This might be attributed to favored oxidation of SO_X and other compounds at lower temperature after cooling stages, increases the parts of other gases per millions at the expense of used up oxygen gas.

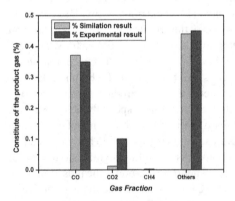

Fig. 11. Simulation vs experimental result

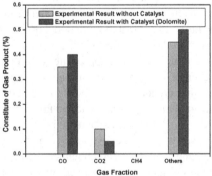

Fig. 12. Comparision of gasification with and without catalyst

The model used an assumption of 1 bar pressure in the gasifier and the pressure gauge at the outlet of the gasifier gave a reading close to 0.82 bar, which makes the assumption valid as the amount of pressure drop observed supports the fact that downdraft gasifier have relatively lower pressure drop.

4 Conclusion

In use of producer gas for IC engines, the most important objective is to produce a cleaner (low tar) gas with high heating value. To achieve the production of gas with relatively high heating value, it is important to convert carbon dioxide and water to as much carbon monoxide, hydrogen and methane as possible, as these constituents contribute relatively high heating values for the gas. Therefore, it can be seen that it is desirable to give emphasis and encourage the two main reduction reactions (Methane formation reaction and Water Gas shift reaction). The optimum LHV of the product gas (8.164 MJ/m^3) is high enough for downdraft gasification as recommended by [26, 27] and is a good yield from downdraft for applications such as utilization of the gas in IC engines for electricity generation. Operating conditions of the gasifier for this best operating condition are at 850 °C and equivalence ratio of 0.2. Tar is observed in the producer gas in lower equivalence ratios and further gas cleaning and conditioning system has to be considered. Non-stoichiometric models give reliable results for producer gas characterization from simple input that can be determined from elemental composition and proximate analysis data. The lower heating value (LHV) of a typical RDF lie in the range 15 MJ/kg to 18 MJ/kg according to the selection process and amount high LHV constituents present [7]. The LHV value of the prepared RDF is 16.63 MJ/kg, which is in the suitable range. A good agreement between modeling and simulation results was achieved for gas characterization at the gasifier outlet, which supports the fact that non–stoichiometric thermodynamic equilibrium model can adequately simplify the computation. Catalytic gasification and the gas cleaning system gives promising results for future advanced investigations on the use of Dolomite as a primary cleaning and more advanced secondary gas cleaning techniques. Generally, the pilot plant is of easy configuration as shown on Fig. 3, which can produce 147 kW of power in an area of less than 3 m^2 and is user-friendly operation, that is, control of the system require only control adequate feed rate than any other technical adjustments on the system.

Acknowledgement. We thank AAU – Vice President for Research and Technology for funding (Under Thematic Research Grant), Ethiopian Minerals, Petroleum and Biofuels Corporation for offering sample Dolomite mineral for free, AUU, Faculty of Natural and Computational Sciences and Department of Chemistry, Geological Survey of Ethiopian laboratories.

Acronyms

E.R	Equivalence Ratio
CFD	Computational Fluid Dynamics
ICEs	Internal Combustion Engines
MW$_{el}$	Mega Watts of electricity

μm	Micro Meter
kW	Kilo Watts
LHV	Lower Heating Value
MSW	Municipal Solid Waste
PDF	Packaging Derived Fuels
PEF	Process Engineered Fuels
ppm	Parts Per Million
RDF	Refuse Derived Fuels
RF	Refused Fuels
WTE	Waste – to – Energy
C, H, O, N	Carbon, Hydrogen, Oxygen, Nitrogen
M_{RDF}	Molecular weight of the RDF
m	Moisture content of the RDF
m_w	Number of moles of water vapor in dry basis
n_i	Number of moles of species 'I' in the producer gas.
n_{tot}	Total number of moles of gases
x, y, z	Normalized coefficient of atomic Hydrogen, Oxygen and Nitrogen for RDF molecule.
X_{air}	Number of moles of air
K_1	Equilibrium Constant for Water – Gas Shift Reaction
K_2	Equilibrium Constant for Methane Formation Reaction
$\Delta G (T)$	Gibbs free energy [KJ/Kmol]
$\Delta g^0_{f,i}(T)$	Change in Gibbs free energy for individual gas, i at a given temperature.
$H^O_{f,i}$	Enthalpy of formation for spices i
a, b, c, d, e, f	Coefficients for Gibbs free energy empirical correlation.
$C_{p,i}$	Specific heat capacity for species i

References

1. Guerrero, L.A., Maas, G., Hogland, W.: Solid waste management challenges for cities in developing countries. Waste Manag **33**(1), 220–232 (2013)
2. Han, Z., et al.: Influencing factors of domestic waste characteristics in rural areas of developing countries. Waste Manag **72**, 45–54 (2018)
3. Bleck, D., Wettberg, W.: Waste collection in developing countries - tackling occupational safety and health hazards at their source. Waste Manag **32**(11), 2009–2017 (2012)
4. Fikreyesus, D., Mika, T., Getane, G., Bayu, N., Mahlet, E.: Ethiopia solid waste and landfill: country profile and action plan. Community Development Research Sponsored by Global Methane Initiative (2011). https://www.globalmethane.org/documents/landfills
5. Bekele, G., Tadesse, G.: Feasibility Study of Small Hydro/PV/Wind hybrid system for off-grid rural electrification in Ethiopia. Appl. Energy **97**, 5–15 (2012)
6. Sever Akdağ, A., Atimtay, A., Sanin, F.D.: Comparison of fuel value and combustion characteristics of two different RDF samples. Waste Manag **47**, 217–224 (2016)
7. Gendebien, A., et al.: Refuse derived fuel, current practice and perspectives. Curr. Pract. **4**, 1–219 (2003)
8. Lombardi, L., Carnevale, E., Corti, A.: A review of technologies and performances of thermal treatment systems for energy recovery from waste. Waste Manag **37**, 26–44 (2015)

9. Beyene, H.D., Werkneh, A.A., Ambaye, T.G.: Current updates on waste to energy (WtE) technologies: a review. Renew. Energy Focus **24**, 1–11 (2018)
10. Bogale, W., Viganò, F.: A preliminary comparative performance evaluation of highly efficient Waste-to-Energy plants. Energy Procedia **45**, 1315–1324 (2014)
11. World Energy Council: World energy resources 2016. World Energy Resour. **2016**, 1–33 (2016)
12. Arnavat, M.P.: Performance modelling and validation of biomass gasifiers. Ors Pr of . Dr . A o Coron Nas D Joan n Carle Es Brun o De Epartme Ent of M Nical En Ngineeri Ing Ta (2011)
13. Kalita, P., Baruah, D.: Investigation of biomass gasifier product gas composition and its characterization. In: De, S., Agarwal, A.K., Moholkar, V.S., Thallada, B. (eds.) Coal and Biomass Gasification. EES, pp. 115–149. Springer, Singapore (2018). https://doi.org/10.1007/978-981-10-7335-9_5
14. Basu, P.: Biomass Gasification and Pyrolysis Handbook. Academic Press, Boston (2010)
15. Reed, T.B., Das, A.: Handbook of biomass downdraft gasifier engine systems. Biomass Energy Foundation, Golden (1988)
16. Aydin, E.S., Yucel, O., Sadikoglu, H.: Development of a semi-empirical equilibrium model for downdraft gasification systems. Energy **130**, 86–98 (2017)
17. Fortunato, B., Brunetti, G., Camporeale, S.M., Torresi, M., Fornarelli, F.: Thermodynamic model of a downdraft gasifier. Energy Convers. Manag. **140**, 281–294 (2017)
18. Patra, T.K., Sheth, P.N.: Biomass gasification models for downdraft gasifier: a state-of-the-art review. Renew. Sustain. Energy Rev. **50**, 583–593 (2015)
19. Mahinpey, N., Gomez, A.: Review of gasification fundamentals and new findings: reactors, feedstock, and kinetic studies. Chem. Eng. Sci. **148**, 14–31 (2016)
20. Marculescu, C., Cenuşă, V., Alexe, F.: Analysis of biomass and waste gasification lean syngases combustion for power generation using spark ignition engines. Waste Manag **47**, 133–140 (2016)
21. Bogale, W.: Preparation of charcoal using flower waste. J. Power Energy Eng. **05**(02), 1–10 (2017)
22. Bhavanam, A., Sastry, R.C.: Modelling of solid waste gasification process for synthesis gas production (2013)
23. Raj, A.B.S., Deepthi, C.: Recycling of municipal solid waste for electricity generation and green earth. Int. J. Sci. Res. Manag. **2**(3), 679–683 (2014)
24. Tobergte, D.R., Curtis, S.: Parametric study of a commercial-scale biomass downdraft gasifier: experiments and equilibrium modeling. J. Chem. Inf. Model. **53**(9), 1689–1699 (2013)
25. Hasler, P., Buehler, R. Nussbaumer, T.: Evaluation of gas cleaning technologies for biomass gasification. In: Tenth European Conference and Technology Exhibition, Biomass for Energy and Industry, Würzburg, Germany, June, pp. 272–275 (1998)
26. Roy, P.C., Datta, A., Chakraborty, N.: An assessment of different biomass feedstocks in a downdraft gasifier for engine application. Fuel **106**, 864–868 (2013)
27. Margaritis, N.K., Grammelis, P., Vera, D., Jurado, F.: Assessment of operational results of a downdraft biomass gasifier coupled with a gas engine. Procedia Soc. Behav. Sci. **48**, 857–867 (2012)
28. Shrivastava, V.: Design and development of downdraft gasifier for operating CI engine on dual fuel mode. Doctoral dissertation (2012)
29. Balas, M., Lisy, M., Skala, Z., Pospisil, J.: Wet scrubber for cleaning of syngas from biomass gasification. Dev. Chem. Adv. Environ. Sci. 195–201 (2014). ISBN 978-1-61804-239-2
30. Singh, R.N., Singh, S.P., Balwanshi, J.B.: Tar removal from producer gas: a review. Res. J. Eng. Sci. **3**, 16–22 (2014). ISSN 2278-9472
31. Kim, J.W., Mun, T.Y., Kim, J.O., Kim, J.S.: Air gasification of mixed plastic wastes using a two-stage gasifier for the production of producer gas with low tar and a high caloric value. Fuel **90**(6), 2266–2272 (2011)

On-Farm Performance and Assessment of Farmers' Perceptions of Hermetic Bags for Farm-Stored Wheat and Maize in Northwestern Ethiopia

Karta Kaske Kalsa[1,2]([✉]), Bhadriraju Subramanyam[3], Girma Demisse[4], Admasu Worku[2], Solomon Workneh[2], and Nigus Gabbiye[2]

[1] Kulumsa Agricultural Research Center, P. O. Box 489, Asella, Ethiopia
kartakaske@gmail.com
[2] Bahir Dar Institute of Technology, Bahir Dar University, Bahir Dar, Ethiopia
[3] Department of Grain Science and Industry, Kansas State University, Manhattan, KS 66502, USA
[4] Holeta Agricultural Research Center, Holeta, Ethiopia

Abstract. Wheat and maize farmers in Ethiopia seldom adopted hermetic storage technologies which can substantially reduce post-harvest losses. Two on-farm storage experiments and a perception survey were conducted to evaluate the effectiveness of the PICS bag and Super GrainPro bag and to assess farmers' perceptions towards the utility of the technologies in two districts of West Gojjam, Northwest of Ethiopia in the years 2016 and 2017. Results showed that live adult weevil densities in hermetic storage bags such as PICS bag and Super GrainPro bag were below five insects per kg of maize after four months of storage. In wheat, there was no live weevil prevalence in hermetic storage bags after four months of storage. Weight loss wheat and maize stored in airtight bags was maintained at <1.0%. A majority of farmers (95.0%, N = 80) perceived that the hermetic bags are effective against weevils, and 87.3% (N = 80) had the tendency to use airtight bags in the future. Farmers' use of PICS bags in the past had a positive influence on their interest in the future use of hermetic containers. In conclusion, the present study showed that hermetic storage bags are practical under on-farm conditions in Ethiopia. Therefore, we recommend the extensive promotion of the technologies and increasing their local availability.

Keywords: Hermetic bags · Farmers' perception · Wheat · Maize · Ethiopia

1 Introduction

Ethiopia is a leading producer of wheat and the 3rd largest producer of maize in sub-Saharan Africa [1]. Yield increasing technologies such as improved varieties, mineral fertilizer, and increased extension education have all contributed for significant improvement in productivity per unit area of grain crops in the country [2]. In Ethiopia, wheat

N. G. Habtu et al. (Eds.): ICAST 2019, LNICST 308, pp. 98–109, 2020.
https://doi.org/10.1007/978-3-030-43690-2_8

and maize yield increased from below 1.5 metric tons per ha before two decades to about 2.7 metric tons per ha and 3.9 metric tons per ha, respectively, in recent years [3]. Currently, wheat and maize are making about 48% of the total cereals and 43% of the total grain production in the country with a total production of 13 million metric tons. However, poor postharvest storage results in loss of about 6.6% of wheat and 11.2% of maize in the country [4].

The farmers' limited awareness and skills on improved post-harvest management options are largely responsible for the food losses in Ethiopia and elsewhere [5, 6]. Smallholder farmers store their grain until the next successful harvest, which might be a year or more. Grain produced by farmers should be stored to meet home consumption, for sale or seed purpose [8, 9]. However, grain stored in traditional structures is subject to deterioration by biological and physical factors [5, 6].

Wheat and maize farmers rarely adopt hermetic grain storage bags that reduce storage losses in Ethiopia [10, 11]. On the other hands, the adoption of recommended post-harvest handling practices is highly correlated with the lower postharvest loss [5]. Hermetic storage techniques can be recommended to farmers without the use of insecticides provided they are inexpensive, and the farmers are trained on a proper application of the technologies [7]. The present study aimed at (1) participatory evaluation of the effectiveness of hermetic storage bags in farmers' houses, (2) assessment of farmer's perceptions towards the utility of hermetic storage bags, and (3) identification of factors related to farmers' tendency of future use of the hermetic storage bags.

2   Materials and Methods

Two on-farm experiments and a survey were conducted to understand the performance of hermetic bags under farmer's conditions and the perception of farmers towards the utility of the improved storage bags. The study was conducted in two districts (Merawi and Wenberma) of West Gojjam, Amhara Regional State.

2.1   Treatment Set Up and Experimental Design

Hermetic storage bags such as Purdue Improved Crop Storage (PICS) bags and Super GrainPro bags (high-density polyethylene bags reducing gas exchange) were compared with traditional storage system (with polypropylene bags at Wenberma and with *gotta* in Merawi district) under farmers' conditions.

The treatments were set up in a randomized complete block design with nine replications. Farmers served as blocks in both wheat and maize studies. Each farmer stored two types of hermetic bags plus his *gotta* (for maize) and polypropylene bags for wheat. Polypropylene bags were purchased from a local market.

2.2   Wheat On-Farm Storage Experiment

At Wenberma, the experiment consisted of three treatments: two hermetic bags (PICS and Super GrainPro bags) and polypropylene bags (control), replicated on seven smallholder farms. Farmers who have grown the maize variety Kakaba had participated in the study and all the farmers had placed untreated wheat in hermetic bags. In this experiment, wheat in polypropylene bag was not treated with any chemical.

Bags were filled with 50 kg of wheat and sealed 30th January 2017, and they were opened on 10th June 2017, after 130 days of storage. The grains in the hermetic bags were kept for about four months, and sampling was carried out by randomly reaching the top, middle, and bottom sections of the bags. The primary samples from a container were then homogenized, and one kg sample per container was brought to the laboratory.

2.3   Maize On-Farm Storage Experiment

At Merawi, the experiment consisted of three treatments: two hermetic bags (PICS and Super GrainPro bags) and one traditional storage structure (*gushgusha*), replicated on nine smallholder farms. Farmers who have grown the maize variety Jabi (Pioneer 3253) had participated in the study, and all the farmers had placed untreated shelled grains in hermetic bags, while the grains in traditional storage structure were treated with Malathion 5% dust or fumigated with Phosphine gas or in combination.

Bags were filled with a naturally infested grain (2 to 4 insects per kilogram, based on samples collected at the beginning of storage) and sealed on 7th to 10th June 2016; they were opened on 10th to 13th October 2016, after 125 days of storage. The grains in the hermetic bags were kept for about four months, and sampling was carried out by randomly reaching the top, middle, and bottom sections of the bags. The same trend was followed to get samples from traditional storage. The primary samples from a container were then homogenized, and one kg sample per container was brought to the laboratory.

2.4   Data Collection from Storage Experiments

Measurements of gas composition (CO_2 and O_2 levels) (done before the hermetic bags were opened), adult insect abundance (both live and dead), grain damage, weight loss, grain moisture content, grain bulk density, and thousand kernel weights were determined after four months of storage for both experiments.

One kg samples were divided following the use of quartering and coning technique until the final sample of around a 100 g of seed was obtained. From the 100 g of whole seeds, damaged and undamaged kernels were counted and weighed.

2.5   Percentage of Weight Loss and Insect-Damaged Kernels

Each of the maize/wheat samples was divided following the quartering and conning technique until a final sample of around a 100 g of maize/wheat was obtained. From a 100 g of sound maize/wheat, damaged and undamaged kernels were separated, counted, and weighed. Mechanical damages were included in dockages (when it was < 50% of the average size). Insect damaged kernels were visually identified based on holes made by boring insects.

Maize/wheat weight loss was estimated using the equation [11, 12]: maize/wheat Weight Loss (%) = [(WU * ND) − (WD * NU)] * 100/[WD * (NU + ND)], where, WU is weight of undamaged maize/wheat, NU is number of intact maize/wheat, WD is weight of damaged maize/wheat, ND is number of damaged maize/wheat.

Grain damage rates were calculated using the equation Percentage of Insect-Damaged Kernels = Number of Insect-Damaged Kernels*100/Number of Kernels in 100 g of maize/wheat.

2.6 Germination Testing

Wheat seed samples were subject to germination testing using the standard method as prescribed for wheat in Rules of Seed Testing of International Seed Testing Association [13] with modifications. Germination test was carried out in two runs of 100 seeds. Seeds (randomly picked damaged and undamaged seeds) were placed in plastic bowls on top of 15 cm diameter sterile germination papers. The germination papers were soaked in distilled water before sowing the seeds. The bowls, then, were covered with a glass lid and placed in a germination room adjusted at 20 °C temperature. Normal and abnormal seedlings and dead seeds were assessed eight days after sowing, and percentages were calculated.

2.7 Perception Survey

A one-page checklist was prepared to assess farmers' perception towards the utility of hermetic bags they used. A total of six villages were included1: one from Merawi and five from Wenberma districts, West Gojjam, Northwest Ethiopia. A total of 80 households, who were provided with hermetic bags during the year 2016 were included in the survey. To cross validate the survey responses, a focus group discussion with development agents and selected farmers was organized at Merawi.

2.8 Data Analysis

All data from the on-farm storage experiments were subject to one-way analysis of variance (ANOVA) using the R Software version 5.3.1. All count data were log transformed where required, and the percentage data were square root transformed before analysis of variance. Where the ANOVA showed an overall significance, Tukey's range test was employed to separate significantly different means at 5% level of significance. Survey data were coded, and descriptive analyses were employed using the IBM SPSS statics version 20. Plots were created using the SigmaPlot Software version 12.5 [14].

3 Results

3.1 Maize On-Farm Storage: Weevil Abundance

There was a significant effect ($P < 0.01$) of storage structures on both live weevil count and total weevil specimen counts per kg of maize (Table 1). The abundance of live weevil specimen was significantly higher in the traditional *gotta* structure compared with the hermetic bags. Hermetic bags substantially decreased the population development of weevils in maize (Fig. 1).

Table 1. Analyses of variance for live weevil counts, total weevil counts, the percentage of insect-damaged kernels and grain weight loss of maize stored in farmers' houses between June and September 2016.

Sources of variation	DF	Live weevils (counts per kg)		Total weevils (counts per kg)		Insect-damaged kernels (%)		Grain weight loss (%)	
		F-value	P-value	F-value	P-value	F-value	P-value	F-value	P-value
Storage structures	2	161	0.00	81.4	0.00	30.6	0.00	27.1	0.00
Farmers	8	0.7	0.70	0.5	0.81	0.9	0.55	0.8	0.58
Error variance	16	0.02		0.01		0.17		0.03	

3.2 Maize On-Farm Storage: Grain Weight Loss and Damage

Percentages of insect-damaged kernels and grain weight loss were significantly influenced ($P < 0.01$) by storage structures (Table 1). The proportion of insect-damaged kernels was significantly higher in *gotta* compared to hermetic bags (Fig. 2). Likewise, the grain weight loss percentage was significantly higher in the traditional *gotta* structure compared to hermetic bags. There was a non-significant difference between the PICS bag and Super GrainPro bag about either the percentage of insect-damaged kernels or the grain weight loss percent.

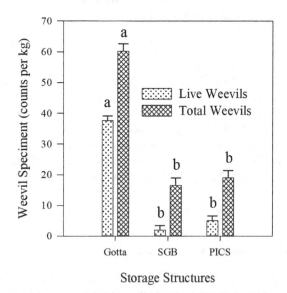

Fig. 1. Mean ($\pm SE$) of weevil abundance (counts per kg of seed) of maize stored in farmers' houses between June and September, 2016. Means followed by the same letter are not significantly different at Tukey's 5% level of significance, and each mean is based on nine farmers.

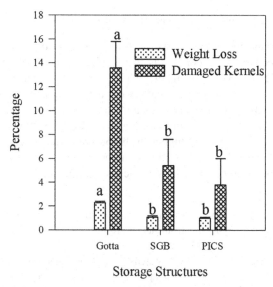

Fig. 2. Mean (±*SE*) percentage of insect-damaged kernels and grain weight loss of maize stored in farmers' houses between June and September 2016. *Note*: Means followed by the same letter are not significantly different at Tukey's 5% level of significance, and each mean is based on nine farmers.

3.3 Wheat On-Farm Storage: Baseline

At the outset of the on-farm storage experiment of wheat, the weevil abundance, test percentage of seed damage and grain weight loss, weight (bulk density), and seed germination and vigor were assessed. There was no live or dead insect specimen detected at the beginning of the storage experiment while a number of insect-damaged seed ranged from 12 to 26 seeds per 100 g with a mean value of 20.1 damaged seeds per 100 g. Likewise, the percentage of insect-damaged kernels ranged from 0.40% to 0.95%, while grain weight loss percentage was between 0.10% and 0.51%. The mean value of percentage insect-damaged kernels and grain weight loss percent were 0.7% and 0.3%, respectively. Test weight (seed bulk density) was between 751 kg m^{-3} and 818 kg m^{-3} with a mean value of 781.8 kg m^{-3}. Percentage seed germination ranged between 87.0% and 99.0% with a mean value of 94.1% whereas the seed vigor index was between 552%.mg to 1786%.mg. The mean value of seedling vigor index at the beginning was 1043.9%.mg.

3.4 Weevil Abundance and Number of Damaged Kernels in Stored Wheat

Significant differences (P < 0.01) between hermetic storage bags and the polypropylene bag were detected in both live insect abundance and the number of insect-damaged kernels (Table 2). The highest mean number of live weevils was detected in wheat stored in polypropylene bags. Likewise, the largest mean number of insect-damaged kernels was observed in the same container.

3.5   Weight Loss and Loss of Bulk Density in Stored Wheat

There were significant differences between hermetic bags and the polypropylene bag regarding their effectiveness of containing losses. Grain weight loss was significantly higher (F = 8.45; DF = 2, 32; P < 0.01) in polypropylene bags compared to the hermetic bags (Fig. 3). There was no such difference between the two hermetic bags. Likewise, the percentage of insect-damaged kernels was significantly higher (F = 16.82; DF = 2, 32; P < 0.01) on wheat stored in polypropylene bags. The loss of test weight (bulk density of the seed) was also significantly higher in the polypropylene bags compared to the hermetic bags. Seed bulk density was slightly higher in Super GrainPro bag compared to PICS bag, but the difference was not statistically significant.

Table 2. Mean (±SE) of weevil abundance and number of insect-damaged kernels of wheat seed stored in farmers' houses at Wenberma from January to June 2017.

Bag Type	Live Weevils (counts per kg)	Damaged Kernels (counts per 100 g)
Super GrainPro Bag	0.6 b	20.1 a
PICS bag	0.1 b	20.1 a
Polypropylene bag	2.6 a	50.1 b
F (DF = 2, 26)	17.07	21.98
P-value	<0.01	<0.01
SEM	0.3	4.2

Means within the same column and followed by the same letter are not significantly different at Tukey's 5% level of significance. Each mean is based on seven farmers and two replications per farmer.

3.6   Seed Quality in Stored Wheat

Table 3 shows seed quality parameters such as the percentage of seed germination, seedling dry-weight, and seedling vigor index of wheat stored in different bag types. There was a non-significant difference among different types of bags regarding seed germination after four months of storage. However, there seedling vigor parameters of wheat stored in Super GrainPro bags was significantly higher compared to the polypropylene bags. There was no significant difference between PICS bag and polypropylene bag during four months of storage.

3.7   Farmers' Perceptions of the Utility of Hermetic Bags

Table 4 shows the descriptive analysis of farmers' perceptions of the utility of hermetic bags. About 95.0% of 80 household heads included in the study had believed that the bags protected their grains from weevil damages. About 93.8% of respondents (N = 80) were indifferent or felt that the price is low, but only 6.3% of all respondents had claimed that

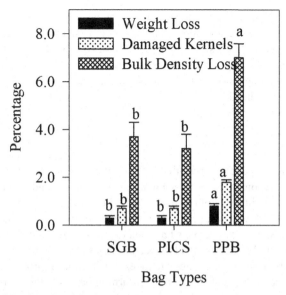

Fig. 3. Mean (±*SE*) of seed weight loss (the %), the percentage of insect-damaged kernels and percentage loss of bulk density (test weight) of wheat seed stored using hermetic bags at farmers' houses in Wenberma from January to June 2017. *Note*: Means followed by the same letter are not significantly different at Tukey's 5% level of significance, and each mean is based on seven farmers and two replications per farmer.

bag prices are costly (the price of PICS bag is ca. $1.47 and that of SuperGrain™ bag is ca. $2.44 at the time of the survey). All farmers who were indifferent about bag price had the likelihood to use the improved bags in the future. However, the possibility of repeated use, reduced amount of loss, and health benefits from reduced/no use of insecticides can be positive drives for future use of hermetic bags by farmers in Ethiopia.

Table 3. Mean (±*SE*) of seed quality characteristics of farm-stored wheat in hermetic bags.

Bag type	Seed germination (%)	Seedling dry weight (mg)	Seedling vigor index (mg. %)
Super GrainPro Bag	94.7	9.4a	885.0a
PICS bag	94.5	8.1ab	763.0ab
Polypropylene bag	94.3	7.3b	687.0b
F (2, 32)	0.10^{NS}	4.88*	4.59*
P-value	0.91	0.01	0.02
SEM	0.8	0.5	46.4

Means within the same column and followed by the same letter are not significantly different at Tukey's 5% level of significance. Each mean is based on seven farmers and two replications per farmer.

There was no significant difference between the ages of those who wanted to use hermetic bags in the future and those who did not want to. However, fishers exact test indicated that there was a significant association (P < 0.05) between sex and the tendency to use hermetic bags in the future (odds ratio = 0.238). Farmers' tendency to use hermetic storage bags did not have any significant association with the education status of the household head.

4 Discussion

In our present study, we have observed that the hermetic bags such as PICS bag and Super GrainPro bag have suppressed weevil population development and reduced the rates of grain damage and weight loss both in maize and wheat under farmers' conditions. The germination capacity of wheat seed was also maintained in a better condition.

Adoption of hermetic storage bags has been driven by the effectiveness, simplicity, low cost, durability, and accessibility of the technologies [15]. Studies showed that some form of exposure by farmers to storage practices is related to improved adoption of the hermetic storage technologies [16]. In our on-farm experimentation with farmers, we have observed that farmers' interest in chemical-free storage technology was heightened. Though farmers were so suspicious to store their maize or wheat in hermetic bags without chemical treatment, they were very happy with the outcomes (Box 1). This shows that once farmers have the chance to look at the difference between their traditional storage method and the improved technologies, they show a better tendency towards using hermetic storage bag.

The main determinants of adoption were household socio-economic characteristics such as age, land ownership, completion of a training course, and quality of basic infrastructure [16]. Our study included only sex, age, and education as a social factor that determined farmers' tendency to use hermetic storage bags. Age and education had no association with farmers' tendency to use hermetic storage bags in the future. Regardless of their age and education status, farmers have applauded the chemical-free hermetic storage technology. The contemporary bag price, with additional awareness of farmers on the reuse of the hermetic bags, does not have a negative influence on farmers' tendency to use the hermetic storage bags in the future. However, the tendency of farmers towards future use of hermetic bags was positively influenced by using PICS bag (Table 5). This might be due to farmers' perception about the triple bagged hermetic technology that it is less susceptible to tears and wears during handling.

Table 4. Farmers' perception of the utility of hermetic bags in Merawi and Wenberma districts

Characters	Frequency (%)	Characters	Frequency (%)
Sex (n = 80)		Level of infestation before bagging (n = 80)	
Male	77.5	High	11.3
Female	22.5	Low	21.3

(continued)

Table 4. (*continued*)

Characters	Frequency (%)	Characters	Frequency (%)
Education (n = 80)		None	67.5
No formal education	57.5	Infested with live weevil after opening (n = 80)	
Primary incomplete	38.8	Yes	21.2
Secondary incomplete	3.8	No	78.8
Bags Used (n = 80)		Level of live weevil infestation after (n = 80)	
PICS	78.8	High	1.3
Super GrainPro	15.0	Low	20.0
Both types	6.3	None	78.8
Types of grain stored (n = 80)		Believe bags effective on weevils (n = 80)	
Wheat	25.0	Effective	95.0
Maize	46.3	Not effective	1.2
Both	28.8	Don't know	3.8
Used chemicals in bags (n = 80)		How do you evaluate bag price? (n = 80)	
Yes	14.7	Costly	6.3
No	86.3	Indifferent	33.8
Type of chemicals (n = 80)		Cheap	60.0
Malathion	2.5	Compare new bags to pp bags (n = 80)	
Phosphine	5.0	Better	95.0
Both	6.3	No difference	5.0
None	86.3	Do you plan to use hermetic bags in the future? (n = 80)	
Infested with live weevil before bagging (n = 80)		Yes	87.3
Yes	67.5	No	12.7
No	32.6		

Box 1:

Ato Demeke Mekonen and W/ro Gedene Demelew are residents of Kudmi kebele in Merawi district, West Gojjam, Amhara. They used hermetic storage bags to store their maize grain from May to September 2016. After four months of storage, the bags were opened in the presence of the spouses, and they saw no damage on the grains while the maize which they fumigated with Phosphine and placed in polypropylene bags had live weevils and certain damages. W/ro Gedene (wife) at the end disclosed that she was so suspicious of storing their maize grain in hermetic bags without treating with chemicals. Ato Demeke and Gedene were one of the families who already have recognized the side effects of chemicals they used against weevil. They were so happy to see a chemical-free technology that preserves their maize grain without damage..

In conclusion, hermetic bags are effective under farmers' conditions, and they can be better alternatives to polypropylene bags which are predominantly used by wheat farmers [7, 17]. Besides, there is a high rate of acceptability of hermetic storage technologies by farmers. The type of hermetic bag used by farmers determined the farmers' tendency to the use of hermetic bags in the future. Introduction of the Super GrainPro bag with an external layer of polypropylene bag might increase farmers' tendency to use it. Besides, local availability of hermetic bags should be improved so that farmers can easily access the bags at the time of their need.

Table 5. Probit analysis of factors influencing farmers' tendency for future use of hermetic bags a,b,c

Variables	Estimate	SE	β- coefficients	t-value	P-value
Intercept	0.516	0.119		4.343	<0.01
Sex (Male = 1; Female = 0)	0.116	0.086	0.189	1.807	0.075
Use PICS (Yes = 1; No = 0)	0.310	0.100	0.321	3.091	0.003
Insect Damaged Before (Yes = 1; No = 0)	−0.083	0.053	−0.167	−1.595	0.115

[a] Null deviance: 9.49 on 79 degrees of freedom
[b] Residual deviance: 7.71 on 76 degrees of freedom
[c] AIC: 49.84

Acknowledgments. The research reported here was also made possible by the partial support of the American people through the United States Agency for International Development (USAID) under the Feed the Future initiative (www.feedthefuture.gov). The contents are the responsibility of the Innovation Lab for the Reduction of Post-Harvest Loss (www.k-state.edu/phl) and do not necessarily reflect the views of USAID or the United States Government.

References

1. FAO. FAOSTAT Database (2019). http://www.fao.org/faostat/en/#home. Accessed 12 July 2019
2. Kotu, B.H., Admassie, A.: Potential impacts of yield-increasing crop technologies on productivity and poverty in two districts of Ethiopia. In: Gatzweiler, F.W., von Braun, J. (eds.) Technological and Institutional Innovations for Marginalized Smallholders in Agricultural Development, pp. 397–421. Springer, Cham (2016). https://doi.org/10.1007/978-3-319-25718-1_20
3. CSA. Report on Farm Management Practices. Agricultural Sample Survey, vol. 3. Addis Ababa, Ethiopia: Central Statistical Agency (CSA) (2018)
4. FAO. Postharvest loss assessment of maize, wheat, sorghum and haricot bean: a study conducted in fourteen selected woredas of Ethiopia. Food and Agriculture Organization (FAO) of the United Nations (2017)
5. Chegere, M.J.: Post-harvest losses reduction by small-scale maize farmers: the role of handling practices. Food Policy **77**, 103–115 (2018)

6. Hengsdijk, H., de Boer, W.J.: Post-harvest management and post-harvest losses of cereals in Ethiopia. Food Secur. **9**(5), 945–958 (2017). https://doi.org/10.1007/s12571-017-0714-y

7. Abass, A.B., Ndunguru, G., Mamiro, P., Alenkhe, B., Mlingi, N., Bekunda, M.: Post-harvest food losses in a maize-based farming system of semi-arid savannah area of Tanzania. J. Stored Prod. Res. **57**, 49–57 (2014)

8. Kalsa, K.K.: Farmers' attitudes and practices towards variety and certified seed use, seed replacement and seed storage in wheat growing areas of Ethiopia. Afr. J. Sci. Technol. Innov. Dev. **11**, 107–120 (2019)

9. Tadesse, A., Eticha, F., Adler, C., Schoeller, M.: Insect pests of farm-stored maize and their management practices in Ethiopia. Integr. Prot. Stored Prod. **23**, 45–57 (2000)

10. Tesfaye, W., Tirivayi, N.: The impacts of postharvest storage innovations on food security and welfare in Ethiopia. Food Policy **75**, 52–67 (2018)

11. Kalsa, K.K., Subramanyam, B., Demissie, G., Mahroof, R., Worku, A., Gabbiye, N.: Evaluation of postharvest preservation strategies for stored wheat seed in Ethiopia. J. Stored Prod. Res. **81**, 53–61 (2019)

12. Mohammed, A., Tadesse, A.: Review of Major Grains Postharvest Losses in Ethiopia and Customization of a Loss Assessment Methodology. USAID/Ethiopia - Agriculture Knowledge, Learning, Documentation and Policy Project, Addis Ababa, Ethiopia (2018)

13. ISTA. International Rules for Seed Testing. Zürichstr. Bassersdorf, Switzerland: International Seed Testing Association (ISTA) (2014)

14. Anonymous, SigmaPlot, version 12.5. Systat Software, Inc., San Jose, California, USA (2013)

15. Moussa, B., Abdoulaye, T., Coulibaly, O., Baributsa, D., Lowenberg-DeBoer, J.: Adoption of on-farm hermetic storage for cowpea in West and Central Africa in 2012. J. Stored Prod. Res. **58**, 77–86 (2014)

16. Bokusheva, R., Finger, R., Fischler, M., Berlin, R., Marín, Y., Pérez, F., Paiz, F.: Factors determining the adoption and impact of a postharvest storage technology. Food Secur. **4**, 279–293 (2012). https://doi.org/10.1007/s12571-012-0184-1

17. Kalsa, K.K., Subramanyam, B., Demissie, G., Worku, A.F., Habtu, N.G.: Major insect pests and their associated losses in quantity and quality of farm-stored wheat seed. Ethiop. J. Agric. Sci. **29**(2), 71–82 (2019)

Water Resource and Environmental Engineering

Developing Domestic Water Security Index in Urban Cities, Bahir Dar City, Ethiopia

Marshet B. Jumber[3]([✉]), Eshetu Assefa[1], Seifu A. Tilahun[1], and Mukand S. Babel[2]

[1] Faculty of Civil and Water Resources Engineering, Bahir Dar Institute of Technology, 26,
Bahir Dar, Ethiopia
esheaa@gmail.com, satadm86@gmail.com

[2] Water Engineering and Management, School of Engineering and Technology, Asian Institute
of Technology, Pathum Thani 12120, Thailand
msbabel@ait.asia

[3] Department of Hydraulic and Water Resources Engineering,
Debre Tabor University, 272, Debre Tabor, Ethiopia
marshetb1@gmail.com

Abstract. Water security is one of the global indicators in sustainable development goals, which becomes the cross-cutting issue worldwide. Studies have been performed at global, national, and city levels to assess the water security issues. Since assessment of water security at domestic scale has not been done yet in developing countries like Ethiopia, it is essential to develop an appropriate framework for the assessment of domestic water security at the city scale and apply it for urban cities of Ethiopia. The study therefore aimed at developing the domestic water security assessment framework and apply the framework to assess domestic water security index for cities in Ethiopia. The developed framework comprises of three dimensions: water supply, sanitation and hygiene; eleven indicators and fifteen variables. These indicators were defined using driver, pressure, state, impact and response (DPSIR) approach. The variables of the indicators were defined by specific, measurable, attainable, relevant and time bound (SMART) criteria and were used to identify and select the composite of the appropriate indicators and variables. Analytical hierarchy process (AHP) and equal weighting methods were used to compute an index by giving different and equal weighting factors for variables, indicators and dimensions respectively. The developed framework was applied for Bahir Dar city to quantify its domestic water security index for the year 2017/18. Generally, Bahir Dar city is found under medium (2.8) domestic water security status with high (3.41), medium (2.29) and very low (1.0) indices of water supply, sanitation and hygiene dimensions respectively.

Keywords: Domestic water security index · Framework · Analytical Hierarchy Process

1 Introduction

Water is at the heart of sustainable development. Its significance for human survival, socio-economic development, and healthy ecosystems cannot be overemphasized [1].

© ICST Institute for Computer Sciences, Social Informatics and Telecommunications Engineering 2020
Published by Springer Nature Switzerland AG 2020. All Rights Reserved
N. G. Habtu et al. (Eds.): ICAST 2019, LNICST 308, pp. 113–125, 2020.
https://doi.org/10.1007/978-3-030-43690-2_9

The threefold increase of the global population during the 20th century has triggered a simultaneous six-fold increase in water use [2]. This has an adverse impact on water security, especially in urban areas. In 2012, approximately 50% of the world population lived in cities, and by 2030 this will be 60% [3]. Securing drinking water supply is one of the fundamental components in urban water security. In related to this, delivery of clean water, adequate sanitation and hygiene is one of the sustainable development goals (SDG6). However, meeting drinking water demands is becoming a big challenge globally, particularly in developing countries due to an increase in consumption that is driven by urbanization, rapid population growth, economic growth, and change in local climate [4]. Thus, water is becoming a critical resource for world's growing urban areas [2].

The recently adopted SDGs has a dedicated global water security. As a result, a number of countries have incorporated national goals in their mid- to long-term policies in order to meet the global targets [1]. Improving water security is, therefore, rapidly becoming a key point on the policy and development agenda both at national and international levels [1]. The definition of water security should be based on the concept of how the city can be water secured [1].

According to Vorosmarty [5], the scale is also critical in assessing water security in analyzed that different disciplines tend to focus on different scales. Hoekstra [6] also described that the concept of water security is used from the household to the global level. Moreover, water security assessment at the national scale can mask significant variations in security at the local scale [5].

Provision of water for human domestic use can be viewed as a fundamental example of water Security [3]. According to Asian Development Bank [7] household water security is the foundation and cornerstone of water security to eradicate poverty and support economic development by providing all people with reliable, safe water, sanitation and hygiene services should as giving a top priority. DPSIR and SMART approaches are a corner stone criterion to select indicators and variables [1].

Definition of Domestic Water Security is therefore the cornerstone to build the assessment of domestic water security on the selected area. It has been defined in relation with how the city become domestically water secured or the water security in household level. As reviewed from literatures, domestic water security has been assessed as one dimension of water security assessment and it is defined as the basic part of water security.

Drinking water supply with adequate quality and quantity, sanitation and hygiene are the basic needs to keep safe human health [8]. However, many countries particularly developing countries are suffering to fulfill those basic needs and water infrastructures. Moreover, urbanization, industrialization, climate change etc. affects water resource. SDG (7) goal dictates to achieve domestic water security; there should be universal and equitable access to safe and affordable drinking water for all and access to adequate and equitable sanitation and hygiene for all and end open defecation [9].

Domestic water security definition for this study: "Every person has to be easily accessed water supply, improved sanitation and hygienic facilities with an affordable price, and drinking water have to be safe quality, sufficient quantity with insignificant water wastage at any time: the sanitation system should be safely managed and every person should be free from water related diseases". The aim of this study is to develop a framework for assessing domestic water security at city scale and to measure the domestic water security index of Bahir Dar city in year 2018/2019.

2 Domestic Water Security Framework Development

2.1 Components of Framework

There are three main components of the domestic water security framework to be developed for the assessment of water security at household level: dimensions, indicators, and variables. Dimensions are main components of domestic water security. Indicators are used to represent the dimensions and answer what to measure. Variables are used to measure indicators. Dimensions was selected from the definition of domestic water security and are water supply, sanitation and hygiene.

Selection of Indicators and Variables: After defining domestic water security and selecting dimensions, the second step is to select indicators that reflect the main characteristics of the key dimensions [10]. Indicators are tools that provide information about something [11]. They are used to express the nature of key dimensions and their selection will depend on the purpose and specific application of the assessment [10]. Variables are used to quantify the indicators and can answer the question "How to measure". They should be acceptable and reliable and are sensitive to changes over space and time [1].

The indicators had been selected from the DPSIR framework, SMART criteria [1]. On the applied DPSIR framework, the impact is the problem on domestic water security and the driver is the cause for the pressure or stress created on. The state is the change due to the stress created or changing the domestic water security status and the response represents the possible solution for solving the problem on domestic water security or to achieve domestic water security.

As the dimensions of water security are water supply, sanitation and hygiene, the driving forces for these dimensions in the Ethiopian context are, anticipated population growth and low-income level. Due to these driving forces, there is a pressure created on the urban community, which is high water demand for drinking, sanitation purpose and hygiene; higher demand of sanitation and hygienic services. The impact of the state of the three dimensions are generally low livelihood security and public health problem. The responses or the solution for those problems are improving water supply system, putting rules and regulations on water, sanitation and hygiene, encouraging good water use habits, personal hygienic practices and wastewater reuse. Monitoring quality of water, water loss, sanitation system management, implementation of hygienic practices are also parts of the responses.

The framework (Fig. 1) was developed by identifying the domestic water security dimensions, indicators and variables.

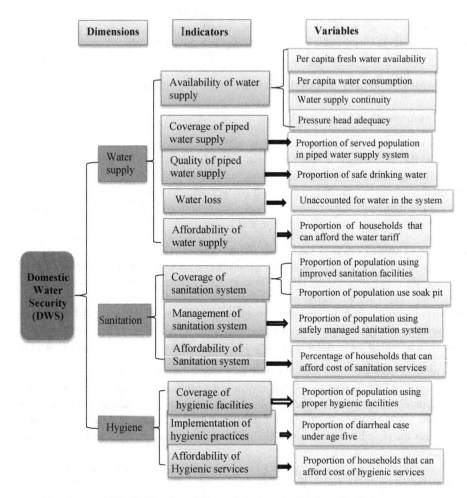

Fig. 1. Developed domestic water security framework

2.2 Representation and Interpretation of the Domestic Water Security Index

In this study, 1 to 5 scale which are <1 very low, 1 to 2 low, 2 to 3 medium, 3 to 4 high and 4 to 5 very high domestic water security was adopted. The very low domestic water security means that the city of the study area is incapable of meeting the basic water supply requirements of its citizens, whereas very high-water security is defined as the city is a model for domestic water secured society.

2.3 Scaling and Bench Marks of Water Security Variables

Developing domestic water security index means expressing it in terms of number or specific value. It is also helpful for the stakeholders to understand the status of the security in easy and understandable way. Growth and Transformation Plan II, SDG and Asian

Water Development Outlook 2013 documents were mostly applied as a benchmark for the assessment of scales of variables. Therefore, to calculate the index, different variables with various measuring units have to be normalized to common scale with interpretation. In this study the value of each variable is classified into a 1 to 5 scale as shown in Table 1.

Table 1. Representation of variable scores in relation to the 1–5 scale adopted

Dimensions	Variables	Unit	Scale					Sources
			1	2	3	4	5	
Water supply	1. Water supply Availability							
	1.1. Per capita water consumption	L/c/d	>25 & <130	[25–40)	[40–60)	[60–80)	[80–130]	[12]
	1.2. Water supply continuity	hr	[0–8)	[8–16)	[16–20)	[20–24)	24	[12]
	1.3. Pressure head adequacy	mH₂O	[0–5)	[5–14)	[14–21)	[21–28)	[28–40]	[13]
	1.4. Per capita water availability	m³/c/yr	[0–500)	[500–800)	[800–1000)	[1000–1700)	≥1700	[14]
	2. Piped water supply coverage	%	[0–50)	[50–60)	[60–80)	[80–100)	100	[12]
	3. Water quality index	WQI	>100	(75–100]	(50–75]	[20–25]	≤25	[14]
	4. Water loss	%	>35	(30–35]	(25–30]	[20–25]	[0–20]	[12]
	5. Affordability	%	≥5	[4–5)	[3–4)	[2–3)	<2	[12, 16]
Sanitation	1. Sanitation coverage	%	[0–60)	[60–70)	[70–80)	[80–90)	[90–100]	[17, 18]
	1.1. Latrine coverage							
	1.2. Coverage of grey water soak pit							
	2. Management of sanitation							
	3. Affordability	%	≥5	[4–5)	[3–4)	[2–3)	<2	[12, 16]
Hygiene	Coverage hand wash facilities	%	[0–60)	[60–70)	[70–80)	[80–90)	[90–100]	[3, 5]
	Implementation of hygienic practices (Diarrheal prevalence)	No.	>760	(500–760]	(200–500]	(100–200]	[0–100]	
	Affordability	%	≥5	[4–5)	[3–4)	[2–3)	<2	[3, 8]

mH_2O appears in row 1.3.

In the calculation of the index, Analytical Hierarchy Process (AHP) approach was employed to set weightage of dimensions. AHP is an effective method for decision analysis and calculation of weighting factors based on multiple criteria to solve computing dimensions. Eleven group of WaSH experts from different organizations were requested to prioritize domestic water security dimensions, indicators and variables in questionnaire form, from 1 to 9 scale of preference and analyzed by saaty scale AHP method. Table 2 shows the result of weights of domestic water security dimensions, indicators and variables.

Table 2. Weight of dimensions, indicators and variables

Domestic water security index

Dimensions	Wt. (%)	Indicators	Wt. (%)	Variables	Wt (%)
Water supply	62.1	Availability	35	Per capita water consmp.	38.8
				Supply continuity	32.3
				Pressure head adequacy	28.9
		Quality	31.1	Water quality index	100
		Coverage	21.1	Proportion of people use piped water supply	100
		Affordability	6.5	Proportion of water tariff from total expenditure	100
		Loss	6.3	Water loss in the system	100
Sanitation	23.6	Management	43.4	Sanitation management	100
		Coverage	56.6	Improved sanitation facility	75.9
				Grey water soak pit	24.1
Hygiene	14.3	Coverage of hygienic facilities	50.7	Coverage of hand wash facilities	100
		Implementation of hygienic practice	49.3	Prevalence of diarrhea under age five children	100

Domestic water security index was then estimated by analyzing each variable weighted to the respective indicators, each indicator weighted to the respective dimensions and finally the weighted arithmetic sum of three dimensions gave domestic water security index. The procedure in calculating domestic water security index can be generally described as,

$$\text{Variable } (V_i) = \frac{\sum W_{vi} * S_{vi}}{\sum W_v} \quad (1)$$

$$\text{Indicator } (I_i) = \frac{\sum V_i * W_{Ii}}{\sum W_I} \quad (2)$$

$$DWSI = \frac{\sum Ii * Wdi}{\sum Wd}$$ (3)

Where: Wvi - weight of variable, Svi - score of variables, WIi - weight of indicator, Wd - weight of dimension and DWSI - domestic water security index.

3 Result and Discussion

First, how the developed framework was applied in Bahir Dar is described and at the end we indicated the overall index. In order to get the index of overall water security, the values of variables, indicators, and dimensions were aggregated. The unequal weight methods (Table 3) to all variables, indicators, and dimensions were applied based on the expert's judgment by using analytical hierarchy process.

3.1 Application of the Developed Framework for Bahir Dar City

Water Supply
According to the data obtained from (Bahir Dar town water and sanitation services office, Bahir Dar health center, Bahir Dar Municipality/Mayor office and Central Statistical Authority), the analyzed and scored results has shown on Table 3. Water tariff affordability (scoring 5) has very high value, which means that current water tariff is affordable and cheap. Whereas, water quality, water supply coverage, water supply continuity and coverage of improved sanitation facilities scored 3.9, 4.0, 3.2 and 4.0 respectively, of which all fall on high domestic water security status. The respective per capita water consumption (scoring 3) and the pressure head adequacy (scoring 1.9)

Table 3. Result of scored variables

Variables	Variable code	Unit	Result	Score
Water supply coverage (% of people)	WSC	%	82.5	4.0
Unaccounted for water in the system	UFW	%	45.5	1.0
Per capita water consumption	PWC	L/c/d	50.6	3.0
Supply continuity	SC	hrs./day	18.2	3.2
Pressure head adequacy	PHA	mH$_2$O	7.98	1.9
Water tariff affordability	WTA	%	1.43	5.0
Water quality index	WQI	Value	40.5	3.9
Improved sanitation coverage	ISC	%	87.7	4.0
Grey water soak pit coverage	GSC	%	57.4	1.0
Proportion of safely managed sanitation	SMS	%	27.0	1.0
Coverage of hand wash facilities	HWF	%	48.5	1.0
Prevalence of diarrhea under age 5	PDU	%	21.8	1.0

show a medium and low domestic water security status. The rest variables having scored values of 1.0 show a very low domestic water security status, which imply that water is used indiscriminately without proper planning and management.

Arithmetic weighted water quality index (AWQI) has done by using selected water quality parameters (pH, turbidity, nitrate, total hardness, E. coli and temperature). Water quality index result in distribution system shows highly satisfactory, but in two of the nine sub- cities Shimbit and Gish Abay, there is still a problem of chlorine dosing, emerging of E. coli and turbidity problem, especially in summer season. The probable reason of this water quality problem for coliform bacteria existence is lack of enough and continuous chlorination and for turbidity there is contamination of the1 water sources by surface water flooding, contamination by storm water from urban areas or may be absorption of mud or soil particles during pumping [19]. Based on the water quality indices and the respective scale values for each sub cities, all sub cities have good water quality status (scoring 4) except Shimbit and Gish Abay (scoring 3), which are under a category of poor water quality.

Improved sanitation coverage isn't in better level as the result shows 12.3% open defecation practices in the city in contrary to the SDG 6.2, which states that there should not be open defecation practices in the city. Water supply coverage (82.5%), is on higher domestic water security status. It showed an improvement from coverage of water supply (55.3%) in 2013 [2]. Average piped water supply coverage of urban cities of Ethiopia (89.7%) in 2015 [20]. But as per Ethiopia Growth and Transformation Plan (GTP-2) and SDG goal, drinking water supply coverage must be 100% with the entire population. Per capita water consumption resulted 50.6 l/c/day falls on medium status which is a satisfactory but still it needs improvement. It does not even meet the GTP-2 plan of minimum per capita water consumption (80 l/c/d) for category two which Bahir Dar City falls in.

Water supply continuity also shows water is available at an average of 18.2 h/day. According to Desalegn [21], 41.6% of the population got water greater than 19 h. where as 17% got water less than 6 h. Though the continuity shows better improvement by meeting the GTP-2 (16 h./day) towards water supply continuity, SDG goal dictates that the community should get water at any time when they need 24 h. to achieve water security. In the study area, water supply continuity differs from one sub city to another. From the average domestic water supply continuity results during the data collection time, people in Gish Abay sub-city get the highest i.e. 21.4 h. water supply time with a scale of 4 whereas in Belay Zeleke sub-city, people get the lowest supplying time of 16.5 h. scaled 2.78 (Fig. 2).

Based on the result of pressure gauge measurements at the customers tap, the pressure head sufficiency shows a low range, which means that there are major gaps on pressure sufficiency and need attention to increase the pressure head. According to some literatures and water supply system design guideline, the minimum water pressure head at ground floor is 5 m, and therefore the average pressure head on tap for the city is 7.98 m, which a little bit higher than the minimum range. Since the city plans for house building is given as ground plus one and above, these pressure head will not be enough. The maximum tap water pressure head is shown in 'Shum Abo' sub city with a value of

9.7 m and scale of 2 whereas the minimum tap water pressure head in 'Gish Abay' with the value of 6.4 m scaled 1.5.

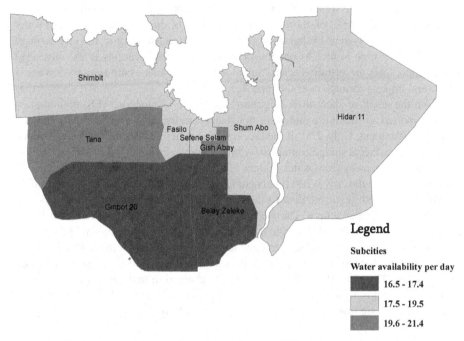

Fig. 2. Average daily domestic water supply availability in hours in each sub-city

Based on the analysis of the collected data, water loss in the system was 45.5% which falls under very low range, which imply incapable of meeting those criterions. High degree of water loss in the system might be due to metering inaccuracies, unbilled metered consumption, unbilled unmetered consumption. In addition, leakage from corroded, old, defective and broken pipes, on service connections up to point of customer metering, due to high pressure, caused by connecting distribution pipes on pressure lines and leakage and overflow at service reservoirs and collection chambers might also be the reasons [21]. This needs strong commitment of the water utility to reduce the high degree of water loss that helps to increase the duration of water availability and coverage in the city which is lagging behind.

Sanitation and Hygiene
Based on the analysis of the collected data, grey water soak pit coverage was 57.4%. The respective proportion of safely managed faecal sludge and coverage of hand wash facilities in the city was 27% and 48.5%. Prevalence of diarrhea under age five was 21.8%. All the above variables fall under very low range, which imply incapable of meeting those criterions. This result clearly indicates that huge proportion of the wastewater generated in the city is discharged in to the local area to the source, neighborhood and within the city (Fig. 3) which might potentially create public health problems. Moreover, the water

sources in and around the city like Abay River and Lake Tana will be unsecured due to the discharging of huge volume of untreated wastewater. As per the interview with water quality experts in the city water utility, more than three deep wells within the boundary of the city, which were source of water for the city population, were abandoned due to contamination. High level of diarrhea in the city might be due to contamination of water in the distribution system by the improper discharged wastewater in the city through leaks and weak pipe joints. As per transient weak in some locations in the city, aged water supply lines are installed across and along storm drains where sanitary sewage is stored and flowing through over the pipe line.

From the result of sheet flow diagram (Fig. 3), the fecal sludge (FS) that emptied and transported to the dump site were not treated, rather discharged to the local and nearby environment. Only 27% of the faecal sludge generated is safely managed which is mainly due to faecal sludge contained within the toilet and not emptied from the toilets and the toilets are away from water sources like hand dug wells. There is still practice of open defecation in the city. When toilets got filled, 46% of the community neither safely buried nor emptied, just over flow to the nearby locality and ends up to water bodies including groundwater source. The faecal sludge not contained is the main contributor for unsafely managed faecal sludge in the city and is the main challenge in the sanitation service chain. The faecal sludge contained and emptied but not delivered to treatment plant rather discharged into the city which has 15% proportion to unsafely managed faecal sludge. The proportion of faecal sludge discharged in to the environment within the boundary of the city administration (unsafely managed faecal sludge) is 73% (Fig. 3). This might have significant influence on the security of domestic water in the city.

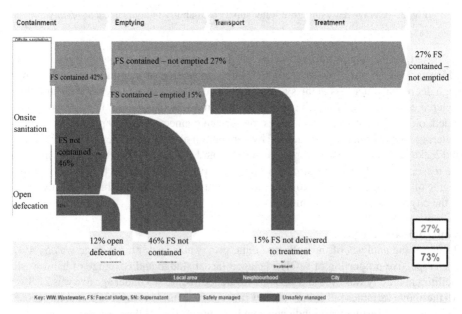

Fig. 3. Existing faecal sludge management situation in the city

The result of coverage of grey water soak pit also shows almost half part of the community does not use it, rather simply pour the grey water into the nearby drainage ditches. On the other hand, both indicators of hygiene have major gaps because of poor coverage of hygienic facilities which are provision of hand wash facilities near to their toilet and implementation of personal hygiene practices. Diarrhea is one of the common indicators that is caused by poor water related hygienic practice. Although all human beings at any age can be affected by diarrhea, its acute effect is usually seen on children under age five. In this study the prevalence of diarrhea in Bahir Dar city on children under age five was estimated as 21.8%, which is very severe that the city health office with other stakeholders need to give strong attention to minimize it.

3.2 Estimation of Water Security Index for Bahir Dar City

The AHP analysis shows that experts give the highest weighting factor to water supply dimension (62.1%), followed by to sanitation dimension (23.6%) and hygiene dimension (14.3%). It results a domestic water security index of medium level (2.8) (Table 4), which implies that the city has a satisfactory system and environment for facilitating domestic water security and still a cause of concern on sanitation (2.29) and hygiene (1.0).

Table 4. Scored result of driver, pressure, state, impact and response by Analytical hierarchy process

Variables	Score	Wt	Indicators	Score	Wt	Dim.	Score	Wt	DWSI
Per capita consumption	3.00	0.39	Water supply availability	2.73	0.35	Water supply	3.41	0.62	**2.8**
Water supply continuity	3.19	0.32							
Pressure adequacy	1.86	0.29							
			Water quality	3.94	0.31				
			Piped water supply coverage	4.00	0.21				
			Water supply affordability	5.00	0.07				
			Water supply loss	1.00	0.06				
Coverage of improved latrine facility	4.00	0.76	Sanitation facilities coverage	3.28	0.57	Sanitation	2.29	0.24	
Coverage of grey water soak pit	1.00	0.24							
Management of sanitation system				1.00	0.43				
Coverage of hygienic facilities				1.00	0.51	Hygiene	1.00	0.14	
Implementation of hygienic practice				1.00	0.49				

4 Conclusion

The developed conceptual domestic water security assessment framework uses an indicator-based approach to carry out an assessment on water supply, sanitation, and hygiene dimensions in Bahir Dar City. The assessment framework would therefore help to identify major challenges of a city in terms of water supply, sanitation, and hygiene situations that are location specific. The developed framework was applied in Bahir Dar City and the result shows considerable difference in domestic water security in different sub-cities in the city. Based on DPSIR result using AHP approach, the water supply dimension is better developed across the city; however, the sanitation dimension shows medium results and hygiene shows poor results. This indicates that the town administration should give the priority to sanitation particularly on the management of wastewater generated but not contained at the point of generation and on the promotion of hygienic practices to enhance the water security level in the city. Generally, the developed framework is applicable, and can be applied to other cities and towns in the country.

Acknowledgement. The work was carried out within the support of Bahir Dar Technology Institute and Exceed Swindon project (http://www.exceed-swindon.org), Joint Research Project within the framework of the DAAD Programme. The researchers are grateful for the support.

References

1. Babel, M.S., Shinde, V.R., Sharma, D., Dang, N.: Developing an operational water security assessment framework for application in diverse regions of Asia (2017)
2. Bogardi, J.J., et al.: Water security for a planet under pressure: interconnected challenges of a changing world call for sustainable solutions. Curr. Opin. Environ. Sustain. **4**(1), 35–43 (2012)
3. Gain, A.K., Giupponi, C., Wada, Y.: Measuring global water security towards sustainable development goals measuring global water security towards sustainable development goals. Environ. Res. Lett. **11**(12), 1–13 (2016)
4. Hardy, D., Cubillo, F., Han, M., Li, H.: Alternative Water Resources: A Review of Concepts, Solutions and Experiences (2015)
5. Vörösmarty, C., McIntyre, P., Gessner, M., Nature, D.: Global threats to human water security and river biodiversity. Nat. Commun. **467**(7315), 555–561 (2010)
6. Hoekstra, A.: Urban water security: a review. Environ. Res. Lett **13**(5), 053002 (2018)
7. Asian Development Bank. Asian Water Development Strengthening Water Security in Asia and the Pacific (2016). www.adb.org
8. Karadirek, I.E.: A Case Study on Evaluation of Household Water Security in Mena Countries (2017)
9. UN. Goal 6: Ensure availability and sustainable management of water and sanitation for all. Sustainable Development Goals, pp. 2–4, March 2016
10. Van Beek, B.E., Arriens, W.L.: TEC Background Papers Water Security : Putting the Concept into Practice. Stockholm Environment Institute (2014a)
11. Global Water Partnership - GWP. Assessing water security with appropriate indicators. Proceedings from the GWP Workshop, p. 113 (2014)

12. Federal Democratic Republic of Ethiopia. Ministry of Water and Energy for Urban Water Utilities Tariff Setting, March 2013 (2013)
13. Adane, M., Mengistie, B., Medhin, G., Kloos, H., Mulat, W.: Piped water supply interruptions and acute diarrhea among under-five children in Addis Ababa slums, Ethiopia: A matched case- control study. PloS One **12**, 1–19 (2017)
14. Falkenmark, M., Lundqvist, J., Widstrand, C.: Macro-scale water scarcity requires micro-scale approaches. Nat. Resour. Forum **13**, 258–267 (1989)
15. Paun, I., Valeria Cruceru, L., Chiriac, F.L., Niculescu, M., Vasile, G., Mirela Marin, N.: Water Quality Indices - Methods for Evaluating the Quality of Drinking Water, pp. 395–402 (2016). https://doi.org/10.21698/simi.2016.0055
16. Hutton, G.: Monitoring Affordability of water and sanitation services after 2015: Review of global indicator options, March 2012 (2015)
17. Asian Development Bank. Asian Water Development Outlook 2016: Strengthening Water Security in Asia and the Pacific; Asian Development Bank: Mandaluyong City, Philippines (2016)
18. Bradley, D.J., Bartram, J.K.: Domestic water and sanitation as water security: monitoring, concepts and strategy. Philos. Trans. R. Soc. Math. Phys. Eng. Sci. **371**(2002), 20120420 (2013)
19. WHO. Progress on Drinking Water, Sanitation and Hygiene. World Health Organization (2017)
20. World Bank. Drinking Water Quality in Ethiopia Drinking Water Quality in Ethiopia (2017)
21. Desalegn. Urban water Supply System performance Assessment, Unpublished, March, 2015 Bahir Dar (2015)

Performance Evaluation and Assessment of Quashni Small Scale Irrigation Scheme, in Amhara Region

Muluedel Aseres[1]([⊠]), Mamaru A. Moges[1], Seifu Tilahun[1], Berhanu Geremew[1,2], Daniel Geletaw[1,2], and Enguday Bekele[1]

[1] Faculty of Civil and Water Resource Engineering, Bahir Dar University,
P.O. Box 26, Bahir Dar, Ethiopia
muluedel.2009@gmail.com
[2] School of Civil and Water Resource Engineering, University of Gondar,
P.O. Box 196, Gondar, Ethiopia

Abstract. Optimizing the use of irrigation water is of vital importance in conserving land and water resources as well as maximizing crop yield utilizing available water. Evaluating an irrigation system performance should measure and show the effectiveness of existing irrigation practice, provide remedial measures if necessary, as well as determining the impacts of the factors which affect the performance parameters. This study attempted to evaluate and assess the performance of Quashni irrigation scheme using internal and external performance indicators. Two irrigation seasons in the 2018 (February–May) and 2018/2019 (October–January) were carried out. Primary data, e.g. soil moisture before and after irrigation, discharge measurements, irrigation depth and soil physical properties, were collected. Secondary data, e.g. meteorological data and irrigated area per crops, were also collected. CROPWAT 8.0 computer model was used to calculate the CWR. The conveyance and application efficiency of the scheme was estimated as 71.8% and 51.2% respectively, which led to an overall scheme efficiency of 36.8%. RWS and RIS of the scheme were 1.24 and 1.12, respectively. Irrigation ratio of Quashni irrigation scheme was found to be 0.84, which implies that 16% of the command area could not be provided with irrigation coverage. In general, the evaluation and assessment indicated a low performance of the Quashni irrigation scheme.

Keywords: Small scale irrigation · Performance evaluation · Efficiency · Quashni irrigation scheme

1 Introduction

1.1 Background

Much of the increase in irrigated area had come as a result of expansion of traditional small-scale irrigation. Yet, the existing irrigation development in Ethiopia, as compared to the resource the country has, is very small. Furthermore, poorly designed, planned and

© ICST Institute for Computer Sciences, Social Informatics and Telecommunications Engineering 2020
Published by Springer Nature Switzerland AG 2020. All Rights Reserved
N. G. Habtu et al. (Eds.): ICAST 2019, LNICST 308, pp. 126–147, 2020.
https://doi.org/10.1007/978-3-030-43690-2_10

managed irrigation undermines efforts to improve livelihoods. The country's irrigation efficiencies are low, of the order of 25 to 50% [1].

Small-scale irrigation has been recognized as a policy priority in Ethiopia for reduction of poverty and climate adaptation [2]. Despite this, the sector has largely been overlooked and not supported through improved water management methods. Due to land and water shortages and the need for food self-sufficiency in the region, it has become essential to improve the productivity of this sector [3].

Irrigation water management is highly expected to play a major role in the realization of Ethiopian food security and poverty alleviation strategy. Irrigation enhances agricultural production and improves the food supply, income of rural population, opening employment opportunities for the poor, supports national economy by producing industrial crops that are used as raw materials for value adding industries and exportable crops. Irrigation projects are widely studied, planed and implemented throughout the country from this important view-point. However, little or no attention is given to the monitoring and evaluation of the performance of already established irrigation schemes [4].

Optimizing the use of irrigation water is vitally important in conserving land and water resources as well as maximizing yield with the available water [5]. [6] states that, Ethiopia has potentially reasonable quantities of irrigable land and water resources, but its agricultural system does not yet fully benefit from irrigated agriculture and proper technologies of agricultural water management; which results in very low agricultural productivity in Ethiopia as a whole. The main factors behind this is low uptake of inputs, such as, adequate irrigation application by farmers with due consideration of the daily crop water requirements and the different crop development stages; as well as the existing soil moisture content. Hence, it is believed that, these production constraints should be reduced using secured access to irrigation and efficient utilization of farming lands.

The performance of many irrigation systems are significantly below their potential due to a number of shortcomings, including poor design, construction, operation, maintenance, well effective water control and measurements misallocation [7] and also According to [8], head tail problems, leaky canals and malfunctioning structures because of delayed maintenance, leading to low water use efficiency and low yields are some of the commonly expressed problems. A large part of low performance may be due to inadequate water management at system and field level.

The performance of irrigation Operation has to be evaluated periodically, both at the system- and at farm-levels, using indicators that have been established. The results and recommendations of the evaluation exercises, when implemented, contribute towards maintaining the sustainability of the farms, for economic utilization of the limited water resource and generation of new data and information for the design and operation of new irrigation schemes. Huge expectation of the irrigation development to alleviate poverty versus inability to sustainably utilize them call for detailed explanation on the relative contribution of technical, support service and institutional problem contributing for the under performance of the irrigation schemes.

Some of the problem observed in Quashni irrigation scheme for motivation of starting these study was, the first secondary canal use pressurized flow system through PVC pipes which crosses the river underneath to irrigate 40 ha command area at right side of the river is totally out of function, the main, secondary and field canals are covered with sediment loads and vegetation, The flow of water at the different segment of the secondary canal is stagnant, Guess work in water allocation; the water committee undertakes water allocation and defines water rights of members not based on study on water requirements of different crops, Lack of satisfactory support from local administrative and legal entities, Tail water users did not receive adequate water, Water users are not willing to register types of crops they grow (vegetables or perennials) and area of their irrigable plots with the committee for clear definition of water rights in spite of the law (bylaws). Even if the scheme has such problems, performance evaluation is not held so far. Therefore the actual performance of Quashni irrigation scheme is not known before this study.

The principal objectives of this study was evaluate and assess the performance of Quashni community managed small scale irrigation scheme. Specifically analyze the overall scheme performance using conveyance and Application efficiency, assess irrigation supply of the scheme satisfy crop water requirement of irrigated area and compare actual efficiency of the scheme with design efficiency. The performances evaluation of the system have the most appropriate tools for abundant save of resources and using them in proper ways; and most likely to increase livelihood of the country. Based on the above facts this study on evaluating the performance of Quashni community managed small scale irrigation scheme are crucial to determine the actual performance of the scheme using performance indicators for conveyances and field water application systems; for the purpose of identifying management practices and systems that can be effectively implemented to improve the irrigation efficiency and also provide relevant information in selecting better performing activity under existing condition.

2 Materials and Methods

2.1 Description of the Study Area

The study was conducted on Quashni small scale irrigation scheme which is found in Dangila woreda at Gayita kebele, geographically located at 36.83° N and 11.25° E having an elevation of 2180–2500 m above sea level. The watershed domain lies in two woredas, namely, Dangila and Fagita Lakma. The kebeles have a long history of traditional irrigation based on the Quashni River. Maize, finger millet, teff, and barely are the main crops grown through rain fed agriculture in the Mehere season in these kebele. In addition, farmers grow a variety of fruits and vegetables during the Bega season through traditional or modern irrigation. Out of 1501 ha of cultivated lands in the kebeles, about 1055 ha of land is irrigated, of which, 250 ha areas benefit from the IFAD built small-scale modern irrigation scheme (Quashni irrigation scheme). The rest is farmed through traditional irrigation (Fig. 1).

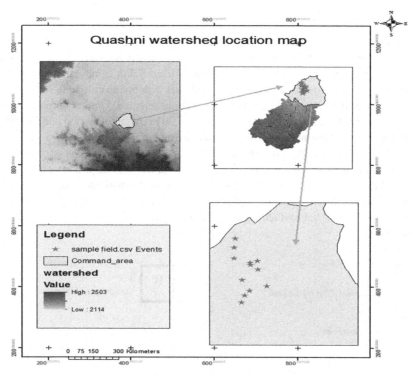

Fig. 1. Location map of Quashni irrigation scheme

2.2 Irrigation Scheme

The weir structure was constructed by financial and technical support of IFAD and become functional in 2013. The designed and actual command areas in irrigation were 250 and 210 ha respectively. It was intended to serve around 343 households found in Gayita kebele. The conveyance system of the irrigation scheme consists of a Main canal (MC1) taking water from the corresponding intake of the weir. The Main canal starts from Water abstraction site on the left side of the weir and conveys water for a length of 1014 m of main canal, for the first 202 m it is masonry lined canal and for the rest it is unlined and delivers water to secondary canals. There are 16 secondary canals in the scheme. Based on functionality of canals divide in three categories, 7 secondary canals functional, 4 secondary canals nonfunctional, 5 secondary canals nearly functional. So for evaluating conveyance efficiency of secondary canals flow measurement was taken on 7 functional secondary canals. The command area available to the left is 205 ha and to the right of it 46.72 ha. However to irrigate the command area at the right side of the river a secondary canal of pressurized pipe crossing the river is installed but until now this secondary canal not functional.

2.3 Sample Size and Techniques

A performance of the schemes was evaluated using both internal and external performance indicators. The internal performance indicators computed were conveyance efficiency, application efficiency and overall scheme efficiency. For computation of absolute performance of application efficiency irrigation fields with potato crop in the first season and pepper crops in the second season were purposely selected. For this purpose, a total of three farmer fields in the first irrigation season in 2018 irrigation period and 9 farmers field in the second season were selected from irrigation scheme as shown in Fig. 2. Farmer's irrigation field selection a technique in this study was based on upper, middle and downstream user's field consideration. Therefore, the first irrigation season select 1farmer's field in upper user, 1in middle user and 1 in downstream user. To increase accuracy of the result repeated data taken prefers so in second irrigation season increase samples for 9 farmers field which means 3 in upper users, 3 in middle users and 3 in downstream users.

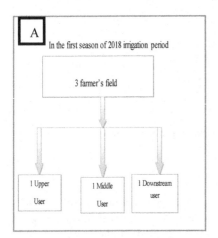
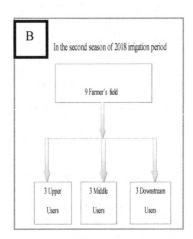

Fig. 2. Sample size flow charts for 1st (A) and 2nd (B) irrigation season

2.4 Data Collection

Measurements of water discharge at diversion points of irrigation scheme was taken and also at the initial and final points of secondary and field canals. Soil moisture before and after irrigation was measured by gravimetric method in the first season and TDR used in the second season. To determine soil texture of farmer's field, six soil samples from three locations of scheme at two different depths were collected. And also using core sampler undisturbed soil samples were collected from different depths and the bulk densities were determined. Secondary data were collected from the Dangila Agricultural and Rural Development Office, Water Resource and irrigation offices at regional and zonal levels. Secondary data includes Irrigated area per crops; meteorological data taken from Dangila and Bahir dar Meteorological Station include rainfall, minimum and maximum air temperature, sunshine hours, wind speeds, relative humidity and solar radiation, books and journals.

Among different canals discharge measurement techniques in this study, floating method (measuring surface velocity) was used in this study. Mean velocity was obtained using a correction factor. In the first irrigation season soil samples at four irrigation events on potato crop were collected to determine the soil moisture content one day before and after irrigation by collecting about 72 soil samples from three farmers field in the schemes with an interval of 0–20, 20–40 and 40–60 cm depths. In the second irrigation season moisture content at two irrigation event of farmers field was measured by using Time Domain Reflectometry (TDR) measuring instrument but this measuring instrument was calibrated by gravimetric method. Measuring depth intervals were the same as oven dry method as listed in the above. Totally 108 times at nine farmers' field was measured. Summary of data collection were listed in Table 1 and Fig. 3.

Table 1. Summary of data collections

No	Data type	Source	Purpose
1	Soil moisture before and after irrigation	Field measurement	For application efficiency evaluation
2	Irrigation depth	>>	To know applied water to the field
3	Flow measurement	>>	Know discharge
4	Soil sample analysis	>>	Physical property of soil
5	Meteorological data	Metrological station	Input for CROPWAT

2.5 Determination Internal Performance Indicator

Conveyance Efficiency
Water conveyance efficiency (Ec) is the ratio in percent of the amount of water delivered by a channel or pipeline to the amount of water delivered to the conveyance system. Ec was computed using the following formula [9].

$$EC = \frac{Qo}{Qi} * 100 \tag{1}$$

Where, E_c is conveyance efficiency (%); Q_o = quantity of water delivered by a conveyance system (outlet); and Q_i = quantity of water delivered to a conveyance system (inflow).

Application Efficiency
The application efficiency (Ea) was computed as the ratio of water stored in the root zone to the water delivered to the farm. The depth of water delivered to the field was measured as an averaged estimate using a Parshall flume designed to measure up to 220 mm. To determine the amount of moisture content stored in the root zone by gravimetric method soil sample four replications of potato crop at three different depths (0–20 cm, 20–40 cm

a) Soil sample taking using core sampler   b) Soil sample dry in oven

c) Soil moisture measurement using TDR   d) Flow measurement (floating method)

Fig. 3. Different data collection techniques.

and 40–60 cm) on three farmers' field in first season was taken and 9 farmers field in the second season was determined by TDR reading. The following equation from Ramulu (1998) was used to estimate Ea.

$$Ea = \frac{\mathbf{Zr}}{\mathbf{D}} \tag{2}$$

Where, Ea is application efficiency (%), Z_r is depth of water store in the root zone (mm), and D is depth of water applied to the field (mm).

Overall Scheme Efficiency

The overall scheme efficiency (Ep) was calculated as the product of conveyance (Ec) and application efficiency (Ea). It was computed using following formula Ramulu (1998):

$$Ep = Ec * Ea \tag{3}$$

2.6 Determination of External Performance Indicator

Water Use Performance Indicators

Two types of indicators namely relative water supply (RWS) and relative irrigation supply (RIS) were used for evaluating irrigation performance. Both indicators (in %) were calculated by using the following formulas of [10].

$$RWS = \frac{TWS}{Crop\ water\ demand} * 100 \tag{4}$$

$$RIS = \frac{Irrigation\ supply}{Irrigation\ demand} * 100 \tag{5}$$

Where, TWS (m^3) is total water supply or diverted water for irrigation plus rainfall, crop water demand (m^3) is the potential crop evapotranspiration (ETp), or The real evapotranspiration (ETc) when full crop water requirement is satisfied, and irrigation supply (m^3) is surface diversions and net groundwater drafts for irrigation, and irrigation demand (m^3) is the crop ET minus the effective rainfall.

Physical Performance Indicator

Physical indicators are related with the changing or losing irrigated land in the command area by different reasons. The selected indicator used for evaluation of physical performance was irrigation ratio which can be expressed as the follows [11]

$$Irrigation\ ratio = \frac{Irrigated\ cropped\ area}{command\ area} \tag{6}$$

Where, Irrigated crop area (ha) is the portion of the actually irrigated land (ha) in any given Irrigation season, and command area (ha) is the potential scheme command area.

2.7 Determination of CWR and IWR

CROPWAT 8.0 computer program was used to estimate the total water requirements of major crops grown in the irrigation schemes on studying season. The model needs climatic, crop and soil data for the determination of crop water and irrigation requirements. 20 years mean monthly minimum and maximum temperature ($^{\circ}$C), relative humidity (%), wind speed (km/day) and sunshine hours (hr) data of Dangila meteorological station were used, while crop data were used based on Food and Agriculture Organization (FAO) recommendations and also soil data derived from laboratory analysis.

3 Results and Discussion

3.1 Determination of Crop and Irrigation Water Requirements

Rainfall Data Analysis
The minimum and maximum rainfall amount occurs in January (2.8 mm) and August (387.6 mm), respectively. The study area has an average total annual rainfall of 1672.8 mm. Scheduling irrigation based on crop demand requires an estimate of effective precipitation or rainfall. Effective rainfall estimates are also important for planning cropping sequences in irrigation crop production. Effective rainfall is the amount of rainfall stored in the crop root zone. Rainfall that runs off the soil surface or passes through the root zone does not contribute to crop growth and yield. As can be seen from Table 2 the highest effective rainfall occurs during August and is about 163.8 mm. The total annual effective rainfall of the area is 945.9 mm.

Table 2. Monthly effective rain fall of the area (USDA S.C Method)

Month	Rain fall depth in (mm)	Effective rainfall (mm)
January	2.8	2.8
February	4	4
March	15.1	14.7
April	47.4	43.8
May	165.9	121.9
June	267.4	151.7
July	366.7	161.7
August	387.6	163.8
September	261.8	151.2
October	117.2	95.2
November	32.7	31
December	4.2	4.2
Total	1672.8	945.9

3.2 Determination of Reference Evapotranspiration (ETo)

As discussed in the methodology, ETo was determined by CROPWAT 8.0 software using Penman-Monteith equation. Table 3 shows a summary of the monthly ETo in the study area. The minimum and maximum monthly ETo values of the irrigation scheme were 2.86 mm/day in July and 3.77 mm/day in April. The annual average value of ETo was 3.23 mm/day (Figs. 4 and 5).

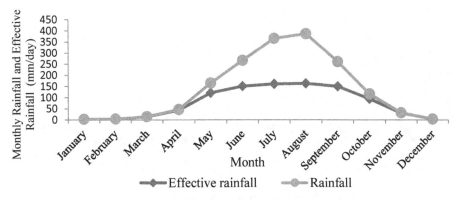

Fig. 4. Relationship between rainfall and effective rainfall

Table 3. Monthly reference evapotranspiration ETo (CROPWAT output)

Month	Min Tem (°C)	Max Temp (°C)	Humidity (%)	Wind (km/day)	Sunshine (hr)	Radiation (MJ/M2/DAY)	ETo (mm/day)
Jan	5	26	50	1	9	20.3	2.96
Feb	7	28	46	1	9	21.7	3.35
Mar	9	29	45	1	8	21.4	3.58
Apr	11	28	46	1	8	21.9	3.77
May	12	26	63	1	7	20	3.63
Jun	12	24	77	1	6	18.2	3.36
Jul	12	22	83	1	4	15.3	2.86
Aug	12	22	83	1	4	15.5	2.87
Sep	12	23	79	1	6	18.4	3.29
Oct	11	24	74	1	6	17.5	3.09
Nov	8	25	66	1	8	19.1	3.09
Dec	5	26	58	1	9	19.7	2.96
Avg.	9.7	25.3	64	1	7	19.1	3.23

Cropping Pattern

There are two irrigation seasons in study area, one from October–January and the other from February–May. The Gayita Kebele agricultural development office reported that about 120 ha of land was cultivated in the 2018 (February–May) irrigation season and 210 ha of land was cultivated in the 2018/2019 (October–January) irrigation season in the study period (Table 4).

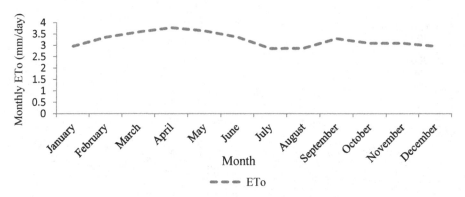

Fig. 5. ETo variation on each month

Table 4. Crop area coverage and LGP of crops in studying season

S.No.	Crop type	Coverage (ha)	% of Coverage	LGP
1	Potato	52	43.34	130
2	Maize	68	56.66	180
Total		120		

3.3 Crop Water Requirements and Irrigation Requirements

The seasonal crop and irrigation water requirements of the major crops (Potato and Maize) grown in the study area during the study period as estimated by the CROPWAT 8 model, are indicated in Tables 5 and 6. The results indicated that the seasonal crop and irrigation water requirement of Potato, which was planted at the beginning of January and harvested during the first decade of May, was estimated as 413.9 mm and 302.5 mm respectively. (Table 5) Similarly, Seasonal crop and irrigation water requirement of Maize, planted at the beginning of January and harvested during May was estimated to be 464.3 mm and 336.4 mm respectively.

Furthermore, irrigated crops in studying season had the highest crop and irrigation water requirement during their mid-season stage. This being so, the water requirement of potato during the initial, developmental, mid-season and late-season stages accounted for 5.5, 31.6, 38.9, and 30.2%, respectively, of the seasonal water requirement of the crop. Similarly, the figures for the same growth stages of tomato were 6.7, 31.6, 38.9, and 22.8%, respectively, of the seasonal water requirement (Table 6).

Table 5. Crop water requirement of Potato crop

Month	Decade	Stage	Kc	ETc (mm/day)	ETc (mm/dec)	Eff. Rain (mm/dec)	Irr. Req (mm/dec)
Jan	1	Init	0.5	1.48	7.4	0.5	6.9
Jan	2	Init	0.5	1.48	14.8	0.8	13.9
Jan	3	Deve	0.5	1.55	17	1	16
Feb	1	Deve	0.64	2.06	20.6	0.9	19.7
Feb	2	Deve	0.86	2.87	28.7	0.9	27.7
Feb	3	Deve	1.05	3.6	28.8	2.3	26.6
Mar	1	Mid	1.15	4.03	40.3	3.1	37.1
Mar	2	Mid	1.15	4.12	41.2	4.1	37.1
Mar	3	Mid	1.15	4.19	46.6	7.6	38.5
Apr	1	Mid	1.15	4.26	42.6	9.8	32.8
Apr	2	Late	1.13	4.26	42.6	12.3	30.3
Apr	3	Late	1.01	3.76	37.6	21.7	15.8
May	1	Late	0.88	3.22	32.2	33.4	0
May	2	Late	0.78	2.82	14.1	21.4	0
					413.9	120	302.5

Table 6. Crop water requirement of Maize crop

Month	Decade	Stage	Kc Coefficient	ETc (mm/day)	ETc (mm/dec)	Eff. Rain (mm/dec)	Irr. Req (mm/dec)
Jan	1	Init	0.7	2.07	10.3	0.5	9.8
Jan	2	Init	0.7	2.07	20.7	0.8	19.8
Jan	3	Deve	0.7	2.16	23.8	1	22.8
Feb	1	Deve	0.78	2.51	25.1	0.9	24.2
Feb	2	Deve	0.91	3.03	30.3	0.9	29.4
Feb	3	Deve	1.02	3.49	27.9	2.3	25.6
Mar	1	Deve	1.13	3.96	39.6	3.1	36.5
Mar	2	Mid	1.2	4.3	43	4.1	38.9
Mar	3	Mid	1.2	4.37	48.1	7.6	40.5
Apr	1	Mid	1.2	4.45	44.5	9.8	34.6
Apr	2	Mid	1.2	4.52	45.2	12.3	32.9
Apr	3	Late	1.16	4.31	43.1	21.7	21.3
May	1	Late	0.9	3.31	33.1	33.4	0
May	2	Late	0.62	2.24	22.4	42.9	0
May	3	Late	0.41	1.44	7.2	20.7	0
					464.3	162.1	336.4

Table 7. NCWR, NIR of the scheme in studying season

Crop name	CWR (mm/season)	IWR (mm/season)	Area (ha)	NCWR (m^3/season)	NIWR (m^3/season)
Potato	413.9	302.5	52	215,228	157,300
Maize	464.3	336.4	68	315,724	228,752
Total			120	530,952	386,052

3.4 Internal Performance Indicators

Conveyance Efficiency

In Quashni irrigation scheme about 202 m length of the main canal (MC11) was lined the rest is unlined. The results of the conveyance efficiency evaluation revealed that this indicator varied within a canal at different points, between main canal & secondary canal in the scheme. The overall conveyance efficiency values which indicate the amount of water lost during transportation of water from the diversion point or source to the cultivated area of Quashni irrigation schemes were found to be 71.8%. However, the values of conveyance efficiency of the schemes are between the recommended value i.e. 70% unlined poorly managed main canals MoAFS (2002) but as compared to the design conveyance efficiency of the scheme it reduced by 18.2% (Table 8).

Table 8. Main canal conveyance efficiency result

Day	MC11 (202 m)			MC12 (406 m)			MC13 (406 m)		
	Inflow (l/s)	Outflow (l/s)	Ec (%)	Outflow (l/s)	Outflow (l/s)	Ec (%)	Outflow (l/s)	Outflow (l/s)	Ec (%)
17-03-18	83	73	88	73	51	69.9	51	37	72.5
24-03-18	108	97	89.8	50	39	78	–	–	–
31-03-18	117	103	88	88	66	75	39	30	76.9
07-04-18	117	103	88	93	71	76.3	–	–	–
14-04-18	105	93	88.6	86	66	76.7	64	47	73.4
21-04-18	104	93	89.4	89	70	78.7	–	–	–
28-04-18	113	91	80.5	82	63	76.8	66	44	66.7
05-05-18	92	82	89.1	75	59	78.7	70	44	62.9
12-05-18	71	61	85.9	59	44	74.6	–	–	–
12-05-18	94	77	81.9	71	50	70.4	56	42	75
29-12-18	161	135	83.9	377	222	58.9	118	75	63.6
05-01-19	174	137	78.7	357	239	66.9	111	74	66.7
12-01-19	172	132	76.7	272	196	72.1	92	62	67.4
19-01-19	169	147	87	236	173	73.3	108	69	63.9

Average Ec (%) = 76.1

In Quashni irrigation scheme totally 1014 m length of main canal. The first 202 m was lined the rest unlined main canal. The distance in the main canal from source to upper, from upper to middle and from middle to lower- end was 202 m, 406 m and 406 m respectively. As we can see in the above Table 4.8, the conveyance efficiency in upper part of lined main canal (MC11) was 85.8%. Middle of main canal (MC12) and Downstream of main canal (MC13) conveyance efficiency was 73.4 and 69% respectively. The mean overall conveyance of the main canal was 76.1%. According to MoAFS (2002) report the minimum recommended main canal water conveyance efficiency was 70%. Main canal water conveyance efficiency in Quashni small scale irrigation scheme is very good in upper part of lined main canal, middle and downstream of main canal as compare to the minimum recommended efficiency value (Fig. 6).

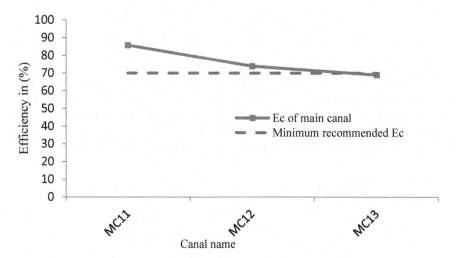

Fig. 6. Conveyance efficiency of main canal with recommended value

As compared to lined and unlined main canal, the conveyance efficiency of lined main canal was higher than unlined main canal. The water loss of main canal was 14.2% at the upper part of main canal, 26.6% at the middle part of main c anal and 31% at the Downstream of main canal as shown in Fig. 4.3. This shows that 23.9% loss of water occurred in the main canal. [4] reported that about 10 to 15% of loss of water in the canal is accepted. When the result was compared to this, it is unacceptable range. The conveyance water loss of the main canal as evaluated during this study is presented as shown below (Fig. 7).

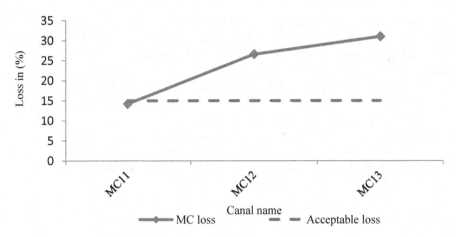

Fig. 7. Main canal water loss with acceptable loss value

The above Figure shows that large amount of water was lost in the downstream of main canal (MC13). The reason for losses in the main canal is mainly related to unauthorized diversions of water by farmers into field ditches, siltation and weeding, seepage, weak section of canal embankment and overtopping of the water from the canal.

The secondary canals conveyance efficiency in the upper, middle and downstream of irrigation scheme was 70.5, 67.6 and 64.3% respectively. The average conveyance

Table 9. Conveyance efficiency (Ec in %) of secondary canals

Day	SC1	SC2	SC3	SC4	SC5	SC6	SC7
17/03/18	65.3	64.6	68.0	62.9	72.5	72.1	69.9
24/03/18	65.4	69.4	76.7	71.9	62.7	–	–
31/03/18	61.8	70.8	61.5	73.9	69.0	67.6	66.4
07/04/18	68.6	74.6	80.2	67.6	66.2	–	–
14/04/18	76.7	76.9	66.1	68.1	68.1	64.4	66.9
21/04/18	72.7	75.9	68.1	71.5	63.7	–	–
28/04/18	62.1	78.7	74.1	66.6	65.5	61.6	62.4
05/05/18	79.6	77.2	76.1	71.8	68.4	64.0	63.6
12/05/18	74.9	71.8	70.1	64.8	60.5	–	–
12/05/18	74.5	71.32	72.9	68.5	66.5	65.4	62.8
29/12/18	56.7	78.2	68.9	70.0	67.1	63.5	63.7
05/01/19	66.5	66.7	65.4	67.7	67.7	58.6	61.3
12/01/19	68.9	64.4	53.4	61.7	51.9	63.9	59.3
19/01/19	66.7	67.1	54.4	66.8	57.1	54.5	60.5
Average	68.8	72.3	69.4	68.2	65.4	64.6	64.0
Secondary canal Ec (%) = 67.5							

efficiency of the secondary canal has 67.5%. According to [12] report the minimum recommended secondary canal water conveyance efficiency was 75%. Therefore secondary canals conveyance efficiency of Quashni irrigation scheme was below recommended value as shown in Table 9 (Fig. 8).

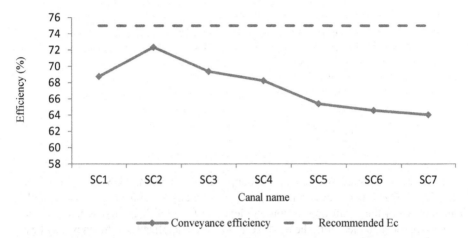

Fig. 8. Conveyance efficiency of secondary canals with recommended value

The water loss was in the upper part 29.5%, 32.4 in the middle and 35.7% in the downstream of secondary canals. The reason for this loss occurs in the secondary canals is due to seepage, evaporation and overtopping flow of water (Fig. 9).

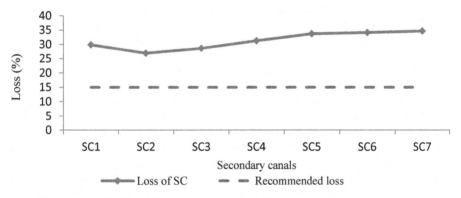

Fig. 9. Secondary canals water loss with acceptable loss value

Application Efficiency
From the result application efficiency of selected farmers' fields at the Quashni irrigation scheme was found to vary from 33.68% to 78.21% with an average of 55.5% in the first season and vary from 24.5.3% to 68.2% with an average of 47% in the second irrigation season. As shown in the Table 10, the water application efficiency of the

farmers was 59.4% at the head, 49.7% at the middle stream, 44.6% at downstream users of the schemes. Therefore, average application efficiency of the scheme was 51.3%. As compared to the design application efficiency of the scheme it was reduced by 18.7%.

Table 10. Application efficiency of the scheme

No	User name	1st season Ea (%)	2nd season Ea (%)
1	U/S	67.3	51.6
2	Middle user	53.3	46.1
3	D/S	46	43.3
Average		55.5	47
Scheme Ea (%) = 51.3			

FAO (2003) reported that the attainable application efficiency in US according ranges from 55%–70%, value below this limit would normally be considered unacceptable. Therefore from the result application efficiency in Quashni irrigation scheme are not between the acceptable limit. The reason for poor water application efficiency may be as small scale irrigations were associated to lack of technical capacity of farmers resulted from absence of extension workers and the required trainings, the type of irrigation system employed which was predominantly wild flooding and furrow irrigation, the slopes of irrigable fields, absence of knowledge of irrigation time and scheduling by farmers and more (Figs. 10, 11, 12 and 13).

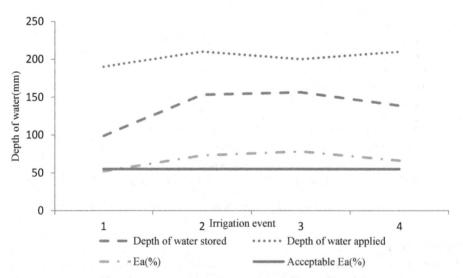

Fig. 10. First season upper user Ea with Acceptable Ea

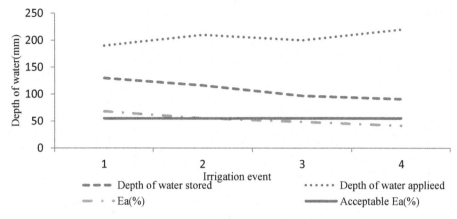

Fig. 11. First season middle user Ea with Acceptable Ea

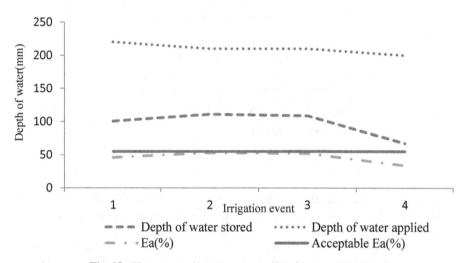

Fig. 12. First season downstream user Ea with Acceptable Ea

Overall Scheme Efficiency

The overall efficiency of the scheme is the ratio of water made available to the crop to the amount released at the headwork. The result indicated that the Quashni irrigation scheme was relatively poor. The overall efficiency of the scheme was not within the range of values (40–50%) commonly observed in other similar African irrigation schemes Savva and Frenken (2002). as compare to the design overall scheme efficiency it was reduced by 13.2%.

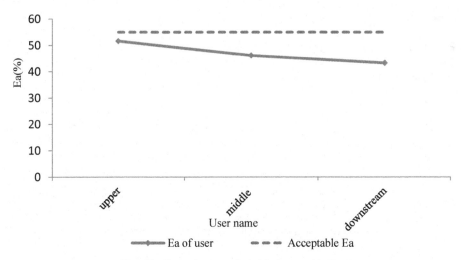

Fig. 13. Second season Ea with Acceptable Ea

Table 11. Actual average irrigation efficiencies of Quashni irrigation scheme

Internal performance indicators	% of efficiency
Conveyance efficiency	71.8
Application efficiency	51.3
Overall scheme efficiency	36.8

Table 11 shows the actual efficiency of the scheme to get overall scheme efficiency by the product of conveyance efficiency with application efficiency. In the present study the overall efficiencies of Quashni irrigation scheme was 36.8% see in the above table. Table 7 shows that designed irrigation efficiency obtained from designed manual. It uses for comparison of actual efficiency with designed efficiency of the scheme. Therefore, as compare to the design efficiency overall scheme efficiency was reduced by 13.2% (Table 12).

Table 12. Design irrigation efficiency of Quashni irrigation scheme

Efficiency	% of efficiency
Conveyance efficiency	90
Application efficiency	70
Overall scheme efficiency	50

(Source: Design manual)

3.5 External Performance Indicators

Relative Water Supply

The relative water supply depicts whether there is enough irrigation water supplied or not. Both the relative water supply and relative irrigation supply relate supply to demand, and give some indication as the condition of water abundance or scarcity, and how tightly supply and demand is matched. The relative water supply value below one normally indicates that the water applied is less than the crop demands and values above one indicate extra water is added to the root zone beyond plant demands. The relative water supply of Quashni irrigation scheme was found to be 1.24.

The result in Table 14 which is greater than one indicates that excess water was used beyond plant demands in the schemes. In order to maximize water use efficiency of the scheme, it is required that the amount of water supplied be reduced in the scheme.

Relative Irrigation Supply

The relative irrigation supply shows whether the irrigation demand is satisfied or not. The relative irrigation supply of Quashni irrigation scheme was found to be 1.1 which is almost 1. During the irrigation season water actually supplied from irrigation for the irrigated land satisfy crop water demand of the scheme. The irrigation requirement was completely to meet irrigation water supply for the irrigated crop area (Table 13).

Table 13. Different parameter used for external performance evaluation

Crop name	Irrigated Land(ha)	CWR (mm)	NCWR (mm)	IR (mm)	NCWR (m)	NCWR (m^3)	IS (m^3)	R.eff (m^3)	TWS (m^3)	Irrigation Demand (m^3)
Potato	52	413.9	179.35	302.5	0.17935					
Maize	68	464.3	263.1	336.4	0.2631	530,952	432,000	224,640	656,640	386,052
Total	120		442.45		0.44245					

3.6 Physical Performance Indicators

Physical indicators are related with the changing or losing irrigated land in the command area by different reasons. The irrigation ratio of Quashni irrigation scheme was 0.84 which means about 16% of command area of the scheme was not under irrigation during the study period. The main reasons for this were the first secondary canal diverted water to right side of the scheme totally non-functional because of pressurized pipe installed underground was out of function.

Table 14. Result external performance indicators at Quashni irrigation Schemes

External indicator	Value
Relative water supply	1.24
Relative irrigation supply	1.12
Irrigation ratio	0.84

4 Conclusions

The Ec of the scheme was 71.8%, Ea 51.3% and overall scheme efficiency were 36.8%. RWS and RIS of the scheme were 1.24 and 1.12 respectively. Irrigation ratio of Quashni irrigation scheme found to be 0.84 which means 16% of the command area was not under irrigation during the study period. The reason of the less conveyance efficiency in canal was absolutely due to lack of proper maintenance of the watercourses hence it may be evaporation, seepage and leakage losses, presence of vegetation and sediments. The loss in conveyance was unavoidable unless the canal was lined or can be minimized with better canal management activities. Therefore the result shows that too low efficiency of the scheme. Irrigation water management requires determining when to irrigate and how much water to apply in each application. Knowledge of CWR and soil properties was essential for management of irrigation water. To enhance efficiency of irrigation and water management it is highly important to pay special attention to the following: adequate planning and proper design of the irrigation system, maintenance of the conveyance and distribution systems, including regular clearing of weeds growing along the main and secondary canals.

Acknowledgments. The author would like to provide her maximum respect and heartfelt thanks to, Dr. Mamaru Moges and Dr. Seifu. Tilahun for their outstanding advisor ship from the initiation of this work to end, as friend and colleague by offering constructive comments end by end continuously without tiresome. We would like to extend our gratitude to staffs in the soil laboratory of Amhara Design and Supervision works Enterprise, all data collectors, farmers in Gayita kebele, all colleagues and friends who contributed for the success of this project. The authors also would like to acknowledge the Ethiopian Road Authority (ERA) and the Ministry of Education of Ethiopia (MOE) for the grant rendered for this project and opportunity given to me.

References

1. Beshir, A., Awulachew, S.B.: Analysis of irrigation systems using comparative performance indicators: a case study of two large scale irrigation systems in the upper Awash Basin (2008)
2. Hazell, P., et al.: The future of small farms: trajectories and policy priorities. World Dev. **38**(10), 1349–1361 (2010)
3. De Schutter, O.: How not to think of land-grabbing: three critiques of large-scale investments in farmland. J. Peasant Stud. **38**(2), 249–279 (2011)
4. Renault, D., Facon, T., Wahaj, R.: Modernizing Irrigation Management: The MASSCOTE Approach-Mapping System and Services for Canal Operation Techniques, vol. 63. Food Agriculture Organization, Rome (2007)
5. Aman, M. Evaluating and Comparing the Performance of Different Irrigation Systems Using Remote Sensing and GIS: A Case Study in Alentejo Region, Portugal. ITC (2003)
6. Misselhorn, A., et al.: A vision for attaining food security. Curr. Opin. Environ. Sustain. **4**(1), 7–17 (2012)
7. Degirmenci, H., Buyukcangaz, H., Kuscu, H.: Assessment of irrigation scheme with comparative indicators in the South Easter Anatolia Project, Kahramanmaras sutcu Imam University, Turk. J. Agricu. **293** (2003)
8. Cakmak, B., et al.: Benchmarking performance of irrigation schemes: a case study from Turkey. Irrig. Drain. J. Int. Comm. Irrig. Drain. **53**(2), 155–163 (2004)

9. Upadhyaya, A., et al.: Performance evaluation of Patna main canal command (2005)
10. Perry, C.J., Narayanamurthy, S.: Farmer response to rationed and uncertain irrigation supplies. vol. 24 (1998). IWMI
11. Molden, D.J., et al.: Indicators for comparing performance of irrigated agricultural systems. vol. 20. (1998). IWMI
12. Brouwer, C., Heibloem, M.: Irrigation water management: irrigation water needs. Training manual 3 (1986)

Evaluation of Shallow Ground Water Recharge and Its Potential for Dry Season Irrigation at Brante Watershed, Dangila, Ethiopia

Daniel G. Eshete[1,3]($\boxtimes$), Seifu A. Tilahun[1], Mamaru A. Moges[1], Schmitter Petra[2], Zoi Dokou[4], Berhanu G. Sinshaw[3], Enguday B. Atalay[1], Muluedel A. Moges[1], Dagne Y. Takele[1], and Wondale A. Getie[1]

[1] School of Civil and Water Resources Engineering, Bahir Dar Institute of Technology, Bahir Dar University, Bahir Dar, Ethiopia
geletawdaniel@gmail.com
[2] International Water Management Institute (IWMI), Yangon, Myanmar
[3] Department of Hydraulic and Water Resources Engineering, Gondar Institute of Technology, Gondar University, P.O. Box 196, Gondar, Ethiopia
[4] Department of Civil and Environmental Engineering, University of Connecticut, 261 Glen-Brook Road, Storrs, Mansfield, CT 06269, USA

Abstract. The estimation of crop water demand and understanding groundwater use is an essential component for managing water effectively. Groundwater is the main source of irrigation in Dangila. However, there is a lack of information in the study area on amount of irrigated land, irrigation water use and demand, groundwater recharge. Consequently, the objective of this study is to determine the groundwater recharge and its potential for dry season irrigation. The study was conducted in Brante watershed of 5678 ha located in Dangila woreda, Ethiopia. Water table data from twenty-five wells and discharge data at the outlet of the watershed used to assess recharge amount in 2017. To calculate irrigation water demand, CROPWAT model was used. Questionnaires were undertaken to assess groundwater use. A KOMPSAT-2 image was used to map shallow groundwater irrigated vegetables in February 2017. From the soil water balance method, the annual groundwater recharge was 17,717,690 m^3 which is 15.8% of annual rainfall, and recharge amount of 14,853,339 m^3 was obtained using water table fluctuation method. From satellite image classification the area coverage of dry season irrigated vegetables (onion, tomato, pepper) below the main road was 4.02 ha. From CROPWAT result, seasonal irrigation water demand for onion, Tomato, and pepper was 333,314, and 261 mm respectively. However, the questioners result indicates that farmers apply in average 20% more water than crop water demand. In the watershed 60,150 m^3, 62,750 m^3 and 41,603 m^3 of water was abstracted for irrigation, domestic and livestock use respectively. The ratio of groundwater use to groundwater recharge at the watershed scale was found to be only 1%. This study indicates that the current use of groundwater was sustainable. For better improvement of household livelihood irrigation can be further expand using ground water. Future work should be performed to determine if the method outlined in this research could be used to accurately estimate available water potential.

Keywords: Recharge · Brante watershed · Water balance · Ethiopia

© ICST Institute for Computer Sciences, Social Informatics and Telecommunications Engineering 2020
Published by Springer Nature Switzerland AG 2020. All Rights Reserved
N. G. Habtu et al. (Eds.): ICAST 2019, LNICST 308, pp. 148–168, 2020.
https://doi.org/10.1007/978-3-030-43690-2_11

1 Introduction

1.1 Background

Irrigation is practicing virtually all over the world, at scales ranging from subsistence farming to large scale national enterprise [1]. Groundwater consider as the main source of water for meeting irrigation, livestock and domestic uses. The driving factors for groundwater use are; its long period of time in the ground, the storage capacity is maximum; level of contamination is low, wide distribution and availability within the reach of the users [2–5]. Groundwater is the worlds most extracted and fresh raw material with withdrawal rates currently estimated to be 1000 cubic kilometers per year [6].

The quantity of water that is extracted from an aquifer without causing significant depletion is primarily dependent on recharge amount and thus, quantification of groundwater recharge using scientific principles is pre-requisite for efficient management of water resource [7–9].

Accurate estimation of crop water demand is an essential component for managing water resource effectively [10]. However, the estimation of the crop water demand requires data on irrigated areas, types of crops grown and cropping calendars. Understanding household groundwater abstraction is important for efficient and effective water resource management [11]. Comparison of actual crop water use against the theoretical irrigation demand is an essential component of irrigation scheduling [12]. The sharper increase in food demands as a result of population pressure and frequent drought has revealed the importance of irrigation development in Ethiopia. Groundwater irrigation is being prioritized recently as the best alternatives for reliable and sustainable food security, income generation, livelihood improvement in the country [13].

With an extended dry season, consumptive water use generates a demand for irrigation in excess of the availability of groundwater. In some cases, inappropriate irrigated agriculture exploits non-renewable groundwater resources or very weakly recharged aquifer systems. The ability to make sound and effective decisions is hampered by a lack of reliable information regarding the renewable groundwater quantity [14]. Groundwater is the ultimate source of water for irrigation at Brante watershed, however, there is lack of enough information on groundwater availability and rates of recharge, and also there is limited information on irrigation water use and demand together with poor documentation of irrigated area. Therefore, the objective of the study was, to evaluate shallow groundwater recharge and it's potential for dry period irrigation by integrating GIS, Remote sensing and CROPWAT model. More specifically, the study was attempted to (1) quantify major hydrologic components and estimate the recharge amount of the watershed using soil water balance and water table fluctuation method, (2) estimate the area of irrigated land in the watershed in the dry season using a satellite image taken in February 2017, (3) determine the irrigation water demand of main vegetables irrigated during the dry season using the CROPWAT model, (4) calculate the groundwater amount used for irrigation, livestock, domestic purpose, and compare with the recharge amount and other standard values.

2 Research Methodology

2.1 Description Study Area

Dangila woreda is located about 80 km south-west from Bahir Dar, along the Addis Ababa-Bahir Dar main road [15] (Fig. 1). This research was conducted in Brante watershed, which is found 10 km from the Dangla town in North West direction, in which the only transport mechanism is using three-wheel vehicles (Bajaj). Geographically, the study area extends from latitude value 11.16° N to 11.3° N and longitude of 36.77° E to 37.0° E. The climate is sub-tropical characterized by large seasonal fluctuations of air temperatures and rainfall [16]. The summer is short and cold, lasting from June through September, with maximum temperature ranging from 22.2 °C to 23.9 °C. Long-term average annual rainfall at the study area is about 1667 mm. The annual potential evapotranspiration (PET) of the study area during the study time was 1190 mm. About 93.2% of the total rainfall occurs between May and October with peaks in June, July, and August that account for 60.4% of the total annual rainfall. At the Brante watershed, crop-livestock mixed subsistence farming is the primary source of livelihood and rain-fed agriculture is predominates [17]. The majority of the land uses type is agricultural, forest, grassing land and residential. The most significant crops that grew are teff, wheat, maize, beans, and sorghum. In addition cultivation of commercial crops in the watershed such as tomato, onion, and pepper is possible during the dry season using shallow groundwater as a source. The livelihood of the community in the catchment is mainly based on mixed farming by growing crops and livestock production.

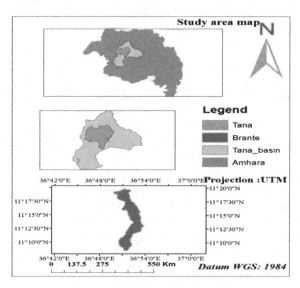

Fig. 1. (A) location of study area

2.2 Materials and Data

Hydro Meteorological Data
To evaluate the groundwater recharge and estimate the crop water requirement various quantitative and qualitative data were collected from both primary and secondary data sources. Climatological data from 1993 to 2017 was collected from Dangila meteorological station and used to estimate the crop water requirement in CROPWAT model. Additionally, climatic data, groundwater level and discharge data were collected for 2017 to estimate the groundwater recharge (see below).

Climatological Data
Missing rainfall data were filled using the arithmetic mean method and the data are checked for mean stability using T-test, variance stability using F-test. Autocorrelation test was performed for checking whether there is persistence or not, and the trend test was conducted using Spearman's rank correlation method. As it is depicted in table below, the average maximum rainfall was recorded in the month of August (387 mm) and the average minimum value obtained in the month of January (3.23 mm). The majority of rainfall in the watershed is concentrated during Ethiopian wet season (Kiremt) and the rainfall is of uni-modal in nature. The rainfall of the watershed is seasonal in which 75.52% of the total annual rainfall was covered in June to September. Climatic data from 1993–2017 is depicted in table below.

Temperatures data in the study area were taken from Dangila stations and analyzed at Microsoft Excel. The mean minimum monthly temperature was recorded in the month of January, which was 4.8 °C and the mean maximum temperature got in March that was 28.46 °C.

Available data of relative humidity were taken from Dangila meteorological station and were analyzed. The maximum and minimum values of relative humidity exist in August (83.6%), and March (45.9%) respectively and this is attributed to the rainy and dry season of Ethiopia respectively (see Table 1).

Table 1. long-term climatic and hydrological data of Brante watershed

Month	Jan	Feb	Mar	Apr	May	Jun	Jul	Aug	Sep	Oct	Nov	Dec
Rf (mm)	3.2	3.5	27.0	55.0	188	273	374	387	275	112	33.3	7.8
RH (%)	51.4	47.9	45.9	47.8	62.4	77.4	83.3	83.6	80.1	75	67.1	58.8
SSH (hr/day)	8.96	8.97	8.14	8.17	7.29	6.08	4.13	4.27	6.01	6	8.17	8.64
U2 (m/s)	0.77	0.88	0.99	1.05	1.07	1.00	0.95	0.92	0.80	0.67	0.60	0.65
T_{min} (°C)	4.80	6.58	8.70	10.8	12.0	12.1	12.1	11.9	11.2	10	7.38	5.10
T_{max} (°C)	26.2	27.9	28.5	28.2	26.3	23.6	21.9	22.0	23.3	23	24.85	24.9

The speed at any height can be approximately obtained from known wind speed at the known heights of observation. Danigla meteorological station workers measure wind speed in the study area and the nearby station at 2 m above the surface of the ground. The analysis indicated the minimum wind speed appeared in November (0.6 m/s) and the maximum wind speed occurred in May (1.07 m/s) (see Table 1).

Sunshine hour plays a significant role in affecting evapotranspiration. Longer sunshine hour within a day increases the evaporation rate and amount that in turn is dependent on the intensity of solar radiation. The minimum hour for the sunshine was 4.13 h per day that was recorded in July. In addition, the maximum sunshine hour was recorded in February (8.97 h/day) (see Table 1).

Ground Water Level Data

Groundwater levels were monitored in 25 hand-dug wells spread in locations within the Brante watershed. Selected farmers are responsible for recording water level in the well using deep meter once per week starting from 2014. A deep meter was used to measure the water level in the well every week since 2014. The change in water level was calculated as the difference between the level measured today and level measured at next time from the ground surface.

Stream Flow Data

The stream flow is the main output from the watershed. Gauging staff was installed at the outlet of Brante watershed to measure the depth of the flow. The stage in the river measured daily. Then the rating curve was prepared in Microsoft excel to calculate the discharge amount. Discharge is one component of the soil water balance of the catchment.

Soil, Crop and Water Use Data Collected

Soil types, common crops that are grown in the area and infiltration capacity of the soil were used for the estimation of potential evapotranspiration and crop water demand. Major crop type, irrigation method, and, date of planting other ancillary data were gathered from the farmers using pretest-structured questioners. Sixty-two farmers were used for questioners. Soil type and infiltration capacity were taken from innovation laboratory for small scale irrigation (ILSSI) project. Crop coefficient, initial soil moisture depletion, number of growing days and maximum root depth of tomato, onion, and green pepper were collected from FAO irrigation and drainage paper 56.

Water use data for irrigation, domestic and livestock were collected using water abstraction survey for 62 farmers. The data was collected from 2016 to 2017 covering one year period. The data includes the source of water for all uses, amount extracted daily for domestic and livestock, the number of households, irrigation technologies used, and vegetables type planted during dry season like tomato, onion and pepper.

2.3 Method of Analysis

Recharge Estimation

The evaluation of the groundwater resources involves several factors of which the groundwater recharge is a key [8]. An understanding of the recharge processes and the quantification of natural recharge rate are basic prerequisites for efficient and sustainable management of the groundwater resources [18, 19]. It is difficult to find a single reliable method for measuring groundwater recharge due to the complexity of the phenomenon and it is recommended to use multiple methods [20].

Quantification of groundwater recharge is a major problem in many water-resource investigations since it is a complex function of meteorological conditions, soil, vegetation, geologic material [7].

Water Balance Method: It is developed in 1948 by Thorn Thwaite and later revised by Thorn Thwaite and Mather [21]. The method is essentially a widely used, which estimates the balance between the inflow and outflow of water. According to [22], the general methodology of computing groundwater balance consists of identification of significant components, evaluating and quantifying individual components

$$R = P - ETa - Q - \Delta S \qquad [22] \tag{1}$$

Potential Evapotranspiration (PET) Estimation Using Penman Modified Method

The evaporation rate formula was modified is given by the following formula which modified by MAFF (1967, as cited in [27].

$$PET = \left(\left(\frac{\Delta}{\gamma} H_t + E_{at} \right) \right) / \left(\frac{\Delta}{\gamma + 1} \right) \tag{2}$$

Where: H_t is the available heat, Δ-is the slope of the curve of saturated vapor pressure plotted against temperature, γ: Hygrometry constant (mm Hg).

Estimation of Actual Evapotranspiration from PET

According to Bakundukize et al. (2011, as cited in [28]), the actual evapotranspiration varies with the temperature and the moisture availability during the year. In the rainy season, when the soil is at field capacity and the amount precipitation is larger than the PET, AET is maximum value

$$\text{IfP\_m} \geq \text{PET\_m, then AET\_m} = \text{PET\_m,} \tag{3}$$

$$\text{IfP\_m} < \text{PET\_m, then AET\_m} = P\_m + \Delta S\_m \qquad [29] \tag{4}$$

Change in Soil Water Storage Calculation

Recharge is estimated in the water balance model based on the accounting of soil water content. The moisture status of the soil depends on the previous day moisture content (S_(m−1)), the difference between precipitation and potential evapotranspiration and the available water capacity (AWC) of the soil [23]. According to Steenhuis and Van Der Molen (1986, as cited in [23]), soil moisture can be calculated in two scenarios.

$$[\text{if P\_m>PET\_m,S}]\_m = [S\_(m-1)+P]\_m - PET\_m \tag{5}$$

$$\text{if } [P\_m<PET\_m,S]\_m = Sm\_(m-1)*e^{\wedge}(((P\_m-PET\_m)/AWC)) \tag{6}$$

Where: S_m is the soil moisture at the current time, S_(m−1) the soil moisture at previous time, P_m is precipitation, PET_m is potential evapotranspiration, AWC available water capacity of the soil.

Discharge Calculation

Rating curve was prepared from the stage reading at the outlet of the watershed. A rating curve is established by making a number of concurrent observations of the stage and discharge over a period of time covering the expected range of stages at the river gauging section [24]. If Q and h are discharge and water level, then the relationship can be analytically expressed as:

$$Q = f(h)$$

Where: f(h) is an algebraic function of the water level. A graphical stage-discharge curve helps in visualizing the relationship and to transform stages manually to discharges whereas an algebraic relationship can be advantageously used. Power type equation, which is most commonly used for rating curve preparation:

$$Q = c[(h+h\_w)]^b \tag{7}$$

Where: Q = discharge (m³/s), h = measured water level (m), h_w = water level (m) corresponding to Q = 0

c = coefficient derived for the relationship corresponding to the station characteristics
b = measure of the geometry of section at various depth [24] (Fig. 2).

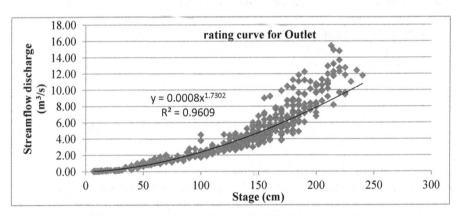

Fig. 2. Stage-discharge relationship of the Brante watershed

Recharge Calculation Using WTF Method

The water table fluctuation method (WTF) is one of the most widely used techniques for estimating groundwater recharge over a wide variety of climatic conditions [20]. The WTF method is based on the assertion that rises in water levels in unconfined aquifers are due to recharge water arriving at the water table, and that all other components of the groundwater budget including lateral flow are zero (Islam et al. 2016). The main limitations of the WTF technique are (1) the need to know the specific yield of the saturated aquifer at a suitable scale. (2) its accuracy depends on both the knowledge and representativeness of monitoring well in the catchment. (3) The method is best applied to shallow water tables that display sharp water-level rises and declines (4) the method cannot account for a steady rate of recharge [25].

$$R = S\_y * A * \Delta h / \Delta t \quad [8]$$ (8)

Where S_y is the specific yield, A is the area influenced by the well and Δh is the difference in water level rise at Δt. The specific yield for the study area was used as 0.08 from Walker et al. 2016 study at Brante watershed. Average area used for groundwater storage was taken as 65% of the watershed from [30] study.

Mapping of Crop Type under Shallow Groundwater Irrigation

Remote sensing has a major advantage over ground surveying methods (theodolite and global positioning system (GPS) surveys), in that images over large areas can be analyzed in a short time and at a relatively cheaper cost. In addition, remote sensing enables the mapping of inaccessible areas [31]. To estimate the area under dry period irrigation of vegetables, data sets that were collected include a KOMPSAT-2 image, ground truth (GT) points, and farmers' surveys of water use. A very high-resolution KOMPSAT_2 image, acquired in February 2017 was used as the primary data source. Korean multi-purpose satellite (KOMPSAT-2) is a high-performance remote sensing satellite, which provides 1.0 m panchromatic image and 4.0 m multi-spectral image resolution [32].

Maximum likelihood classification algorithm was used. It is an efficient method to classify pixels of the satellite image, it is available in image analysis environment, it is unlikely to yield abnormal result [26] (Fig. 3). The confusion matrix is an established method to assess the accuracy of the classification [33].

Estimation of Crop Water Requirement Using CROPWAT Model

Crop water requirement is defined as the depth of water needed to meet the water loss through evapotranspiration (ETcrop) of a disease free crop growing in a large field under non-restricting soil conditions, including soil water and fertility, and achieving full production in a given growing environment [23]. The FAO Penman-Monteith method to estimate ETo was derived.

$$ET_o = \frac{0.408\Delta(R_n - G) + \gamma \frac{900}{T+273}U_2(e_s - e_a)}{\Delta + \gamma(1 + 0.43U_2)}$$ (9)

Where: ETo: reference evapotranspiration [mm day^{-1}], $R\dot{}_n$: Net radiation at the crop surface [MJ m^{-2} day^{-1}], G: soil heat flux density [MJ m^{-2} day^{-1}], T: mean daily air temperature at 2 m height [°C], u_2: wind speed at 2 m height [m s^{-1}], e_s: Saturation vapor pressure [kPa], ea: Actual vapor pressure [kPa], e_s-e_a: Saturation vapour pressure deficit [kPa], Δ: Slope vapor pressure curve [kPa °C^{-1}] γ: psychrometric constant [kPa °C^{-1}].

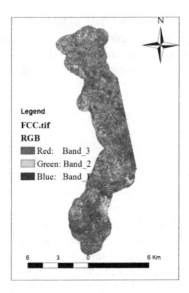

NDVI map

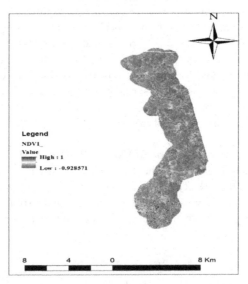

Fig. 3. Image enhancement (A) false color composite (B) NDVI

It was assumed that for each month, if the total quantity of water available, given by the sum of monthly rainfall and water stored in the root zone was sufficient to satisfy the monthly crop water need, no irrigation is needed. Otherwise, if the rainfall is insufficient and soil water storage is depleted, the difference is the deficit that should be supplied by irrigation. Irrigation water requirement is calculated as

$$IWR = \sum\nolimits_{i=1}^{n} (ET_o * K_c - P_{eff}) \tag{10}$$

Where: IWR = irrigation requirement, A = irrigate area, $[ET]\_o$ = reference evapotranspiration, = K_c crop coefficient, P_eff = effective precipitation.

Groundwater Use Calculation

The total amount of withdrawal groundwater in the study area throughout the catchment consists of irrigation, domestic and livestock water uses. Apart from the evaluation of the groundwater potential, this study also attempted to quantify the groundwater use. This objective was fulfilled by collecting data using questioners. Calculations for livestock water consumption were using the following equation [34]. By assuming livestock water consumption from Brante river is negligible.

$$NA * CR \text{ per animals} = \text{average daily use} \left(m^3/day \right) \qquad (11)$$

Where: NA was a number of animals, CR was consumption rate

During the rainy season, agriculture was supported by precipitation and surface water, but once the rain had stopped, gardens needed watering. The daily volume of water applied for irrigation of major vegetable was calculated from farmer response on the number of buckets used and calibration amount the bucket holds. Irrigation water use calculated as,

$$IA \left(m^2 \right) * \text{Daily water applied (m)} * \text{growth season (days)} = IWR \left(m^3/season \right) \qquad (12)$$

Where IA is irrigated crop area, IWR is irrigation water requirement.

Calculation for domestic use: Shallow hand dug well, bored hole and springs provide access for drinking water for Brante watershed. However, most of the domestic water demand is supplied from shallow hand dug well. Water demand for human consumption was estimated by the following formula [29].

$$AED \, (mm/year) = (DC \left(m^3/(day.Well) \right)) * \text{number of well}$$
$$* \, 365 \text{ days/year} * 1000 \, mm/m)/Area \left(m^2 \right) \qquad (13)$$

Where AED is annual equivalent depth, DC is daily consumption.

3   Result and Discussion

3.1   Groundwater Recharge Estimation

Rainfall and Potential Evapotranspiration

Rainfall is the principal means for replenishment of moisture in the soil water system and it was the only input to the moisture water balance. Since the irrigated area was small and farmer use bucket to irrigate, percolation due to dry season irrigation was assumed to be negligible. Rainfall was the main hydrological parameter for water balance approaches to estimate the recharge in the study area. In the Brante watershed, Dangila meteorological station rainfall data is recording daily and this data was used for this study. From the analysis, the annual rainfall amount during 2017 was 2000 mm or 113575000 m^3 (Fig. 4).

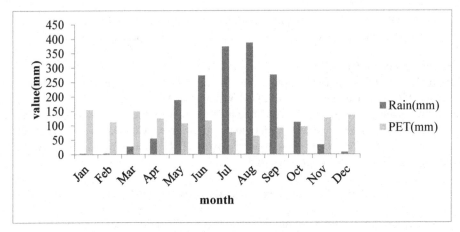

Fig. 4. Monthly rainfall and potential evapotranspiration of the watershed in 2017

Table 2. Monthly potential evapotranspiration value

Month	Jan	Feb	Mar	Apr	May	Jun	Jul	Aug	Sep	Oct	Nov	Dec
T	27	28	29.3	28.2	24.9	24.5	22.6	22	23	24.5	25.4	26.6
e_s	16.5	17.4	19.0	19.4	17.4	17.2	15.9	15.4	16	16.7	16.2	15.8
RH	0.4	0.6	0.4	0.6	0.7	0.8	0.8	0.8	0.8	0.8	0.6	0.5
e_a	6.8	9.5	8.4	11.1	12.3	13.0	12.7	12.8	12	12.6	10.1	8.1
N	9.9	7.2	7.8	6.7	6.0	6.9	4.6	3.9	5.4	5.8	8.5	9.3
N	11.4	11.6	11.9	12.3	12.5	12.7	12.6	12.4	12	11.7	11.5	11.3
n/N	0.87	0.62	0.65	0.55	0.48	0.54	0.36	0.31	0.5	0.50	0.74	0.82
Fa (n/N)	0.70	0.54	0.57	0.50	0.46	0.50	0.39	0.35	0.4	0.47	0.62	0.67
H_t	4.26	3.90	4.51	4.31	3.96	4.24	3.29	3.04	3.7	3.55	3.99	3.91
Eat	1.15	1.2	1.72	1.17	0.7	0.8	0.63	0.42	0.6	0.5	0.72	0.68
Δ/γ	4.1	4.0	4.4	4.1	3.6	3.6	3.2	3.1	3.4	3.5	3.7	3.8
PET(mm/month)	149.9	116	168	128	91	87	62	49	71	73	102	101

In 2017, maximum rainfall was recorded in August, which was 376 mm, and from the graph, it is clear that there was no rainfall during November, December, and January which is corresponding to Ethiopia dry season (Table 2).

The annual potential evapotranspiration of the watershed was calculated as 1190 mm. The maximum potential evapotranspiration i.e. 168.5 mm was obtained in March, which was the dry season and also it is related to the highest ambient temperatures (29.3 °C) of the area. However, relative humidity was minimum when the potential evapotranspiration was high.

Actual Evapotranspiration Estimation by Soil Water Balance Method
The average actual evapotranspiration in the study area was calculated as 698 mm or 39637675 m^3. The graph below highlights surplus soil moisture was existed when the

rainfall amount was higher than potential evapotranspiration and these phenomena were appeared in Ethiopian wet season only. Consequently in dry season, for replacing soil moisture deficit in the soil profiles and for better crop production, irrigation has no substitute (Fig. 5).

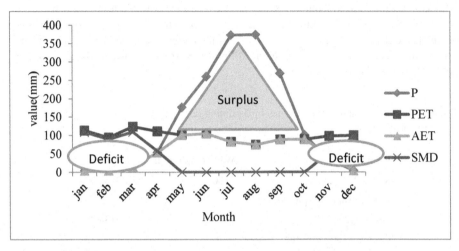

Fig. 5. Graphs shows the annual soil water balance of Brante watershed

Stream Discharge Calculation: From the prepared rating curve, the estimated stream-flow during 2017 was 970 mm or 55083875 m^3 per year, which accounts for 48% annual rainfall. Contrary to the findings of Bizimana et al. 2016 on the surface runoff potential, which was 500 mm (46% rainfall) the current result seems higher (Fig. 6).

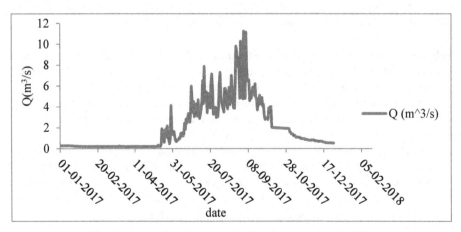

Fig. 6. Stream flow hydrograph of Brante watershed in 2017

As the above hydrograph shows, the discharge rate was increased from May to the end of August and it tends to decline at September and follows the same pattern up to

December that is associated with amount of rain fall. In August 2017, maximum rainfall was recorded compared to the other months that were 376 mm. This result indicates the excess amount of water almost half of the rainfall was taken out from the watershed through the stream flow.

Daily soil moisture calculations were made from 1st of January to December 30th 2017 using initial soil moisture of 8.5 mm. The available water holding capacity of the area was calculated as 70 mm, 120 mm and 140 mm for different soil type and root depth. The change in storage was calculated as the difference in available water at final and at initial time. The annual change in soil moisture storage was calculated as 20 mm or 1135755 m^3 (Table 3).

Table 3. Soil water balance components by assuming during recharge (wet season) there is no significant abstraction

Parameters	Water depth (mm)	Volume (m^3)
Rainfall	2000	113,575,000
Actual evapotranspiration	698	39,637,675
Discharge	970	55,083,875
Change in soil moisture storage	20	1,135,755
Ground water recharge	312	17,717,690

From water balance equation, recharge was 17717690 m^3 or 312 mm. Even though this result is below the previously reported 504 mm recharge using SWAT as simulator by Binziman et al. (2016), it suggests that there is a significant amount of recharge. A difference between values could be attributable to the difference in the method used, variation of rainfall, and uncertainty in determination of parameter.

Recharge Calculation Using WTF Method: Based on Walker et al. (2016, as cited in Walker et al. 2018), specific yield could be taken as 0.08; the area used for ground water recharge was 0.65 * 56787500 m^2, which yields 36911875 m^2. The water levels fluctuations in the monitoring wells showed that the water levels rose and fell according to rainfall events and withdrawal until the end of the rainy season wherein the absence of input of water, the water level continuously fell.

The water level in the well was measured from the ground surface. In Fig. 7, a slight rise of ground water in well number eight start in June and continue to rise up to August. However, when there is no rain, the depth to water was dropped 10 m below the ground. The amount of water reach ground water table during the wet season was calculated as the sum of June, July and August i.e. 15384870 m^3, or 416 mm.

Limitations of the Approach
Because of the lack of meteorological station distributed over the water, the spatial distribution of the recharge over the study area not investigated. Another limitation in

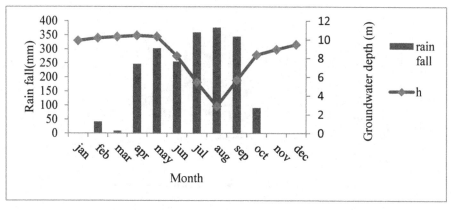

Fig. 7. Well Hydrograph for well number 8, in 2017

the methodology involves the issue of using multiple recharge estimation mechanisms since the result was based on only water balance approach and WTF method. Although the water balance approach widely accepted, it suffers from some limitations due to consider locally renewable groundwater availability as the major controlling parameter for groundwater irrigation potential. In addition, it assumes non-limiting conditions in terms of other fundamental physical properties, e.g. soil and water quality, terrain slope, and groundwater accessibility for the implementation of groundwater irrigation. In addition, there was short period of data in water level monitoring and stage measurement that prohibit to do long term ground water recharge analysis. The assumption for WTF may not always valid.

3.2 Mapping Groundwater Irrigated Crop and Area Estimation

The irrigated vegetables during dry season were mapped in Arc map environment from satellite image using supervised maximum likelihood classification and accordingly their area was estimated and displayed below.

Figure 8 depicted most of the area in the watershed below the main road which have ground truth data was covered by bare land and grazing land during February 2017. Irrigated vegetables (onion, tomato, green pepper) cover 4 hectare i.e. only 0.18% of the watershed area. Overall land use classification accuracy was 79% (Table 4).

3.3 CROPWAT Model Result

Reference Evapotranspiration Calculation
The lowest ET_o was obtained in July and it was about 2.97 mm/day or 90.2 mm per month; while the highest ET_o occurs during April and was about 4.56 mm/day or 136.8 mm/month. The average ET_o of the area was calculated as 3.62 mm/day or 109.9 mm/month.

Effective Rainfall: From the CROPWAT result, effective rainfall was obtained as 52% of the rainfall i.e. 1036 mm per annum out of the total average annual rainfall 2000 mm,

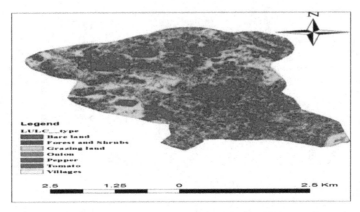

Fig. 8. Land use land cover map of Brante watershed below main road

Table 4. Area coverage of each land use type in the watershed below the main road

Land use type	Area (ha)	Percentage
Grazing land	803.6	34.35
Bare land	1150.4	49.23
Residential	135.7	5.80
Onion	1.59	0.067
Tomato	1.09	0.046
Pepper	1.34	0.057
Forest and Shrubs	245.2	10.48

and the losses estimated as 48% of rainfalls in the study area. The minimum amount of effective precipitation was found in January that is 3.3 mm. during the dry period effective rain fall was almost equal to the rain fall the water shed received due to the reason that the rain fall is too small and could not generate significant amount of loses. Comparison of the mean monthly rainfall and evapotranspiration indicates that, for the maximum crop production in the area during the dry season, irrigation is the most important choice (Table 5).

3.4 Calculation of Irrigation Water Applied

The water use questioner was conducted below the main road that divides the watershed in to two. So that groundwater use for irrigation was calculated for the watershed that found below the main road. From Table 6, it was observed that during irrigation season excess depth of water was applied for tomato, onion, and green pepper than the demand estimated by CROPWAT model.

Table 5. Irrigation water requirement (mm/month)

Month	Onion	Tomato	Pepper
Jan	17.1	25.7	4.5
Feb	87.4	67	64.5
Mar	116.7	103.5	91.9
Apr	103.4	105.1	91.9
May	8.6	12.6	8.4

Table 6. Actual quantities of water applied by farmer and CROPWAT result

Crops	Area (m^2)	Applied (mm/day)	Growing per (dy)	Applied water (mm/seas)	Applied (M^3/season)	IWR (mm/season) (CROPWAT)	M^3/Season (CROPWAT)
Tomato	10948	2.5	145	377	4112	314	3425.7
Onion	15920	2.7	150	400	6384	333	5269.5
Pepper	13408	2.5	120	312	4183.3	261	3499.5

Calculation of Water Used for Livestock

The total volume of water used by livestock was 196.2 m^3 per day. Even though Brante river is perennial, From the questioners, the information was that the farmer use hand dug well for livestock for months starting from November to May, which counts 211 days. So that the total water demand for livestock per the operating season is 41603 m^3. This result now provides evidence to manage groundwater for animal watering.

Calculation of Water Used for Domestic Use

The total number of functional hand-dug well and borehole is 925. The average daily domestic consumption per well in a single day was calculated as 160 L (0.16 m^3), for eight households which is equivalent to 20 L per capita per day. The annual equivalent depth for domestic consumption represents approximately 1.7 mm per year or 62750.19 m^3 per year. Generally, Seasonal change in water use was due to the changing availability of groundwater in wells, surface water, and the frequency of rain events. The water use is the highest during the autumn season due to high availability and increased demand for water by agriculture.

Comparing Groundwater Use and Recharge

It was necessary to determine whether shallow groundwater recharge could support for all ground water uses. The groundwater use for irrigation, livestock and domestic was calculated as 164503 m^3, which were (60150 m^3 + 41603 m^3 + 62750.19 m^3). The annual recharge in the watershed was 17717690 m^3. Therefore, the groundwater use in the study area was 1% of the annual recharge. Barring other influencing factors, the quantities of groundwater available in study areas are capable of sustaining groundwater-irrigated vegetable production for now and in the near future without affecting long-term groundwater storage (Table 7).

Table 7. Computation of the stage of ground use for irrigation during 2017

No	Description	Values
1	Annual rainfall in the watershed	113,745362.5 m^3
2	Annual recharge from rainfall	17,717690 m^3
3	Percentage of recharge to rainfall (2/1) * 100	15.9%
4	Domestic water use for the watershed during the whole year	62,750 m^3
5	Livestock water use for the dry season	41,603 m^3
6	Irrigation water use for the dry season	60,150 m^3
7	Total groundwater draft during the year (4 + 5 + 6)	164,503 m^3
8	Percentage of groundwater draft to recharge (7/2) * 100	1%
9	Utilizable water for irrigation (2 − (4 + 5)	1,636421 m^3
10	Level of groundwater development for irrigation (6/9) * 100	4%
11	Stage of groundwater development	Underexploited

From this evaluation, it could be stated that the water withdrawals within the watershed are very unlikely to deplete the groundwater aquifers in the Brante watershed. Considerable opportunities, therefore, exist for improving the population's livelihood through the development of the watershed water resources if the estimations elsewhere are considered reliable.

Meanwhile, if for any reason (e.g., underestimation of the daily withdrawal volumes reported by the surveyors, or even inconsistent assumptions in the withdrawal estimation, an estimation error of 100% of the withdrawal volume is considered, a correction will merely bring it to 329,006 m^3, which is still remarkably low compared to the 17,717690 m^3 of recharge.

Comparing the recharge volumes and the crop water requirement for the main vegetable grown in both study areas, there exist the potential to increase groundwater-irrigated land up to 1000 ha.

Accuracy Assessment of Water Use
Individual variations of water use were noticed during the water use interviews. However, for simplicity, these changes in water use were omitted from the results because they were observed as an inconsistent or insignificant addition to the total village water use. occasionally less water was used from ground water for domestic use during the wet season seasons the farmer washes their clothes using river water and by collecting rain in the pot. Seasonal production of products such as coffee required a couple of buckets

of water at each production session. More buckets were extracted occasionally when there were weddings and other ceremonies.

Benefits and Constraints of Groundwater Irrigation in the Study Area

They use the river and shallow well as a water source for their livestock watering purpose. Groundwater from shallow well is the main for irrigated production of vegetables and fruit during the dry period. Moreover, the ease of access to shallow groundwater sources and the erratic variability of rainfall distribution of the area made the communities depend highly on it. Most of the irrigators use hand-dug wells and dugouts produce vegetables on plot sizes between 0.01 and 0.025 ha.

The area cultivated varies from one year to another, and is influenced by the profitability of the previous season, access to credit facilities, availability of land, and the rainfall situation of the preceding season are among other factors. Most of the landowners engage solely in rain-fed agriculture and do not cultivate in the dry season.

Mostly buckets and cans are used for watering of crops, though a few of the irrigators have invested in small-capacity motorized pumps. In addition, 54.5% of irrigation users take credit for accessing technologies for water lifting and delivering to site. 48.9% of groundwater used for irrigation is at January, February, March, and April; 81% of irrigators use shallow hand dug wells. Many of the irrigators in the study areas mentioned that groundwater-irrigated vegetable production is profitable and an important source of income to the household. However, they do take losses in years of poor rainfall or low recharge, which results in less water being available in the shallow aquifers. Despite this study did not include in-depth data collection and analysis to determine the level of revenue irrigators get from groundwater irrigation, an attempt was made at quantifying the profits through an extensive informal discussion with an irrigator at the watershed who is a well-known landowner and cultivated about 0.02 ha of onion and pepper.

The net revenue, based on the 2017 irrigation season, was 3000 birr, which is equivalent to united state dollar 115, based on the June 2017 exchange rate. Most of the irrigators are full-time farmers in the rainy season, but some of them are employing in animal rearing and therefore profits from groundwater irrigation are considering additional income. Notwithstanding that groundwater, irrigation was profitable, it was constrained by many challenges; including lack of access to credit facilities, seed access limitations, lack of appropriate drilling technology, market access, and extension services.

Moreover, the farmer willingness to use groundwater for irrigation is weak. This is due to the reason that it takes a long time to transport water from hand dug well to irrigation site manually that is tedious and labor intensive. One of the farmers has three shallow groundwater well but still, he did not use for irrigation purpose. The reason was that rather than searching for, he waits someone to give him seed, and advice to use irrigation.

4   Conclusions

The annual recharge to the groundwater aquifers in the study area was estimated to be 312 mm (15.7% of the mean annual rainfall). This allows concluding that a simple water balance formula could be used to quantify the point recharge due to rainfall. The image classification result indicates that bare land was the dominant type of land use followed by grazing land during February 2017. The perennial crops such as forest, bare land, grazing land were classified with reasonable accuracy, while seasonal irrigated vegetation is poorly distinguished on the image.

The CROPWAT model analysis leads to conclude crops require more amount of water at their development or flowering stage. From the abstraction survey analysis, it is possible to conclude that most of the farmer applied more water for irrigated vegetables. The communities abstract 41603 m^3 of water from the hand dug well for livestock, 60150 m^3 of water abstract by the farmer to irrigate vegetables at the dry season, and 62750 m^3 of water for domestic. In conclusion, the actual water withdrawals from the Brante aquifers for all uses were relatively low compared to the annual recharge. Estimated groundwater use was 1% of the annual recharge to the watershed. These low withdrawals mean possibilities for further groundwater irrigation expansion.

5 Recommendations

Future work should be performed to determine if the water balance method outlined in this research, or a close variation of this method, could be used to accurately estimate monthly available water potential. If funding is not readily available to communities' for the construction of pumping wells, water containment projects might be the only option.

Although the results of this study can be considered substantial for preliminary steps in the watershed ground water resources management, additional studies need to be carried out for their validation and for the planning of sustainable water management.

The following are recommended

- Successful identification of agricultural crop could have required multi-temporal image at least at the middle and late growth stage. Combining images of a very high resolution with images of a medium resolution (e.g., LandSat-TM) could be the way forward to assess the existing as well the potential of shallow groundwater irrigation in Brante watershed.
- For most agricultural crops, especially short season crops and areas with multiple crops grown per season, it is suggested that mapping should be done closely as possible as acquisition time of the image
- Groundwater abstraction for irrigation should increase by expanding irrigation area.
- The amount of water applied for the crop by the farmer should be in accordance with the demand for better production.
- Encouraging the use of common dug wells or community irrigation wells, and maintain an equitable and fair distribution of water between the users particularly in areas where elders are lives and unable to dig wells.
- Soil and water conservation has to be implemented to reduce runoff as much as possible. In addition, sometimes the obtained information of farmer during fieldwork has not enough reliability. Consulting with local agriculture agent is suggested.
- Satellite image for irrigated area identification and classification should use for irrigation which have large area.

Acknowledgments. The corresponding author would like to thanks the Almighty Lord, Jesus Christ and his mother Saint Mary, for his mercy, Grace, and Guidance for all my life and the achievement of this work. I give special thanks for SIPS-IN project, Ethiopia Coordinator for providing the satellite image and support through my study. My thanks also goes to PIRE project for their funding for data collection. I have no word to say thank you for my main advisor who gives me genuine help, inspiration, and continuous advice for the completion of my work in any time regardless of the time allocated for consultation. My grateful thanks also go to the co- advisor who sacrifices his valuable time to give me critical and constructive comments. And finally Gondar University and Bahir Dar University are acknowledged for giving the chance for pursuing my master study.

References

1. Ozdogan, M., et al.: Remote sensing of irrigated agriculture: opportunities and challenges. Review. Remote Sens. **2**, 2274–2304 (2010)
2. Qablawi, B.: A comparison of four methods to estimate groundwater recharge for Northeastern South Dakota (2016)
3. Villholth, K., Jordano, M.: Ground water use in global perspective can it be managed? (2007)
4. Pavelic, P., et al.: Water-balance approach for assessing potential for smallholder groundwater irrigation in Sub-Saharan Africa. International Water Management Institute, Colombo, Sri Lanka (2012)
5. Shah, T., Burke, J., Villholth, K.: Groundwater: a global assessment of scale and significance. In: Water for Food, Water for Life: A Comprehensive Assessment of Water Management in Agriculture, International Water Management Institute (IWMI), Colombo, Sri Lanka, Earthscan, London (2007). Chapter 10
6. Margat, J., Gun, J.V.D.: Groundwater Around the World. CRC Press/Balkema, London (2013)
7. Kumar, C.P.: Estimation of ground water recharge using soil moisture balance approach (n.d)
8. Orji, A.E., Egboka, B.C.E., Oko, O.S.: Estimation of groundwater recharge in Sokoto Basin, using the watertable fluctuation method. J. Sci. Eng. Res. **3**(1), 25–33 (2016)
9. Kindie, A.T., Enku, T., Moges, M.A., Geremew, B.S., Atinkut, H.B.: Spatial analysis of groundwater potential using GIS based multi criteria decision analysis method in Lake Tana Basin, Ethiopia. In: Zimale, F.A., Enku Nigussie, T., Fanta, S.W. (eds.) ICAST 2018. LNICST, vol. 274, pp. 439–456. Springer, Cham (2019). https://doi.org/10.1007/978-3-030-15357-1_37
10. Naidu, C.R., Giridhar, M.V.S.S.: Irrigation demand VS supply-remote sensing and GIS approach. J. Geosci. Environ. Prot. **4**, 43–49 (2016)
11. Allen, W.H., Sinclair, S.V., Bryant, T.P.: An analysis of groundwater use to aquifer potential yield in Illinois (2003)
12. Rajanayaka, C., Fisk, L.: Irrigation water demand & land surface recharge assessment for Heretaunga Plains, Irrigation report (2018)
13. Awulachew, S.B., et al.: Water resources and irrigation development in Ethiopia. Working Paper 123. International Water Management Institute, Colombo, Sri Lanka (2007). 78 p.
14. Kendy, E., et al.: A soil-water-balance approach to quantify groundwater recharge from irrigated cropland in the North China Plain. Hydrol. Process. **17**, 2011–2031 (2003)
15. Tesema, M., et al.: Evaluating irrigation technologies to improve crop and water productivity of onion in Dangishta watershed during the dry monsoon phase (2016)
16. Mehretie, B., Woldeamlak, B.: Stakeholder linkages for sustainable land management in Dangila woreda, Amhara Region, Ethiopia. Ethiop. J. Environ. Stud. Manag. **6**(3), 253–262 (2013)

17. Bizimana, J.C., et al.: Ex Ante Analysis of Small-Scale Irrigation Interventions in Dangila. Feed The Future Project (n.d)
18. Healy, R.W., Cook, P.G.: Using groundwater levels to estimate recharge. Hydrogeol. J. **10**, 91–109 (2002)
19. Islam, S., Singh, R.K., Khan, R.A.: Methods of estimating ground water recharge. Int. J. Eng. Assoc. **5**(2), 6–13 (2016)
20. Scanlon, B.R., Healy, R.W., Cook, P.G.: Choosing appropriate techniques for quantifying groundwater recharge. Hydrogeol. J. **10**, 18–39 (2002)
21. Badr, Q.: A comparison of four methods to estimate groundwater recharge for Northeastern South Dakota (2016)
22. Kumar, C.P.: Assessment of groundwater potential. Int. J. Eng. Sci. **1**(1), 64–79 (2012)
23. Endalamaw, A.M.: Optimum utilization of ground water in Kobo valley, Eastern Amhara, Ethiopia. Master of Science, Graduate School of Cornell University (2009)
24. Marg, O.P., Khas, H.: Hydrology project Training module #SWDP - 29 how to establish stage discharge rating curve New Delhi. World Bank & Government of the Netherlands Funded (1999)
25. Beekman, H.E., Xu, Y.: Review of ground water recharge estimation in arid and semiarid Southern Africa. Council for Scientific and Industrial Research (South Africa) and University of the Western Cape Report (2003)
26. Karlsson, A.: Classification of high resolution satellite images (2003)
27. Elizabeth, S.M.: Hydrology in Practice, 3rd edn. Taylor & Francis e-Library, New York (1994)
28. Van Landtschoote, A.: Hydrogeological investigation and recharge estimation of Gumera river catchment in lake Tana basin, Northern Ethiopia, The Degree of Master of Science Geology (2017)
29. Wohlgemuth, A.: Evaluating groundwater recharge in the Saloum Region (2016)
30. Tilahun, S.A., et al.: An efficient semi-distributed Hillslope erosion model: the Anjeni Watershed in the sub-humid Ethiopian highlands (2015)
31. Barry, B., Kortatsi, B., Forkuor, G., Gumma, M.K., Namara, R., Rebelo, L.-M.: Shallow groundwater in the Atankwidi catchment of the white Volta Basin: current status and future sustainability. International Water Management Institute, Colombo (IWMI Research Report 139) (2010). https://doi.org/10.5337/2010.234. 30 p.
32. Seo, D.C., Yang, J.Y., Lee, D.H., Song, J.H., Lim, H.S.: Kompsat-2 direct sensor modeling and geometric calibration/validation international archives of the photogrammetry. Remote Sensing and Spatial Information Sciences, vol. XXXVII. Part B1 (2008)
33. Chris, B.: Supervised and unsupervised land use classification (2002)
34. De Loe, R.C.: Agricultural water use: a methodology and estimates for Ontario. Can. Water Resour. J. **30**(2), 111–128 (2005)

Evaluating the Impacts of Climate Change on the Stream Flow Events in Range of Scale of Watersheds, in the Upper Blue Nile Basin

Gerawork F. Mulu[1], Mamaru A. Moges[2(✉)], and Bayu G. Bihonegn[1]

[1] Department of Hydraulic and Water Resource Engineering,
Kombolcha Institute of Technology, Wollo University, Dessie, Ethiopia
`geru302@gmail.com`
[2] Faculty of Civil and Water Resources Engineering, Bahir Dar Technology Institute,
Bahir Dar University, Bahir Dar, Ethiopia
`mamarumoges@gmail.com`

Abstract. The main focus on three watersheds in the upper Blue Nile. The study used the Representative concentration pathway (RCP) climate model scenarios with 50 km resolution. The CORDEX-Africa model output of RCP2.6 and RCP8.5 scenarios were used. The Parameter Efficient Semi Distributed Water Balance model (PED-WM) was calibrated and validated to project the climate change impacts on the stream flow events. The future climate projection results were presented by dividing in to three future time horizons of 2030s (2021–2040), 2060s (2051–2070) and 2090s (2081–2100). The bias corrected maximum and minimum temperature increases in all months and seasons in the selected watersheds. The change in magnitude in RCP8.5 emission was higher than RCP2.6 scenario. The study resulted considerable average monthly, seasonal and annual precipitation change variability in magnitude and direction. In 2030s, the average annual Stream flow projection decreases up to −32.18% for RCP2.6 and up to −19.44% for RCP8.5 scenarios. In 2060s also the average annual stream flow decreases by −12.3% and −32.18% for RCP2.6 and RCP8.5 emission scenarios, respectively. Similarly, in 2090 s, the average annual Stream flow change decreases by −20.67 and −51.78% for RCP2.6 and RCP8.5 respectively. For the future time horizon, the maximum Stream flow changes in wide range from (−56.4 to 81.1%) and minimum flow from (−61.72 to 8.17%) in both RCP2.6 and RCP8.5.

Keywords: Blue Nile · CORDEX · RCP · Scenario · PED-WM

1 Introduction

For centuries, the environment has been influenced by human beings. In any case, it is just since the start of the modern unrest that the effect of human exercises has started to reach out to a worldwide scale [1]. Today, environmental issue turns into the greatest worry of humankind as an outcome of logical proof about the expanding centralization of ozone harming substances in the environment and the changing atmosphere of the Earth. All

© ICST Institute for Computer Sciences, Social Informatics and Telecommunications Engineering 2020
Published by Springer Nature Switzerland AG 2020. All Rights Reserved
N. G. Habtu et al. (Eds.): ICAST 2019, LNICST 308, pp. 169–192, 2020.
https://doi.org/10.1007/978-3-030-43690-2_12

around, temperature is expanding and the sum and appropriation of precipitation is being changed [2]. The effect of environmental change on water assets are the most critical research plan in overall dimension [3]. This change in climate causes a significant impact on the water resource by disturbing the normal hydrological processes. Future change in overall flow of magnitude, variability and timing of the main flow event are among the most frequently cited hydrological issues. According to the International Panel on Climate Change (IPCC) Scientific Assessment Report, the increased concentrations of CO_2 and other greenhouse gases in the atmosphere since 1750 have been comprised the prominent causes of climate change. The combined land and sea surface temperature in worldwide has expanded by 0.85 °C (0.65 °C to 1.06 °C), over the period from 1880 to 2012. Crosswise over a lot of Africa, for instance, projections dependent on the high Representative Concentration Pathway (RCP), suggests that a mean yearly temperature peak will occur in mid-century and could riches 3 °C and 6 °C and before the finish of the 21st century and ocean level rise up to 100 cm by 2100 [4].

The IPCC finding indicated that in developing countries, such as Ethiopia there will be more vulnerability to climate change. This is due to less flexibility to adjust the economic structure and being largely dependent on agriculture, the impact of climate change has far reach implications in Ethiopia. The upper Blue Nile Basin is one of the largest basins in the country with high population pressure, degradation of land and highly dependent on agricultural economy. The increase in population growth, economic development and climate change have been proven by IPCC, 2007 [5] to cause rise in water demand, necessity of improving flood protection system and drought (water scarcity). The Upper Blue Nile River catchments are the main sources for the Blue Nile River basin and their water resources are an important input for the different water development projects and the livelihood support of the people in the basin.

The climate in this basin is variable from region to region. Due to variable climatic regions this impact might not be similar throughout the upper Blue Nile basin. Some studies on climate change impacts on the Upper Blue Nile region was conducted using fourth assessment report [6–11]. Most the above studies focusing on annual and seasonal total precipitation and stream flow. Studies that considered extreme conditions are limited. However, the results of these investigations are often divergent and inconsistent. This study differs from the previous, the study used (i) Parameter Efficient semi Distributed (PED-W) hydrological saturation excess water balance model which was tested for Ethiopian highlands having monsoonal climate (ii) to dated Representative Concentration Pathway (RCP) scenarios and (iii) different scale of ranges of watersheds. The study of the changes of hydro-climatic extreme events occurring at local and regional levels using to dated RCP scenario was necessary in order to provide valuable information which assists all stakeholders and policy makers to build up an innovative thinking on water resource availability and productivities as response to climate change risks and make appropriate decisions and to adapt the current situation and changes in water resources that might occur due to climate change. Gilgel Abbay, Temcha and Anjeni watersheds are the selected watersheds in the Upper Blue Nile basin in which currently, different multipurpose water resources development projects are proposed and constructed in the river basin. So, it is critical to determine the hydrological responses to climate change for the sustainability of the projects and looking for the possible mitigation measures.

The objective of this study is to evaluate the impacts of climate change on stream flow events in different ranges of watersheds in the upper Blue Nile river basin using PED-W model. The precipitation and temperature scenarios have been bias corrected to the fine resolution required by the hydrological model from RCM using change factor bias correction method.

2 Description of the Study Area

The locations of the selected catchments are lie in the upper Blue Nile basin, between 7°45′ and 12°45′ N, and 34°05′ and 39°45′ E.

Anjeni watershed is situated about longitude of 37°31′ E and latitude of 10°40′ N, in the Northern part of Ethiopia. It is bordered by the DebreMarkos-Bahir Dar road, 15 km north of Dembecha town on the rural road to Feres Bet and 65 km north-west of DebreMarkos [12–14] and the size of the hydrological catchment is about 113.4 ha. Temcha watershed is located in the Amhara Region near Dembecha town. It lies in between 10°23′ to 10°41′ N latitude and 37°16′ to 37°45′ E longitude with an average elevation of 2083 m and lies 350 km NW of Addis Ababa and have an area of 406 km². Gilgel Abbay watershed which is found in Tana basin and lies between (10°56′ to 11°51′ N) latitude and (36°44′ to 37°23′ E) longitude. Gilgel Abbay catchment is the biggest of the four main sub-basins of Lake Tana Basin. It depletes the southern part of Lake Tana basin to perennially feed lake tan River which empties itself in Lake Tana.

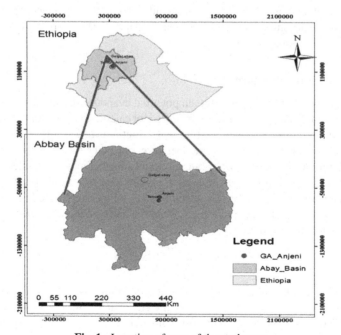

Fig. 1. Location of map of the study area

Being the main tributary of Lake Tana, Gilgel Abbay River originates from springs, considered as sacred water by the local people, located at an elevation 2750 m a.m.s.l near Mt. Gish. The hydrological catchment covers an area of 1650 km^2 (Fig. 1).

3 Methodology

3.1 Data Sources and Availability

Meteorological data collected from National Metrological Station Agency (NMSA), in Bahir Dar branch. SRTM 30 m × 30 m DEM data was used as an input data for Arc GIS software for catchment delineation. Hydrological data (stream flow) for the selected rivers in the upper Blue Nile River basin were used for model calibration and validation. These data were collected from the Ethiopia Ministry of Water Energy and Water Resources (MoWIE).

3.2 Climate Scenario Data

The future Precipitation and temperature (maximum and minimum) CORDEX-Africa GCM output 0.5 degree by 0.5 degree resolution RCP2.6 and RCP8.5 data was downloaded from Earth System Grid Federation (ESGF) Website http://www.csag.uct.ac.za/cordex-africa. Daily precipitation and temperature are taken from a set of simulations (historical and scenario) conducted with the CORDEX-Africa climate model. The projection depends on the bases of the new greenhouse gas concentration emission of representative concentration pathways (RCP).

The climate data ranges from 1st January 1976 until 31st December 2005 as historical period and for RCP4.5 and RCP8.5 which include data from 1st January 2006 until 31st December 2100. The temperature and precipitation data were bias corrected using change factor method developed by [15].

3.3 Potential Evapotranspiration (PET)

There are a number of methods to estimate potential evapotranspiration. The estimation methods vary based on climatic variables required for calculation. These are temperature-based method which use only temperature and sometimes day length; radiation-based method which uses net radiation and temperature and other formulas like [16] where it requires both temperature and net radiation and other climatic variables like wind speed and relative humidity. In area where there are data scarce, temperature method such as Enku's are required. For this specific study temperature based Enku's simple temperature method [17] is adopted to calculate the daily potential evaporation during model calibration and validation.

$$ET_o = \frac{(T\text{max})^n}{K} \tag{1}$$

Where, ET_o is the reference evapotranspiration (mm day^{-1}), n is 2.5 which can be calibrated for local conditions, k is Coefficient which can be calibrated for local conditions. The coefficient, k could be approximated as k = 48 * T_{mm} − 330 where T_{mm} is the mean annual maximum temperature.

3.4 Parameter Efficient Semi Distributed Watershed (PED-W) Model

The Parameter Efficient semi Distributed watershed (PED-W) model is a conceptual semi-distributed watershed model for continuous daily time step simulation of catchment runoff [18]. The model input requirement for PED model are daily rainfall, evapotranspiration, the areal fraction, maximum storage for each zone and the inter flow and base flow time. In PED-W the watershed is subdivided into three zones, degraded hill slope with little or no soil cover and the two runoff producing zone distinguished as the bottom lands that potentially saturate in the rainy monsoon phase, and one zone which contributes interflow and base flow of the watershed is permeable hill slope zone. PED-W model used to simulate future stream flow. The hydrological model was calibrated and validated using observed stream flow data of the selected watersheds in the basin. The model was selected because of its simplicity, suitability for monsoonal climate, easily availability, and widely acceptance.

PED-W Model Calibration and Validation
The PED-W model was calibrated manually, first by fitting the runoff volumes and followed by calibrating the shape of the hydrograph. The data record of 1990–2000, 1986–1994 and 1986–1994 was used for calibration for Gilgel Abbay, Temcha and Anjeni respectively. The calibrated model was validated using the independent set of observed from 2001–2005, 1996–1998 and 1995–1998 for Gilgel Abbay, Temcha and Anjeni respectively.

PED-W Model Performance Criteria
The performance of the model was evaluated by the Nash–Sutcliffe efficiency, (NSE) [19] Root Mean Square, RMS and Coefficient of Determination (R^2). NSE is a standardized measurement that determines the relative magnitude of the residual variance compared to the measured observed flow variance. NSE ranges from negative infinite to 1. Generally, NSE value between 0.6 and 0.8 indicates fair to good performance and when NSE is above 0.8 a model is said to be very good [20].

$$NSE = 1 - \frac{\sum\limits_{i=1}^{n}(Q_{oi} - Q_{si})^2}{\sum\limits_{i=1}^{n}(Q_{oi} - Q_o)^2}$$

Where Q_{oi} = observed discharge, Q_{si} = simulated discharge, Q_o = mean of observed discharge.

RMSE determines the degree to which the model predictions deviate from the observed data. The model efficiency (ENS) values ranges from 1.0 (best) to negative infinity.

R^2 is indicates how the simulated data correlates to the observed values of data. The range of R^2 is extends from 0 (unacceptable) to 1(best).

$$R^2 = \frac{\left[\sum\limits_{i=1}^{n}(Q_{si} - \overline{Q}_s)(Q_{oi} - \overline{Q}_o)\right]^2}{\sum[Q_{si} - \overline{Q}_s]\sum[Q_{oi} - \overline{Q}_o]}$$

Where Q_{si} is the simulated value, Q_{oi} is the measured values, $\overline{Q}_s$ is the average simulated value, $\overline{Q}_o$ is the average measured value.

4 Results and Discussion

In this investigation, 0.5 degree by 0.5-degree grid resolution CORDEX-Africa bias corrected GCM model outputs based on RCP2.6 and RCP8.5 emission scenarios for three watersheds in the upper Blue Nile Basin used for analysis. Period from 1976–2005 taken as a base period and three future periods considered for impact investigation of 2030s (2021–2041), 2060s (2051–2070) and 2090s (2081–2100). In order to check the exactness replication of the multimodal prediction for the basin the CORDEX-Africa model historical climate data output compared against observation data for each catchment. The mean monthly precipitation, maximum and minimum temperature observed (1986–2005) and GCMs (1976–2005) compared for three catchments (Anjeni, Temcha and Gilgel Abbay) for Upper Blue Nile Basin. All changes in projected climate variables under this study have been evaluated bias corrected base line climate variable. The climate change analysis was first by evaluating climate variables with corrected base line period. Secondly stream flow change evaluation due to climate change by simulating discharge using base line period and projected climate variables.

4.1 Historical GCMs Output Comparison with Observed Data

The raw RCM (CORDEX-Africa) out of long term daily and mean monthly precipitation and temperature indicated that there is relatively good agreement in trend and pattern with the observed data. The daily and monthly correlation of the selected grid point RCM model out puts with the observed station data was in the range of (0.35–0.44) and (0.85–0.90) respectively over the historical period. The observed data indicated that mean annual precipitation over the Gilgel Abbay watershed was 1380.92, 1490.25 and 2300 mm/year for Bahir Dar, Dangila and Injibara respectively, while the CORDEX-Africa climate model output have 2220.75 mm/year. For Anjeni and Temcha watersheds the mean annual observed precipitation was 1608 and 1393 mm/year and climate model output 1385.96 and 1385.96 mm/year respectively. The model out have little variation with the observed data, therefore the bias correction was inevitable to decrease the discrepancy between cordex output and observed data. The outputs of CORDEX model maximum and minimum temperature data have daily and monthly correlations of (0.53–0.63) and (0.85–0.90) over the historical period with observed respectively. From the observed records, average maximum temperatures 26.8 °C and 24.4 °C and average minimum temperatures 12.27 °C and, 8.5 °C for Bahir Dar and Dangila respectively. For Anjeni and Temcha watershed the observed average maximum temperature have 23.36 °C and 24.5 °C and minimum temperature 9.15 °C and 10.69 °C respectively. Like the precipitation records, CORDEX-Africa model outputs generally had little variation between the annual mean maximum temperature 23.47 °C and 22.4 °C, and mean minimum temperature 13.96 °C and 12.35 °C of grid. Hence the CORDEX- Africa model datasets present different historical means and distributions from the observed dataset; the decision to perform bias correction was inevitable. Due to these reason relatively simple bias correction method could be used to shift and adjust the data to the observed mean and standard deviation.

4.2 Projected Changes in Climate Variables

Precipitation

The projected average monthly precipitation indicated a decreasing trend from march–September and increasing from October–February except during the month of December, from the base line period for all three catchments. In Anjeni watershed, the projected average monthly precipitation change ranging from (−25.4% to 92.2%), (−69.4% to 103.1%) and (−39.9% to 34.3%) in 2030s, 2060s and 2090s for RCP2.6 respectively. The maximum change was observed in month of November (92.2%) in 2030s and October (103.1% and 34.3%) in 2060s and 2090s. Similarly, for RCP8.5, the projected average monthly precipitation change ranges from (−51.1% to 79.2%), (−64.1% to 76.8%) and (−84.2% to 92.7%) in 2030s, 2060s and 2090s respectively. The maximum change was observed in month of February (79.2%), November (76.8%) and December (92.3%) in 2030s, 2060s and 2090s respectively. For both RCPs the increment of precipitation change was observed mostly in dry months (October–February). However, the reduction was observed in wet months (March–September) (Fig. 2a).

In Temcha watershed, the projected average monthly precipitation change ranging from (−30.47% to 64.26%), (−65.53% to 48.35%) and (−31.05% to 68.8%) in 2030s, 2060s and 2090s for RCP2.6 respectively. The maximum change was observed in month of January (64.26%) in 2060s and October (48.35% and 68.8%) in 2030s and 2090s. Similarly, for RCP8.5, the projected average monthly precipitation change ranges from (−48.2% to 61.1%), (−1.95% to 36.5%) and (−70.4% to 65.8%) in 2030s, 2060s and 2090s respectively. The maximum change was observed in month of February (61.1%) in 2060s January (36.5%) and (65.8%) in 2030s and 2090s respectively. For both RCPs the increment of precipitation change was observed mostly in dry months (October–February). However, the reduction was observed in wet months (march–September) (Fig. 2b).

In Gilgel Abbay watershed, the projected average monthly precipitation change ranging from (−2.5% to 42.8%), (−40.4% to 106.8%) and (−50% to128%) in 2030s, 2060s and 2090s for RCP2.6 respectively. The maximum change was observed in month of March (42.8%, 106.8% and 128.6%) in 2030s, 2060s and 2090s. Similarly, for RCP8.5, the projected average monthly precipitation change ranges from (−43.6% to 156.0%), (−65.7% to 103.6%) and (−68.3% to132.9%) in 2030s, 2060s and 2090s respectively. The maximum change was observed in month of February (156.6%), March (103.6%) and November (132.9%) in 2030s, 2060s and 2090s respectively. For both RCPs the increment of monthly precipitation change was observed mostly in dry months (October–February). However, the reduction was observed in wet months (march–September) (Fig. 2c). In general, in main rainy season (June to September) the rainfall exhibits decreasing scenario from base line period in RCP2.6 and RCP8.5 in all watersheds and future time horizons (Fig. 2). In general, the projected monthly change of future precipitation decreases in the month of March to September.

The average seasonal precipitation result indicated that in the future, the precipitation decreases in summer and spring in both RCP2.6 and RCP8.5. However, it increases in winter and autumn. The average annual precipitations presented in Table 1 and Fig. 3 shows, over each watershed the precipitation decreases in the future period for both RCPs. The maximum annual change was observed in 2090s for both RCPs and all watersheds.

The projected mean monthly precipitation shows similar pattern with the work of [21] which, describes the impact of climate change on Gilgel Abbay watershed using A2 and B2 scenarios. Gebre and Ludwig [22] indicated in their studies the mean monthly precipitation increased in a positive direction particularly in August, September, and October under both in 2030s and 2070s using both scenarios. A 24% increment in precipitation projection in the late 21st century (2070–2099) was reported by [6] using 11 GCMs, while [7] reported insignificant precipitation change by using 17 GCMs in Blue Nile basin. Conway [23] and [3] also indicated that there is large inter-model difference in the detail of rainfall changes over Ethiopia. These inter-model differences in projection of future precipitation is due to the diversity of African climates, high rain fall variability, very sparse observational network makes the prediction difficult at sub regional and local scales. This study shows the projected precipitation for the future period decrease in the main rainy season (June–September) as compared to base period but, the monthly magnitude of rain fall was high from June to September, due to the summer monsoon climate which brings atmospheric moisture into the basin, leading to large amounts of rainfall during the wet season. Generally, the variation of the projected future precipitation for the future period in the Upper Blue Nile basin is due to the variation of GCM model, scenarios used downscaling and bias correction methods, variability of the precipitation in the basin and limited and very sparse observational network availability.

Projected Maximum Temperature
The projected average monthly maximum temperature significantly increases in future periods in both RCPs scenarios. In Anjeni watershed, the maximum change in maximum

Table 1. Shows the change in percentage of projected annual average precipitation

Catchment	Factor	Observed	Projected					
			RCP2.6			RCP8.5		
			2030s	2060s	2090s	2030s	2060s	2090s
Anjeni	AARF(mm)	1608.3	1567.3	1478.1	1396.3	1378.5	1345.1	1114.0
	R^2		0.91	0.89	0.94	0.93	0.92	0.86
	Change (%)		−2.55	−8.10	−13.18	−14.29	−16.36	−30.74
Gilgel Abbay	AARF(mm)	1970.0	1793.0	1812.0	1758.5	1764.4	1717.8	1539.1
	R^2		0.93	0.92	0.89	0.83	0.82	0.76
	Change (%)		−8.98	−8.02	−10.73	−10.44	−12.80	−21.88
Temcha	AARF(mm)	1393.1	1335.9	1288.3	1284.2	1216.2	1251.2	1089.0
	R^2		0.94	0.94	0.95	0.95	0.93	0.91
	Change (%)		−4.10	−7.52	−7.81	−12.70	−10.19	−21.83

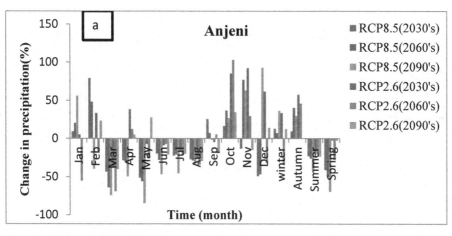

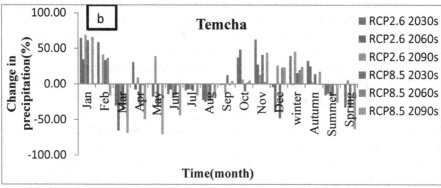

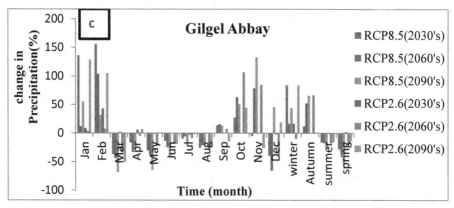

Fig. 2. Relative percentage change of average monthly and seasonal precipitation for 2030s. 2060s and 2090s as compared to the base line period

temperature was observed in January (7.03 °C, 7.22 °C and 8.2 °C) in 2030s, 2060s and 2090s for RCP8.5 respectively. Similarly, for RCP2.6 the maximum change was observed in January (6.8 °C, 7.2 °C, and 6.4 °C) in 2030s, 2060s and 2090s respectively.

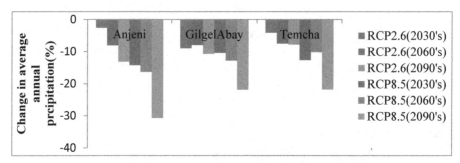

Fig. 3. Relative changes in average annual precipitation on Anjeni, Temcha and Gilgel Abbay watersheds based on RCP2.6 and RCP8.5 for 2030s, 2060s and 2090s as compared to the base period

The minimum change in maximum temperature was observed in July (0.2 °C) in 2030s RCP2.6 (Fig. 4a). Annually, the change of maximum temperature varies from (1.82 °C to 2 °C), (2.9 °C to 3.2 °C) and (5.24 °C to 5.7 °C) in 20305, 2060s and 2090s for RCP8.5. Similarly, for RCP2.6 the change varies from (1.28 °C to 1.42 °C), (1.52 to 1.66 °C) and (1.52 °C to 1.69 °C) in 2030s, 2060s and 2090s respectively.

For Temcha watershed, the maximum change of maximum temperature was observed in January (7.02 °C, 7.4 °C and 7.27 °C) in 2030s, 2060s and 2090s for RCP2.6 respectively. For RCP2.6 the change was observed in January (7.22 °C, 8.4 °C and 10.4 °C) in 2030s, 2060s and 2090s respectively. The minimum change was observed in July in 2030s and 2090s and December in 2060s for RCP2.6 (Fig. 4b). Annually, the change of maximum temperature varies from (1.27 °C to 1.43 °C), (1.51 °C to 1.67 °C) and (1.51 °C to 1.68 °C) in 2030s, 2060s and 2090s for RCP2.6 respectively. Similarly, for RCP8.5 the change varies from (1.82 °C to 2.0 °C), (2.94 °C to 3.22 °C) and (5.24 °C to 5.7 °C) in 2030s, 2060s and 2090s respectively.

For Gilgel Abbay watershed, the maximum change of maximum temperature was observed in January (7.4 °C, 7.7 °C and 7.6 °C) in 2030s, 2060s and 2090s for RCP2.6 respectively. For RCP8.5 the change was observed in January (7.6 °C, 8.7 °C and 10.78 °C) in 2030s, 2060s and 2090s respectively. The minimum change was observed in July in 2030s, August in 2090s and December in 2060s for both RCP2.6 and RCP8.5 (Fig. 4c). Annually, the change of maximum temperature varies from (1.34 °C to 1.48 °C), (1.41 °C to 1.59 °C) and (1.45 °C to 1.63 °C) in 2030s, 2060s and 2090s for RCP2.6 respectively. Similarly, for RCP8.5 the change varies from (1.78 °C to 2.01 °C), (2.86 °C to 3.23 °C) and (5.17 °C to 5.75 °C) in 2030s, 2060s and 2090s respectively.

The change in maximum temperature in dry season was higher than wet season in all future time horizons for both RCP2.6 and RCP8.5 in all watersheds (Fig. 4a–c). This is due to in wet season peak temperatures reduced because of rainfall, cloudy conditions and energy use for evapotranspiration [23]. In all Projection periods the magnitude is higher for the higher emission scenarios of RCP8.5 than for the low emission scenarios of RCP2.6. The projected maximum temperature in all time horizons was within the range projected by IPCC which indicate the average temperature will be rise 1.4–5.8 °C towards the end of the 21st century.

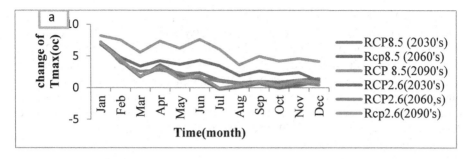

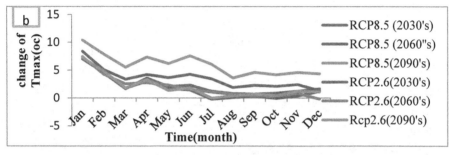

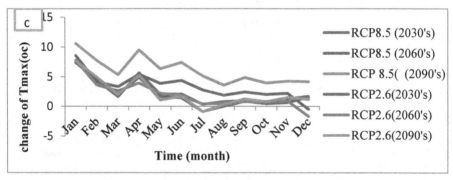

Fig. 4. Projected change in mean maximum temperature at (a) Anjeni (b) Temcha (c) Gilgel Abbay, watershed for 2030s, 2060s and 2090s time windows under RCP 2.6 and RCP8.5.

Projected Minimum Temperature

The minimum temperature showed an increasing trend in all three of future time horizons. In Anjeni watershed, the maximum change in minimum temperature was observed in January (4.9 °C, 5.32 °C and 5.14 °C) in 2030s, 2060s and 2090s for RCP2.6 respectively. Similarly, for RCP8.5 the maximum change was observed in January (3.7 °C, 4.92 °C, and 7.37 °C) in 2030s, 2060s and 2090s respectively. The minimum change in minimum temperature was observed in July (0.02 °C) in 2030s RCP2.6 (Fig. 5a). Annually, the change of minimum temperature varies from (1.32 °C to 1.38 °C), (1.53 °C to 1.62 °C) and 1.55 °C to 1.62 °C) in 2030s, 2060s and 2090s for RCP2.6. Similarly, for RCP8.5 the change varies from (1.46 °C to 1.59 °C), (2.93 to 3.17 °C) and (5.14 °C to 5.55 °C) in 2030s, 2060s and 2090s respectively.

For Temcha watershed, the maximum change of minimum temperature was observed in January (3.12 °C, 3.5 °C and 3.36 °C) in 2030s, 2060s and 2090s for RCP2.6 respectively. For RCP8.5 the change was observed in January (3.27 °C, 4.82 °C and 7.26 °C) in 2030s, 2060s and 2090s respectively. The minimum change was observed in July in 2030s and 2060s and December in 2090s for RCP2.6 (Fig. 5b). Annually, the change of minimum temperature varies from (1.22 °C to 1.34 °C), (1.46 °C to 1.6 °C) and (1.4 °C to 1.5 °C) in 2030s, 2060s and 2090s for RCP2.6 respectively. Similarly, for RCP8.5 the change varies from (1.46 °C to 1.59 °C), (2.94 °C to 3.17 °C) and (5.14 °C to 5.55 °C) in 2030s, 2060s and 2090s respectively.

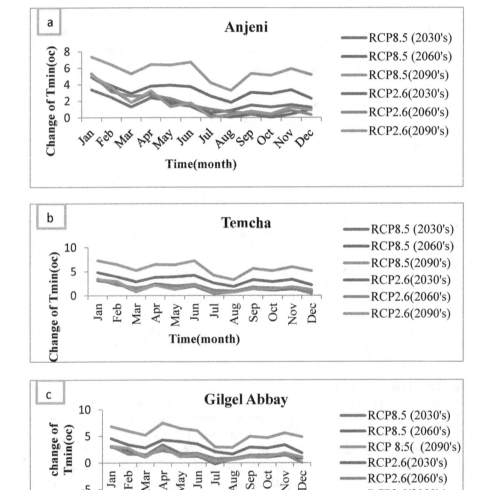

Fig. 5. Projected changes in mean minimum temperature at (a) Anjeni (b) Temcha (c) GilgelAbbay watershed for 2030s, 2060s and 2090s time windows under RCP2.6 and RCP8.5

For Gilgel Abbay watershed, the maximum change of minimum temperature was observed in January (3.1 °C, 3.18 °C and 4.16 °C) in 2030s, 2060s and 2090s for RCP2.6 respectively. For RCP8.5 the change was observed in January (3.25 °C, 4.6 °C and 6.8 °C) in 2030s, 2060s and 2090s respectively. The minimum change was observed in July in 2030s, and 2090s and December in 2060s for both RCP2.6 and RCP8.5 (Fig. 5c). Annually the change of minimum temperature varies from (1.23 °C to 1.34 °C), (1.35 °C to 1.5 °C) and (1.35 °C to 1.5 °C) in 2030s, 2060s and 2090s for RCP2.6 respectively. Similarly, for RCP8.5 the change varies from (1.43 °C to 1.56 °C), (2.83 °C to 3.09 °C) and 4.84 °C to 5.25 °C) in 2030s, 2060s and 2090s respectively. The minimum relative change of temperature is observed in July in all climate periods and emission scenarios except in 2060s in RCP2.6 which occurs in December. The projected minimum temperature increases an average of 1.47 °C and 1.7 °C, over the short-term period 2030s, 1.6 °C and 3.7 °C over midterm period 2060s and 1.68 °C and 5.6 °C over the long-term period 2090s in both RCP2.6 and RCP8.5 respectively for all three watersheds (Fig. 5a–c).

Potential Evapotranspiration
The projected change in average monthly potential evapotranspiration indicated an increasing for RCP2.6 and RCP8.5 for all watersheds. In Anjeni watershed, the maximum change in potential evapotranspiration was observed in January for (51.6%, 38 mm/month), (57.1%, 42 mm/month) and (63.3%, 46.6 mm/month) in 2030s, 2060s and 2090s for RCP8.5 respectively. Similarly, for RCP2.6 the change was observed in January (53.6%, 39.4 mm/month), (57.3%, 42.2 mm/month) and (54.9%, 40.4 mm/month) in 2030s, 2060s and 2090s respectively. The minimum evapotranspiration change was observed in August (0.25%, 0.13 mm/month), (6.3%, 2.8 mm/month) and (15%, 6.8 mm/month) in 2030s, 2060s and 2090s for RCP8.5 respectively. In RCP2.6 the minimum change was observed in August and September (less than 1.68%, 0.9 mm/month) in all future time horizons. Annually, the change of potential evapotranspiration varies from (92.6 to 111.5 mm/year), (102.4 to 119.2 mm/year) and (106 to 122.7 mm/year) in 2030s, 2060s and 2090s for RCP2.6. Similarly, for RCP8.5 the change varies from (116.2 to 133.6 mm/year), (174.7 to203.44 mm/year) and (315.4 to 361mm/year) in 2030s, 2060s and 2090s respectively (Fig. 6).

In Temcha watershed, the maximum change in potential evapotranspiration was observed in January (49.6%, 60.45 mm/month), (50.89%, 61.94 mm/month) and (53.1%, 64.65 mm/month) in 2030s, 2060s and 2090s for RCP2.6 respectively. Similarly for RCP8.5 the change was observed in January (48%, 58.5 mm/month), (53.34%, 64.9 mm/month) and (59.47%, 72.47 mm/month) in 2030s, 2060s and 2090s respectively. The minimum evapotranspiration change was observed in August (0.39%, 0.26 mm/month), (7.4%, 5.07 mm/month) and (17.3%, 11.72 mm/month) in 2030s, 2060s and 2090s for RCP8.5 respectively. In RCP2.6 the minimum change was observed in August and December (less than 3%, 3.8 mm/month) in all future time horizons (Fig. 6). Annually, the change of potential evapotranspiration varies from (96.2 to113.2 mm/year), (101.99 to 122.9 mm/year) and (106.9 to 127.3 mm/year) in 2030s, 2060s and 2090s for RCP2.6. Similarly, for RCP8.5 the change varies from (117.8 to 137.6 mm/year), (181 to 209 mm/year) and (326.8 to 376 mm/year) in 2030s, 2060s and 2090s respectively.

In Gilgel Abbay watershed, the maximum change in potential evapotranspiration was observed in January (53.75%, 56.6 mm/month), (57.1%, 60.2 mm/month) and (55%, 58 mm/month) in 2030s, 2060s and 2090s for RCP2.6 respectively. Similarly, for RCP8.5 the change was observed in January (49.9%, 52.6 mm/month), (49.4%, 52.04 mm/month) and (63.4%, 66.8 mm/month) in 2030s, 2060s and 2090s respectively. The minimum evapotranspiration change was observed in August (0.78%, 0.58 mm/month) and (13.9%, 10.31 mm/month) in 2006s and 2090s for RCP8.5 respectively. In 2030s the minimum change was observed in September (0.6%, 0.65 mm/month) for RCP8.5. In RCP2.6 the minimum change was observed in September, November and October (less than 1.2%, 1.32 mm/month) in 2030s, 2060s and 2090s respectively (Fig. 8). Annually the change of potential evapotranspiration varies from (105.8 to 117.7 mm/year), (102.8 to 126 mm/year) and (105.7 to 127.5 mm/year) in 2030s, 2060s and 2090s for RCP2.6. Similarly, for RCP8.5 the change varies from (113.1 to 130.8 mm/year), (112.6 to 130.8 mm/year) and (315.2 to 367.5 mm/year) in 2030s, 2060s and 2090s respectively.

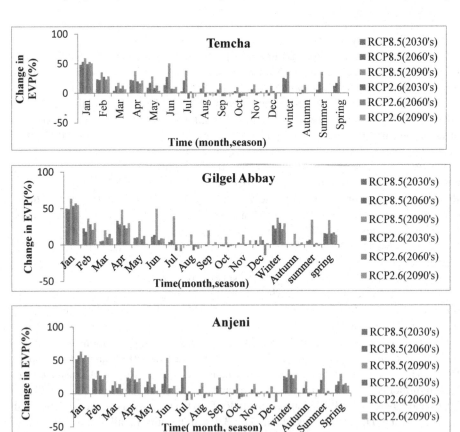

Fig. 6. Relative percentage change of average monthly and seasonal potential evapotranspiration for 2030s, 2060s and 2090s as compared to the base line period

In all-time windows the reduction of percentage change is observed in the months of July to October except in 2060s and 2090s for RCP8.5. The projected average seasonal potential evapotranspiration increases in all seasons for both emission scenarios. Generally, a positive potential evaporation change resulted both seasonally and annually for all future time horizons as compared to the base line period (Fig. 6). The increment of evapotranspiration is due to increment of temperature [23]. The decreasing of rainfall and increasing of temperature result the increasing of evapotranspiration. This also results decrement of stream flow.

4.3 Hydrological Modeling of the Watersheds

The hydrology of the watershed was modeled by using the parameter efficient semi- distributed watershed (PED-W) model. The PED-W model were calibrated manually, first by fitting the Discharge followed by calibrating the shape of the hydrograph from 1990 to 2000 for Gilgel Abbay, 1986 to 1994 for Temcha and Anjeni. The calibrated model was validated from 2001 to 2005, 1996 to 1998 and 1995–1998 for three of watersheds respectively. The discharge was simulated at a daily time step with NSE of 0.78 and 0.74 for Gilgel Abbay, 0.60 and 0.56 for Temcha, and 0.76 and 0.5 for Anjeni watershed during calibration and validation period respectively. On the monthly time scale the model was simulated with NSE of 0.91 and 0.89 for Gilgel Abbay, 0.91 and 0.89 for Temcha and 0.91 and 0.88 for Anjeni watershed for calibration and validation respectively. The initial points of parameters used for calibration and validation were dependent up on the value of the previous studies of PED-W model on the upper Blue Nile basin by [18] and [24]. Manually changing the parameters until the observed and predicted discharge hydrograph fits. The calibration and validation result of Gilgel Abbay was consistently in the range with earlier studies of PED-W discharge simulation for Ethiopian high lands watershed by [25]. In Anjeni and Temcha watershed the NSE and R^2 results are consistent with previous similar studies ([18, 25, 26] in range of (0.53 < NSE < 0.78) at daily time step, during calibration and validation periods (Table 2). The difference of parameters in values and model performance indicators from the previous studies in the same area might be due to recorded length of observed discharge in calibration and validation. During calibration and validation the PED-W model parameters of the fractional

Table 2. Shows the calibration and validation performance of the PED –W model

Watershed	Description	Daily			Monthly		
		R^2	NSE	RMSE	R^2	NSE	RMSE
Gilgel Abbay	Calibration	0.80	0.78	0.49	0.94	0.91	0.31
	Validation	0.78	0.74	0.53	0.93	0.89	0.33
Temcha	Calibration	0.61	0.60	0.63	0.92	0.9	0.30
	Validation	0.60	0.56	0.67	0.86	0.82	0.43
Anjeni	Calibration	0.78	0.76	0.49	0.93	0.91	0.30
	Validation	0.53	0.5	0.71	0.93	0.88	0.34

areas, the half-life of the base flow, and duration of the interflow after a rainstorm and Maximum soil storage for base flow (Bsmax) are sensitive for the forecasting of stream discharge.

4.4   The Impacts of Climate Change on Stream Flow

The projected change of mean monthly discharge for the three future time horizons: 2030s, 2060s and 2090s has indicated an increasing from October–February and decreasing from March–September except, Temcha watershed in RCP2.6 in May in 2060s (Fig. 7). The simulated stream flow with both scenarios from bias corrected climate model indicated a reduction and increment of discharge in the watersheds. This was directly related to the reduction and increment in precipitation, but there was also reduction of precipitation and increment in potential evapotranspiration in a season, these factors are anticipated to decrease the runoff on that season, however there was an increment of runoff in winter and autumn seasons from the base period.

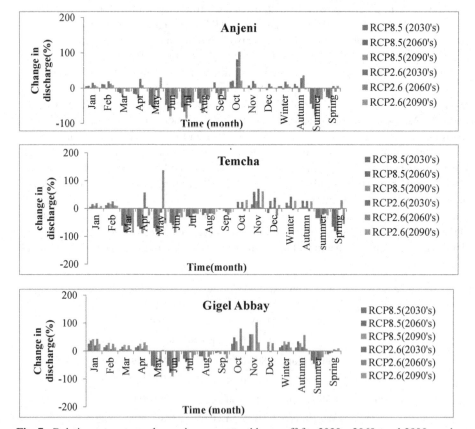

Fig. 7. Relative percentage change in mean monthly runoff for 2030s, 2060s and 2090s under RCP2.6 and RCP8.5 scenarios as compared to the baseline period.

In 2090s even though the change of precipitation with respect to the base period for this future time series has the same value in range with the first future time series 2030s and 2060s, high reduction stream flow was anticipated in RCP2.6 in Gilgel Abbay watershed because there is high increment of potential Evapotranspiration. In this period, the evapotranspiration have high increment rather than the first future time series (2030s) and (2060s). This increment of evapotranspiration results high decrements of runoff in this period.

In Anjeni watershed, the maximum change of increment of stream flow was observed in October (81%, 0.55 m³/s), (102.64%, 0.74 m³/s) in 2030s and 2060s for RCP2.6. In 2090s, the maximum change was observed in May (30.6%, 0.03 m³/s). The maximum change of decrement of stream flow was observed in July (0.58 m³/s, 0.79 m³/s and 0.75 m³/s) in 2030s, 2060s and 2090s respectively. Similarly, for RCP8.5, the maximum change was observed in October (18.25%, 0.12 m³/s), (21.1%, 0.14 m³/s) and (3.76%, 0.025 m³/s) in 2030s, 2060s and 2090s respectively. The maximum reduction was observed in July in all time future.

In Temcha watershed, the maximum change of increment was observed in October (70.4%, 49 m³/s) and (61.4%, 43.3 m³/s) in 2030s and 2090s for RCP2.6. In 2060s the change was observed in May (137.58%, 26 m³/s). Similarly for RCP8.5 the maximum change was observed in November (14.5%, 10.2 m³/s), (59.6%, 42 m³/s) and (26.4%, 18.6 m³/s) in 2030s, 2060s and 2090s respectively. The maximum reduction was observed in May (98.4%, 18.6 m³/s) in 2090s.

In Gilgel Abbay watershed, the maximum change of increment was observed in November (102.64%, 25 m³/s) and (30.5%, 7.7 m³/s) in 2060s and 2090s for RCP2.6 respectively. In 2030s, the change was observed in January (19.2%, 0.98 m³/s). Similarly, for RCP8.5 the maximum change was observed in November (59.2%, 15 m³/s) in both 2060s and 2090s. In 2030s also the change was observed in October (25.98%, 19.6 m³/s). The maximum reduction was observed in June (90.7%, 40 m³/s) in 2090s.

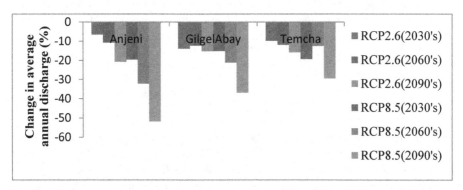

Fig. 8. Relative percentage change in mean annual runoff for 2030s, 2060s and 2090s under RCP2.6 and RCP8.5 scenarios as compared to the baseline period

Figure 7 indicated all watersheds have reduced value of Streamflow in all future time horizon 2030s, 2060s and 2090s in summer and spring season except RCP2.6 in all future time in spring season Gilgel Abbay (3.37%, 5.06% and 9.75%), Anjeni (6.16 in

2030s and in 2090s 6.4%), Temcha (29.37% in 2060s). In winter and autumn season, the projected Streamflow showed increment in all time horizons except RCP2.6 in 2030s for Temcha and RCP8.5, 2090s for Anjeni watershed.

The average annual stream flow showed a decreasing in the future time horizon for both RCPs in all three watersheds. The average annual flow shows maximum reduction of 51.78% at Anjeni, 36.77% at Gilgel Abbay and 29.40% at Temcha watershed in 2090s (Fig. 8).

4.5 The Impacts of Climate Change on the Stream Flow Events

Maximum Flow Analysis Using Annual Maximum Method
The maximum flow analysis was carried out using annual maximum method. This method evaluates the maximum annual flow by selecting the maximum flow from a year. The change of maximum annual flow for the first future time series 2030 s indicated an increasing in RCP2.6 scenario for Anjeni, Gilgel Abbay and Temcha catchments which have more than 4.5% change with respect to the base period maximum flow (1986–2005). However, in RCP8.5 scenario Gilgel Abbay and Temcha catchments show decrement mainly which have reduction more than 4.98%. In Anjeni watershed, the highest increment was (81.07%) for RCP2.6. In Gilgel Abbay watershed the highest reduction (10.15%) was observed for RCP8.5 for the first future time series with respect to the base period maximum annual flow (Table 3).

Table 3. Change of high stream flow for future periods in two scenarios as compared to base period

Watershed	RCP2.6							RCP8.5					
	Annual maximum flow				Percentage change			Annual maximum flow			Percentage change		
	Base period	2030s	2060s	2090s	2030s	2060s	2090s	2030s	2060s	2090s	2030s	2060s	2090s
Anjeni	0.3	0.5	0.5	0.3	81.1	101.4	19.0	0.3	0.3	0.3	28.9	19.8	7.4
Gilgel Abbay	388.5	406.0	486.2	434.0	4.5	25.2	11.7	349.0	406.0	379.3	−10.2	4.5	−2.4
Temcha	68.2	77.9	68.9	62.2	14.1	1.0	−8.9	64.8	75.2	65.0	−5.0	10.2	−4.8

For the second future time horizon 2060s, the percentage change of maximum annual flow showed an increment in all catchments in both RCP scenarios. The maximum increment (101.4%) was seen for Anjeni watershed in Rcp2.6. The change of maximum annual flow in the long -term future time horizon 2090s indicated an increasing for Anjeni and Gilgel Abbay watershed in RCP2.6. Whereas in RCP8.5 only increase for Anjeni watershed. For Temcha watershed, the maximum decrement was showed in both RCPs. A maximum change in 2090s was observed in Anjeni (7.43%) and Temcha (−8.89%) watersheds (Table 3). For all catchments the percentage change of maximum annual flow indicated an increment in RCP2.6 for all future time horizons except, 2090 s for Temcha. In RCP8.5 scenario for Gilgel Abbay and Temcha watershed indicated a decrement for 2030 and 2090s. However, Gilgel Abbay, and Temcha catchments indicated an increment for 2060s future time horizon and Anjeni for all future time horizons. In general, the increasing of high flow extremes in the future causes flooding and ground water reduction.

Maximum Flow Analysis Using Flow Duration Curve

For 5% probability (Q_5) of exceedance, the percentage change of maximum daily flow in 2030 s was changed from −2% to 36.1% in RCP2.6 scenario for Anjeni, Gilgel Abbay and Temcha catchments with respect to the base period flow (1986–2005). However in RCP8.5 scenario all catchments indicated decrement mainly which have reduction less than 10.2% (Table 4). For the future time horizon 2060s and 2090s the 5% probability of exceedance change from (−1.5% to −56.4%) for both RCPs. The maximum change of increment was observed at (Gilgel Abbay 36.1%) in 2030s and reduction at (Temcha 56.4%) in 2090s. Generally the extreme high flow (Q_5) changed in wide range from (−56.4% to 36.1%) (Table 4).

Table 4. Change of high stream flow (Q5) for future periods under two scenarios as compared to base period

Watershed	RCP2.6			RCP8.5		
	Percentage change			Percentage change		
	2030s	2060s	2090s	2030s	2060s	2090s
Anjeni	−2.0	7.4	8.2	−2.9	−13.1	−27.9
Gilgel Abbay	36.1	−1.5	−8.9	−10.2	−15.8	−40.0
Temcha	0.0	0.0	0.0	0.0	0.0	−56.4

This study supports the studies [27–29] which showed wide projections, from (1%–10%) probability of exceedance, with an overall changes in high stream flows was (−43% to 60%), prompting a reduction in drought events for the 2020 s, 2050 s and 2080 s at the Upper Blue Nile basin scale. Also there is little variation in range from the above studies, due to scale of watersheds, climate model used, emission scenario differences and hydrological model.

Low Flow Analysis Using Flow Duration Curve

Climate change affects both the high flows and low flows owing to variability in the precipitation and temperature. In this investigation, to describe low flow conditions in the stream a 95% exceedance probability was considered. The effect at 95% exceedance probability in 2030s, 2060s and 2090s the low flow indicated a decrement in both RCP scenarios for all catchments except RCP2.6 for Anjeni catchment with respect to the baseline situation. Table 5 and Fig. 9(a–c) indicated that the extreme low flow statistics at 95% exceedance probability decreased in all watersheds and RCPs. The maximum change of low flow was observed at (Temcha −61.7%) watershed in 2090s and the minimum change was at (Anjeni 1.43%) in 2090s (Table 5).

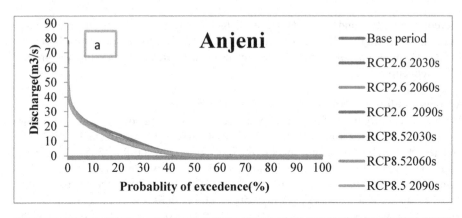

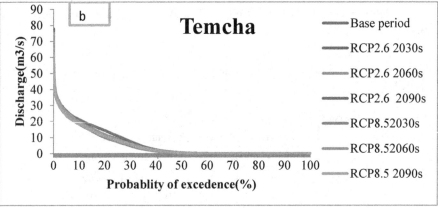

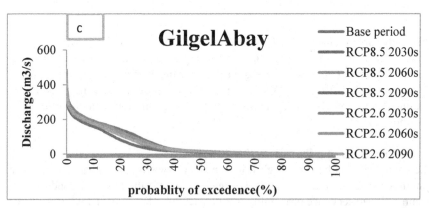

Fig. 9. Flow duration curve for RCP2.6 and RCP8.5 scenario for different time periods (a) Anjeni (b) Temcha (c) Gilgel Abbay

At the yearly scale, statistically significant declines in stream flow are reported by [30], However, [27] indicated an increasing trend in low stream flow statistic (Q_{90})

Table 5. Change of low stream flow (Q95) for future periods under two emission scenarios as compared to base period

Watershed	RCP2.6			RCP8.5		
	Percentage change			Percentage change		
	2030s	2060s	2090s	2030s	2060s	2090s
Anjeni	7.73	3.37	1.43	−7.22	−15.20	−48.44
Gilgel Abbay	−25.92	8.17	−1.04	−9.53	−7.18	−27.47
Temcha	−4.65	−11.25	−31.11	−33.49	−21.93	−61.72

using six GCM with A2 scenario in range of −25% to 60% for the 2050 horizon. Using 17 GCMs with A1B and B1 scenarios for the same 2050s horizon, [11] discover that changes low stream flows vary from −61% to +56%. Similarly, using three GCMs, [31] reported that projections of drought characteristics for future periods do not agree on the direction or magnitude for the Lake Tana sub-basin. However, [10] study on Gilgel Abbay sub basin using hadCM3 model, the low stream flow (Q_{95}) did not show any effects in 2020s, 2050s and 2080s. But Q_{70} flow decrease in 2020s and 2050s and increase for 2080s. This study analyzed the low stream flow Q95 using the Coordinated Regional Climate Downscaling Experiment in Africa (CORDEX Africa) outputs based on RCP2.6 and RCP8.5 scenarios for the future 2030s, 2060s and 2090s time horizon and the result indicated similar trends [10, 11, 27]. The decrement of low flow (Q_{95}) for the future period indicated the availability of water in the watershed for the future will reduced. The reason for this was due to changes in precipitation and temperatures can affect the magnitude and timing of runoff, which in turn affect the frequency and intensity of hydrologic extreme events such as floods and droughts.

5 Conclusions

This study evaluated the impacts of climate change on extreme state of hydrology using the downscaled bias corrected output and Hydrological model simulation approach of PED-W model. So the study reached on the following conclusions. The projected precipitation for the future time horizon increases from October to February and decrease from March to September for both scenarios Rcp2.6 and RCP8.5. For RCP2.6 the monthly maximum increment of precipitation reaches up to 92.2% at Anjeni in 2030s and (106.8% and 128%) at Gilgel Abbay 2060s and 2090s. For RCP8.5, the increment reaches 156%, 103.6% and 132.8% at Gilgel Abbay in 2030s, 2060s and 2090s respectively. The monthly maximum precipitation reduction reaches up to 30.47% and 51.1% for 2030s, 69% and 65.7% for 2060s and 70% and 84.8% for 2090s both in RCP2.6 and RCP8.5 respectively. Seasonally, the projected precipitation increase in winter and autumn, however, it decreases in summer and spring. The average increment reaches a maximum of 84.26% for RCP2.6 and 84.04% for RCP8.5 in Gilgel Abbay watershed. The annual precipitation shows decreasing trend for both RCP2.6 and RCP8.5 scenarios in all watersheds with the maximum decrement of 30.74% at Anjeni towards the end

21st century. The results of the projected monthly, seasonal and annual maximum and minimum temperature indicated an increasing trend in all future time horizons for both RCP2.6 and RCP8.5 scenarios. For RCP2.6 the maximum monthly increment of maximum and minimum temperature was observed in January reaches up to 7.4 °C and 4.9 °C in 2030s, 7.7 °C and 5.32 °C in 2060s and 7.6 °C and 5.14 °C in 2090s respectively. For RCP8.5, the maximum increment of maximum and minimum temperature reaches up to 7.6 °C and 3.7 °C in 2030s, 8.7 °C and 4.92 °C in 2060s and 10.78 °C and 7.37 °C in 2090s. In all projection period the maximum monthly increment was observed at Gilgel Abbay and minimum temperature at Anjeni watershed. The projected average annual maximum temperature changes (1.9, 3.05 and 5.46 °C) in 2030s, 2060s and 2090s for RCP8.5 in all watersheds respectively. For RCP2.6 the maximum change (1.35, 1.59 and 1.6 °C) in 2030s, 2060s and 2090s projection period. The projected annual maximum temperature in all time horizons is with the range projected by IPCC which indicate the average temperature will be rise 1.4–5.8 °C towards the finish of the century. The model performance criterion which was used to evaluate the model result indicates that the daily and monthly Nash and Sutcliffe efficiency criteria (NSE) within the ranges 0.6 to 0.78 and 0.9 to 0.91 during calibration and 0.5 to 0.74 and 0.82 to 0.89 during validation period respectively. The result indicated that the average projected monthly, seasonal and annual stream flow changes mainly corresponding to the change in precipitation except in month of March and April and spring season in Gilgel Abbay catchment which the flow increases even though the precipitation decreases. The maximum reduction of the average monthly flow reaches up to 85.76% at Anjeni, 90.7% at Gilgel abbey and 98.4% at Temcha watershed in 2090s for RCP8.5 and the maximum increment of the average monthly stream flow reaches up to 102.64% at Anjeni and Gilgel abbey and 137.58% at Temcha watershed in 2060s for RCP2.6. The average annual stream flow showed decreasing in the future time horizon for both RCPs in all three watersheds. The average annual flow shows maximum reduction of 51.78% at Anjeni, 36.77% at Gilgel Abbay and 29.40% at Temcha watershed in 2090s. The result indicated that the maximum flow event in both maximum annual and flow duration curve method changes in wide ranges from (−56.4 to 81.1%) in both scenarios for the future time and the minimum flow (Q_{95}) changes from (−61.72% to 8.17%). In general, the results from this study have clearly indicated that there would be variability in rainfall on the monthly and seasonal variation. Besides there would be also increasing trend in temperature and decreasing low flows. This indicates that there would be higher demand of evapotranspiration in dry season which additional water resource developments need to be planned for irrigation to sustain the already fragile food security of the country. Hence the water resource management and planning in the Blue Nile basin should address thesis phenomenon. Therefore, prevention and adaptation strategies in and around these watersheds have to be developed so as to maintain sustainability of available water resources and to prevent extreme events.

References

1. Baede, A.P.M.: The climate system: an overview. In: Climate Change 2001: The Scientific Basis, pp. 38–47 (2001)

2. Cubasch, U., et al.: Projections of future climate change. Climate change 2001: the scientific basis. Contribution of Working Group I to the Third Assessment Report of the Intergovernmental Panel on Climate Change. In: Ding, Y., et al. (eds.), pp. 526–582. Cambridge University Press, New York (2001)
3. Latta, G., Temesgen, H., Adams, D., Barrett, T.: Analysis of potential impacts of climate change on forests of the United States Pacific Northwest. For. Ecol. Manage. **259**, 720–729 (2010)
4. Pachauri, R.K., et al.: Climate change 2014: synthesis report. Contribution of Working Groups I, II and III to the fifth assessment report of the Intergovernmental Panel on Climate Change. IPCC (2014)
5. IPCC (2007). https://scholar.google.com/scholar?hl=en&as_sdt=0%2C5&q=IPCC%2C+2007+&btnG. Accessed 1 Nov 2019
6. Beyene, T., Lettenmaier, D.P., Kabat, P.: Hydrologic impacts of climate change on the Nile River Basin: implications of the 2007 IPCC scenarios. Clim. Change **100**, 433–461 (2010)
7. Elshamy, M., Seierstad, I.A., Sorteberg, A.: Impacts of climate change on Blue Nile flows using bias-corrected GCM scenarios. Hydrol. Earth Syst. Sci. **13**, 551–565 (2009)
8. Kim, U., Kaluarachchi, J.J.: Climate change impacts on water resources in the upper Blue Nile River Basin, Ethiopia 1. JAWRA J. Am. Water Resour. Assoc. **45**, 1361–1378 (2009)
9. Adem, A.A., et al.: Climate change projections in the upper Gilgel Abay River catchment, Blue Nile Basin Ethiopia. In: Melesse, A.M., Abtew, W., Setegn, S.G. (eds.) Nile River Basin, pp. 363–388. Springer, Cham (2014). https://doi.org/10.1007/978-3-319-02720-3_19
10. Dile, Y.T., Berndtsson, R., Setegn, S.G.: Hydrological response to climate change for Gilgel Abay River, in the Lake Tana basin-upper Blue Nile Basin of Ethiopia. PLoS One **8**, e79296 (2013)
11. Taye, M.T., Ntegeka, V., Ogiramoi, N.P., Willems, P.: Assessment of climate change impact on hydrological extremes in two source regions of the Nile River Basin. Hydrol. Earth Syst. Sci. **15**, 209–222 (2011)
12. Ashagre, B.B.: SWAT to identify watershed management options: Anjeni Watershed, Blue Nile Basin, Ethiopia. Ph.D. thesis, Citeseer (2009)
13. Herweg, K., Gebre, M.Y.: Adaptation or adoption? Integrating different perceptions of soil and water conservation in Ethiopia. Local Environ. In: Flury, M., Geiser, U. (eds.) Local Environmental Management in a North-South Perspective: Issues of Participation and Knowledge Management, pp. 181–190. Vdf Hochschulverlag AG ETH Zurich, Zurich (2002)
14. Ludi, E.: Economic Analysis of Soil Conservation: Case Studies from the Highlands of Amhara Region, Ethiopia. Geographica Bernensia, Bern (2004)
15. Anandhi, A., et al.: Examination of change factor methodologies for climate change impact assessment. Water Resour. Res. **47**, W03501 (2011)
16. Penman, H.L.: Natural evaporation from open water, bare soil and grass. Proc. R. Soc. Lond. Ser. Math. Phys. Sci. **193**, 120–145 (1948)
17. Enku, T., Melesse, A.M.: A simple temperature method for the estimation of evapotranspiration. Hydrol. Process. **28**, 2945–2960 (2014)
18. Steenhuis, T.S.: Predicting discharge and sediment for the Abay (Blue Nile) with a simple model. Hydrol. Process. Int. J. **23**, 3728–3737 (2009)
19. Nash, J.E., Sutcliffe, J.V.: River flow forecasting through conceptual models Part I—A discussion of principles. J. Hydrol. **10**, 282–290 (1970)
20. Moriasi, D.N., Arnold, J.G., Van Liew, M.W., Bingner, R.L., Harmel, R.D., Veith, T.L.: Model evaluation guidelines for systematic quantification of accuracy in watershed simulations. Trans. ASABE **50**, 885–900 (2007)
21. Abdo, K.S., Fiseha, B.M., Rientjes, T.H.M., Gieske, A.S.M., Haile, A.T.: Assessment of climate change impacts on the hydrology of Gilgel Abay catchment in Lake Tana basin Ethiopia. Hydrol. Process. Int. J. **23**, 3661–3669 (2009)

22. Gebre, S.L., Ludwig, F.: Hydrological response to climate change of the upper Blue Nile River Basin: based on IPCC fifth assessment report (AR5). J. Climatol. Weather Forecast. **3**, 121 (2015)
23. Conway, D.: From headwater tributaries to international river: observing and adapting to climate variability and change in the Nile basin. Glob. Environ. Change **15**, 99–114 (2005)
24. Collick, A.S., et al.: A simple semi-distributed water balance model for the Ethiopian highlands. Hydrol. Process. Int. J. **23**, 3718–3727 (2009)
25. Tilahun, S.A., et al.: Distributed discharge and sediment concentration predictions in the sub-humid Ethiopian highlands: the Debre Mawi watershed. Hydrol. Process. **29**, 1817–1828 (2015)
26. Moges, M.A., et al.: Suitability of watershed models to predict distributed hydrologic response in the awramba watershed in Lake Tana Basin. Land Degrad. Dev. **28**, 1386–1397 (2017)
27. Kim, U., Kaluarachchi, J.J., Smakhtin, V.U.: Climate change impacts on hydrology and water resources of the upper Blue Nile River Basin, Ethiopia, vol. 126. IWMI, Colombo (2008)
28. Aich, V., et al.: Comparing impacts of climate change on streamflow in four large African River Basins. Hydrol. Earth Syst. Sci. **18**, 1305–1321 (2014)
29. Nawaz, N.R., Bellerby, T., Sayed, M., Elshamy, M.: Blue Nile runoff sensitivity to climate change. Open Hydrol. **4**, 137–151 (2010)
30. Setegn, S.G., Rayner, D., Melesse, A.M., Dargahi, B., Srinivasan, R.: Impact of climate change on the hydroclimatology of Lake Tana Basin, Ethiopia. Water Resour. Res. **47** (2011)
31. Enyew, B.D., Van Lanen, H.A.J., Van Loon, A.F.: Assessment of the impact of climate change on hydrological drought in Lake Tana catchment, Blue Nile basin, Ethiopia. J. Geol. Geosci. **3**, 174 (2014)

Soil Water Dynamics on Irrigated Garlic and Pepper Crops Using Hydrus–1D Model in the Lake Tana-Basin, Northwestern Ethiopia

Enguday Bekele[1(✉)], Seifu Tilahun[1], Abebech Beyene[1], Sisay Asres[1], Berhanu Geremew[1,2], and Haimanot Atinkut[3]

[1] Faculty of Civil and Water Resource Engineering,
Bahir Dar University, 79, Bahir Dar, Ethiopia
`enguday18@gmail.com`
[2] Gondar Institute of Technology, University of Gondar, 196, Gondar, Ethiopia
[3] College of Agriculture and Environmental Science, University of Gondar,
196, Gondar, Ethiopia

Abstract. Soil water is an important variable in regulating and predicting hydrological process for optimal irrigation. Hydrus-1D was used to simulate soil water dynamics under overhead irrigation in Dengeshita watershed at the plot level. Experiments were carried out from October-February 2017/2018 and from March – June 2018. The treatments were conservation agriculture (CA) and conventional tillage (CT). Irrigation depth, crop phenology, meteorological and soil parameters were determined. Soil parameters were estimated using a K-nearest neighbor approach (KNN) pedotransfer functions for tropical soils and fitted using retention curve optimization program. Sensitivity analysis result showed saturated soil water content (θs), saturated hydraulic conductivity (Ks), and pore size distribution (n) were the most important parameters for the model. The model performance using measured soil water content (SWC) was good with R^2 of (0.64–0.77) and errors; RMSE of 0.021–0.063 and ME of 0.0013–0.040. Based on overall evaluation, CA plots had higher average SWC (0.39–0.40 cm^3.cm^{-3}) than CT plots (0.36–0.37 cm^3.cm^{-3}). The average seasonal actual transpiration was lower for CT (88.76%) than CA (93.46%) plots due to higher evaporation loss (CT = 7.69% and CA = 1.15%); the difference is statistically insignificant. Seasonal deep percolation from CT and CA plots was 0.38% and 3.15% respectively. Therefore, CA was better than CT due to store more water for plants.

Keywords: Soil water dynamics · Hydrus-1D · Hydraulic parameters · Conservation agriculture · Conventional tillage · Overhead irrigation

1 Introduction

1.1 Background

Using water efficiently by improving water management is the primary objective of irrigated agriculture to minimize risks on available water resources (Siebert et al. 2010).

N. G. Habtu et al. (Eds.): ICAST 2019, LNICST 308, pp. 193–209, 2020.
https://doi.org/10.1007/978-3-030-43690-2_13

To improve the irrigation water management, the major losses of irrigation water should be pointed out and quantified by relatively accurate methods. Soil water is water stored in the unsaturated part of the soil profile, i.e. between the soil surface and ground water level (Van der Kwast 2009). Analyzing the spatial and temporal distribution of soil water is essential in regulating and predicting a range of hydrological processes like Plant water availability (Böhme et al. 2016, Mulebeke et al. 2013, Qiu et al. 2001). Soil water flow prediction in the unsaturated zone is important for efficient agricultural water use (Yadav et al. 2009). Optimal irrigation water management, design, and management of irrigation regimes required a comprehensive knowledge of the distribution and movement of soil water in the root zone (Mei-Xian et al. 2013). Soil water content information is an important variable for the estimation of plot-catchment scale water balance (Sánchez et al. 2012). Soil water in the unsaturated zone is also important resource of water for plants and helps to monitor plant water consumption for crop growth (Liang et al. 2015).

For a better understanding of soil water dynamics, good quality soil moisture time series data is required (Gabiri et al. 2018). Therefore, continuous and exhaustive field measurement of soil water content is necessary for investigation and understanding of soil water dynamics (Espejo-Pérez et al. 2016). As stated by Jurik et al. (2012) and Šimunek et al. (2012), realization of field soil water monitoring could be characterized as extremely time and money consuming. Water movement in the unsaturated zone is an incredibly complex process due to the heterogeneous nature of the soil and variable atmospheric boundary conditions at the soil surface over a short period (Saifadeen and Gladneyva 2012). Li et al. (2014) also stated that water flow in the soil is the interaction of complex processes, their observation and evaluation under field condition is relatively difficult, costly, and time consuming. Besides, Šimunek et al. (2012) pointed out that direct field soil water monitoring could be characterized as extremely time and money consuming.

Tools such as TDR, neutron probes and capacitance probes, which are used to measure soil water with high temporal resolution, are instructive and lack the necessary spatial resolution to capture heterogeneities in soil properties (Kuhl et al. 2018). As the acquisition of field data is costly and time consuming, models are alternative ways to manage systems once they are well validated (Arnold and Allen 1996). Numerical simulations are efficient approaches to investigate soil water dynamics for optimal irrigation management practices (Chauhan et al. 2003). In this study, a widely used soil water model, Hydrus-1D by Simunek et al. (2005), which simulates one dimensional water, heat and solute transport in variably saturated and unsaturated media, was applied to simulate the soil water dynamics.

Models such as MODular Hydrologic Modeling System (MODHMS) (Varut et al. 2011) and Hydrus-2D and-3D (Šimunek et al. 2012) can be adopted to simulate soil water dynamics. However, they are data demanding, required considerable computer resources, and are difficult to adapt to the investigated study area because of complex boundary condition (Gabiri et al. 2018). Hydrus-1D, in comparison, is less data demanding and useful tool for evaluating various water fluxes in agricultural fields with different crops and various irrigation schemes (Kandelous et al. 2012). It has been successfully applied in numerous studies for predicting soil water content and movement under different conditions (Beyene et al. 2018, Chen et al. 2014, González et al. 2015, Zhang et al. 2016).

Therefore, the purpose of the present study was to evaluate the soil water dynamics using Hydrus-1D on irrigated Garlic and pepper crops under overhead irrigation application method to quantify the significant losses of irrigation water in the plant root zone. Specifically to analyze the vital soil water balance components in the root zone, to evaluate the effect of CA on soil water dynamics and test the applicability of Hydrus-1D model for the study area.

2   Materials and Methods

2.1   Study Site

This study was conducted at Dengeshita watershed located in Dangila district in Amhara region of Awi Administrative zone. Dangila is one of Agricultural Growth Program (AGP) and feeds the future woredas in the region. It is located about 80 km south west from Bahir Dar (the capital city of Amhara region), having latitude and longitude of 36.83° N and 11.25° E respectively with a mean elevation of 2137 m above sea level. The study area was within Dengeshita watershed. Experimental plots were selected from farmer's fields within the watershed; plots have surface soils of clay texture (0–60 cm) and very high clay content (heavy clay soil) to a depth of 90 cm. The watershed covers an area of 57 km^2 with mainstream length of 43 km and is 8 kms away from Dangila town. The livelihood of the area is based on both crop and livestock production. Crop production mainly includes cereals like maize, teff, and finger millet; legumes like beans; irrigated crop production such as garlic, onion and pepper. Ground water is the primary water source for irrigation. Pulleys together with manual water lifting device are widely used in the area (Fig. 1).

2.2   Field Experimentation and Data Collection

For this study on-farm research experiment was designed to evaluate soil water dynamics under smallholder irrigated plots. The plot size was set to be a 10 m x 10 m, just for manageability depending on water resources of the study area. Accordingly, five experimental plots were selected by purposive sampling technique during the first irrigation period. Garlic and pepper crops produced during the first and second season, respectively. Each plot divided in to CA and CT subplots. Farmers used ground water for irrigation. Eight raised beds designed in each plot having a length of 10 m, width of 80 cm with 40 cm bed spacing were prepared. CA, with overhead irrigation conducted on the half of the scenarios (4 beds) and CT with overhead irrigation was performed on the remaining half (4 beds). Fertilizer and other manure applications were set common for both treatments.

Daily soil water content was measured at the top 10 cm depth at 8 points (4 times from CA and 4 times from CT) from each plot using Time Domain Reflectometer (TDR probe). For this study 1 m × 1 m × 1 m pit was excavated from one of the representative plot to determine soil physical properties. Soil physical properties such as texture, bulk density, field capacity (FC), permanent wilting point (PWP), organic matter, cation exchange capacity (CEC) and PH were determined by taking soil samples

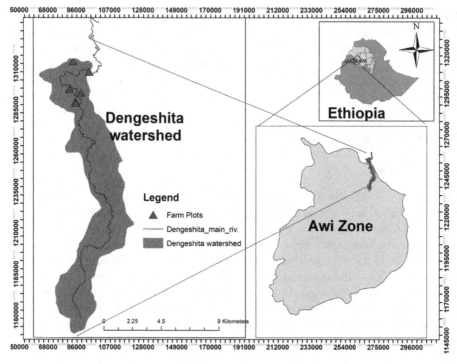

Fig. 1. Location of study area

at each horizon to estimate model parameters. Bulk density determined from undisturbed soil samples taken at each horizon using core sampler having a diameter of 4.38 cm and length of 5.14 cm. Soil samples analyzed at Amhara design and supervision works enterprise soil laboratory.

Seasonal plant height and root depth were measured using the meter at each development stage from CA and CT plots. The amount of irrigation determined by counting the number of already measured container (10 L bucket) by which the farmers apply irrigation. Therefore, multiply the number of buckets by 10 L to get the total volume of flooding. Then convert irrigation volume (m^3) to irrigation depth dividing it by plot size (area); assuming the water uniformly distributed throughout the plots. The effective root depth (the depth within which most plant roots are concentrated) of garlic is 0.3–0.5 m and maximum root depth for pepper is 0.5–1.0 m (Allen et al. 1998).

Because ground water table was in-depth during the experiment it does not have any contribution to crop soil-water use and an effect on soil water variation around the root zone of the plant; therefore ground water level variation was not monitored during the simulation periods. Due to lack of water resource and manual overhead irrigation system at the study area excess water was not generated as surface runoff due to irrigation from experimental plots.

2.3 Hydrus-1D Model

2.3.1 Model Description

The one dimensional Hydrus-1D computer program (Šimůnek et al. 2008) which based on Richards equation was selected to simulate soil water dynamics in experimental plots. Hydrus-1D model was freely available for download from PC PROGRESS website. Since water flow in the soil profile between the soil surface and groundwater table (unsaturated zone) is predominantly in the vertical direction, there was no need to use a model such as Hydrus (2D or 3D) that would consider multiple dimensions (Li et al. 2015, Van Dam et al. 2005). Therefore Hydrus-1D model can be used to study soil-water dynamics. Several researchers like (Chen et al. 2014, Daniel et al. 2017, Li et al. 2015, Rubio and Poyatos 2012) preferred Hydrus-1D and successfully applied it for unsaturated zone soil water dynamics.

The governing one dimension water flow equation for partially saturated porous medium is described using the modified form of the Richards equation, under the assumptions that air phase plays an insignificant role in the liquid-flow process and that water flow due to heat gradient neglected:

$$\frac{\partial \theta}{\partial t} = \frac{\partial}{\partial z}\left[k(h)\left(\frac{\partial h(\theta)}{\partial z}\right) + \cos \alpha\right] - s \tag{1}$$

Where, θ is the volumetric soil-water content [$cm^3\ cm^{-3}$], t is time [day], z is the vertical coordinate [cm] (positive upward and its origin is the soil surface), h is the water pressure head [cm]. S is the sink term in the flow equation [$cm^3 cm^{-3}\ day^{-1}$] accounting for root water uptake by plants (transpiration), α is the angle between the flow direction and the vertical axis (i.e., $\alpha = 0°$ for vertical flow, $90°$ for horizontal flow, and $0° < \alpha < 90°$ for inclined flow), and k (h) is the unsaturated hydraulic conductivity function [$cm\ day^{-1}$]. The sink term (S) in Eq. (1) is defined as the volume of water derived from a unit volume of soil per unit time by plant roots. It accounts for actual root water uptake equivalent to actual transpiration, calculated by the model using Feddes equation (Soylu et al. 2011).

2.3.2 Estimation of Soil Hydraulic Parameters

The van Genuchten soil hydraulic parameters θs, θr, α, n and m (Table 1) required by Hydrus-1D were estimated using KNN pedotransfer function and optimized using the retention curve parameter optimization (RETC) software by fitting retention data, θ (h). Points on the soil water retention curves for each soil horizons were estimated with KNN pedotransfer functions of tropical soils (Botula et al. 2013). The service requires the measured particle size distribution, organic matter content, bulk density, soil water content at field capacity, at permanent wilting point, CEC, and PH. Then the RETC program was used to fit the predicted data and to derive the unsaturated soil hydraulic parameters (θr, θs, n, α, and m). Retention curve uses a nonlinear least-squares optimization approach to estimate unknown model parameters from observed retention data (Van Genuchten et al. 1991). The pore connectivity parameter (l) was assumed equal to the average value of 0.5 for many soils.

2.3.3 Initial and Boundary Conditions of Hydrus-1D

The initial condition was defined using SWC measured during the crop planting period. The soil surface subjected to the atmosphere with specified values of irrigation and evaporation. The upper boundary condition in the model defined by an atmospheric boundary condition with surface runoff using potential evapotranspiration (ETo). ETo was calculated using the Penman-Monteith equation (Allen et al. 1998) using recorded meteorological data. Ground water table was deep enough so exclude its influence on water movement in the plant root zone by capillary rise. Due to this reason, free drainage (irrigation water infiltrates beneath plant root zone) was specified to describe lower boundary conditions of the soil profile. Daily meteorological data such as maximum air temperature, minimum air temperature, relative humidity, sunshine hour, and wind speed, which used as an input to Hydrus-1D obtained from Dangila meteorological stations located in the study site of Dengeshita watershed. During simulation measured irrigation depths were considered as time variable boundary condition. Two soil layers (0–30 cm of thickness 1 and 30–60 cm of width 2) found for simulation purpose.

3   Result and Discussion

3.1   Hydraulic Parameters Used for Hydrus-1D Model

Hydrus-1D soil hydraulic parameters (i.e., θr, θs, a, n, and Ks) derived from the observed soil physical properties using the K-nearest neighborhood pedotransfer function for tropical soils used to evaluate soil water dynamics stated in Table 1. The retention curve parameter optimization program for unsaturated soils was used to optimize the parameters. Calibration for Hydrus-1D was performed by fitting the observed soil water contents using the retention curve parameter optimization program (RETC).

Table 1. Hydrus-1D optimized soil hydraulic parameters

Depth (cm)	Soil type	$\theta r(cm^3/cm^3)$	$\theta s(cm^3/cm^3)$	$\alpha(cm^{-1})$	n	Ks(cm/day)	R^2	SSQ
0–30	Clay	0.1808	0.4874	0.0524	1.1440	4.8	0.997	0.00023
30–60	Clay	0.1817	0.4962	0.0498	1.1440	4.8	0.996	0.00032

Where θr-Residual soil water content, θs-Saturated soil water content, α-Shape parameters, n-pore size distribution parameter, Ks-Saturated hydraulic conductivity, R^2-Coefficient of determination and SSQ-sum square of error.

3.2   Sensitivity Analysis of Model Parameters

Sensitivity analysis was performed to analyze the influence of each parameter variations on the model outputs and then to select the most sensitive settings (Chang et al. 2007). For this study Local sensitivity analysis (LSA) using a one-at-a-time (OAT) approach was used to understand the effect of each parameter to the model output since this approach allows a clear identification of single parameter effects. From the result, saturated soil water content, saturated hydraulic conductivity, and pore size distribution parameters were the most critical hydraulic parameters that affect model output (Fig. 2).

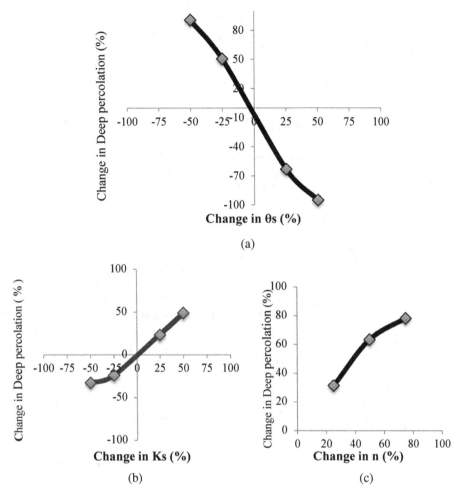

Fig. 2. Sensitivity analysis of saturated water content (θs) (A), saturated hydraulic conductivity (Ks) (B), and pore size distribution parameter (C).

3.3 Hydrus-1D Model Validation

For evaluating the accuracy of model, predicted soil water content from the observation node (at 10 cm soil depth) by Hydrus-1D compared with the observed SWC for all experimental plots (Figs. 3a, b and 4). Also, the model validated by graphical technique which provides a visual comparison of measured and simulated soil water content. The result showed that the model underestimates soil water in CA experimental plots averagely by 0.025 cm^3cm^{-3} during the first simulation period. Hydrus-1D model does not have parameters especially consider for CA in addition to soil hydraulic parameters and initial condition. Due to this reason, Hydrus-1D underestimates daily soil water content in CA plots. The observed and simulated soil water content matched well and showed reasonably similar trends for both CT and CA plots.

Comparison of observed and simulated soil water content at different times during crop growth in 2017/2018 and 2018 showed a good correlation. A good correlation was indicated by high R^2 (0.64–0.77) and low RMSE (0.021–0.063), ME (0.0013–0.040) values. The R^2, RMSE and ME between observed and simulated soil water content indicated that the model performed well in simulating soil water dynamics.

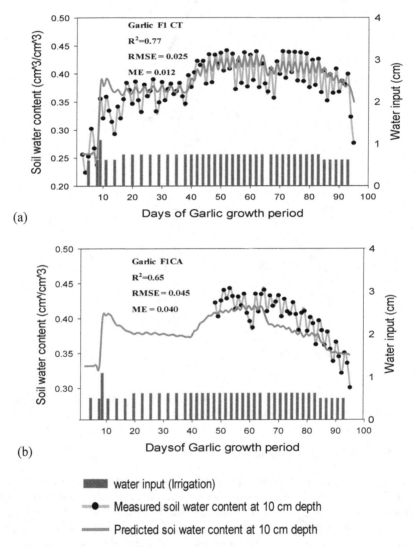

(a)

(b)

water input (Irrigation)

Measured soil water content at 10 cm depth

Predicted soi water content at 10 cm depth

Fig. 3. Comparison of observed and simulated soil water content for CT and CA

During 2017/2018 simulation period, more fluctuations of soil water content in CT plot (Fig. 3a) than in the CA plot (Fig. 3b) were due to more irrigation water applications in CT compared to CA plot. Compared to growth stage, the soil system stored higher water content from the end of development to the beginning of late stage due to high irrigation applications. The result clearly showed that soil water content was gradually increase starting from the end of the development stage (immediately when irrigation interval is small) in CT and CA experimental plots. The model validation result clearly showed Hydrus-1D can simulate soil water dynamics in CA and CT experimental plots. However, the model underestimates soil water content in CA experimental plots, and the correlation coefficients were smaller compared to CT plots, even measured and simulated values had similar trend. There were discrepancies between the observed and predicted soil water content during most days of plant growth season, especially in CA plots, and the observed soil water contents were greater compared to predicted values. No soil hydraulic parameters were estimated for CA plots, and measurement errors at the field condition inevitably led to the difference between observed and simulated soil water content. Hydrus-1D does not have parameters consider only for CA, which may also cause for mismatch of observed and simulated water contents.

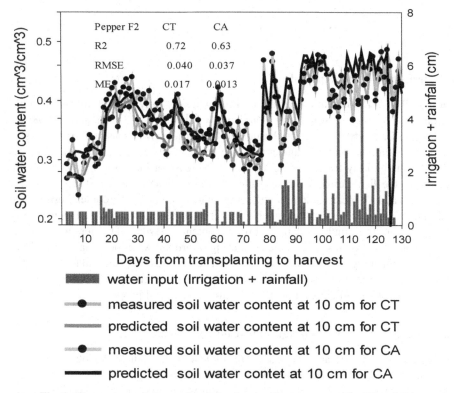

Fig. 4. Comparison of observed and simulated soil water content for CT and CA

Hydrus-1D also could simulate soil water dynamics (SWD) successfully during pepper growth season. Change in the soil water content between observed and simulated values matched well during this season. Daily Soil water content also responded positively to irrigation and rainfall events. Due to frequent rainfall events, the soil system store higher water content from 80–125 days after transplanting of pepper (DAT). Even though an equal amount of water was applied, both observed and predicted soil water content in CA was higher than in CT plots, especially at the early stage (Table 2).

Table 2. Average daily soil water content for experimental plots during simulation period

| Plot code | Average observed daily soil water content ($cm^3.cm^{-3}$) | | Average simulated daily soil water content ($cm^3.cm^{-3}$) | |
| | Garlic | | Pepper | |
	CT	CA	CT	CA
F1	0.376	0.400	0.392	0.398
F2	0.374	0.389	0.386	0.395
F3	0.371	0.384	0.425	0.432
F4	0.331	0.349		
F5	0.384	0.401		

3.4 Irrigation Water Applied

During 2017/2018 simulation period, crop growth was fully through irrigation applications. The average seasonal irrigation depths used were 278.86 mm and 241.68 mm for CT and CA plots respectively throughout the garlic growth season. During the second experimental period, average cumulative water input (irrigation plus rainfall) was 773.03 mm similarly for CT and CA plots. A decrease or increase of irrigation depth applied to the fields directly impacts the amount of water stored in the soil system (Figs. 3a, b and 4). Means that higher water input gives higher water content result in the soil system and vice versa. Also, smaller irrigation applications could not significantly affect and vary the simulated daily soil water content of Hydus-1D. There was a shortage of water for irrigation due to the decreasing of ground water potential staring from pepper transplanting to the coming of rainfall. The rain was onset around the beginning of pepper development stage even though the amount was minimal. However, the rain was occurred with sufficient amount during the mid-stage of pepper.

3.5 Effects of Conservation Agriculture on Soil Water

During 2017/2018 simulation period, the result demonstrated that CA plots stored more water in the soil system compared with CT plots; even irrigation applications in the former treatments were less. Similarly, daily soil water contents at the top 10 cm soil depth for CA plots were higher than CT plots during 2018 period. However, unlike the first equal amount of irrigation water was applied to the soil system for both tillage systems up to the beginning of rainfall during experimental pepper period. This clearly indicated that CA has the potential to conserve soil moisture due to the effect of mulch cover on the soil surface producing less evaporation and delay the drying of soil moisture. These results are consistent with those of others (Han et al. 2015, Thierfelder and Wall 2009, Ward et al. 2006).

Soil water in CA plots was higher throughout the whole growth period of garlic. Similarly, at the beginning of second experimental period just after transplanting – the mid stage of pepper measured and simulated soil water for CA were greater. However, during some days of plant growth, especially after pepper mid stage soil water difference between two treatments (CA and CT) was insignificant. This was probably due to the size of garlic leaf canopy was smaller, and its variation throughout its growth season was also lower. Therefore under garlic experiment, the top surfaces of CT plots were exposed to sunlight because of little leaf area coverage compared to CA plots, which has mulch cover. However, during second experimental period as pepper matured, plants expand their leaf canopy and shading the soil surface starting to mid-growth stage so that the top surfaces of CT plots were protected from direct interaction with solar radiation by large leaf canopy of pepper (compared to garlic) the same as CA which protected by mulch.

Based on the t-test equal variance statistical analysis result of observed soil water content for CA and CT of 2017/2018 simulation period have a significance difference with 95% confidence interval t cri (1.98) was less than t stat (2.82), therefore reject the non-rejection region of the probability distribution function. Means that the difference detected was statistically significant, as shown in Table 3.

Table 3. T-Test: Two-sample assuming equal variances for measured SWC of 2017/2018

Statistics	CA	CT
Mean	0.38	0.36
Variance	0.0014	0.0011
t Stat	2.82	
P(T < = t) one-tail	0.0028	
t Critical one-tail	1.66	
P(T < = t) two-tail	0.0055	
t Critical two-tail	1.98	

During 2018 simulation period, t-test equal variance statistical analysis result of average simulated SWC using Hydrus-1D in CA and CT experimental plots clearly indicated that the difference was significant statistically with t cri (1.97) was much less than t stat (2.65), reject non rejection region (Table 4).

3.6 Transpiration and Evaporation

Hydrus-1D model simulate daily plant transpiration and soil evaporation for two simulation periods. The simulation result showed that during the beginning of crop growth evaporation was higher since the plant was small with low soil coverage. Then evaporation was reduced with time for all experimental plots when plants mature, expanding their leaf canopy and shading the soil surface completely. The simulated transpiration was smaller at the early stage and continuously increases following plant growth. During

Table 4. T-Test: Two-sample assuming equal variances for simulated SWC of 2018

Statistics	CA	CT
Mean	0.38	0.37
Variance	0.00064	0.00087
t Stat	2.65	
P(T < = t) one-tail	0.00455	
t Critical one-tail	1.65	
P(T < = t) two-tail	0.0091	
t Critical two-tail	1.97	

2017/2018 the actual transpiration was first little then increases gradually and reaches an absolute peak value. Then the amount was reduced rapidly at the end stage of the plant following to absence of irrigation. The evaporation result for CT was more significant as compared to CA throughout the season. Therefore, CA has the potential to reduce water evaporation by interfering solar radiation falling on the soil surface and act as a barrier between the soil surface and atmospheric air above.

Actual root water uptake (mm/day) for CA showed more water uptake by roots compared with CT even though more irrigation water applied in the CT treatments. The actual transpiration result was an average of 93.5% and 88.8% of water input for CA and CT, respectively during the first simulation period. During pepper average cumulative transpiration resulted in CA plots (365.65 mm) were higher compared to those in CT plots (353.67 mm) even both treatments had equal water inputs. The results indicated that plants in CA plots were used water through their root system effectively compared to those in the CT experimental plots. Compared with simulation periods, the actual transpiration and soil evaporation resulted during 2017/2018 was lower than during 2018 period.

Also, the percentage of average seasonal evaporation result from CT plots was higher (7.69%) compared to those from CA plots (1.15%) during garlic growth period. Likewise, during experimental pepper period average seasonal evaporation greater for CT plots (5.83%) than CA plots (1.09%). The reason was presumably mulch cover on the soil surface of CA has the potential to reflect an incident solar radiation falling on the topsoil surface and act as a barrier between the soil surface and atmospheric air above. However, the top surface of conventionally tillage plots was open and exposed to solar radiation. Due to this reason, more water was evaporated from CT plots. Therefore, CA has the potential to reduce water evaporation by interfering solar radiation falling on the soil surface.

The simulated actual transpiration and potential transpiration was almost equal throughout most of the plant growth period (Fig. 5) during 2017/2018 period. This indicated that garlic crop was not under stress. However, during pepper growth season, actual root water uptake results were smaller compared to potential transpiration (Fig. 5) in most days throughout the growth period. Therefore pepper crops were under stress due to insufficient irrigation application during the experiment compared to garlic crops.

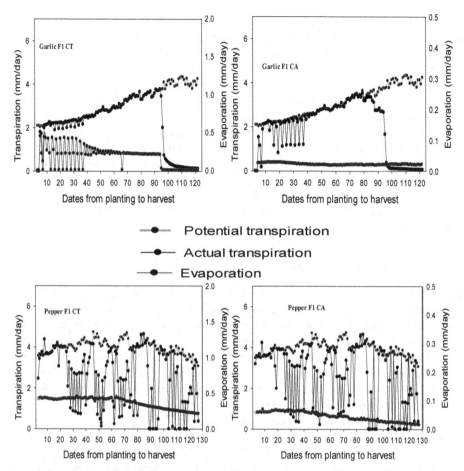

Fig. 5. Simulated potential transpiration, actual transpiration and soil evaporation throughout crops growth periods

3.7 Evapotranspiration (ET) Estimation

The maximum and minimum daily Potential evapotranspiration was approximately 6.088 mm/day and 2.742 mm/day respectively throughout garlic experimental period. The simulation result shown that excess water generated as surface runoff from experimental plots was insignificant (zero). The result was similar to the observed value during the field monitoring period i.e. Excess water was not generated as surface runoff from experimental plots during irrigation.

Reflecting global crop growth, simulated actual ET (sum of transpiration and evaporation) was initially small during seed germination stage of garlic. Actual evapotranspiration then gradually increased and reached its maximum value between 50 and 95 days almost similarly for all experimental plots. Cumulative actual evapotranspiration for CT plots was higher than CA plots due to higher evaporation from CT. The seasonal actual evapotranspiration results vary from 228.87–288.49 mm and 184.18–244.54 mm respectively in CT and CA plots throughout the season. During the late stages of garlic, actual daily evapotranspiration gradually declined and near to zero immediately starting 104 days of simulation because absence of irrigation caused water stress in the plant root zone.

During pepper, the maximum and minimum daily Potential evapotranspiration was approximately 6.033 mm/day and 1.096 mm/day, respectively. Actual ET results during garlic growth season were lower compared to those in pepper growth season due to higher water consumption of pepper. The seasonal simulated actual transpiration values for CA plots were more significant than CT plots; even the trend was similar. However, evapotranspiration for CT was greater than CA because of more evaporation from the former plot. The minimum and maximum cumulative AET results throughout pepper growth season were 363.85 mm and 422.13 mm respectively for CT plots. Under CA plots, the minimum of 344.00 mm and maximum of 391.03 mm seasonal actual evapotranspiration was resulted.

3.8 Deep Percolation Estimation

The simulated daily deep percolation value for each experimental plot by Hydrus-1D was plotted as a function of plant growth period (Fig. 6). Deep percolation closely corresponded with irrigation and rainfall events. During garlic and most of pepper growth stages when water input was predominantly through irrigation, the deep percolation was very insignificant for all experimental plots. Due to intensive rainfall (compared to irrigation applied before rain coming) relatively higher percolation was mainly observed during the later growth stages of pepper. This indicated that water management system used during the experiment was sound.

During 2017/2018 simulation period, the percentage of average seasonal deep percolation from CT and CA were 3.15% and 0.38% of water input respectively. Cumulative percolation was 29.95% and 34.51% for CT and CA respectively during 2018 (pepper) period. The result indicated that water percolation from CA plots was higher than CT plots. Overall, even though total water input for the CA was substantially lower than CT during garlic growth period cumulative deep percolation from CA was slightly higher than CT plots. Similarly, cumulative percolation result of CA was higher than CT pots during 2018 when seasonal water input was equal for both treatments.

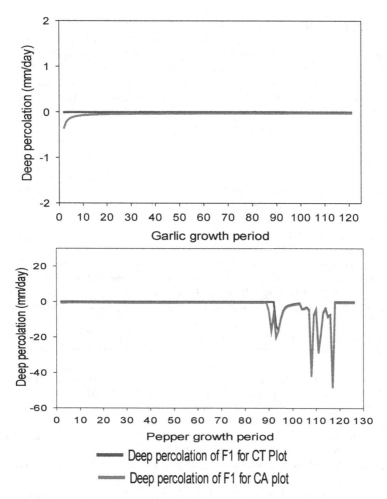

Fig. 6. Simulated deep percolation throughout the simulation periods

4   Conclusions

The result of this study showed Hydrus-1D could simulate root zone soil water dynamics in the CT and CA experimental plots. Soil water dynamics computed by the model fit well with the observed value at the top surface 10 cm soil depth. The daily soil water content stored in CA plots was higher compared with CT plots. Generally, more actual transpiration was observed in CA plots than CT due to high evaporation loss of later. The seasonal deep percolation from CA treatments was higher compared to those from CT treatments. However, evaporation loss for CT was more significant. The actual evapotranspiration was affected by water management substantially increase and decrease with irrigation/rainfall events. From the analysis of soil water dynamics during cop development period conclude that CA can increase infiltration and store more water in the soil system by reducing water loss through evaporation. Generally, CA practice used less water and had higher actual root water uptake; and recommended for farmers irrigation practice in the study area.

Acknowledgements. This research was financially supported by Appropriate Scale Mechanization Continuum (ASMC) project, a cooperative research project implemented through the United States Agency for International Development (USAID) to support the Feed the Future program in Collaboration with Bahir Dar University Institute of Technology (BIT). We would like to thank Amhara Design and Supervision works Enterprise, Soil Laboratory experts. We also thank the data collector Ato GirmaYihune. I am thankful for Ethiopian road authority (ERA) for full sponsorship of my Master's degree education.

References

Allen, R.G., Pereira, L.S., Raes, D., Smith, M.: Crop Evapotranspiration-Guidelines for Computing Crop Water Requirements-FAO Irrigation and Drainage Paper 56, vol. 300, D05109. Fao, Rome (1998)

Arnold, J., Allen, P.: Estimating hydrologic budgets for three Illinois watersheds. J. Hydrol. **176**, 57–77 (1996)

Beyene, A., et al.: Estimating the actual evapotranspiration and deep percolation in irrigated soils of a tropical floodplain, northwest Ethiopia. Agric. Water Manag. **202**, 42–56 (2018)

Böhme, B., Becker, M., Diekkrüger, B., Förch, G.: How is water availability related to the land use and morphology of an inland valley wetland in Kenya? Phy. Chem. Earth Parts A/B/C **93**, 84–95 (2016)

Botula, Y.-D., Nemes, A., Mafuka, P., Van Ranst, E., Cornelis, W.M.: Prediction of water retention of soils from the humid tropics by the nonparametric k-nearest neighbor approach. Vadose Zone J. **12** (2013)

Chang, C.-W., Wu, C.-R., Lin, C.-T., Chen, H.-C.: An application of AHP and sensitivity analysis for selecting the best slicing machine. Comput. Ind. Eng. **52**, 296–307 (2007)

Chauhan, N., Miller, S., Ardanuy, P.: Spaceborne soil moisture estimation at high resolution: a microwave-optical/IR synergistic approach. Int. J. Remote Sens. **24**, 4599–4622 (2003)

Chen, M., Willgoose, G.R., Saco, P.M.: Spatial prediction of temporal soil moisture dynamics using HYDRUS-1D. Hydrol. Process. **28**, 171–185 (2014)

Daniel, S., et al.: Spatial distribution of soil hydrological properties in the Kilombero floodplain, Tanzania. Hydrology **4**, 57 (2017)

Espejo-Pérez, A.J., Brocca, L., Moramarco, T., Giráldez, J.V., Triantafilis, J., Vanderlinden, K.: Analysis of soil moisture dynamics beneath olive trees. Hydrol. Process. **30**, 4339–4352 (2016)

Gabiri, G., Burghof, S., Diekkrüger, B., Leemhuis, C., Steinbach, S., Näschen, K.: Modeling spatial soil water dynamics in a tropical floodplain, East Africa. Water **10**, 191 (2018)

González, M.G., et al.: Modelling soil water dynamics of full and deficit drip irrigated maize cultivated under a rain shelter. Biosyst. Eng. **132**, 1–18 (2015)

Han, M., Zhao, C., Feng, G., Yan, Y., Sheng, Y.: Evaluating the effects of mulch and irrigation amount on soil water distribution and root zone water balance using HYDRUS-2D. Water **7**, 2622–2640 (2015)

Jurik, L., Kaletova, T., Huska, D.: Soil water regime of agricultural areas in small experimental catchment. J. Landscape Manag. (Czech Republic) (2012)

Kandelous, M.M., Kamai, T., Vrugt, J.A., Šimůnek, J., Hanson, B., Hopmans, J.W.: Evaluation of subsurface drip irrigation design and management parameters for alfalfa. Agric. Water Manag. **109**, 81–93 (2012)

Kuhl, A.S., Kendall, A.D., Van Dam, R.L., Hyndman, D.W.: Quantifying soil water and root dynamics using a coupled hydrogeophysical inversion. Vadose Zone J. **17** (2018)

Li, H., et al.: Modeling of soil water and salt dynamics and its effects on root water uptake in Heihe arid wetland, Gansu, China. Water **7**, 2382–2401 (2015)

Li, Y., Šimůnek, J., Jing, L., Zhang, Z., Ni, L.: Evaluation of water movement and water losses in a direct-seeded-rice field experiment using Hydrus-1D. Agric. Water Manag. **142**, 38–46 (2014)

Liang, Z., Zhang, J., Guo, B.: Research on the dynamic soil moisture contents using Hydrus-3D model (2015)

Mei-Xian, L., Jing-Song, Y., Xiao-Ming, L., Mei, Y., Jin, W.: Numerical simulation of soil water dynamics in a drip irrigated cotton field under plastic mulch. Pedosphere **23**, 620–635 (2013)

Mulebeke, R., Kironchi, G., Tenywa, M.M.: Soil moisture dynamics under different tillage practices in cassava–sorghum based cropping systems in eastern Uganda. Ecohydrol. Hydrobiol. **13**, 22–30 (2013)

Qiu, Y., Fu, B., Wang, J., Chen, L.: Soil moisture variation in relation to topography and land use in a hillslope catchment of the Loess Plateau, China. J. Hydrol. **240**, 243–263 (2001)

Rubio, C.M., Poyatos, R.: Applicability of Hydrus-1D in a Mediterranean mountain area submitted to land use changes. ISRN Soil Sci. **2012** (2012)

Saifadeen, A., Gladneyva, R.: Modeling of solute transport in the unsaturated zone using HYDRUS-1D (2012)

Sánchez, N., et al.: Water balance at plot scale for soil moisture estimation using vegetation parameters. Agric. For. Meteorol. **166**, 1–9 (2012)

Siebert, S., et al.: Groundwater use for irrigation–a global inventory. Hydrol. Earth Syst. Sci. **14**, 1863–1880 (2010)

Simunek, J., Van Genuchten, M.T., Sejna, M.: The HYDRUS-1D software package for simulating the one-dimensional movement of water, heat, and multiple solutes in variably-saturated media. Univ. Calif. Riverside Res. Rep. **3**, 1–240 (2005)

Šimunek, J., Van Genuchten, M.T., Šejna, M.: HYDRUS: model use, calibration, and validation. Trans. ASABE **55**, 1263–1274 (2012)

Šimůnek, J., Van Genuchten, M.T., Šejna, M.: Development and applications of the HYDRUS and STANMOD software packages and related codes. Vadose Zone J. **7**, 587–600 (2008)

Soylu, M., Istanbulluoglu, E., Lenters, J., Wang, T.: Quantifying the impact of groundwater depth on evapotranspiration in a semi-arid grassland region. Hydrol. Earth Syst. Sci. **15**, 787–806 (2011)

Thierfelder, C., Wall, P.C.: Effects of conservation agriculture techniques on infiltration and soil water content in Zambia and Zimbabwe. Soil Tillage Res. **105**, 217–227 (2009)

Van Dam, J., De Rooij, G., Heinen, M., Stagnitti, F.: Concepts and dimensionality in modeling unsaturated water flow and solute transport. Frontis, 1–36 (2005)

Van Der Kwast, J.: Quantification of top soil moisture patterns: evaluation of field methods, process-based modelling, remote sensing and an integrated approach. Utrecht University, Royal Dutch Geographical Society (2009)

Van Genuchten, M.V., Leij, F., Yates, S.: The RETC code for quantifying the hydraulic functions of unsaturated soils (1991)

Varut, G., Wei, X., Huang, D., Shinde, D., Price, R.: Application of MODHMS to simulate integrated water flow and phosphorous transport in a highly interactive surface water groundwater system along the eastern boundary of the Everglades National Park, Florida. In: Proceedings of the MODFLOW and More (2011)

Ward, J., et al.: Effects of conservation systems on soil moisture and productivity in cotton. In: 2006 ASAE Annual Meeting, American Society of Agricultural and Biological Engineers, p. 1 (2006)

Yadav, B.K., Mathur, S., Siebel, M.A.: Soil moisture flow modeling with water uptake by plants (wheat) under varying soil and moisture conditions. J. Irrig. Drain. Eng. **135**, 375–381 (2009)

Zhang, X., Zhao, W., Liu, Y., Fang, X., Feng, Q.: The relationships between grasslands and soil moisture on the Loess Plateau of China: a review. CATENA **145**, 56–67 (2016)

Evaluation of Stream Flow Prediction Capability of Hydrological Models in the Upper Blue Nile Basin, Ethiopia

Bayu G. Bihonegn[1], Mamaru A. Moges[2]($\boxtimes$), Gerawork F. Mulu[1], and Berhanu G. Sinshaw[3]

[1] Department of Hydraulic and Water Resource Engineering, Kombolcha Institute of Technology, Wollo University, P.O.Box 208, Kombolcha, Ethiopia
[2] Faculty of Civil and Water Resource Engineering, BiT, Bahir Dar University, P.O.Box 26, Bahir Dar, Ethiopia
mamarumoges@gmail.com
[3] Department of Hydraulic and Water Resource Engineering, Institute of Technology, University of Gondar, P.O.Box 196, Gondar, Ethiopia

Abstract. This study aims to evaluate stream flow predication capability of three hydrological models including Parameter Efficient Semi-Distributed Watershed Model (PED-WM) model, Hydrologiska Byrans Vattenbalansavdelning (HBV) and Hydraulic Engineering Center-Hydrologic Modeling System (HEC-HMS) in range of sizes of watersheds, Upper Blue Nile Basin, Ethiopia. The model efficiency on daily time scale during calibration period for PED-W (NSE = 0.76, 0.81 and 0.57), HBV-IHMS (NSE = 0.68, 0.79 and 0.59) and HEC-HMS (NSE = 0.63, 0.68 and 0.48) were obtained for Anjeni, Gumara and Main Belles watersheds respectively. Similarly, for validation period PED-W (NSE = 0.6, 0.73 and 0.37), HBV-IHMS (NSE = 0.56, 0.79 and 0.55) and HECHMS (NSE = 0.52, 0.74 and 0.37) were obtained for Anjeni, Gumara and Main Belles watersheds respectively. Similarly, the model performances on monthly time steps were also varied among three hydrological models and the results better than the daily time scale. In PED-W, saturation excess is the main direct runoff process. The overall model performance indicated that PED-W model was better than the other two models. The result indicates that the models in the highlands of Ethiopia are dominantly dependent on the runoff mechanism dominantly on saturation excess runoff mechanism. Hence, there should be an approach to integrate climate region specific model in our water resource development system for predicting stream flow for ungagged catchments.

Keywords: HBV · HEC-HMS · Hydrological model · PED-W · Upper Blue Nile basin

© ICST Institute for Computer Sciences, Social Informatics and Telecommunications Engineering 2020
Published by Springer Nature Switzerland AG 2020. All Rights Reserved
N. G. Habtu et al. (Eds.): ICAST 2019, LNICST 308, pp. 210–227, 2020.
https://doi.org/10.1007/978-3-030-43690-2_14

1 Introduction

1.1 Background

Hydrological models are simplified, conceptual representation of the hydrological cycle. As the hydrologic cycle consists of many complex components, hydrologic models are highly preferred to capture the associated issues. It also plays a great role in planning, designing, operation and monitoring of water resources. In number of models, simulating the discharge from watersheds in the Blue Nile basin has increased exponentially [1]. This type of watersheds require very suitable models are vital for understanding the change in catchment dynamics [2].

Hydrological models like physical based models that give a sound description of hydrological cycle process can be used to predict stream flow and sediment transport. However, in countries like Ethiopia, adequate data for hydrological modeling are different to access or not available. Specifically, the problem of the upper Blue Nile basin is also scarcity of data for prediction of the stream flow of the basin and for planning, design and implementation of numerous national developments projects in the area. However, models with the existing scarce data that could be capable of predicting the hydrologic models are needed. But choosing right watershed model for stream flow predication has always been a challenge [3]. Different researcher has been conducted which is related to estimate stream flow in the Upper Blue Nile basin using different hydrological distributed models. For instance, a number of models have been developed and applied to study the water balance, soil erosion, climate and environmental changes in the Blue Nile Basin. Steenhuis et al. [4] has been studied on the issue of prediction discharge in the Blue Nile Basin using PED-W model. The study found that the model performance to predicate discharge in Abbay (Blue Nile) basin was (NSE = 0.98). It is also found that PED-W model is an applicable in large watershed. But the calibration period is too short to evaluate the model performance. Collick et al. [5] has also been studied on the issue related to develop simple water balance model for the Ethiopia highlands. The study indicates that to develop a realistic simple model that is useful as a tool for planning watershed management and conservation activities so that the effects of local interventions on stream flow can be predicted at large scale. The study found that daily discharge values were predicted reasonably well with NSE values ranging from 0.56 to 0.78. The study conclude that the model could be used to predicted discharge in ungagged basins in the humid highlands. According to Tilahun et al. [6] studies on the catchments of Ethiopia highlands (Anjeni, Andit Tid, Enkulal and the Blue Nile basin) to predict discharge and sediment using PED state that the value of NSE for validation of the discharge predicting had resulted NSE = 0.77 and 0.92. The study concludes that this type of model, which requires a few calibration parameters to simulate runoff and sediment transport is important in data scarcity environment.

The study of Geberye et al. [7] showed that modeling the Upper Blue Nile basin catchments using HEC-HMS for better assessment and prediction of simulation of hydrological responses. However, this study was the run off estimation is not considering the land use basin. The runoff processes in the Upper Blue Nile basin are found to be affected much by rainfall, as the performance of model was better for those study catchments where coverages of rainfall station were good Dessie et al. [8]. The basic intention of this study was to evaluate the suitable hydrological model for stream flow prediction at various watershed scales using PED-W, HEC-HMS, HBV-IHMS models.

2   Materials and Methods

2.1   Description of the Study Area

The study was conducted in Anjeni, Gumara and Main Belles watershed, a tributary of Blue Nile River Basin which are located in the western part of the Ethiopia highland (Fig. 1). The study area lies at an altitude of 2405–2500 m, 1790–3600 m and 990–2725 m above sea level and located at latitude range $10°\ 40'$ N to $10°\ 50'$ N and longitude range of $37°\ 31'$ to $37°\ 45'$, $11°\ 34'\ 41.41''$ N to $11°\ 56'\ 36.95''$ N & $37°\ 29'\ 30.48''$ E to $38°\ 10'\ 58.01''$ E longitude for Anjeni, Gumara and Main Belles Watersheds respectively. The study was concentrated on the upper/gaged part of the Gumara watershed, which has area coverage of 1280.73 km^2 and the study also covered the Anjeni and Main Belles watersheds which have area coverage 1.13 km^2 and 3431 km^2 respectively. The annual rainfall of the study area ranges between 1550 to 1695 mm, 1600 to 1800 mm and 1500 to 1700 mm for Anjeni, Gumara and Main Belles watersheds respectively.

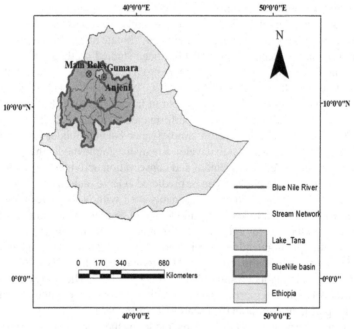

Fig. 1. Location of study area

2.2 Data Collection

In this study, all the metrological data were collected from National Meteorological Service Agency (NMSA) for nearest stations of the watersheds. Therefore, Mekaneyesus, Wanzaye, Deberatbor and Amedber, Wereta, Mekaneyesus and Lewaye metrological stations were used for Gumara watershed study (Fig. 1). The Only Station was Anjeni that used to represent the Anjeni watershed. Lastly, Pawe, Dangila, Shawra and Yismala stations are used for Main Belles watershed study.

2.3 Model Input

The model input requirements for semi distributed watershed models are daily rainfall and temperature, daily observed flow, potential evapotranspiration, digital elevation model and catchment characteristic of the area.

2.3.1 Determination of Area Rainfall

For this study, the thiessen polygon method was used for this study due to its sound theoretical basis and availability of computational tools. However, the method is dependent on a good network of representative rain gauges (Fig. 2).

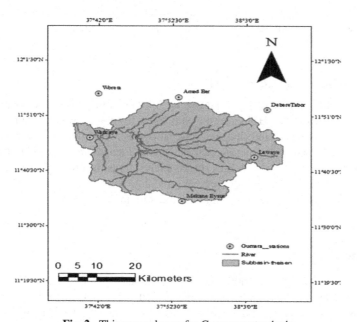

Fig. 2. Thiessen polygon for Gumara watersheds

2.3.2 Evapotranspiration

The potential evapotranspiration as a model input in this study was estimated based on simple temperature method approach showed by Enku and Melesse by [8] as indicated in equation in below. This method are used for estimation of daily evapotranspiration where they are insufficient data.

$$ET_0 = (T_{max})^n/K \qquad (1)$$

Where ETo is the reference evapotranspiration (mm/day); n = 2.5, which can be calibrated for local conditions; k is the coefficient, which can be calibrated for local conditions ranging from about 600 for lower mean annual maximum temperature areas to 1300 for higher mean annual maximum temperature areas. The coefficient, could be approximated as k = 48 * Tmm-330 for combined wet and dry conditions, k = 73 * Tmm-1015 for dry seasons, and k = 38 * Tmm-63 for wet seasons, where Tmm (°C) is the long-term daily mean maximum temperature for the seasons under consideration.

2.3.3 Stream Flow Data

The daily discharge of the study area is collected from Ethiopia Ministry of Water Irrigation and Electricity (EMoWIE). Unlike the daily precipitation, the daily discharge has full data composition for the considered stations to represent the study area.

2.3.4 Catchment Characteristics

Since HBV-Light model works as semi distributed model, the catchment area can be divided in to different sub basins and the sub basins further in to different elevation and vegetation zone.

2.3.5 HEC-GeoHMS Data Processing

The point of many data are preprocessing using Arc-Hydro tools was to create input files for the GeoHMS tools. GeoHMS uses the output files from Arc Hydro and automatically create sub basins, longest and centroid flow paths, basin centroid and other watershed properties. Additionally, parameters such as slope and length are assigned to flow lines and basins. In general, GeoHMS uses spatial analyst tools to convert geographic information into parameters for each of the basins and flow lines. These parameters are used to create a HEC-HMS model that can be used within the HEC-HMS program (Figs. 3, 4 and Table 1).

2.4 Watershed Models

The methodology were used three hydrological model such as PED-W, HBV-IHMS and HEC-HMS to predicate stream flow in selected watersheds of the upper blue Nile basin. Sensitivity analysis, model calibration and validation and evaluating the model efficiency were used to select suitable hydrological models to predicate stream flow.

2.4.1 PED-W Model

PED-W (Parameter efficient semi distributed watershed) model is a conceptual semi distributed model and firstly was developed by Collick and Steenhuis. Tilahun et al. [6]

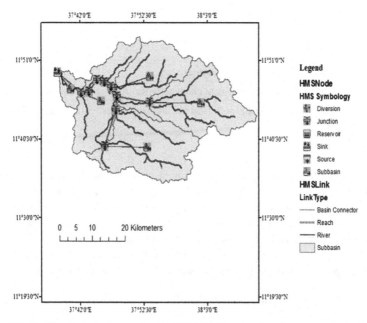

Fig. 3. Hec-Geoms processing for HEC-HMS set up for Gumara watershed

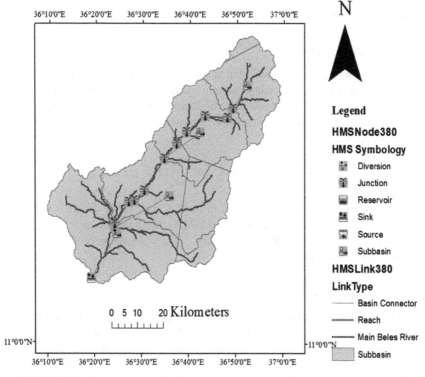

Fig. 4. Hec-Geoms processing for Hec-Hms set up for Main Belles watershed

Table 1. The input data and output of different models

Model type	Model input	Model output
PED-W	Daily RF, Temp and observed discharge	Simulated Q & sediment
HBV-IHMS	Daily RF, Temp, Q, catchment characteristics, AET	Simulated Q and sediment
HEC-HMS	DEM, RF, Temp, Q and soil, land use and land cover data	Simulated discharge

are then extended the model to predict sediment concentration in Anjeni Watershed. In PED-W model, the watershed subdivided in to three regions, two surface runoff producing zones consisting of areas near the river that becomes saturated during the wet monsoon period and the degraded hillsides with little or no soil cover. The remaining hillside areas have infiltration rates in excess of the rainfall intensity [9].

The amount of water stored in the root zone of the soil, S (mm), for hill slopes and the saturated and degraded areas were estimated separately with a water balance Eq. 2.

$$S = S_{t-\Delta t} + (P - AET - R - Perec)\Delta t \tag{2}$$

Where P is precipitation, (mm d^{-1}); AET is the actual evapotranspiration, (mm d^{-1}), $S_{t-\Delta t}$, previous time step storage, (mm), R saturation excess runoff (mm d^{-1}), Perc is percolation to the subsoil (mm d^{-1}) and Δt is the time step.

2.4.2   HBV-IHMS Model

It is a conceptual hydrological model, which means it attempts to cover the most important runoff generating processes using a simple and robust structure, and a small number of parameters. The model simulates daily discharge using daily rainfall, temperature and potential evaporation as input. The general water balance equation of HBV model is illustrated under equations

$$P - E - Q = \frac{d}{dt}[SP + SM + UZ + LZ + L] \tag{3}$$

Where recharge is input from soil routine (mm day^{-1}), SUZ is storage in upper zone (mm), SLZ is storage in lower zone (mm) and UZL is threshold parameter (mm), PERC is maximum percolation to lower zone (mm day^{-1}), Ki = recession coefficient (day^{-1}), Qi is runoff component (mm day^{-1}).

2.4.3   HEC-HMS Model

HEC-HMS model setup consists of a basin model, meteorological model, control Specifications and input data (time series data). The basin Model, for instance, contains information relevant to the physical attributes of the model, such as basin areas, river reach connectivity, or reservoir data. Likewise, the Meteorological Model holds rainfall data. The Control Specifications section contains information pertinent to the timing of the model such as when a storm occurred and what type of time interval is to be used in the model, etc. Each of the HEC-HMS model provides a variety of options for simulating precipitation-runoff processes.

SCS Curve Number (CN) method is more preferable to determine the runoff volume of each watershed. Because it is simply, widely used and efficient for determining the approximate amount of runoff from rainfall, even in particular area. The model approach used to determine the runoff volume was the SCS-CN method. The standard SCS curve number method is based on the under Eqs. 4 and 5 relationship between rainfall depth, P, and runoff depth Q [11]

$$Q = (P - 0.2S)^2/(P + 0.8S), \text{ for } P > \text{ otherwise } Q = 0 \tag{4}$$

$$S = 25400/CN - 254(\text{in mm}) \tag{5}$$

$$I_a = 0.2S \tag{6}$$

Where Q is the surface runoff (mm), P is precipitation; S is the soil retention (mm), Ia is the initial abstraction loss (mm), and CN is the curve number.

2.5 Sensitivity Analysis

Sensitivity analysis explores how changes in parameter values affect the overall change in the output of the model. This can be done by using simple sensitivity analysis, where only one parameter is changed or more complex arrangements that explore the relationships between multiple parameters. Thus, a sensitivity analysis for PED-W, HBV-IHMS and HEC-HMS models were performed for the entire data. Then, the most sensitive parameters were identified and used for calibration of the model.

2.6 Model Calibration and Validation

After sensitivity analysis was carried out, the calibration of PED-W, HBV-IHMS and HEC-HMS models were done manually. The calibration was carried out using the output of the sensitivity analysis of the model and by changing the more sensitive parameter at a time while keeping the rest. PED Model was calibrated through using nine input parameters. Initial values for calibrating parameters were based on different researcher done in this study area [4, 5, 12, 13]. These initial values were changed manually through randomly varying input parameters in order that the best "closeness" or "goodness-of-fit" was achieved between simulated and observed subsurface flow and overland flow in the watershed.

Model Validation is the process of testing the model ability to simulate observed data, Other than those used for the calibration, within acceptable accuracy. The model performance is evaluated by three objective functions consisting of the Nash Sutcliffe efficiency (NSE), percent bias (PBIAS), and coefficient of determination (R^2).

3 Results and Discussion

The finding of this study was presented based on model sequence as PED-W, HBV-IHMS and HEC-HMS hydrological models. Firstly, the stream flow predication was presented using PED-W, HBV-IHMS and HEC-HMS models on Anjeni, Gumara and Main Belles watersheds. Subsequently, model suitability for Anjeni, Gumara, and Main Belles watersheds in Upper Blue Nile basin was assessed by first evaluating the simulated and observed discharge at the outlet.

3.1 Sensitivity Analysis Results

Determination of the sensitive parameters is one of the most important tasks in rainfall-runoff modeling in order to reduce the parameters and the time of the calibration. Before, the calibration one parameter at a time was varied an analyses from −50% to 50% with increments of 10%, keeping all other parameters constant. The boundary condition of PED-W model in case of calibration process is the area of watershed with the range of zero up to one fraction number.

In PED-W, manual sensitivity analysis for stream flow prediction at the outlet resulted in the identification of six most sensitive parameters: the areal hill-side coverage (Ah), the saturated area (As), degraded area (Ad), Maximum base flow soil storage (BSmax), the recession coefficient (k) and half life time. From nine input PED-W model parameter five parameters were found most sensitivity such as area hillside (Ah), saturated area (As), degraded area (Ad), maximum soil storage in saturated area (Smax) and recession coefficient (K). These results of parameter sensitivity were similar as identified by Moges et al. [13] study for Awramba watershed in the Blue Nile Basin. From the five most sensitive parameters, the area of hillside is the most sensitive parameter that affect the model output. However, the rank of other parameters were varying from one watershed to another. The reason that were varying the rank due to catchment characteristics variation, topography and rainfall pattern.

HBV-IHMS had more than 13 parameters but seven model parameters that used to control the total volume and shape of the hydrograph used in this study [14]. The remaining parameters are not influencing the total volume of water and shape of the hydrograph. Out of those 7 parameters, five were found most sensitivity: field capacity (fc), soil drainage (beta), limiting for evapotranspiration (LP), storage coefficient and percolation. In HBV-Light model parameters of soil moisture routine, response function and routing routine were sensitivity for to predicate discharge for each watershed.

It was found that the most suitable method was so accounting SCS loss method, which has 10 parameters for calibrating HEC-HMS model. The most sensitive parameters in this method were Curve Number, Time of concentration, Muskingum routing and soil coefficient storage.

3.2 PED-W Calibration and Validation

For the PED-W model, all nine input parameters were calibrated. The starting values for calibrating parameters were based on the study of Collick et al. and Staneehuis et al. [4] and [5]. These starting values were changed manually through randomly varying input parameters in order that the best "closeness" or "goodness-of-fit" was achieved between simulated and observed subsurface flow and surface flow in the watershed. The optimal value of calibration parameters for different watersheds were varying (Table 2).

The calibrated model parameters for the subsurface flow represented by the half-life $(t_{1/2})$ and interflow calibration parameter t* for the different rainfall input data are almost the same for all simulations as expected and consistent with values used in simulation of Anjeni watershed and other watersheds in the Blue Nile Basins [6]. The fractional regions contributing to rapid subsurface and overland flow have different values for stream flow simulation. The total contributing area for the gauged rainfall adds up to 100% for Gumara, 78% for Main Belles and 57% for Anjeni. It is also consistent with earlier studies of PED simulation for a wide scale of watersheds study areas by [15].

The observed and simulated hydrograph in Anjeni watershed using the optimum parameter was shown in Fig. 5a. Visually inspection of the observed and simulated hydrograph shows that the performances of the model in simulating the base flow, rising and recession limb of hydrograph was good. The model simulation for peak flow was satisfactory although it under estimates very high single peak. The model results as shown below in Fig. 5b indicated that the observed and simulated hydrograph do have better agreement in mean monthly flow compared to daily flow. The hydrograph pattern in monthly time step indicated that the good relationship between observed and simulated discharge and the model efficiency was 0.94, which was higher than daily model efficiency. The calibrated PED model using gauged rainfall could represent the observed daily stream flow reasonably well for the both calibration and validation for Anjeni (0.76 > NSE > 0.6), Gumara (0.81 > NSE > 0.75) and Main Belles (0.57 > NSE > 0.5).

Table 2. Optimal calibrate parameters of watershed for PED-WM model

Description	Parameters	Gumara	Main Belles	Anjeni
Fraction of saturated area	$Area_1$	0.051	0.04	0.02
	S_{max} in A_1	73	100	200
Fraction of degraded area	$Area_2$	0.09	0.01	0.1
	S_{max} in A_2	15	15	15
Fraction of hill side area	$Area_3$	0.95	0.73	0.45
	S_{max} in A_3	150	150	115
$t_{1/2}$ (days)		12	40	60
τ_* (days)		6	55	10
B_{Smax}		210	100	115

Increase the time step showed increases the performance of PEW-W model was high for flow simulation in Gumara catchment during calibration period. The monthly PED-W model Calibration indicated that relation between observed and simulated discharge were good agreement. The model results as shown in the Fig. 6b indicated that the observed and simulated hydrograph do have better agreement in mean monthly flow compared to daily flow. The Nash and Sutcliffe efficiency and the correlation coefficient during the monthly calibration period were 0.93 and 0.92 respectively, which could take as high satisfactory. The model efficiency indicated that in Main Belles watershed was highly satisfactory.

The hydrograph pattern showed that in Fig. 7, the relation between daily observed and simulated stream flow hydrograph was very good. Because the performance of the model in simulating the base flow, rising, and recession limb hydrograph was good. The daily peak simulated discharge and observed peak discharge for Gumara watershed almost were the same. Due to seasonal variability and monthly average discharge were generally at some points over estimated with low flow period and peak flow.

3.3 HBV-Model Calibration and Validation

Manual calibration was done by making optimization of the parameters of different routines of HBV-Light hydrologic model based on existing catchment characteristics. A total of 15 years (2000–2014) period data was used for both model calibration and validation. Here the first year (2000) data was used for warming up period to initiate the model and the remained 14 years of data from which 2/3 data period (2000–2009) was used for model calibration and the remaining 1/3 data period (2010–2014) was also used for the validation purposes for Gumara watershed. Accordingly, running the model for a number of times was made to have the correspondent values of observed and simulated discharge. For the Anjeni watershed 14 years (1986–1998) was used for both calibration and validation. Parameter optimization was made for the Monte Carlo runs of the model by supplying the lower and upper ranges to get an optimum value for the three routine (Soil moisture, Response and Routing) except snow routine, which was left due to the absence of the snow in the watershed. The optimized parameters are described in Table 3.

Some of the peak flows were under predicated by the model in the period of between 1990 to 1994. The mean difference between the observed and simulated was 86 mm/year. Compared to the performance of models calibrated on daily time step, the simulated and observed hydrograph shows poor agreement when compared from PED-W model result hydrograph.

From the results showed in Figs. 8 and 9, it can be concluded that it is difficult to predicate discharge properly during peak flow. This can be caused by spatial average

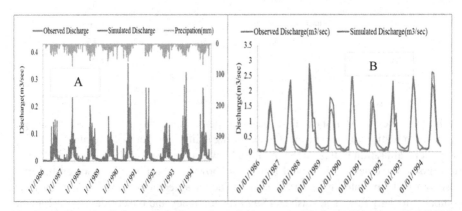

Fig. 5. Predicated and observed discharge for Anjeni watershed during calibration period (1986–1994) (a) daily and (b) monthly

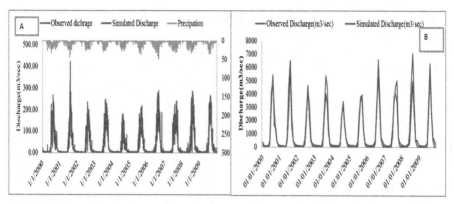

Fig. 6. Predicated and observed discharge for Gumara watershed during calibration period (2000–2009)

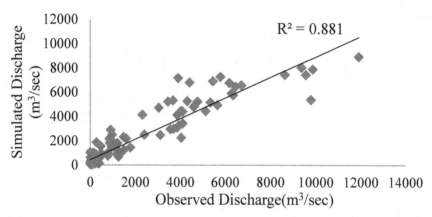

Fig. 7. Observed and simulated monthly for discharge for Main Belles watershed during calibration period (1994–2003)

precipitation that does not represent the real rainfall property. On the other hand, the constant and relative high discharge during dry periods not a realistic representation (Fig. 10).

3.4 HEC-HMS Calibration and Validation

HEC-HMS calibration was performed for a period of ten years (1986 to 1994), (2000 to 2009), (1994 to 2003) for Anjeni, Gumara and Main Belles watersheds on the daily basis. The flow was calibrated automatically using the observed flow at the outlet of Gumara, Anjeni and Main Belles watersheds. Optimization of the parameter values was carried out within the allowable ranges recommended by the US Army corps of Engineers Hydrologic Engineering Center [16]. The model results as obtained from the final manual

Table 3. The input parameters that was involved and optimized in the calibration process

Description	Parameters	Gumara	Main Belles	Anjeni
Soil Moisture Routine				
Field Capacity	FC	1500	347	1950
Beta	β	0.8	0.11	0.24
Soil moisture value	LP	2	2.99	1
Response Routine				
Maximum Percolation Rate	PERC	0.5	15.2	5.5
Threshold for the k_0 outflow	UZL	15	120	20
Recession Coefficient (Upper)	K_0	0.04	0.8	0.02
Recession Coefficient (Upper storage)	K_1	0.09	0.012	0.46
Recession Coefficient (Lower storage)	K1	0.01	0.15	0.2
Routing routine				
Length of triangular weighting Function MAXBAS		1	1	1

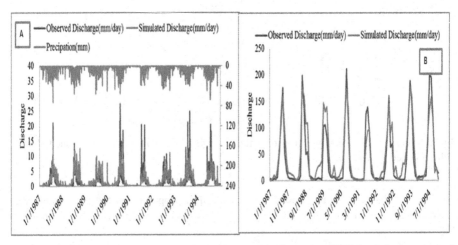

Fig. 8. Daily and monthly observed and predicate stream flow using HBV for Anjeni watershed

calibration showed that there was a good agreement between the simulated and observed flow for Anjeni, Gumara and Main Belles catchments. This was demonstrated by the correlation coefficient and the Nash-Sutcliffe (1970) efficiency values for catchments (Fig. 11).

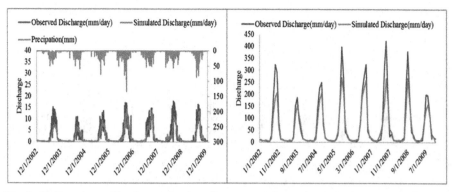

Fig. 9. Daily and monthly observed and predicate stream flow using HBV for Gumara watershed

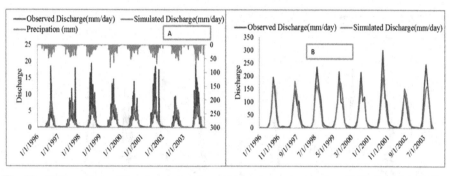

Fig. 10. Daily and monthly observed and predicate stream flow using HBV for Main Belles watershed

As shown in figure above, the daily hydrograph, simulated stream flow caught the observed flow during calibration period (1986–1994) was good simulated. However, the peak flow is under predicated in the model. The model efficiency for Anjeni watershed was 0.603. In HEC-HMS simulating hydrograph for Gumara watershed, it can be concluded that the daily observed and simulated stream flow hydrograph have a good agreement between them when we compared the other two watersheds. The model performance was checked using NSE and R^2 where these results obtained were satisfactory and acceptable to simulate the basin runoff for future projection (Fig. 12).

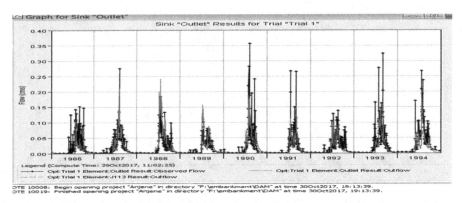

Fig. 11. Flow hydrographs for the observed and simulated flows at Anjeni gaging station

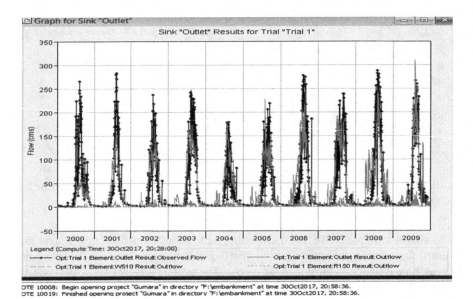

Fig. 12. Flow hydrographs for the observed and simulated flows at Gumara gaging station

The validation result indicated that how to the model efficiency evaluate to simulated discharge for different year of data. Based on the calibrated parameters values the model was validated and the model performance a little bit decreasing. So that the validation result presented as shown below in figures (Figs. 13, 14 and 15).

3.5 Model Performance and Comparison

A daily time step of the observed discharge was simulated using PED with NSE of 0.76 and 0.6 whereas for HBV-IHMS NSE was 0.68 and 0.56 and for HEC-HMS 0.63 and 0.52 during calibration and validation period respectively for Anjeni watershed. For Gumara watershed, the daily-observed discharge was simulated using PED with NSE of

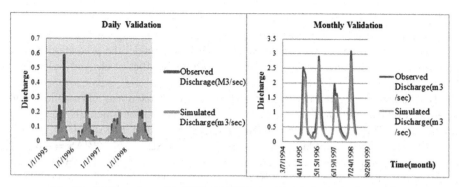

Fig. 13. Daily and monthly PED–W Validation Result for Anjeni watershed

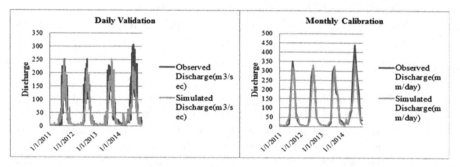

Fig. 14. Daily and monthly HBV Validation Result for Gumara watershed

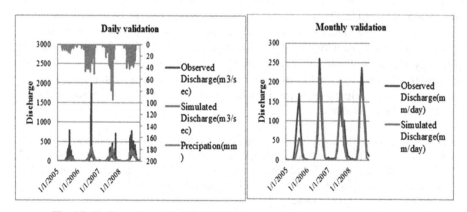

Fig. 15. Daily and monthly HBV Validation Result for Main Belles watershed

0.81 and 0.73 whereas for HEC-HMS was 0.68 and 0.73 and for HBV-IHMS was 0.79 and 0.79 during calibration and validation period in respectively. Lastly, the daily time step the observed discharge for Main Belles watershed was simulated using HBV-IHMS of 0.59 and 0.55 whereas for PED was 0.57 and 0.53 and for HEC-HMS was 0.48 and

0.37 during calibration and validation period respectively. This result of PED-W model were within the range of similarity studies: done Tilahun et al., Dagnew et al., Steenhuis et al. [4, 5, 17–20] and [13];. Similarly, for HBV-IHMS model the prediction model performance results were consistent with the study of Rientjes et el. And wale et al. [14]; and [21].

The value of Nash Sutcliffe, Root mean square error, percent bias and coefficient of determination using PED-W model during calibration period for Anjeni (NSE = 0.76, RMSE = 0.49, PBIAS = 22%, R^2 = 0.78), Gumara (NSE = 0.81, RMSE = 0.44, PBIAS = 14.14%, R^2 = 0.82) and Main belles (NSE = 0.57, RMSE = 0.66, PBIAS = −6.8%, R^2 = 0.57) in respectively watersheds and performance indicators. For HBV-IHMS model in the Anjeni (NSE = 0.68, PBIAS = −18.04%, R^2 = 0.69), Gumara (NSE = 0.79, PBIAS = 10.63%, R^2 = 0.82) and Main belles (NSE = 0.59, PBIAS = 13.62%, R^2 = 0.59) in respectively watersheds. For HEC-HMS model in the Anjeni (NSE = 0.63, PBIAS = −8.41%, R^2 = 0.78), Gumara (NSE = 0. 68, PBIAS = −4.21%, R^2 = 0.68) and Main belles (NSE = 0.48, PBIAS = 2.42%, R^2 = 0.48) in respectively watersheds.

4 Conclusion

The model efficiency on daily time step during calibration period for PED-WM (NSE = 0.76, 0.81 and 0.57), HBV-IHMS (NSE = 0.68, 0.79 and 0.59) and HEC-HMS (NSE = 0.63, 0.68 and 0.48) were obtained for Anjeni, Gumara and Main Belles watersheds respectively. Similarly, for validation period the results were PED-W (NSE = 0.6, 0.73 and 0.37), HBV-IHMS (NSE = 0.56, 0.79 and 0.55) and HECHMS (NSE = 0.52, 0.74, 0.37). PED-W (a semi distributed saturation excess runoff model) was relatively better in predicating stream flow in the three watersheds. HBV-IHMS was the next best, while HEC-HMS based on infiltration excess and was setting as last. PED-W model was also the most appropriate model to predicate stream flow for watershed scale size when we compared from the other two models. However, the PED-W model was relative less efficiency for determination of peak discharge. In generally, the results showed that all models can reproduce historical daily runoff series with an acceptable accuracy on the monthly time scale however for daily times scale model selection based on runoff mechanism was advisable.

Acknowledgements. The financial source of this study primally has been supported by Ethiopia government such as Minister of education, Ethiopia Road Authority. The first authors would like to thanks Bahir Dar University for their supporting every aspect for needed study. We would like to also thanks to National Meteorological Agency (NMA) Bahir Dar branch for their help by providing necessary data for this study.

References

1. Awulachew, S.B., McCartney, M., Steenhuis, T.S., Ahmed, A.A.: A review of hydrology, sediment and water resource use in the Blue Nile Basin; IWMI (2009). ISBN 978-92-9090-699-5

2. Johnson, M.S., Coon, W.F., Mehta, V.K., Steenhuis, T.S., Brooks, E.S., Boll, J.: Application of two hydrologic models with different runoff mechanisms to a hillslope dominated watershed in the Northeastern US: a comparison of HSPF and SMR. J. Hydrol. **284**, 57–76 (2003)
3. Moges, M.A., Schmitter, P., Tilahun, S.A., Steenhuis, T.S.: Watershed modeling for reducing future non-point source sediment and phosphorus load in the Lake Tana Basin, Ethiopia. J. Soils Sediments, **18**(1), 309–322 (2017). https://doi.org/10.1007/s11368-017-1824-z
4. Steenhuis, T.S., et al.: Predicting discharge and sediment for the Abay (Blue Nile) with a simple model. Hydrol. Process. Int. J. **23**, 3728–3737 (2009)
5. Collick, A.S., et al.: A simple semi-distributed water balance model for the Ethiopian Highlands. Hydrol. Process. Int. J. **23**, 3718–3727 (2009)
6. Tilahun, S.A., et al.: An efficient semi-distributed hillslope erosion model for the subhumid Ethiopian Highlands. Hydrol. Earth Syst. Sci. **17**, 1051–1063 (2013)
7. Gebre, S.L.: Application of the HEC-HMS model for runoff simulation of upper Blue Nile River Basin. Hydrol. Curr. Res. **6**, 1 (2015)
8. Enku, T., Melesse, A.M.: A simple temperature method for the estimation of evapotranspiration. Hydrol. Process. **28**, 2945–2960 (2014)
9. Bayabil, H.K., Tilahun, S.A., Collick, A.S., Yitaferu, B., Steenhuis, T.S.: Are runoff processes ecologically or topographically driven in the (sub) humid Ethiopian Highlands? The case of the Maybar watershed. Ecohydrology **3**, 457–466 (2010)
10. Thornthwaite, C.M., Mather, J.R.: The Water Balance. Publica Tions Climatol, Centerton (1955)
11. Hammouri, N., El-Naqa, A.: Hydrological modeling of ungauged wadis in arid environments using GIS: a case study of Wadi Madoneh in Jordan. Rev. Mex. Cienc. Geológicas **24**, 185–196 (2007)
12. Tilahun, S.A., et al.: An efficient semi-distributed hillslope sediment model: the Anjeni in the sub humid Ethiopian Highlands. Hydrol. Earth Syst. Sci. Discuss. **8**, 2207–2233 (2011)
13. Moges, M.A., et al.: Suitability of watershed models to predict distributed hydrologic response in the Awramba watershed in Lake Tana Basin. Land Degrad. Dev. **28**, 1386–1397 (2017)
14. Wale, A., Rientjes, T.H.M., Gieske, A.S.M., Getachew, H.A.: Ungauged catchment contributions to Lake Tana's water balance. Hydrol. Process. Int. J. **23**, 3682–3693 (2009)
15. Tilahun, S.A., et al.: Distributed discharge and sediment concentration predictions in the sub-humid Ethiopian Highlands: the Debre Mawi watershed. Hydrol. Process. **29**, 1817–1828 (2015)
16. U.A.C. Engineers of Hydrologic modeling system HEC-HMS technical reference manual. Hydrol. Eng. Cent. (2000)
17. Easton, Z.M., et al.: A multi basin SWAT model analysis of runoff and sedimentation in the Blue Nile. Ethiopia. Hydrol. Earth Syst. Sci. **14**, 1827–1841 (2010)
18. Tilahun, S.A., et al.: Spatial and temporal patterns of soil erosion in the semi-humid Ethiopian Highlands: a case study of Debre Mawi watershed. In: Melesse, A.M., Abtew, W., Setegn, S.G. (eds.) Nile River Basin, pp. 149–163. Springer, Cham (2014). https://doi.org/10.1007/978-3-319-02720-3_9
19. Tilahun, S.A., et al.: A saturation excess erosion model. Trans. ASABE **56**, 681–695 (2013)
20. Dagnew, D.C., et al.: Impact of conservation practices on runoff and soil loss in the sub-humid Ethiopian Highlands: the Debre Mawi watershed. J. Hydrol. Hydromech. **63**, 210–219 (2015)
21. Rientjes, T.H.M., Haile, A.T., Kebede, E., Mannaerts, C.M.M., Habib, E., Steenhuis, T.S.: Changes in land cover, rainfall and stream flow in Upper Gilgel Abbay catchment, Blue Nile Basin–Ethiopia. Hydrol. Earth Syst. Sci. **15**, 1979–1989 (2011)

Dynamics of Eutrophication and Its Linkage to Water Hyacinth on Lake Tana, Upper Blue Nile, Ethiopia: Understanding Land-Lake Interaction and Process

Minychl G. Dersseh[1]([✉]), Aron Ateka[2], Fasikaw A. Zimale[1], Abeyou W. Worqlul[3], Mamaru A. Moges[1], Dessalegn C. Dagnew[4], Seifu A. Tilahun[1], and Assefa M. Melesse[5]

[1] Faculty of Civil and Water Resources Engineering, Bahir Dar Institute of Technology, Bahir Dar University, P.O. Box 26, Bahir Dar, Ethiopia
minychl2009@gmail.com, fasikaw@gmail.com, mamarumoges@gmail.com, satadm86@gmail.com
[2] Bureau of Water Resources, Irrigation and Energy, Bahir Dar, Ethiopia
atekaaron@gmail.com
[3] Texas A&M AgriLife Research, Temple, TX 76502, USA
Abeyou_wale@yahoo.com
[4] Institute of Disaster Risk Management and Food Security Studies, Bahir Dar University, P.O. Box 5501, Bahir Dar, Ethiopia
cdessalegn@yahoo.com
[5] Department of Earth & Environment, Florida International University, Miami, FL 33199, USA
melessea@fiu.edu

Abstract. The increasing population has put an immense pressure on our natural resources leading to water pollution and land degradation. The need for new agricultural areas, urbanization and industrial development have been responsible for resources degradation and pollution. Eutrophication can be resulted due to substantial driven enrichment of seasonal cycle of nutrients like phosphorus and nitrogen. So, this study is aimed at evaluating the (1) spatial and temporal dynamics of eutrophication on Lake Tana, (2) linkage between eutrophication and water hyacinth infested area (3) lake-land linkage of nutrients and water hyacinth infestation. To evaluate the dynamics of eutrophication, the samples were taken from 143 points at 0.5 m depth of the lake in August (2016), December (2016) and March (2017). To see the lake-land linkage of nutrients, two major nutrients (P and N) were collected at the major tributary rivers. The trophic status index of TP, SDD and Chl-s was determined by adopting Carlson's model by using spatial analyst tool of ArcGIS. The result of this study showed that the trophic status index of the lake is shifting from mesotrophic to eutrophic condition. The growth of the invasive weed in the northeastern part of the lake is caused by the spatial distribution of nutrient and eutrophication as well as the depth, wind direction

The original version of this chapter was revised: The affiliation of the author's has been corrected. The correction to this chapter is available at https://doi.org/10.1007/978-3-030-43690-2_56

© ICST Institute for Computer Sciences, Social Informatics and Telecommunications Engineering 2020, corrected publication 2020
Published by Springer Nature Switzerland AG 2020. All Rights Reserved
N. G. Habtu et al. (Eds.): ICAST 2019, LNICST 308, pp. 228–241, 2020.
https://doi.org/10.1007/978-3-030-43690-2_15

and the extent of large floodplain. This study will help to manage and control the pollution of Lake Tana and the expansion of water hyacinth.

Keywords: Eutrophication · Spatial distribution · Trophic sate index · Geographic information system (GIS) · Lake Tana · Water hyacinth

1 Introduction

Increasing population is the main cause of water pollution through the increased sewage and garbage, expanding agriculture practices (application of pesticides, herbicides and fertilizer) and rapid industrialization (effluents and hazardous waste) (Sheela et al. 2011). Water can play a great role in transformation energy within an ecosystem, facilitate the weathering process of rocks during the formation of soil, transport nutrients, regulate temperature in the atmosphere and used as a detergent of pollutants and particulate matters (Khan and Ansari 2005). The basic pollutants of water bodies, which can be extracted from different sources of water bodies are Phosphorus and Nitrogen (Penelope and Charles 1992; Hinsely and Jones 1990; Cunha et al. 2013; Teshale et al. 2002).

In etymology, eutrophic meant "good nourishment" and eutrophication meant the process by which water bodies being more productive for the growth of phytoplankton (Ferreira et al. 2011). Eutrophication is the sum of the effects of the excessive growth of phytoplankton caused by nutrient enrichment through runoff that carried down excessive application of fertilizers in agroecosystem and human wastes from settlements or it is a plant growth facilitating process resulting from accumulation of nutrients in lakes or other water bodies (Khan and Ansari 2005; Harper et al. 2008). Eutrophication changes the status of water quality parameters substantially and significantly (Penelope and Charles 1992).

Eutrophication is caused by enrichment of seasonal cycle of nutrients like P and N in water bodies (Bricker et al. 2003). Chlorophyll-a is a biological indicator of eutrophication in coastal and deep-water bodies (Bricker et al. 1999, 2003, 2005, 2008; Kowalewska et al. 2004). Turbidity affects the eutrophication and its process of water bodies. The reduction of water transparency can shift macrophyte communities from submergent to canopy forming, to floating leaved and then to emergent vegetation (Chambers 1987; Moss 2009; Niemer and Hubert 1984; Sand-Jensen 1997; Van Den Berg et al. 1999). Lakes in turbid stable state can shift from dominant of submergent species and clear water to dominant of emergent species and high turbidity (Scheffer et al. 2001). High total dissolved solids (TDS) indicates the cultural eutrophication which is the process that speeds up natural eutrophication because of human activity (Vijayvergia 2007). According to Vijayvergia (2007), lakes which have less than 100 mg l-1 TDS could be classified as Oligotrophic whereas lakes which have more than 100 mg l-1 TDS could be classified as Eutrophic lakes.

The release of phosphorus from aerobic sediment surface to the trophogenic zone in summer, which is made up the major fraction of the total phosphorus load in shallow lakes can be influenced by temperature and pH (Jensen and Andersen 1992). The internal loading of phosphorus is an important mechanism in delaying the recovery of shallow lakes which is followed by reduced external loading of phosphorus (Ryding 1985).

Previous studies showed that substantial amount of sediment is transporting from its catchments to the lake (Setegn et al. 2010; Zimale et al. 2016; Lemma et al. 2018).

According to Lemma et al. (2018), the rate of sedimentation of Lake Tana is 11.7 $\pm$ 0.1 kg m-1 yr-1 and its trap efficiency is estimated about 97%. The sediment load transported from the to the lake and flood plains has implications on nutrient transportation and facilitates the eutrophication process of the lake.

Lakes can be classified as Oligotrophic, Mesotrophic and Eutrophic with sub classifications within each class according to the Trophic Status Index (TSI) of Total phosphorus (TP), Chl-a and Secchi Disc Depth (SDD) (Carlson 1977; Sheela et al. 2011). According to Carlson (1977); Sheela et al. (2011), lakes can be classified in to three main categories (Oligotrophic, Mesotrophic and Eutrophic) and four possible classes (Oligotrophic, Mesotrophic and Eutrophic and hypereutrophic). The classification of lakes based on the values of Trophic State Index (TSI) is oligotrophic for TSI <30−40, Mesotrophic for TSI 40−50, Eutrophic for TSI 50−70 and Hypereutrophic for TSI 70−100+. In the other hand, the trophic status of water bodies can be classified based on the numerical values of TP and Chl-a concentration of lakes (Jolankai and Biro 2008).

The dynamic nature of the trophic status of Lake Tana and its linkage with water hyacinth infesting area was not well known. Even though the data was limited, a few previous studies showed that the trophic status of the lake was in transition condition from Oligotrophic to Mesotrophic (Moges et al. 2017; Nagelkerke 1997; Teshale et al. 2002; Wondie et al. 2007; Wubneh 1998). The study will play a great role in designing strategic plan to control and manage the infestation of water hyacinth in Lake Tana. The objectives of this study were to (1) valuate the spatial and temporal dynamics of eutrophication on Lake Tana (2) evaluate the linkage between eutrophication and water hyacinth infested area and (3) evaluate the lake-land linkage of nutrients and water hyacinth infestation using the nutrient concentration of major rivers.

2   Materials and Methods

2.1   Study Area

The Lake Tana region is situated in the northern part of the Ethiopian Highlands in Amhara National Regional State, Ethiopia. Lake Tana is the largest lake in Ethiopia and is the third largest lake in Africa. The Lake is registered as a World Natural Biosphere Reserve Heritage by UNESCO in June 2015. Its basin has a total area of 1.5 million hectares and out of this, 55% is cultivated, 21% is water, 10% is grassland and 1.6% is the wetland (Heide 2012). Geographically it is situated between latitude 10°58′–12°47′N and longitude 36°45′–38°14′E (Fig. 1), the watershed consists of 347 Kebeles and 21 Woredas (districts) in four administrative zones (IFAD 2007). The surface area of the lake is approximately 3078 to 3080 km^2 and stretching approximately 84 km north-south and 66 km east-west. Located at an elevation of 1840 masl it is also the highest lake in Africa. Its maximum depth is 15 m with a decreasing trend due to siltation and lowering water level.

Lake Tana Basin accounts for 50% of the inland water to the Blue Nile. The lake basin has a drainage area of approximately 15,096 km^2. The lake has 40 tributaries (rivers and streams), on which Gilgel Abay, Ribb, Gumara and Megech account for 93% of the total inflow (Setegn et al. 2008). According to UNESCO 2011, the lake was formed 20 million years ago by a lava extrusion that functions as a natural reservoir.

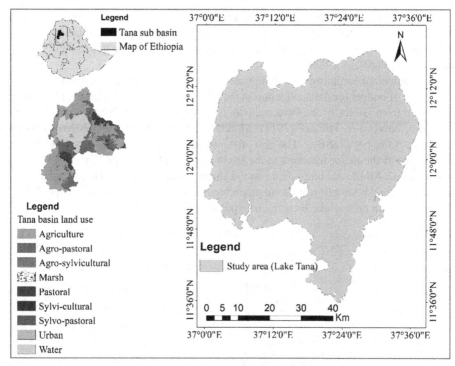

Fig. 1. Lake Tana and the land use map of its Basin in the Upper Blue Nile area, North Western Ethiopia

2.2 Dataset and Data Collection Methods

To achieve the objectives of this study, three water quality parameters such as total phosphorus (TP), Chl-a and Sechi Disc Depth (SDD) on the lake and two water quality parameters (phosphate and nitrate) on major tributary rivers were collected from primary and secondary sources. The water quality data on the lake was collected from 143 sampling points in August, December (2016) and March (2017) in 5 km interval and 0.5 m depth from the surface of the lake.

Transparency of the water was measured by a Secchi disc of 20 cm in diameter. The maximum depth at which the disc can be seen when lowered into the water is marked and measured. Total phosphorus (TP) concentrations were determined using PhosVer®3 based on Acid per sulfate digestion method in the range of 0.06–3.50 PO_4^{3-} mgP.L^{-1}. Digestion was realized at 150 °C for 30 min respectively for TP. The absorption was then measured using HACH product DR.2008 and DR.3900 spectrophotometer at the wave length of 410 nm and 890 nm for TN and TP respectively.

Chlorophyll-a concentrations were determined by acetone extraction method after sample filtration on 0.47 μm glass fiber filter (Whatman GF/C) using Gellman polycarbonate filtration towers, under low to moderate vacuum (10–40 cm Hg). Extracts were clarified by centrifugation at 4000 rpm for 20 min. Sample and standard absorbance were read at 750 and 664 nm before acidification (750b and 664b) and 750 and 665 nm after acidification (750a and 665a). Chlorophyll-a concentration in the extract was determined with spectrophotometer using the standard method of Perkin-Elmer Lambda 35 UV/VIS spectrophotometer with a 1 nm spectral band width and optically matched 4 cm plastic micro-cuvettes (APHA 1988).

The number of sampling was determined based on its representativeness and the availability of budget for data collection in the lake and laboratory expenses. Phosphate and nitrate from Gilgel Abay, Gumara, Rib, Megech and Dirma rivers were collected in August, November, January (2011), March, May (2012) and July (2013) by Tana Sub Basin Authority (TaSBo). The aim of the data from the river was to see the land-lake linkage of the major nutrients in the basin and the infested area of the lake by the invasive weed. Additional input data was the shape file of the lake and the geographical coordinates of each sampling points to predict and display the spatiotemporal variability of eutrophication on the lake by using interpolation techniques.

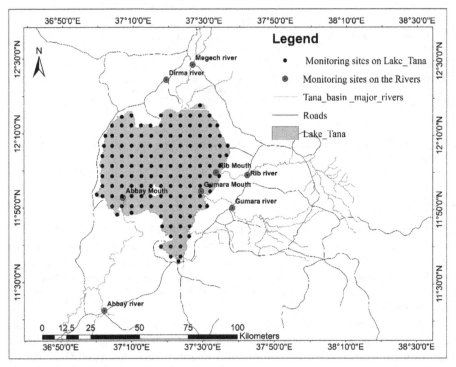

Fig. 2. Data collection sites on the lake (black spot) and on the rivers (red spot) (Color figure online)

The spatial and temporal trophic state index of Lake Tana was computed by using measured data on 143 sampling points all over the lake. To observe the spatial distribution of trophic status of the lake, first we calculated the indexes of the three parameters (TP, SDD and Chl-a) based on the Carlson numerical model which is mentioned in part 2.3.1. Using spatial analyst tool in Arc GIS 10.1, the spatial and temporal values were predicted by interpolation of the measured data using Kriging method.

Carlson's Numerical Model

The trophic state index of the lake was evaluated by using Carlsen's Trophic State Index numerical model applied by (Devi Parasad 2012). The reason we used this model is that its simplicity and good indicator of eutrophication status of lakes in limnology if there is available data. The result of each Trophic State Index (TSI) parameters on each sampling points were interpolated by Arc GIS 10.1. version using surface analyst tools.

$$TSI(Chl\text{-}a) = 9.81 \ln Chl\text{-}a\left(mg/m^3\right) + 30.6 \tag{1}$$

$$TSI\ (SDD) = 60 - 14.41 \ln SDD(m) \tag{2}$$

$$TSI(TP) = 14.42 TP\left(mg/m^3\right) + 4.15 \tag{3}$$

Where TSI is Carlson Trophic State Index and ln is Natural logarithm. Carlson's trophic state index (CTSI):

$$CTSI = [TSI(TP) + TSI(Chl\text{-}a) + TSI(SDD)]/3 \tag{4}$$

In addition to Carlson's numerical model, the trophic state classification of the lake also can be evaluated according to numerical values of two parameters (TP and Chl-a) as described in Table 1 (Jolankai and Biro 2008).

Table 1. Eutrophic status classification based on numerical values of TP and Chl-a adopted from (Jolankai and Biro 2008).

Eutrophication	TP (mg/m^3)	Chl-a max (mg/m^3)	Chl-a mean (mg/m^3)
Ultraoligotrophic	<4	<2.5	<1
Oligotrophic	<10	<8	<2.5
Mesotrophic	10–30	8–25	2.5–8
Eutrophic	35–100	25–75	8–25
Hypereutrophic	>100	>75	>25

3   Result and Discussion

3.1   Spatiotemporal Distribution of Trophic Status of Lake Tana

Spatial and Temporal Distribution of TSI(TP) and CTSI on Lake Tana

Lake eutrophication cannot be evaluated by a single physical, chemical and biological parameter because of its multidimensional nature (Xu et al. 2001). According to Carlson's (1977) range of trophic status index values, the result of TSI (TP) and CTSI from Fig. 3(a and b) the lake laid on eutrophic condition in all the sampling months and/or

seasons. This indicates that the lake is becoming enrich with phosphorus and other nutrients which can limit the growth of aquatic plants. In terms of TSI(TP), in August, the
north eastern and north western shore of the lake is highly eutrophic whereas the south
corridor and the center of the lake in lower eutrophic condition. In December, in the
same parameter, all the shore of the lake is highly eutrophic and in March, only the north
eastern part of the lake is highly eutrophic. From the perspective of CTSI values, the
eutrophication became highest in the western shore of the lake in the rainy season and
shifts towards Eastern shore in the dry season.

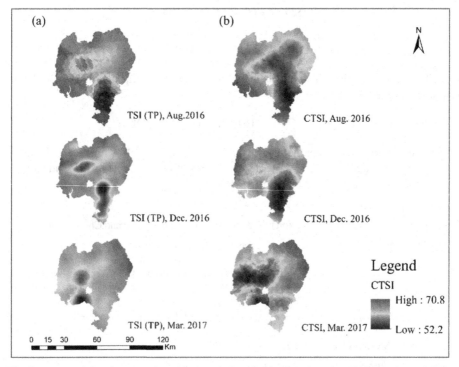

Fig. 3. The spatial and temporal trophic state index of Lake Tana based on TSI (TP) (a) and CTSI
(b).

Spatiotemporal Distribution of TSI (Chl-a) and TSI (SDD) on Lake Tana

According to the spatial and temporal values of trophic state index of SDD in Fig. 4(a),
the trophic status of the lake in the wet season (August) is eutrophic and in the dry season
(December and March), large area of the lake is eutrophic and the north east shore of
the lake indicates hypereutrophic condition.

According to the values of trophic state index of Chl-a in Fig. 4(b), in the wet season
(August), the north and south western part of the lake is eutrophic whereas the northeast part is mesotrophic. In December, the central and north-west areas of the lake have
been eutrophic and the north-east and south corridors of the lake were in mesotrophic
condition. In March, the lake was in eutrophic condition except in some areas of the

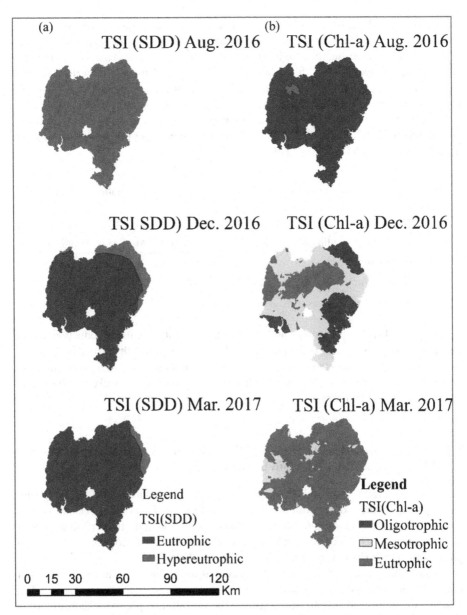

Fig. 4. The spatial and temporal trophic state index of Lake Tana based on TSI (SDD) (a) and TSI (Chl-a) (b).

lake. Generally, according to the values of TSI of Chl-a, the lake's trophic status laid on the range of mesotrophic to eutrophic status in increasing order from wet season to dry season.

This result indicates that in the dry season, the lake is being suitable for microphytes and in the wet season the lake is being suitable for macrophytes (emerging aquatic plants). In the wet season, the lake is turbid (less light transparency) and rich in nutrient which is being favorable for the growth of floating aquatic plants like water hyacinth and in the dry season the lake is less turbid (high light transparency) which is favorable for the growth of submergent species (algae and other micro aquatic plants).

To evaluate the trophic status classification of Lake Tana according to (Jolankai and Biro 2008) fixed scale, the values of determinant parameters (TP and Chl-a) of Lake Tana was summarized in Table 2 below.

Table 2. The numerical values of Total phosphorus and Chl-a concentration on Lake Tana

Parameters	August			December			March		
	Min	Max	Mean	Min	Max	Mean	Min	Max	Mean
TP (mg/m^3)	47	290	140	68	350	180	36	630	210
Chl-a (mg/m^3)	0.05	19.36	2.26	1.38	35.8	13.6	7.99	40.4	20.9

In the fixed scale of Jolankai and Biro which is described in the introduction part of this study, the measured numerical values of the TP showed that the lake is in the range of Eutrophic and Hypereutrophic status in both spatially and temporally. The values of Chl-a showed that the Lake is mesotrophic in wet season (August) and eutrophic in dry season (December and March).

3.2 Nutrient Concentration of the Major Tributaries of Lake Tana and Their Linkage with Water Hyacinth Infested Areas

The nutrient concentration of the major tributaries of Lake Tana can affect the eutrophication process of the lake. To evaluate the lake-land linkage of major nutrients (phosphate and nitrate) and water hyacinth infestation, the contribution of each river had to be analyzed in clusters (North eastern and North western Rivers). The concentration of total phosphorus in the rivers was summarized in Table 3 below.

From Table 3, the highest phosphate concentration was recorded in July in all major rivers. The mean values have been found in the decreasing order of July to August, May, March, November and January respectively. The overall total phosphors concentration of the North Eastern rivers (Megech, Rib, Gumara and Dirma) is higher than the North Western rivers (Gilgel Abay). The concentration of phosphate in the lake was lower in the wet season than the dry season with mean values of 0.14 mg l^{-1} in August and 0.21 mg l^{-1} in March whereas higher in wet season than in the dry season in the Rivers as shown in Table 3. This result showed that the nutrient that comes from the sub basin might sink on the large flood plains or it might sink on the lake bed as in the form of particulate phosphate. The infestation of the lake by water hyacinth has been on the northeastern shores. The northeastern rivers and the large flood plain in this cluster might

Table 3. Phosphate concentration of the Tributaries rivers of Lake Tana

Cluster	Major Rivers	TP (mg/l)					
		2011		2012			2013
		Aug.	Nov.	Jan.	Mar.	May	Jul.
North and south eastern Rivers	Ribb River	9.71	0.65	0.51	1.41	1.02	12.3
	Gumara River	4.4	0.62	0.28	0.40	0.98	8.9
	Megech River	2.2	0.02	0.42	0.32	0.84	7
	Dirma River	6.1	0.02	0.2	0.89	0.54	9.1
North and south western Rivers	G/Abay River	5.01	0.50	0.22	0.43	0.71	7.5

be the main causes for unevenly expansion of water hyacinth and the main source of the phosphate is the sub basin. The other nutrient which is useful for the growth of water hyacinth is nitrate. The concentration of nitrate in the rivers was described in Table 4 below.

Table 4. Nitrate Concentration of the Tributaries of Lake Tana

Clusters	Major rivers	Nitrate (mg/l)					
		2011		2012			2013
		Aug.	Nov.	Jan.	Mar.	May	Jul.
North and south eastern rivers	Rib River	0.64	0.13	0.04	0.07	0.45	3.1
	Gumara River	0.6	0.26	0.07	0.12	0.25	6.17
	Megech River	0.54	0.45	0.24	0.43	0.43	4.52
	Dirma river	0.75	0.22	0.21	0.1	0.09	1.99
North and south western river	G/Abay river	0.53	0.14	0.13	0.22	0.37	3.02

Table 4 shows that the maximum value of the nitrate concentration was observed mainly in July followed by August and it was minimum in the dry season. On the lake, the value of nitrate concentration is higher than phosphate concentration in both the dry and rainy season. The concentration nitrate in the lake was higher in the wet season than the dry season with mean values of 2.73 mg l^{-1} in August and 1.92 mg l^{-1} in march and had the same trend in the rivers. This result indicated that the main source of nitrate is the catchments in addition to the lake process. The overall nitrate concentration of northeast rivers is higher than the northwest and southwest rivers.

Generally, the expansion and growth of water hyacinth in northeast shore of the lake is due to high concentration of phosphate and nitrate in the north and south eastern cluster rivers but further studies shall be done about the other factors which can affect the spatial expansion of the weed such as wind direction and lake morphology.

3.3 Linkage of Eutrophication and Water Hyacinth Expansion on Lake Tana

In the current situation, the lake is severely infested by water hyacinth and the expansion of water hyacinth is on northeast shore of the lake with peak growing rate at the end of the rainy season (September–November) (Fig. 5). In terms of trophic state index of TP, SDD and the average trophic sate index (CTSI), in all the sampling months, the lake was in eutrophic condition with an exception of hypereutrophic condition in the northeast corridor of the lake due to TSI (SDD) in the dry months (December and March). This result indicates that the dynamics of eutrophication process is fundamentally suitable for the growth and expansion of the lake.

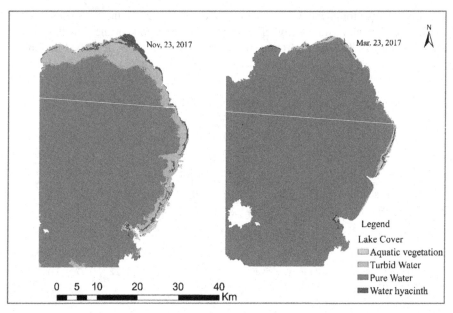

Fig. 5. Water hyacinth infestation at the end of the rainy season and dry season using SENTINEL2 Satellite Imagery and Google Earth Engine for supervised classification at the most infested shore of Lake Tana.

4   Conclusion

According to this study, the lake is being polluted and its trophic state is shifting to eutrophic condition as the result, reduction of dissolved oxygen may occur in the lake and being suitable for the growth of aquatic plants. The lake is turbid in the wet season and this becoming suitable for the growth and expansion of emerged and floating aquatic plants rather than the submerged ones. The infestation of the invasive weed in the north eastern part is the nutrient contribution of north and south eastern cluster rivers but the depth, wind direction, wind induced wave and large flood plain might affect its expansion and growth.

In the rivers, the concentration of phosphorus and nitrogen are higher in the rainy season than in the dry season. The concentration of total phosphorus was higher in the dry season than in rainy season in the lake due to its low flushing rate and high resident time, and wind induced resuspension of the particulate phosphorus in the dry season when the temperature of the water surface is high. The source of phosphorus in the dry season might be the resuspension of particulate phosphorus with sediment which deposits on the lake bed during the wet season or it might be the bed rock and decomposition of residue materials in the lake bed. This needs further investigation by collecting data in depth integration. Whereas the concentration of nitrate was higher in the rainy season than in the dry season in both the lake and in the rivers.

Acknowledgement. The data used were collected by Bahir Dar University Ethiopia and International Water Management Institute (IWMI) as part of the Feed the Future innovation Lab for Sustainable Intensification (AID-OAA-L-14-00006) through the Sustainably Intensified Production Systems Impact on Nutrition (SIPSIN). We thank Tana Sub Basin Office (TaSBO) and Amhara Design and Supervision Works Enterprise, ADWE) to give us additional secondary data.

Author Contributions. Minychl contributed in computation of the overall GIS work, data analysis, writing the manuscript and improving the manuscript based on the comments and suggestions of the coauthors. Aron contributed in the data collection and laboratory work. Fasikaw contributed in improving this manuscript by reviewing and editing the language as well as the images. Assefa contributed in conceptualization of the manuscript, giving comments, suggestions and improving the writing up and result interpretation. Seifu A. contributed in conceptualization of the manuscript, shaping the objectives, the methods and in giving comments and suggestions for the overall work as well. Abeyou played a great role in the GIS part for example in improving the quality of images. Mamaru contributed in shaping the overall contents, English, structure of the paper and giving significant comments. Desalegn Contributed in editing, improving the English and in giving significant comments for the paper.

Conflict of Interest. The authors have declared no conflict of interest.

References

Bricker, S.B., Clement, C.G., Pirhalla, D.E., Orlando, S.P., Farrow, D.R.: National estuarine eutrophication assessment: effects of nutrient enrichment in the nation's estuaries. US National Oceanographic and Atmospheric Administration, National Ocean Service, Special Projects Office and the National Center for Coastal Ocean Science (1999)

Bricker, S.B., Ferreira, J.G., Simas, T.: An integrated methodology for assessment of estuarine trophic status. Ecol. Model. **169**(1), 39–60 (2003)

Bricker, S.B., Smith, S.V., Ferreira, J.G., Nobre, A.M., Dettmann, E., Latimer, J.: Assessment of eutrophication: a comparison of methods applied to Barnegat Bay. Estuarine Research Federation 2005, Session SYM-06: Managing River Basins and Estuaries: An International Assessment of Approaches and Progress (2005)

Bricker, S.B., et al.: Effects of nutrient enrichment in the nation's estuaries: a decade of change. Harmful Algae **8**(1), 21–32 (2008)

Carlson, R.E.: A trophic state index for lakes 1. Limnol. Oceanogr. **22**(2), 361–369 (1977)

Chambers, P.A.: Light and nutrients in the control of aquatic plant community structure. II. In situ observations. J. Ecol. **75**, 621–628 (1987)

Devi Prasad, A.G.: Carlson's trophic state index for the assessment of trophic status of two lakes in Mandya district. Adv. Appl. Sci. Res. **3**(5, Cop), 2992–2996 (2012)

Cunha, D.G.F., do Carmo Calijuri, M., Lamparelli, M.C.: Atrophic state index for tropical/subtropical reservoirs (TSItsr). Ecol. Eng. **60**, 126–134 (2013)

Ferreira, J.G., et al.: Overview of eutrophication indicators to assess environmental status within the European Marine Strategy Framework Directive. Estuar. Coast. Shelf Sci. **93**(2), 117–131 (2011)

Harper, D.M., Zalewski, M., Pacini, N. (eds.): Ecohydrology: Processes, Models and Case Studies: An Approach to the Sustainable Management of Water Resources. Cabi, Wallingford (2008)

Hinesly, T.D., Jones, R.L.: Phosphorus in waters from sewage sludge amended lysimeters. Environ. Pollut. **65**(4), 293–309 (1990)

IFAD: Community-Based Integrated Natural Resources Management Project in Lake Tana Watershed-Ethiopia. IFAD project document (third draft: 31 August 2007), Government of the Federal Democratic Republic of Ethiopia & International Fund for Agricultural Development (2007)

Jensen, H.S., Andersen, F.O.: Importance of temperature, nitrate, and pH for phosphate release from aerobic sediments of four shallow, eutrophic lakes. Limnol. Oceanogr. **37**(3), 577–589 (1992)

Jolánkai, G., Bíró, I.: Nutrient budget modelling for lake and river basin restoration. In: Harper, D.M., Zalewski, M., Pacini, N. (eds.) Ecohydrology: Processes, Models and Case Studies: An Approach to the Sustainable Management of Water Resources, p. 138. Cabi, Wallingford (2008)

Khan, F.A., Ansari, A.A.: Eutrophication: an ecological vision. Bot. Rev. **71**(4), 449–482 (2005)

Kowalewska, G., Wawrzyniak-Wydrowska, B., Szymczak-Żyła, M.: Chlorophyll a and its derivatives in sediments of the Odra estuary as a measure of its eutrophication. Mar. Pollut. Bull. **49**(3), 148–153 (2004)

Lemma, H., et al.: Revisiting lake sediment budgets: How the calculation of lake lifetime is strongly data and method dependent. Earth Surf. Proc. Land. **43**(3), 593–607 (2018)

Moges, M.A., et al.: Water quality assessment by measuring and using landsat 7 ETM+ images for the current and previous trend perspective: lake Tana Ethiopia. J. Water Resour. Prot. **9**(12), 1564 (2017)

Moss, B.R.: Ecology of Fresh Waters: Man, and Medium, Past to Future. Wiley, New York (2009)

Nagelkerke, L.: The barbs of Lake Tana, Ethiopia: morphological diversity and its implications for taxonomy, trophic resource partitioning, and fisheries (1997)

Niemeier, P.E., Hubert, W.A.: The aquatic vascular flora of Clear Lake, Cerro Gordo County, Iowa. Proc. Iowa Acad. Sci. **91**(2), 57–66 (1984)

Penelope, R.V., Charles, R.V.: Water Resources and the Quality of Natural Waters. Jones and Bartbett Publishers, London (1992)

Ryding, S.O.: Chemical and microbiological processes as regulators of the exchange of substances between sediments and water in shallow eutrophic lakes. Internationale Revue der gesamten Hydrobiologie und Hydrographie **70**(5), 657–702 (1985)

Sand-Jensen, K.: Eutrophication and plant communities in Lake Pure during 100 years. In: Sand-Jensen, K., Pedersen, O., Sand-Jensen, K. (eds.) Freshwater Biology: Priorities and development in Danish research, pp. 26–38. Gad, Copenhagen (1997)

Scheffer, M., Carpenter, S., Foley, J.A., Folke, C., Walker, B.: Catastrophic shifts in ecosystems. Nature **413**(6856), 591 (2001)

Setegn, S.G., Srinivasan, R., Dargahi, B.: Hydrological modelling in the Lake Tana Basin, Ethiopia using SWAT model. Open Hydrol. J. **2**, 46–62 (2008)

Setegn, S.G., Srinivasan, R., Melesse, A.M., Dargahi, B.: SWAT model application and prediction uncertainty analysis in the Lake Tana Basin, Ethiopia. Hydrol. Process. Int. J. **24**(3), 357–367 (2010)

Sheela, A.M., Letha, J., Joseph, S., Ramachandran, K.K., Sanal Kumar, S.P.: Trophic state index of a lake system using IRS (P6-LISS III) satellite imagery. Environ. Monit. Assess. **177**(1–4), 575–592 (2011)

Teshale, B., Lee, R., Zawdie, G.: Development initiatives and challenges for sustainable resource management and livelihood in the Lake Tana region of Northern Ethiopia. Int. J. Technol. Manag. Sustain. Dev. **1**(2), 111–124 (2002)

UNESCO: Concept MAB (Man and the Biosphere) Strategy for the Federal Republic of Ethiopia. First draft report. Paris, France (2011)

Van den Berg, M.S., Scheffer, M., Van Nes, E., Coops, H.: Dynamics and stability of Chara sp. and Potamogeton Pectinatus in a Shallow lake changing in eutrophication level. Hydrobiologia **408**, 335–342 (1999)

Vijayvergia, R.P.: Eutrophication: a case study of highly eutrophicated lake Udaisagar, Udaipur (Raj.), India with regards to its nutrient enrichment and emerging consequences. In: Proceedings of Taal2007: The 12th World Lake Conference, vol. 1557, p. 1560 (2007)

Wondie, A., Mengistu, S., Vijverberg, J., Dejen, E.: Seasonal variation in primary production of a large high-altitude tropical lake (Lake Tana, Ethiopia): effects of nutrient availability and water transparency. Aquat. Ecol. **41**(2), 195–207 (2007)

Wudneh, T.: Biology and management of fish stocks in Bahir Dar Gulf, Lake Tana, Ethiopia. Wageningen Agricultural University, The Netherlands, Doctoral dissertation, Ph.D. dissertation (1998)

Xu, F.L., Tao, S., Dawson, R.W., Li, B.G.: A GIS-based method of lake eutrophication assessment. Ecol. Model. **144**(2–3), 231–244 (2001)

Zimale, F.A., et al.: Calculating the sediment budget of a tropical lake in the Blue Nile basin: Lake Tana. SOIL Discuss. (2016). https://doi.org/10.5194/soil-2015-84

Zur Heide, F.: Feasibility Study for a Lake Tana Biosphere Reserve, Ethiopia. Bundesamt für Naturschutz, BfN, Bonn (2012)

Multi-purpose Reservoir Operation Analysis in the Blue Nile Basin, Ethiopia

Dereje M. Ayenew[1], Mamaru A. Moges[2,3($\boxtimes$)], Fasikaw A. Zimale[3], and Asegdew G. Mulat[2,3]

[1] Water, Irrigation and Energy Development Bureau, Bahir Dar, Ethiopia
[2] Blue Nile Water Institute, Bahir Dar University, Bahir Dar, Ethiopia
mamarumoges@gmail.com
[3] Bahir Dar Institute of Technology, Bahir Dar University, Bahir Dar, Ethiopia

Abstract. This study focused on developing rule curves for multi-purpose cascade reservoirs operation to optimize the available water for hydropower production, irrigation development, water supply, and environmental flow in Blue Nile Basin using HEC-ResSim reservoir simulation model. The model tried to represent the physical behavior of cascade reservoirs in the basin with its high speed hydraulic computations for flows through control structures, and hydrologic routing to represent the lag and attenuation of flows through the main and tributaries of the river based on the current projects operation, and future likely development projects implementation period. Therefore, the management of multi-purpose cascade reservoirs is complex due to conflicting interests between these objectives. Thus, the optimal operation of cascade reservoirs is important to address trade-offs between multiple objectives to achieve the water management goals. From the simulation of cascade reservoirs operation, Hydropower power guide curve operation rule was selected to optimize the basin's available water.

Keywords: Cascade · HEC-ResSim · Optimize · Simulation · Blue Nile Basin

1 Introduction

Reservoir operation is a complex problem that involves many decision variables, multiple objectives as well as considerable risk and uncertainty [1]. In addition, the conflicting objectives lead to significant challenges for operators when making operational decisions. Different reservoir operation models have been developed and applied for planning studies to formulate and evaluate for solving water resources management problems; for feasibility studies of proposed projects as well as for re-operation of existing reservoir systems. However, the selection of an appropriate model for the derivation of reservoir operation is difficult and there is a scope for further improvement [2]. For this study, HEC-ResSim reservoir simulation model was used. Since its versatility, freely available, interface with other HEC models and applicable for both series and parallel reservoirs operation [3].

© ICST Institute for Computer Sciences, Social Informatics and Telecommunications Engineering 2020
Published by Springer Nature Switzerland AG 2020. All Rights Reserved
N. G. Habtu et al. (Eds.): ICAST 2019, LNICST 308, pp. 242–257, 2020.
https://doi.org/10.1007/978-3-030-43690-2_16

There are a number of existing, under construction, and planed development projects in Abbay basin. According to the Abbay basin master plan [4], joint multi-purpose projects upstream of Grand Ethiopian Renaissance Dam (i.e. Karadobi, Beko Abo and Mendaya) projects were identified. There were no recent studies directly in Blue Nile basin on optimal multi-purpose cascade reservoirs operation. But, few investigations have been conducted on the hydrology of the upper Blue Nile basin due to absence of data and other limitations. In the past, some related research and development projects were conducted in the Blue Nile basin [4–8] investigated that the total hydropower generation in the basin is about 13,000 MW [4] and around 815,581 ha of irrigable command area [9]. However, all of the studies were conducted at feasibility level and are not detail studies.

Thus, the objective of this study was to develop optimum rule curves for multi-purpose cascade reservoirs system for Blue Nile basin, this study has the importance of the implementation of good water resources management and allocation among the upstream and downstream users (water supply, irrigation, power generation requirement and environmental releases for downstream ecosystem).

2 Description of Blue Nile Basin

The Ethiopia part of Blue Nile also called Abbay basin in Ethiopia is located in the northwestern region of Ethiopia between 847705 m N and 1420688 m N latitude, and 656255 m E and 588616 m E longitude. It covers an area of approximately 199,812 km2 and it shares a boundary with the Tekeze basin to the north, the Awash basin to the east and southeast, the Omo-Gibe basin to the south, and the Baro-Akobo basin to the southwest. The Blue Nile River is the most important tributary of the Nile River, providing over 62% of the Nile's flow at Aswan [10]. Both Egypt, and to a lesser extent Sudan, are almost wholly dependent on water that originates from the Nile. This dependency makes the challenges of water resources management in this region an international issue [11].

From its source Gish (approximately 2744 masl) in West Gojam, flows northward as the Gilgel into Lake Tana. The Blue Nile River exits from the south east of Lake Tana and flows south and then westwards cutting a deep gorge towards the western part of Ethiopia. The basin accounts for a major share of the country's irrigation and hydropower potential. It has an irrigation potential of 815,581 ha and a hydropower potential of 78,820 GWh/y [9]. A number of tributaries joined River in Ethiopia: Beshilo, Derame, Jema, Muger, Finchaa, Didessa and Dabus from the east and south; and the Suha, Chemoga, Keshem, Dera and Beles from the north. The Dinder and Rahad rise to the west of Lake Tana and flow westwards across the border joining the Blue Nile below Sennar. In the Sudan, the Blue Nile flows on the plain desert until it reaches the confluence, where it meets with White Nile in Khartoum.

The topography of the Blue Nile basin signifies two distinct features; the highlands, ragged mountainous areas in the center and eastern part of the basin and the lowlands in the western part of the basin. The altitude in the basin ranges from 498 masl in the lowlands up to 4261 masl in the highlands. The Ethiopian highlands extend from 1500 masl up to as high as 4260 masl, with a slope of greater than 25% in the eastern part. Whereas the Ethiopian lowlands flatten 1000 masl to 500 masl with a slope of less than 7%, in Dinder and Rahad sub basins [12].

Lake Tana is Located at an altitude of 1,786 m above sea level. The catchment area at the lake outlet is 15,321 km^2. Geographically, it extends between 1211257 m N and 1412924 m N in latitude and from 269408 m E to 418595 m E in longitude. The elevation ranges between 914 m to 4096 m above sea level. More than 40 rivers and streams feed Lake Tana; but 93% of the water comes from four major rivers: Gilgel Abbay, Ribb, Gumara and Megech [13].

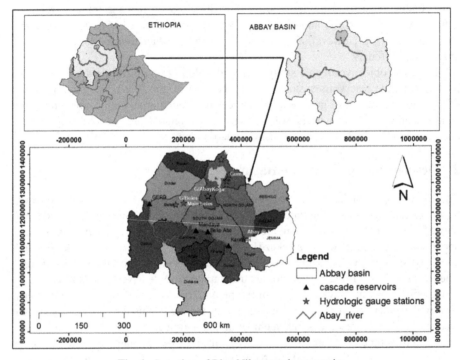

Fig. 1. Location of Blue Nile cascade reservoirs

3   Materials and Methods

3.1   HEC-ResSim Model Approach and Data Sets

The tool used in this study was HEC-ResSim reservoir simulation software with the intensive data needs for reservoir simulation and flow routing in the river basin system. The model used times series (observed and local flow) data, physical and operational reservoir (elevation-storage-area, dam elevation and length data).

HEC-ResSim has a graphical user interface which utilizes the HEC data storage system (HEC-DSS) for storage and retrieval of input and output time series data. HEC-DSS is designed as the data base system, which effectively store and retrieve data, such as time series data, and spatially oriented girded data and more [3]. It is unique among reservoir simulation models because it attempts to reduce the decision making process that human reservoir operators must use to set releases. The program represents the physical behavior of reservoir system with a combination of hydraulic computations for flows through control structures and hydrologic routing to represent the lag and attenuation of flows through segments of streams. It represents operating goals and constraints with an original system of rule based logic that has been specifically developed to represent the decision-making process reservoir operation [3].

Stream flows are needed and estimated at each site where management decisions are being considered based on the results of rainfall-runoff models or on measured historical flows at gage sites. Since, there are no stream flow gauge stations at the inlet of Lake Tana and river flow did not fully reach at the mouth of the Lake due to the effect of flood plains and back water effect in the catchments, the stream flow were simulated using a semi-distributed conceptual Parameter Efficient Distributed Watershed Model (PED-W) rainfall runoff and sediment loss model applied to catchments ranging from a few square kilometers to hundreds of thousands of square kilometers with minimum calibration parameters based on the saturation excess runoff process [13–15] and input for HEC-ResSim model simulation. The ungauged parts of the major watersheds as well as additional ungauged areas of the Lake Tana basin were simulated using [16]. Below Lake Tana sub basin, stream flow gauge stations in the basin are poorly distributed in the area of interest; gauged stream flows were transferred to ungauged sites using the recommended area ratio method [17] described in Eq. (1). This method uses the drainage areas to interpolate flow values between or near gauged sites on the same stream. Flow values are transferred from a gauged site, either upstream or downstream to the ungauged site. Having these, the inflow regime of the downstream reservoirs are governed by the upstream hydropower reservoirs and contributing catchments (incremental flow) and tributaries.

$$Q_{site} = Q_{gaug}[\frac{DA_{site}}{DA_{gaug}}]^n \tag{1}$$

where DAsite is drainage area of site of interest, DAgauge drainage area of the gauge site, Qsite discharge at site of interest (m³/s), Qgauge discharge at gauge (m³/s), and n a parameter typically varies between 0.6 and 1.2.

If the DAsite is within 20% of the DAgauge (0.8 < -[DAsite/DAgauge] < -1.2). Then n = 1 to be used. The estimated discharge at the site will then be within 10% of actual discharge. When DAsite is within 50% of the DAgauge two station data are considered for data transferring. Relation can be developed to estimate a weighted average flow at a site lying between upstream and downstream gauges.

$$Q_{site} = \frac{(DA_{gaug1} - DA_{gaug2gaug1} + (DA_{site} - DA_{gaug2}))}{(DA_{gaug1} - DA_{gaug2})} \tag{2}$$

where gauge1 upstream gauging site and gauge2 downstream gauge site. These methods were applied to transfer all river discharge to the proposed dam site and river confluence locations (mainly confluence to Abay River).

The aim of this study was to develop the optimal reservoir operation rule curves, reservoir and power guide curves using the three reservoir operation rules under HEC-ResSim simulation for the period of 1973–2014 on monthly basis of stream flow data;

the total stream flow (including rainfall over the reservoir surface area and the total demand (irrigation releases, hydropower releases, environmental release, water supply), water losses (evaporation), useful storage, water spilled and water stress analysis were also undergo using excel spreadsheet.

Simulation was performed to select the optimal reservoir operation rule that optimize the available water resources of the basin for hydropower energy generation, environmental release and irrigation demand satisfaction as well as flood control each year. Accordingly, simulation was performed using the defined three reservoir operation alternatives for each four scenarios taking into account the present reservoirs operation and future likely development projects considering similar future hydrologic condition of the basin using monthly time series of inflow data from 1973–2014 (Fig. 2).

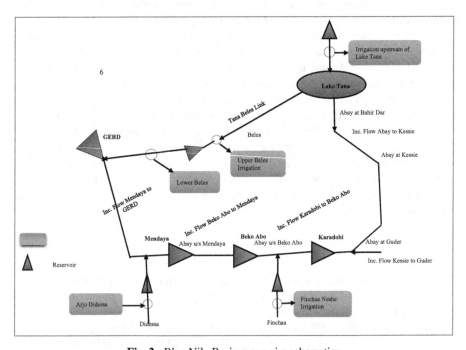

Fig. 2. Blue Nile Basin reservoirs schematics

Scenarios for Blue Nile Basin cascade multi-purpose reservoirs were set based on the present and likely future projects implementation in the basin to see their future likely effects when they are operational in similar time periods. The scenarios are:

Scenario one: Lake Tana only,
Scenario two: Lake Tana, GERD,
Scenario three: Lake Tana, GERD, Karadobi,
Scenario four: Lake Tana, GERD, Karadobi, Bekoabo, Mendaya

Based on this, the simulation results were presented below for the four scenarios based on the three alternatives for the reservoirs operation to optimize the available water resources in the Blue Nile River Basin. Lake Tana was developed basically for the Lake's future situation by considering Beles transfer project, irrigation projects directly pumped from the Lake, environmental flow requirement for Tis Isat fall and irrigation projects upstream of Lake Tana basin.

On the basis of modeling of the cascade reservoirs in the basin to optimize the available water for hydropower, irrigation water demand satisfaction, water supply, environmental and flood controlling in the cascade reservoir system, the alternatives were drawn for each scenario to select the best reservoir operation which provides the maximum power generation. The reservoir operation rules applied on cascade dam/reservoirs for the three alternatives are tandem reservoir operation (alt-1), hydropower schedule (alt-2) and hydropower guide curve (alt-3). Tandem reservoir operation rule operates the reservoir operation in the system and storage distribution among the reservoirs on the same river system. In tandem reservoir operation rule; the model determines the volume of water release from the upper reservoir in such a way that the downstream reservoir is operating to achieve a storage balance. For every decision interval an end-of-period, storage is first estimated for each reservoir based on the sum of the beginning of period storage and period average inflow value, minus all potential outflow volumes. The estimated end of date storage for each reservoir is computed to a de-sired storage that's determined by using a system storage balance scheme. The priority for release is then given to the reservoir that is furthest above the desired storage. When a final release decision is made, the end of period storage is recomputed. Depending on other constraints or higher priority rules, system operation strives for a storage balance such that the reservoirs have either reached their guide curve or they are operating at the desired storage [3]. On the other hand, Hydropower schedule operation rule has an option to define a regular monthly or user specified seasonally varying hydropower requirements while power guide curve rule permits defining a function that describes the hydropower generation requirement with respect to the available storage in the power pool.

Water Demand

Water demand is the sum of all water requirements for the different water uses served by the reservoir for the time period t. The demand varies with time (e.g., due to seasonal agricultural demand or due to some rule, usually based on the quantity of water in the reservoir). The possibility of supplying as much water to the irrigation area as is needed during each period of the irrigation season depends primarily on the availability of the water at its source. Availability may vary within a year, or from year to year. For this study, the computation of irrigation water demand for each dam was done using crop wat model and ENTRO tool kit and presented in Table 1.

Table 1. Water demand of current, proposed and under development projects (ENTRO, 2009)

Water demand (MCM)	Jan	Feb	Mar	Apr	May	Jun	Jul	Aug	Sep	Oct	Nov	Dec
Ribb (19920 ha)	37.3	42.7	26.4	14	21	0	0	0	0	0	5.4	18.6
Koga (7000 ha)	14.2	15	6.4	0	0	0	0	0	0	0	4.1	9
Megech (7310 ha)	16.6	26.4	21.5	10.3	2.4	0	0	0	0	0.5	4.9	8.3
G/Abbay (14552 ha)	34.2	39.6	31.9	5	4.8	12.3	3.9	1.7	1.8	1.9	7.1	24.7
Gumara (14000 ha)	20	26.4	26.6	14	0	0	0	0	0	0	18	18.1
Arjo Didessa (13665)	18.9	23.5	12.7	1.9	0	0	0	0	0	0	12	15.3
Finchaa Nesh (21000 ha)	18.9	20.5	13.5	10.6	1	0	0	0	3.3	14.3	23.9	23.4
Upper Beles (53720 ha)	84.1	87.9	75.8	72.9	23.1	0	0	0	0	0	81.4	39
Lower Beles (85000 ha)	148.3	185	173.2	91.7	5.2	0	0	0	0	0	121.6	47.1
NE Tana (5475 ha)	8.2	10.5	11.0	5.1	0.0	0.0	0.0	0.0	0.0	0.0	6.2	6.9
SW Tana (11632 ha)	16.2	23.5	23.4	13.6	0.0	0.0	0.0	0.0	0.0	0.0	10.9	16.2
NW Tana (6720 ha)	8.9	11.9	13.2	6.5	0.0	0.0	0.0	0.0	0.0	1.6	8.5	9.2
Megech Pump (24510 ha)	32.0	42.9	47.6	23.2	0.0	0.0	0.0	0.0	0.0	5.3	30.8	33.3

Hydropower Energy Requirement

The monthly energy requirement is input data for the model for the allocation of the release through the outlet of the hydropower based on the reservoir operation and these monthly energy requirements were considered as constant throughout the simulation period by the assumption that the hydropower projects were designed at least for 50 years (Table 2).

Table 2. Monthly energy generation requirements in GWh for the hydropower reservoirs

Reservoir	Jan	Feb	Mar	Apr	May	Jun	Jul	Aug	Sep	Oct	Nov	Dec
Lake Tana	–	–	–	–	–	–	–	–	–	–	–	–
Karadobi	235	161	195	187	200	286	2208	4374	2090	937	486	326
Bekoabo	328	236	286	271	310	434	2371	5325	2506	1268	600	423
Mendaya	260	187	220	208	254	456	1598	3935	2285	1322	521	335
GERD	342	244	279	254	326	605	2174	4678	3191	1865	760	468

3.2 HEC-ResSim Simulation Model

HEC-ResSim represents a significant advancement in the decision support tools available to the water managers and used to model reservoir operations at one or more reservoirs for a variety of computational goals and constraints. The software simulates reservoir operations for flood risk management, low flow augmentation and water supply for planning studies, and real-time decision support. The software can be used as a decision support tool that meets the needs of modelers performing reservoir project studies as well as meeting the needs of reservoir regulators during the real time events.

The model has three separate modules which are watershed setup, reservoir network definition and simulation scenario management each with unique purpose and an associated set of functions accessible through means, toolbars, and schematic elements. The model development began with the establishment of watershed schematics followed by establishment of reservoir network that represents a collection of watershed elements connected by routing reaches. The network includes reservoirs, reaches and junctions. Finally, the model development was completed by defining the development of alternatives for each scenarios and running simulations and analyzing results accordingly and best alternative was selected for cascade dams and reservoirs operation.

4 Result and Discussion

4.1 Reservoir Inflow Generation

4.1.1 Calibration and Validation of PED-W Model

The PED-W model was calibrated and validated on the daily basis from 2000–2009 and 2010–2014 respectively for the major gauged watersheds of the Lake Tana basin (Ribb, Gumara, Megech, and Gilgel Abbay) by adjusting all the nine parameters of the physical model parameters repeatedly until the model performs well. The initial values were based on the previous model runs of [13] and [14], and these initial values were changed manually through randomly varying calibrated parameters in order that the best "closeness" or "goodness-of-fit" was achieved between simulated and observed subsurface and overland flow in the watersheds. The goodness-of-fit and the model performance were measured and evaluated using the Nash–Sutcliffe efficiency (NSE) coefficient [18], coefficient of determination (R^2) and the root mean squared error (RMSE), percent bias (Pbias) and relative volume error (RVE) (Table 3).

Table 3. Calibrated parameters used in the PED model for the major gauged watersheds of Lake Tana basin at river gauge stations

Parameter	Unit	Watersheds			
		Gumara at Bahir Dar	Gilgel Abbay at Merawi	Ribb at Addis Zemen	Megech at Azezo
Area A1	%	0.05	0.05	0.05	0.05
Smax-A1	Mm	43	45	100	100
Area A2	%	0.11	0.1	0.1	0.02
Smax-A2	Mm	95	70	30	25
Area A3	%	0.84	0.85	0.5	0.58
Smax-A3	Mm	105	135	125	150
Bsmax	mm	85	115	75	75
t1/2	days	40	50	40	20
τ^*	days	45	60	60	30

A calibrated model should be valid before it is recommended for use. For validation, the simulated data as predicted by the model must be computed with the observed data and statistical tests of error functions must be created on. The overall results for PED model validation were summarized in Table 4 below.

As we see the tabular values (Table 4), the PED-W model performed quite well for the three watersheds both at daily and monthly basis except Megech watershed. This is due to the regulating effect of the Angereb dam that was used for Gondar town water supply purpose. Due to this, Megech River flow was attenuated as this was described in [13].

The total inflow in to the Lake mouth was determined after having the inflow from gauged, ungauged and incremental flow from each catchments separately and later the total inflow was taken as the aggregate of inflow series from gauged and ungauged catchments. From the model result obtained, the annual inflow to Lake Tana reservoir was estimated to be 5.6 BCM.

Detail description for the inflow for the Abbay river basin below the Lake Tana was discussed in Sect. 3.1. The inflow for each reservoirs is described in such a way that, reservoirs will get inflow from the contributing catchments (i.e. incremental flow) and from tributaries. Due to the release of water from upstream reservoirs, the downstream reservoirs will get higher amounts of water (Fig. 3).

4.2 Simulation in HEC-ResSim

As the simulation result showed that, the guide pool of the Lake Tana was above the conservation pool and overflow over the spillway. This is due to the high river flows which attributes of high rainfall pattern in August, September and in some extent on October that increased its reservoir level to the flood zone. This clearly showed average, maximum

Table 4. Model Efficiency for calibration and validation of discharge in mm/day for the major watersheds at river gauge stations

Watershed	Description		Calibration		Validation	
			Daily	Monthly	Daily	Monthly
Gumara	Mean	Predicted	2.05	62.41	1.89	57.56
		Observed	2.46	74.88	2.39	72.98
		R^2	0.74	0.89	0.78	0.94
		NSE	0.73	0.88	0.76	0.89
		RMSE	1.5	37.8	1.8	35.4
		RVE	0.2	0.2	0.21	0.2
		Pbias	16.7	16.7	21.1	21.1
Ribb	Mean	Predicted	1.5	45.99	1.05	32.05
		Observed	1.28	38.98	0.82	24.84
		R^2	0.79	0.91	0.76	0.95
		NSE	0.78	0.90	0.6	0.84
		RMSE	1.2	28.02	0.85	14.3
		RVE	−0.28	−0.18	−0.3	−0.3
		Pbias	−18	−27.6	−29	−29
G/Abay	Mean	Predicted	3.271	99.56	3.226	98.2
		Observed	2.96	90.1	2.675	81.4
		R^2	0.72	0.93	0.73	0.87
		NSE	0.70	0.92	0.64	0.80
		RMSE	2.14	30.7	2.22	46.5
		RVE	−0.11	−0.11	−0.2	−0.2
		Pbias	−10.5	−10.6	−20.6	−20.6
Megech	Mean	Predicted	1.19	36.308	1.49	45.4
		Observed	1.13	34.55	1.43	43.6
		R^2	0.41	0.77	0.46	0.88
		NSE	0.40	0.76	0.45	0.83
		RMSE	1.9	27.3	2.18	24.3
		RVE	−0.2	−0.05	−0.04	−0.04
		Pbias	−19.5	−5.1	−4	−4

and minimum reservoir level of 1786.76 m, 1787.29 m and 1785.66 m respectively for scenario one, scenario two, and scenario3. However, scenario four showed the average, maximum and minimum water surface level of 1784.56 m, 1786 m, and 1782.76 m respectively.

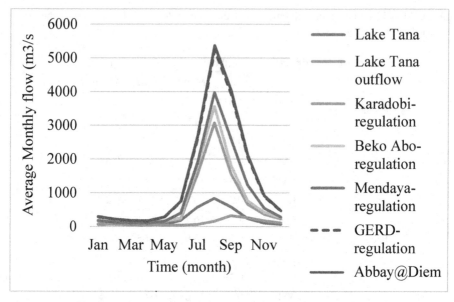

Fig. 3. Discharge of Abbay River at Blue Nile basin (1973-2014)

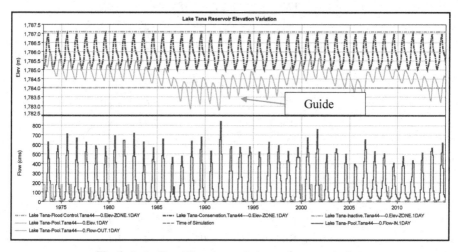

Fig. 4. Lake Tana Elevation variation under scenario four

A simple water balance was done on the system and the total useful volume of the reservoir was checked in balance of the total water requirement of the project under the each scenario. From these, scenario one, two, and scenario three has no deficit in its water balance. Since the allowable lake level for Navigation is 1784.75 m; but, in scenario four, the Lake's water level was lowered by 1.99 m and this will impose and cease hydropower, irrigation as well as navigation purposes in the Lake in the future and shown graphically in Fig. 4.

Using the three reservoir operation rules for the four cascade hydropower projects, different reservoir simulations were computed for each scenario and average the simulation results of the all the scenarios were based on the three alternatives shown in Table 5 below.

Table 5. Simulation results of scenario two, three and four for each alternatives

Scenarios	Scenario 2			Scenario 3			Scenario 4		
Location/parameter	alt1	alt2	alt3	alt1	alt2	alt3	alt1	alt2	alt3
GERD-Power Plant									
Energy generated per time step (MWh)	–	46892	39339	16318	57488	44560	21600	71271	49307
Power generated (MW)	–	1954	1639	680	2395	1857	900	2970	2054
Karadobi-Power Plant									
Energy generated per time step (MWh)				36774	36188	34857	21181	31714	31819
Power Generated (MW)				1532	1507	1452	883	1321	1326
Bekoabo-Power Plant									
Energy generated per time step (MWh)							34929	46493	43407
Power generated (MW)							1455	1937	1809
Mendaya-power plant									
Energy generated per time step (MWh)							35271	35940	32928
Power generated (MW)							1470	1498	1372

From Table 5 above, alternative two gives higher values of average energy generation per simulation daily time step for the three alternatives which are significantly larger value than the remaining alternatives. Thus, Hydropower power generation guide curve was selected for modeling of the cascade reservoirs operation in the basin to optimize the available water for hydropower, water supply, environmental and flood control in the cascade reservoirs system.

The GERD reservoir showed a lowered pool level shown in Fig. 5 in hydropower power guide curve operation rule in which the reservoir released more water to produce high amount of energy (Fig. 6).

Scenario three considered both GERD and Karadobi hydropower projects and the reservoir operations are defined by the same rule as scenario two. From the simulation results shown in Table 5 above, the hydropower power guide curve (alt2) generates 57488, and 36774 MWh of energy per simulation daily time step for GERD and Karadobi respectively. Hence, hydropower power guide curve was selected for modeling the cascade reservoirs to optimize the water for hydropower in the basin.

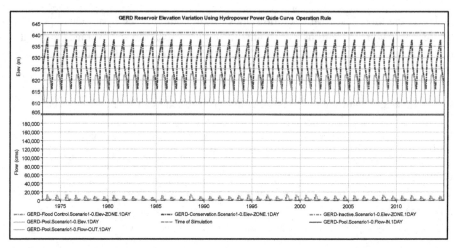

Fig. 5. GERD reservoir elevation variation using Hydropower power guide curve for scenario two

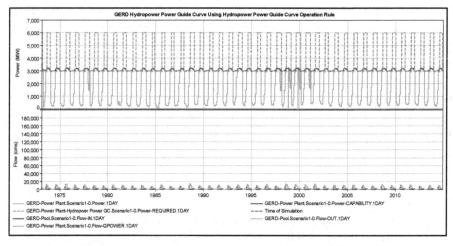

Fig. 6. GERD hydropower power guide curve using scenario two

Using the same approach of simulation, scenario four considered GERD, Karadobi, Bekoabo and Mendaya cascade dam/reservoirs. As the simulation result showed, alt2 generates 71271, 31714, 46493 and 35940 MWh of average energy per simulation day time step for GERD, Karadobi, Bekoabo and Mendaya hydropower projects. The average energy generated per daily time step for each alternatives showed that, alternative two gives the higher value of average energy generation per simulation day time step which are considerably higher values than the other alternatives. Along this, 38745 GWh/yr. of average energy will be produced when Karadobi, Bekoabo, Mendaya and GERD are in operation simultaneously. However, this finding didn't consider and incorporate all the proposed development projects of the Abbay River sub basins (only considered Finchaa,

Beles, and Didessa projects). Thus, the hydropower power guide curve operation rule was selected on the basis of modeling of the cascade reservoirs in the basin to optimize the available water for hydropower, environmental and flood controlling in the cascade reservoir system and increased the reservoir power guide curve average yearly energy generation than the others. When we compare the average total energy production; total energy of the Blue Nile basin was increased by 27% from the basin's master plan study with the newly updated operation rule.

In terms of energy generated in the basin, from previous studies by [19], considering the economic benefits of energy production and irrigation water demand satisfaction in the Eastern Nile, Ethiopia could have maximum energy (38200 GWh/yr.) could be achieved when Karadobi, Bekoabo low, Mendaya and GERD are in operation simultaneously. The maximum energy of 36525 GWh/yr. could be also achieved when Bekoabo high, Mendaya and GERD are combined. Energy in the eastern Nile will increase at least by 126% for GERD only case and could increase by 258% for Karadobi, Bekoabo low, Mendaya and GERD combination. On the other hand, considering the economic benefits energy production and irrigation water demand satisfaction in the Eastern Nile [20] investigated that, upstream storage in Ethiopia (and their regulation capacity) will generate positive externalities in Ethiopia and Sudan. In Ethiopia, the production of hydroelectricity is boosted by 40 TWh (+1666%), amongst which 14.3 TWh due to the regulation capacity of Karadobi, Beko-Abo, Mendaya and Border.

5 Conclusion

Water resource planning and management has become more important to maximize benefits, these need to be managed and operated in best possible manner due to perceivable overall increase in water demand for various needs and attempts have been made to establish an operation guide rules that would enable operation of Blue Nile cascade dam using HEC-ResSim simulation model. Thus, The ways in which management of the available and water resources of the basin is achieved by improving the operation of reservoirs using the updated guide curves which brings substantial benefits. Indeed, this can be achieved by selecting the reservoir operation rule which optimizes the available water resources of the Blue Nile River Basin. Three alternatives were established for three scenarios to simulate the cascade dams and reservoirs operation based on the simulation outputs of the average energy generation per daily time step and the best reservoir operation rule was selected from the three alternatives in which that optimizes the available water resources. From the three scenarios simulation results obtained, hydropower power guide curve operation rule gives maximum average energy generation and availability of water. Thus, hydropower power guide curve was selected for cascade dam/reservoirs operation of Blue Nile Basin.

The scenarios were applied for each reservoir operation to determine current operational and the likely future development projects impact on the cascade reservoirs operation. From the simulation result in scenario four, Lake Tan reservoir showed the Lake level is lowered by 1.99 m and thus, the upstream irrigation projects will have significant effect on the Lake's operation. On the other hand, if the planned development occurs on average, GERD hydropower operation was not influenced by the proposed development projects.

As the simulation result indicated, the average yearly energy generation using Tandem reservoir operation rule, hydropower schedule operation rule and hydropower power guide curve increased from the designed reservoir operation. Of these, the hydropower power guide curve operation rule increased the reservoir and power guide curves average yearly energy generation than the others.

The overall results of the study showed that, the model improves the performance of the cascade hydropower plants to generate more than the expected design of the previous studies in the basin.

In the Abbay basin, the development water infrastructures were at feasibility stage and did not studied well in detail. So, further study will be necessary taking into account the time of construction and all the existing and proposed small, medium, and large scale multipurpose projects in the basin.

Acknowledgment. The authors would like to thanks the Blue Nile Water Institute for the financial Aid to accomplish this study. We would like to thanks the Ministry of Water, Irrigation and Electricity for providing the stream flow data and the National Meteorology Agency for meteorological data. We also would like to thanks also the Ethiopian Electricity Corporation (EEPC) for providing us the hydropower and hydropower related data.

Conflicts of Interest. The authors declare no conflict of interest.

References

1. Oliveira, R., Loucks, D.P.: Operating rules for multi reservoir systems. Water Resour. Res. **33**(4), 839–852 (1997)
2. Jothiprakash, V., Ganesan, S.: Single reservoir operating policies using genetic. Water Resour. Res. **20**, 917–929 (2006)
3. Hydrologic engineering center: HEC-ResSim, Reservoir System Simulation, User's Manual Version 3.1. U.S. Army corps of Engineers (2013)
4. BCEOM: Abbay River Basin Integrated Development Master Plan Project, Phase 2 Section II, Vol. III: Part 1 – Climatology and Part 2–Hydrology, Ethiopia (1999)
5. SMEC: Hydrological Study of The Tana – Beles Sub-basins, main report, Ministry of Water Addis Ababa Ethiopia (2008)
6. Pietrangeli, S.: Tana-Beles Project part 2. hydrological report, Addis Ababa (1990)
7. USBR: Land and Water Resources of the Blue Nile Basin Main Report, United States Department of Interior Bureau of Reclamation, Washington, DC (1964)
8. Lahmeyer Consulting Engineers: Gilgel Abbay Scheme, Imperial Ethiopian Government, Ministry of Public Works, Addis Ahaba, Ethiopia (1962)
9. Awulachew, S.B., Yilma, A.D., Loulseged, M., Loiskandl, W., Ayana, M., Alamirew, T.: Water resources and irrigation development in Ethiopia Colombo, Sri Lanka. International Water Management Institute. Working Paper 123 (2007)
10. World Bank: Managing Water Resources to Maximize Sustainable Growth: A Country Water Resources Assistance Strategy for Ethiopia. World Bank, Washington DC (2006)
11. Waterbury, J.: The Nile Basin: National Determinants of Collective Action. Yale University Press, New Haven (2002)

12. Yilma, D.A., Awulachew, S.B.: Characteristics and atlas of the Blue Nile Basin and its sub basins, the improved water and land management in the Ethiopian highlands: its impact on downstream stakeholders dependent on the Blue Nile. In: Awulachew, S.B., Erkosa, T., Smakhtin, V., Ashra, F. (eds.) Intermediate Results Dissemination Workshop Held at the International Livestock Research Institute (ILRI), 5–6 February, Addis Ababa, Ethiopia (2009)
13. Steenhuis, T.S., et al.: Predicting discharge and erosion for the Abay (Blue Nile) with a simple model. Hydrol. Process. **23**, 3728–3737 (2009)
14. Tilahun, S., et al.: An efficient semi-distributed hillslope erosion model for the sub humid Ethiopian Highlands. Hydrol. Earth Syst. Sci. **17**, 1051–1063 (2013). https://doi.org/10.5194/hess-17-1051-2013
15. Tilahun, S., et al.: Distributed discharge and sediment concentration predictions in the sub-humid Ethiopian highlands: the Debre Mawi watershed. Hydrol. Process. **29**, 1817–1828 (2015)
16. Fasikaw, A.Z., et al.: Budgeting suspended sediment fluxes in tropical monsoonal watersheds with. J. Hydrol. Hydromech. **66**(1), 65–78 (2017)
17. Ries and Friesz: Development of regression equations to estimate flow durations and low-flow frequency statistics in New Hampshire streams U.S. Geological survey (2000)
18. Nash, J.E., Sutcliffe, J.V.: River flow forecasting through conceptual models part I-a discussion of principles. J. Hydrol. **10**(3), 282–290 (1970)
19. Mulat, A.G., Moges, S.A., Moges, M.A.: Evaluation of multi-storage hydropower development in the upper Blue Nile River (Ethiopia). J. Hydrol. Reg. Stud. **16**, 1–14 (2018)
20. Goor, Q., Halleux, C., Mohamed, Y., Tilmant, A.: Optimal operation of a multipurpose multi-reservoir system in the Eastern Nile River Basin. Hydrology Earth System Sciences **14**(10), 1895–1908 (2010)

Evaluation of Co-composting Methods Using Effective Microorganisms

Tilik Tena[1]([✉]), Atikilt Abebe[1], Endawoke Mulu[1], and Kefale Wagaw[2]

[1] Faculty of Civil and Water Resources Engineering, Bahir Dar Institute of Technology,
26, Bahir Dar, Ethiopia
tenatilik@gmail.com, atikiltabebe@gmail.com,
endawoke.mulu12@gmail.com
[2] Faculty of Chemical and Food Engineering, Bahir Dar Institute of Technology,
26, Bahir Dar, Ethiopia
zdkefale@gmail.com

Abstract. Organic matter is indispensable for increasing crop yield, fertility and water holding capacity of the soil. Using organic fertilizer or compost promotes circular economy and resource recovery. Conversely, the method of composting is very important to enhance the quality of compost and simplify further complication on the final users. In this study the co-composting methods were evaluated by adding effective microorganisms with municipal solid waste i.e., food waste (31.2%), wet and dry grass (44.21%), soil (22.45%), sugarcane straw (0.09%) and urine separated excreta (44.21%). The composting methods was comparatively evaluated in terms of composting period, pH, temperature, moisture content and chemical parameters composted for 60 days. The experiment was performed for pit and heap composting methods with and without effective microorganisms. Both composting methods were turned periodically once in a week and to increase the reliability of the experiment, each treatments method was replicated two times for similar effective microorganism and composting matter. The analysis showed that using effective microorganism has significant change among the composting methods in moisture content, organic matter, temperature, total nitrogen, and exchangeable cations (Ca and Mg). In this regard, pit and heap aided with effective microorganism co-composting process matured on 39th and 45th day respectively.

Keywords: Co-composting · Pit · Heap · Effective microorganisms · Excreta · Municipal solid waste

1 Introduction

Compact eco-city is one of the national urban agenda currently adapted to promote urban agriculture through organized small business groups. Ethiopia is a member of this agenda of sustaining the agriculture and working toward waste recovery (NUA 2035). Rapid urbanization and population growth generates a huge organic waste. The shift to ecological sanitation opens an opportunity to recover the valuable nutrients and reduce the impacts on the global environment (Bong et al. 2019). Due to environmental

N. G. Habtu et al. (Eds.): ICAST 2019, LNICST 308, pp. 258–267, 2020.
https://doi.org/10.1007/978-3-030-43690-2_17

compatibility and waste stabilization compositing have significant impact on quantity and quality of agricultural yield (Onwosi et al. 2017). The organized groups in Ethiopia particularly in Bahir Dar the case study doesn't have the proper skill to choose the effective and healthier composting methods, rather using the conventional composting methods. Moreover, the material used for co-composting were selected based on the preliminary research surveyed from the organized groups and own study.

Co-composting is a method used to enhance and counterbalance the degradation and nutrient recovery and produce safe and valuable quality compost (Camargo 2017; Olufunke et al. 2009). In addition to co-composting the use of microbial inoculums facilitate the maturation period, increase compost quality and reduces the impact on the environment due to its strong assimilative capacity (Laskowska et al. 2018). In Laskowska et al. 2018 and Shao et al. 2008 depicted the use of effective microorganisms controls and prevents secondary soil salinity. Effective microorganism (EM) is a mixture of groups of organisms that has a reviving action on humans, animals and the natural environment (Higa 1995; Balogun et al. 2016) and has also been described as a multi-culture of coexisting anaerobic and aerobic beneficial microorganisms.

Co-composting of excreta and organic solid along with activated effective microorganism contributed towards producing good quality and large quantity of compost (Olufunke et al. 2009; Yousefi et al. 2012). More importantly the selection of appropriate composting methods is crucial for drawing the final decision. Thus, in this study an integrated evaluation of co-composting scenarios in line with composting methods is valuable for efficiently and effectively recover the waste in to wealth.

2 Materials and Methods

2.1 Raw Material

Organic solid waste consisted of food waste, municipal grass (wet and dry), and sugarcane straw collected from the city while urine separated excreta was collected from 14 ecosan-urine diverted dry toilets (UDDT) located in the City. Form the preliminary research conducted, the type of co-composting materials and compositions have been calculated and used for this study. In this regard, 81.2 kg (31.2%) food waste, 115.2 kg (44.21%) excreta, 2.4 kg (0.09%) dry grass, 58.5 kg (22.45%) soil, 0.9 kg (0.034%) sugarcane, and 2.4 kg (0.09%) wet grass were properly mixed to prepare mixed organic co-composting waste for four (two pits and heaps) experimental scenarios and two controls. The dimension of the composting pit and heaps were 1 m * 1 m * 1 m. The construction procedure adopted from Nzdl.org. 1992.

A widely used commercially available microbial inoculum (EM1) which contains lactic acid bacteria, yeast and phototrophic bacteria (Jusoh et al. 2013), was purchased from Woljjeji Industrial Plc. 2 kg of EM1 was activated with 20 L of water and 2 kg molasses and sprayed over the mixed waste after fermented for 8 to 10 days as per the experimental design.

2.2 Experimental Procedures

The co-composting of mixed waste was performed using three (one control) 1 m * 1 m * 1 m (1m3) unlined pits and three heaps (one control) composting methods.

The stick was provided in the middle of all composting scenarios for proper mixing and control. Moreover, simplify compost samplings which are collected from top, middle and bottom considering vertical - horizontal distribution and uniformly mixed before the sample has been measured.

For this set of experiments, two pits and two heaps experiments with two controls. Initially, sugarcane straw, wet and dry grass was chipped in to uniform sizes, food waste was added and all the waste thoroughly mixed layer by layer and the mixed waste was turned once in week. Moreover, effective microorganism was added in all the experimental scenarios as per the experimental design. Suitable site were selected for piloting the co-composting process and similar waste material were used for both methods shown in Fig. 1.

Fig. 1. (a) Brown dry grass, (b) Soil, (c) Green wet grass, (d) Effective microorganisms, (e) Urine separated feaces, (f) Mobil ecosan toilets, (g) Food waste

A 260.6 kg of mixed co-composting waste was subjected to compost in pit and heaps for 60 days. Before the compost become matured a total of well mixed and homogenous waste samples (228.57 gm) were withdrawn once in three days and at maturation for measuring various main physical and chemical parameters. While composting the waste in pits and heaps temperature, moisture content and pH were measured regularly at three days interval for the first 39 days. Moreover, for the remaining 45, 50, 55 and 60 days were also recorded. The samples were analyzed for checking the maturity and its quality.

2.3 Data Analysis

The experimental data were measured during composting process at site and laboratory. Temperature, moisture content and pH was measured during the composting period for 60 days at site. Using the standard procedure shown in Table 1, laboratory test was conducted for the selected physico-chemical parameters to determine; total nitrogen, Ca, K, Mg, Na, C:N and organic carbon in the laboratory. Analysis of variance (ANOVA) was used to identify whether there was significant difference between co-composting methods and with respect to measured parameters.

Table 1. Experimental methods and standards for the measured parameters (Ozores-Hampton 2017; Seal et al. 2012)

No.	Parameters	Experimental method	Standards
1.	Total nitrogen	Kjeldahl method	0.4–3.5%
2.	Phosphorous	Standard test	0.3–3.5%
3.	Temperature	Teramo meter	
4.	Moisture content	Standard test	35–40%
5.	pH	pH meter	7–8
6.	Exchangeable base (Ca, Mg)	Atomic absorption spectrophotometer	0.1–2 cmol (+)/kg, 1.2–8 cmol (+)/kg respectively
7.	Exchangeable K and Na	Flame -photometer	
8.	Organic carbon	Standard test	>19.4%
9.	C/N	Mathematical model	10:1 to 15:1

3 Results and Discussion

3.1 Temperature, Moisture Content and PH Profile of Co-composting Process

In this study the pH value while measured during co-composting process varied in the range of 5.4 to 7.75 for both methods. The optimum pH range is 7–8 and the microbial activity highly depends on the pH and the organic matter present in the waste (Seal et al. 2012). For pit and heap experiments pH starts increasing on 9th (6.75 & 5.75) to 21st (7.4 & 6.4) day respectively. From 22nd the pH value starts to decline until 27th day. Decrease in pH depicted that the formation of carbon dioxide gas and organic acid during the co-composting process (Kharrazi et al. 2014; Meng et al. 2017). The pH value slightly increase on 30th (7.5) to 39th (7.75) day for pit and extends till 45th (7) day for heap experiment. Even though, for pit and heap control no significant difference in pH values with in the interval, starts increasing on 27th (6.4 & 5.4) to 45th (7.15 & 6.8) day respectively shown in Fig. 2. The increase in pH for all scenarios indicated that the decomposition of organic matter was occurred and the formation of ammonia (Meng et al. 2017). These imply the compost becomes matured. The pit experiment in terms of pH attained maturity on day 39, while heap experiment, control and pit control reached maturity at the 45th and 50th days respectively. Hence, from the result of pH value obtained pit composting with effective microorganism method has attained the optimum pH value compared to all other scenarios.

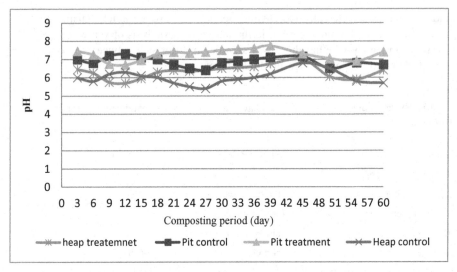

Fig. 2. pH profile in the co- composting process

The average temperature of the composting methods (pit and heap) was within the intervals (three days) showed no significant ($p > 0.05$) difference, but compared with control and experimental sample of both pits and heaps observed significant ($p < 0.05$) difference shown in Fig. 3.

The maximum temperature measured for pit and heap experiments were obtained on the 15th (40.25 °C) and 18th (37.5 °C) days respectively, have a significant difference ($p < 0.05$). While pit and heap control samples were reached a maximum temperature on the 27th day (40.6 °C & 38 °C respectively). From Fig. 3 showed that after 27th day the temperature for heap treatment is greater than pit treatment because in pit the compost reached maturation very fast while heap matures very late. The highest temperature represents thermophilic phase of the composts and influenced by the microbial activity which depend on the physico-chemical characteristics of the co-composted material (Van Fan et al. 2018). Conversely, the change in temperature also affected by the frequency of mixing (Hosseini et al. 2013).

The increase in temperature showed that highest microbial activity for the experiment treated with effective microorganism compared to the co-composting process without effective microorganism (control). The temperature for pit experiment from a maximum of 40.25 °C on day 15 declined to 32 °C on day 39. While heap experiment showed 37.5 °C on day 18 dropped to 32 °C on day 50. On the hand for pit and heap control the temperature from 40.6 °C and 38 °C on day 27 decreased to 33 °C on day 50 and 55 respectively. The decrease in temperature showed that the microbial activity become slow down and the organic matter present in the compost exhausted and the composting process reached cooling stage (Zakarya et al. 2019).

The maximum average moisture content for pit and heap experiments was recorded at 3rd day (52.5% & 47.5%) respectively. For pit experiment the moisture content declines to 45.6% on day 15 and slightly rises to 49% on day 21 and decline to 45.25% on day

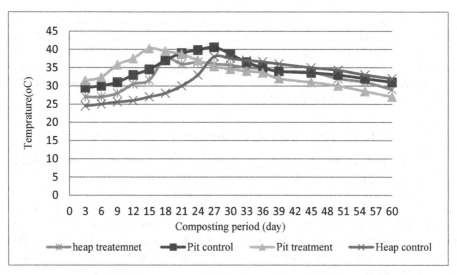

Fig. 3. Temperature profile in the co-composting process

30, rises to 47% on day 36 and finally decline for the reaming composting periods. Hence, the maximum and final moisture content decline was 43.9% recorded on day 39. While heap experiment also experienced the moisture content fluctuation over the co-composting period. The final maximum decline was obtained 38.9% on day 39. For pit and heap control samples there was a fluctuation in moisture content and the final maximum decline reading on day 39 was 42% & 37% shown in Fig. 4.

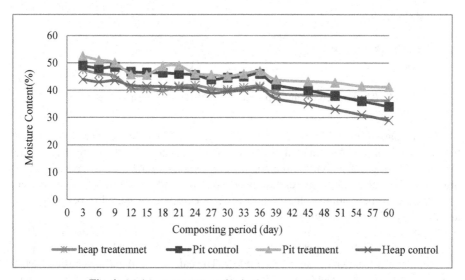

Fig. 4. Moisture content profile in the co-composting process

The moisture content fluctuation happened due to temperature variation over the composting period (Zakarya et al. 2019). In this regard, the moisture losses when the temperature rises in the composting process. Conversely, the co-composting materials used play an important role by increasing the moisture content. From this study the experiment performed with the addition of effective microorganisms attained relatively higher moisture content than controls.

3.2 Physico-Chemical Properties of the Compost

The organic carbon content and C:N of pit experiment (14:1) compared to other scenarios has a significant (p < 0.05) difference. For pit experiment the organic carbon is 33.5% on day 39, however heap control showed the smallest organic carbon content 18.5%. As shown in Fig. 5 pit and heap experiments treated with effective microorganism ranked first and second respectively compared to other scenarios. Compared to the standard value pit and heap control have the smallest C:N (8.7:1 & 8.4:1 respectively) than others. The C:N showed that the uptake of carbon content for the decomposition of organic matter by the microorganisms.

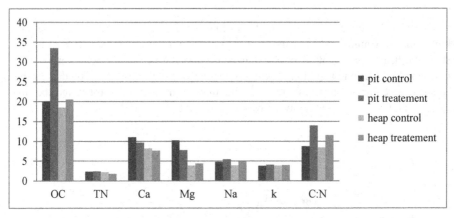

Fig. 5. The physico-chemical properties of the compost measured at 39 day

The increase in carbon indicated that in the co-composting process there was reduced the release of carbon (Ameen et al. 2016; Varma and Kalamdhad 2014a, b). Hence, the presence of microbial activity in the composting process would lead to the increase of organic carbon and reduce the emission of ammonia and volatilization of ammonia. Since pit experiment attained the highest organic carbon contributed to better quality and maturity of the final compost.

In pit and heap experiment at day 39 recorded the total nitrogen 2.4% and 1.75% respectively, in which pit experiment was significantly (p < 0.05) higher than heap experiment and control shown in Fig. 5 and Table 2. The calcium (Ca) and magnesium (Mg) content of pit experiment (9.64 & 7.75 cmolc/kg) and control (11 & 10.2 cmolc/kg) has significant (p < 0.05) difference compared to heap experiment (7.65 & 4.35 cmolc/kg) and control (8.2 & 3.86 cmolc/kg) respectively.

Table 2. The mean result for physico-chemical properties at 39 day and maturity date

Composting methods	pH	OC	TN	Ca	Mg	Na	K	C:N	Moisture content (%)	Temperature (°C)	Maturity date
Pit treatment	7.75	33.5	2.4	9.64	7.75	5.45	4.05	14.0	43.9	32.0	39.0
Heap treatment	6.75	20.5	1.77	7.65	4.35	4.9	3.95	11.5	38.9	34.0	45.0
Pit control	7.1	20	2.3	11	10.2	4.8	3.75	8.7	42.0	34.0	50.0
Heap control	6.2	18.5	2.2	8.2	3.86	3.87	3.83	8.4	37.0	36.0	50.0

The decline in Ca indicated that the reduction of ash content in the final compost. But potassium (K) has no significant ($p > 0.05$) difference compared to all scenarios. Highly stabilized and decomposed compost has high potassium content (Varma and Kalamdhad 2014a, b). In this regard, pit experiment (4.05 cmolc/kg) has better composting capability compared to others.

3.3 Co-composting Maturity

The maturity of compost measured primarily using ammonia to nitrogen and carbon to nitrogen (C:N) ratio (Guo et al. 2012). The carbon to nitrogen ratio for pit treatment has significant ($p < 0.05$) difference compared to heap experiment and controls. This is the critical indicator to measure the maturity of the compost. But the controls have carbon to nitrogen ratio out of the standard value and this implies the compost need more decomposition period for better maturation. The compost maturity varies from 39 to 60 days depending on the co-composting methods and experiments. Pit and heap control doesn't show any significant difference between each other. However, pit experiment aided with effective microorganism attained maturation on 39 days has significant difference compared to heap experiment (45 days) shown in Table 2.

4   Conclusion

Co-composting using excreta from mobile ecosan toilets and municipal solid waste (food waste, grass and sugarcane straw) with the help of microbial inoculum (EM1) achieved the maturity of compost in 39 days for pit, while 45 days for heap experiments and 50 days for controls.

In this research, the co-composting of excreta and municipal solid waste (food waste, sugarcane straw, municipal grass) using effective microorganism was evaluated for pits and heaps composting methods. The compost quality, maturation period and physico-chemical properties of the final compost were evaluated and from this result pit method performs better than heap. Hence the usage of effective microorganism and co-composting of organic waste in pit is the most appropriate composting method than heap and conventional methods.

References

Ameen, A., Ahmad, J., Munir, N., et al.: Physical and chemical analysis of compost to check its maturity and stability. Eur. J. Pharm. Med. Res. **3**, 84–87 (2016)

Balogun, R.B., Ogbu, J.U., Umeokechukwu, E.C., Kalejaiye-Matti, R.B.: Effective micro-organisms (EM) as sustainable components in organic farming: principles, applications and validity. In: Nandwani, D. (ed.) Organic Farming for Sustainable Agriculture. SDB, vol. 9, pp. 259–291. Springer, Cham (2016). https://doi.org/10.1007/978-3-319-26803-3_12

Bong, C.P.: Towards low carbon society in Iskandar Malaysia: Implementation and feasibility of community organic waste composting. https://www.ncbi.nlm.nih.gov/pubmed/27267145. Accessed 8 Feb 2019

Camargo Millán, G.: Co-composting of solid waste organic urban with sludge. J. Int. Area Stud. **21**(2), 23–36 (2017)

Guo, R., et al.: Effect of aeration rate, C/N ratio and moisture content on the stability and maturity of compost. Bioresour. Technol. **112**, 171–178 (2012)

Higa, T.: What is EM Technology, College of Agriculture, University of Ryukyus, Okinawa, Japan (1995)

Hosseini, S., Aziz, H.: Evaluation of thermochemical pretreatment and continuous thermophilic condition in rice straw composting process enhancement. Bioresour. Technol. **133**, 240–247 (2013)

Jusoh, M., Manaf, L., Latiff, P.: Composting of rice straw with effective microorganisms (EM) and its influence on compost quality. Iran. J. Environ. Health Sci. Eng. **10**(1), 17 (2013)

Laskowska, E., Jarosz, Ł.S., Grądzki, Z.: Effect of the EM Bokashi® multimicrobial probiotic preparation on the non-specific immune response in pigs. Probiotics Antimicrob. Proteins **11**(4), 1264–1277 (2018). https://doi.org/10.1007/s12602-018-9460-5

Meng, L., Li, W., Zhang, S., Wu, C., Lv, L.: Feasibility of co-composting of sewage sludge, spent mushroom substrate and wheat straw. Bioresour. Technol. **226**, 39–45 (2017)

National Urban Agenda (2035) United Nations Development Programme. Plan 2018–2035

Nzdl.org: Learn how to Make and Use Compost Manure in Farming (Friends-of-the-book Foundation, 1992, 54 p.): (introduction…) (2019). http://www.nzdl.org/gsdlmod. Accessed 8 Feb 2019

Olufunke, C., Doulaye, K., Silke, R., Daya, M., Chri, Z.: Co-composting of faecal sludge and organic solid waste for agriculture: process dynamics. Water Res. **43**, 4665–4675 (2009)

Onwosi, C., et al.: Composting technology in waste stabilization: on the methods, challenges and future prospects. J. Environ. Manage. **190**, 140–157 (2017)

Ozores-Hampton, M.: Guidelines for assessing compost quality for safe and effective utilization in vegetable production. HortTechnology **27**(2), 162–165 (2017)

Seal, A., Bera, R., Chatterjee, A.K., Dolui, A.K.: Evaluation of a new composting method in terms of its biodegradation pathway and assessment of compost quality, maturity and stability. Arch. Agron. Soil Sci. **58**(9), 995–1012 (2012)

Shao, X., Tan, M., Jiang, P., Cao, W.: Effect of EM Bokashi application on control of secondary soil salinization. Water Sci. Eng. **1**(4), 99–106 (2008)

Varma, V.S., Kalamdhad, A.S.: Evolution of chemical and biological characterization during thermophilic composting of vegetable waste using rotary drum composter. Int. J. Environ. Sci. Technol. **12**(6), 2015–2024 (2014a)

Varma, V.S., Kalamdhad, A.S.: Stability and microbial community analysis during rotary drum composting of vegetable waste. Int. J. Recycl. Org. Waste Agric. **3**(2), 52 (2014b)

Yousefi, J., Younesi, H., Ghasempoury, S.M.: Co-composting of municipal solid waste with sawdust: improving compost quality. CLEAN Soil Air Water **41**(2), 185–194 (2012)

Zakarya, I., Khalib, S., Mohd Ramzi, N.: Effect of pH, temperature and moisture content during composting of rice straw burning at different temperature with food waste and effective microorganisms. In: E3S Web of Conferences, vol. 34, p. 02019 (2019)

Impact of Land Use and Landscape on Runoff and Sediment in the Sub-humid Ethiopian Highlands: The Ene-Chilala Watershed

Nigus H. Tegegne[1]([⊠]), Temesgen Enku[1], Seifu A. Tilahun[1], Meseret B. Addisea[1], and Tammo S. Steenhuis[1,2]

[1] Faculty of Civil and Water Resources Engineering, Bahir Dar Institute of Technology, Bahir Dar University, Bahir Dar, Ethiopia
Nihailu2011@gmail.com, temesgenku@gmail.com, satadm86@gmail.com, meseret.belachew21@gmail.com
[2] Biological and Environmental Engineering, Cornell University, Ithaca, NY, USA
tammo@cornell.edu

Abstract. The effect of land cover and landscape on runoff and sediment yield was evaluated in the Ethiopian highlands. We selected three small catchments: agriculture dominated watershed, bush & agriculture dominated watershed and agriculture dominated but with higher coverage of bush & grass watershed compared to the other two watersheds with in 399 ha Ene-chilala watershed. Hydrometric, sediment concentration and rill erosion data were measured for two years (2015 and 2016). The result showed that; sediment yield were statistically significant different between watershed one and watershed two. Moreover, the sediment concentration in watershed three varies statistically when compared with watershed one and watershed two. The greater runoff, suspended sediment concentration and yield in the agriculture dominated but with higher coverage of bush & grass catchment (WS3) results from saturated areas and gully erosion in the bottomlands. Since the agricultural land is highly degraded no more soil is transported due to rill erosion (detachment limited) by generated runoff. The bedrocks at the upland of these watersheds generate high runoff. Shallow and deep active gullies at the bottomlands contributed for higher sediment concentration. Our results support that watershed management that involve gully treatment on bottom lands and increase ground cover on degraded agricultural areas to reduce runoff and soil loss.

Keywords: Ene-chilala watershed · Erosion · Ethiopian highlands · Landscape land use

1 Introduction

Soil erosion hinders agricultural productivity in the Ethiopian highlands (Hurni et al. 2005; Mitiku et al. 2006; Vanmaercke et al. 2010). Rill and gully erosions are typical form of soil losses that reduced soil productivity, sedimentation of water infrastructures

© ICST Institute for Computer Sciences, Social Informatics and Telecommunications Engineering 2020
Published by Springer Nature Switzerland AG 2020. All Rights Reserved
N. G. Habtu et al. (Eds.): ICAST 2019, LNICST 308, pp. 268–278, 2020.
https://doi.org/10.1007/978-3-030-43690-2_18

and water-quality deterioration in streams and reservoirs (Sun et al. 2013). Around 1.5 to 2 billion tons yr-1 soil is lost from Ethiopia highlands it is equivalent to 35 to 42 tons ha-1 yr-1 (Constable and Belshaw 1986; Hurni 1978; Hurni 1983; Hurni and Tato 1992; Tamene and Vlek 2008). Crop production is decreasing due to the removal of fertile soil by erosion (Sertsu 2000). Soil degradation can be regarded as a direct result of a change in the landscape within the Ethiopian highlands.

Land use and land cover has largely influenced runoff and soil loss dynamics in a watershed (Dagnew et al. 2015). The increased demand for land resources as a result of increasing population changes the natural state of land cover distribution in the highlands of Ethiopia. Soil erosion is highly influenced by land uses and land cover as compared to other factors (Kosmas et al. 1997; Thornes 1990). Degraded highland areas are subjected to high surface runoff and low infiltration capacity (Steenhuis et al. 2009). Land use changes like deforestation aggravates soil erosion (Ayele et al. 2016; Dagnew et al. 2015; García-Ruiz 2010). The cause for the excessive rate of soil loss is the unsustainable use of the land resource (Bewket and Sterk 2003). Land use change after deforestation affects rates of runoff (Bewket and Sterk 2005; Symeonakis et al. 2004).

Rill erosion is a result of surface runoff and associated sheet wash, which is a process that selectively removes fine material and organic matter (Bewket and Sterk 2003). Upland rill and sheet erosion rates can contribute up to 125 t ha-1 y-1 in the humid areas (Bewket and Teferi 2009). Rills and gullies are erosion features that often indicate hot spots and affected by soil erosion (Mitiku et al. 2006). Rills are temporary features and can be easily destroyed during plowing but gullies are more permanent features in the landscape (Zegeye 2009). Rills from wetted agricultural fields or gullies from local saturated areas are sources of sediment (Tilahun 2012).

Runoff and soil loss from a given catchment vary depending on the type of land uses (Adimassu and Haile 2011; Girmay et al. 2009; Taye et al. 2013). Understanding the effect of land uses on runoff and soil erosion processes is used for sustainable land use management (Kang et al. 2001). In Ethiopia mostly the land use change is caused by human activities for the expansion of agricultural area, for forest production purpose (Zeleke and Hurni 2001). Moreover, other studies focused land use changes in a watershed can impact water supply by altering hydrological processes (Ndulue et al. 2015) and results land degradation (Bewket 2002; Tekle and Hedlund 2000; Zeleke and Hurni 2001).

This study is focused on comparing and evaluating the effect of land use and landscape on runoff and sediment yield based on measured data collects in different three sub catchments. The overall objective of this study is therefore to understand how land uses and landscape affects runoff and soil losses within the Ene-chilala watershed. The specific objectives are to: (1) assess the effect of land uses and landscape on runoff and sediment/soil loss from three sub watersheds in Ene-chilala watershed, (2) understand the spatial differences of runoff and sediment losses among three small watersheds, and (3) quantify the rate of soil loss due to rill erosion in the three small watersheds.

2 Materials and Methods

2.1 Description of Study Area

Ene-chilala is a small watershed is located in the upper Blue Nile Basin, in the sub-humid Ethiopian highlands (Fig. 1). The watershed has an area 399 ha and characterized by highly rugged topography ranging between 1996 m and 2414 m elevations. Ene-chilala has three sub water sheds where gauging stations (weirs) installed at the outlets (Fig. 1). The slopes of the three sub watersheds are almost similar. Generally it has an average slope of 35% and steeply upland bedrock (Ayele et al. 2016).

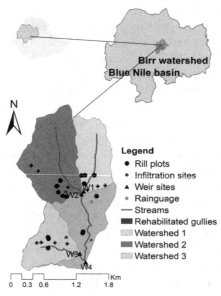

Fig. 1. Location map of Ene-chilala watershed and flow & sediment monitoring (Weirs), Rill and infiltration sites

The average annual rainfall from June to September in Ene-chilala watershed is about 1,225 mm and the dominant soil type is chromic luvisol (Ayele et al. 2016). Ene-chilala watershed had 98 household heads and a total population of 525. The agricultural system is mixed farming system. The dominant crops are 'Teff' (Eragrostis tef), maize (Zea mays), barley and wheat (Triticum aestivum), Livestock is the important productive asset for the households. Forest in the watershed was cleared during the Derg regime in the early 1980s, and crop yields have steadily declined since that time (Ayele et al. 2016). Gullies are formed in the periodically saturated bottomlands to carry off the additional direct runoff (both interflow and subsurface water) from agricultural lands (Ayele et al. 2016).

2.2 Data and Methodology

Precipitation, runoff, suspended sediment and rill erosion were measured during the rainy seasons of 2015 and 2016 and infiltration tests were conducted in 2016 (Fig. 2).

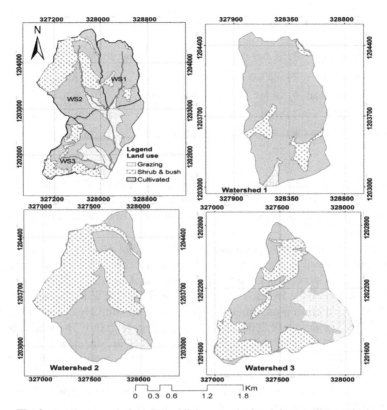

Fig. 2. Land use map of the Ene-chilala watershed and three sub watersheds

The study was conducted in three small watersheds in the Ene-chilala watershed for monitoring runoff and sediment yield. The proportion of land use types of the three watersheds were measured using hand held GPS (Table 1).

NB: numbers in brackets refers to the % coverage of each land use type.

For rainfall measurement a tipping bucket raingauge was installed in the Ene-chilala which recorded in 5-min interval. In addition to this, local raingauge and the nearby "Genet Abo" metrological station data was also used.

Soil infiltration measurements were applied on 11 sites based on land use and landscapes (Fig. 1) throughout the watershed using a 25-cm diameter single-ring infiltrometer in September 2016. A floater was used to read water depth fluctuations in the infiltrometer during the test. The constant infiltration rate at the end of the test was taken as the infiltration capacity of the soil.

The runoff amounts were collected in the three selected sub watersheds after rainfall generates runoff (at the outlets). The observation periods were from June 15th to September 23rd in 2015 and from June 8th to October 1st 2016. The flow velocity was determined by a floating method. The floating materials were released at a fixed distance on the upstream away from the outlet of the weir. The time taken for the floating materials to reach the outlet of the weir was recorded. In addition to this flow depth values were

Table 1. Land use type and area of the three sub watersheds

Land use area (ha)	WS1 area in ha (%)	WS 2 area in ha (%)	WS3 area in ha (%)
Cultivated land	74.2(89.4)	79.6(53.1)	48.5(63.7)
Shrub & bush land	7.2(8.7)	64.2(42.9)	15.8(20.8)
Grazing land	1.6(1.9)	6.0(4.0)	11.9(15.6)
Total	**83**	**149.8**	**76.2**

measured for 15 min time intervals for each storm events. Those measurements were continued until the runoff/discharge has stopped. The mean flow volume was computed by multiplying wetted cross sectional area with two-third of the measured flow velocity (Tilahun 2012).

Rills measurement 15 fields were selected from the 399.3 ha Ene-chilala watershed, based on landscape and land cover types. The erosion rates from rills in these fields were determined after 8 storm events between the periods of June 27, 2016 to August 28, 2016. The total area of the 15 fields was 3 ha (almost 1% of the watershed area, Table 3). The method of rill erosion measurement was conducted similarly as explained in the studies of (Bewket and Sterk 2003; Tilahun 2012; Zegeye 2009). The total volume of soil loss by rill was obtained by summing the volumes of all homogenous rill segments in each field. The total soil loss (t ha^{-1}) was computed by multiplying the computed volume with the measured bulk density (1.31 g cm^{-3}) and then dividing by the area of the agricultural land. Rill density (m ha^{-1}) was calculated by dividing the total rill length (all rill length measurements) by the total area of the agricultural fields.

For Sediment concentration data the sampling periods were similar to runoff. For each three sub watersheds the sediment data were obtained by taking samples using one litter bottles continuously every 15 min from the beginning of runoff to the end (Fig. 1). This sediment sample was filtered by using Whatman 320 mm diameter with a pore size of 2.5 μm filter papers. Finally it oven dried at 105 °C for 24 h and weights it to quantify the sediment weight per liter of sample volume. This was converted to mg/L in each sub-watershed.

2.3 Data Analysis

After collecting the raw data; rainfall, runoff, sediment concentration and sediment yield were analyzed. Stage - discharge (rating curve) was developed from runoff value versus flow depth by using power function. The overall results are described using Statistical Package for the Social Sciences (SPSS) version 20, descriptive statistics like mean, median, mode, minimum, maximum, variance, and standard deviation. Runoff and soil loss data from three watersheds were analyzed separately in order to understand the effect of land use on runoff and soil loss.

3 Results and Discussion

3.1 Rainfall

Ene-chilala watershed received uni-modal rainfall pattern which occurs usually from May to October. Most of the rainfall with higher intensities occurs in July and August. Total precipitation in the four months of the rainy season (June–September) was 588 mm in 2015 and 904 mm in 2016.

3.2 Infiltration Rates of Soils

The average infiltration rates for the upper, mid and downslopes were 85.2, 56 and 23 mm hr^{-1}, respectively at 11 samples of measurement. The maximum measured infiltration capacity was 240 mm hr^{-1} at upslope of watershed two. Moreover in uplands of cultivated lands the soil type is sandy loam which has generally higher infiltration. The median infiltrations were 36 mm hr^{-1}, 63 mm hr^{-1} and 27 mm hr^{-1} for watershed one, watershed two, and watershed three respectively. This also corresponds with the land use type. Watershed two had high median infiltration capacity as compared to watershed one and three.

Low infiltration was measured in bottom landscape positions due to compaction of soils. In bottom landscape of grazing lands the soil type is clay, the infiltration is low. Infiltration rates of the cultivated land in the upland vary greatly. Cultivated land with low infiltration rates represents the degraded soils while the soils with high infiltration rates are not degraded. When the rainfall is intense, the degraded soils produce surface runoff but some amount of runoff might infiltrate down.

Water infiltrated better in the upper fields than the downslope fields (Zegeye 2009). But in this infiltration tests water infiltrated in the upper slopes than the down slope only at watershed one. Due to the presence of impervious layer of shrub & bush land at uplands on watershed two and watershed three, the infiltration rates of midslope were higher than upslope and downslope in the Ene-chilala watershed.

3.3 Runoff

The amount of runoff from all watersheds during the rainy phase of 2015 was lower than the 2016 rainy phase (Table 2). This is due to the lower amount of precipitation in 2015 compared to 2016. WS2 and WS3 have more area coverage of shrub and bush which have impervious layer underneath, which results in large volume of runoff. In both 2015 and 2016 runoff volume generated from WS1 is slightly greater than that of WS2 because WS1 had less median infiltration capacity compared with WS2; these differences were not statistically significant at 1% significance level using F-test.

In addition, the runoff volume generated from watershed three was smaller than watershed one and watershed two in 2015 but it was almost similar in 2016 due to high coverage of locally saturated areas. However the differences were statistically significant at 1% significance level using F-test. In the Ene-chilala watershed, the bottomlands are saturated and runoff source areas. These results indicated that land use and landscape determine the storm runoff process.

Table 2. Monthly runoff, sediment concentration and sediment yield for 3 weirs

Weirs		Storm runoff (mm)		Mean suspended sediment concentration ($g\ l^{-1}$)		Sediment yield ($t\ ha^{-1}$)	
		2015	2016	2015	2016	2015	2016
Weir 1	June	1.4	11.3	1.8	12.6	0.0	2.2
	July	10.4	21.3	4.6	3.2	0.6	1.1
	Aug.	35.8	26.5	3.3	2.6	1.5	0.9
	Sep.	4.8	19.1	0.4	2.0	0.0	0.6
	Annual	52.4	78.2	3.6	4.9	2.1	4.7
Weir 2	June	0.2	5.3	6.0	4.2	0.0	0.3
	July	9.6	16.7	1.7	5.7	0.2	1.0
	Aug.	8.9	24.6	3.2	1.8	0.2	0.6
	Sep.	1.3	13.1	0.4	2.2	0.0	0.3
	Annual	20.1	59.6	2.4	3.7	0.4	2.3
Weir 3	June	0.3	3.6	15.5	13.9	0.0	0.6
	July	2.8	29.5	11.5	7.7	0.6	4.1
	Aug.	1.7	13.0	10.8	4.1	0.3	0.8
	Sep.	1.8	10.1	1.0	6.6	0.0	1.2
	Annual	6.6	56.2	10.7	7.2	0.9	6.7

3.4   Rill Measurement as Affected Soil Loss

Rill soil loss and rill density are higher in the early July 2016. The maximum measured rill soil loss was 30 t ha^{-1}. Rainfall intensity has a great role on rill erosion formation. Rills from 15 agricultural fields were filled by inter rill and sheet erosion after only two storm events in 2015 year because of low rainfall volume.

The soil loss rate and the rill density from 15 agricultural fields increase from June 27, 2016 to July 2, 2016 (Table 3). Rills were developed after a higher rainfall storm event and increased rill dimensions up to July 2. The main driving forces for an increase in length, depth and width of rill are head erosion, flow shear and collapse of channel wall, respectively. There was a gradual decrease after July first week until the end of August when rills were filled up by soil from sheet & inter-rill erosions. Therefore we will use the rate of soil loss in July first week as the volume of soil lost when there is maximum rill depth, width and length were recorded.

The cumulative soil loss rate from rills in the watershed is 11 t ha^{-1}. Field 5, 8 and 9 has values of zero soil loss for all days at time of observation (Table 3). Because those fields were sowed at the early rainy season. Upslope fields 1, 2, 11, 12 and 13 which had an average soil loss of 16 t ha^{-1} while the bottom fields such as 3, 6, 14 and 15 were 8.8 t ha^{-1}. This difference between upslope and downslope is not statistically significant at 1% significance level using F-test. The result is not in line with the findings of (Tilahun 2012; Zegeye 2009). This reason rises from Ene-chilala watershed is highly degraded as compared with other watershed. Fields such as 2, 3, 4 and 5 which are located on watershed 1 had an average cumulative soil loss of 10 t ha^{-1}, Fields 6, 7, 8, 9 and 10

Table 3. Soil loss rate from agricultural fields monitored in 2016

Field ID	Crop types	Field size	Cumulative soil loss (t ha^{-1})							
			27-Jun	2-Jul	15-Jul	24-Jul	1-Aug	9-Aug	16-Aug	24-Aug
1	Maize	0.124	0.0	8.4	8.2	5.4	3.9	3.6	4.4	2.8
2	Teff	0.353	3.4	25.1	0.0	4.8	13.8	4.7	7.2	2.9
3	Maize	0.24	0.0	5.0	3.1	0.0	0.0	0.0	0.0	0.0
4	Bean	0.144	0.0	10.8	17.4	11.4	0.5	0.0	14.4	0.0
5	Bean	0.144	0.0	0.0	0.0	0.0	0.0	0.0	0.0	0.0
6	Nut	0.08	0.0	9.3	8.1	3.8	3.8	2.1	4.1	2.5
7	Maize	0.328	5.1	17.3	7.2	9.1	4.2	1.9	2.2	2.0
8	Bean	0.169	0.0	0.0	0.0	0.0	0.0	0.0	0.0	0.0
9	Barely	0.124	0.0	0.0	0.0	0.0	0.0	0.0	0.0	0.0
10	Maize	0.161	1.8	21.8	15.1	9.3	4.8	0.0	0.0	0.0
11	Barely	0.327	3.0	2.5	3.2	5.9	1.8	1.3	0.0	0.0
12	Teff	0.137	0.0	30.7	0.0	0.0	0.0	0.0	0.0	0.0
13	Barely	0.189	0.5	14.6	12.1	7.4	1.2	0.6	0.6	0.0
14	Chick pea	0.24	0.0	0.0	0.0	0.0	2.0	1.1	2.2	0.0
15	Teff	0.282	5.7	21.0	23.7	0.0	0.0	0.0	0.0	0.0

which are located on watershed two had an average cumulative soil loss of 9 t ha^{-1} and fields 11, 12 and 13 which are located on watershed 3 had an average cumulative soil loss of 16 t ha^{-1} (Table 3). This difference between sub watersheds is not statistically significant at 1% significance level using F-test.

3.5 Sediment Concentration

The mean annual suspended sediment concentration for watershed one and watershed two during the rainy phase of 2015 was lower than that of 2016 rainy phase (Table 2). This is due to the lower amount of precipitation in 2015 compared to 2016. But the sediment concentration for watershed three is decreased in 2016 due to gully head treatment in 2015. When storm runoff amount increased the sediment concentration also increased. But it in some case suspended sediment concentration was decreased for high amount of runoff from three sub watersheds. Sediment concentration increased at the first rainy season and then gradually decreased particularly at cultivated dominant land use watershed (WS1). Watershed with gullies had higher sediment concentration at the end of rainy season (WS3). Because when water table raised gully was expanded. The main reason was the effect of land use, land cover, rainfall intensity and gully formation within Ene-chilala watershed. Lowering both the water table and protecting the gully heads decreased soil loss due to gully erosion (Addisie et al. 2016). The sediment concentration was greater in WS3 than WS1 and WS2 for both years due to shallow and deep active gullies. The differences were significant. In addition, the sediment concentration for watershed one in two years is greater than that of watershed two due to the contribution of upland rill erosion to WS1; the differences were not significant. Most sediment is generated from the bottom land; because the bottom lands for watershed three has gullies (the shrub and bush land at upper elevation and cultivated land were limited to gully formation in Ene-chilala watershed).

3.6 Sediment Yield

The annual sediment yield for the three watersheds during the rainy phase of 2015 was lower than that of 2016 rainy phase. This is due to the lower amount of precipitation in 2015 compared to 2016 (Table 2). Similarly to the suspended sediment concentration, the sediment yield was greater in watershed three than watershed one and watershed two in 2016 due to shallow and deep active gullies. These differences were not statistically significant. The sediment yield for watershed one is greater than watershed two for the two years. These differences were statistically significant. Because cultivated land dominated watershed contributes rill erosion to the total soil loss. Rill erosion on cultivated land at early rainy season and gully erosion in saturated grazing land at the bottoms were main sources of sediments in Ene-chilala watershed.

The soil loss from Donkorowoniz at bottom slope of watershed two and Lay Enset Bet Village gully on the remaining part of Ene-chilala watershed was 110 and 90 t ha^{-1} respectively (Ayele et al. 2016). The soil losses from gullies are five times or more higher than the average cumulative soil loss from rill erosion (upslope 16 t ha^{-1} and down slope 9 t ha^{-1}).

4   Conclusion

This study was conducted to examine the patterns of runoff, sediment concentration and sediment loads at Ene-chilala watershed. The results showed that upper shrub and bush, saturated grazing land at the bottom and upland rill erosion in the early rainy season were the source of the runoff and sediment. The sediment yield was statistically significant different between watershed one and watershed two. This indicates that the influence of land use was significant impact on runoff and sediment yield. Intensive investigations have been conducted to explain the development processes of rill erosion. In this study, runoff erosivity and soil erodibility have main impacts on rill erosion process.

Sediment yield were generally greater in the mainly grass watershed as compared with watershed with cultivated land and shrub & bush dominance land use. The sources of sediment were rills from agricultural fields and/or gullies from local saturated grazing areas. Gullies on grazing land are erosion hot spot areas in Ene-chilala watershed. Soil conservation practice should be given priority to saturated grazing lands with active shallow and deep gullies than agricultural lands for better soil conservation results in the area. After gully treatment, SWC practices should be done on agricultural fields.

Acknowledgement. The research was made possible through the CGIAR Research Program on Water, Land and Ecosystem's East Africa focal regional program.

References

Addisie, M.B., et al.: Gully head retreat in the sub-humid Ethiopian highlands: the ene-chilala catchment. Land Degrad. Dev. **28**(5), 1579–1588 (2016)

Adimassu, Z., Haile, N.: Runoff, soil loss and their relationships under different land uses in the central highlands of Ethiopia. Ethiop. J. Appl. Sci. Technology **2**, 39–49 (2011)

Ayele, G.K.: Physical and economic evaluation of participatory gully rehabilitation and soil erosion control in the (sub) humid Ethiopian highlands: birr river headwaters, Ethiopia (2016)

Bewket, W.: Land cover dynamics since the 1950s in Chemoga watershed, Blue Nile basin, Ethiopia. Mt. Res. Dev. **22**(3), 263–269 (2002)

Bewket, W., Sterk, G.: Assessment of soil erosion in cultivated fields using a survey methodology for rills in the Chemoga watershed, Ethiopia. Agr. Ecosyst. Environ. **97**(1), 81–93 (2003)

Bewket, W., Sterk, G.: Dynamics in land cover and its effect on stream flow in the Chemoga watershed, Blue Nile basin, Ethiopia. Hydrol. Process. **19**(2), 445–458 (2005)

Bewket, W., Teferi, E.: Assessment of soil erosion hazard and prioritization for treatment at the watershed level: case study in the Chemoga watershed, Blue Nile Basin. Ethiop. Land Degrad. Dev. **20**(6), 609–622 (2009)

Constable, M., Belshaw, D.: The Ethiopian highlands reclamation study: major findings and recommendations. In: Proceedings of the National Workshop on Food Strategies for Ethiopia ONCCP (Office of the National Committee for Central Planning) Towards a Food and Nutrition Strategy for Ethiopia, pp. 8–12 (1986)

Dagnew, D.C., et al.: Impact of land use and topography on catchment runoff and soil loss in the sub-humid Ethiopian highlands: the Debre Mawi watershed (2015)

García-Ruiz, J.M.: The effects of land uses on soil erosion in Spain: a review. Catena **81**(1), 1–11 (2010)

Girmay, G., Singh, B., Nyssen, J., Borrosen, T.: Runoff and sediment-associated nutrient losses under different land uses in Tigray, Northern Ethiopia. J. Hydrol. **376**(1), 70–80 (2009)

Hurni, H.: Soil erosion forms in the Simen mountains-Ethiopia (with map 1: 25 000). Geographica Bernensia G **8**, 93–100 (1978)

Hurni, H.: Soil erosion and soil formation in agricultural ecosystems: Ethiopia and Northern Thailand. Mt. Res. Dev., 131–142 (1983)

Hurni, H., Tato, K.: Erosion, conservation, and small-scale farming. Geographica Bernensia, c/o Group for Development and Environment (1992)

Hurni, H., Tato, K., Zeleke, G.: The implications of changes in population, land use, and land management for surface runoff in the upper Nile basin area of Ethiopia. Mt. Res. Dev. **25**(2), 147–154 (2005)

Kang, S., et al.: Runoff and sediment loss responses to rainfall and land use in two agricultural catchments on the Loess Plateau of China. Hydrol. Process. **15**(6), 977–988 (2001)

Kosmas, C., et al.: The effect of land use on runoff and soil erosion rates under Mediterranean conditions. Catena **29**(1), 45–59 (1997)

Mitiku, H., Herweg, K., Stillhardt, B.: Sustainable land management–a new approach to soil and water conservation in Ethiopia, Land Resource Management and Environmental Protection Department, Mekelle University, Mekelle, Ethiopia. Center for Development and Environment (CDE), University of Bern and Swiss National Center of Competence in Research (NCCR) North-South, Bern, Switzerland (2006)

Ndulue, E., Mbajiorgu, C., Ugwu, S., Ogwo, V., Ogbu, K.: Assessment of land use/cover impacts on runoff and sediment yield using hydrologic models: a review. J. Ecol. Nat. Environ. **7**(2), 46–55 (2015)

Pimentel, D., et al.: Soil erosion and agricultural productivity. In: World Soil Erosion and Conservation, pp. 277–292 (1993)

Pimentel, D., et al.: Environmental and economic costs of soil erosion and conservation benefits. Science-AAAS-Weekly Paper Edition **267**(5201), 1117–1122 (1995)

Sertsu, S.: Degraded soils of Ethiopia and their management. In: Proceedings of the FAO/ISCW Expert Consultation on Management of Degraded Soils in Southern and East Africa 2nd Network Meeting, pp. 18–22 (2000)

Steenhuis, T.S., et al.: Predicting discharge and sediment for the Abay (Blue Nile) with a simple model. Hydrol. Process. **23**(26), 3728–3737 (2009)

Sun, L., Fang, H., Qi, D., Li, J., Cai, Q.: A review on rill erosion process and its influencing factors. Chin. Geogr. Sci. **23**(4), 389–402 (2013)

Symeonakis, E., Koukoulas, S., Calvo-Cases, A., Arnau-Rosalen, E., Makris, I.: A landuse change and land degradation study in Spain and Greece using remote sensing and GIS. In: Proceedings of XXth ISPRS Congress, Istanbul, Turkey, 15 January 2006. Citeseer (2004). http://www.isprs.org/istanbul2004/comm7/papers/110.pdf

Tamene, L., Vlek, P.L.: Soil erosion studies in northern Ethiopia. In: Braimoh, A.K., Vlek, P.L.G. (eds.) Land Use and Soil Resources, pp. 73–100. Springer, Dordrecht (2008). https://doi.org/10.1007/978-1-4020-6778-5_5

Taye, G., Poesen, J., et al.: Effects of land use, slope gradient, and soil and water conservation structures on runoff and soil loss in semi-arid Northern Ethiopia. Phys. Geogr. **34**(3), 236–259 (2013)

Tekle, K., Hedlund, L.: Land cover changes between 1958 and 1986 in Kalu District, Southern Wello, Ethiopia. Mt. Res. Dev. **20**(1), 42–51 (2000)

Thornes, J.B.: The interaction of erosional and vegetational dynamics in land degradation: spatial outcomes. In: Vegetation and Erosion Processes and Environments, pp. 41–53 (1990)

Tilahun, S.A.: Observations and modeling of erosion from spatially and temporally distributed sources in the (semi) humid Ethiopian highlands. Citeseer (2012)

Vanmaercke, M., Zenebe, A., Poesen, J., Nyssen, J., Verstraeten, G., Deckers, J.: Sediment dynamics and the role of flash floods in sediment export from medium-sized catchments: a case study from the semi-arid tropical highlands in Northern Ethiopia. J. Soils Sediments **10**(4), 611–627 (2010)

Zegeye, A.D.: Assessment of Upland Erosion Processes and Farmer's Perception of Land Conservation in Debre-Mewi Watershed, Near Lake Tana. Cornell University, Ethiopia (2009)

Zeleke, G., Hurni, H.: Implications of land use and land cover dynamics for mountain resource degradation in the Northwestern Ethiopian highlands. Mt. Res. Dev. **21**(2), 184–191 (2001)

Urban Growth and Land Use Simulation Using SLEUTH Model for Adama City, Ethiopia

Yanit Mekonnen[1]([✉]) and S. K. Ghosh[2]

[1] Department of Architecture, Dilla University, SNNPR, Dilla, Ethiopia
tinayeth@gmail.com
[2] Department of Civil Engineering, Indian Institute of Technology Roorkee, Roorkee, Uttarakhand, India

Abstract. Urban Growth Model has been adapted to study the urban growth and its impact on the surrounding environment. Here a cellular automaton model known as SLEUTH has been standardize using multi historical digital maps of areas to forecast the future coverage of an urban and land use. The model will use the best fit growth rule parameters by narrowing coefficients throughout calibration mode and passed down to predict future urban growth pattern, generate various probability map and LULC map. As per SLEUTH modelling, the generated future urban growth pattern prediction of Adama city shows that nearly 42.89% urban rise in 2020, 46.85% in 2030, 49.15% in 2040 and 50.49% in 2050. Generally, the expansion of the urban growth pattern is exhibiting new spreading centre which are indication of a city to expand also the result present useful information for future urban planning and improvement.

Keywords: Urban growth · GIS and remote sensing · SLEUTH

1 Introduction

Modelling urban growth is a significant information for analysis and evaluation towards the sustainable improvement of a city. The ecological effects and degree of urban issues have been developing and producing solid imbalance between the city and its environment. The need to address this intricacy in evaluating and checking the urban arranging and the executive's procedures and practices is unequivocally felt in the recent years (Lavalle 2002).

The international contributors are progressively connected with the critical ecological errands for the feasible improvement of their urban areas, the planning difficulties looked by the nearby authorities, and the significance of remote sensing data and GIS techniques in the investigation of urban growth to address these difficulties. Deciding the rate of urban spatial arrangement and urban growth, from remote sensing data, is a pervasive approach in contemporary urban geographic studies. Characterized urban structure, map of growth from remotely sensed data can help planners to visualize the directions of the urban, basic frameworks, functions, and structures (Bhatta et al. 2010). However, despite the fast improvement of remote sensing technologies, there is no end phases of intriguing

© ICST Institute for Computer Sciences, Social Informatics and Telecommunications Engineering 2020
Published by Springer Nature Switzerland AG 2020. All Rights Reserved
N. G. Habtu et al. (Eds.): ICAST 2019, LNICST 308, pp. 279–293, 2020.
https://doi.org/10.1007/978-3-030-43690-2_19

logical inquiries to be posed about urban areas and their growth, however at times these inquiries don't coordinate the operational exertion and uneasiness of a given city. This requires increasingly engaged research and discussion in the territories of urban growth analysis, in perspective on their applications (Bhatta 2012).

The study aims to predict future urbanization, by compiling remote sensing, GIS, and SLEUTH model with cygwin as a tool with the intention that the urban growth and the land transformations.

2 Study Area

Adama (see Fig. 1) is a central city in Oromiya regional state and a major city of Ethiopia. It is about 98 km away from Addis Ababa in the southeast direction. Its approximate location is 8°33′35′ N–8°36′46′ N latitude and 39°11′57′ E–39°21′15′ E longitude in a UTM/WGS84, zone 37 N projected coordinate system. The city has an average altitude of 1,712 m (5,617 ft) above mean sea level (a.m.s.l.).

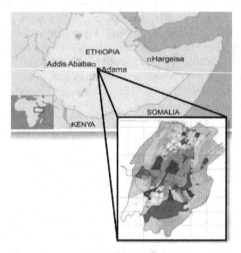

Fig. 1. Study area.

3 The SLEUTH Model

Sleuth is a cellular automata (ca) based model that recreates urban growth and land use changes through time. The model has been applied to various urban areas and in many regions of the world (Chaudhuri et al. 2013; Clarke 2008; Clarke and Gaydos 1998; Clarke et al. 2007; Clarke et al. 1997). The name sleuth originates from GIS input data images that are incorporated into model: slope, land use, exclusion layer (where development can't happen), urban, transportation, and hill shade (Gazulis and Clarke 2006).

SLEUTH is a firmly coupled model including two modules, the Urban Growth Model (UGM) and the DELTATRON Land Cover (LCD) Model. The UGM is a C program running under UNIX that uses the standard GNU C Compiler (GCC) and might be executed in parallel. The LCD model is incorporated inside the code and will be called and driven by the UGM. The LCD is firmly tied with an urban rule, while UGM can run autonomously. Together, these joined models are called to as SLEUTH.

In the structure of the SLEUTH model as appeared in Fig. 2, the urban territory inside this CA model work as a living organism trained by a limited arrangement of transition rules that impact the state changes inside the two modules in a set of nested loops. During model adjustment, the outer control loops executes Monte Carlo iterations on chronicled maps and scans for the parameters that best repeat the changes between input data of the first year (the seed layer) and the last year, holding aggregate factual data. The second or the internal loop executes the growth rules to imitate the growth and advances between the individual input time frames (Clarke and Gaydos 1998; Sietchiping 2004; Gazulis and Clarke 2006; Dietzel and Clarke 2007).

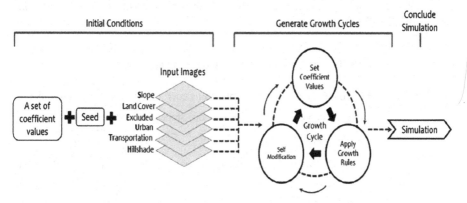

Fig. 2. Structure of the SLEUTH model (Chaudhuri and Clarke 2013).

SLEUTH modelling start by calibrate the historical input data to derive a set of five control parameter coefficients (dispersion coefficient, breed coefficient, spread coefficient, road gravity, and slope resistance) which control the behaviour of the system and encapsulate the past urbanization trends of that region. The impact of these coefficient values determines the degree to which each of the four growth rules influences urban growth in the system (Clarke et al. 1997; Gazulis and Clarke 2006).

The most generally utilized calibration procedure is known as brute force calibration, and during this mode of the modelling, a set of control parameters are refined by three consecutive calibration stages: coarse, fine and final calibrations (Silva and Clarke 2002; Dietzel and Clarke 2007).

The Optimal SLEUTH Metric (OSM) (Dietzel and Clarke 2007) is utilized to determine the best fit (level of closeness between simulated images and control years) and to give the most robust outcomes to SLEUTH calibration (Clarke 2008). The ideal arrangement of parameters dependent on the OSM produces a yield map that most intently looks like the control data (Dietzel and Clarke 2007; Clarke 2008) and is utilized in the subsequent stage of calibration. The mix of parameters with the most noteworthy OSM value in the final calibration stage is then utilized for prediction, after adjustment to reflect their values at the end of the calibration period rather than the start. At long last, the accuracy of the anticipated maps is estimated outside the model utilizing distinctive map correlation techniques and an observed map of the anticipated year (if accessible).

The model simulation is comprised of a progression of growth cycles and four sorts of growth can occur in the model: Spontaneous, Diffusive, Organic, and Road influenced growth of the non-urbanized cells (Clarke and Gaydos 1998). Aside from the initial growth rules there is a second degree of rules, which controls the conduct of the large-scale framework called the 'self-modification' rules. These rules react to the total growth rate, they begin to increment or abatement the growth control parameters in every one of the accompanying growth cycles (Sietchiping 2004). Self-modification is imperative to keep away from straight or exponential growth of the zone in the model (Silva and Clarke 2002). Table 1 shows the relation between every growth rule with growth coefficients that control the growth rules.

Table 1. Type of growth rules and controlling coefficients.

Growth cycle order	Growth rules	Controlling coefficients	Summary descriptions
1	Spontaneous	Dispersion, Slope	Simulates random urbanization of new growth cells
2	New Spreading Center	Breed, slope	Simulates development of new urban growth cells
3	Edge	Spread, slope	Branched growth from existing urban centers
4	Road-Influenced	Road-Gravity, Dispersion, Breed, slope	Simulates development pattern along transportation network
Throughout	Slope Resistance	Slope	Slope effect on urbanization
Throughout	Excluded Layer	User-Defined	Excluded development areas specified by users

3.1 Input Data

For measurable calibration of SLEUTH model, six different input layers are required. From Table 2, input data shows that the topographic data (slope and hill shade) got from Aster digital elevation model; two land use layers of the year 1984 and 2014 utilized for anticipating area use in the deltatron land use model; regions over 25% slope fined as undevelopable in the excluded layer; four urban layers (arranged from Landsat 5 TM (1984 and 1994), Landsat 7 ETM+ (2004 and 2014); and four weighted street system maps utilized from various timeframes (Chaudhuri and Clarke 2013). All information must be in grey scale.gif image files with a steady number of lines and segments.

A supervised classification was performed on the images for land use grouping. The study area has been sorted into five distinctive LULC classes, in particular, urban, agriculture, shrub and bushes, barren area and hilly area. The target of supervised classification is to arrange each image pixel into one of a few pre-characterized land type classes (Harris 1965). For the urban layer, the developed regions was considered as urban and the rest of the region was classified as non-urban and the street layers were made from 1984 to 2014 topographic maps.

Table 2. Detail of input data sets for SLEUTH modelling.

Input data	Input data type	Format & input data years
Slope layer	DEM	Raster (in percent) (1)
Land cover layer	Landsat TM, ETM	Raster, 1984 & 2014 (2)
Exclusion layer	Landsat TM	Rasterized from vector (1)
Urbanization layer	Landsat MSS, TM, ETM	Raster, 1984, 1994, 2004, 2014 (4)
Transportation layer	Shapefiles	Rasterized from vector, 1984, 1994, 2004, 2014 (4)
Hill shade layer	DEM	Raster (1)

4 Methodology

The flow chart of the proposed technique embraced in SLEUTH modelling for simulation of urban growth and land use appeared in Fig. 3. In the first place, readiness of input data is carried out i.e. preparation of slope map, land use map, exclusion map, urban map, transportation map and hill shade map. Since SLEUTH has the ability to consider different factors and limitations responsible for urban growth, urban growth has been determined utilizing best in class SLEUTH model. Further, examination utilizing SLEUTH has three consecutive steps, which are Calibration mode and Prediction mode utilizing various spatial lattices. The input data were adjusted utilizing data up to 2014 and anticipated from 2020 to 2050. After thorough calibration of the SLEUTH model, the best-fit parameter esteems were utilized to run predictions from 2014 to 2050 (Chaudhuri and Clarke 2013).

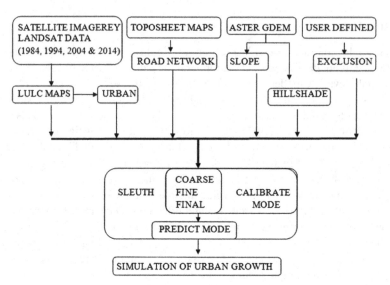

Fig. 3. Flowchart of methodology adapted for SLEUTH.

5   Result Analysis

5.1   Input Data Preparation

Two types of datasets have been prepared. One category belongs to GIS obtained dataset using satellite imagery including ASTER DEM and the other one is prepared using topo sheet map. From satellite imagery different types of maps have been prepared one is LULC map, urban map, slope map, exclusion map and hill shade map. Using topo sheet transportation map have been prepared. (See Fig. 4). Shows different input map in a different years.

5.2   Model Calibration

Calibration is the most mind-boggling mode in SLEUTH. Every blend of coefficient set is created by START, STOP and STEP values so as to introduce a run (R). Each run will be executed by MONTE CARLO ITERATIONS number of times. Generally, calibration is practiced in three stages: coarse, fine and final, which is reflected in the best scope of model's coefficients.

In Table 3, the result of model calibration coefficient are appeared. In the coarse stage, the underlying parameter go for all growth coefficient is 0–100 which is the incentive for start and stop respectively. Consequently, in the fine stage, coefficients' diminished to the estimations of 0–20, 50–100, 25–75, 0–25 and 0–100, representing the dispersion, breed, spread, slope resistance and road gravity coefficients, respectively. The following stage, final calibration, utilized the yield of fine alignment growth coefficient as input coefficient and gave the diminished estimations of 0–20, 50–100, 25–65, 0–20 and 0–100 indicated to the model parameters' values respectively. This values prompts final

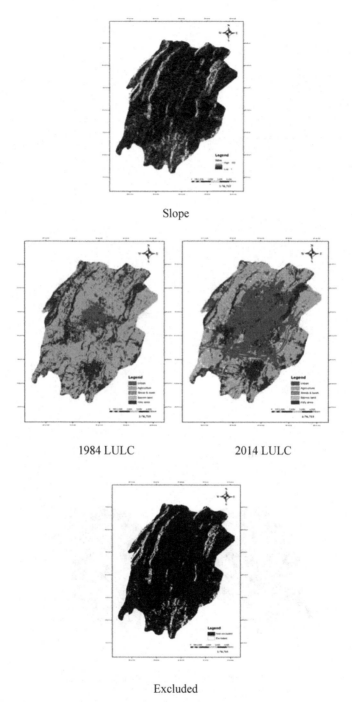

Slope

1984 LULC   2014 LULC

Excluded

Fig. 4. Input layer (Color figure online).

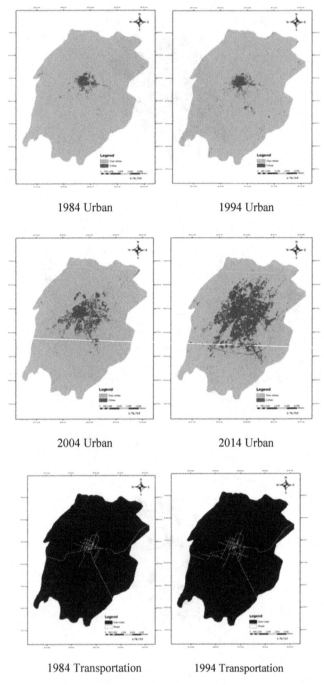

1984 Urban   1994 Urban

2004 Urban   2014 Urban

1984 Transportation   1994 Transportation

Fig. 4. (*continued*)

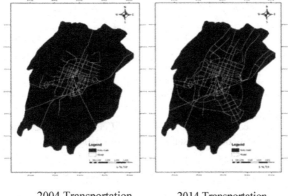

2004 Transportation   2014 Transportation

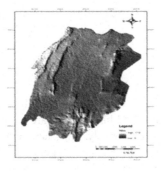

Hill shade

Fig. 4. (*continued*)

mode coefficient values of predict mode. The predict mode gave the estimation of 1, 67, 55, 2 and 26 respectively for the SLEUTH model forecasting.

5.3 Prediction

Models are frequently made a decision by their prescient power (Silva and Clarke 2002). As appeared in Table 3, coefficient of expectation has a high estimation of 67. The high breed parameter indicated that Adama city significant growth is new spreading from centers. The spread coefficient has a moderately high estimation of 55, that edge growth is another significant growth type. In this city, the estimation of slope coefficient of 2 shows that the topography has low dynamic for urban growth. Consistent low diffusion coefficient estimation of 1 shows that no irregular urbanization of land, that occurred close to the current urban regions and new urban focuses. The relatively even road gravity coefficient estimation of 26 shows that the street systems has influence the urban growth.

The predicted urban growth map of simulated years' and the probabilities of urbanization for years' of 2020, 2030, 2040 and 2050 has shown in different colors in Figs. 5 and 6. Red shaded are areas that has 81–100% certainty of growth. Most conservatively,

Table 3. Summary of growth coefficient values during each process.

Mode	Coarse		Fine		Final		Prediction mode
Pixel dimension	(1732 * 2204)		(866 * 1102)		(433 * 551)		(433 * 551)
Growth parameter	MC iteration = 4		MC iteration = 7		MC iteration = 9		MC iteration = 100
	Lee sallee statistic = 0.23		Lee sallee statistic = 0.23		Lee sallee statistic = 0.29		Lee sallee statistic = 0.3
	Range	Step	Range	Step	Range	Step	Best fit value
Dispersion	0–100	25	0–20	5	0–20	4	1
Breed	0–100	25	50–100	10	50–100	10	67
Spread	0–100	25	25–75	10	25–65	8	55
Slope	0–100	25	0–20	5	0–20	4	2
Road gravity	0–100	25	0–100	25	0–100	25	26

this area most likely growth zones which include infilling of existing settlement, and outward expansion. Pink, yellow and blue shaded are areas with a range of 61–80%, 41–60%, and 21–40% certainty respectively. This class of prediction has an even chance of growth probabilities. Finally, a projection category of 1–20% certainty is shown in light green. In this zone, the combination of the extent of the city and new urban centers are included. When a new spreading center forms in repeated model run, it could be identified as a 'city waiting to happen', a site so potentially ripe for growth that it is merely a matter of time before urbanization arrives (Clarke and Gaydos 1998).

Land use change studies usually compare the landscape at two points in time and model the transition quantities and proportions of change both across the landscape and among land use and cover classes (Lambin and Geist 2008). Due to involvement of remote sensing, GIS and SLEUTH modeling it is also possible to simulate LULC map as shown in Fig. 7 and also possible to calculate the area and percentage of each LULC distribution as shown in Table 5. Table 4 shows the percentage of annual transition probabilities for simulated years and probability of urban change from different land use classes are;

1. About 23.75% area of agriculture cover has probability of conversion into urban;
2. About 12.45% area of Shrub and bushes cover has probability of conversion into urban;
3. About 6.08% area of Barren area cover has probability of conversion into urban;
4. About 18.59% area of hilly area cover has probability of conversion into urban.

(a) 2020

(b) 2030

(c) 2040

(d) 2050

Fig. 5. SLEUTH model prediction for Adama city in different years (Color figure online).

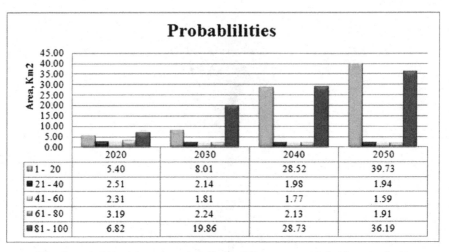

Fig. 6. Probability of number of pixels for different years (Color figure online).

Table 4. Logging annual transition probabilities in percent.

Class name	Urban	Agriculture	Shrub and bushes	Barren area	Hilly area
Urban	82.13	5.17	5.55	0.21	6.93
Agriculture	23.75	58.50	3.73	4.78	9.25
Shrub and bushes	12.45	23.52	38.35	1.05	24.64
Barren area	6.08	62.05	8.11	14.86	8.90
Hilly area	18.59	38.78	8.86	3.53	30.24

Table 5. Area of different LULC categories

Class name	Area, km^2							
	2020	%	2030	%	2040	%	2050	%
Urban	57.67	42.89	63.00	46.85	66.09	49.15	67.9	50.49
Agriculture	47.41	35.26	41.68	31.0	38.48	28.62	36.67	27.27
Shrub and bushes	9.18	6.83	10.25	7.62	10.68	7.94	10.88	8.09
Barren area	4.17	3.10	3.67	2.73	3.34	2.48	3.15	2.34
Hilly area	16.03	11.92	15.86	11.8	15.87	11.80	15.87	11.80
Total	134.46		134.46		134.46		134.46	

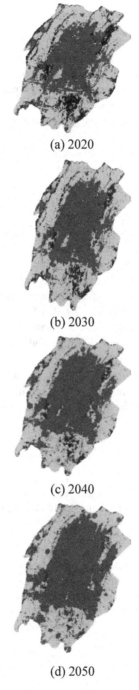

(a) 2020

(b) 2030

(c) 2040

(d) 2050

Fig. 7. Simulated LULC in Adama city of different years (Color figure online).

6 Conclusion

This study intended to consolidate simulation of urban growth and LULC of Adama city utilizing SLEUTH model. SLEUTH model simulated Adama city urban growth of the year 2020, 2030, 2040 and 2050. Simulation of urban expansion, land use land cover change detection, zoning policies change, town planning and land use planning, growth-control strategies, waste disposal management, road network modelling, utility line supply i.e. electricity, water supply, sewerage disposal and so on.

1. The analysis of thirty years' of Landsat satellite imagery illustrate that urban area has been drastically increased through- out the years. From SLEUTH model analysis, the calibrate mode is quite complex and require careful adjustment. A possible combination of coefficients is seriously explored through each combination step that lead to best fit of the model coefficients. Prediction mode of SLEUTH model shows that about 81–100% probability of other class being converted into urban area. About 6.82 km^2 area has been converted into urban in 2020, about 19.86 km^2 area has been converted in urban in 2030, about 28.73 km^2 area has been converted in urban in 2040 and about 36.19 km^2 area has been converted in urban in 2040.
2. It is further predicted that in the future 36 years' from 2014, there will be nearly 42.89% urban rise in 2020, 46.85% in 2030, 49.15% in 2040 and 50.49% in 2050. The annual transition probability of LULC shows that the major likelihood of urban area growth will be 23.75% from agriculture land, 12.45% shrub and bushes, 6.08% from barren land and 18.59% from hill shade.
3. Generally, the repeated model run for future urbanization patterns are exhibiting new spreading center i.e. outward expansion and infilling of existing settlement, are indication of a city to expand in spontaneous growth manner.

References

Bhatta, B.: Urban Growth Analysis and Remote Sensing: A Case Study of Kolkata, India 1980–2010. Springer, Dordrecht (2012). https://doi.org/10.1007/978-94-007-4698-5

Bhatta, B., Saraswati, S., Bandyopadhyay, D.: Quantifying the degree-of-freedom, degree-of-sprawl, and degree-of-goodness of urban growth from remote sensing data. Appl. Geogr. **30**(1), 96–111 (2010)

Chaudhuri, G., Clarke, K.C.: How does land use policy modify urban growth? A case study of the Italo-Slovenian border. J. Land Use Sci. **8**(4), 443–465 (2013)

Clarke, K.C.: Mapping and modelling land use change: an application of the SLEUTH model. In: Pettit, C., Cartwright, W., Bishop, I., Lowell, K., Pullar, D., Duncan, D. (eds.) Landscape Analysis and Visualization, pp. 353–366. Springer, Heidelberg (2008). https://doi.org/10.1007/978-3-540-69168-6_17

Clarke, K.C., Gaydos, L.J.: Loose-coupling a cellular automaton model and GIS: long-term urban growth prediction for San Francisco and Washington/Baltimore. Int. J. Geogr. Inf. Sci. **12**(7), 699–714 (1998)

Clarke, K.C., Gazulis, N., Dietzel, C., Goldstein, N.C.: A decade of SLEUTH modeling: lessons learned from applications of a cellular automaton land use change model. Classics IJGIS Twenty Years Int. J. Geogr. Inf. Sci. Syst., 413–427 (2007)

Clarke, K.C., Hoppen, S., Gaydos, L.: A self-modifying cellular automaton model of historical urbanization in the San Francisco Bay area. Environ. Plann. B Plann. Des. **24**(2), 247–261 (1997)

Dietzel, C., Clarke, K.C.: Toward optimal calibration of the SLEUTH land use change model. Trans. GIS **11**(1), 29–45 (2007)

Gazulis, N., Clarke, K.C.: Exploring the DNA of our regions: classification of outputs from the SLEUTH model. In: El Yacoubi, S., Chopard, B., Bandini, S. (eds.) ACRI 2006. LNCS, vol. 4173, pp. 462–471. Springer, Heidelberg (2006). https://doi.org/10.1007/11861201_54

Harris, B.: New tools for planning. J. Am. Inst. Planners **31**(2), 90–95 (1965)

Lambin, E.F., Geist, H.J. (eds.): Land-Use and Land-Cover Change: Local Processes and Global Impacts. Springer, Heidelberg (2008). https://doi.org/10.1007/3-540-32202-7

Lavalle, C.: Towards an Urban Atlas: Assessment of Spatial Data on 25 European Cities and Urban Areas, vol. 30. European Environment Agency, Copenhagen (2002)

Sietchiping, R.: A geographic information systems and cellular automata-based model of informal settlement growth (Doctoral dissertation) (2004)

Silva, E.A., Clarke, K.C.: Calibration of the SLEUTH urban growth model for Lisbon and Porto, Portugal. Comput. Environ. Urban Syst. **26**(6), 525–552 (2002)

Integration of SWAT and Remote Sensing Techniques to Simulate Soil Moisture in Data Scarce Micro-watersheds: A Case of Awramba Micro-watershed in the Upper Blue Nile Basin, Ethiopia

Berhanu G. Sinshaw[1]([✉]), Mamaru A. Moges[2], Seifu A. Tilahun[2], Zoi Dokou[3],
Semu Moges[3], Emmanouil Anagnostou[3], Daniel G. Eshete[1], Agumase T. Kindie[1],
Engudye Bekele[2], Muludel Asese[2], and Wondale A. Getie[2]

[1] Department of Hydraulic and Water Resource Engineering, IOT, University of Gondar,
P.O. Box 196, Gondar, Ethiopia
berhanugeremew0@gmail.com
[2] Faculty of Civil and Water Resource Engineering, BiT,
Bahir Dar University, 26, Bahir Dar, Ethiopia
[3] Department of Civil and Environmental Engineering, University of Connecticut,
261, Glen-Brook Road, Storrs, CT 06269, USA

Abstract. Understanding soil moisture at a small scale is beneficial for predicting productivity and management of both rained and irrigated agriculture in mostly smallholder communities. This study aims to accurately represent micro-watershed scale soil moisture using the optimization capability of SWAT (SUFI2) model and soil information derived from Sentinel 2 A level 1 C satellite images with OPtical TRApezoid Model (OPTRAM) and MNDWI. The study was carried in the 700 ha Awramba watershed in the Upper Blue Nile, Ethiopia. Calibration and validation of SWAT were performed using in-situ stream flow data to enable the accurate simulation of water balance components such as soil moisture. The spectral water index was evaluated using MNDWI from the green band (560 nm) and short wave infrared band (2190 nm). The Results were evaluated based on the runoff response n and soil moisture fit to measured values. The runoff fit against the measured data using Nash Sutcliffe Efficiency (NSE) and R^2 criteria is 0.7 is and 0.75, respectively. The simulated daily soil moisture against the in-situ constant soil moisture provided NSE $= 0.51$, $R^2 = 0.77$, RMSE $= 0.19$ and PBIAS $= -0.242$. The simulation results indicate that validation of SWAT, OPTRA M and MNDWI models with in situ soil moisture data leads to acceptable accuracy with 0.0027 cm^3 cm^{-3}, 0.0022 cm^3 cm^{-3} and 0.034 cm^3 cm^{-3} standard errors, respectively. Furthermore, Sentinel 2A imagery is found to have a higher potential to simulate soil moisture compared to TDR data. The overall study indicates satellite-based soil moisture provides an encouraging pathway to setting up soil moisture-based prediction for smallholder agriculture in Ethiopia.

Keywords: Sentinel -2 · OPTRAM · SWAT · TDR · Gravimetric method · Soil moisture

© ICST Institute for Computer Sciences, Social Informatics and Telecommunications Engineering 2020
Published by Springer Nature Switzerland AG 2020. All Rights Reserved
N. G. Habtu et al. (Eds.): ICAST 2019, LNICST 308, pp. 294–314, 2020.
https://doi.org/10.1007/978-3-030-43690-2_20

1 Introduction

1.1 Background

Globally, 65% of water received as precipitation returns to the atmosphere as green water flow and the rest remain in the soil and flow as a runoff. The green water storage (soil moisture) is the amount of water in the soil profile at the end of a period [1]. Surface soil moisture controls the partition of rainfall into runoff, infiltration and other hydrological variables. Soil moisture directly influences the rate of evaporation, groundwater recharge and runoff generation and has an essential influence on climate [2]. Soil moisture can be estimated using in situ networks, hydrological models and remote sensing technique. However, an integrated approach can overcome the drawbacks of every single method and produce more big data [3]. Traditional in situ measurements provide valuable information at different soil depths. Many field techniques are available including; gravimetric, tension measuring, neutron probe, Time Domain Reflectometry (TDR) and capacitance measurements [4]. Hydrological SWAT model can estimate soil moisture in HRU/sub-basin/level up to vertical root depth (60 cm) of plants. For the data-scarce region, the model effectively calibrated and validated using stream flow data for the proper partition of hydrological water balance components [5].

Remote sensing technique enables to monitor soil moisture over a large area. The recently launched Sentinel two satellite has the potential to improve soil moisture product up to a resolution of 10 m. Soil moisture content is a critical hydrological and climatic variable in various application domains but the retrieval from local direct measurements of distributed, quantitative and accurate information relative to the moisture level of soils on a global scale is almost impracticable, due to the high spatial variability of the target variable, time, and expensive nature of devices. Sustainable agriculture and water resource management need accurate information on surface soil moisture. Low soil moisture for sustained periods results in drought and plant water deficit and potentially leading to wild Fire [6].

Conversely, high soil moisture leads to increased risk of flood. Also, the evaporation rate is strongly correlated to soil moisture that makes a secure connection between the land surface and atmosphere [7]. Continuous observation of soil moisture is difficult in a large area, but we can monitor effectively and conveniently by using remote sensing technology. Despite the importance of soil moisture, in situ measurement is very difficult and requires resources, both labour and finance. The only limited area can be controlled by in situ point observation, which cannot be representative for the broader region. Nowadays, direct views of soil moisture were restricted to discrete measurements at a specific location, and such point-based measures do not represent the spatial distribution, because soil moisture is highly variable both in spatially and temporal scale. The depth at which soil moisture is sensed by satellites depends on the sensor frequency but usually does not exceed 30 cm in order to access root zone soil moisture hydrological model is needed and several approaches have been developed such as techniques based on the energy balance approach based on thermal infrared soil moisture or simplified water balanced approaches [8]. Passive remote sensing instruments can be used to determine the surface soil moisture with a temporal resolution of different days. The European Space Agency (ESA) Soil Moisture and Ocean Salinity (SMOS) mission [9] and the National Aeronautics and Space Administration (NASA) Soil Moisture Active and Passive (SMAP) mission have a low spatial resolution around 25 km. According to [10] the current Sentinel-2 purpose, active onboard C-band sensor offers regular temporal coverage (about five days for both A and B satellites) together with a spatial resolution of 10 m from the optical image.

1.2 Objective

1.2.1 General Objective

- The main aim of the study is to simulate soil moisture using SWAT and Remote Sensing Techniques in Data Scarce Micro-Watersheds.

1.2.2 Specific Objective

- To simulate spatial and temporal soil moisture content using SWAT hydrological model at sub-basin level
- To generate a time series satellite image-based soil moisture index from Sentinel 2 A images
- To evaluate satellite-based water index from Sentinel 2 A picture with in situ soil moisture data.

2   Materials and Methods

2.1 Description of the Study Area

The study was carried out in upper Blue Nile, Ethiopia, in small watershed called Awramba. Geographically located between 11.886° N–11.9253° N and 37.781° E–37.806° E having elevation difference between 1887 m and 2305 m above sea level. It located in the south-east of part Lake Tana, 75 km North West of Bahir Dar city. Awramba watershed covers an area of 700 ha that receive 1497 mm rainfall depth and 21 °C average temperature (Fig. 1).

Soil type: In Awramba, the type of soil is volcanic in origin range from mainly clay texture throughout the mid and down slope positions (near the outlet) and clay to sandy clay soils on the top slopes [22]. More than 99% of the watershed based on the classification of the Food and Agriculture Organization (FAO) consists of Haplic Luvisols.

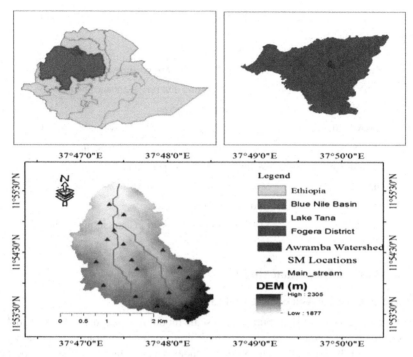

Fig. 1. Location map of Awramba watershed

2.2 Materials

The materials used for this study were presented in (Tables 1 and 2).

Table 1. Different data sources used for this study

No	Type data	Source	Purpose
1	STRM DEM	https://earthexplorer.usgs.gov/	Delineation and slope map
2	Soil	MoWRIE	Soil map
3	Sentinel 2 image	(https://scihub.copernicus.eu/dhus/ # /home)	OPTRAM, MNDWI and LULC map
4	Weather data	Metrological stations	Input for the SWAT model

Soil Moisture: In-situ soil moisture measurements were collected seven-day basis over 2017/2018 at 18 representative locations in the Awramba watershed. In-situ soil moisture observations collected for SWAT model and satellite soil moisture product validation purpose. In each site, the measurement was carried out at 10 cm depth using TDR. The assembled TDR probe soil moisture products calibrated with commonly used gravimetric soil moisture content.

Table 2. Different decision support tools used for this study and their purposes

No	Software name	Purpose
1	Arc GIS 10.1	Preparation of daily soil moisture maps
2	ENVI 5.1	Lee sigma filtering and image enhancement
3	EndNote X6	Citation and references
4	SNAP 6.0	Sentinel 2 image-processing, NDVI and MNDWI
5	Arc SWAT 2012	Act as a GIS interface for SWAT modeling
6	WAGEN.excel macro	Weather generator preparation
7	dew02.exe	Monthly dew point computation
8	XLSTAT	Hydrological data quality
9	SWAT CUP 2012	SWAT calibration, validation and sensitivity analysis

2.3 Soil Moisture Estimation Models

2.3.1 Soil and Water Assessment Tool (SWAT)

It is a physical based semi-distributed basin scale model that uses different data such as DEM, soil, land use, and climatic data for hydrological and climatological modeling on the daily or monthly bases [11]. The model includes weather, hydrology, soil properties, and plant growth, nutrients, and land management practices. The first stage of-of modeling involves watershed delineation. The delineated watershed further subdivided into hydrologic response units (HRU), which is a unique combination of land use management, soil, and slope. Each HRU in the model behaves differently for precipitation and temperature input [12].

The conversion of sub-basin to the single basin made by changing the threshold limit in the model. After simulating SWAT output, soil moisture ($m^3\ m^{-3}$) determined by using Eq. 1.1

$$\Delta SMC = \sum_{i=1}^{t} (Rday - Qsurf - Ea - Wseep - Qgw) \tag{1.1}$$

Where; SW_T is the final soil water content (mm), Rday is the simulation time (days), R_{ay} is the amount of daily precipitation (mm), Qsurf is the amount of daily surface runoff (mm), Ea is the amount of daily evapotranspiration (mm), Wseep is the amount of water entering into the vadose zone from the soil profile on a given day (mm), and Qgw is the amount of return flow on a given day (mm).

2.3.2 SWAT Model Calibration and Validation

An automatic SWAT- CUP computer program was implemented for calibration and validation of the SWAT model. This program links GLUE, Parasol, SUFI 2, and MCMC and PSO procedures to SWAT. It enables sensitivity analysis, calibration and validation of SWAT model parameters. This method uses a Bayesian framework to determine the uncertainties with a sequential uncertainty fitting process in which iteration and unknown parameter estimates were achieved before final forecast. It considers difficulties of model input, structure, parameters and observed data. Global Sensitivity analysis method (using t-Stat and p-Value to assess sensitivity) during the calibration process was to avoid the equifinality phenomenon.

2.4   Sentinel Image Soil Moisture Estimation

Sentinel-2 is a European wide-swath, high-resolution, multi-spectral imaging mission. The full mission specification of the twin satellites flying in the same orbit but phased at 180°, is designed to give a high revisit frequency of 5 days at the equator. Sentinel-2 carries an optical instrument payload that has 13 spectral bands: four bands at 10 m, six bands at 20 m and three bands at 60 m spatial resolution. The novel optical trapezoid model is a physical based model designed to estimate soil moisture content from a visual image by replacing Land surface temperature from a thermal band with a measure for soil moisture in the optical domain develop OPTRM from flux radiative transfer model formulate a physical model that exhibits a linear relationship between surface soil moisture content and SWIR transformed reflectance using Eq. 1.2 [13, 14]

$$SMI = \frac{\theta - \theta d}{\theta w - \theta d} = \frac{STR - STRd}{STRw + STRd} \tag{1.2}$$

Where STR is the SWIR transformed reflectance, STR_d and STR_w are STR at θd and θw respectively. The STR is related to SWIR reflectance, RSWIR, computed using Eq. 1.3

$$STR = \frac{(1 - RSWIR)^2}{2RSWIR} \tag{1.3}$$

Based on the assumption of a linear relationship between soil and vegetation water contents, we expect that the STR-NDVI space forms a trapezoid as well. Therefore, the parameters of the can are obtained for a specific location from the dry and wet edges of the optical trapezoid using linear regression system determined using Eqs. 1.4 and 1.5

$$STR_d = i_d + S_d NDVI \tag{1.4}$$

$$STR_w = i_w + s_d NDVI \tag{1.5}$$

The normalized difference water index (NDVI) computed from band 4 (Red) and band 8 (NIR) using Eq. 1.6;

$$NDVI = \frac{NIR - Red}{NIR + Red} \tag{1.6}$$

Where; NIR is the TOA reflectance value of the NIR band (band 8), and red is the TOA reflectance value of the red group (group 4). The freely available sentinel -2 Levels 1C dataset is a standard product of TOA reflectance [15].

The NDVI was determined from the contribution of visible and NIR band. Healthy and well-nourished vegetation absorbs most of the visible wavelengths and reflects a large proportion of NIR light, whereas sparse plant reflects more visible wavelength light and less NIR light. Combining Eqs. 1.4 and 1.5, the soil moisture for each pixel can be estimated as a function of STR and NDVI determined as Eq. 1.7

$$SMI = \frac{id + SdNDVI - STR}{(id - iw) + (sd - sw)NDVI} \tag{1.7}$$

Where; i_d and s_d are dry parameters of NDVI – STR scatter plot, i_n and SW are wet parameters of NDVI – STR scatter plot and NDVI is the average vegetation index of the satellite. The Sentinel 2A level 1 C band 12 images with 20 m spatial resolutions were resample to 10 m resolution with the nearest neighbor method to match the spatial resolutions of group 4 and 8.

2.4.1   OPTRA M Model Validation and Sensitivity Analysis

The parameter removal sensitivity analyses, according to [16, 17] and [18] were used to identify the factors that profoundly affect the soil moisture content.

$$s = \left[\frac{\frac{SM}{N} - \frac{SM'}{n}}{SM} \right] \tag{1.8}$$

where; S is Sensitivity index analysis associated with the removal of one parameter; SM is the soil moisture index computed using all the settings; SM' is the soil moisture index calculated by excluding one thematic parameter at a time; N a n are the numbers of parameters used to calculate SM and SM' respectively.

2.4.2   Satellite Data Bias Correction

The bias from satellite image soil moisture retrieval was removed using cumulative density function CDF function.

$$\theta = \mu_{ground} + \frac{\sigma sat + \sigma ground}{2} \times \frac{Sat - \mu sat}{\sigma sat} \tag{1.9}$$

Where; θ is the final corrected soil moisture, the μ_{ground} ground is in situ soil moisture, σ_{sat} is the standard deviation of satellite soil moisture, the σ_{ground} is the standard deviation of in situ soil moisture, sat is satellite soil moisture, sat is satellite soil moisture.

2.4.3   Spectral Water Index Extraction Using MNDWI

The spectral Normalized difference water index proposed by [19] designed to maximize the reflectance of the water body in the green band and minimize the reflectance of the water body in the NIR band. McFeeters's NDWI determined as;

$$NDWI = \frac{\rho Green - \rho NIR}{\rho Green + \rho NIR} \tag{2.0}$$

Where; $\rho Green$ is the TOA reflectance value of the green band and ρNIR is the TOA reflectance value of the NIR band. Comparing to the raw Digital Numbers (DN), TOA reflectance is more suitable in calculating NDWI. The freely available Sentinel 2A Level 1C dataset is already a standard product of TOA reflectance. Therefore, no additional pre-processing is required.

2.4.4 Model Performance Evaluation

Based on [19], four quantitative statistics were used to assess model performance in catchment simulation (Table 3).

Table 3. SWAT model performance range

Rank	NSE	PBIAS	RMSE
Very good	$1 \geq \mathrm{NSE} \geq 0.75$	$\mathrm{PBIS} < 10$	$0 \leq \mathrm{RMSE} \leq 0.5$
Good	$0.75 \geq \mathrm{NSE} \geq 0.65$	$15 \geq \mathrm{PBIS} > 10$	$0.5 \leq \mathrm{RMSE} \leq 0.6$
Satisfactory	$0.65 \geq \mathrm{NSE} \geq 0.5$	$25 \geq \mathrm{PBIS} > 15$	$0.6 \leq \mathrm{RMSE} \leq 0.7$

3 Results and Discussion

3.1 Land Use Land Covers Classification

Thirty-four ground truth spatial points were used to classify pixel based land use land cover classification.

According to Table 4, the image classified in to four major classes; agriculture ($3.53 \ \mathrm{km}^2$), forest ($2.21 \ \mathrm{km}^2$), grassland and shrubs ($1.16 \ \mathrm{km}^2$) and village ($0.067 \ \mathrm{km}^2$). Agriculture was the dominant type of land use practice which covers half of the total area of the watershed. The study had an overall classification accuracy of 85.5% and a kappa coefficient of 80% that indicated very good classification (Fig. 2).

Table 4. Performance evaluation of Sentinel 2 for land LULC classification

Land use	Producer accuracy (%)	Omission error (%)	User accuracy (%)	Commission error (%)	Overall accuracy (%)	Kappa coefficient (%)
Cultivated	82	18	90	10	85	80
Village area	100	0	83	17		
Forest land	71	29	71	29		
Grass land	91	9	91	9		

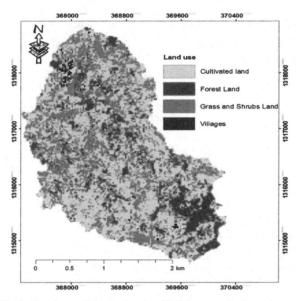

Fig. 2. Land use of Awramba classified from sentinel two images

3.2 SWAT Model Configuration

The SWAT model has configured with DEM 30 m resolution and discredited based on the maximum areal threshold value into 330 Hydrological Response Unit (HRU) and 35 sub-basins to get detail information about the topographic characteristics. The maximum area of the sub basin was 1.732 Km^2 (sub basin 32), and the minimum was 0.0164 Km^2 (sub basin 8). The HRUs were defined using land use, soil and slope with a threshold value of 10%, 20%, 10% respectively [20]. The input tables were defined based on the daily time step climatic data collected from within and around the watershed with their relevant location files. The model was run from 2013–2017 seasons by considering 2013 data to warm up the model and the rest three and one year's data were considered as calibration and validation at the outlet point using stream discharge daily observation.

During the simulation of the SWAT model, there was a discrepancy between measured data and simulated results. Therefore, to minimize this inconsistency, selecting sensitive parameters which affect the outcome and the extent of variation is mandatory for better hydrological modeling. Global sensitivity analysis in SWAT CUP 2012 is the favorite tool to show the rank and relative sensitivity. In the present study, initially, 30 parameters were used to know the status of each parameter. Among the 30 benchmarks, the top nineteen parameters were used for the calibration and validation process. Parameter sensitivity and ranking in SWAT CUP was measured using the t-stat and p-values. Where t-stat is the coefficient of a parameter divided by its standard error. The p-value is used to determine the significance of the sensitivity. Parameters are significant for a larger absolute t-stat and lower p-values. The T-stat measures sensitivity with larger absolute values, while the P-value considers zero cost to determine sensitivity [21]. A more significant p-value suggests that changes in the predictor values are not associated with changes in the response variable.

3.3 Sensitivity Analysis, Calibration and Validation of SWAT Model

According to Global sensitivity analysis result indicates that curve number II, alpha base flow recession constant, and groundwater delay were the three top sensitive parameters that determine the water balance of Awramba catchment. The sensitivity rank is in line with [20, 22] tested in the upper Blue Nile basin. Curve number method is one of the most popular ways for computing the runoff volume from a rainstorm. Soil and groundwater parameters are found to be the most sensitive parameters in lowland catchments [23] (Table 5).

Table 5. SWAT parameters used for calibration and their sensitivity ranks in Awramba

Parameter Name	File Extra	Fitted Value	Min Value	Max Value	t Stat	P Value	Sensitivity Rank
R__CN2	mgt	−0.165	−0.2	0.2	−29.2	0	1
V__ALPHA_BF	Gw	0.104	0	1	−0.28	0.78	2
V__GW_DELAY	Gw	164.583	0	500	1.51	0.14	3
V__GWQMN	Gw	1437.5	0	5000	−0.16	0.88	4
R__ESCO	hru	0.188	0	1	1.55	0.12	5
R__ESCO	bsn	0.671	0	1	−0.64	0.52	6
R__CH_N2	rte	0.021	0	0.3	−0.03	0.98	7
R__CH_K2	rte	95.104	5	130	−1.77	0.08	8
R__SOL_AWC	sol	0.283	−0.2	0.4	0.13	0.9	9
R__SOL_BD	sol	0.138	−0.5	0.5	2.54	0.01	10

3.4 SWAT Stream Flow Modeling

Stream discharge in Awramba watershed was collected from 2013–2017 for watershed management evaluation purpose in daily time step. The rating curve developed by [22] from 2013–2015 was used to estimate the discharge in 2016 and 2017. To evaluate the SWAT model performance stream-discharge relationship at gage station historical time series data from 2013–2017 is considered. Calibration and validation were performed on measured stream flow from a gagging station for the year 2014–2016 and 2017 respectively (Tables 6, 7 and Fig. 3).

Table 6. Daily stream flow modeling statistical performance

Flow (m^3/s)	p-factor	r-factor	R^2	NSE	PBIAS	RMSE
Calibration	1	0.64	0.75	0.7	−2.1	0.55
Validation	0.98	0.49	0.91	0.9	−9.7	0.31

Table 7. Monthly stream flow model performance

Flow (m^3/s)	R^2	NSE	PPBIAS	RMSE
Calibration	0.98	0.94	−16.432	1.07
Validation	0.97	0.96	−0.07367	1.075

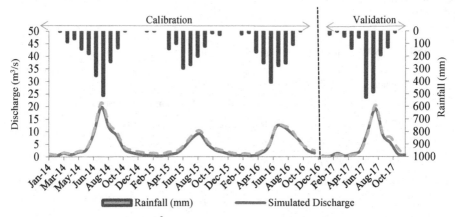

Fig. 3. Monthly stream flow (m^3/s) during calibration and validation versus monthly rainfall depth (mm)

3.5 SWAT Soil Moisture Modeling

The moisture content was calibrated and validated by stream flow data due to lack of long term gagged soil moisture data at sub-basin level because the simulation of soil moisture content using SWAT model is highly dependent on simulation of runoff generation process [24].

As indicated in (Fig. 4) SWAT model results the amount of soil moisture reduces from 2014–2017 with annual rainfall depth (Table 8).

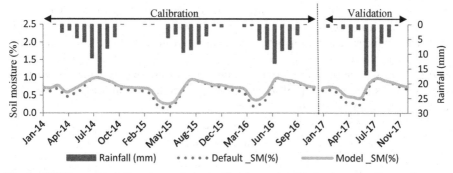

Fig. 4. SWAT monthly soil moisture during calibration and validation by using Stream flow data from 2014–2017

Table 8. Water balance of Awramba watershed using SWAT model (2014–2017)

Year	Rainfall	PET	ET	Q_GW	WYLD	SM	Q
	(mm)	(mm)	(mm)	(mm)	(mm)	(mm)	m³/s
2014	1713.92	1233.6	560.3	355.96	1124.49	119.34	795
2015	1171.05	1339	569.6	193.4	575.22	98.34	447
2016	1505.53	1287.7	537.9	295.66	946.73	107.72	662
2017	1599.3	1306.7	597.4	281.52	972.35	105.15	649
Mean	1497.45	1291.7	566.3	281.64	904.7	107.64	638

The rainfall depth in 2014 was 1713 mm respond an average soil moisture value of 119.33 mm. In 2015 season, the rainfall depth was 1171.05 mm response 98.34 mm amount of water stored in root depth of the plant. The amount of rainfall in 2016 and 2017 were 1505 mm and 1599 mm, which responses 107.72 mm and 105.14 mm soil moisture content. SWAT modeling results indicated the amount of soil content around the watershed was determined by the amount of rainfall value directly. Both hydrological variables reduced with time, especially in 2015 there was a small amount of rainfall annually; as a result, the amount of water stored and available for plants were lower than the rest years. But, the partition of soil moisture from the total rainfall was higher in 2015 because the soil can absorb the incident rainfall by reducing runoff generation potential. SWAT model calibration using stream flow data improve the soil moisture product in daily time step.

3.6 Sentinel 2 Satellite Soil Moisture Estimation Methods

A physically-based trapezoidal space termed the "Optical TRApezoid Model" (OP-TRAM) to estimate surface soil moisture remote from Sentinel two satellites based on optical data only [13]. The concept is based on the pixel distribution between STR-NDVI spaces, where STR is the SWIR transformed reflectance, and NDVI is the Normalized difference vegetation index, thereby replacing LST in the conventional trapezoid model. Considering a linear relationship between soil moisture content, SMI (0 for completely dry and 1 for saturated soil) and STR [25] Normalized Difference Vegetation Index (NDVI): Most vegetation indices combine information contained from the red and near-infrared (NIR) spectral bands [26]. The index was higher in the rainy season and lowered in the dry season (April and May) (Fig. 5).

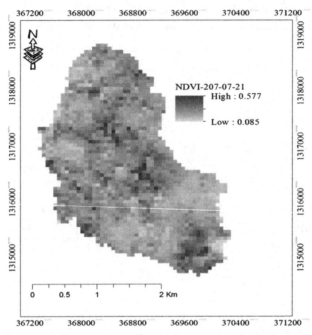

Fig. 5. Normalized difference vegetation index map

3.6.1 Shortwave Infrared Transformed Reflectance (STR) Map

Shortwave infrared transformed reflectance (STR) is one of the parameter used to determine the soil moisture status of a soil by replacing the land surface temperature (NDVI, LST) in thermal triangular model with a linear relationship between (NDVI, STR) in optical tripartite model because LST is computed from thermal band of the satellite imagery (Fig. 6).

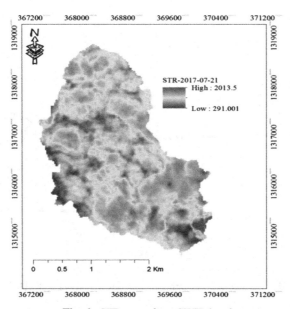

Fig. 6. STR maps from SWIR band

STR map in the study area varies both spatially and temporally in 2017 season. Most of the STR map result reveals that the highest elevation part of the watershed has a lower value of STR whereas lower elevation part of the basin was the higher value of STR like that of land surface temperature (Table 9 and Fig. 7).

Table 9. Daily OPTRA M parameters

Date	NDVI max	NDVI min	STR max	STR min	i_d	i_w	s_d	s_w
2-Jan-17	0.75	0.05	1326	239.5	190.5	1142.98	76.23	457.37
11-Feb-17	0.59	0.01	1450.5	287	262.88	1328.6	79.63	402.44
23-Mar-17	0.4	0.06	1242	455.5	433.27	1181.4	98.13	267.58
22-Apr-17	0.64	0	1528	350	317.18	1384.71	102.03	445.44
11-Jun-17	0.66	−0.08	3226	211.5	194.82	2971.51	57.01	869.62
1-Jul-17	0.58	0.12	1616.5	306	272.46	1439.3	95.6	505.02
21-Jul-17	0.58	0.09	2013.5	290	287.89	1510.18	24.63	871.84
30-Aug-17	0.55	0.13	2013.5	291	261.46	1809.06	87.89	608.14
29-Sep-17	0.79	0.15	1487.5	111.5	108.89	923.47	16.86	721.71
9-Sep-17	0.77	0.12	1280	154	128.62	1069.02	57.14	474.91
9-Oct-17	0.78	0.13	1823	221	182.88	1508.52	83.5	688.77
29-Oct-17	0.82	0	1266	203	173.66	1083.03	71.38	445.15
28-Nov-17	0.63	0.16	1719	212.5	183.71	1486.1	32.69	588.31
28-Dec-17	0.67	0.05	1591.5	233	206.28	1408.97	74.24	507.13

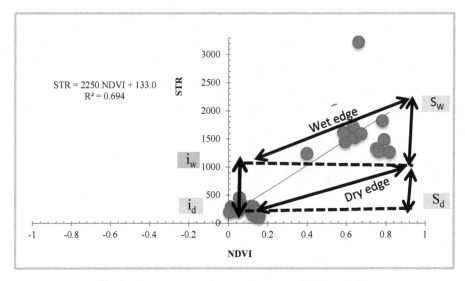

Fig. 7. Standardized rating curve between NDVI and STR

3.6.2 Sensitivity Analysis of Optical Trapezoidal Model Parameters

The highest variation index with mean −7.97 associated with soil moisture index value. Soil moisture index also sensitive to STR and NDVI with a mean variation index value of −1.09 and −1.01 respectively next to i_w. It is less susceptible to S_d and S_w with a mean variation of 0.19 and 0.02, respectively (Table 10).

Table 10. Map removal sensitivity analysis statistical value of the OPtical TRApezoidal Model

Date	NDVI	STR	i_d	i_w	s_d	s_w
2-Jan-17	−1.02	−1.08	−0.77	−30.1	0.03	0.2
11-Feb-17	−0.94	−1.1	−0.76	−8.05	0.02	0.12
23-Mar-17	−0.91	−1.23	−0.73	−2.99	0.03	0.08
22-Apr-17	−0.96	−1.12	−0.76	−6.7	0.03	0.14
1-Jul-17	−0.98	−1.09	−0.77	−11.2	0.02	0.16
29-Sep-17	−1.23	−1.03	−0.79	4.12	0	0.42
9-Oct-17	−1.07	−1.06	−0.78	16.14	0.02	0.24
29-Oct-17	−1.03	−1.08	−0.77	−54.1	0.03	0.21
28-Nov-18	−0.99	−1.05	−0.78	41	0.01	0.18
28-Dec-17	−0.97	−1.07	−0.77	−27.9	0.02	0.16
Average	−1.01	−1.09	−0.77	−7.97	0.02	0.19
Sensitivity rank	3	2	4	1	6	5

3.6.3 Soil Moisture Index Map

Mapping soil moisture index in small watershed level is difficult due to satellites poor resolution and quality of imagery. The Sentinel 2 A levels 1 C image has 13 spectral bands that can detect our environment in the different spectral band from 443 nm–2190 nm. Group 4 (665 nm) and band 8 (740 nm) were used for normalized difference vegetation index (NDVI) computation in sentinel application platform(SNAP Version 6.0), and the short wave infrared (SWIR) band 12 (2190 nm) was used for computing STR in band math. Finally, the soil moisture mapping process were done using OPtical TRApezoidal Model after calculating the daily dry edge (i_d and S_d) and wet edge (i_w and S_w) parameters in linear regression program using Microsoft excel solver. The daily time series dry and wet edge parameters are presented in Table 11 below (Fig. 8).

Table 11. Spatial and temporal MNDWI product in Awramba watershed

Date	2-Jan-17	11-Jan-17	23-Mar-17	22-Apr-17	12-May-17	11-Jun-17	1-Jul-17	30-Aug-17	9-Sep-17	9-Oct-17	28-Nov-17	8-Dec-17	Mean
SM_1	−0.44	−0.31	−0.32	−0.43	−0.28	0.02	−0.29	−0.09	−0.25	−0.28	−0.41	−0.44	−0.28
SM_2	−0.38	−0.38	−0.25	−0.34	−0.21	−0.1	−0.14	−0.01	−0.24	−0.28	−0.31	−0.34	−0.24
SM_3	−0.25	−0.22	−0.2	−0.23	−0.22	−0.07	−0.13	−0.02	−0.18	−0.25	−0.35	−0.34	−0.19
SM_4	−0.39	−0.26	−0.27	−0.39	−0.18	−0.23	−0.22	0	−0.2	−0.19	−0.43	−0.43	−0.25
SM_5	−0.29	−0.18	−0.24	−0.3	−0.2	−0.12	−0.15	−0.01	−0.24	−0.31	−0.39	−0.32	−0.22
SM_6	−0.26	−0.13	−0.18	−0.22	−0.18	−0.12	−0.03	−0.01	−0.18	−0.25	−0.3	−0.28	−0.17
SM_7	−0.3	−0.25	−0.18	−0.3	−0.18	−0.18	−0.17	−0.03	−0.11	−0.2	−0.33	−0.32	−0.2
SM_8	−0.34	−0.21	−0.23	−0.3	−0.16	−0.15	−0.04	−0.02	−0.16	−0.23	−0.28	−0.25	−0.19
SM_9	−0.35	−0.31	−0.25	−0.35	−0.17	−0.22	−0.17	−0.04	−0.24	−0.31	−0.35	−0.33	−0.25
SM_10	−0.25	−0.12	−0.18	−0.25	−0.17	−0.2	−0.13	−0.09	−0.15	−0.18	−0.25	−0.24	−0.18
SM_11	−0.22	−0.21	−0.18	−0.25	−0.16	−0.12	−0.11	−0.03	−0.15	−0.21	−0.3	−0.28	−0.18
SM_12	−0.21	−0.14	−0.15	−0.2	−0.18	−0.18	−0.14	0.05	0.04	−0.23	−0.3	−0.28	−0.15
SM_13	−0.29	−0.23	−0.2	−0.28	−0.16	−0.1	−0.13	0.06	−0.19	−0.23	−0.34	−0.32	−0.19
SM_14	−0.38	−0.15	−0.26	−0.36	−0.17	−0.25	−0.14	0.02	−0.19	−0.29	−0.4	−0.4	−0.23
SM_15	−0.21	−0.18	−0.14	−0.21	−0.2	−0.13	−0.09	−0.01	−0.15	−0.2	−0.23	−0.22	−0.16
SM_16	−0.28	−0.19	−0.19	−0.29	−0.16	−0.1	−0.16	−0.01	−0.21	−0.25	−0.27	−0.25	−0.19
SM_17	−0.31	−0.25	−0.2	−0.28	−0.18	−0.26	−0.14	−0.03	−0.11	−0.11	−0.18	−0.13	−0.19
SM_18	−0.25	−0.21	−0.19	−0.28	−0.29	−0.23	−0.14	0.04	−0.17	−0.22	−0.24	−0.21	−0.2
Mean	−0.3	−0.22	−0.21	−0.29	−0.19	−0.15	−0.14	−0.01	−0.17	−0.23	−0.31	−0.3	−0.2

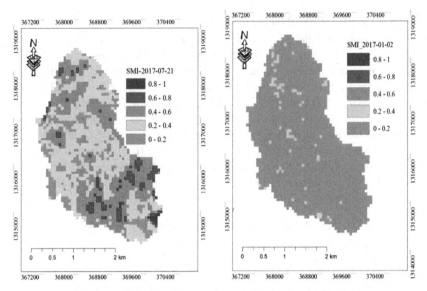

Fig. 8. Daily soil moisture maps estimated using OPTRAM

3.6.4 Bias Correction

There is a discrepancy in estimating soil moisture form sentinel 2 A satellite image. To account any bias between the two sets of data is removed using a simple cumulative density function (CDF) that the standard deviation of both the ground station data and the satellite data. The percentage bias was estimated at -0.094, which is very insignificant.

3.6.5 Spectral Water Index Extraction Using MNDWI

The average product of spectral water index is less than -0.013 cm^3 cm^{-3} thus indicates that water is not the dominant land use coverage. Spectral water index approaches to zero in the rainy season especially July – end of September and lowers in the dry season in November – May. The average value of MNDWI (-0.212) was more significant than the average NDVI (0.3). The result is agreed with a five years analysis of MODIS image in the vast central plain of the United States (NDVI $= 0.5$ and NDWI $= 0.3$) [27]. The time series MNDWI data in (Fig. 9) indicates that water index was higher in the rainy season (June – September) and decline starting the dry season from October – May. The water index has a similar pattern with soil moisture time series data extracted from Sentinel 2 A image, but the product of soil moisture is higher than 0 cm^3 cm^{-3}, and MNDWI is less than 0.

3.7 Model Accuracy Assessment

A comparison between SWAT, OPTRA M soil moisture and MNDWI spectral water index with in situ soil moisture measured at 10 cm depth data is depicted in Fig. 9. The result indicates that validation of three models with in situ soil moisture data generally leads to acceptable accuracy having 0.0027 cm^3 cm^{-3} and 0.0022 cm^3 cm^{-3}

and 0.034 cm^3 cm^{-3} standard errors respectively. Overall, the accuracy of sentinel two images using OPtical TRApizoidal Model and SWAT hydrological model are grater then MNDWI spectral water index. All models were agreed with result of soil moisture content less than 0.04 cm^3 cm^{-3} standard error [13] (Table 12).

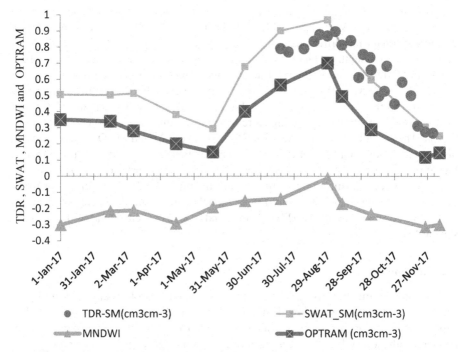

Fig. 9. Time series soil moisture product in TDR, SWAT, MNDWI and OPTRAM

Table 12. Model evaluation

Model	NSE	R^2	PBIAS	RMSE
SWAT	0.51	0.77	−0.24	0.19
OPTRAM	0.61	0.73	0.19	0.025
MNDWI	0.75	−7.98	0.81	132.83

According to the common performance criteria's OPTRAM is relatively the best method to estimate soil moisture in the catchment.

4 Conclusions and Recommendation

4.1 Conclusion

SWAT model sensitivity analysis, it indicated that CN2, ALPHA_BF, GWQMN and ESCO were the most sensitive parameters and has a great impact on stream flow and soil moisture content. The new OPtical TRApezoid Model (OPTRA M) proposed in this study offers a novel approach to satellite-based remote sensing of soil moisture. OPTRA M has been derived based on the linear relationship between STR and surface soil moisture in bare or vegetated soils. OP-TRAM parameters for a given area can be determined either based on the pixel distribution with-in the STR-NDVI space or with least square regression of the model to field observations. The achievable prediction accuracy of OPTRA M is comparable with the TDR probe. OPTRA M using sentinel 2A level 1C image perform well having NSE (0.61), R^2 (0.73), PBIAS (0.19) and RMSE (0.025). The ESA Sentinel Data Hub at the level 1C processing level (Top-of-Atmosphere radiance) MNDWI spectral index extracted from green (560 nm) and SWIR (2160 nm) bands. NDVI and MNDWI values are well correlated even though the mean vegetation index was less than 0.49, whereas the MNDWI spectral index was less than -0.013. But in all cases, the spectral index has higher reflectance in summer season and low in the dry season. The overall results revealed that SWAT, OPTRA M and MNDWI were capable of simulating soil moisture in daily base. The spatial variation of soil moisture was higher in the TDR probe, and the temporal variation was higher for the MNDWI model. The satellite soil moisture underestimates the In-situ and SWAT modeled moistures. The result indicates that validation of three models with in situ data generally leads to acceptable accuracy having $0.0027\,\mathrm{cm}^3\,\mathrm{cm}^{-3}$ and $0.0022\,\mathrm{cm}^3\,\mathrm{cm}^{-3}$ and $.034\,\mathrm{cm}^3\,\mathrm{cm}^{-3}$ standard errors respectively.

4.2 Recommendation

Soil moisture estimation using SWAT semi distributed hydrological model will give accurate result with stream flow data with successful calibration and validation. The depth of soil moisture measurement can be reduced to 5 cm and better approximation can be found with the satellite. Formulating universal dry and wet edge parameter is essential for the better optical trapezoidal model using long term NDVI and STR indexes. Sentinel 2 soil moisture product using visual trapezoidal model should be used to calibrate and validate hydrological models for soil moisture estimation. Even though MNDWI is designed to extract the water body, the index also used to monitor soil moisture status.

Acknowledgements. The authors gratefully acknowledge Bahir Dar University and university of Connecticut for the research fund through its PIRE project. The authors also acknowledge European satellite agency (ESA) for enabling free sentinel images, National Meteorology Agency (NMA) of Ethiopia, and university of Gondar. The three anonymous reviewers and editors are gratefully acknowledged for their valuable comments on our manuscript.

References

1. Falkenmark, M., Rockström, J.: The new blue and green water paradigm: breaking new ground for water resources planning and management. J. Water Resour. Plann. Manage. **132**(3), 129–132 (2006)
2. Chen, H., Shao, M., Li, Y.: The characteristics of soil water cycle and water balance on steep grassland under natural and simulated rainfall conditions in the Loess Plateau of China. J. Hydrol. **360**(1–4), 242–251 (2008)

3. Brocca, L., et al.: Soil moisture estimation through ASCAT and AMSR-E sensors: an inter-comparison and validation study across Europe. Remote Sens. Environ. **115**(12), 3390–3408 (2011)
4. Zhang, Q., Shi, Y., Zhu, R.: The study on landslide monitoring with TDR technology. Chin. J. Geol. Hazard Control **6**(2), 67–69 (2001)
5. Narasimhan, B., Srinivasan, R.: Development and evaluation of soil moisture deficit index (SMDI) and evapotranspiration deficit index (ETDI) for agricultural drought monitoring. Agric. For. Meteorol. **133**(1–4), 69–88 (2005)
6. Abate, M., et al.: Morphological changes of Gumara River channel over 50 years, upper Blue Nile basin, Ethiopia. J. Hydrol. **525**, 152–164 (2015)
7. Koster, R.D., et al.: On the nature of soil moisture in land surface models. J. Clim. **22**(16), 4322–4335 (2009)
8. Alexandridis, T.K., et al.: Spatial and temporal distribution of soil moisture at the catchment scale using remotely-sensed energy fluxes. Water **8**(1), 32 (2016)
9. Baghdadi, N., et al.: Analysis of TerraSAR-X data and their sensitivity to soil surface parameters over bare agricultural fields. Remote Sens. Environ. **112**(12), 4370–4379 (2008)
10. Entekhabi, D., et al.: The soil moisture active passive (SMAP) mission. Proc. IEEE **98**(5), 704–716 (2010)
11. Arnold, J.G., et al.: Large area hydrologic modeling and assessment part I: model development 1. JAWRA J. Am. Water Resour. Assoc. **34**(1), 73–89 (1998)
12. Yacoub, C., Foguet, A.P.: Slope effects on SWAT modeling in a mountainous basin. J. Hydrol. Eng. **18**(12), 1663–1673 (2012)
13. Sadeghi, M., et al.: The optical trapezoid model: a novel approach to remote sensing of soil moisture applied to Sentinel-2 and Landsat-8 observations. Remote Sens. Environ. **198**, 52–68 (2017)
14. Kubelka, P., Munk, F.: An article on optics of paint layers. Z. Tech. Phys. **12**(593–601) (1931)
15. Korhonen, L., Packalen, P., Rautiainen, M.: Comparison of Sentinel-2 and Landsat 8 in the estimation of boreal forest canopy cover and leaf area index. Remote Sens. Environ. **195**, 259–274 (2017)
16. Babiker, I.S., et al.: A GIS-based DRASTIC model for assessing aquifer vulnerability in Kakamigahara Heights, Gifu Prefecture, central Japan. Sci. Total Environ. **345**(1–3), 127–140 (2005)
17. Kindie, A.T., Enku, T., Moges, M.A., Geremew, B.S., Atinkut, H.B.: Spatial analysis of groundwater potential using GIS based multi criteria decision analysis method in Lake Tana basin, Ethiopia. In: Zimale, F.A., Enku Nigussie, T., Fanta, S.W. (eds.) ICAST 2018. LNICST, vol. 274, pp. 439–456. Springer, Cham (2019). https://doi.org/10.1007/978-3-030-15357-1_37
18. Lodwick, W.A., Monson, W., Svoboda, L.: Attribute error and sensitivity analysis of map operations in geographical informations systems: suitability analysis. Int. J. Geogr. Inf. Syst. **4**(4), 413–428 (1990)
19. McFeeters, S.K.: The use of the normalized difference water index (NDWI) in the delineation of open water features. Int. J. Remote Sens. **17**(7), 1425–1432 (1996)
20. Setegn, S.G., Srinivasan, R., Dargahi, B.: Hydrological modelling in the Lake Tana Basin, Ethiopia using SWAT model. Open Hydrol. J. **2**(1), 49–62 (2008)
21. Abbaspour, K.C., et al.: Modelling hydrology and water quality in the pre-alpine/alpine Thur watershed using SWAT. J. Hydrol. **333**(2), 413–430 (2007)
22. Moges, M.A., et al.: Suitability of watershed models to predict distributed hydrologic response in the Awramba watershed in lake Tana basin. Land Degrad. Dev. **28**(4), 1386–1397 (2017)
23. Asres, M.T., Awulachew, S.B.: SWAT based runoff and sediment yield modelling: a case study of the Gumera watershed in the Blue Nile basin. Ecohydrol. Hydrobiol. **10**(2–4), 191–199 (2010)

24. Han, E., Merwade, V., Heathman, G.C.: Implementation of surface soil moisture data assimilation with watershed scale distributed hydrological model. J. Hydrol. **416**, 98–117 (2012)
25. Babaeian, E., et al.: A novel optical model for remote sensing of near-surface soil moisture. In: AGU Fall Meeting Abstracts (2016)
26. Gitelson, A.A., et al.: Novel algorithms for remote estimation of vegetation fraction. Remote Sens. Environ. **80**(1), 76–87 (2002)
27. Szabó, S., Gacsi, Z., Balázs, B.: Specific features of NDVI, NDWI and MNDWI as reflected in land cover categories. Acta Geogr. Debrecina Landsc. Environ. **10**(3–4), 194–202 (2016)

Pilot-Scale Horizontal Subsurface Flow Constructed Wetland for Removal of Chromium from Tannery Waste Water with Suitable Local Substrate Material

Gemechu Kassaye[1]($\boxtimes$), Agegnehu Alemu[2], and Nigus Gabbiye[1]

[1] Faculty of Chemical and Food Engineering, Bahir Dar Institute of Technology,
Bahir Dar University, P.O. Box 26, Bahir Dar, Ethiopia
gzabera@gmail.com
[2] Department of Chemistry, College of Science, Bahir Dar University, P.O. Box 79,
Bahir Dar, Ethiopia

Abstract. The aim of this study was to investigate the performance of pilot scale horizontal subsurface flow constructed wetlands (HSSFCW) for removal chromium containing industrial wastewater with locally available two plant species (Cyprus Papyrus) and Para grass (Brachiara mutica). Twenty-one constructed wetland systems half-filled with coarse aggregate were built. Eighteen of them were used to study the efficiency of chromium (VI) removal with both plants in three replicates and the other three units were used as a control. The experiments were performed at different bed depth of 0.20 m, 0.40 m, and 0.60 m. It was found that HSSFCW with papyrus at constructed wetland bed depth of 0.20 m was the best performed for chromium removal with an efficiency of 98.41%. Comparing efficiency for chromium (VI) removal at the same bed depth, papyrus plant was better than Para grass. On one hand, the growth rate of the plant species was unaffected by the depth of the constructed wetland wastewater system.

Keywords: Constructed wetlands · Tannery wastewater · Para grass · Papyrus grass · Horizontal subsurface flow

1 Introduction

Water scarcity is becoming a global issue since industrial evolution which is manifest by global warming [1]. The world population growth and the trend in industrial revolution have led to environmental degradation especially by the release of partially treated or untreated wastewater into the water body. Due to such activities, the global freshwater resource is at risk and the majority of the problems that humanity face in recent years is related to access to clean water [1]. Thus, the treatment of wastewater is a basic component to protect the health and the environment of the communities [2]. However, many developing countries lack adequate and low-cost wastewater treatment facilities.

© ICST Institute for Computer Sciences, Social Informatics and Telecommunications Engineering 2020
Published by Springer Nature Switzerland AG 2020. All Rights Reserved
N. G. Habtu et al. (Eds.): ICAST 2019, LNICST 308, pp. 315–324, 2020.
https://doi.org/10.1007/978-3-030-43690-2_21

One such promising technology for wastewater treatment is the constructed wetland system [3].

Constructed wetland system for the removal of heavy metal from wastewater effluent is becoming a focus of many investigations in recent years. Constructed wetlands are considered as a technical, economical, and environmentally sustainable solution for wastewater treatment in small communities since they are efficient with diverse pollutants removal [4–11].

Subsurface flow wetlands are engineered systems, which mostly employ gravel as a substrate to support the growth of plants, and wastewater flows vertically or horizontally through the substrate where it comes into contact with microorganisms, living on the surfaces of plant roots and substrate.

Subsurface flow constructed wetlands are further divided into two groups, according to the flow direction inside the packed media: (1) vertical flow, and (2) horizontal flow systems [12–14].

Horizontal Wetland system is a cost-effective, environmentally friendly, aesthetically pleasing approach and most suitable for developing countries. It is a multi-beneficial system for environmental protection. Subsurface flow constructed wetlands, which are commonly seen as low cost, green treatment technologies [11, 15].

The removal mechanism of chromium in constructed wetlands is a complex combination of physicochemical and biological processes including sedimentation, binding to porous media, plant uptake, and precipitation as insoluble forms. The efficient reaction zone in constructed wetlands is the root zone area (rhizosphere) where physicochemical and biological processes take place by the interaction of plants, microorganisms, and pollutants [16, 17].

Currently, Ethiopia is focusing on industries majorly textile and tannery sector. These factories release toxic chemicals to the environment. In practical, leather industries release toxic heavy metal that cannot be treated by conventional treatment methods. Currently, about 54% of leather industries reported that they have treatment facilities (12% secondary and 42% primary), which can treat their wastewater to a certain degree [18]. The rest are discharge the wastewater directly into the nearby water bodies without any form of treatment.

The objective of the present study is therefore to evaluate the performance of pilot-scale constructed wetland system with two plant species at three different bed depth for the removal of chromium from leather wastewater effluent, since the influence of water depth has received a relatively less attention and the information available is presently limited to a few reports [19–21]. Since the depth of the wetland will affect the performance of the plant by stressing its root. The significance of this study is to help the industries to use green wastewater treatment technologies of constructed wetland with suitable plants (C. papyrus and Para grass) to remediate wastewater.

2   Materials and Methods

2.1   Experimental Setup and Operating Conditions of Wetlands

The experimental study was conducted in HSSFCW system at Bahir Dar University, Bahir Dar Institute of Technology Campus Bahir Dar, Ethiopia. The system consists of twenty-one analogous treatment beds aligned in parallel and is designed with a range of wastewater flow-rate from 14 L/d to 42 L/d measured using a bucket and stopwatch method and theoretical hydraulic residence time (HRT) of 3 days. The substrate or plant growth media used for the 21 HSSFCW systems was 20 to 30 mm diameter sized gravel [22]. The substrate was filled to a height of 0.45 m. Fragments of rhizomes about 10 cm long carrying young shoots of C. papyrus and Para grass plants selected according to Dr. Heike [23] were taken from the natural wetlands of Lake Tana and transplanted into their respective treatment beds with a surface area of 4.2 m^2 at a density of four rhizomes/m. For each depth (0.2 m, 0.4 m, and 0.6 m) there were seven constructed wetlands which were planted with C. papyrus and Para grass with three replicates and a control. Each treatment bed was fed with the influent water which was taken from Lake Tana with their respective average flow rate from the equalization tank through pipes after 3 months acclimation period. During the acclimation period, the nutrient was prepared and feed into the system once per week [24]. The Wastewater used in the study was prepared via Chromium six with a concentration of 1 mg/L and added to the storage tank. After the plants were well grown the prepared wastewater was pumped to the wetland at a rate of 20 L/d.

2.2 Wetland Design

Constructed wetlands are classified according to whether the water level is above or below the substrate surface [23, 25] (Fig. 1).

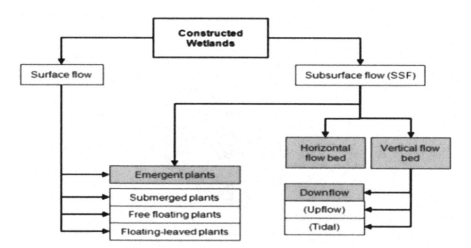

Fig. 1. Classification of constructed wetlands for wastewater treatment [23].

Because of its low cost and widely used, we selected horizontal flow and the hydraulic retention time is calculated according to Eq. (1) [25].

$$t = \frac{\eta h l w}{Q} \tag{1}$$

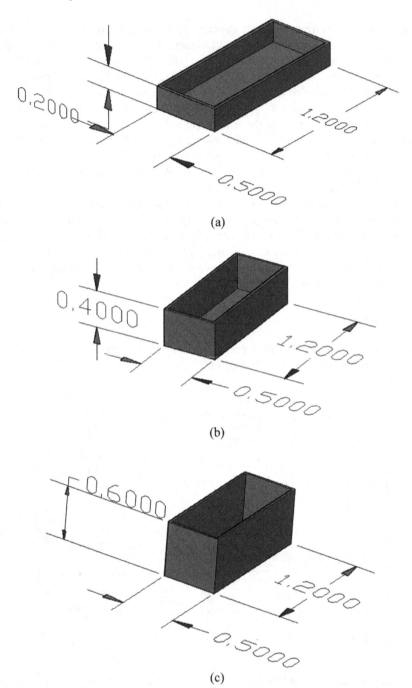

(a)

(b)

(c)

Fig. 2. A schematic diagram of the wetland system (a) with a depth of 0.2 m, (b) with depth 0.4 m and (c) with a depth of 0.6 m and the other entire dimension were the same.

Where t is hydraulic detention time, is the porosity of the substrate material, l is the length, Q is the average flow rate and w is the width of the treatment cell.

It is widely reported, those small aspect ratios are preferable because they offer reduced construction costs and improved hydraulic control [25]. So we select the aspect ratio between 0.2–3 which was (l: w) 2.4. Figures 2, 3, 4 shows the scheme of the wetlands.

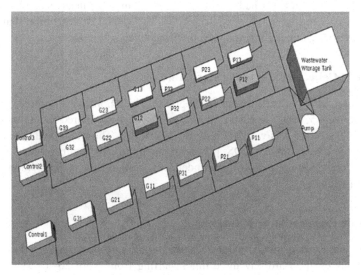

Fig. 3. Setup of the constructed wetlands showing the twenty-one sampling sites

Fig. 4. Photo of Pilot scale constructed wetlands at BiT, Bahir Dar

2.3 Construction of the Wetlands

The wetlands were constructed with concrete at the bottom and hollow concrete block for the walls and an approximate 1% slope at the bottom. All sides of the bed and the bottom were covered by geo-membrane to prevent leakage. Leakage was tested by keeping water within the system one weeks and monitoring the water level change. The outlet and the level of the effluent were controlled with pipes typically used for drip irrigation. Each wetland tank had a surface area of 1.2 m × 0.5 m and a depth of 0.20 m, 0.40 m, and 0.60 m from shallow to deep beds. The wetted depths of the shallow and deep beds were 0.18 m, 0.35 m and 0.55 m, respectively.

2.4 Sample Collection and Laboratory Analysis

Water samples were collected manually in 500 ml clean bottles every three days since April 23- to May 5, 2018. In each CW, two points were monitored (inlet, outlet) once a day since, the pump was working only for 12 h a day. The water quality parameters analyzed were chromium six, TDS, pH and temperature. To confirm steady state flow water was collected in a measuring cylinder for a certain time using a stopwatch and calculate the flow rate.

2.5 Sample Preparation and Analyses

Samples of wastewater (influent) and treated water (effluent) were collected by 500 mL plastic bottles on the third day three times starting from April 23- to May 5, 2018, each day at 12:00 PM. The sample was filtered through 0.45 μm Watt man paper and 100 ml of the filtered sample was rinsed with sulphuric acid. The analyses were done immediately after sample collection [26]. PerkinElmer UV-Vis XLS single beam UV-visible spectrophotometer with 10 mm quartz cell was used for Cr6+ measurements at $\lambda = 540$ nm. The pH meter (HANNA Instruments) was calibrated at pH of 4, 7, and 10 with appropriate buffer solutions and use for the adjustment of sample pH.

Reagents and Standard Preparations. Astandard stock solution was prepared according to [27]. By dissolving 141.4 mg dried K2Cr2O7 to 1 L distilled water. 10.00 mL of potassium dichromate stock solution was added to 100 mL of distilled water. Phosphoric acid and sulfuric acid was used to adjust the pH below 2 and 250 mg 1, 5-diphenylcarbazidein dissolved in 50 mL acetone and added to the sample to form the complex reaction which shows violet color.

UV Vis Spectrometric Analysis of samples. Acalibration equation ($y = 0.688x + 0.035$, R2 $= 0.990$, where y is absorbance and x is concentration in ppm) derived from a calibration curve was plotted from standards (0.2 ppm, 0.4 ppm, 0.5 ppm, 0.8 ppm and 1 ppm) for the determination of Cr(VI) in wastewater samples. However, due to the low sensitivity to low Cr (VI) concentrations and low detection limits of Cr (VI) in wastewater samples, no pink color developed on complexation with 1, 5-diphenylcarbazide. According to Harris [28].wastewater samples were spiked with 2 mL, 7 mL, and 9 mL of a 0.5 ppm Cr (VI) standard to determine the Cr (VI) in the wastewater samples.

Statistical Analyses. Comparison of the efficiency and growth of the two plants in each unit for chromium (VI) removal was by using one-way ANOVA at 95% confidence. All statistical analyses were performed with Microsoft Office EXCEL 2007 and SPSS program (version 20).

3 Results and Discussion

3.1 The Chromium Removal Efficiency of the Horizontal Subsurface Flow Constructed a Wetland

The effect of bed depth on the removal efficiency of chromium by the two plants was investigated. The efficiency of the pilot units subject to the different depth with two plants was monitored through their operation, and the characteristics of the wastewater collected from the inflow and outflow of each pilot unit are determined. The results are presented in Fig. 6, Tables 1 and 2. As it can be seen in Fig. 6 higher removal efficiency of chromium was achieved in a bed with a depth of 0.2 m by C. papyrus (98.41%). While lower removal efficiency was in the planted wetland was by Para grass (94.21%) in the 0.2 m depth. From Fig. 5 we can see that the concentration of chromium (VI) for all depths at the outlet of the treatment bed were below 0.1 ppm which is the permissible standard limit [29].

3.2 The Growth Rate of Plants

The experiment took eight months starting from the planting of the C. papyrus and Para grass to the end of the analysis period. It was initially observed that, in all water depths, the growth rate of both plants was low. This is due to the accumulation period needed by the plant to adopt the new environment. In the first 10 days, leaves were narrow and the upper surface had a yellow pale color. The growth rate after 10 days was the same as the control unit. After the accumulation period, it was found that the growth rate of C. Papyrus was higher than Para grass in all of the water depths. On the other hand, statistical analysis by ANOVA demonstrated that water depth had no significant effect on the growth rate of the plant (Tables 2 and 3).

Table 1. Influent wastewater characteristics

Analysis items	Average ($\pm$SD)
Temperature	21.6 ± 4.9
pH	7.66 ± 0.36
BOD5	210 ± 25
TDS	100 ± 4.56
Cr6+	1 ± 0.008

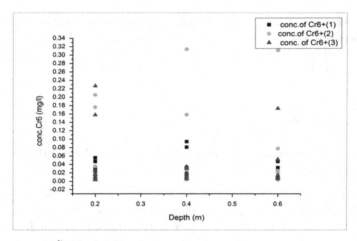

Conc. of Cr^{6+} (1) for depth 0.2m
Conc. of Cr^{6+} (2) for depth 0.4m
Conc. of Cr^{6+} (3) for depth 0.6m

Fig. 5. Chromium concentration at the three wetland depths

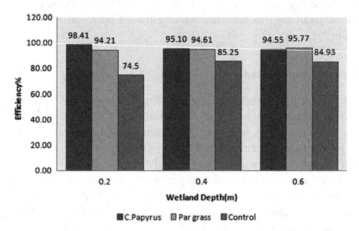

Fig. 6. Average removal efficiency of plants for chromium six at three wastewater depths

Table 2. Average height of experimental plants at three wastewater depths

Water depth (m)	C. Papyrus		Para grass	
	Experiment (cm)	Control (cm)	Experiment (cm)	Control (cm)
0.20	116.2	100.3	65.6	70.3
0.40	106.0	106.0	70.0	85.2
0.60	104.6	110.5	91.2	98.0
	ns	ns	ns	ns

ns no significant difference at 95%

Table 3. Overall influent and effluent concentrations and removal efficiencies in each unit

	Influent concentration (mg/L)	Effluent concentration (mg/L)			Effluent concentration (mg/L)			Removal efficiency (%)					
		C. Papyrus at different depth			Para grass at different depth			C. Papyrus at different depth			Para grass at different depth		
		0.2 m	0.4 m	0.6 m	0.2 m	0.4 m	0.6 m	0.2 m	0.4 m	0.6 m	0.2 m	0.4 m	0.6 m
Cr 6+	1	0.016	0.049	0.054	0.058	0.054	0.042	98.41	95.10	94.55	94.21	94.61	95.77
BOD	215	40.02	52.01	49.54	43.00	41.23	39.12	81.39	75.81	76.96	80.00	80.82	81.80

Total number of sample 63

4 Conclusions

In this study, the removal efficiency of 98.4% was achieved with C. papyrus at constructed wetland depth of 0.20 m. Comparison of the efficiency for chromium (VI) removal of wetland at 0.20 m, 0.40 m and 0.60 m depth was found that papyrus and Para grass have better efficiency for chromium (VI) removal at 0.20 m and 0.60 m pilot-scale constructed wetland depth respectively.

On the other hand, it was found that the growths of both plants were not affected by three wetland depths when compared with the control. It can be suggested in general that horizontal subsurface flow constructed wetland system with Papyrus plant species could be a potential candidate for removal of chromium at large discharge volume.

References

1. Kivaisi, A.K.: The potential for constructed wetlands for wastewater treatment and reuse in developing countries: a review. Ecol. Eng. **16**, 545–560 (2001)
2. Andreo-Martínez, P., García-Martínez, N., Quesada-Medina, J., Almela, L.: Domestic wastewaters reuse reclaimed by an improved horizontal subsurface-flow constructed wetland: A case study in the southeast of Spain. Biores. Technol. **233**, 236–246 (2017)
3. Werker, A.G., Doughtery, J.M., McHenry, J.L., Van Loon, W.A.: Treatment variability for wetland wastewater treatment design in cold climates. Ecol. Eng. **19**, 1–11 (2002)
4. Dierberg, F.E., DeBusk, T.A., Jackson, S.D., Chimney, M.J., Pietro, K.: Submerged aquatic vegetation-based treatment wetlands for removing phosphorus from agricultural runoff: response to hydraulic and nutrient loading. Water Res. **36**, 1409–1422 (2002)
5. Pastor, R., Benqlilou, C. Paz, D., Cardenas, G., Espun, A., Puigjaner, L.: Design optimization of constructed wetlands for wastewater treatment. Resour. Conserv. Recycl. **37**, 193–204 (2003)
6. Matamoros, V., Puigagut, J Garci, J., Bayona, J.M.: Behavior of selected priority organic pollutants in horizontal subsurface flow constructed wetlands: a preliminary screening. Chemosphere **69**, 1374–1380 (2007)
7. Toscano, A., Langergraber, G., Consoli, S., Cirelli, G.L.: Modelling pollutant removal in a pilot-scale two-stage subsurface flow constructed wetlands. Ecol. Eng. **35**, 281–289 (2009)
8. Konnerup, D., Koottatep, T., Brix, H.: Treatment of domestic wastewater in tropical, subsurface flow constructed wetlands planted with Canna and Heliconia. Ecol. Eng. **35**, 248–257 (2009)
9. Vymazal, J.: The use constructed wetlands with horizontal sub-surface flow for various types of wastewater. Ecol. Eng. **35**, 1–17 (2009)

10. Dotro, G., Larsen, D., Palazolo, P.: Preliminary evaluation of biological and physical-chemical chromium removal mechanisms in gravel media used in constructed wetlands. Water Air Soil Pollut. **215**, 507–515 (2011)
11. Zidan, A.R.A., El-Gamal, M.M., Rashed, A.A., El-Hady Eid, M.A.A.: Wastewater treatment in horizontal subsurface flow constructed wetlands using different media (setup stage). Water Sci. **29**, 26–35 (2015)
12. Vymazal, J.: Removal of nutrients in various types of constructed wetlands. Sci. Total Environ. **380**, 48–65 (2007)
13. Rousseau, D.P.L., Lesage, E., Story, A., Vanrolleghem, P.A., De Pauw, N.: Constructed wetlands for water reclamation. Desalination **218**, 181–189 (2008)
14. Saeed, T., Sun, G.: Kinetic modeling of nitrogen and organics removal in vertical and horizontal flow wetlands. Water Res. **45**, 3137–3152 (2011)
15. Saeed, T., Afrin, R., Al Muyeed, A., Sun, G.: Treatment of tannery wastewater in a pilot-scale hybrid constructed wetland system in Bangladesh. Chemosphere **88**, 1065–1073 (2012)
16. Mthembu, M.S., Odinga, C.A., Swalaha, F.M., Bux, F.: Constructed wetlands: a future alternative wastewater treatment technology. Afr. J. Biotechnol. **12**(29), 4542–4553 (2013)
17. Sultana, M.-Y., Akratos, C.S., Pavlou, S., Vayenas, D.V.: Chromium removal in constructed wetlands: a review. Int. Biodeterior. Biodegradation **96**, 181–190 (2014)
18. Terfie, T.A.: Post Treatment of Tannery Wastewater in Horizontal Subsurface Flow Constructed Wetland Connected to Sequence Batch Reactor: Performance, Nutrient Profile and Effluent Reuse for Irrigation Doctor of Philosophy in Environmental Sciences Addis Ababa University (2017)
19. Vymazal, J.: The use of sub-surface constructed wetlands for wastewater treatment in the Czech Republic: 10 years of experience. Ecol. Eng. **18**, 633–646 (2002)
20. Garcia, J., Aguirre, P., Barragán, J., Matamoros, V., Bayona, J.M.: Effect of key design parameters on the efficiency of horizontal subsurface flow constructed wetlands. Ecol. Eng. **25**, 405–418 (2005)
21. Torrens, A., Molle, P., Boutin, C., Salgot, C.: Impact of design and operation variables on the performance of vertical-flow constructed wetlands and intermittent sand filters treating pond effluent. Water Res. **43**, 1851–1858 (2009)
22. USEPA. Methodology for Deriving Ambient Water Quality Criteria for the Protection of Human Health, U. S. E. P. Agency (2000)
23. Heike, et.al.: Review of subsurface flow constructed wetlands for greywater and domestic wastewater treatment in developing countries, Deutsche Gesellschaft für Technische Zusammenarbeit GmbH (GTZ) (2010)
24. Yadav, A.K., Abbassi, R., Kumar, N., Satya, S., Sreekrishnan, T.R., Mishra, B.K.: The removal of heavy metals in wetland microcosms: effects of bed depth, plant species, and metal mobility. Chem. Eng. J. **211–212**, 501–507 (2012)
25. Buchberger, S.G., Shaw, G.B.: An approach toward the rational design of constructed wetlands for wastewater treatment. Ecol. Eng. **4**, 249–275 (1995)
26. Calheiros, C.S., Rangel, A.O., Castro, P.M.: Constructed wetland systems vegetated with different plants applied to the treatment of tannery wastewater. Water Air Soil Pollut. **41**, 1790–1798 (2007)
27. 7196 A, M. CHROMIUM, HEXAVALENT (COLORIMETRIC)
28. Harris, D.C.: Quantitative Chemical Analysis. W.H. Freemanand, New York (2007)
29. EPA, E. the provisional standard for industrial pollution control in Ethiopia. E. P. Authority (2005)

Assessment of Industrial Effluent Pollution on Borkena River, Kombolcha, Ethiopia

Alemayehu Ali Damtew[1,2], Atikilt Abebe Ketema[1,2(✉)],
and Beshah Mogesse Behailu[3]

[1] Kombolcha Institute of Technology, Wollo University, Kombolcha, Ethiopia
alexemanali@gmail.com, atikiltabebe@gmail.com
[2] Bahir Dar Institute of Technology, Bahir Dar University, Bahir Dar, Ethiopia
[3] Arbaminch Water Technology Institute, Arbaminch University, Arba Minch, Ethiopia
beshahnb@yahoo.com

Abstract. In this study the effect of untreated and partially treated industrial wastewater on Borkena River was assessed. Six sampling sites were chosen spatially along the tributary of Borekena River and the River itself. The results indicated significant water quality deterioration, which characterized by Temperature, TSS, TDS, DO, BOD_5, COD and Phosphate with the mean concentration range from 45.27 ± 6.0 to 302.00 ± 10.56 °C, 571.67 ± 94.34 to 1633.33 ± 175.46, 450.00 ± 30 to 2422.33 ± 431.2, 6.40 ± 0.61 to 2.77 ± 0.35, 10 ± 0.50 to 190 ± 1.01, 34 ± 3.00 to 508 ± 4.00 and $12.93 \pm 4.41\_329.33 \pm 43.03$ mg/L respectively. The magnitude of these values were found above the permissible limits of ambient surface water quality stated by Ethiopia Environmental Protection Authority at all sampling sites, except upstream of Borkena River (SP_6). Significant increment of these parameters was evidenced at the downstream (SP_5) in comparison with the upstream (SP_6) of Borkena river ($P < 0.05$). The mean concentration of pH, EC, Sulphate, and Nitrate nitrogen were ranged from 6.84 ± 0.35 to 9.75 ± 0.43, 0.92 ± 0.27 to 9.07 ± 0.43, 7 ± 5.20 to 59.67 ± 11.52 and 3.57 ± 0.16 to 28.68 ± 4.91 mg/L were found under the permissible limits, except pH at sampling point 1 and 3. It was therefore concluded that Huaxu textile and BGI-brewery industry's effluents are polluted, from which Huaxu textile industry's effluent was contributed more for Borkena River contamination.

Keywords: Borkena River · Untreated wastewater · Partially treated wastewater

1 Introduction

Population growth, urbanization, and industrialization are adversely affect the quality of most of surface water globally (Walakira and Okot-okumu 2011; Owa 2013). This is due to extensive anthropogenic inputs of nutrients and sediments through unmonitored disposal of municipal-, institutional- and industrial solid and liquid wastes (Annalakshmi and Amsath 2012; Tessema et al. 2014). Rivers crossing urban and peri-urban areas of the developing countries are become the most polluted water source, since they are the

© ICST Institute for Computer Sciences, Social Informatics and Telecommunications Engineering 2020
Published by Springer Nature Switzerland AG 2020. All Rights Reserved
N. G. Habtu et al. (Eds.): ICAST 2019, LNICST 308, pp. 325–333, 2020.
https://doi.org/10.1007/978-3-030-43690-2_22

formal and informal disposal sites of Treated, Partially-treated and Untreated municipal and industrial wastewater (Bernard 2010; Suthar et al. 2010; Ljee 2011). As the result, the rivers and streams are highly polluted and hardly satisfy environmental demands for aquatic life. Studies also show that people lives near to polluted rivers, which carrier toxic chemicals and pathogens are exposed to acute and chronic diseases.

Physicochemical water quality monitoring is essential to characterize the quality of the rivers/streams with time and space. It also helps to identify the point and source of contamination.

In Ethiopia, Most of Industries are located near to rivers/streams in order to easily dispose their untreated and partially treated wastewater in to them. Likewise, Loyal and Workie streams are receiving untreated industrial wastewater from Huaxu textile and BGI-brewery industries and municipal wastewater from surrounding community from Kombolcha town. These streams tribute in to Borekena river that is used for cleaning, construction of buildings, irrigation of vegetables, swimming by children, drinking by animals and birds. Currently people living in near and downstream of the industries disposal points are facing many health related problems such as asthma, bronchial disease, dysentery, cholera, typhus, skin ulcer and chronic disease. So it is necessary to evaluate the extent of pollution on the streams and Borkena river in order to discover the effect of untreated and partially treated wastewater. Therefore, this study is aimed to assess the quality of Huaxu textile's and BGI-brewery's wastewater effluent, sewage from the surrounding community and receiving water bodies and to assess the pollution magnitude with respect to the national wastewater discharge standards.

2 Methods and Material

2.1 Study Area Description

Kombolcha town is one of the industrial towns of Amhara region. It is situated 24 km of south-west of Dessie town and 380 km north of Addis Ababa, the capital city of Ethiopia. Kombolcha town is geographically located in the latitude of $11°5'$ N and longitude of $39°44'$ E with an elevation ranges from 1842 masl to 1945 masl. The average annual temperature is 23 °C. Borekena river crosses the town from east to west directions. Most of the industries are located very closely to the center of the town and along the streams and Borekena river. Untreated and partially treated industrial and domestic wastewater is discharged in to Borkena river through its tributaries: Workie and Loyal streams.

2.2 Data Collection

Sampling points and sampling time are selected by surveying the location where and when Industrial and domestic wastewaters are discharged to the streams and where the streams join the river. In addition, upstream and downstream of the Borkena River was sampled to evaluate the water quality variation before and after wastewaters are discharged, respectively. Based on these criteria, Six (6) sampling locations are selected on the streams and the river. Sample point 1 (SP_1) at the outlet canal of Huaxu textile industry's untreated wastewater; Sample point 2 (SP_2) is at the point where Huaxu textile wastewater joined Loyal stream; Sample point 3 (SP_3) is at the point just before the loyal stream joined the Borekena river; Sample point 4 (SP_4) is at outlet canal of BGI-brewery industry partially treated wastewater to Workie stream, Sample point 5 (SP_5) is at the point after Loyal and Workie streams joined Borekena river and Sample point 6 (SP_6) is on the upstream of Borkena river before these industrial and domestic wastewater pollution (Fig. 1).

Grab sample was collected two times for each sampling point. Sample collection and handling procedure were performed according to American Public Health Associations recommended procedures (APHA 1999). The samples were collected by 2 L polystyrene bottle. The bottles were washed out thoroughly with the detergent, acid (1: 1 HNO_3 and H_2O by V/V), tap water, and then with distilled water before sampling. The actual samplings were done at midstream depth by dipping each sample bottle at approximately 5–10 cm below the water surface, projecting the mouth of the container against the flow direction.

The sample was taken twice (on March 24 and April 7/2018 at 6:00 AM) with three replicates to evaluate the effect of different wastewater effluent colors (i.e. Red and Grey color) from Huaxu textile industries. Samples were transported to the Bahir Dar Institute of technology water treatment laboratory in ice box within 8 hrs. The samples kept in the refrigerator at 4 °C till analyzed.

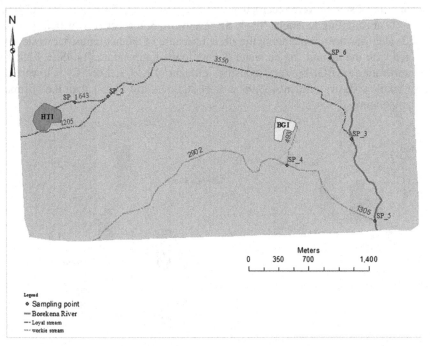

Fig. 1. Sampling location in the study area (length of stream segments in meter) (Color figure online)

2.3 Data Analysis

The water quality sample taken from each sampling points were tested at Bahir Dar Institute of Technology water treatment laboratory. The twelve (12) physicochemical water quality parameters were analyzed with descriptive statistics methods using SPSS-PC statistical package (SPSS 20 for Windows version). The mean value of each parameter was compared with Ethiopian Environmental Protection Authority ambient environment standards (EEPA 2003). ANOVA test was conducted to evaluate the significance of the water quality variation among sampling point with 95% confidence interval. Geographic Information System (GIS) software was used for data analysis and interpretation.

3 Result and Discussion

The Physicochemical water quality parameters analysis results revealed that the effluents discharged by Huaxu textile and BGI-brewery industries polluted the respective receiving streams and Borkena river in large. Domestic sewage discharged in to Loyal stream is also contributed to the pollution.

The mean temperature value were ranged from its highest value of 20.95 ± 0.94 °C at sampling location of SP_1 and lower value of 14.95 ± 1.39 °C at sampling location SP_6 (Fig. 2 and Table 1). The mean temperature values from Huaxu textile industry Effluent to loyal stream were recorded as 20.95 ± 0.94 °C, 18.93 ± 1.18 °C and 16.05 ± 0.39 °C at sampling locations SP_1, SP_2 and SP_3, respectively, which indicates that the value was decreasing along the stream because of the hot industrial wastewater is diluted with the natural stream water having lower temperature (14.95 ± 1.39 °C). The temperature of BGI-brewery industries effluent (19.20 ± 1.06 °C) is lower than Huaxu textile industry effluent (20.95 ± 0.94 °C), but still higher than the upstream river temperature.

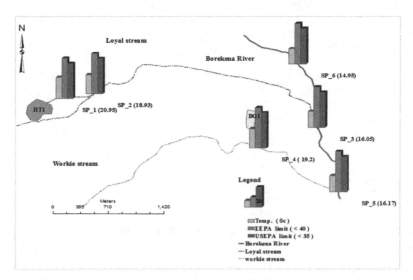

Fig. 2. Mean values of temperature (in °C) at different sampling point.

Table 1. Physicochemical and Biological water quality parameters (n is sample number, HTI: Huaxu Textile Industry, BGI: BGI-Brewery Industry, Upstream: Borkena river upstream and Downstream: Borkena river downstream)

Parameter	SP_1 (n = 6)- HTI effluent	SP_2 (n = 6)	SP_3 (n = 6)	SP_4 (n = 6) BGI effluent	SP_6 (n = 6) Upstream	SP_5 (n = 6)- Downstream	EEPA (2003) standard
Temp (°C)	20.95 ± 0.94	18.93 ± 1.18	16.05 ± 0.39	19.20 ± 1.06	14.95 ± 1.39	16.17 ± 1.04	≤(Upstream Tem ± 3 °C)
EC (μS/cm)	8.46 ± 5.49	7.47 ± 5.54	6.80 ± 1.09	9.07 ± 0.43	0.92 ± 0.27	4.02 ± 0.90	≤1000 @20 °C
pH (pH unit)	9.55 ± 0.44	8.98 ± 0.52	9.75 ± 0.43	7.43 ± 0.06	6.84 ± 0.35	8.22 ± 0.2	6–9
TSS	1633.33 ± 175.46	1474.17 ± 92.21	963.67 ± 155.64	1114.33 ± 182.97	571.67 ± 94.34	997 ± 23.30	≤25 & 50 Max value
TDS	2422.33 ± 431.2	1591.17 ± 211.65	1868.50 ± 158.28	1770 ± 26.46	450.00 ± 30	1383 ± 15.27	≤15% change from upstream
DO	3.19 ± 0.65	3.46 ± 0.42	2.87 ± 0.53	2.77 ± 0.35	6.40 ± 0.61	3.52 ± 0.50	50% Samples ≥9
BOD_5	109.83 ± 13.33	115.67 ± 15.92	136.00 ± 25.3	190 ± 1.01	10 ± 0.50	150 ± 2.50	≤5 mg/L O_2
COD	473.83 ± 66.32	453.67 ± 64.53	487.50 ± 20	155 ± 5.57	34 ± 3.00	508 ± 4.00	≤40 mg/L O_2*
NO_3^--N	13.23 ± 3.61	17.28 ± 6.56	28.68 ± 4.91	15 ± 5.25	3.57 ± 0.16	12.56 ± 0.07	≤50 NO_3^- (11.3 NO_3^--N)
PO_4^{-3}	329.33 ± 43.03	140.00 ± 45.64	165.50 ± 35.06	47.9 ± 3.97	12.93 ± 4.41	106.67 ± 46.09	≤25
SO_4^{2}	59.67 ± 11.52	40.67 ± 14.81	42.50 ± 31.97	14.86 ± 3.9	7.00 ± 5.2	18 ± 2.20	≤200
Hardness (of $CaCO_3$)	658.33 ± 24.22	202.93 ± 19.92	226.25 ± 7.5	54.17 ± 6.29	110 ± 2.5	298.83 ± 29.62	No limit is stated

Units in mg/L unless otherwise state

The analysis result revealed that a significant temperature variation between the point SP_2, where Huaxu textile industry effluent mixed with loyal stream (20.95 ± 0.94 °C) and the upstream of Borkena river (14.95 ± 1.39 °C) (P = 0.035 < 0.05). However, no significant temperature variation (P = 0.29 > 0.05) between upstream (14.95 ± 1.39 °C) and downstream of Borkena river (16.17 ± 1.04 °C), this is because of larger volume effect of Borkena than Loyal river. The temperature values at the Upstream and downstream of Borkena river and at SP_3 are under the permissible limit of EEPA (2003), such as below upstream temperature ±3 °C.

The maximum mean value of BOD_5 was recorded as 190 ± 1.01 mg/L at SP_4. This highest value is mainly attributed to the availability of large amount organic matter in the partially treated BGI wastewater. The result showed that a significant increment of BOD_5 value (Fig. 3 and Table 1) along the Loyal stream (P = 0.04 < 0.05), this is caused by the additional domestic sewage discharge in to Loyal river from the surrounding community. These leads to a significantly increment of BOD_5 (P = 10^{-6} < 0.05) at the downstream, SP_5 (150 ± 2.5 mg/L) in comparison with the upstream of the river, SP_6 (10.00 ± 0.5 mg/L).

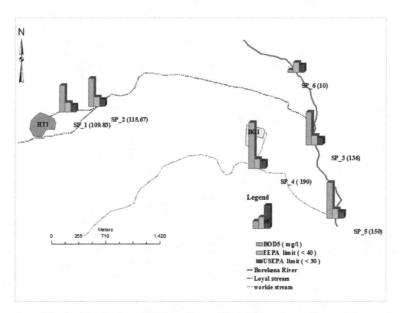

Fig. 3. Mean values of BOD_5 (in mg/L) at different sampling point.

All the measured values of BOD_5 except the value on the upstream location of Borkena River (SP_6) were found higher than EEPA (2003) permissible surface water BOD_5 limit (below 25). Higher BOD_5 concentration at the downstream of Borekena river is resulted primarily from an excess amount of biodegradable organic matter contents of partially treated BGI industrial wastewater (190 ± 2.01) than the untreated Huaxu textile industrial wastewater and sewage released from the surrounding community (136.00 ± 25.3). Large organic matter presence maximize the availability of decomposers, which uses much amount of oxygen for their growth and deplete dissolved oxygen concentration (Table 1).

All the measured values of COD except the value at the upstream of Borkena river were found higher than EEPA (2003) permissible (below 40). There is a significant COD value increment between upstream and downstream sampling location of Borkena river ($P = 8 * 10^{-9} < 0.05$), which is because of much chemical waste release from Huaxu textile industry and considerable addition from BGI waste (Fig. 4 and Table 1). Desta (1997) and Mammo (2004) studies also confirmed the high magnitude of COD from Ethiopian textile factories effluent. The red and gray colour of Huaxu textile industry effluent and algae blooms downstream of loyal rives are reasoned out with the availability of large concentration of dissolved solid (2422.33 ± 431.2) and PO_4^{-3} (165.50 ± 35.06), respectively (Fig. 5). Maximum concentration of PO_4^{-3} was recorded at Huaxu textile industry effluent sample site (329.33 ± 43.03). This results significant increment of PO_4^{-3} concentration ($P = 0.024 < 0.05$) at the downstream of Borkena river (106.67 ± 46.09) from the upstream sampling site (12.93 ± 4.41). At all sampling site the PO_4^{-3} concentration is higher than the EEPA (2003) permissible limit (below 25 mg/L) except SP_6 Temperature, BOD5, COD and Phosphate.

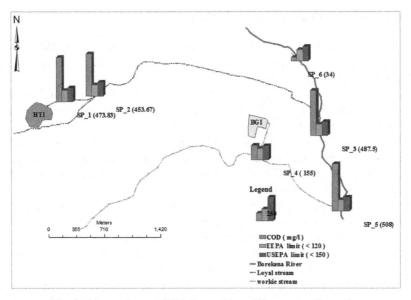

Fig. 4. Mean values of COD (in mg/L) at different sampling point.

The mean concentration magnitude of TSS, TDS, DO were found above the permissible limits of ambient surface water quality value stated by EEPA (2003) at all sampling sites, except at the upstream of Borkena river (SP_6). Significant increment of these parameters was identified at the downstream sampling point (SP_5) comparing with upstream sampling point (SP_6) of Borkena river (P < 0.05). The mean concentration of pH, EC, Sulphate, and Nitrate nitrogen were found within the permissible limits, except pH at SP_1 and SP_3.

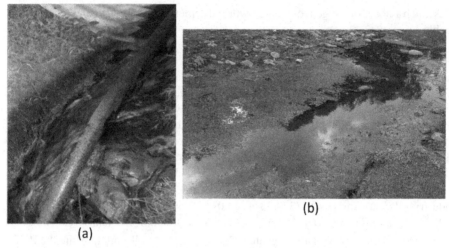

Fig. 5. (a) Red colour Huaxu textile industry effluent (b) Algae blooms at downstream of Loyal stream (Color figure online)

4   Conclusion and Recommendation

The physicochemical parameters analysis results confirmed that untreated Huaxu textile industry and partially treated BGI brewery industrial wastewater are hardly satisfied EEPA (2003) and US EPA (1994) discharging standard.

It was therefore concluded that Huaxu textile and BGI-brewery industry's effluents are polluted, in which Huaxu textile industry effluent was highly contaminated than BGI. As the consequence aquatic life and surrounding livelihood of Borkena River in large and respective tributary rivers (Loyal and Workie streams) were adversely affected.

In general, the result of this study give us insight about the high level of Borkena river contamination due to untreated and/or partially treated industrial and domestic effluent discharge from Kombolcha Industrial zone.

It is recommended to conduct Heavy metals concentrations in Huaxu textile industry effluent for future work so as to quantify types and strength of the pollution in detail, to predict its impact on the environment and target for pollution prevention. It is also important to make periodic quantity and quality measurement of the effluent, since the type, concentration and parameters load can differ with process type and production variation. Enforcement of environmental protection rules and periodic monitoring program is mandatory to decrease the industrial pollution level.

References

Annalakshmi, G., Amsath, A.: An assessment of water quality of river Cauvery and its tributaries Arasalar with reference to physico-chemical parameters at Tanjore DT, Tamilnadu, India. Int. J. Appl. Biol. Pharm. Technol. **3**(1), 269–279 (2012)

APA: Standard Methods for the Examination of Water and Wastewater, 20th edn., American Public Health Association/American Water Works Association/Water Environment Federation, Washington, D.C. (1999)

Bernard, A.: Assessing the performance of Dompoase wastewater treatment plant and its effect on water quality of the Oda River in Kumasi. Unpublished M.Sc. thesis, Kwame Nkrumah University of Science and Technology, Ghana (2010). http://wwwdatad.aau.org/handle/123456789/8636

Mammo, D.: An assessment of downstream pollution profile of Sebeta River and its surroundings. M.Sc. thesis, School of Graduate Studies, Addis Ababa University (2004)

EEPA (Ethioian Environmental Protection Authority): Guideline Ambient Environment Standards for Ethiopia. Prepared by EPA and UNIDO under ESDI project US/ETH/99/068/Ethiopia. Addis Ababa, Ethiopia (2003)

Ljee, T.: Revue scientifique et Technique, pp. 100–115, Décembre 2011 (2011)

Owa, F.D.: Water pollution: sources, effects, control and management. Mediterr. J. Soc. Sci. **4**(8), 65–68 (2013)

Suthar, S., Sharma, J., Chabukdhara, M., Nema, A.K.: Water quality assessment of river Hindon at Ghaziabad, India: impact of industrial and urban wastewater. Environ. Monit. Assess. **165**(1–4), 103–112 (2010)

Tessema, A., Mohammed, A., Birhanu, T., Negu, T.: Assessment of physico-chemical water quality of Bira dam, Bati Wereda. J. Aquac. Res. Dev. **5**(6), 1–4 (2014)

US EPA (United States Environmental Protection Agency): National recommended Water quality criteria correction-EPA-822/z-99-001, Washington, D.C. (1994)

Walakira, P., Okot-okumu, J.: Impact of industrial effluents on water quality of streams in Nakawa-Ntinda, Uganda. Appl. Sci. Environ. Manag. **15**(2), 289–296 (2011)

Desta, Z.: Industrial environmental management: the case of Awassa Textile Factory, Ethiopia. M.Sc. thesis, Wageningen Agricultural University, The Netherlands (1997)

Electrical, Electronics and Computing

Planning, Designing and Performance Evaluation of Micro Wave Link Case Study from Wegeda to NefasMewucha

Gashaw Mihretu[1]([⊠]), Pushparaghavan Annamalai[1], and N. Malmurugan[2]

[1] Faculty of Electrical and Computer Engineering,
Bahir Dar Institute of Technology, Bahir Dar University, POB 26, Bahir Dar, Ethiopia
gashite2009@gmail.com, aprshamu@gmail.com
[2] Mahindra College of Engineering, Salem, Tamilnadu, India
n.malmurugan@gmail.com

Abstract. The Microwave link is an alternative link for fiber optics or for the area which is difficult to practically implement fiber optics and satellite link access. It has different properties like line of sight, environmental constraints, including rain fade and many obstacle issues such as hills, buildings and trees. In Ethiopia, Amhara region, South Gondar, currently the hill station in between Wegeda Amanuel areas, microwave link severely affected and equipment failure due to the environmental interferences. Because of interruption of this link, most of the times stop the connection of this area. Due to the above limitation of the rural access to this area, this paper is specially intended to provide and fulfill the needs by planning and designing microwave link between NefasMewucha to Wegeda. The traffic from and to Wegeda is likely to increase in future as it is one of the important potential area in Amhara region. Hence, it needs reliable and efficient alternate communication link. In overall, this paper deals the site survey, system margins, frequency planning, power budget calculation and performance evaluation activities and the results are simulated using Global mapper 12.

Keywords: Path clearance · Signal Radiation Loss · System Margin · Power budget · Link reliability

1 Introduction

Microwave link is very important in the Ethiopia Amhara region because most of the geographical areas are not suitable for wired communications systems. Wegeda is one of the most inconvenient areas for copper wire and optical fiber link, but these areas are highly productive and it should have an uninterrupted telecommunication network to access these products and increase the development. An alternative link has required to connect Wegeda to other parts of Amhara region and whole country. Preferably, micro wave link is a choice to achieve this objective in appropriate way for the cost effective, more convenient for the proposed link access better than optical link [7].

© ICST Institute for Computer Sciences, Social Informatics and Telecommunications Engineering 2020
Published by Springer Nature Switzerland AG 2020. All Rights Reserved
N. G. Habtu et al. (Eds.): ICAST 2019, LNICST 308, pp. 337–354, 2020.
https://doi.org/10.1007/978-3-030-43690-2_23

The following Fig. 1 illustrates the flow chart approach for the proposed microwave link system and its design process. Mainly, the proposed link focus on the path performance for stage by stages per the system design process [2].

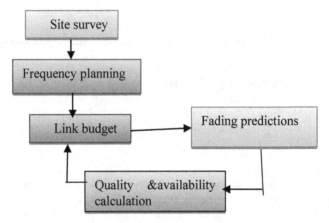

Fig. 1. System design process flow chart

2   Site Planning and Selection

The two sites of proposed link are, one is NefasMewucha and the other is Wegeda. From these sites, most of the real time data are collected by pilot surveying approach. These data are helped to know the path clearance, the coordinates of the sites, distance between path link, antenna height and the location and height of obstacles [3].

2.1   Path Wegeda to NefasMewucha

Figure 2 shows a geographical map of the two proposed terminals (Wegeda to NefasMewucha).

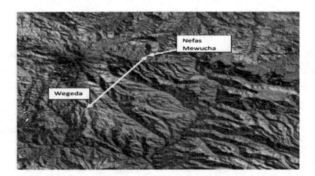

Fig. 2. Map of area of interest of the link

The proposed link is from Wegeda to NefasMewucha and its coordinate is measured at the presently existing tower of the two sites by using Global Positioning System (GPS) receivers and possible hop distance is determined by Global mapper 12 software by using these coordinates. Table 1 given below shows the coordinates and possible hop distance of the proposed link.

Table 1. Co-ordinates and hop distance of Wegeda and NefasMewucha

Path profile	Radio terminals sites	
	Wegeda	NefasMewucha
Latitude	11°23'50.0580"N	11°44'505"N
Longitude	38°14'18.173"E	38°28'665"E
Elevation	2560.84 m	3010 m
Maximum Hop length	45.1 km from NefasMewucha	45.1 km from Wegeda

Note: the hop length from the above Table 1 is line of sight length not road distance.

Based on the above data, path profile between two sites, the maximum hop length, elevation of the two sites and the maximum height of obstacles are obtained and shown in Fig. 3.

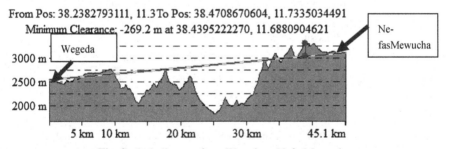

Fig. 3. Path distance from Wegeda to NefasMewucha

As shown in Fig. 3. It is observed that the link is not a clear line of sight. So an alternative link is required.

2.2   Recommended Hop Link: Wegeda to Guna and Guna to NefasMewucha

The two recommended hop links are from Wegeda to Guna and from Guna to Nefas-Mewucha with repeater at Guna. The map shown in Fig. 4 illustrates the two alternative links.

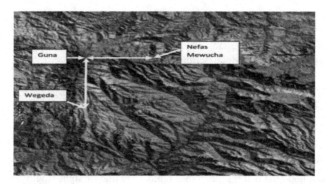

Fig. 4. Illustrate the hop from Wegeda to Guna and Guna to NefasMewucha

Coordinates of the two hops such as latitude, longitude and elevation are measured using GPS receivers at the existing towers (Table 2).

Table 2. Co-ordinates of sites and their path length

Path profile	Link sites		
	Wegeda	NefasMewucha	Guna
Latitude	11°23′50.0580″N	11°44′505″N	11°42′39″N
Longitude	38°14′18.173″E	38°28′665″E	38°14′31.9605″E
Elevation	2560.84 m	3010 m	4122 m
Maximum hop length	35.0 km from Guna	25.5 km from Guna	35.0 km to Wegeda & 25.5 km from NefasMewucha

Note:- The hop distance in the above table is line of sight distance.

The path profile of the two alternative links, from Wegeda to Guna and Guna to NefasMewucha are shown in Figs. 5 and 6 below. The path profile of the hop from Wegeda to Guna and Guna to NefasMewucha needs minimum 28.8 m and 21.4 m height antennas respectively for line of sight.

From Pos: 38.2382793111, 11.3!To Pos: 38.2419421103, 11.7115266539
Minimum Clearance: -5.4 m at 38.2419313794, 11.7105984347

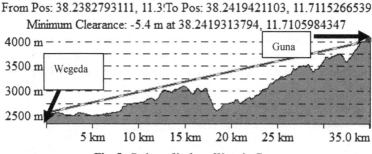

Fig. 5. Path profile from Wegeda-Guna

From Pos: 38.2382793111, 11.7To Pos: 38.4708670604, 11.7389976479
Minimum Clearance: -10.3 m at 38.2391878570, 11.7134582081

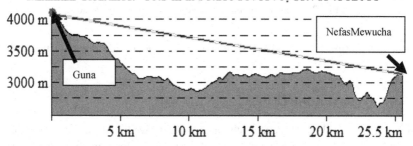

Fig. 6. Path link length from Guna to NefasMewucha

2.3 Frequency Planning

The operating frequency bands of existing link at the Guna station in the direction of the proposed link is 8 GHz. So, that the frequency to be selected should be different from this band. In the design link 7 GHz frequency band is used for both transmitter and receiver frequency for each hop as per Table 3 shown below

Table 3. Frequency arrangement

Station	Unit	Tx module	Rx module	LO	IF (Tx/Rx)	T/R (Duplex)
Guna	MHz	7550	7850	5550	2000/2161	161 MHz
NefasMewucha to/from Guna	MHz	7850	7550		2161/2000	
Guna to/from Wegeda	MHz	7125	7425	5125	2000/2161	161/154 MHz
Wegeda	MHz	7425	7125		2161/2000	

3   Use of Repeaters

As shown in Fig. 3 below, it is already seen that there is no possibility of establishing the direct microwave link between the stations Wegeda to NefasMewucha due to LOS obstruction. Hence a repeater station in Guna is suggested in between [11].

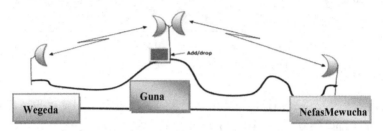

Fig. 7. Repeaters between Wegeda and NefasMewucha

At Guna station adds/drops of data, voice and videos are done by using ADM equipment.

4   First Fresnel Zone (FFZ)

After getting a feasible link, the next step in the microwave link design is calculating the (FFZ) radius, in order to know at least 60% of the FFZ free from any type of obstruction in the hop [6].

It depends on the hope length and the operating frequency [1]. For no obstructions between two sites, the maximum first Fresnel zone radius is calculated using the following formula [6].

$$F = 8,657\sqrt{l/f} \tag{1}$$

Where

F = first Fresnel zone
l = the maximum hop length in meter
f = operating frequency of the link

4.1   FFZ –Wegeda to Guna

The maximum 60% FFZ of this path is calculated using Eq. (1) with,

l = Hop length from Wegeda to Guna in meter = 35 km = 35000 m
f = operating frequency of link = 7.125 GHz

$$F = 8,657\sqrt{35000/7.125 * 10^9} = 19.187$$

4.2 FFZ– Guna to NefasMewucha

The 60% radius of the FFZ for the above link is calculated using Eq. (1) with,

l = Hop length from Guna to NefasMewucha 25.5 km = 25500 m
f = operating frequency of path = 7.55 GHz

$$F = 8,657\sqrt{25500/7.55 * 10^9} = 15.9\,\text{m}$$

5 Antenna Height Calculation

Antenna height of the microwave link is calculated based on the Rec. ITU-R P.530-14 [10]. For the first hop antenna height, $(A_h) = 1.0 * F_1 = 1 * 19.187\,\text{m} = 19.187\,\text{m}$, we must consider the height of trees and growth of vegetables 12 m and 3 m respectively. Where F_1 is First Fresnel Zone radius, so the antenna height, $(A_h) = 19.187\,\text{m} + 12\,\text{m} + 3\,\text{m} = 34.187\,\text{m}$ (this is the minimum antenna height for the first hop).

Similarly, the same procedure can be repeated for the second hop.

Antenna height, $(A_h) = 1.0 * F_1 + 12\,\text{m} + 3\,\text{m} = 15.9\,\text{m} + 12\,\text{m} + 3\,\text{m} = 30.9\,\text{m}$ (this is the minimum antenna height for the second hop). In the two hops, the antenna should not be mounted less than the calculated height.

In our design, the antennas can be mounted at 40 m and 35 m for the first hop and the second hop on the existing tower heights respectively to have more clearance.

The first and second hop path profiles with the recommended antenna heights have 34.6 m and 24.7 m give clearance from any obstacle and they are shown in Figs. 8 and 9 respectively. These indicate the feasible path of the two hops.

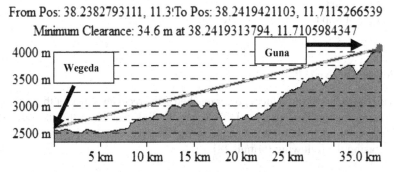

From Pos: 38.2382793111, 11.3!To Pos: 38.2419421103, 11.7115266539
Minimum Clearance: 34.6 m at 38.2419313794, 11.7105984347

Fig. 8. Path clearance from Wegeda to Guna with 40 m antenna height

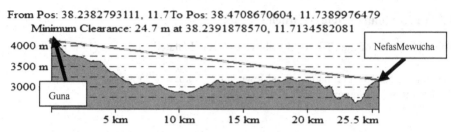

From Pos: 38.2382793111, 11.7 To Pos: 38.4708670604, 11.7389976479
Minimum Clearance: 24.7 m at 38.2391878570, 11.7134582081

Fig. 9. Path from Guna to NefasMewucha with 35 m antenna height

6 Micro Wave Link Path Analysis

Microwave link path analysis is carried out to dimension the link and it is a calculation involving the gain and loss factors associated with the antennas, transmitters, transmission lines and propagation environment [2].

6.1 Signal Radiation Losses (SRL)

Signal radiation loss is the degradation of transmitting signals, when it propagates through a free space. This loss depends on the length of links and the operating frequency of path [4].

If the frequency and the distance are expressed in terms of Kilometer and Giga Hertz, the signal radiation loss is given by the following equation [6, 8].

$$L_{SRL} = 92.45 + 20\log(f) + 20\log(d) \text{ [dB]} \tag{2}$$

Where

f = frequency (GHz)
d = distance of hop between transmitter and receiver (Km)

6.2 Power Received (P$_r$)

The receive power is the amount of power reached at the receiver unit after the transmitted power pass through a free space [5]. To assure the link feasibility the received power magnitude must be greater than or equal to the Receiver sensitivity threshold. P_r can calculate using the following formula [8].

$$P_r = P_t - L_{ctx} + G_{atx} - L_{crx} + G_{arx} - SRL - R_t \text{ [dBm]} \tag{3}$$

Where

P_r = Power received
P_t = Output power of the transmitter (dBm)
$L_{ctx,}$ = Connectors, branching Loss (cable unit) b/n Transmitter and Transmitter antenna (dB)
L_{crx} = Connectors, branching Loss (cable unit) b/n Receiver and Receiver antenna (dB)
G_{atx} = Gain of transmitter antenna (dBi)
G_{arx} = Gain of receiver antenna (dBi)
SRL = Signal Radiation Loss (dB)
R_t = Rain attenuation (dB)
$P_r \geq R_s$ (receiver sensitivity threshold)

6.3 Rain Attenuation Calculation for the First Hop (Wegeda to Guna)

The rain data were taken from National Metrology Agency Bahir Dar branch which is collected from NefasMewucha, Simada (Wegeda) and Gassay rain fall sites.

The rain attenuation calculations are calculated based on ITU-R Model of Rain Attenuation because the rain attenuation is minimum in this model when compare to other methods. It is calculated by using the following steps [9].

Step 1: Obtain the rain rate R0.01 exceeded in 0.01% of the time (with an integration of 1 min) [9]. The maximum rain rate at the two sites are taken from the collected data. But in Guna there is no rainfall station, we use the rainfall data from Gassay station, which is near to Guna and it has almost the same rain data. The maximum rain rate at Wegeda and Gassay record in July 2013 and mar 2014, and the values are 444.9 mm/h and 719.6 mm/h respectively. The average rain ratings are used.

$$\text{Average rain rate} = (444.9\,\text{mm/h} + 719.6\,\text{mm/h})/2$$
$$= 582.25\,\text{mm/h}$$
$$R_{0.01} = 582.25\,\text{mm}/60\,\text{min} = 9.7\,\text{mm/min}$$

Step 2: Compute the specific attenuation, γ (dB/km) for 7 GHz frequency band, vertical polarization and the above rain rate. It can be expressed as follows [9].

$$\gamma = KR^\alpha \tag{4}$$

Where

γ = rain rate at p% of probability
K, α = functions of frequency, f (GHz) in the range 1 to 1000 GHz.

The specific attenuation is computed by using $k = 0.00265$ and $\alpha = 1.312$, these values are tabulated values by different publications for 7 GHz frequency. Therefore, specific attenuation is calculated by using Eq. (4).

$$\gamma = KR^\alpha = 0.00265 * 9.7^{1.312} = 0.0522 \, dB/km$$

Step 3: Compute the effective path length, d_{eff}, of the link by multiplying the actual path length (1) by a distance factor(r). Before computing effective path length, distance factor is given by [9].

$$r = 1/1 + 1/d_0 \tag{5}$$

Where

$r =$ distance factor
$l =$ path length

Where, for $R_{0.001} \leq 100$ mm/h [10].

$$d_0 = 35e_{0.01}^{-0.015R} \tag{6}$$

With actual path length of 35 km and d_0 is calculated by Eq. (6)
But in our design $0.01 \, R \geq 100$ mm/h, we use the value 100 mm/h in place of $0.01R$.

$$d_0 = 35e^{-0.015*100} = 3.448 \, km$$

Therefore, distance factor and effective distance become.

$$\text{And} \quad d_{eff} = 35 \, km * 0.0897 = 3.1395 \, km$$

Step 4: An estimate of the path attenuation exceeded in 0.01% of the time is given by [9]

$$A_{0.01} = \gamma d_{eff} = \gamma l.r \, (dB) \tag{7}$$

Where

$l =$ path length
$r =$ reduction factor

By using the values of effective distance and specific attenuation from the above analysis the estimated path attenuation exceeded 0.01% becomes

$$A_{0.01} = 0.0522 * 3.1395 = 0.164 \, dB$$

6.4   Rain Attenuation Calculation for the Second Hop (Guna to NefasMewucha)

The rain attenuation calculations are calculated based on ITU-R Model of Rain Attenuation because the rain attenuation is minimum in this model when compare to other methods [9]. It is calculated by using the following steps.

Step 1: The rain rate R0.01 exceeded in 0.01% of the time (with an integration of 1 min) [9]. The data were collected by the national metrology agency, Bahir Dar branch. We take the maximum rain rate at the two sites from the collected data. But at Guna there is no rainfall station, we use the rainfall data from Gassay station which is near to Guna. The maximum rain rate at Guna and NefasMewucha are recorded in March 2014 and July 1998, and the values are 719.6 mm/h and 510.0 mm/h respectively. The average rain ratings are used.

$$\text{Average rain rate} = (510.0\,\text{mm/h} + 719.6\,\text{mm/h})/2$$
$$= 614.8\,\text{mm/h}$$
$$R_{0.01} = 614.8\,\text{mm}/60\,\text{min} = 10.25\,\text{mm/min}$$

Step 2: Computation of the specific attenuation, γ (dB/km) for 7 GHz frequency band, vertical polarization and the above rain rate. The specific attenuation is computed by using k = 0.00265 and α = 1.312, these values are tabulated values by different publications for 7 GHz frequency. The calculation is done by using Eq. (4) as follow.

$$\gamma = KR^{\alpha} = 0.00265 * 10.25^{1.312} = 0.056\,\text{dB/km}$$

Step 3: Computation of the effective path length, d_{eff}, of the link by multiplying the actual path length (l) by a distance factor r. Before computing effective path length, we must calculate the distance factor by using Eq. (5) with actual path length of 25.5 km and d_0 is calculated by Eqs. (6).

But In our design 0.01 R $\geq$ 100 mm/h, we use the value 100 mm/h in place of 0.01R.

$$d_0 = 35e^{-0.015*100} = 3.448\,\text{km}$$

Therefore, distance factor and effective distance become.

$$r = 1/(1 + 25.5\,\text{km}/3.448\,\text{km}) = 1/8.3956 = 0.119$$
$$\text{And} \quad d_{eff} = 25.5\,\text{km} * 0.119 = 3.037\,\text{km}$$

Step 4: An estimate of the path attenuation exceeded in 0.01% of the time is calculated by using Eq. (7)

$$A_{0.01} = 0.056 * 3.037 = 0.17\,\text{dB}$$

The rain attenuation of the first hop and the second hop are 0.164 dB and 0.17 dB respectively. This result shows the rain attenuation is directly proportional to the rain rate because the rain rate in the second hop is greater than the first hop.

6.5 System Margin (SM)

System margin is an essential parameter in microwave link path which is to evaluate the performance of the link to be established and it can be expressed as

$$SM = P_r - R_{th} \tag{8}$$

Where

SM = System margin
P_r = Received Signal Level
R_{th} = Receiver threshold

7 Power Budget of the Proposed Link

Before establishing the path of the proposed link we should determine the equipment's used at the transmitter and the receiver site and select that equipment's with appropriate ratings to have a reliable system [2].

The specification of the equipment's used at the transmitter and receiver site is shown in Table 4 below.

Table 4. Rating of equipment used in transmitters and receivers site

Frequency bands (GHz)		7
Full-duplex		FDD
Operating frequency		7125 MHz to 7900 MHz
Standby mode configuration		$1 + 0$ or $1 + 1$
Power supply (V)		DC: −48 V (+24 V), 10%
RF output power (dBm)		27
Receiver threshold (dBm)		−84
Antenna gain (dBi) medium (0.9 m diameter)		34.8
Type of cable	Operating frequency	Loss in dB per 100 feet
LMR-900	7 GHz	2.9

7.1 Power Budget from Wegeda to Guna

In order to calculate the Power budget, we use the specifications of the equipment given in Table 4.

Signal Radiation Loss (SRL)
Signal Radiation Loss in free space *is* calculated using Eq. (2) with f = frequency (GHz) = 7.125 and d = distance of the hop between *Wegeda to Guna* (Km) = 35

$$L_{SRL} = 92.45 + 20\log(7.125) + 20\log(35) \text{ [dB]}$$
$$= 92.45 + 17.055 + 30.88 = 140.386 \text{ dB}$$

Power Received P_r
Received power at the receiver side can be calculated using Eq. (4) with P_t = output power of the transmitter (dBm) = 27 and Lctx, = Loss (cable, connectors, branching unit at Tx) = 5.766 dB + 0.025 dB = 5.79 dB, because the cable length at the transmitter side is 60 m, it has 5.766 dB loss and 0.025 dB is connector loss.

L_{crx} = Loss (cable, connectors, branching unit at Rx) 5.766 dB + 0.025 dB = 5.79 dB, because the cable length at the receiver side is 60 m, it has 5.766 dB loss and 0.025 dB is connector loss between transmitter/receiver and antenna.

G_{atx} = Gain of transmitter antenna (dBi) = 34.8
G_{atx} = Gain of transmitter antenna (dBi) = 34.8
G_{arx} = Gain of receiver antenna (dBi) = 34.8
L_{SRL} = Signal Radiation Loss (dB) = 140.386
R_t = Rain attenuation (dB) = 0.164

$$P_r = 27 \text{ dBm} + 34.8 \text{ dBi} - 5.79 \text{ dB} + 34.8 \text{ dBi} - 5.79 \text{ dB} - 140.386 \text{ dB} - 0.164 \text{ dB}$$
$$= -55.53 \text{ dBm}$$

System Margin (SM)
The system margin of the above path can be calculated as follows using Eq. (8).
With P_r = power Received = −55.53 dBm and R_{th} = Receiver threshold = −84 dBm

$$SM = P_r - R_{th}$$
$$= -55.53 \text{ dBm} - (-84 \text{ dBm}) = 28.47 \text{ dB}$$

7.2 Link Budget from Guna to NefasMewucha

In order to calculate the power budget, we use the specifications of the equipment given in Table 4.

Signal Radiation Loss (SRL)
Signal Radiation Loss in free space *is* calculated using Eq. (3) with f = frequency (GHz) = 7.55 and d = distance of the hop between Guna to NefasMewucha (Km) = 25.5

$$L_{SRL} = 92.45 + 20\log(7.55) + 20\log(25.5) \, [dB]$$
$$= 92.45 + 17.559 + 28.13 = 138.14 \, dB$$

Power Received (P_r)
Received power at the receiver side in the second hop can be calculated using Eq. (4) with P_t = output power of the transmitter (dBm) = 27, L_{ctx}, = Loss (cable, connectors, 55 m, it has 5.23 dB loss and 0.025 dB is connector loss between transmitter/receiver and antenna (dB) = 5.23 dB + 0.025 dB = 5.255 dB, L_{crx} = Loss (cable, connectors, branching unit at Rx) 5.23 dB + 0.025 dB = 5.255 dB, because the cable length at the transmitter side is 55 m, it has 5.23 dB loss and 0.025 dB is connector loss between transmitter/receiver and antenna, G_{atx} = gain of the transmitter antenna (dBi) = 34.8, G_{arx} = gain of receiver antenna (dBi) = 34.8, L_{SRL} = Signal Radiation Loss s (dB) = 138.14 and R_t = rain attenuation (dB) = 0.17 dB.

$$P_r = 27 \, dBm + 34.8 \, dBi - 5.255 \, dB + 34.8 \, dBi - 5.255 \, dB - 138.14 \, dB - 0.17 \, dB$$
$$= -52.22 \, dBm$$

System Margin
The system margin of the above path can be calculated as follows using Eq. (8) with P_r = power Received = −52.22 dBm and R_{th} = Receiver threshold = −84 dB.

$$SM = P_r - R_{th}$$
$$= -52.22 \, dBm - (-84 \, dBm) = 31.78 \, dB$$

Note: in the power budget analysis of the above two hops, Wegeda to Guna has system margin of 28.47 dB and the second Guna to NefasMewucha has 31.78 dB. These results are greater than 10 dB (threshold value) which shows the link has the ability to provide guaranteed quality of service.

8 Link Availability

The path availability also called link reliability is the percentage of time that the received signal is above the required threshold, P_{req}. It is sometimes expressed as the expected minutes of outage per year and the percentage of time represents the outage time for a given link budget [8]. The path availability is function of the radio frequency, diversity, fade margin, path length, and local climate. The International Telecommunication Union publishes reports with empirical models of required fade margin for different parts of the world [10].

The percentage of time (P_w) that fades depth (A) (dB) is exceeded in the average worst month is calculated by using the following equation [10].

$$P_w = k * l^{3.6} * f^{0.89} (1 + |\varepsilon_p|)^{-1.4} * 10^{-A/10} \tag{9}$$

Where

k = geoclimatic factor
l = path length in km
f = frequency in GHz
ε_p = path slope
A = fade margin [dB]

The path inclination $|\varepsilon_p|$ (mrad) of the link is calculated from the antenna heights of the transmitter and receiver (above sea level or some other reference height) and it is calculated as follows [10],

$$\varepsilon_p = (h_A - h_B)/l \tag{10}$$

Where

h_A = antenna height + ground elevation at the transmitter in m
h_B = antenna height + ground elevation at the receiver in m
l = path length in Km

Another parameter that determines the percentage of the time average worst month is geoclimatic (k) factor.

It can be calculated using

$$K = 10^{-(6.5 - Clat - Clon)} P_L^{1.5} \tag{11}$$

The above equation is because of that the proposed link is Overland links for which the lower of the transmitting and receiving antennas is less than 70 m above mean sea level.

ITU recommendation calculations for K, there are four K categories, two of which are for overland inks and two for over-water links. K can be estimated from the contour maps given in Figures of ITU-R PN.453-4, from Figs. 7, 8, and 9. For the percentage of time P_L that the average refractivity gradient in the lowest 100 m of the atmosphere is less than 100 N-units per km [8].

The value of P_L is determined by using figures of ITU-R PN.453-4. From these figures the value of P_L is determined to be 5, 20, 10 and 1 for the months of November, August, May and February respectively and we take the highest value. Hence 20 is used as P_L value, and 0 (dB), and 0.3 (dB) are taken as the value of C_{Lat} and C_{Lon} respectively.

By using Eq. (11).

$$K = 10^{-(6.5-0-0.3)}20^{1.5} = 5.64 * 10^{-5}$$

8.1 Link Availability from Wegeda to Guna

After we determine geoclimatic (k) factors, path inclination will be calculated by using Eq. (10) with $h_A = 2610.08$ m, $l = 35$ km and $h_B = 4162$ m

$$\varepsilon_p = (2610.08 - 4162) \text{ m}/35 = -44.34$$

Hence, the percentage of time (P_w) can be calculated by using Eq. (9) with fade depth (A) = 28.47 dB

$$P_w = 5.64 * 10^{-5} * 35^{3.6} * 7^{0.89}(1 + |-44.34|)^{-1..4} * 10^{-28.47710}$$
$$= 77.45 * 10^{-5} = 0.0007745\%$$

We can consider the above outage (unavailability) is due to equipment failure and propagation outage. The outage is expressed in terms of hour, minute and second. Let us consider a 1-year or 8760-h interval. A year has 525,600 min or 31,536,000 s. Then the annual expected outage of this link with unavailability of 0.0007745% is

$$8760 \text{ h} * 0.000007745 = 0.06784 \text{ h}$$
$$525,600 \text{ min} * 0.000007745 = 4.070772 \text{ min}$$
$$31,536,000 \text{ s} * 0.000007745 = 244.2463 \text{ s}$$

Therefore, unavailability occurs in this hop 0.06784 h, 4.070772 min or 244.24632 s annually.

The availability of this link is determined based on the outage of the worth month or time percentage and it can be calculated as follows.

$$\text{Link availability } (P_A) \% = 100\% - P_w\%$$
$$= 100\% - 0.0007745$$
$$= 99.9992255\%$$

From the above unavailability and availability values we can say the link is reliable.

8.2 Link Availability from Guna to NefasMewucha

After we determine geoclimatic (k) factors, path inclination will be calculated. By using Eq. (10) with $h_A = 4157$ m, $l = 25.5$ km and $h_B = 3045$ m

$$\varepsilon_p = (4157\,m - 3045\,m)/25.5 = 43.6$$

Hence, the percentage of time (p_w) can be calculated by using Eq. (9) with fade depth (A) = 31.78 dB

$$P_w = 5.64 * 10^{-5} * 25.5^{3.6} * 7^{0.89}(1 + |43.6|)^{-1..4} * 10^{-31.78/10} = 8.51 * 10^{-5}$$
$$= 0.0000851\%$$

We can consider the above outage (unavailability) is due to equipment failure and propagation outage. The outage is expressed in terms of hour, minute and second. Let us consider a 1-year or 8760-h interval. A year has 525,600 min or 31,536,000 s. Then the annual expected outage of this link with unavailability of 0.0000851% is

$$8760\,h * 0.000000851 = 0.007455\,h$$
$$525,600\,min * 0.000000851 = 0.447286\,min$$
$$31,536,000\,s * 0.000000851 = 26.837\,s$$

Therefore, unavailability occurs in this hop 0.007455 h, 0.447286 min or 26.837 s annually.

The availability of this link is determined based on the outage of the worth month or time percentage and it can be calculated as follows.

$$\text{Link availability } (P_A) \% = 100\% - P_W\%$$
$$= 100\% - 0.0000851\%$$
$$= 99.9999149\%$$

From the above unavailability and availability values we can say the design system is reliable.

9 Conclusion

A direct microwave link between Wegeda to NefasMewucha was initially proposed because of the importance of Wegeda as one socioeconomic growth area in Amhara region. This direct link could not be designed due to Non-clear line of sight propagation. An alternative proposal consisting of two paths from Wegeda to Guna and from Guna to NefasMewucha has been considered and power budget, signal radiation loss, rain attenuation, system margin and reliability of the link are calculated and simulated. The results are found to be consistent with practice.

The link availability of the two hops was calculated based on ITU recommendations, which is 99.9992255% in the first hop and 99.9999149% in the second hop. The fade margin is 28.47 dB and 31.78 dB in the first and second hop respectively which are greater than the recommended fade margin, in other words as the outage or unavailability percentage is very small, the designed link is more reliable and quality of service will be established.

References

1. Moreno, L.: Point-To-Point Radio Link Engineering (2001–2010)
2. Freeman, R.L.: Telecommunication System Engineering, 4th edn. Wiley, Hoboken (2004)
3. Balanis, C.A.: Antenna Theory, Analysis and Design, 3rd edn. Wiley, Hoboken (2005)
4. Young, M.F.: Planning a Microwave Radio Link (2002)
5. Garlington, T.: Microwave Line-of-Sight Transmission Engineering (2006)
6. Lehpamer, H.: Microwave Transmission Networks, Planning, Design and Deployment, 2nd edn, p. 106. McGraw-Hill Professional Engineering, New York (2004)
7. Rakib Al Mahmud, M.D., Khan, Z.S.: Analysis and planning microwave link to established efficient wireless communications. Blekinge Institute of Technology, September 2009
8. Ul Islam, M.R., et al.: Fade margins prediction for broadband fixed wireless access (BFWA) from measurements in tropics. Prog. Electromagn. Res. C 11, 199–212 (2009)
9. Rec. ITU-R p.530-12: Propagation data and prediction methods required for the design of terrestrial line-of-sight systems. ITU, Geneva (2007)
10. ITU-R P.530-14: Propagation data and prediction methods required for the design of terrestrial line-of-sight systems. ITU, February 2012
11. Shaoying, C.:Digital Microwave Communication Principles V1.1. Huawei Technologies Co., Ltd., Shenzhen (2006)

Enhancement of Power Flow with Reduction of Power Loss Through Proper Placement of FACTS Devices Based on Voltage Stability Index

Yeshitela Shiferaw$^{(\boxtimes)}$ and K. Padma

College of Engineering (A), Andhra University, Visakhapatnam 530003, Andhra Pradesh, India
Yeshitela2010@gmail.com, padma315@gmail.com

Abstract. One of the significant problems in the power system network is the overloading of the transmission system which increases stress on transmission lines. This problem can be mitigated by the addition of isolated and individually controlled devices such as FACTS to the existing networks. Thus, the main objective of this paper is determining the optimal placement of SVC and TCSC FACTS device at bus and lines and minimizing the total power loss & enhances the transferred power by applying these SVC and TCSC FACTS devices. To this end, first, load flow analysis was done using the Newton Raphson technique. Then, the optimal location was found by the voltage stability index (L-indices) and fast voltages stability indices (FVSI). The critical bus has the lowest voltage and the critical line has the largest value of FVSI. Consequently, SVC and TCSC FACTS device is installed on both the critical bus and the critical line respectively. To validate the methodology, we use IEEE-30 bus standard test system network and the simulation is done on PSAT (power system analysis toolbox) in MATLAB. Finally, based on the finding of the simulation result, the best locations for SVC and TCSC FACTS devices for improving power transfer, voltage profile and loadability are the weakest bus and line of the system.

Keywords: Optimal placement · Thyristor control series compensator · Static var compensator · Loadability · Voltage stability index

1 Introduction

The major problem of a heavily loaded system is that the transmission network operates near to its limit. This, in turn, leads to the increment of stress on the transmission. This problem was solved by the addition of isolated and individually controlled devices such as FACTS to the existing networks.

The power flow analysis is necessary for power system planning, new power generation, new transmission line and load scheduling. It is crucial in placing FACT devices in the weak bus and weak lines. FACTS devices can be fully utilised if the optimal location is determined through specific techniques. Here, the voltage stability index calculation method was used for the optimal position of the TCSC and SVC FACTS devices [1].

© ICST Institute for Computer Sciences, Social Informatics and Telecommunications Engineering 2020
Published by Springer Nature Switzerland AG 2020. All Rights Reserved
N. G. Habtu et al. (Eds.): ICAST 2019, LNICST 308, pp. 355–365, 2020.
https://doi.org/10.1007/978-3-030-43690-2_24

The purpose of this study is to illustrate the applications of voltage stability indexes. In line with these indexes were found to be effective in detecting the weakest bus and line in the system. Moreover, the addition of SVC and TCSC FACTS devices on the weakest bus and line has improved the voltage profile, total power loss and loadability of the system. Standard IEEE-30 bus test system network and MATLAB/PSAT were used to validate the methodology.

Criteria for selection of optimal locations.

During steady-state operation, FACTS devices can be considered as a Controllable reactance connected in series with the line and with the bus. The effects of the insertion of FACTS devices [2, 3]:

- Reduces transfer reactance between the two buses.
- Increases transfer capability of the line.
- Reduces reactive power loss.
- Improves the voltage profiles.

The criteria for the optimal placement of FACTS devices are as follows [3, 4, 5]:

- The device should be placed in a line which has the least sensitivity concerning the magnitude of static reactance.
- The sending end bus must be either a load bus or a generator bus with no regulating generation.
- The device should be placed in a line which has the most substantial absolute value of the sensitivity concerning the phase angle.
- The device should not be placed in the line containing generation buses even if the sensitivity is the highest.
- The terminal end bus should not have a switched shunt connected to it.
- Multiple devices sending end on the same bus can be allowed.

2 Voltage Stability Analysis Using Bus and Line Index

The main goal of voltage stability indices is to determine voltage instability within the system network [6, 7]. These indices are referred either to a bus or a line.

2.1 Voltage Stability Index (L-Index)

The load flow algorithms incorporate load and generator control characteristics. The voltage stability indices value is changed between zero (no load) and one (voltage collapse) based on the solution of load flow using Newtown Raphson, the L index [8] can be calculated as:

$$L_j = \left| 1 - \sum_{i=1}^{ng} F_{ji} \frac{V_i}{V_j} \right| \tag{1}$$

Where $ng \in [0, n]$. F_{ji} is attained from the Y bus matrix as follows:

$$\begin{pmatrix} I_G \\ I_L \end{pmatrix} = \begin{pmatrix} Y_{GG} & Y_{GL} \\ Y_{LG} & Y_{LL} \end{pmatrix} \begin{pmatrix} V_G \\ V_L \end{pmatrix} \tag{2}$$

Where I_G, I_L, V_G, V_L, represents current and voltages at the generator and load buses.
Rearranging (2), it can be written as

$$\begin{pmatrix} V_L \\ I_G \end{pmatrix} = \begin{pmatrix} Z_{LL} & F_{LG} \\ Y_{GL} & Y_{GG} \end{pmatrix} \begin{pmatrix} I_L \\ V_G \end{pmatrix} \tag{3}$$

Where $F_{LG} = -[Y_{LL}]^{-1}[Y_{LG}]$ are the necessary values, the L indices for a given load condition are computed for all load buses.

The equation for the L index for the node can be written as

$$L_j = \left| 1 - \sum_{i=1}^{ng} F_{ji} \frac{V_i}{V_j} \angle \theta_{ij} + \delta_i - \delta_j \right| \tag{4}$$

Where θ_{ij} is the power factor angle and δ_i & δ_j are voltage angle of the ith and j^{th} bus respectively.

Algorithm to obtaining voltage stability indices are [6, 9].

Step one: form admittance matrix (Y-bus) for the system
Step two: find the element of F_{LG} from Eq. (3)
Step three: find the value of L-indices using Eq. (4) by applying step two

2.2 Line Stability Index (Fast Voltage Stability Index)

The line stability index (fast voltage stability index) projected by Musirin *et al.* [10] is based on a conception of power flow through a single transmission line. For a significant transmission line, the fast voltage stability index is defined by:

$$FVSI_{ij} = \frac{4Z^2 Q_j}{V_i^2 X_{ij}} \tag{5}$$

Where Z = line impedance, X_{ij} = line reactance, Q_j = reactive power at the receiving end and V_i = sending end voltage.

The line voltage stability indices which show that FVSI is very close to unity (1.0) implies that it is approaching the point of instability. If FVSI is starting to be higher than unity, this is the indication of voltage collapse in the system network due to a sudden drop in voltage [11].

3   SVC Thyristor Modeling (B = Bscv)

The SVC can be variable reactance by using firing-angle limits or reactance limits, as it is shown in Fig. 1. The SVC nonlinear power equation is derived from variable shunt compensator modelling and changed to the linear equation by Newton's method.

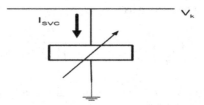

Fig. 1. Variable shunt susceptance

From Fig. 1 the current drawn by SVC and reactive power injected at bus K is

$$I_{SVC} = jB_{SVC} * V_K \tag{6}$$

$$Q_{SVC} = Q_K = -V_k^2 * B_{SVC} \tag{7}$$

The linearised equation is given by Eq. (7) where the equivalent susceptance B_{SVC} is taken to be the state variable

$$\begin{bmatrix} \Delta P_K \\ \Delta Q_K \end{bmatrix}^i = \begin{bmatrix} 0 & 0 \\ 0 & Q_K \end{bmatrix}^i \begin{bmatrix} \Delta\theta_K \\ \Delta B_{SVC}/B_{SVC} \end{bmatrix}^i \tag{8}$$

The variable shunt susceptance B_{SVC} is updated at the end of the iteration (i) is

$$B_{SVC}^i = B_{SVC}^{(i-1)} + \left(\frac{\Delta B_{SVC}}{B_{SVC}}\right)^{(i)} B_{SVC}^{(i-1)} \tag{9}$$

This changing susceptance characterises the total SVC susceptance essential to keep the nodal voltage magnitude at the specific value. Once the level of compensation has been determined, the firing angle required to achieve such compensation level can be calculated.

4   TCSC Variable Series Impedance Modeling

The variable series compensation is hugely effective in both controlling power flow in the line and in improving the stability of the power system within the ranges of the system [12, 13].

The amount of reactance is determined efficiently using Newton's method.

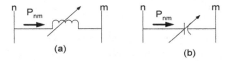

Fig. 2. TCSC equivalence circuit: (a) inductive and (b) capacitive type.

The transfer admittance matrix of the variable compensator shown in the Fig. 2 is

$$\begin{bmatrix} I_n \\ I_m \end{bmatrix} = \begin{bmatrix} j\,B_{nn} & j\,B_{nm} \\ j\,B_{mn} & j\,B_{mm} \end{bmatrix} \begin{bmatrix} V_n \\ V_m \end{bmatrix} \tag{10}$$

The active and reactive power equations at bus n are:

$$P_n = V_n V_m B_{nm} \sin(\theta_n - \theta_m) \tag{11}$$

$$Q_k = -V_k^2 B_{nn} - V_n V_m B_{nm} \cos(\theta_n - \theta_m) \tag{12}$$

The set of linearised power flow equations are:

$$\begin{bmatrix} \Delta P_n \\ \Delta P_m \\ \Delta Q_n \\ \Delta Q_m \\ \Delta P_{nm}^{XTCSC} \end{bmatrix} = \begin{bmatrix} \frac{\partial P_n}{\partial \theta_n} & \frac{\partial P_n}{\partial \theta_m} & \frac{\partial P_n}{\partial V_n}V_n & \frac{\partial P_n}{\partial V_m}V_m & \frac{\partial P_n}{\partial X_{TCSC}}X_{TCSC} \\ \frac{\partial P_m}{\partial \theta_n} & \frac{\partial P_m}{\partial \theta_m} & \frac{\partial P_m}{\partial V_n}V_n & \frac{\partial P_m}{\partial V_m}V_m & \frac{\partial P_m}{\partial X_{TCSC}}X_{TCSC} \\ \frac{\partial Q_n}{\partial \theta_n} & \frac{\partial Q_n}{\partial \theta_m} & \frac{\partial Q_n}{\partial \theta_n}V_n & \frac{\partial Q_n}{\partial \theta_m}V_m & \frac{\partial Q_n}{\partial X_{TCSC}}X_{TCSC} \\ \frac{\partial Q_m}{\partial \theta_n} & \frac{\partial Q_m}{\partial \theta_m} & \frac{\partial Q_m}{\partial \theta_n}V_n & \frac{\partial Q_m}{\partial \theta_m}V_m & \frac{\partial Q_m}{\partial X_{TCSC}}X_{TCSC} \\ \frac{\partial P_{nm}^{XTCSC}}{\partial \theta_n} & \frac{\partial P_{nm}^{XTCSC}}{\partial \theta_m} & \frac{\partial P_{nm}^{XTCSC}}{\partial \theta_n}V_n & \frac{\partial P_{nm}^{XTCSC}}{\partial \theta_m}V_m & \frac{\partial P_{nm}^{XTCSC}}{\partial X_{TCSC}}X_{TCSC} \end{bmatrix} \begin{bmatrix} \Delta \theta_n \\ \Delta \theta_m \\ \frac{\Delta V_n}{V_n} \\ \frac{\Delta V_m}{V_m} \\ \frac{\Delta X_{TCSC}}{X_{TCSC}} \end{bmatrix} \tag{13}$$

Where ∂P_{nm}^{XTCSC} is the active power flow mismatch for the series reactance calculate as follow

$\partial P_{nm}^{XTCSC} = P_{nm}^{reg} - P_{nm}^{XTCSC,cal}$, and ΔX_{TCSC} is given by $\Delta X_{TCSC} = X_{TCSC}^{(i)} - X_{TCSC}^{(i-1)}$

The state variable XTCSC of the series controller is updated at the end of each iterative step according to

$$X_{TCSC}^{(i)} = X_{TCSC}^{(i-1)} + \left(\frac{\Delta X_{TCSC}}{X_{TCSC}} \right)^i X_{TCSC}^{(i-1)} \tag{14}$$

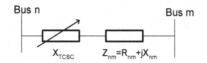

Fig. 3. Modelling of transmission line with TCSC

The model of transmission line with a TCSC connected between bus n and bus m is shown in Fig. 3

$$X_{line} = X_{nm} + X_{TCSC} \tag{15}$$

Where X_{nm} is the reactance of the line between bus n and m without TCSC reactance, and the reactance X_{TCSC} is restricted to the domain.

$X_{TCSC,min} \leq X_{TCSC} \leq X_{TCSC,max}$ Where the values of X_{TCSC}, *min* and X_{TCSC}, *max* are determined by the size of the TCSC device and the characteristics of the line in which it is placed.

5 Continuous Power Flow

A conventional power flow has a problem during a Jacobian matrix which becomes singular at the voltage stability limit; this problem can be overcome by using continuous power flow [13]. The graph obtained using continuous power flow methods between bus voltage, and the loading factor λ is a P-V curve. It determines the loadability of margins. The flow chart describes in Fig. 4 shows the steps to solve continuous power flow analysis.

5.1 Mathematical Reformulations

Reformulating Newton Raphson load flow Equations to include loading factor λ.
The conventional Newton Raphson load flow equations can be as follow

$$P_i = V_i \sum_{j=1}^{n} V_j Y_{ij} \cos(\theta_i - \theta_j - \delta_{ij}) \tag{16}$$

$$Q_i = V_i \sum_{j=1}^{n} V_j Y_{ij} \sin(\theta_i - \theta_j - \delta_{ij}) \tag{17}$$

Conventional power flow equations modified by incorporating of λ

$$P_{Li} = P_{Li0}(1 + \lambda K_{Li}) \tag{18}$$

$$Q_{Li} = Q_{Li0}(1 + \lambda K_{Li}) \tag{19}$$

$$P_{Gi} = P_{Gi0}(1 + \lambda K_{Gi}) \tag{20}$$

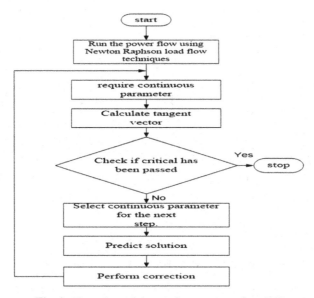

Fig. 4. Flow chart of the continuous power flow [13]

Applying continuous power flow algorithm to these equations, and the whole set of equations can be written as:

$$F(\theta, V, \lambda) = 0 \tag{21}$$

Predict, and corrector steps can be given by the following Eqs. (22) and (23) respectively.

$$\begin{bmatrix} F_\theta & F_V & F_\lambda \end{bmatrix} \begin{bmatrix} d\theta \\ dV \\ d\lambda \end{bmatrix} = 0 \tag{22}$$

$$\begin{bmatrix} F(x) \\ x_k - \eta \end{bmatrix} = 0 \tag{23}$$

6   Result and Discussion

The system simulation and load flow equations are solved; voltage stability indices (L-indices) and fast voltage stability indices (FVSI) are simulated to determine the weakest bus and line in the system. The results of the comparison and the performance of the system with and without FACTS devices are presented in this section.

IEEE 30 bus system network consists of six generating units interconnected with 41 branches of a transmission network with a total load of 283.4 MW and 126.2 MVAR, four transformers with off-nominal tap ratio, as its shown in Fig. 5. The bus data and the branch data are taken from [14].

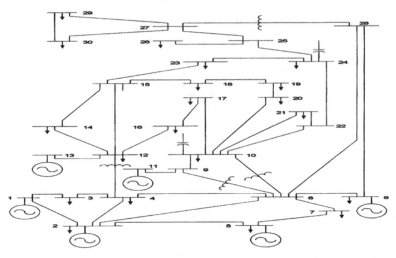

Fig. 5. IEEE-30 bus standard test system diagram [14]

For incorporating power flow with FACTS devices, power system analysis toolbox (PSAT) is used in MATLAB software. This power system analysis toolbox is helpful for power system analysis and control including optimal power flow as well as continuous power flow analysis [5].

6.1 P-V Curve

Before analysing P-V curves, we have to find out the weakest bus and line using voltage stability index computation. From Table 1, it is observed that the five most critical bus and lines are selected. Besides, as it can be seen from Fig. 6, bus number 26 exhibits the highest voltage stability index which means it is the weakest bus in the system. From Table 1, it is noted that the line which connects between bus 3 and 4 is the most critical based on the stability indices of lines. Voltage collapse can be accurately predicted when the index is more than one. The line that gives index value closest to one should be the most critical line of the bus and may lead to the instability of the whole system.

Table 1. Voltage stability index

Line stability index			Bus stability L-index	
From bus	To bus	Voltage stability index (FVSI)	Bus no	L-index
3	4	0.20585	26	0.0761
2	6	0.11878	30	0.0729
2	4	0.09494	24	0.0715
4	12	0.09014	19	0.0715
1	3	0.08590	18	0.0697

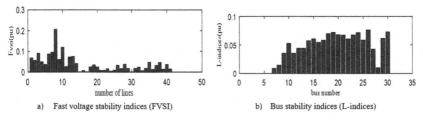

a) Fast voltage stability indices (FVSI)   b) Bus stability indices (L-indices)

Fig. 6. Voltage stability index

The variations of bus voltage with the loading factor λ were obtained for IEEE-30 bus system network. The loading factor was one at the base case and gradually increased until the loading point reached the maximum. It was found that bus number 26 was the most insecure bus as the voltage at each reactive load of bus 26 was minimum. Figure 7(a) shows the P-V curve for the lowest five voltage buses without SVC, and the loading parameter is 3.4362 pu. Figure 7(b) shows the P-V curve for five most economical voltage buses with SVC at bus 26, and the loadability setting (λ) increased to 3.447 pu. It clearly showed that the load ability margin had risen significantly.

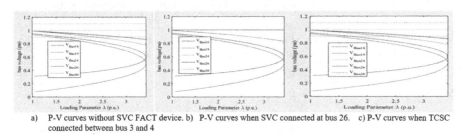

a) P-V curves without SVC FACT device. b) P-V curves when SVC connected at bus 26.   c) P-V curves when TCSC connected between bus 3 and 4

Fig. 7. P-V curve without and with SVC FACTS device

6.2 Performance of the System with TCSC and SVC Facts Devices

The consolidated comparative bus voltage results have been represented in Fig. 8(a). The use of SVC shunt compensator has improved network voltage profile and keeps the voltage magnitude at 1 p.u at bus 26. The real power flow for thirty bus system was analysed without and with FACTS device in Fig. 8(b) from the result the TCSC series compensator model is to maintain the active power flow between bus 3 and 4 as compared to SVC shunt compensator. Similarly, in Fig. 8(c) the TCSC series compensator was more applicable to reduce the real power loss in the line.

As clearly shown in Table 2. The instalment of SVC is not only improving the system voltage profile but also reduces total real power losses. The actual power loss after installing SVC at bus 26 is reduced by 0.124%. Similarly, TCSC FACTS device reduce total power loss by 2.813%. While as result TCSC FACTS device is more significant for total real power loss.

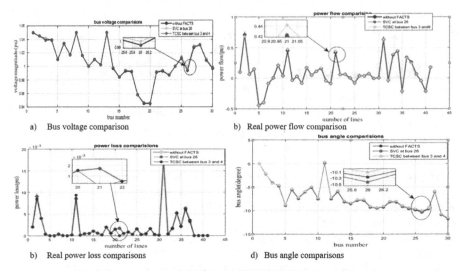

a) Bus voltage comparison   b) Real power flow comparison

b) Real power loss comparisons   d) Bus angle comparisons

Fig. 8. Performance of TCSC and SVC FACTS devices comparison

Table 2. Total power loss comparison with and without SVC and TCSCFACTS device

No	Power loss (pu) without FACTS devices	Power loss (pu), SVC @bus 26	Power loss (pu), TCSC b/n 3 and 4 bus
	0.075576	0.075482	0.07345
Reduced by		0.124%	2.813%

7 Conclusion

The paper analyzed voltage stability indices for selecting the weak bus and line and put the SVC and TCSC FACTS device on this weak bus and line for the improvement of bus voltage and power flow on the line. Here are the main contributions.

- Weak bus and line are identified using voltage stability indexes
- The voltage profile for all the buses was obtained.
- Power transfer in each line was attained.
- Loadability was compared with and without SVC FACTS device.
- TCSC FACTS device which was connected between bus-3 and bus-4 showed great improvement in reducing total real and reactive power loss.
- SVC FACTS device which was connected on bus-26 has improved real power loss and loadability.
- The use of FACTS device in both at bus and line reduces power loss and improves system voltage profile

Acknowledgements. We would like to acknowledge the support of Defense University, Engineering College, research and development Centre, Ethiopia and Andhra University, Electrical Engineering Department, India.

References

1. Liu, Q., You, M., Sun, H., Matthews, P.: L-index sensitivity based voltage stability. School of Engineering and Computing Sciences, Durham, UK (2017)
2. Kazemia, B.B.A.: Modeling and simulation of SVC and TCSC to study. Electr. Power Energy Syst. **26**, 381–388 (2004)
3. Padhy, N.P., Abdel-Moamen, M.A.: Optimal placement of FACTS devices for practical utilities. Int. J. Power Energy Syst. **27**(2), 193–204 (2007)
4. Vanfretti, L., Milano, F.: The experience of PSAT (power system analysis toolbox) as a free and open source software for power system education and research. Int. J. Electr. Eng. **25**(12), 1–28 (2008)
5. Milano, F.: An open source power system analysis toolbox. IEEE **25**(2), 1–8 (2004)
6. Chengaiah, Ch., Satyanarayana, R.V.S., Mrutheswar, G.V.: Location of UPFC in electrical transmission system: fuzzy contingency ranking and optimal power flow. Int. J. Eng. Res. Dev. **1**(12), 10–20 (2012)
7. Kumar, S., Kumar, A., Sharma, N.K.: A novel method to investigate voltage stability of IEEE-14 bus wind integrated system using PSAT. Front. Energy (6), 2–8 (2016). https://doi.org/10.1007/s11708-016-0440-8
8. Reddy, V.R.K., Lalitha, M.P.: Identification of instability and its enhancement through the optimal placement of facts using L-index method. J. Theor. Appl. Inf. Technol. **60**(3), 616–622 (2014)
9. Chakrabarti, A.: Electricity Pricing Regulated, Deregulated and Smart Grid Systems. Taylor & Francis Group, Kolkata (2014)
10. Musirin, I.: Novel fast voltage stability index (FVSI) for voltage stability analysis. In: Research and Development Proceedings, Shah Alam Malaysia (2002)
11. Ambriz-Perez, H., Acha, E.: Advanced SVC models for Newton-Raphson load flow and Newton optimal power flow studies. IEEE Trans. Power Syst. **15**(1), 129–131 (2000)
12. Lakshan Piyasinghe, Z.M.: Impedance-model-based SSR analysis for type 3 wind generator and series-compensated network. IEEE Trans. Sustain. Energy **5**(1), 179–187 (2015)
13. Ajjarapu, V.: The continuation power flow: a tool for steady state voltage stability analysis. IEEE Trans. Power Syst. **7**(1), 416–423 (1992)
14. Üney, M.Ş.: Optimal power flow and load flow analysis with considering different DG integration rates. Asian J. Appl. Sci. Technol. (AJAST) **1**(9), 542–549 (2017)

Designing and Modeling of a Synchronous Generator Using AGC, PSS, and AVR Case Study on Tis Abay II Hydroelectric Power System

Abdulkerim Ali[(✉)] and B. Belachew

Faculty of Electrical and Computer Engineering, İnstitute of Technology,
Bahir Dar University, Bahir Dar, Ethiopia
abduali548@gmail.com

Abstract. This paper explains the design, modeling, and control of a synchronous generator using Automatic Generation Control (AGC) and Power System Stabilizer (PSS) with a combination of Automatic Voltage Regulator (AVR) for a hydroelectric power system. In the proposed system the damping torque and another source of negative damping of the generator can be reduced by the AVR. A classical PID controller is used in the AVR system. Interconnecting (synchronizing) the generator in a tie system, the overall system fluctuation due to a large disturbance in one of the interconnections is mathematically analyzed and the transient & steady state performance of the controller are evaluated.

Generally the work intended in designing and modeling the controller for enhancement of power system stability with steady-state and transient analysis, the application to the sudden increase in power input, and the application of three-phase fault have been examined using Matlab/Simulink. The model is also used to simulate the performance of tie line system under the same phase faults as well as load disturbance conditions. Power system stabilizers designed to enhance the damping of power system oscillations.

The designed PSS and AGC improved the performance of power system dynamic stability. Besides, the desired frequency and power interchange with the neighboring system is maintained by the AGC. The total system generation against system load and losses could be balanced.

Keywords: Synchronous generator · Automatic Generation Control · Automatic Voltage Regulator

1 Introduction

The ability of power system to recover from faults is becoming more important nowadays because of the complexity of the system. Then, in the power system voltage and frequency should be maintained within narrow and rigid values, and In case of interconnected operation, the tie line power flows must be maintained at the specified values in practical applications because of generation must adequate to meet the load demand.

© ICST Institute for Computer Sciences, Social Informatics and Telecommunications Engineering 2020
Published by Springer Nature Switzerland AG 2020. All Rights Reserved
N. G. Habtu et al. (Eds.): ICAST 2019, LNICST 308, pp. 366–381, 2020.
https://doi.org/10.1007/978-3-030-43690-2_25

The electric power system is often subjected to various disturbances, caused by, for example, fault activating, capacitor switching, large load changing, transmission line switching, etc. With appropriate operations on power system controls such as correct circuit breaker operations and proper generator excitation controls, the disturbing power system can either regain the pre-disturbance operating state or reach a new stable operating state after the disturbances [10].

The generator excitation system maintains the generator voltage and controls the reactive power flow. It is known that a change in the real power demand affects essentially the frequency, whereas a change in the reactive power affects mainly the voltage magnitude. The interaction between voltage and frequency controls is generally weak enough to justify their analysis separately. In this paper the reactive power control is achieved by manipulating the generator excitation system using PID controlled AVR. An increase in the reactive power load of the generator is accompanied by a drop in the terminal voltage magnitude. The voltage magnitude is sensed through a potential transformer on one phase. This voltage is rectified and compared to the DC setpoint signal. The amplified error signal controls the exciter field and increases the exciter terminal voltage. Thus, the generator field current is increased, which results in an increase in the generated emf. The reactive power generation is increased to a new equilibrium, raising the terminal voltage to the desired value.

The purposes of AGC are to maintain system frequency very close to a specified nominal value, to maintain the generation of individual units at the most economic value, to keep the correct value of tie-line power between different control areas. Automatic Generation Control (AGC) is define by IEEE as the regulation of the power output of electric generators within a prescribed area in response to changes in system frequency, tie line loading, or the regulation of these to each other, so as to maintain the scheduled system frequency and/or the established interchange with other areas within predetermined limits.

In addition, Automatic Generation Control (AGC) is a very important issue in power system operation and control for supplying sufficient and both good quality and reliable electric power. A sudden load change or disturbances in a single area or multi-area power system, the frequency and power undergo a fluctuation which persists for a very long time. This fluctuation is very poorly damped. Since these oscillations are the result of an imbalance of power. The generation is adjusted automatically by Automatic Generation Control to restore the frequency to the nominal value as the system load changes continuously [5].

2 Designing and Modeling of Controller

2.1 Automatic Voltage Control (AVR)

The main elements of AVR include excitation circuit, generator field, sensor and first order amplifier. Figure 1 below depicts the block diagram of AVR with PID controller.

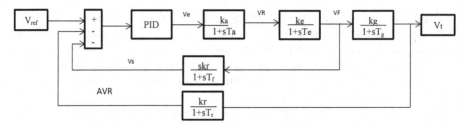

Fig. 1. Block diagram of AVR with PID and stabilizer

Equations (1) to (5) shows the mathematical model of amplifier, exciter, generator field, and PID respectively. The transfer function of first order amplifier is:

$$\frac{V_R(s)}{V_e(s)} = \frac{Ka}{1 + sTa} \tag{1}$$

Where: Ka and Ta are the dc gain and time constant respectively.

The transfer function of the exciter circuit is also first order and it is given in Eq. (2) where Ke and Te are dc gain and time constant of the exciter,

$$\frac{V_F(s)}{V_R(s)} = \frac{Ke}{1 + sTe} \tag{2}$$

The transfer function relating the generator terminal voltage to its field voltage can be represented by a gain Kg and a time constant Tg is formulated as:

$$\frac{Vt(s)}{V_F(s)} = \frac{Kg}{1 + sTg} \tag{3}$$

A potential transformer used as feedback sensor is accompanied by bridge rectifier. It is modeled by a simple first-order transfer function given by:

$$\frac{Vs(s)}{Vt(s)} = \frac{Kr}{1 + sTr} \tag{4}$$

Where Kr sensor gain constant and Tr be Sensor time constant.

PID Control: Determination of the proportional, integral and derivative constants of the controller is called the tuning-in process. The transfer function of a PID controller can be written as:

$$G_{PID}(s) = K_p + \frac{K_i}{s} + K_d = \frac{K_d s^2 + K_p s + K_i}{s} \tag{5}$$

The value of K_p, K_d and K_i is obtained by matlab tuning method.

2.2 Automatic Generation Control (AGC)

The objective of AGC is to minimize the transient deviations and to provide zero steady-state errors of these variables in a very short time [2–5]. The AGC involves *Load Frequency Control (LFC)* to achieve real power balance by adjusting the turbine output and the *Supplementary loop* to maintain a zero frequency deviation. The block diagram of the AGC for a single power system is shown in Fig. 2 below.

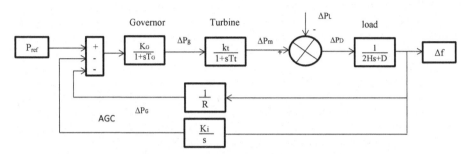

Fig. 2. Block diagram of AGC for a single power system

And a two area interconnected power system is shown in Fig. 3.

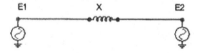

Fig. 3. Single line diagram of two area interconnected system

Tie line power flow from area 1 to area 2 can be written as:

$$P_{tie,12} = \frac{E_1 E_2}{X} sin(\delta_1 - \delta_2) \qquad (6)$$

Where δ_1 and δ_2 are power angles.
Linearizing about an initial operating point we have

$$\Delta P_{tie,12} = T_{12}\Delta\delta_{12} = T_{12}(\delta_1 - \delta_2) \qquad (7)$$

Where,

$$T_{12} = \frac{|E_1||E_2|}{P_{r1}X} cos(\delta_1 - \delta_2) = \text{Synchronizing coefficient} \qquad (8)$$

$$\Delta P_{tie,12} = 2\pi T_{12}(\Delta f_1 - \Delta f_2) \qquad (9)$$

And Tie line power flow from area 2 to area 1 can be written as:

$$\Delta P_{tie,21} = 2\pi T_{21}(\Delta f_2 - \Delta f_1) \tag{10}$$

Where

$$T_{21} = \frac{|E_1||E_2|}{P_{r2}X} \cos(\delta_2 - \delta_1) = \text{Synchronizing coefficient} \tag{11}$$

Then from the above equation:

$$\Delta P_{tie,21} = a_{12}\Delta P_{tie,12} \tag{12}$$

Where,

$$a_{12} = \frac{-P_{r1}}{P_{r2}} \tag{13}$$

That is $\Delta f = \Delta f1 = \Delta f2$. Thus, for area 1, we have

$$\Delta P_{m1} - \Delta P_{D1} - \Delta P_{12} = D_1 \Delta f \tag{14}$$

Where, ΔP_{12} is the tie-line power flow from Area 1 to Area 2, and for Area 2:

$$\Delta P_{m2} + \Delta P_{12} = D_2 \Delta f \tag{15}$$

The mechanical power depends on regulation. Hence

$$\Delta P_{m1} = -\frac{\Delta f}{R_1} \quad \text{And} \quad \Delta P_{m2} = -\frac{\Delta f}{R_2} \tag{16}$$

Substituting these equations, yields

$$\left(\frac{1}{R_1} + D_1\right)\Delta f = -\Delta P_{12} - \Delta P_{D1} \quad \text{And} \quad \left(\frac{1}{R_2} + D_2\right)\Delta f = \Delta P_{12} \tag{17}$$

Solving for Δf, we get

$$\Delta f = \frac{-\Delta P_{D1}}{\left(\frac{1}{R_1} + D1\right) + \left(\frac{1}{R_2} + D2\right)} = \frac{-\Delta P_{D1}}{\beta_1 + \beta_2} \tag{18}$$

$$and \qquad \Delta P_{12} = \frac{-\Delta P_{D1}\beta_2}{\beta_1 + \beta_2} \tag{19}$$

Where $\beta_1 = (D_1 + 1/R_1)$ and $\beta_2 = (D_2 + 1/R_2)$.

The area controls error (ACE) is met when the control action maintains frequency at the scheduled value and net interchange power (tie-line flow) with neighboring areas at the scheduled values.

The ACE of the two areas are given by

For area 1 : $ACE_1 = \Delta P_{12} + \beta_1 \Delta f$ For area 2 : $ACE_2 = \Delta P_{12} + \beta_1 \Delta f$
$$\tag{20}$$

The overall block diagram of when two areas interconnected with AGC and HTG as shown below figures (Fig. 4):

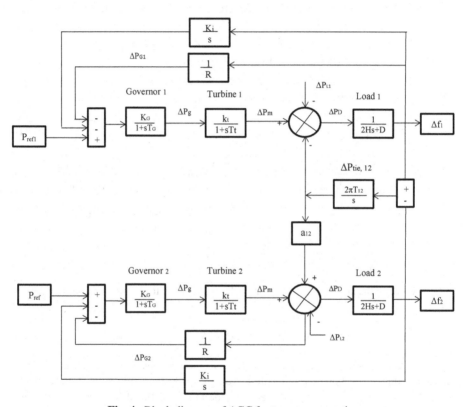

Fig. 4. Block diagram of AGC for two-area operation

2.3 AGC with AVR and PSS

The interaction between voltage and frequency controls is generally weak enough to justify their analysis separately. The methods of improving the voltage profile in the electric systems are transformer load tap changers, switched capacitors, step voltage regulators and static var control equipment. The controller of voltage or reactive power of generator is excitation control using the automatic voltage regulator (AVR). The main objective of an AVR is to hold the terminal voltage magnitude of a synchronous generator at a desired value [6]. This e.m.f determines the magnitude of real power and hence the AVR loop felt in the AGC loop. When we include the small effect of voltage on real power, we get the following equation:

$$\Delta P_e = P_s \Delta \delta + K_2 E' \tag{21}$$

Where, $K_2 = \frac{\Delta P_e}{E'}$ with constant $\Delta \delta =$ is load angle, and $P_s = \frac{\Delta P_e}{\Delta \delta}$ with constant E' is synchronizing power coefficient.

Generally, all the variables with subscript 0 are values of variables evaluated at their pre-disturbance steady-state operating point from the known values of P_0, Q_0, and V_{t0}.

$$i_{q0} = \frac{P_0 V_{to}}{\sqrt{(P_0 x_q)^2 + (V_{t0}^2 + Q_0 x_q)^2}} \qquad v_{d0} = i_{q0} x_q \tag{22}$$

$$v_{qo} = \sqrt{V_{t0}^2 - v_{t0}^2} \qquad i_{d0} = \frac{Q_0 + x_q i_{q0}^2}{v_{q0}} \tag{23}$$

$$E_{q0} = v_{q0} + i_{d0} x_q \qquad E_0 = \sqrt{(v_{d0} + x_e i_{q0})^2 + (v_{q0} - x_e i_{d0})^2} \tag{24}$$

$$\delta_0 = \tan^{-1} \frac{(v_{d0} + x_e i_{q0})}{(v_{q0} - x_e i_{d0})} \qquad K_1 = \frac{x_q - x_d'}{x_e + x_d'} i_{q0} E_0 \sin \delta_0 + \frac{E_{q0} E_0 \cos \delta_0}{x_e + x_q} \tag{25}$$

$$K_2 = \frac{E_0 \sin \delta_0}{x_e + x_d'} \qquad K_3 = \frac{x_d' + x_e}{x_d + x_e}, \qquad K_4 = \frac{x_q - x_d'}{x_e + x_d'} E_0 \sin \delta_0 \tag{26}$$

$$K_5 = \frac{x_q}{x_e + x_q} \frac{v_{d0}}{V_{t0}} E_0 \cos \delta_0 - \frac{x_{d'}}{x_e + x_d'} \frac{v_{q0}}{V_{t0}} E_0 \sin \delta_0 \qquad K_6 = \frac{x_e}{x_e + x_d'} \frac{v_{q0}}{V_{t0}} \tag{27}$$

By including the small effect of rotor angle upon generator terminal voltage, we may write

$$\Delta V_t = K_5 \Delta \delta + K_6 E' \tag{28}$$

Where K_5 is changed in terminal voltage for a small change in rotor angle at constant stator e.m.f and K_6 is a change in terminal voltage for a small change in stator e.m.f at constant rotor angle. Finally, modifying the generator field transfer function to include the effect of rotor angle, we may express the stator e.m.f as

$$E' = \frac{K_g}{1 + T_g} (V_f - K_4 \Delta \delta) \tag{29}$$

The constants K_1, K_2, K_3, K_4, and K_6 are usually positive; however, K_5 may take either positive or negative value depending on the impedance $R_E + j X_E$.

The overall block diagram of AGC, AVR, and stabilizer is (Fig. 5):

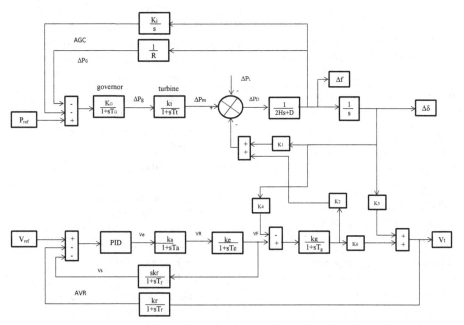

Fig. 5. Block diagram of AGC and PSS with AVR

3 Simulation Results and Discussion

While doing this paper, we have two conditions to run Tis Abay II hydroelectric power system these are at:

1. Steady-state condition
2. Fault condition

The following operating conditions for a synchronous machine connected to an infinite bus through a transmission line of the Tis Abay II hydroelectric power system (Tables 1 and 2).

Table 1. Nameplate rating data of generator

Rating data for generator	Type
Manufacture	Kvaerner hangar
Rated capacity (S)	40 MVA
Rated power (S)	36.8 MW
Rated voltage (V_{LL})	13.8 kV
Rated current (I_L)	2.1994 kA
No of phase, power factor (cos Φ)	0.9
Rated speed	214.3 rpm
Runaway speed	428 rpm
Rated frequency	50 Hz
Direction of rotation	Clockwise viewed from above
Insulation class	F
Type of excitation	Static SCR

Table 2. Parameter of AVR and exciter

Elements	Parameters	Data for simulation
Amplifier	Regulator gain Ka	10–400
	Regulator amplifier time constant Ta(s)	0.02 s
Exciter	Exciter constant related to self-excited field Ke	1
	Exciter time constant Te(s)	0.5 s
Feedback stabilizer	Generating stabilizing circuit gain K_F	0.03
	Regulator stabilizing The time constant T_F(s)	1
Generator	Generator terminal voltage to its field voltage K_g	1
	Generator time constant T_g(s)	2 s
Sensor (Low-pass filter)	Gain (K_R)	1
	Time constant (T_R)	0.05 s

3.1 System Running at Steady State Condition

A. ***The synchronous generator block diagram with AVR, FS and PID controller shown below:***
See Fig. 6.

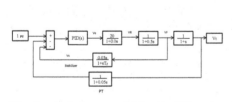

Fig. 6. Block diagram of SG with AVR and PID

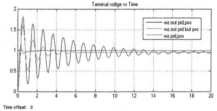

Fig. 7. Terminal voltage response

Result and Discussion 1:

From the simulation result in Fig. 7 the generator shows

i.   With only AVR the terminal voltage is not controlled to the desired value (1 Pu = 13.8 kV) which is 0.9 Pu (12.42 kV) after almost 8 s and also the overshot value is 1.8 Pu.

ii. With AVR and stabilizer the oscillation is decreased (1.6 Pu) and the settling time is decreased which is 4 s and the overshoot values are 1.2 Pu but it does not reduce the steady-state error.

iii. With AVR, stabilizer and PID the terminal voltage is controlled which is the settling time, overshoot and steady-state errors are almost zero.

B.   *The complete block diagram of the AGC model and its simulation of an isolated power system:*
     See Figs. 8 and 9.

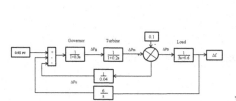

Fig. 8. Block diagram of AGC

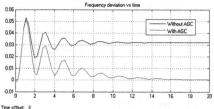

Fig. 9. Frequency deviation response

Result and Discussion 2:

i.   With only LFC the frequency deviation (change) is not controlled to the desired value (0 Pu = 50 Hz) that is 0.03 Pu (1.5 Hz) have an error after almost 8 s and the overshot value is 0.056 Pu.

ii. However, LFC with supplementary that means with AGC is controlled which is the steady-state error is zero Pu (new frequency = 50 Hz) after 10 s and the overshoot is decreased by almost 0.05 Pu.

C.   *The block diagram and its simulation of AGC Including AVR and Stabilizer*
     See Figs. 10.

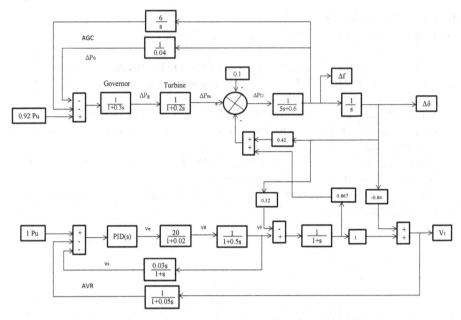

Fig. 10. Matlab/Simulink block diagram of AGC and PSS with AVR

Simulation Results:

See Figs. 11 and 12.

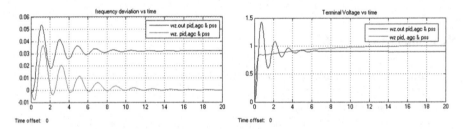

Fig. 11. Frequency deviation response   **Fig. 12.** Terminal voltage response

Result and Discussion 3:

a. With only LFC the frequency deviation (change) is not controlled to the desired value (0 Pu = 50 Hz) that is 0.03 Pu (1.5 Hz) have an error after almost 8 s and also the overshot value is 0.056 Pu.

b. However, LFC with supplementary that means with AGC is controlled which is the steady-state error is zero Pu (new frequency = 50 Hz) after 10 s and the overshoot is decreased by almost 0.05 Pu (Fig. 14).

c. With only AVR the terminal voltage is not controlled to the desired value (1 Pu = 13.8 kV) which is 0.9 Pu (12.42 kV) after almost 8 s. and also the overshot value is 1.8 Pu (Fig. 15).

d. With AVR and stabilizer the oscillation is decreased (1.6 Pu) and the settling time is decreased which is 4 s and the overshoot values are 1.2 Pu but it does not reduce the steady-state error.

e. With AVR, stabilizer and PID the terminal voltage is controlled which is the settling time, overshoot and steady-state errors are almost zero (Fig. 15).

Note: Therefore, the Automatic generation controller is controlled or maintained the frequency from the equation if the frequency is controlled the output power; the rotor angle and speed are controlled. In addition, the automatic voltage controller with PID will be controlled the terminal voltage also the reactive power.

D. *The block diagram and its simulation of the two areas interconnected*
   See Fig. 13.

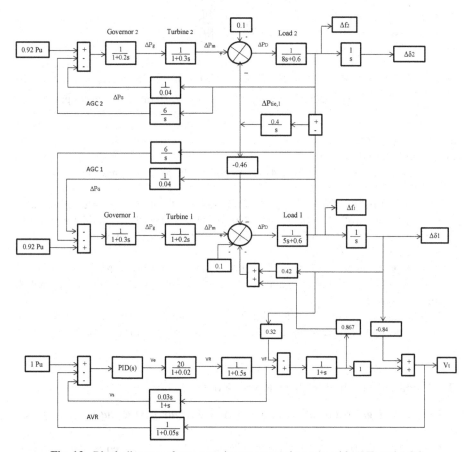

Fig. 13. Block diagram of two areas interconnected system with AVR and AGC

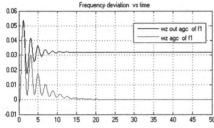

Fig. 14. Frequency deviation response

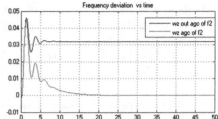

Fig. 15. Frequency deviation response

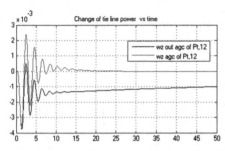

Fig. 16. Tie line power response

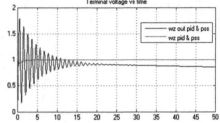

Fig. 17. Terminal voltage response

Simulation Results:
Result and Discussion 4:
From the simulation result in Figs. 14, 15, 16 and 17 the generator shows

i.   With only LFC the frequency deviation (change) of both power systems one and two are not controlled to the desired value (0 Pu = 50 Hz) that is 0.032 Pu (1.6 Hz) have an error after almost 8 s but with AGC the steady-state will be eliminated after almost 10 s (Figs. 17 and 18).

ii.   From Fig. 16 the tie-line power without AGC (only LFC) have error (unstable state) but with AGC, it will be stable and decrease the steady state error almost eliminated after almost 15 s.

iii. In addition, from Fig. 17 AVR, with PID the terminal voltage is controlled which is the settling time, overshoot and steady state errors are almost zero.

3.2   Simulation Result of the System with Fault

E. *The block diagram and its simulation of AGC Including AVR and PSS with fault*:

Let, the fault (pulse generator) is occurred at t = 15 s is occurred on the input and the fault duration is 250 ms.

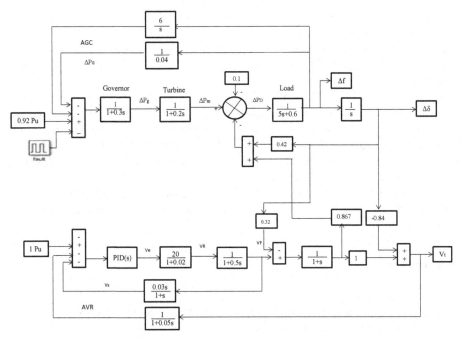

Fig. 18. Block diagram of SG including AGC and AVR with fault

Simulation Results:
Result and Discussion 5:

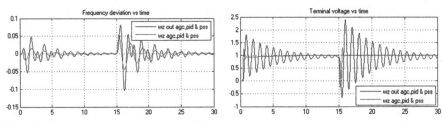

Fig. 19. Frequency deviation response with fault

Fig. 20. Terminal voltage response with fault

In the above Figs. 19, 20 when the fault occurs at 15 s in the power system it will be cleared quickly (fault duration time is 0.25 s) and became at normal value with and without a controller.

4   Conclusion

Based on the simulation result, it is possible to conclude that:

- This paper focuses on the improvement of power system stability in the power system by connecting a synchronous generator to the controller.
- Due to the connection of AGC and PSS in the grid, it is seen that the change of frequency (error), and output power are achieved at the nominal or desired value and decreasing the oscillation.
- When there is sudden load change in a single synchronous generator (power system) or any interconnected area, the frequency and tie-line power are affected. It is essential to minimize these errors for economic and reliable operation of the power system. Therefore, the AGC designed here to meet the stated demand.
- AGC Controller designed here minimizes the change in frequency in the single power system area as well as in multi-area.
- AVR with PID and PSS, it is seen that the terminal voltage as well as the reactive power also controlled and is achieved at the nominal or desired value and damping the oscillation of the system.

Acronyms

B: Frequency Bias factor
D: Percent change in load divided by the percent change in frequency
Ki: Supplementary control constant
H: Inertia Constant
ΔP: Change in power
ΔP_m: Change in mechanical power input
ΔP_D: Change in power demanded by the load
ΔP_{tie}:   Tie-line power deviations
ΔP_V: Change in valve position from nominal
R: Speed Droop Characteristic
Tg: Speed governor time constant
Tt: Turbine time constant
f: Frequency of system
Δf: Change in system frequency

References

1. Kundur, P.: Power System Stability and Control, 4th edn. McGraw-Hill Inc., New York (1994)
2. Teshager, G.: Optimal power generation expansion planning for Ethiopian electric power system. Addis Ababa University (2011)
3. Anderson, P.M., Fouad, A.A.: Power System Control and Stability. Iowa State University Press, Ames (1977)
4. Arshad, M.F.B.H.M.: Model and Performance of Power System Stabilizer Using Matlab. Malasia University (2009)
5. Memon, A.P.: Artificial neural network applications in electrical alternator excitation systems. Mehran University of Engineering and Technology (2002)
6. Surjan, B.S., Garg, R.: Power system stabilizer controller design for SMIB stability study. IJEAT 2, 209–214 (2012)

7. Singh, G., Bala, R.: Automatic generation & voltage control of interconnected thermal power system including load scheduling strategy. IJEAT **1**, 1–7 (2011)
8. Tanwani, N.K.: Simulation Techniques of Electrical Power System Stability Studies Utilizing. Quaid-e-Awam University of Pakistan, March 2014
9. Abdel-Magid, Y.L., Abido, M.A.: Coordinated design of a PSS and an SVC-based controller to enhance power system stability. Electr. Power Energy Syst. **25**, 695–704 (2003)
10. Dabur, P., Yadav, N.K., Avtar, R.: Matlab design and simulation of AGC and AVR for single area power system with fuzzy logic control. IJEAT **1**, 44–49 (2012)
11. Dabur, P., Yadav, N.K., Tayal, V.K.: Matlab design and simulation of AGC and AVR for multi-area power system and demand side management. IJECE **3**, 259 (2011)
12. Mon, T.W., Aung, M.M.: Simulation of synchronous machine in stability study for power system. World Acad. Sci. Eng. Technol. **39**, 128–133 (2008)
13. Tanwani, N.K.: Analysis and Simulation Techniques of Electrical Power System Stability Studies (2013)
14. Narne, R., Panda, P.C., Therattil, J.P.: Transient stability enhancement of SMIB system using PSS and TCSC-based controllers. In: IEEE PEDS (2011)
15. Suhail, K.: Feedforward neural network-based power system stabilizer for excitation control system. M.E. Thesis, Department of Electrical Engineering (2011)
16. Memon, A.P.: Design of FFNN AVR for Enhancement of Power System Stability Using Matlab/Simulink. Mehran University (2012)
17. Aziz, A., Mto, A., Stojsevski, A.: Automatic generation control of multigeneration power system. J. Power Energy Eng. **2**, 312–333 (2014)

Generator Excitation Loss Detection on Various Excitation Systems and Excitation System Failures

Alganesh Ygzaw[✉], Belachew Banteyirga, and Marsilas Darsema

Bahir Dar Institute of Technology, Bahir Dar University, Bahir Dar, Ethiopia
alganeshy196@gmail.com

Abstract. Generating steadiness of synchronous generator is highly dependent on their exciter as the direct current from excitation system sustains stator and rotor windings magnetically coupled. But generator loss of excitation weakens stator and rotor coupling which result in mechanical and electrical power imbalance and rotor speed rise beyond synchronous speed. And this phenomenon is able to damage both the generator and the grid if an early protection is not issued through excitation loss relay. This paper presents performance evaluation of excitation loss relay for DC, AC and static (ST) type exciters and various causes of excitation loss. Comparatively the relay shows a good performance in all causes of full loss of excitation than in partial field voltage loss in any type of excitation systems. But the relay detection time in static type exciter is short compare to DC and AC type exciters.

Keywords: Excitation loss protection · Excitation system failures · Generator excitation loss

1 Introduction

The efficacy of electrical energy transmission in all part of power system is highly dependent on the reliability of synchronous generating machines as these machines are the main source of energy for the whole system. Generally synchronous generator has two inputs; mechanical input from turbine and field voltage from excitation system [1]. And at normal condition generator is able to produce and deliver active power due to the mechanical input and reactive power due to the field voltage. Excitation system is part of generating unit which produces flux by passing current in the field winding to supply its output through either brushes or slip rings to run synchronous machines [1, 2]. Generally excitation system consists of two relatively independent components, excitation regulator (AVR) and the exciter itself [3]. Excitation system regulation should include these three main characteristics: speed of system operation which identifies the reliability of stability in power system in terms of over voltage limitation in under load condition or de-excitation in internal failure condition, autonomy of excitation system that insure reliability of exciter at any condition and maximal drive security that ensures reliability function of integrated components [4, 5].

© ICST Institute for Computer Sciences, Social Informatics and Telecommunications Engineering 2020
Published by Springer Nature Switzerland AG 2020. All Rights Reserved
N. G. Habtu et al. (Eds.): ICAST 2019, LNICST 308, pp. 382–394, 2020.
https://doi.org/10.1007/978-3-030-43690-2_26

Thus, excitation system is able to control voltage and reactive power flow by ensuring if the machine does not exceed the capability limits. Excitation systems can be classified in terms of their construction as static or rotating and according to excitation energy source as separate or self-excited systems [1]. In static exciters energy is brought through slip rings and carbon brushes to the generator field winding. To perceived use of brushes in large synchronous machines, use of brushes in static excitation systems have been eliminated in rotating excitation systems [1]. Generally excitation system can be classified as (DC), AC or static (ST) type.

DC type exciters uses direct current generators as sources of excitation power and provide current to the rotor of the synchronous generator through slip rings. This type of exciter mainly have replaced by the other two types except a few synchronous machines are equipped with DC exciters. This group consists of four models as described in [6]. In AC type of exciters Alternating Current machines are used as source of the main generator excitation power and rectification of AC voltage is carried out through controlled or non-controlled rectifiers to provide DC to the generator field winding. However, except AC4A model, DC exciters did not allow negative field current flow which does not allow them de-excitation in case of internal failures in the generator. This is the main disadvantage of this type of systems because it does not allow de-excitation of generator. In static exciters however, energy is brought through slip rings and carbon brushes to the generator field winding. In such systems generator itself is power source or the generator is self-excited. This type of excitation system consist of seven models and the possibility to produce negative excitation current is their significant advantage. Thus, it provides quick de-excitation which may be needed in case of generator internal fault. In this paper, DC1A, AC1A and ST1A exciters will be used to study performance of excitation loss relay detection for various excitation fault type scenarios.

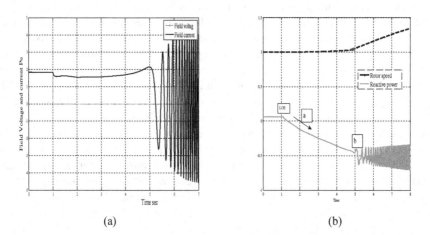

Fig. 1. Generator (a) field current and voltage (b) rotor speed and reactive power

Any failure in excitation system directly interrupts the generating capability of the synchronous generator and transmission of power to the system. The phenomenon where the generators lose its excitation is called excitation loss. In excitation loss event, the excitation system fails to deliver DC current and the generator seek a way to stay excited which causes the faulty generator to absorb a large amount of reactive power from the system connected with it. And consequently reduces reactive power delivery from generator to system and lead to power system voltage and current instability and if it continues to blackout of the whole system [6, 7]. Generator excitation loss can be summarized as two stages as shown in Fig. 1b as point (a) and (b). Region-(a) is the first stage of excitation loss event and the generator starts to consume reactive power from the system. In this stage, the system is capable of feeding reactive power to the generator and the generator remains in synchronism. The reactive power amplitude consumed by the generator could be as large as 1.56 times rated power of the generator which indicates the machine is trying to run the faulted generator and to keep the system stable. On the second stage shown point (b), the system reaches the maximum limit of reactive power delivering and the generator speed rises rapidly beyond synchronous speed due to power imbalance. In this stage, the relation between the stator and rotor is already very week due to under-excitation limit is achieved. And over speed of the generator consequences the generator to loss synchronism and bring a huge damage to the system [3, 8]. In this condition the generator must be isolated from the remaining system.

Generator terminal voltage and terminal current measurement is used to protect against excitation loss event. In 1949, Mason [9] suggests a negative off-set mho-type distance relay to sense the impedance variation of generator terminal point due to excitation loss. When the impedance trajectory falls under predefined protective zone in R-X plane for a reasonable pre-set time delay, excitation loss will be detected. Shortly afterwards, in 1975, Berdy [10] presents a two off-set mho circle protection zones by addition of another mho unit to this protection scheme proposed in [6] to reduce detection duration of lightly loaded generators. These two methods are the base of excitation loss detection algorithms proposed ever since but mal-operating in stable power swing is the main threat for the algorithms. Some years later, the above methods have been modified using modern computational methods, such as neural networks [11], decision tree [12] and fuzzy algorithms [13] in protection against loss of excitation. These methods may present good results, however require a considerable amount of training and vast simulation scenarios. With the advent of digital relays, a Space Vector Machine (SVM) technique is proposed to differentiate system and excitation failures [14] but the algorithm needs a significant amount of data for training. In 2016, Mahamedi and Zhu [15] present a setting free approach using generator terminal resistance variations where if the derivative values of the resistance remains negative for predefined time delay, excitation loss will be detected. However, the oscillatory nature of terminal resistance is speed variation the algorithm may reset in excitation loss events with high slip frequencies. On the same year, Abedini et al. [16], proposes a method using the rate decay of the generator internal voltage with the field flux linkage variation. An adaptive and threshold loss of excitation index is introduced such if the generator achieve greater excitation loss index for a given samples, then loss of excitation will be detected. A combined index based on generator terminal voltage, reactive power and power angle variations is presented in [6]. Although this technique can be implemented by considering a special case of the network operation, regarding the network combination is inevitable. A flux based method is presented in [17], which it uses the installed search coils in stator slots to measure the air-gap flux. This scheme however should normally be implemented by the generator manufacturer.

Still the actual excitation loss protection in power system industries is so called impedance type protection proposed almost four decades ago. Since the protective relays should be designed with requirements of sensitivity to sense all possible failures of excitation systems for all types of excitation systems and accuracy and reliability as should be easy and less complex to set the threshold of the protective devices after a possible failure. In this paper, the actual excitation loss relay in power system industries will be studied on various type of excitation loss and excitation system.

Excitation Loss Relay

The main indicator in capturing the probability of excitation failure is the significant flow of reactive power into the generator. The most common excitation loss protection is based on the calculation of the impedance at generator terminal. In modern power system industries, Berdy method [10] is the most popular which has two protection circle zones plotted on the R-X plane of the terminal impedance as can be observed in Fig. 2 [6, 10]. The protection zones are positioned in the negative reactance coordinate of the R-X plane with offset value $X'd/2$ and with circle zone diameter of 1 pu and Xd for zone-1 and zone-2 respectively. As can be seen from Eq. (1) in normal operating condition, both generator resistance (R) and reactance (X) are positive and the terminal impedance is located in the first quadrant in R-X plane. However, when the generator loses excitation the generator starts to draw reactive power from the system and reactance becomes negative from the relay point of view. As a result, the terminal impedance trajectory in R-X plane moves to the forth quadrant and the relay is able to detect excitation loss event when the impedance trajectory enter in the protection zones. A reasonable time delay is proposed to distinguish between a recoverable swings and loss of excitation. For zone-2, 0.5 s and 1 s time delay is suggested to send alarm and trip signals consequently. But for zone-1 no delay is suggested.

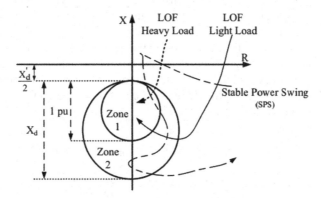

Fig. 2. Excitation loss relay

$$Z = \frac{V}{I} = R + jX = \frac{V^2 P_t}{P_t^2 + Q_t^2} + j\frac{V^2 Q_t}{P_t^2 + Q_t^2} \qquad (1)$$

Where $R = \frac{V^2 P_t}{P_t^2 + Q_t^2}$ and $X = \frac{V^2 Q_t}{P_t^2 + Q_t^2}$

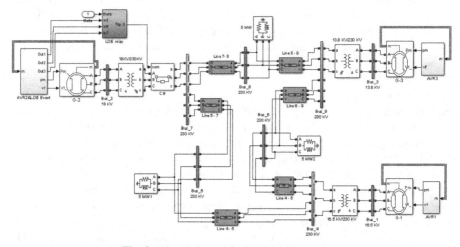

Fig. 3. Simulink model of IEEE 9-bus system

2 Excitation Loss Types

Generator loses its excitation completely when the field voltage or field current supplied to the generator is totally lost and the exciter fails to run the synchronous generator completely. In this condition the synchronous generator is able to produce active power due to the mechanical input but it starts consuming reactive power from the system. Full loss of excitation is initiated either due to field winding failure, poor brush contact, AVR control failure, slip ring flash over, main circuit breaker failure or sudden AC voltage loss to exciter [2, 7]. Despite the cause of excitation loss, either the field voltage or field current reduce in value or to zero depend on the type of excitation loss cause or sever of the failure. To study excitation loss event, IEEE nine bus system shown in Fig. 3 has modeled in MATLAB/SIMULINK and excitation loss is created on G-2 of the system as its parameter values has given in Table 1.

Table 1. Parameter values of generator under study (G-2)

Generator	MVA	kV	X_d	X'_d	T'_{do}
9-Bus G-2	192	18	1.72	0.23	8

2.1 Field Winding Short Circuit

A short circuit on field winding is the most common type of excitation system fault. In field winding short circuit the field voltage literally decline to zero as shown in Fig. 1a. But the field current remains high and it is able to swing when the generator lose synchronism due to self-exciting excitation system is used and field current is dependent on parameters of generator.

Figure 4 shows the impedance trajectory of G-2 for field winding short circuit in different loading effects; heavy load, medium load and light load conditions. In heavy load condition excitation loss relay detect field winding short circuit at 4.16 s for DC1A, 4.33 s for AC1A and 4.037 s for ST1A exciters through zone-1 since the first zone of impedance protection is modelled to protect heavy loaded generators. On the other hand, when the loading effect starts to decrease, zone-2 is capable of detecting excitation loss event with a reasonable time delay. In medium load the event is detected after 5.804 s through zone-2 for DC1A exciter. On the same manner, in light load condition, the generator delivers 30% of the rating power, and field winding short circuit is detected after 6.286 s. But, the impedance trajectory enters zone-1 after 13.43 s which is much slower than in heavy load case.

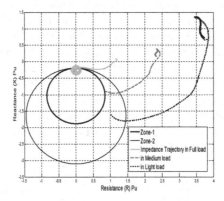

Fig. 4. G-2 impedance trajectory in field winding short circuit

2.2 Sudden Failure of Main Circuit Breaker

When the main circuit breaker between the exciter and generator opened due to sudden failure, the exciter and the generator totally isolated and the generator loses its field voltage totally. Due to this the generator field voltage reduce to zero and results in complete loss of excitation but the exciter remains at normal state. Also AVR failure reduces field voltage of the generator to null. These causes of excitation loss have similar characteristics to field winding short circuit due the field voltage generator is terminated to null. And excitation loss relay detect sudden failure of main circuit breaker and AVR failure scenarios with in similar length of time as their impedance trajectory given in Fig. 5. For both cases, heavy load condition is detected through zone-1 after 4.16 s for DC1A exciter similar to field winding short circuit.

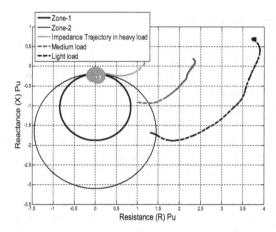

Fig. 5. G-2 impedance trajectory in sudden main circuit breaker failure

2.3 Sudden Loss of AC Voltage to Excitation System

Despite the variety of excitation system, any exciter has its own starting means either separate source or direct from the machine connected with it (self-exciting) depend on the type of excitation system. However, if the AC voltage that run the exciter interrupted by any means, excitation system and also the generator connected with the exciter will be faulted. In this work self-excited exciter is used, so sudden loss of AC voltage to the exciter is studied when the generator terminal voltage run the exciter is suddenly interrupted. Thus, AC voltage loss to the exciter also results in full loss of excitation in generator as can be shown in Fig. 6a below. Complementary to other causes of excitation loss, excitation system got support from the other components of the exciter in sudden

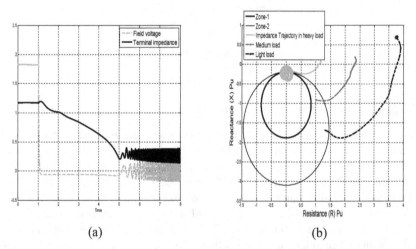

(a)   (b)

Fig. 6. G-2 (a) field voltage and terminal impedance (b) impedance trajectory in sudden AC voltage loss to exciter

AC voltage loss to exciter since the field voltage is dependent on the initial value of field voltage and the terminal voltage of the generator.

For simulation, let the excitation system of G-2 suddenly loss AC voltage at 1 s. The relay detects the event at 4.223, 4.418 and 4.109 s for DC1A, AC1A and ST1A exciters consequently through zone-1 in heavy load condition which is about 0.63 s longer than the above causes.

2.4   Field Winding Open Circuit

In field winding open circuit, field current is terminated to null. It is associated with inserting of an infinite discharge resistance which tends to reduce the field current to almost null. This is the worst cause of excitation loss event that generator lose synchronism in fraction of microseconds in any loading conditions. As can be observed from Fig. 7a, comparing the courses of generator values during loss of excitation in field winding open circuit, system reactive power feeding limit is reached at 0.06 s after fault which is almost 4 s before in other causes of excitation loss. And it can be noticed that the peak value reactive power is smallest in open-circuit case comparing to other causes of excitation loss as can observed from Figs. 1b and 7a.

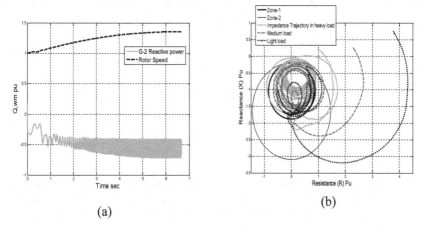

(a)

(b)

Fig. 7. G-2 (a) field current and reactive power (b) impedance trajectory in field winding open circuit

From Fig. 7b, after the fault is initiated the seen impedance by the relay moves from quadrant-one toward the fourth-quadrant of the R-X plane and then moves back to the third-quadrant. For DC1A excitation type, LOE relay detect field winding open circuit in 0.0835 s for heavy load, 0.0467 s for medium and 1.131 s for light initial load conditions which is faster than the other causes of excitation loss.

Table 2 summarizes excitation loss relay performance on various causes of full excitation loss on the three types of excitation systems. Generally, excitation loss relay detect field winding open circuit in very short period of time than the other causes in any generator initial loading condition. On the other hand in AC excitation system the relay has longer detection time than the other two exciter. And it can also observe that, impedance protection of excitation loss is highly dependent on initial generation ability of the generator. But, the relay was able to detect full loss of excitation in less than 6.5 s in all loading conditions.

Table 2. Excitation loss relay detection ability in main causes of full excitation loss

Initial loading (in pu)	Types of excitation	Type of LOE and Generator tripping time (second)			
		FW short circuit	AC voltage loss	Main CB failed	FW open circuit
0.8485 + j0.06307	DC1A	4.160	4.223	4.160	0.0835
	AC1A	4.281	4.450	4.160	0.2638
	ST1A	4.037	4.223	4.160	0.0687
0.7604 + j0.04781	DC1A	4.961	5.027	4.160	0.06485
	AC1A	5.03	5.236	4.160	0.0783
	ST1A	4.850	5.109	4.160	0.0783
0.6792 + j0.03679	DC1A	5.165	5.236	4.160	0.05115
	AC1A	5.482	5.703	4.160	0.0618
	ST1A	5.095	5.296	4.160	0.0584
0.2547 + j0.3	DC1A	6.286	6.348	4.160	1.131
	AC1A	6.400	6.634	4.160	1.237
	ST1A	6.163	6.267	4.160	0.994
0.3396 + j0.03424	DC1A	5.773	5.853	4.160	0.0341
	AC1A	5.903	6.004	4.160	0.0508
	ST1A	5.560	5.752	4.160	0.0327

2.5 Partial Loss of Excitation

Partial loss of excitation is happen when field winding voltage of the generator decrease in value by any reason. In this case, the filed voltage does not subject to null, so there will be some reactive power generation but not enough to feed the system so the generator still consumes reactive power from the system even if that is slower than full loss of excitation The detection ability of excitation loss relay will be studied for different percentage losses of field voltage starting from the worst partial loss which is decrease Efd by 1.6497 pu till the least loss 0.1833 pu field voltage reduction as can be scrutinized in Table 3.

When the field voltage reduced to 30% of its normal value, the system is able to feed reactive power to the synchronous generator for about 15 s after fault happen. On the other hand, when the generator lost 50% and 70% of the field voltage, the synchronous generator was able to consume reactive power from the system for about 9 s and 7 s respectively without loss of synchronism as shown in Fig. 8a. Thus, the field voltage reduction only affects the reactive power consumption duration and variable changing rate of the machine and the initial condition determines the generator output during loss of excitation.

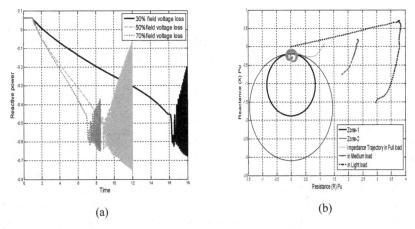

(a)   (b)

Fig. 8. G-2 (a) reactive power reduction (b) impedance trajectory in 30% field voltage loss

Figure 8b shows the impedance trajectory of G-2 in 30% field voltage loss. Excitation loss relay successfully detects 30% diminishing of field voltage only for heavy loaded generator after 15.210 s for DC1A exciter. Similarly, reduction of half field voltage remains un-detected for 24.15 s in medium load and not detected at all in light condition. This threat system stability and may lead to blackout of the whole system. But in heavy load the field voltage reduction is detected after 8.563 s.

Table 3. Excitation loss relay detection ability in partial loss of excitation

| Initial loading (in pu) | Types of excitation | Field voltage percentage loss (% Efd loss) and G-tripping duration [Y(sec)/N] | | | | |
		30%	40%	50%	70%	90%
0.8485 + j0.06307	DC1A	15.210	10.940	8.563	5.913	4.592
	AC1A	16.021	4.450	8.932	6.209	4.927
	ST1A	15.082	4.016	8.202	5.731	4.320
0.7604 + j0.04781	DC1A	18.210	12.51	9.563	6.816	5.493
	AC1A	18.864	13.042	10.06	7.023	5.780
	ST1A	18.109	12.302	9.392	6.590	5.285
0.6792 + j0.03679	DC1A	22.29	14.100	10.48	7.161	5.659
	AC1A	22.940	14.905	10.960	7.823	5.828
	ST1A	21.102	13.89	10.362	7.008	5.406
0.2547 + j0.3	DC1A	N	N	N	13.41	7.37
	AC1A	N	N	N	13.894	7.893
	ST1A	N	N	N	13.058	7.031
0.3396 + j0.03424	DC1A	N	N	24.15	10.04	6.644
	AC1A	N	N	24.602	10.592	6.942
	ST1A	N	N	23.883	9.704	6.172

Excitation loss relay have a good performance in detecting field voltage loss greater than half of the rated field voltage as have been shown in Table 3. On the other hand, for partial excitation loss less than half of the rated field voltage of the synchronous generator, it fails detecting field voltage diminishing except for heavily loaded generators for each type of excitation types.

2.6 Power Swings

Power swing is the oscillation of machine rotor angle due to power system disturbances like a fault, generator or line outages and load propagation that alters the mechanical equilibrium of one or more machines. Table 4 summarizes excitation loss relay performance on various system disturbances. In order to ensure the reliable operation of LOE relay there is a short time delay between entering time to the operating zone and the initiation of a tripping signal. Comparing to critical transmission line outage, main load rejection worsens the impedance trajectory closeness to the relay characteristics (Fig. 9).

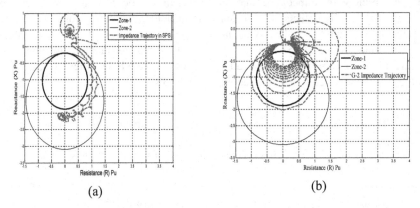

(a)   (b)

Fig. 9. G-2 impedance trajectory in (a) SPS (B) Unstable swing

Table 4 shows LOE relay performance on various system disturbances including SPS and OOS on heavy, medium and lightly load generators. As can be observed from the results, LOE relay had actually detected a loss of synchronism which was caused by prolonged fault clearing times even in short period of time than LOE event for all type of exciters.

Table 4. Performance of excitation loss relay on system disturbances

Initial loading (in pu)	Types of excitation	System disturbances			
		SPS	OOS	Line outage	G-outage
Heavy load	DC1A	1.105	0.856	N	N
	AC1A	0.902	0.508	N	N
	ST1A	1.05	0.884	N	N
Medium load	DC1A	1.25	0.601	N	N
	AC1A	1.3	0.573	N	N
	ST1A	1.008	0.693	N	N
Light load	DC1A	1.053	0.638	N	N
	AC1A	1.058	0.601	N	N
	ST1A	1.118	0.750	N	N

3 Conclusion

The performance of excitation loss relay was assessed for various type of excitation system by simulating the test system with different excitation loss type. From the results, it has shown that field current reduction detected faster than field voltage reduction and comparatively excitation loss in static type exciter detects in less time than the remaining exciters. Based on the simulation and results obtained for the above test cases, the time available to trip loss of excitation depends on various conditions such initial loading of the generator, type of excitation loss, reactive power support from interconnected systems and type of excitation system. More generator active power output and full excitation loss implies that there is less time before the excitation loss protection detected and vice versa for weak MVAR support from the system and partial excitation loss.

References

1. Kundur, P.: Power System Stability and Control. McGraw-Hill, New York (1994)
2. Bialek, J.W., Robak, S., Bumby, J.R., Machowski, J.: Excitation control system for use with synchronous generators. In: IEEE Proceedings - Generation, Transmission and Distribution, vol. 145, no. 5, September 1998
3. Méster, M., Krištof, V.: Loss of excitation of synchronous generator. J. Electr. Eng. **68**, 54–60 (2017)
4. Jolevski, D.: Excitation system of synchronous generator. University of Split, Faculty of Electrical, Mechanical Engineering and Naval Architecture (2009)
5. IEEE Power Engineering Society: IEEE Recommended Practice for Excitation System Models for Power System Stability Studies. IEEE Std. 421.5-2005. IEEE, New York (2006)
6. Hasani, A., Haghjoo, F.: A secure and setting free technique to detect loss of field in synchronus generators. IEEE Trans. Energy Convers. **32**, 1512–1522 (2017)
7. Naser, N., et al.: Analytical technique for synchronous generators loss of excitation protection. IET Gener. Trans. Disturb. **11**, 2222–2231 (2017)
8. Platero, C.A., et al.: Review of loss of excitation protection setting and coordination to the generator capacity curve. IEEE (2017)

9. Mason, C.R.: New loss-of-excitation relay for synchronous generators. Trans. Am. Inst. Electr. Eng. **68**(2), 1240–1245 (1949)

10. Berdy, J.: Loss of excitation protection for modern synchronous generators. IEEE Trans. Power Appar. Syst. **94**(5), 1457–1463 (1975)

11. Fan, B., et al.: The research UL-P of loss-of-excitation protection for generator based on the artificial neural networks. In: Asia-Pacific Power and Energy, pp. 1–4 (2009)

12. Amraee, T.: Loss of field detection in synchronous generators using decision tree technique. IET Gener. Trans. Distrib. **7**(9), 943–954 (2013)

13. de Morais, A.P., et al.: An innovative loss-of-excitation protection based on the fuzzy inference mechanism. IEEE Trans. Power Delivery **25**(4), 2197–2204 (2010)

14. Gokaraju, R., Sachdey, M.S., Ajuelo, E.: Identification of generator loss-of-excitation from power-swing conditions using a fast pattern classification method. IET Gener. Trans. Distrib. **7**(1), 24–36 (2013)

15. Zhu, J.G., Mahamedi, B.: A setting-free approach to detecting loss of excitation in synchronous generators. IEEE Trans. Power Delivery **31**, 2270–2278 (2016)

16. Sanaye-Pasand, M., Abedini, M.: An analytical approach to detect generator loss of excitation based on internal voltage calculation. IEEE Trans. Power Delivery **32**, 2329–2338 (2017)

17. Sanaye-Pasand, M., Abedini, M.: Flux linkage estimation based loss of excitation relay for synchronous generator. IET Gener. Trans. Distrib. **11**(1), 280–288 (2017)

Performance Enhancement of Distribution Power System by Optimal Sizing and Sitting of Distribution Statcom

Nebiyu Yisaye$^{(\boxtimes)}$, Elias Mandefro, and Belachew Bantyirga

Faculty of Electrical and Computer Engineering, Bahir Dar Institute of Technology,
Bahir Dar University, Bahir Dar, Ethiopia
nyissaye@gmail.com, eliasmandefro01@gmail.com,
belchwbbg1j1@gmail.com

Abstract. In this paper, an approach for optimal sizing and sitting of D-STATCOM in radial distribution network is proposed with multi objective functions of power loss minimization, voltage stability, and voltage profile enhancement subjected to equality and inequality constraints. Voltage stability index is used to pre-determine the candidate bus for optimal sitting of D-STATCOM. Genetic algorithm is proposed to determine the optimal size and sit of D-STATCOM. The performance of the proposed method is tested on the two IEEE 33-bus and 69-bus radial distribution feeders. The test systems are analyzed with different loading and sizing condition of D-STATCOM. The simulation result shows that optimal sitting and sizing of D-STATCOM in the proposed networks effectively upgrade the performance of the system.

Keywords: D-STATCOM · Genetic algorithm · Loss minimization · Sitting · Sizing · Voltage profile · Voltage stability

1 Introduction

Power system networks are become very complex, dynamic, nonlinear, and are prone to various types of disturbances. The distribution system is part of a power system that distributes power to end users. It is the most extensive part of the electrical system as a result of being responsible for energy losses. Different studies indicated that 13% of the total power generated is wasted in the form of losses at the distribution network. The distribution system is constantly being faced with an ever-growing load demand; thus increasing load demand results in increasing system loading and reduced the voltage profile. The voltages at buses reduce if we moved away from substation, and under critical loading it may lead to voltage collapse. Thus to improve the voltage profile and to avoid voltage collapse reactive power compensation is required. Improving the overall efficiency of power delivery has forced the power utilities to reduce the losses at the distribution level [1].

Voltage instability problem occurs in a power system when a disturbance causes a progressive and uncontrollable decrease in acceptable voltage levels. A disturbance

© ICST Institute for Computer Sciences, Social Informatics and Telecommunications Engineering 2020
Published by Springer Nature Switzerland AG 2020. All Rights Reserved
N. G. Habtu et al. (Eds.): ICAST 2019, LNICST 308, pp. 395–414, 2020.
https://doi.org/10.1007/978-3-030-43690-2_27

such as a fault or change in operating conditions leads to increased demand for reactive power. This increase in electric power demand makes the power system to operate close to their limit conditions, which indicates that the system is operating under heavy loading conditions. As a result, voltage stability becomes one of the major concerns and an appropriate solution must be found to avoid the voltage collapse in a operated system network [2].

The main causes of voltage instability problems are:

- High reactive power consumption at load center
- Generating stations located far from load center
- Difficulties in the transmission of reactive power under heavy loads
- Due to improper locations of FACTS controllers
- Poor coordination between multiple FACTS controllers

The voltage instability problem has the following effects:

- Loss of load in specific areas
- Tripping of distribution lines
- Voltage collapse in the system

Voltage stability can be improved using:

- Placement of FACTS controllers
- Co-ordination of multiple FACTS controllers
- Installation of synchronous condensers
- Placement of series and shunt capacitors/reactors

Series voltage regulator and shunt capacitor are the two convectional FACTS devices for enhancing voltages profile of the distribution system at an acceptable range but they have some operational limitations. Thus Series voltage regulators cannot generate reactive power and have a slow response due to their step by step operations. Shunt capacitors also cannot generate continuously variable reactive power and their natural oscillatory behavior when they are connected with the same circuits to inductive components [3]. In order to increase system performance in loss minimization, improvement of voltage profile and stability there should be an installation of highly advanced equipment; Such equipment's are capacitor banks, shunt and series reactors, Automatic Voltage Regulator (AVR) or recently developed Distribution Network Flexible AC Transmission (FACTS) such as Distribution Static Compensator (D-STATCOM), Unified Power Flow Conditioner (UPQC), and Static Synchronous Series Compensator (SSSC). D-STATCOM has unique features, such as low cost, compact size, less harmonic production, low power losses, and high regulatory capability as compared with other FACTS device [4].

D-STATCOM is one of a shunt FACTS device that can inject and absorb real or reactive power at the bus thereby removing the sag in bus voltages. It consists of a three phase inverter controlled by SCRs, MOSFETs or IGBTs, a D.C capacitor which provides the D.C voltage for the inverter, a link reactor which links the inverter output to the AC supply side, filter components to filter out the high frequency components due to the

PWM inverter. From the DC Side capacitor, a three phase voltage is generated by the inverter. This is synchronized with the AC supply. The link inductor links this voltage to the AC supply side. The magnitude of voltage sources used in D-STATCOM decides the direction and magnitude of reactive current flow at the point of connection. If a voltage magnitude is higher than the magnitude of the voltage source, it works as a reactor and absorbs the excess reactive power; otherwise, it will inject reactive power and works as a capacitor at point of connection [5].

2 Related Works

Recently, authors have been working on the optimal sizing and sitting of D-STATCOM for improving the performance of the distribution network with a different objective functions and system constraints [6].

Seraj et al. presented an optimal location of STATCOM in the transmission network using the PSO method. This work states a single objective function which is RMS voltage deviation. The simulation result showed that there is a minimization in the voltage deviation of the system network. The effectiveness of the proposed control scheme has been verified experimentally using a laboratory prototype system [7]. Kumarasamy and Raghavan proposed a cost-effective solution for optimal placement and size of multiple Statcom units using particle swarm optimization. The objective function incorporates system parameters like voltage profile, system loss, reactive compensation, and system voltage stability. The proposed work shows a clear improvement in system performance in voltage deviation, size of Statcom, real power loss, and maximum load ability limit as compared with conventional methods [8]. Saket and Ifran proposed a method of optimal placement of Statcom for improving the system voltage stability using a genetic algorithm. The objective function considers the improvement of voltage stability and loss reduction. The result showed that a reduction in system loss, and cost of generation besides improving the voltage at the buses [9]. Yuvaraj et al. investigated an optimal location and size of D-STATCOM using harmony search algorithm for power loss minimization. The result showed that total annual cost and power loss reduction compared with an immune algorithm [6]. Gupta and Kumar presented an analytical approach for determining the optimal placement and size of D-STATCOM for radial distribution network with the aim of reducing loss, improving voltage profile and overall energy saving. Two different sensitivity methods were applied to determine the optimal location of D-STATCOM and its size was calculated using vibrational technique [10]. Devabalaji and Ravi proposed a novel approach to the optimal location and sizing of multiple DGs and D-STATCOMs in radial distribution system based on the combination of LSF and BFOA algorithm. This research considered a predetermined location for DGs and D-STATCOM using LSF; while the optimal size is determined using BFOA [11]. Gowtham and Lakshmi presented power loss reduction and voltage profile improvement of radial distribution networks using particle swarm optimization. First fuzzy logic approach is predetermined the optimal location and then PSO algorithm determined optimal size of D-STATCOM. The result showed that the reduction in power loss and system voltage profile is maintained within acceptable limits [12]. Atma et al. presented a modified power loss index method for optimal placement and size of D-STATCOM. An objective function of power loss reduction and improvement of voltage profile is considered. The result showed that the reduction in power loss as well as improvement in voltage profile and various aspects [13].

Tanmoy et al. proposed an approach for optimal placement of Statcom using a gravitational search algorithm. The proposed system reduces power loss, the installation cost of D-STATCOM, and improves system voltage profile [14]. Sanam et al. presented an optimal allocation of D-STATCOM and DG units in a radial distribution network using the exhaustive search algorithm with an objective function of power loss minimization and voltage profile improvement. The performance of the proposed method showed a great reduction in system power loss and improvement of voltage profile [15]. Mohammed and Srinivasula proposed an optimal placement of STATCOM using an artificial bee colony (ABC) algorithm. In this work, an objective function of minimizing power losses, installation cost, voltage deviation and fuel cost minimization of the network. The simulation result showed that the optimal placement of D-STATCOM by the ABC algorithm was effective [16]. Some of the limitations of reviewed literatures are convergence limitations of the optimization algorithm, unconstrained objective function, single objective fitness function, and either placement or sizing of D-STATCOM was done.

3   Genetic Algorithm

Genetic algorithm (GA) is one of the stochastic search algorithms based on the mechanics of natural genetics. It allows a population composed of many individuals to evolve under specified selection rules to a state that maximizes the fitness (minimizes the cost function). A solution variable for the problem is first represented using artificial chromosomes (strings). A string represents one search point in the solution space. After convergence, strings are decoded to the original solution variables and the final solutions are obtained [17, 18].

In the GA algorithm, the population has n chromosomes that represent candidate solution and its implementation steps are:

Step 1: (Initialization): Set the iteration counter $k = 1$ and generates randomly n chromosomes.
Step 2: (Fitness): Evaluate each chromosome in the initial population using the objective function. The fitness $f(x)$ of each chromosome/individual x in the population.
Step 3: (Selection): Depending on individual chromosome fitness and using a given selection Scheme. The rank method is applied for the selection process. It first ranks the population and then every chromosome receives fitness from this ranking. Select two parent chromosomes from a population according to their Fitness (the better fitness, the bigger chance to get selected).
Step 4: (Elitism): Make a copy of selected parents.
Step 5: (Cross over): Cross over the selected parents to form a new child with a crossover probability. Two points cross over process is applied for crossover.
Step 6: (Mutation): Mutate new offspring at each locus (position in chromosome) with mutation probability. Interchanging Mutation process is applied for mutation.

Step 7: (New population): A new population is created with better fitness value.
Step 8: If the stopping criteria is satisfied go to step 10 else go to step 9.
Step 9: (Iteration updating): Update the iterations counter k = k + 1 and go to step 2.
Step 10: Stop, the optimized solution is the chromosome with the best fitness in the present Population (Table 1).

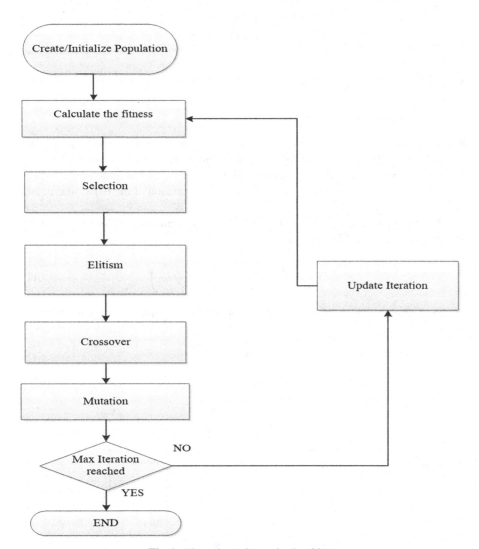

Fig. 1. Flow chart of genetic algorithm

Table 1. Input parameters of the GA algorithm

No	GA parameters	Values
1	Population size	40
2	Maximum iteration	30
3	Mutation probability	0.03
4	Cross-over probability	0.8

4 Problem Formulations

4.1 Power Flow Analysis

Newton rapson, Gauss seidel, and the two decoupled load flow solution techniques are unsuitable for solving load flow for radial distribution networks because of their high R/X ratio of branches. A direct load flow analysis is executed to find system voltage and loss at any bus by calculating load current, the formation of the BIBC matrix and forward sweep across a line [19, 20].

The single line diagram of a simple distribution system is shown in Fig. 2 and the load current at any bus t is given as:

$$I_t = \left(\frac{P_t + jQ_t}{V_t}\right)^* = \left(\frac{P_t - jQ_t}{V_t^*}\right) \tag{1}$$

Kirchhoff's current law used to calculate the branch current in the Line section between buses t and t + 1

$$J_{t,t+1} = I_{t+1} + I_{t+2} \tag{2}$$

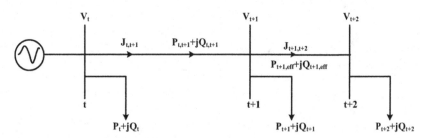

Fig. 2. Simple distribution system

The relationship between load current (I) and branch current (J) can found using simple KCL equations as follows where BIBC is bus injected to branch current matrix:

$$[J] = [BIBC][I] \tag{3}$$

The receiving end voltages can be calculated by forward sweeping method across the line by subtracting the line section drop from the sending end voltages of the line section:

$$V_{t+1} = V_t - J_{t,t+1}(R_{t,t+1} + jX_{t,t+1}) \tag{4}$$

The active and reactive power loss in the line section between t and t + 1, which is given as follows:

$$P_{Loss(t,t+1)} = (\frac{P_{t,t+1}^2 + Q_{t,t+1}^2}{|V_{t,t+1}|^2}) * R_{t,t+1} \tag{5}$$

$$Q_{Loss(t,t+1)} = (\frac{P_{t,t+1}^2 + Q_{t,t+1}^2}{|V_{t,t+1}|^2}) * X_{t,t+1} \tag{6}$$

The total active and reactive power loss of the distribution systems is found by adding each branch current line losses:

$$Q_{TLoss} = \sum_{t=1}^{nb} Q_{Loss(t,t+1)} \tag{7}$$

$$P_{TLoss} = \sum_{t=1}^{nb} P_{Loss(t,t+1)} \tag{8}$$

Percentage reduction in active power loss with D-STATCOM

$$\%P_{Loss\,reduction} = \left(\frac{P_{loss}^{Base} - P_{loss}^{DSTATCOM}}{P_{loss}^{Base}}\right) * 100 \tag{9}$$

Percentage reduction in reactive power loss with D-STATCOM

$$\%Q_{Loss\,reduction} = \left(\frac{Q_{loss}^{Base} - Q_{loss}^{DSTATCOM}}{Q_{loss}^{Base}}\right) * 100 \tag{10}$$

4.2 Modeling of D-STATCOM

The steady state modeling of D-STATCOM which is installed at the radial distribution feeder bus is shown in Fig. 3 below. After integration of D-STATCOM at the candidate bus the voltage values where it is installed and at the neighboring buses changes. The new voltages are V_n' at the candidate bus and V_m' at the previous bus. Current changes to I_m' which is the summation of I_m and I_{DS}. Where I_{DS} is the current injected by D-STATCOM and is in quadrature with the voltage [20].

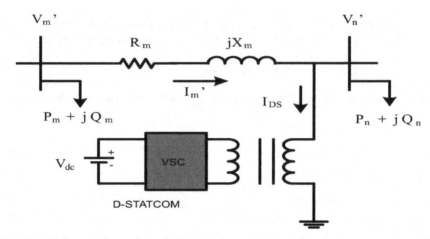

Fig. 3. Single line diagram of two-bus distribution system with D-STATCOM integration

Therefore, the expression for new voltage after installing D-STATCOM is given as

$$V_n' \angle \theta_n = V_m' \angle \theta_m' - (R_m + jX_m)(I_m \angle \delta + I_{DS} \angle (\frac{\pi}{2} + \theta_n')) \tag{11}$$

Here θ_n', θ_m' and δ are the phase angles of V_n', V_m' and I_m respectively.

By separating real and imaginary parts of Eq. (11) and manipulating the equations we get

$$t = \frac{-B \pm \sqrt{D}}{2A} \tag{12}$$

Where

$$t = \sin \theta' \tag{13}$$

$$A = (h_1 h_3 - h_2 h_4)^2 + (h_1 h_4 + h_2 h_3)^2 \tag{14}$$

$$B = 2(h_1 h_3 - h_2 h_4) + (V_n')(h_4) \tag{15}$$

$$C = (V_n' \cdot R_m)^2 - (h_1 h_4 + h_2 h_3)^2 \tag{16}$$

$$D = B^2 - 4AC \tag{17}$$

Where

$$h1 = \text{Real}(V_m' \angle \theta_m') - \text{Real}(Z_m I_m \angle \delta) \tag{18}$$

$$h2 = \text{Imag}(V_m' \angle \theta_m') - \text{Imag}(Z_m I_m \angle \delta) \tag{19}$$

$$h3 = -X_m \tag{20}$$

$$h4 = -R_m \tag{21}$$

Now there are two roots of t to determine the correct value of roots, the boundary conditions are examined as:

$$V_n' = V_n \Rightarrow I_{DS} = 0 \text{ And } \theta_n' = \theta_n \tag{22}$$

Results show that $t = \frac{-B \pm \sqrt{D}}{2A}$ it is the desired root of the Eq. (12).

D-STATCOM current angle and magnitude is:

$$\angle I_{DS} = \frac{\pi}{2} + x_2 = \frac{\pi}{2} + \sin^{-1} t \tag{23}$$

$$|I_{DS}| = x_1 = \frac{V_n' \cos \theta_n - h_1}{-h4 \sin \theta_n' - h3 \cos \theta_n'} \tag{24}$$

Finally, the reactive power injected is:

$$jQ_{DS} = (V_n' \angle \theta_n') . (I_{DS} \angle (\frac{\pi}{2} + \theta_n'))^* \tag{25}$$

Where * denotes the complex conjugate.

4.3 Objective Function

The objective of D-STATCOM allocation in the radial distribution system is to minimize the total active power losses, enhancement of voltage profile and voltage stability index while satisfying the equality and inequality constraints.

Loss Minimization

The total active power losses in the distribution system can be calculated as follows:

$$F_1 = \sum_{i=1}^{NBr} R_i \times I_i^2 \tag{26}$$

Where F_1 is the first objective function associated with the system power loss minimization

I_i is the current of line i

R_i is the resistance of ith line

NBr is the number of system branches.

Voltage Profile Improvement

The second objective function is improving the voltage profile of the network:

$$F_2 = \sum_{i=1}^{NBus} (1 - V_i)^2 \tag{27}$$

Where

V_i is the voltage of the ith bus

NBus is the number of the system bus.

Voltage Stability Improvement

A new steady state bus based voltage stability index method is used to identify the node, which has more chance to voltage collapse. The stability index at each node is calculated using Eq. (28). The node which has the low value of VSI is the weakest node and the voltage collapse phenomenon will start from that node. VSI is calculated from the load flow for all the buses of the given system and the values are arranged in ascending order. The VSIs choose the sequence in which the buses are to be considered for D-STATCOM placement. Therefore to avoid the possibilities of voltage collapse, the VSI of nodes should be maximized [11, 21] (Fig. 4).

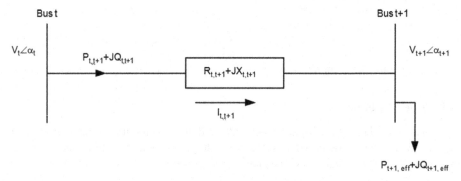

Fig. 4. Two-bus distribution system for VSI analysis

$$VSI(t+1) = |V_t|^4 - 4[P_{t+1,eff} \times X_t - Q_{t+1,eff} \times R_t]^2 - 4[P_{t+1,eff} \times R_t + Q_{t+1} \times X_t]|V_t|^2 \tag{28}$$

$$F_3 = \min(VSI(t+1)) \tag{29}$$

Where VSI $(t + 1)$ is the voltage stability index at bus $t + 1$, t and $t + 1$ are the sending and receiving bus number. $P_{t+1, eff}$ and $Q_{t+1, eff}$ are active and reactive power demands at bus $t + 1$, respectively, V_t is the voltage of the sending bus, $R_{t, t+1}$, $X_{t, t+1}$ are the resistance and reactance of branch between bus t, and $t + 1$ (Table 2).

The mathematical formulation of the general objective function (F) is given by

$$Minimize\,(F) = min\,(w_1 * F_1 + w_2 * F_2 + w_3 * \frac{1}{F_3}) \tag{30}$$

Where

$$\sum_{n=1}^{3} wn = 1 \tag{31}$$

Table 2. Weighting value representation

No	Objective functions	Weighting value
1	Power loss (w_1)	0.4
2	Voltage profile (w_2)	0.3
3	Voltage stability index (w_3)	0.3

4.4 System Constraint

Voltage Deviation Limit
The system voltage in all buses should be in an acceptable range:

$$V_m^{\min} \leq |V_m| \leq V_m^{\max}$$

Reactive Power Compensation
The reactive power injected by D-STATCOM to the system is limited by lower and upper bounds as given in following:

$$Q_m^{\min} \leq |Q_m| \leq Q_m^{\max}$$

Thermal Limit
The power flow through the lines is limited by the thermal capacity of lines:

$$|S_{ij} \leq S_{ij}\text{max}|$$

4.5 Methodology for the Proposed Optimization Algorithm

The proposed optimization algorithm is implemented using the following steps:

1. Read line and load data for test network of radial distribution feeders.
2. Set the lower and upper bounds of system constraints, genetic algorithm control parameters (population size, mutation probability, and cross-over probability) and maximum iteration.
3. Generate an initial random population.
4. Run the base case load flow algorithm and compute voltage profile at each bus, the real and reactive power loss of lines.
5. Developing bus based voltage stability index method for selecting candidate buses for sitting D-STATCOM.
6. Apply all steps for genetic optimization algorithm from Fig. 1 steps from (1–10), and optimized the fitness function using Eq. 30.
7. Select an optimal solution (Optimal sizing and sitting).
8. Display optimal solutions.

5 Result and Discussion

The performance of the proposed work is tested on the two IEEE-33 and IEEE-69 bus system in Matlab simulation software. The optimal sizing and sitting of D-STATCOM for test systems are considered under different test cases and loading conditions.

5.1 IEEE 33-Bus Test System

This is a medium scale radial distribution feeder with 33 buses and 32 branches. The single line diagram for the test system is shown in Fig. 5 below with bus voltage = 12.66 kV, base MVA = 100 MVA, total active power load 3.715 MW, and reactive power load 2.3 MVAr. The optimal sizing and sitting of D-STATCOM for the test system are considered with different system constraints and cases. The line and load data of the test system are taken from [22].

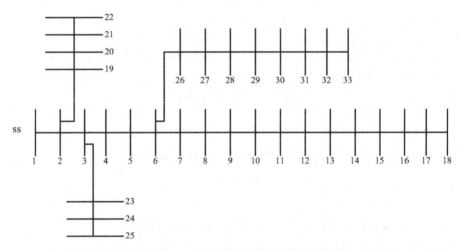

Fig. 5. Single line diagram for IEEE 33-bus radial distribution network

Case 1: System with D-STACOM the reactive power injected by D-STACOM is constrained with the maximum value of 1000 kVAr and the bus voltage is in range of $0.91 < V_m < 1.05$ with maximum power transfer capability of $S_{max} = 100$ MVA.

In Table 3 it shows that comparison of reactive and real power losses, voltage profile, voltage stability index, location, optimal size (kVAr) for the proposed method. In case 1, the real and reactive power losses have been reduced to 145.88 kW (percentage of reduction is 28.02%), 97.43 kVAr (percentage of reduction is 27.9065%), minimum voltage with a compensating device improves to 0.9230 p.u, and minimum VSI increases to 0.7258 p.u after installing the D-STATCOM. The optimal size of D-STACOM is 1000 kVAr and sits in bus 30 of the test network.

Case 2: System with D-STACOM the reactive power injected by D-STACOM is constrained with the maximum value of 2000 kVAr and the bus voltage is in range of $0.91 < V_m < 1.05$ with maximum power transfer capability of $S_{max} = 100$ MVA.

In Table 3 it shows that comparison of reactive and real power losses, voltage profile, voltage stability index, locations, optimal size (kVAr) for proposed method. In case 2, the real and reactive power losses have been reduced to 143.62 kW (percentage of reduction is 29.14%), 96.30 kVAr (percentage of reduction is 28.74%), minimum voltage with compensating device improves to 0.9251 p.u, and minimum VSI increases to 0.7325 p.u after installing the D-STATCOM. The optimal size of D-STATCOM is 1232 kVAr and sits in bus 30 of the tested network.

Table 3. Performance evaluation of IEEE-33 bus system

No	Parameters	Base case	Case-1	Case-2	PSO [22]
1	Active power loss	202.68 kW	145.88 kW	143.62 kW	148.8 kW
2	Reactive power loss	135.14 kVAr	97.43 kVAr	96.3070 kVAr	…………..
3	Minimum VSI	0.6950 p.u	0.7258 p.u	0.7325 p.u	0.74 p.u
4	Minimum voltage	0.9131 p.u	0.9230 p.u	0.9251 p.u	…………..
5	D-STATCOM location	…………..	30	30	30
6	D-STATCOM size	…………..	1000 kVAr	1232 kVAr	887 kVAr
7	Active power loss %	…………….	28.0219%	29.14%	26.00%
8	Reactive power loss %	…………..	27.9065%	28.74%	………..

Case 3: System with D-STACOM considering different loading conditions with the maximum size of 1000 kVAr and the bus voltage of $0.91 < V_m < 1.05$ with maximum power transfer capability of $S_{max} = 100$ MVA.

The proposed system is tested under different loading conditions 90%, 95%, 105%, and 110% of the normal loading conditions. From Table 4 it shows that as system loading increases system performance decrease and the installation of D-STATCOM improves its performance. Therefore distribution network operators can easily select the size of D-STATCOM as the load changes for the efficient operation of the network.

From the simulation result, it is shown that the comparative performance analysis of the proposed methods with a GA optimization algorithm for case 1 and case 2 in Power loss, voltage profile, and stability index. The proposed method shows an improvement as compared with PSO tested results. For the existing PSO method, the real power losses have been reduced to 148.8 kW (percentage of reduction is 26.00%), and minimum VSI

Table 4. IEEE 33-bus loading condition

No	Loading (%)	Ploss base case (kW)	Sitting (bus)	Sizing (kVAr)	Ploss with D-STATCOM (kW)	Reduction (%)
1	90%	161.6419	29	984	117.52	27.29%
2	95%	181.4935	30	1000	130.13	28.30%
3	105%	225.2272	30	962.25	163.77	27.28%
4	110%	249.1815	29	1000	184.30	26.03%

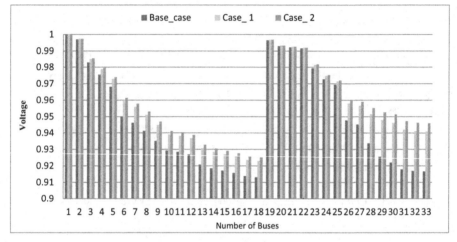

Fig. 6. Voltage profile for IEEE-33 bus

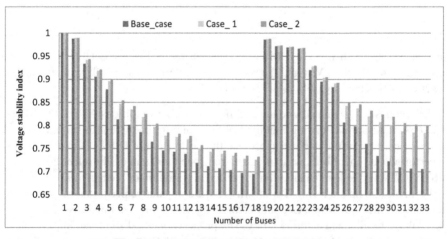

Fig. 7. Voltage stability index for IEEE-33 bus

increases to 0.74 p.u after installing the D-STATCOM. The optimal size of D-STATCOM is 887 kVAr and sits in bus 30 of the radial distribution network [22]. From Figs. 6 and 7 it shows a comparative voltage profile and voltage stability index for the base case, case 1, and case 2 of the test network respectively. It has shown clearly that as the size of D-STATCOM increases there is an improvement in system voltage profile magnitude and bus voltage stability index.

5.2 IEEE 69-Bus Test System

This is a large-scale radial distribution feeder with 69 buses and 68 branches. The single line diagram for the test system showed in Fig. 8 below with bus voltage = 12.66 kV, base MVA = 100 MVA, total active power load 3.8 MW, and reactive power load 2.69 MVAr. The optimal sizing and placement of D-STATCOM for the test system are considered under different system constraints. The line and load data are taken from [22].

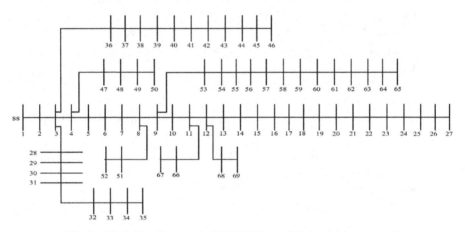

Fig. 8. Single line diagram for IEEE 69-bus radial distribution network

Case 1: System with D-STACOM the reactive power injected by D-STACOM is constrained with the maximum value of 1000 kVAr and the bus voltage is in range of $0.91 < V_m < 1.05$ with maximum power transfer capability of $S_{max} = 100$ MVA.

In Table 5 it shows that comparison of reactive and real power losses, voltage profile, voltage stability index, location, optimal size (kVAr) for the proposed method. In case 1, the real and reactive power losses have been reduced to 156.7897 kW (percentage of reduction is 30.3035%), 72.8594 kVAr (percentage of reduction is 28.6720%), minimum voltage with compensating device improves to 0.9259 p.u, and minimum VSI increases to 0.7349 p.u after installing the D-STATCOM. The optimal size of D-STATCOM is 1000 kVAr and sits in bus 62 of the test network.

Case 2: System with D-STACOM the reactive power injected by D-STACOM is constrained with the maximum value of 2000 kVAr and the bus voltage is in range of $0.91 < V_m < 1.05$ with maximum power transfer capability of $S_{max} = 100$ MVA.

In Table 5 it shows that comparison of real and reactive power losses, voltage profile, Voltage stability index, location, optimal size (kVAr) for proposed methods. In case 2, the real and reactive power losses have been reduced to 152.2115 kW (percentage of reduction is 32.3386%), 70.6490 kVAr (percentage of reduction is 30.8360%), minimum voltage with compensating device improves to 0.9293 p.u, and minimum VSI increases to 0.7459 p.u after installing the DSTATCOM. The optimal size of DSTATCOM is 1258.6 kVAr and sits in the bus 61 of the test network.

Table 5. Performance evaluation of IEEE-69 bus system

No	Parameters	Base case	Case-1	Case-2	PSO [22]
1	Active power loss	224.96 kW	156.7897 kW	152.2115 kW	158.8 kW
2	Reactive power loss	102.1470 kVAr	72.8594 kVAr	70.6490 kVAr	....
3	Minimum VSI	0.6828 p.u	0.7349 p.u	0.7459 p.u	0.734 p.u
4	Minimum voltage	0.9090 p.u	0.9259 p.u	0.9293 p.u	....
5	D-STATCOM location	....	62	61	63
6	D-STATCOM size	....	1000 kVAr	1258.6 kVAr	947 kVAr
7	Active power loss %	....	30.3035%	32.3386%	29%
8	Reactive power loss %	....	28.6720%	30.8360%	....

Case 3: System with D-STACOM considering different loading conditions with the maximum size of 1000 kVAr and the bus voltage of $0.91 < V_m < 1.05$ with maximum power transfer capability of $S_{max} = 100$ MVA.

The proposed system is tested under different loading conditions 90%, 95%, 105%, and 110% of the normal loading conditions. From Table 6 it shows that as system loading increases system performance decrease and the installation of D-STATCOM improves its performances. Therefore distribution network operators can easily select the size of D-STATCOM as the load changes for the efficient operation of the network.

Table 6. IEEE 69-bus loading conditions

No	Loading (%)	Ploss base case (kW)	Sitting (bus)	Sizing (kVAr)	Ploss with D-STATCOM (kW)	Active power loss reduction (%)
1	90%	178.9130	61	1000	122.9430	31.28%
2	95%	201.1623	63	966.37	140.7865	30.01%
3	105%	250.3566	61	1000	175.130	30.04%
4	110%	277.4018	64	1000	199.9365	27.93%

From the simulation result, it is shown that the comparative performance analysis of the proposed method with a GA optimization algorithm for case 1 and case 2 in Power loss, voltage profile, and stability index. For the existing PSO method, the real power losses have been reduced to 158.8 kW (percentage of reduction is 29.00%), and minimum VSI increases to 0.734 p.u after installing the D-STATCOM. The optimal size of D-STATCOM is 947 kVAr and sits in bus 30 of the radial distribution network [22]. From Figs. 9 and 10 shows a comparative voltage profile and voltage stability index for the base case, case 1, and case 2 of the test network respectively. It has shown clearly that as the size of D-STATCOM increases there is an improvement in system voltage profile and voltage stability index.

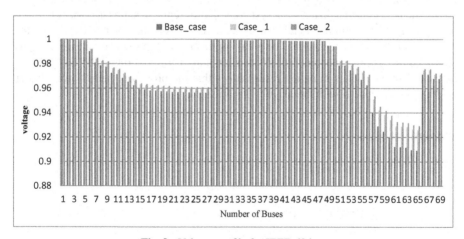

Fig. 9. Voltage profile for IEEE-69 bus

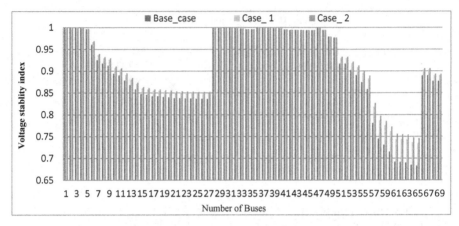

Fig. 10. Voltage stability index for IEEE-69 bus

6 Conclusion

A combined method of VSI and GA is proposed for optimal sitting and sizing of D-STATCOM with a multi-objective function of minimizing power loss, enhancing the voltage profile, and stability of the system. The bus-based voltage stability index method is used to predetermine the candidate bus for optimal sitting, and GA algorithm selects for optimal sitting and sizing of D-STATCOM. The proposed method is tested on IEEE 33-bus and 69-bus radial distribution system with different cases. It is necessary to place the D-STATCOM at optimal location with optimal size to ensure the maximum benefits of the system from its integration. The great improvement in system voltage profile, loss minimization, and enhancement of VSI is shown after installation of D-STATCOM at the candidate bus. The simulation result shows that the proposed method gives better results when compared with the existing Pso method.

Nomenclature

ABC	Artificial Bee Colony
AVR	Automatic Voltage Regulator
BFOA	Bacterial Foraging Optimization algorithm
BIBC	Bus Injected to Branch Current
DC	Direct current
DG	Distribution Generator
D-STATCOM	Distribution Static synchronous compensator
ESA	Exhaustive Search algorithm
FACTS	Flexible AC Transmission System
GA	Genetic Algorithm
IEEE	Institute of Electrical and Electronics Engineers
kV	Kilovolt
kVA	Kilovolt Ampere

kVAr	Kilo volt ampere reactive
KVL	Kirchhoff's Voltage Law
kW	Kilowatt
LSF	Loss sensitivity factor
MVA	Mega volt ampere
MVAr	Mega volt ampere reactive
MW	Megawatt
PSO	Particle Swarm Optimization
p.u	Per unit
R	Resistance
RDS	Radial distribution system
SSSC	Static synchronous series compensator
UPQC	Unified power quality control
VSC	Voltage source converter
VSI	Voltage stability index
X	Reactance

References

1. Yuvaraj, T., Ravi, K., Devabalaji, K.R.: DSTATCOM allocation in distribution networks considering load variations using bat algorithm. Ain Shams Eng. J. **8**(3), 391–403 (2017)
2. Pujara, A.J., Vaidya, G.: Voltage stability index of radial distribution network. In: 2011 International Conference on Emerging Trends in Electrical and Computer Technology, ICETECT 2011, no. 3, pp. 180–185 (2011)
3. Hussain, S.M.S., Subbaramiah, M.: An analytical approach for optimal location of DSTAT-COM in the radial distribution system. In: 2013 International Conference on Energy Efficient Technologies for Sustainability, ICEETS 2013, pp. 1365–1369 (2013)
4. Yuvaraj, T., Devabalaji, K.R., Ravi, K.: Optimal placement and sizing of DSTATCOM using Harmony search algorithm. Energy Procedia **79**, 759–765 (2015)
5. Iqbal, F., Khan, M.T., Siddiqui, A.S.: Optimal placement of DG and DSTATCOM for loss reduction and voltage profile improvement. Alex. Eng. J. **57**(2), 755–765 (2018)
6. Sirjani, R., Rezaee Jordehi, A.: Optimal placement and sizing of distribution static compensator (D-STATCOM) in electric distribution networks: a review. Renew. Sustain. Energy Rev. **77**, 688–694 (2017)
7. Ahamad, S., Ahmed, P.A., Khan, P.M.A.: Optimal location of STATCOM using PSO in IEEE 30 bus system. Int. J. Adv. Res. Sci. Eng. **8354**(2), 156–165 (2013)
8. Kumarasamy, K., Raghavan, R.: Cost effective solution for optimal placement and size of multiple STATCOM using particle swarm optimization. J. Theor. Appl. Inf. Technol. **67**(3), 701–708 (2014)
9. Saurabh, S.: Optimal placement of STATCOM for improving voltage stability using GA. Int. J. Sci. Eng. Technol. **2**(6), 1349–1353 (2014)
10. Gupta, A.R., Kumar, A.: Energy savings using D-STATCOM placement in radial distribution system. Procedia Comput. Sci. **70**, 558–564 (2015)
11. Devabalaji, K.R., Ravi, K.: Optimal size and siting of multiple DG and DSTATCOM in radial distribution system using Bacterial Foraging Optimization Algorithm. Ain Shams Eng. J. **7**(3), 959–971 (2016)

12. Gowtham, G., Devi, A.L.: Power loss reduction and voltage profile improvement by DSTATCOM using PSO. Int. J. Eng. Res. Technol. **4**(02), 192–196 (2015)
13. Gupta, A.R., Jain, A., Kumar, A.: Optimal D-STATCOM placement in radial distribution system based on power loss index approach. In: 2015 International Conference on Energy, Power and Environment: Towards Sustainable Growth, ICEPE 2015, p. 4 (2016)
14. Deb, T., Siddiqui, A.S.: Optimal placement of STATCOM using gravitational search algorithm for enhanced voltage stability. WSEAS Trans. Power Syst. **11**, 271–275 (2016)
15. Sanam, J., Ganguly, S., Panda, A.K.: Allocation of DSTATCOM and DG in distribution systems to reduce power loss using ESM algorithm. In: 1st International Conference on Power Electronics, Intelligent Control and Energy Systems, ICPEICES 2016, pp. 1–5 (2017)
16. Shaik, M.R., Reddy, A.S.: Optimal placement of STATCOM with ABC algorithm to improve voltage stability in power systems. In: International Conference on Signal Processing, Communication, Power and Embedded System, SCOPES 2016 - Proceedings, pp. 648–652 (2017)
17. Balaji, S.: Voltage stability enhancement by optimal placement of STATCOM using genetic algorithm. Int. J. Sci. Res. Dev. **3**(2), 27–33 (2017)
18. Man, K.F., Tang, K.S., Kwong, S.: Genetic algorithms: concepts and applications. IEEE Trans. Industr. Electron. **43**(5), 519–534 (1996)
19. Teng, J.-H.: A direct approach for distribution system load flow solutions. IEEE Trans. Power Deliv. **18**(3), 882–887 (2003)
20. Jain, A., Gupta, A.R., Kumar, A.: An efficient method for D-STATCOM placement in radial distribution system. In: India International Conference on Power Electronics, IICPE, vol. 2015, May 2015
21. Prada, R.B., et al.: Identification of weak buses using Voltage Stability Indicator and its voltage profile improvement by using DSTATCOM in radial distribution systems. IEEE Trans. Power Syst. **2**(4), 392–396 (2013)
22. Okati, M., Aminian, M.: Distribution system loss reduction, voltage profile and stability improvement by determining the optimal size and location of D-STATCOM. **4**(2), 67–80 (2017)

Power Distribution System Reliability Assessment and Improvement Case of Jimma Town, Ethiopia

Eyasu Berhanu Abrha[1]($\boxtimes$), Getachew Biru Worku[2], and Tadele Abera Abose[2]

[1] Raya University, Raya, Tigray, Ethiopia
eyuhashenge@gmail.com
[2] Addis Ababa University, Addis Ababa, Ethiopia
gbiru@yahoo.co.uk, tadenegn@gmail.com

Abstract. A frequent and long lasting power interruption has become a serious problem in Ethiopia. This problem has highly affected the life and economic activity of the society. The cost of power interruption to the power utility and also to the industry is very significant. This research has made an assessment of this problem and explored potential mitigation techniques. The reliability assessment has been done on the 15 kV city feeder. The interruption data of years 2010 to 2015 has been evaluated to determine the customer interruption indices. The study has evaluated different mitigation alternatives to look at the possibilities of reliability improvement. ETAP software has been used to test the improvement potential of the reliability indices for the distribution system. Various alternatives have been assessed using heuristic method. Reliability indices such as SAIFI, SAIDI and EENS have been reduced by 84.75%, 85% and 88.651% respectively as compared with the base year average values.

Keywords: Power distribution system · Power reliability · Protection system coordination · ETAP software

1 Introduction

Jimma is the oldest city of Oromia region in Ethiopia. It is located at the geographical coordinates of $7°\,40'\,22.1''$ N and $36°\,50'\,32.9''$ E and is 354 km away from Addis Ababa, capital of Ethiopia. The life of the people is highly dependent on electricity. Electricity is needed for lighting, cooking, water supply, educational activities, health sectors, etc. Assessment of the power reliability problem and exploration of cost effective problem mitigation techniques are the focus of the research. Many researches had been worked in different areas of the globe, to improve power distribution system reliability. The author of this research has been reviewed many researches and has got many ideas and techniques of solving such real existing problems.

Koval and Chowdhury [1] recommended a basic new restoration methodology for distribution system configurations that maximizes the amount of load that can be restored

© ICST Institute for Computer Sciences, Social Informatics and Telecommunications Engineering 2020
Published by Springer Nature Switzerland AG 2020. All Rights Reserved
N. G. Habtu et al. (Eds.): ICAST 2019, LNICST 308, pp. 415–423, 2020.
https://doi.org/10.1007/978-3-030-43690-2_28

after a grid blackout, substation outage and distribution feeder line section outages and evaluates the cost of load point interruptions considering feeder islanding and substation capacity constraints. Several case studies with restoration procedures are presented and discussed to clearly reveal the impact of distribution system capacity constraints on load point reliability indices and the cost of load point interruptions.

Merlin and Back [2] proposed a branch and bound type heuristic method to determine the network configuration to enhance distribution system reliability and for minimum line losses. Its solution scheme starts with a meshed network by initially closing all switches in the network. The switches are then opened one at a time until a new radial configuration is reached. In this process the switch to be opened at each stage is selected in order to enhance distribution system reliability and to minimize line losses of the resulting network.

2   Distribution System Reliability Assessment

The old and simple radial power distribution system topology is used in Ethiopia dominantly. The primary distribution system of Jimma town takes 132 kV and steps down to 15 kV and 33 kV. There are seven outgoing feeders (two 33 kV and five 15 kV) which supplies the town and surrounding Woredas. This study focuses on the one, 15 kV feeder, with the highest rate of interruption and supplies the largest part of the town (Fig. 1).

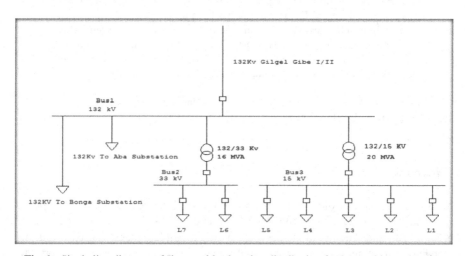

Fig. 1. Single line diagram of Jimma old substation distribution feeders and incoming line

The power distribution system reliability of the case study area is assessed by using different reliability indices. The indices for power distribution system analysis include customer-oriented indices and energy-oriented indices as defined in IEEE Standard 1366™-2012 [3].

2.1 Customer Oriented Indices

System Average Interruption Frequency Index (SAIFI): It is the average frequency of sustained interruptions per customers over a predefined area. Total number of customer interruptions per year divided by the total number of customers served.

$$\text{SAIFI} = \frac{\sum N_i}{N_t} \tag{1}$$

Where, Ni is the number of interrupted customers for each interruption event i during the reporting period, N_t is the total number of customers served in the area.

System Average Interruption Duration Index (SAIDI): It is commonly referred to as customer minutes of interruption or customer hours and provides information as to the average time the customers are interrupted.

$$\text{SAIDI} = \frac{\sum r_i N_i}{N_t} \tag{2}$$

Where, N_i is the number of interrupted customers for each interruption event i during the reporting period, N_t is the total number of customers served in the area and r_i is outage duration for event i.

Customer Average Interruption Frequency Index (CAIFI): This index gives the average frequency of sustained interruptions for those customers experiencing sustained interruptions. It is the value of total number of customer interruptions divided by total number of customers affected.

Customer Average Interruption Duration Index (CAIDI): It is the average time needed to restore service to the average customer per sustained interruption. It is the sum of customer interruption durations divided by the total number of customer interruptions.

$$\text{CAIDI} = \frac{\text{SAIDI}}{\text{SAIFI}} \tag{3}$$

Average Service Availability Index (ASAI): This index represents the fraction of time (often in percentage) that a customer has power provided during one year or the defined reporting period.

2.2 Load or Energy Oriented Indices

Expected Energy Not Supplied Index (EENS): This index represents the total energy not supplied by the system.

$$\text{EENS} = \sum_i L_i r_i \tag{4}$$

Where L_i the average load is connected to load point i and r_i is the outage duration for event i.

Table 1. Summary of reliability indices of city feeder for years 2010–2015

Reliability indices	Unit	2010	2011	2012	2013	2014	2015	Average of six years
SAIDI	Hrs./customer/yr.	237	181	238	203	302	471	272
SAIFI	Int./customer/yr.	241	302	480	424	461	705	435.5
CAIDI	Hrs./Interruptions	0.9	0.6	0.49	0.48	0.66	0.67	0.62
EENS	MWH	311	335	441	721	851	1458	686.2

The summary of the reliability indices for the years from 2010 to 2015 for the site are selected as base years and shown in Table 1.

In Jimma, each interruption, interruption duration and loads of each feeder per hour is recorded in the substation but the causes of interruptions are not recorded. As per the information from the technicians at the substation, the most common causes of interruptions are: overload, trees, windy rain, lightning, accidents, animals, scheduled operational interruptions, human error, grid outage, equipment malfunction and others. Among the causes, feeder overloading ranked first followed by tree contact and windy rain with operational scheduled interruptions and unknown causes ranked fourth and fifth place respectively.

The power outage frequency is as high as 435 and service restoration duration is as long as 272 h per year for the selected feeder. The data clearly indicates that power interruption per day is a common phenomenon in the case study area and due to this problem day to day activities of the society are highly affected and hence the customers' complaints to the utility have been strong and frequent.

To predict the reliability indices of a distribution system, values of failure rates and mean time to repair for each component are necessary. To estimate the failure rate of the line per kilometer, the total number of outages should be divided by the feeder length (Kilo meters) as indicated in Eq. (5). The average mean time to repair (MTTR) of each failure is computed using Eq. (6).

$$\mu_A = \frac{\text{Total Number of Interruptions}}{(\text{Total feeder length(km)}) \times (\text{Number of years})} \tag{5}$$

$$\text{MTTR} = \frac{\text{Total Repair Time}}{\text{Total Number of Interruptions}} \tag{6}$$

Where, μ_A is active failure rate of a component.

The calculated average failure rate of the line and average repair times per km of the existing feeder are 7.96 (Interruptions/(km·year)) and 0.62 (Hrs./interruption) respectively. By using the above two equations, the basic reliability parameters used in ETAP software for reliability analysis are calculated.

3   System Modeling

In this thesis, ETAP 12.6.0 has been used as a design, simulation and reliability assessment analysis tool. Figure 2 shows the project editor view, with the reliability page opened. Length of feeder, rating and type of each transformer, topology and layout of the system, conductor type, topography and others are used as input in modeling the system.

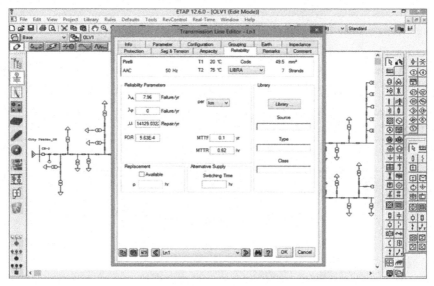

Fig. 2. Window of Etap 12.6.0 software as reliability page opened

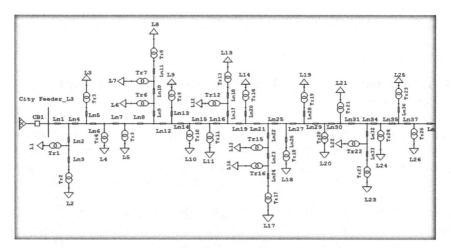

Fig. 3. Single line diagram of the existing system partially

Figure 3 shows single line diagram for some part of the existing feeder. In the diagram L1–L68 indicates Load Points on each transformer, Tr1–Tr68 are Transformers, Ln1–Ln90 represents Segmented Lines of the Feeder and CB is for Circuit Breaker.

Table 2 reveals that the simulation result has given the reliability indices values with minimum deviation from the average of six years interruption data. The two basic reliability indices, system average yearly interruption duration and system average yearly interruption frequency are 272.02 and 435.5 respectively.

Table 2. Results of reliability indices for the existing system

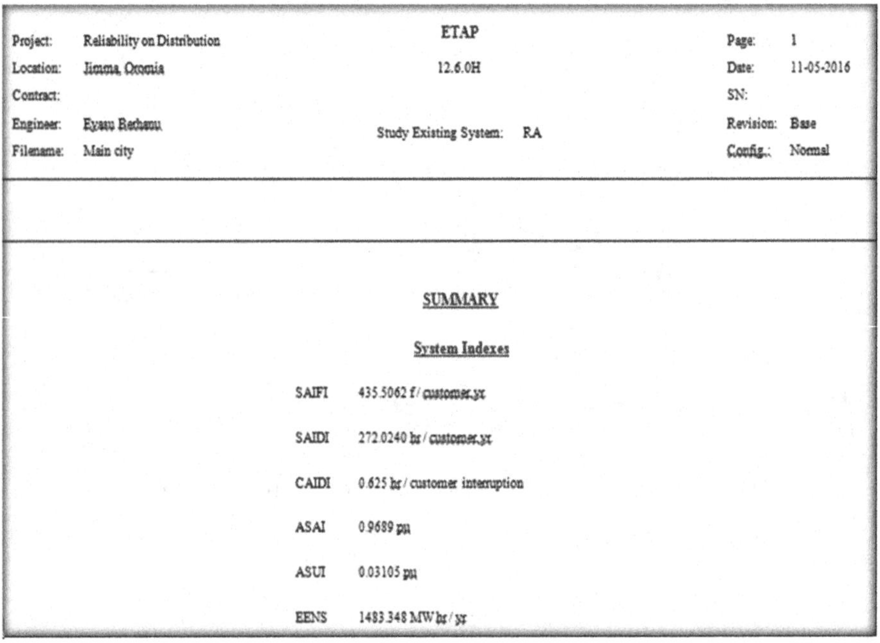

Project:	Reliability on Distribution	ETAP	Page:	1
Location:	Jimma, Oromia	12.6.0H	Date:	11-05-2016
Contract:			SN:	
Engineer:	Eyasu Bacheou	Study Existing System: RA	Revision:	Base
Filename:	Main city		Config.:	Normal

SUMMARY

System Indexes

SAIFI   435.5062 f / customer.yr

SAIDI   272.0240 hr / customer.yr

CAIDI   0.625 hr / customer interruption

ASAI   0.9689 pu

ASUI   0.03105 pu

EENS   1483.348 MWhr / yr

4   Evaluation of the Reliability Improvement for Different Scenarios

The above analysis clearly shows how the power reliability of Jimma town is very poor and does not meet the requirements set by the Ethiopian Electric Agency (EEA). A new substation is under construction in Jiren about 8 km away from the center of **Jimma** town. The 230 kV incoming lines are from Gilgal Gibe I & II and also planned to get power from Fincha power plant via Nekemt - Bedele - Agaro HV power line during outages of Gilgal Gibe I & II. There are 40 MVA, 230/132 kV and 40 MVA, 230/15 kV large power transformers in the substation. The breakers are vacuum and SF6 types. The main purpose of the new substation is to upgrade the old 132 kV to 230 kV system.

The new substation is located on the other end of the town almost in the opposite side of the old substation, which will make reconfiguration of the existing distribution system simple and also uses mainly to overcome the overloading of the existing substation.

Starting from the existing system design and the reliability indices of the base years, the study has evaluated different mitigation alternatives to improve the system reliability at reasonable cost. Five different cases have been analyzed by computer simulation. The simulation focuses on evaluating the impact of using reclosers, tie switches and reconfiguration of the feeder on reliability of the system.

Recloser allows utilities to implement automatic back feed restoration (loop automation), fault finding and fault isolation. The device is also equipped with precise timing parameters allowing protection coordination time between devices to be minimized. Automatic circuit reclosers are designed for use on overhead distribution lines as well as distribution substation applications for different voltage classes like 15 kV, 27 kV and 38 kV [4].

Place and number of automatic re-closers are chosen by considering number of customers, feeder length, sensitivity of the area and economic benefits. The reliability indices SAIFI, SAIDI and cost benefits are the main drivers for comparison of the alternatives and this is done using heuristic technique.

For a fault occurred anywhere in the system, different protection devices may operate differently as a result of varying sensitivities, operating times and tolerances. When a fault occurs, the protection device closest to the fault should operate first to isolate the faulty circuit. If a protection device higher in the hierarchy trips first, multiple loads may unnecessarily lose service. To accommodate for the varying tolerances and to ensure that multiple protection devices do not unnecessarily trip for the same fault current, the protection devices should be coordinated to each other based on their settled pickup currents and tripping times [5]. The five alternatives are arranged as below, and their results are tabulated and compared.

Case-1: Using One Auto Recloser
Case-2: Using Two Auto Reclosers
Case-3: Reconfiguring the system using Tie switch
Case-4: Using Tie Switch and Isolating Dedo Woreda
Case-5: Using Two Auto reclosers, Tie Switch and Isolating Dedo Woreda

As a sample, the case-5 is shown with the reclosers and Tie-switch in Fig. 4. The model shows that two reclosers and a tie switch integrated in the system with the line to Dedo woreda is being isolated from the 15 kV city feeder. The two reclosers in both sides of the normally open tie-switch are placed by considering length of the feeder, number of customers and criticality of the location. Recloser (Rec-1) has been placed almost at a midpoint by considering the length and number of the customers connected to the new substation. The same thing was considered for Recloser (Rec-2) which has been placed at the old substation side.

Table 3 (Case-5) shows the value of reliability indices obtained from the simulation. As can be seen from the Table, the two reclosers together with the tie switch significantly enhance the reliability of the system. The expected number of outages per year per

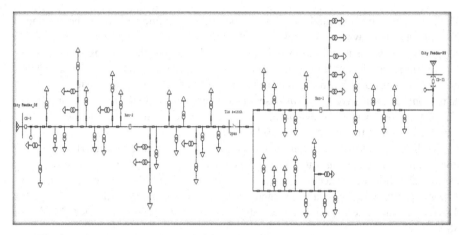

Fig. 4. Using two auto reclosers and tie switch with Dedo Woreda isolated (Case-5)

Table 3. Reliability indices of simulation results for case-5

Project:	Reliability on Distribution	ETAP	Page: 1
Location:	Jimma, Oromia	12.6.0H	Date: 22-02-2017
Contract.			SN:
Engineer:	Eyasu Berhanu	Study Case: RA…Case 5	Revision: Base
Filename:	Main city		Config.: Normal

SUMMARY

System Indexes

SAIFI	66.4190	f / customer. yr
SAIDI	40.8441	hr. / customer. yr
CAIDI	0.615	hr. / customer interruption
ASAI	0.9953	pu
ASUI	0.00466	pu
EENS	168.339	MW hr. / yr

customer has been reduced from 435.5062 to 66.42 (84.75% system reliability improvement), and the annul outage duration has been reduced from 272 to 40.844 h (85% reduction in outage duration) as compared with the values at the selected base years. Table 4 summarizes reliability indices values for all the five cases mentioned above.

As it is observed from Table 4, both the SAIFI value in interruptions per year per customer and the SAIDI value in hours per year per customer of city feeder has been improved by almost 85% as compared with the values at the base years.

Table 4. Summary of reliability indices values for all cases

Cases	SAIFI	SAIDI	EENS (MWh/yr.)	ECOST (US Dollar)	% Reduction in SAIFI	% Reduction in SAIDI	% Reduction in EENS
Existing	435.5	272	1483.3	29406.7	0	0	0
Case-1	297.6	185.2	863.2	17112.3	31.7	31.9	41.8
Case-2	199.1	123.8	529.5	10497.9	54.3	54.5	64.3
Case-3	161.5	99.4	418.9	8305.1	62.9	63.5	71.8
Case-4	88.05	54.2	227.8	4515.4	79.8	80.1	84.6
Case-5	66.42	40.844	168.339	3337.246	84.75	85	88.651

5 Conclusion

In this research, the reliability assessment of Jimma distribution system has been done. Primary data from the field and secondary data from Jimma substation have been collected and analyzed. In order to explore reliability improvement options, the system is modeled and simulated using ETAP12.6.0 software for five different cases. SAIFI, SAIDI and cost have been used as driving parameters. From the cases, the system with two auto reclosers, tie switch and isolating the long line goes to Dedo woreda has been selected as an effective mitigation solution from the cases studied. For this case, SAIFI has been reduced by 84.75% as compared with the average reliability indices value of the base year. In the same case SAIDI and EENS have been reduced by 85% and 88.651% respectively. The proposed solution can save 579523.96 ETB per year from the unsold energy of the selected feeder with 2.03 years payback period for the recloser investment. Satisfaction of the society has been considered as a priceless advantage.

References

1. Koval, D.O., Chowdhury, A.A.: Reliability analysis of the isolation and restoration procedures of distribution feeders. IEEE (2006). 0-7803-9193-4/06/$20.00
2. Merlin, A., Back, H.: Search for a minimal loss operating spanning tree configuration for an urban power distribution system. In: Proceedings of the 5th Power System Computation Conference (PSOC), Cambridge, pp. 1–18 (1975)
3. IEEE Guide for Electric Power Distribution Reliability Indices, IEEE Std. 1366™-2012, 31 May 2012
4. O'Sullivan, N., Kimura, B.: Only Smart Reclosers Build Smart Grids, 10 May 2013. http://www.nojapower.co.uk/dl/.../only-smart-reclosers-build0smartgrids.pdf
5. Interlocking of protection devices (2016). http://www.freepatentsonline.com/.../Interlockingofprotectiondevices.html

Joint Evaluation of Spectral Efficiency, Energy Efficiency and Transmission Reliability in Massive MIMO Systems

Tewelgn Kebede[1]([✉]), Amare Kassaw[1], Yihenew Wondie[1],
and Johannes Stenibrunn[2]

[1] Addis Ababa Institute of Technology, Addis Ababa, Ethiopia
tewelgn@gmail.com, amex2121@gmail.com, yiheneww@gmail.com
[2] Kempten University of Applied Science, Kempten, Germany
josteinbrunn@hotmail.com
http://www.aait.edu.et
http://www.hs-kempten.de

Abstract. The main goals planned to achieve in fifth generation (5G) networks are to increase capacity, improve data rate, decrease latency, improve energy efficiency and provide a better quality of service. To achieve these goals, massive multiple input multiple output (MIMO) is considered as one of the competing technologies that provide high spectral efficiency (SE) and energy efficiency (EE). Hence, energy efficiency, spectral efficiency and transmission reliability are the main performance metrics for massive MIMO systems. Although these performance metrics are thoroughly studied independently, their joint effects are not considered and evaluated for massive MIMO systems. Hence, in this work, we investigate a mathematical model that jointly evaluates the spectral efficiency, energy efficiency and transmission reliability in downlink massive MIMO systems with linear precoding techniques. Closed-form analytical formulation is derived that jointly evaluates the impacts of spectral efficiency and transmission reliability on energy efficiency. Finally, numerical results are provided to validate the theoretical analysis.

Keywords: Massive MIMO · Spectral efficiency · Energy efficiency · Precoding techniques · Transmission reliability

1 Introduction

By using large numbers of small physical size and inexpensive low-power antennas at the base station (BS), massive MIMO improves spectral efficiency and energy efficiency [1]. Deploying a large number of antennas at the BS helps to focus the transmission energy into a smaller region of space. With a very large number of antenna arrays, things that were random before start to look deterministic so that the effect of small-scale fading is averaged out [2]. Besides, when

N. G. Habtu et al. (Eds.): ICAST 2019, LNICST 308, pp. 424–435, 2020.
https://doi.org/10.1007/978-3-030-43690-2_29

the number of BS antennas grows large, the random channel vectors between the users become pair-wisely orthogonal. In the limit of an infinite number of BS antennas, with simple matched filter processing at the BS, uncorrelated noise and intra-cell interference disappear completely [2].

The authors in [3] evaluate the achievable spectral efficiency and energy efficiency in downlink multiuser MIMO systems. To reap the benefits provided by large number of BS antennas, accurate channel state information (CSI) is necessary which makes possible to have a reliable communication. With perfect CSI, downlink precoding is employed to maximize link the performance. Equipping large number of antennas at the BS makes linear precoding techniques to perform nearly the same as nonlinear precoding techniques [4]. A comprehensive review of precoding techniques in massive MIMO systems is provided in [5]. The authors in [6] compares the performance of maximum ratio transmission (MRT) and zero forcing (ZF) precoding in downlink massive MIMO systems under perfect CSI. The results show that when the number of BS antennas increases, linear precoding techniques give near optimal performance with low complexity. To study the trade-off on energy efficiency and spectral efficiency, a new metric called resource efficiency is proposed in [7,8]. The resource efficiency helps to balance the spectral efficiency and energy efficiency through optimization algorithms.

To the best of our literature, there are no recent works that jointly evaluate the spectral efficiency, energy efficiency and transmission reliability in massive MIMO systems. Thus, in this work, we develop a more general analytical expression for energy efficiency in terms of spectral efficiency and transmission reliability. In this regard, the contributions of this work are summarized as follows:

- Develop a mathematical model that relates the spectral efficiency, energy efficiency and transmission reliability in single cell downlink massive MIMO system.
- Formulate analytical expression to the proposed model with linear precoding techniques.
- Perform numerical simulation to validate the theoretical analysis.

The rest of this paper is organized as follows. In Sect. 2, the system model for single cell downlink massive MIMO system is provided. Spectral efficiency and system power consumption is formulated in Sects. 3 and 4, respectively. Energy efficiency is formulated in Sect. 5. Transmission reliability and its impact on energy efficiency is provided in Sects. 6 and 7, respectively. Simulation results and discussions are presented in Sect. 8 and conclusions are drawn in Sect. 9.

2   The Massive MIMO System Model

We consider a single-cell downlink massive MIMO system shown in Fig. 1, where the BS is equipped with M antennas to support K single-antenna users in the same time-frequency resource. Let $\mathbf{x}$ denotes the complex valued $M \times 1$ transmitted signal vector from the M antennas, the $K \times 1$ received signal vector $\mathbf{y}$ at the users is given by [9]

$$\mathbf{y} = \sqrt{p_d}\mathbf{H}\mathbf{x} + \mathbf{n} \tag{1}$$

where $\mathbf{H} \in \mathbb{C}^{K \times M}$ is a channel matrix between the BS antennas and K users [2, 21]. The channel is assumed to be a Rayleigh fading and ergodic with perfect CSI at the BS. Thus, the elements of $\mathbf{H}$ are assumed to be independent and identically distributed (i.i.d) complex Gaussian random variables with zero mean and unit variance. $\mathbf{x} = \mathbf{W}\mathbf{s}$ is the precoded signal at the BS, $\mathbf{s} \in \mathbb{C}^{K \times 1}$ is the information bearing signal with $\mathbb{E}\{\mathbf{s}\mathbf{s}^H\} = \mathbf{I}_K$, $\mathbf{W} \in \mathbf{C}^{M \times K}$ is the precoding matrix at the BS and p_d is the downlink transmit power for user k. $\mathbf{n}$ is additive white Gaussian noise vector at the users with zero mean and unit variance elements.

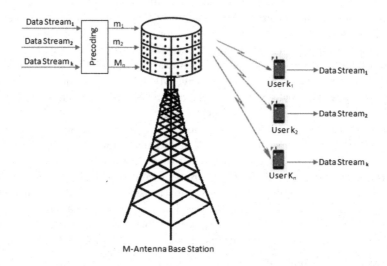

Fig. 1. Downlink massive MIMO system model [9].

Then, the received signal at the kth user is given by [8]

$$y_k = \sqrt{p_d}\mathbf{h}_k\mathbf{w}_k s_k + \sum_{i=1, i \neq k}^{K} \sqrt{p_d}\mathbf{h}_k\mathbf{w}_i s_i + n_k \tag{2}$$

where $\sqrt{p_d}\mathbf{h}_k\mathbf{w}_k s_k$ is the desired signal for user k and $\sum_{i \neq k}^{K} \sqrt{p_d}\mathbf{h}_k\mathbf{w}_i s_i$ is the multi-user interference signal. The signal to interference plus noise ratio (SINR) at user k is given by [12]

$$\text{SINR}_k = \frac{p_d|\mathbf{h}_k\mathbf{w}_k|^2}{p_d\sum_{i=1, i \neq k}^{K} |\mathbf{h}_k\mathbf{w}_i|^2 + 1} \tag{3}$$

which is a function of the channel $\mathbf{h}_k$ and transmit precoding vector $\mathbf{w}_k$.

3   Spectral Efficiency in Massive MIMO Systems

One of the metrics to quantify the performance of a massive MIMO system is the achievable rate. It gives the lower bound on the spectral efficiency that the massive MIMO systems can transmit over the fading channel [10]. Based on the Shannon's channel capacity theory, the achievable rate per user in a single cell downlink massive MIMO system is given by [10]

$$R_k = B \log_2(1 + \text{SINR}_k) \tag{4}$$

and the achievable sum rate of the system with K users is given by [6]

$$R_s = B \sum_{k=1}^{K} \log_2(1 + \text{SINR}_k) \tag{5}$$

where B is the bandwidth of the system.

3.1 Spectral Efficiency with Linear Precoding Techniques

Spectral Efficiency with ZF Precoding: Zero forcing or null-steering precoding is a method of spatial signal processing by which multiple antenna transmitter can null multiuser interference signals. That is, with ZF precoding the inter-user interference can be average out at each user. The ZF precoding matrix is generated by implementing the pseudo-inverse of the channel matrix. Hence, the ZF precoding matrix employed by the base station is given by [9]

$$\mathbf{W}_{\text{ZF}} = \mathbf{H}^H (\mathbf{HH}^H)^{-1}. \tag{6}$$

For large values of M and K, the SINR of a user in (3) with ZF precoding is given by [9]

$$\text{SINR}_k^{\text{ZF}} \approx p_d \Big(\frac{M - K}{K}\Big). \tag{7}$$

Thus, the achievable sum rate in (5) with ZF precoding is

$$R_s^{\text{ZF}} \approx K \log_2 \Big(1 + p_d(\frac{M - K}{K})\Big). \tag{8}$$

Spectral Efficiency with MRT Precoding: By implementing the conjugate transpose of the channel matrix, MRT precoding aims to maximize the signal to interference plus noise ratio at the intended user. Thus, the MRT precoding matrix employed by the BS is given by [9]

$$\mathbf{W}_{\text{MRT}} = \mathbf{H}^H. \tag{9}$$

For large values of M and K, the SINR of a user in (3) with MRT precoding is given by [6]

$$\text{SINR}_k^{\text{MRT}} \approx \frac{p_d M}{K(p_d + 1)}. \tag{10}$$

Thus, the achievable sum rate of the system in (5) with MRT precoding is become

$$R_s^{\text{MRT}} \approx K \log_2 \Big(1 + \frac{p_d M}{K(p_d + 1)}\Big). \tag{11}$$

4 Power Consumption in Massive MIMO Systems

Accurate modeling of the system power consumption is required to formulate the energy efficiency and to obtain reliable guidelines on energy efficiency optimization with respect to the system parameters. The total power consumption of the proposed downlink massive MIMO system is given by the sum of transmitted power and circuit power consumption as [3]

$$P_t = \mu \sum_{k=1}^{K} p_k + MP_c + P_{\text{fix}} \tag{12}$$

where μ is the inverse of the power amplifier efficiency at the BS, p_k is the downlink transmitter power allocated to each user, P_c is the constant circuit power consumption per antenna that includes power dissipation in the transmit filter, mixer, frequency synthesizer and digital-to-analog converter, P_{fix} is the fixed power consumption at the BS which is independent of the number of transmit antennas.

5 Energy Efficiency in Massive MIMO Systems

The energy efficiency (in bits/Joule) of the massive MIMO system is commonly defined as a benefit-cost ratio where the achievable rate is compared with the associated energy consumption of the system [7,8]. One of the well known established metrics to measure this benefit-cost ratio is the global energy efficiency (GEE) which is given by [7,8,19]

$$EE = \frac{\text{Achievable sum rate}}{\text{Total power consumption}}. \tag{13}$$

Plugging (5) and (12) into (13), the energy efficiency of a downlink massive MIMO system is given by

$$EE = \frac{B \sum_{k=1}^{K} \log_2(1 + \text{SINR}_k)}{\mu \sum_{k=1}^{K} p_k + MP_c + P_{\text{fix}}}. \tag{14}$$

Generally, increasing the transmit power increases the achievable sum-rate. But, the energy efficiency is a unimodal function with the transmit power and thus, it increases until some transmit power and then decrease after that power.

6 Transmission Reliability in Massive MIMO Systems

The transmission reliability or symbol transmission success rate of a communication system describes the probability of receiving a symbol correctly over the communication link. Since any symbol error results in loss of the symbol, the symbol transmission success rate is defined in terms of the bit error probability as [15]

$$f(\gamma) = (1 - P_e(\gamma))^{\frac{L}{b}} \tag{15}$$

where γ is the received SINR of the communication link, P_e is the bit error probability, L is the information bits in the transmitted symbol and b is the number of bits per symbol which is determined based on the modulation type.

6.1 BER in Massive MIMO Systems

The bit error rate (BER) which is also termed as the bit error probability measures the errors in received bits over a communication channel that is altered due to noise, distortion, interference, or synchronization errors. It is the ratio of the numbers of bits in error to the total number of transmitted bits during a predefined time interval [16]. For the proposed massive MIMO system, the BER is determined based on the modulation scheme employed for the transmission. When the massive MIMO system employs ZF precoding and Gray-coded square NQAM modulation, the average BER for the kth user can be expressed as [17, 18, 20]

$$P_e(\gamma_k) \approx \frac{c_N}{2d_N} \frac{\Gamma(\tau + \frac{1}{2})/\Gamma(\tau + 1)}{(\gamma_k d_N^2 + 1)^{(\tau + \frac{1}{2})} \sqrt{\pi \gamma_k}} \tag{16}$$

where $\tau = M - K$ is the degree of freedom, $\gamma_k = \frac{P_T}{K\sigma^2}$ is the transmission SNR of the user, P_T is the total transmission power at the BS which is divided equally for each user and $\Gamma(.)$ is the Gamma function. The constant c_N and d_N is derived from the modulation level as

$$(c_N, d_N) = \begin{cases} (1, 1) & N = 2 \\ (2\frac{1 - 1/\sqrt{N}}{\log_2(\sqrt{N})}, \sqrt{\frac{3/2}{N-1}}) & N \geq 4. \end{cases} \tag{17}$$

The effect of $\Gamma(\tau + \frac{1}{2})/\Gamma(\tau + 1)$ is negligible and if we omit it, the bit error rate is approximated as

$$P_e(\gamma_k) \approx (\gamma_k d_N^2 + 1)^{-(\tau + \frac{1}{2})} \gamma_k^{-\frac{1}{2}}. \tag{18}$$

The result in (18) shows that the BER is improved by deploying large number of antennas at the BS; where as the BER is become worse when the scheduled users become very large.

7 Impact of Transmission Reliability on Energy Efficiency

In this section, different from the previous works that only focus on the relationship between spectral efficiency and energy efficiency, we develop a framework that relates the spectral efficiency, energy efficiency and transmission reliability.

The proposed formulation defines an energy efficiency expression that incorporates all necessary wireless performance metrics. Mathematically, the problem of interest is formulated as [22,23]

$$\text{EE} = \frac{[\text{Achievable sum rate}] \times [\text{Transmission reliability}]}{\text{Total power consumption}}. \tag{19}$$

By using the results from (5), (12) and (15), the proposed formulation for the energy efficiency interms of the spectral efficiency and transmission reliability is given by

$$\text{EE} = \frac{B \sum_{k=1}^{K} \log_2(1 + \text{SINR}_k)(1 - P_e(\gamma))^{\frac{L}{b}}}{\mu \sum_{k=1}^{K} p_k + M P_c + P_{\text{fix}}}. \tag{20}$$

With ZF precoding, the energy efficiency of the proposed system is expressed as

$$\text{EE}^{\text{ZF}} \approx \frac{KB\left(\log_2(1 + P_d(\frac{M-K}{K}))\right)(1 - P_e(\gamma))^{\frac{L}{b}}}{\mu \sum_{k=1}^{K} p_k + M P_c + P_{\text{fix}}}. \tag{21}$$

Similarly, with MRT precoding, the energy efficiency of the proposed system is expressed as

$$\text{EE}^{\text{MRT}} \approx \frac{KB\left(\log_2[1 + \frac{P_d M}{K(P_d+1)}]\right)(1 - P_e(\gamma))^{\frac{L}{b}}}{\mu \sum_{k=1}^{K} p_k + M P_c + P_{\text{fix}}}. \tag{22}$$

8   Simulation Results and Discussions

In this section, we validate the theoretical analysis via numerical simulation. For the simulation, we consider single cell downlink massive MIMO system with perfect CSI. To evaluate the spectral efficiency, energy efficiency and transmission reliability for the proposed system, we use the mathematical expressions that are formulated in the previous sections. Performance analysis is done for both ZF and MRT precoding techniques under different systems and propagation parameters. The spectral efficiency with Monte-Carlo realizations from (5) is added to validate the tightness of the asymptotic lower bound spectral efficiency expressions in (8) and (11). Some of the standard simulation parameters are summarized in Table 1 [2].

Figure 2 shows the achievable sum rate versus the number of BS antennas for both precoding techniques. The result shows that as the number of BS antennas increases, the achievable sum rate increases for both precoding techniques. As expected when the BS antennas grows large, ZF achieves better sum rate than MRT. Because, at large number of BS antennas, ZF precoding can completely null-out the inter-user interference. The result also shows that the gaps between analytical approximation and the simulated values are very small. Thus, it is quite reasonable to formulate the system energy efficiency by using the closed-form lower bound achievable sum rate approximations in (8) and (11).

Table 1. Some of the simulation parameters

Parameter	Value
Circuit Power Consumption per BS Antenna (P_c)	2 W
Fixed Power Consumption P_{fix}	10 W
Downlink Transmit Power (P_d)	1 W
Power Amplifier Efficiency (η_{UE})	0.38
System Bandwidth (B)	20 MHz
Information Bits (L)	64
Number of bits per symbol (b)	2, 4, 6
Modulation level (NQAM)	4, 16, 64

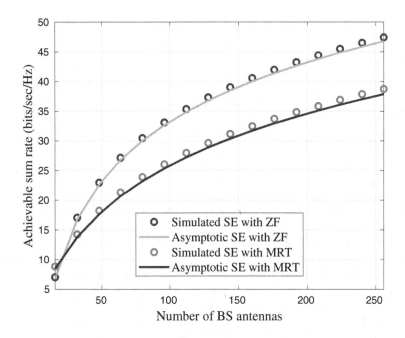

Fig. 2. Spectral efficiency versus the number of BS antennas.

Figure 3 shows the energy efficiency with the number of BS antennas. The result shows that the energy efficiency increases until some number of BS antennas and then decreases with the number of BS antennas. This is because as shown in (12) when the number of BS antennas grows large, the total circuit power consumption of the BS increases and this results in a lower energy efficiency. Thus, although increasing the number of BS antennas can help to reduce the transmission power for the system, it decreases the energy efficiency due to the increment on internal power consumption. Hence, a design trade-off is required to obtain the optimal number of BS antennas that give maximum spectral efficiency and energy efficiency simultaneously.

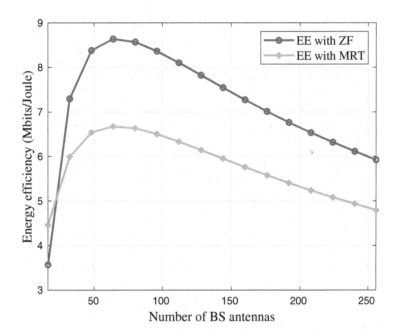

Fig. 3. Energy efficiency versus the number of BS antennas. We assume $\gamma = 1$ dB and 16 QAM.

The energy efficiency versus the spectral efficiency performance of the proposed massive MIMO system is shown in Fig. 4. The results shows that in lower spectral efficiency regime, when the spectral efficiency increases, the energy efficiency is also increased. Whereas at high spectral efficiency regime, the energy efficiency decreases. This is because, the spectral efficiency grows in logarithm function whereas the power consumption grows linearly and thus after a certain time the increment on the power consumption overtakes the spectral efficiency increment and the energy efficiency starts to decrease.

Finally, Fig. 5 shows the impact of the modulation level on the energy efficiency of the system. As shown in (15), when the modulation level increases, the symbol transmission success rate is decreased. This shows that under fixed bandwidth when the modulation level increases, the reliable data transmission function is deteriorated. Thus, the energy efficiency decreases with modulation level.

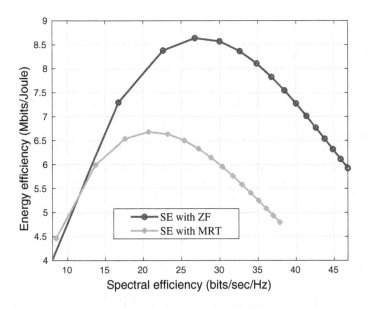

Fig. 4. Spectral efficiency versus energy efficiency. We assume $\gamma = 1\,\mathrm{dB}$ and $16\,\mathrm{QAM}$.

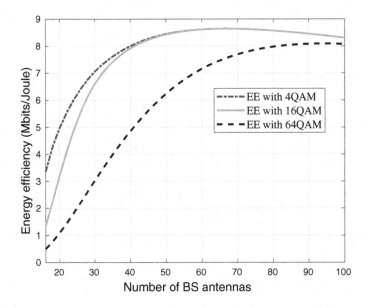

Fig. 5. Impact of the modulation level on energy efficiency. We consider ZF precoding.

9   Conclusion

In this work, we have investigated a mathematical model that jointly evaluates the spectral efficiency, energy efficiency and transmission reliability in downlink massive MIMO systems with linear precoding techniques. Closed-form analytical formulation is derived that jointly evaluates the impacts of spectral efficiency and transmission reliability on energy efficiency. Numerical results have been done to validate the effectiveness of the proposed analytical expression for energy efficiency. The impacts of system and propagation parameters on the spectral and energy efficiency are evaluated. The result shows that energy efficiency is a uni-modal function that increases until some value and decreases above that value. Hence, a design trade-off is required to obtain the optimal system and propagation parameters that maximize the spectral efficiency and energy efficiency simultaneously.

References

1. Adnan, N.H.M., Rafiqul, I.Md., Zahirul Alam, A.H.M.: Massive MIMO for fifth generation (5G): opportunities and challenges. In: International Conference on Computer and Communication Engineering (2016)
2. Ngo, H.Q., Larsson, E.G., Marzetta, T.L.: Energy and spectral efficiency of very large multiuser MIMO systems. IEEE Trans. Commun. **61**(4), 1436–1449 (2013)
3. Tan, W., Jin, S., Yuan, J.: Spectral and energy efficiency of downlink MU-MIMO systems with MRT. China Commun. **14**(5), 105–111 (2017)
4. Pappa, M., Ramesh, C., Kumar, M.N.: Performance comparison of massive MIMO and conventional MIMO using channel parameters. In: IEEE WiSPNET 2017 Conference (2017)
5. Fatema, N., Hua, G., Xiang, Y., Peng, D., Natgunanathan, I.: Massive MIMO linear precoding: a survey. IEEE Commun. Syst. **12**(4), 3920–3931 (2018)
6. Mohammad, M.A.B., Osman, A.A., Elhag, N.A.A.: Performance comparison of MRT and ZF for single cell downlink massive MIMO system. In: IEEE International Conference on Computing, Control, Networking, Electronics and Embeddeds Systems Engineering (2015)
7. Huang, Y., He, S., Wang, J., Zhu, J.: Spectral and energy efficiency tradeoff for massive MIMO. IEEE Trans. Veh. Technol. **67**(8), 6991–7002 (2018)
8. Tang, J., So, D.K.C., Senior, E.A., Hamdi, K.A.: Resource efficiency: a new paradigm on energy efficiency and spectral efficiency trade-off. IEEE Trans. Wirel. Commun. **13**(8), 4656–4669 (2014)
9. Parfait, T., Kuang, Y., Jerry, K.: Performance analysis and comparison of ZF and MRT based downlink massive MIMO systems. In: 6th International Conference on Ubiquitous and Future Networks (ICUFN) (2014). Chengdu, Kumasi
10. Selvan, V.P., Iqbal, M.S., Al-Raweshidy, H.S.: Performance analysis of linear precoding schemes for very large multi-user MIMO downlink system. In: 4th International Conference on the Innovative Computing Technology (INTECH 2014) (2014)
11. Xiao, Z., Li, Z.: Analysis of massive MIMO systems downlink precoding performance. In: IEEE International Conference on Communications and Networking in China (2014)

12. Mohammed, A.B.: Performance evaluation of linear precoding techniques for downlink massive MIMO. IEEE Syst. J. (2016)
13. Shimamoto Laboratory: Non orthogonal multiple access employing multiple power levels for 5G wireless communication networks. Global Information and Telecommunication Studies Waseda University Japan (2015)
14. Hao, U., Song, Z., Hou, S., Li, H.: Energy and spectral efficiency tradeoff in massive MIMO systems with inter-user interference. In: IEEE Indoor and Mobile Radio Communications (2015)
15. Fakhri, Y., Nsiri, B., Aboutajdine, D., Vidal, J.: Throughput optimization for wireless OFDM system in downlink transmission using adaptive techniques. In: International Conference on Wireless Communications, Networking and Mobile Computing (2006)
16. Padmaja, C., Malleswari, B.L.: Bit error rate analysis of 4G communication systems. In: 13th International Conference on Wireless and Optical Communications Networks (WOCN) (2016)
17. Hilario-Tacuri, A., Tamo, A.: BER Performance of mm-Wave based systems in rainfall scenarios. In: IEEE International Conference on Electronics, Electrical Engineering and Computing (INTERCON) (2018)
18. Zhang, Y., Cui, Q., Wang, N.: Energy efficiency maximization for CoMP joint transmission with non-ideal power. In: 28th Annual International Symposium on Personal, Indoor, and Mobile Radio Communications (PIMRC) (2017)
19. Kassaw, A., Hailemariam, D., Zoubir, A.M.: Review of energy efficient resource allocation techniques in massive MIMO systems. In: 9th International Conference on Information and Communication Technology Convergence (ICTC), October 2018
20. Zhao, L., Zheng, K., Long, H., Zhao, H.: Trans. Emerg. Telecommun. Technol. Performance analysis for downlink massive MIMO system with ZF precoding $25(12)$, 1219–1230 (2013)
21. Kassaw, A., Hailemariam, D., Zoubir, A.M.: Performance analysis of uplink massive MIMO system over Rician fading channel. In: 26th European Signal Processing Conference (EUSIPCO), pp. 1272–1276 (2018)
22. Kassa, H.B., Hailemariam, D., Astatke, Y., Moaz-zami, F., Dean, R.: Energy efficiency evaluation in downlink cellular communication networks. In: IEEE AFRICON International Conference (2015)
23. Meriaux, F., Valentin, S., Lasaulce, S., Kieffer, M.: An energy efficient power allocation game with selfish channel state reporting in cellular networks. In: 6th International ICST Conference on Performance Evaluation Methodologies and Tools (2012)

Optimal Allocation of Distributed Generation for Performance Enhancement of Distribution System Using Particle Swarm Optimization

Elias Mandefro[✉] and Belachew Bantiyrga

Faculty of Electrical and Computer Engineering, Bahir Dar Institute of Technology,
Bahir Dar University, Bahir Dar, Ethiopia
eliasmandefro01@gmail.com, belchwbbg1j1@gmail.com

Abstract. The rapid growth of power demand and urbanization needs a quality
and reliable power supply system. On the other hand, the existing passive distribution network and high cost of power transmission from generation can't meet
the fast-growing power demand. The weak performance of the utility like high
power interruption and poor voltage profile affect the living standard of individual
consumers which are the most serious problems of Ethiopian power distribution
system. This type of problem can be minimized by integrating optimally allocated
renewable distributed generations with the existing distribution system which are
environmentally friend. Optimal sizing and siting of DG done by applying PSO
for multi-objective function using MATLAB software. The significant process is
how to minimize the power loss, reduce power interruption and improve the voltage profile of distribution systems. The voltage profile and power loss evaluation
are done using a power flow method of forward-backward for radial networks.
The reliability indices of the network like SAIDI, SAIFI, and EENS are evaluated
using ETAP software. The proposed method is tested at Gihon 25-bus feeder of
Bahir Dar distribution system. The simulation result indicates appropriate sizing
and placement of solar based DG improves the performance of the distribution
system.

Keywords: Distributed generation · Reliability indices · Power losses · Particle
swarm optimization · Voltage profile

1 Introduction

The electric power produced from generation can be delivered to end-users through
transmission and distribution systems. Utilities contain a complex structure of power
system consisting of transmission lines, generating plants, substations, distribution systems, and the load. The fundamental purpose of the power system is to give an economic
and reliable channel for electrical energy to transfer from points of generation to customer locations. The complex structure of the power system challenges the quality and
reliability of power supply system [1]. Distribution systems directly connected to end

© ICST Institute for Computer Sciences, Social Informatics and Telecommunications Engineering 2020
Published by Springer Nature Switzerland AG 2020. All Rights Reserved
N. G. Habtu et al. (Eds.): ICAST 2019, LNICST 308, pp. 436–453, 2020.
https://doi.org/10.1007/978-3-030-43690-2_30

users. The responsibility of electric power distribution systems are to deliver the electrical energy from the complex power systems to the consumers with the desired quality and reliability but the imbalance between power demand and supply, inaccurate design and operation practices, aging infrastructures, radial type network and high exposure to external environment are the main agents for reliability problems in distribution system [2]. In radial distribution network, there is high power loss which diminishes the quality of power supply. The power loss affects the voltage profile of the system which results in loads not to get the nameplate value.

The existing power distribution systems are not flexible to handle the power demand [2]. This problem diverts the idea of power engineers to change the existing passive distribution systems to active distribution systems. The passive distribution system cannot satisfy the interest of consumers in terms of quality and reliable power supply system. The installation of new generation power plants and transmission lines needs high capital and long time. This problem reduced by using renewable distributed energy sources. The renewable energy sources like wind and PV take the attention of power world to minimize the impact of other energy sources on the environment [3]. Ethiopia which is the country near to the equator that has a good solar irradiance for solar power installation. Due to high solar irradiance available in the country using solar power based DG is preferable. The main performances that determine the efficiency of the distribution system are high reliability, minimum power loss, and desired voltage profile. There are different economical and technical contributions that can be obtained from the integration of renewable based DG such as [4],

- Voltage profile improvement
- Reduction of reserve requirements
- Improved power quality
- Energy loss reduction
- Reliability enhancement
- Increased energy security
- Emissions reduction

On the other hand, improper installation of renewable based DG in the distribution system may reduce the system performance like the voltage profile to be under voltage or overvoltage, decrease system overall efficiency and enable system feeders to be overloaded. Consequently, DG units' placement and sizing into an existing distribution system must be designed and planned precisely.

1.1 Renewable Energy Resource Assessment of Bahir Dar City Ethiopia

Ethiopia is located near the equator and has abundant renewable energy resources. Even though, the available resources are not used sufficiently to the manner that eliminates the problem of power demand. So, before integrating renewable DG to the system the first task is identifying the feasible type of source in the site. From the Table 1 below the solar irradiance of the country is from 4–6 Kwh/m^2/day [5]. This shows Ethiopia has high renewable energy resource as compared to other countries. Bahir Dar is the capital city of the Amhara region which has solar irradiance of 4.0 to 5.5 Kwh/m^2/day throughout the year [6].

Table 1. Ethiopian energy resource potential [5]

Type of resource	Unit	Maximum capacity	Used
Solar irradiance/day	KWh/m^2	4–6	<0.01
Wind: power speed	GW m/s	100 > 7	<0.01
Hydropower	MW	45,000	<0.05
Geothermal	MW	<10,000	<0.01
Wood	Million tons	1120	0.5
Agricultural waste	Million tons	15–20	0.3
Coal	Million tons	300	0
Natural gas	Billion m3	113	0
Oil shale	Million tons	253	0

The insolation of Bahir Dar city is more than enough because the solar irradiance that reaches the surface of Bahir Dar city is from 4.0 to 5.5 Kwh/m^2/day [6]. As compared to developed countries like Germany which uses 40% of renewable distributed generation the renewable energy resource of Ethiopia is untouched. Ethiopia has much enough resource to shift towards solar based distributed generation but still, it is less than 1%.

The average wind speed of the country at 50 m height is around 6 m/s. Bahir Dar which is more suitable for solar power as compared to wind power from the resource availability. But the other part of Ethiopia like Adama and Mekele are also suitable for wind power. For Bahir Dar city solar based DG is preferable since the solar irradiance throughout the year is 4.0–5.5 Kwh/m^2/day as shown in Fig. 1 above. The output of wind power depends on different factors in addition to wind speed. In large cities like Bahir Dar which have large buildings and trees installing wind power faces some challenges. Lower places have higher obstructions from the surrounding and this reduces the wind speed of the area. The monthly average wind speed at 40 m is shown in Fig. 2 below and indicates the wind speed of Bahir Dar city is not enough to generate high power.

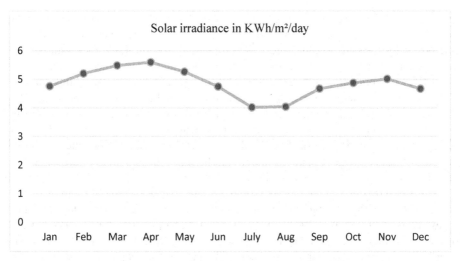

Fig. 1. Average monthly insolation of Bahir Dar city

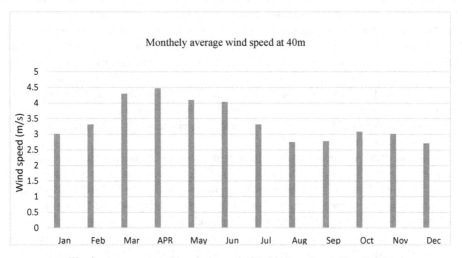

Fig. 2. Average monthly wind speed of Bahir Dar city at 40 m height

2   Related Works

There have been numerous studies on DG optimal sizing and placement techniques. The power loss and voltage deviation index minimization are one of the objectives to be achieved. Particle Swarm Optimization (PSO) and Genetic algorithm (GA) were used to place and size DG. PSO is preferred due to its fast convergence and its flexibility to handle multi-objective function. PSO is used to size and place DG so as to satisfy a multi-objective function with different constraints. Solar based DG injects real power to the system so that the voltage profile should be in the limit by minimizing the loss.

Arazghlich Igderi et al. [7] suggested on the problem of sizing and allocating of DG. Proper allocating and sizing of DG improves several parameters of the network like power loss, voltage profile, and total harmonic distortion. PSO algorithm is used to place and size DG by considering different constraints. The objective function is formulated by combining different single objective functions using weighting factors. The proposed system is implemented on Tehran 12 bus radial distribution network. The result indicates the optimal placing and sizing of DG improves several parameters. The installation and operating cost of DG are reduced without affecting the power loss and voltage profile of the network. PSO method is preferable than the genetic algorithm interims of fast convergence and low iteration. The contribution of DG on the reliability of the distribution system was not studied.

Raji Rahul [8] done on optimal sizing and placement of DG using PSO to improve the voltage profile of the distribution system with the objective function of voltage stability index. The connection of DG with Grid is in parallel, and the placement depends on the resource availability. Installing DG units may have a negative effect on performances of distribution system like reliability, power quality and voltage profile of the system. The proposed method is simulated in MATLAB software by implementing on IEEE 33 and 69 bus distribution systems. This research addresses only on voltage profile improvement. It did not address power loss minimization and reliability indices enhancement.

Musa and Adamu [9] done on performance enhancement of the distribution network by minimizing the power loss and improving the voltage profile. The optimal place of DG installation is found using the objective function. A combination of evolutionary programming and PSO is used to place and size DG by searching the minimum voltage stability index. The method was developed on IEEE 33 bus system. The result indicates the method used improves the voltage profile by minimizing the power loss. It did not say about the effect of DG on other performance parameters like reliability, protection, operation and installation cost of DG.

Prasanna et al. [10] proposed on reduction of power loss and improvement of voltage profile by optimal allocating and sizing of distributed generation using a genetic algorithm. A multi-objective function is make up by combining the tail-end node voltage deviation index and power loss reduction index using weighting factors. The method was implemented on standard IEEE 69 and 33 bus radial distribution network. The result indicates that the method brings good result on reduction of power loss and improvement of voltage profile. Even if the result on improvement of voltage profile and power loss reduction is good but the research did not address the outcome of DG on reactive power loss and reliability. And also it did not consider the environmental impact and stochastic nature of DG. Economic feasibility and protection problem of integrating DG is not studied.

Ajay Bansal et al. [11] done on voltage profile and efficiency improvement of the distribution system by minimizing real power loss. Selective PSO technique is used to allocate and size DG by considering distributed generation capacity and voltage limit. The objective function is to minimize the active power loss by obtaining the appropriate size and location of DG. The proposed method was tested on IEEE 33 and 69 bus radial distribution network which brings a better performance improvement when compared to genetic algorithm technique. This technique reduces the number of distributed generation by allocating optimally and meets the objective. The objective function did not include reactive power loss. Reliability of the network is not considered when distributed generation installed. Cost analysis and a payback period of the DG is not analyzed. Renewable energy sources are motivated to install as distributed generation. It did not suggest the significance of renewable energy on the environment.

Tiwari et al. [12] done on distribution system performance enhancement using the optimal allocation of DG and DSTATCOM in order to minimize branch losses with the improvement of voltage profiles. The weak bus was identified by fast voltage stability index to size and place DG with the power loss minimization and voltage profile enhancement of the system as the objective function. The method was implemented on IEEE 33 bus radial distribution network and the result compares the voltage profile and power loss of the system with the base case. This research did not address the effect of DG on the reliability of a radial distribution network.

Mohamed et al. [3] suggested to minimize operating cost and power loss by keeping the voltage profile in the desired value. A hybrid PSO is used to allocate DG effectively by combining loss sensitive factor, operating cost of installing DG and VSI. The weighting factors were used to form objective functions. Power flow analysis is done using the forward-backward method due to the special feature of radial network. The method was tested by IEEE 33 and 69 bus radial distribution network. The convergence of HPSO technique is fast when compared to the GA and PSO. This method achieves the objective with better output relatively to the previous techniques. Reactive power loss and environmental problems were not studied. The effect of integrating DG on the short circuit current level of protection devices were not evaluated in this research. Only the operating cost of distributed generation is considered related to reliability evaluation.

Laksmi Kumari et al. [13] done on efficiency enhancement of distribution network by optimally sizing DG. PSO was used for DG optimization. Finding the optimal size and location of DG plays a very important and effective role in the distribution system to improve the overall efficiency by reducing the active power loss. The developed method was tested on IEEE 33 Bus and IEEE 15 Bus radial distribution systems. The obtained result shows the NPSO optimized system is more effective than the PSO optimized and the non-optimized system for voltage profile improvement and system loss reduction. This research did not suggest the contribution of renewable DG on system reliability of the network.

Hussein Abdel-mawgoud et al. [14] done on optimal DG allocation in radial distribution networks using the loss sensitivity factor and moth-flame optimization algorithm. The objective of the study was to reduce the power loss, to improve the voltage profile and the voltage stability of the system by optimally sizing and siting of wind and PV-based DG. The method was implemented on standard IEEE 33 and 69 bus system. The result shows wind and PV-based DG enhances system performance. The stochastic nature of solar irradiance and wind speed were not studied in this research. The impact of PV and wind-based DG on the reliability of the system was not studied.

From previous related works they mostly study on voltage profile improvement and real power loss minimization by optimally placing and sizing of DG. This research addresses placing and sizing of renewable DG by minimizing active power loss, reactive power loss and voltage deviation index by considering as multi-objective function using weighting factors. The particle swarm algorithm has been coded as well as the power flow forward-backward method using MATLAB. The effect of DG on reliability studied before and after DG placement using ETAP software. Feasibility of wind and solar power resource also studied on Bahir Dar city.

3   Proposed System Model

A standard and efficient power flow technique is required for real-time applications such as planning, switching, optimization of network, load shading, and so on. Load flow analysis of radial distribution system is done using the Backward/Forward Sweep(BFS) algorithm since it is fast, flexible, simple to implement, powerful in convergence and the high ratio of R/X nature of radial distribution system [3].

A.   Power flow analysis

The power flow analysis is done using a load flow method of BFS. A simple radial distribution system which connects bus "i" and "k" through a line "M" in Fig. 3 is used for modeling of radial network.

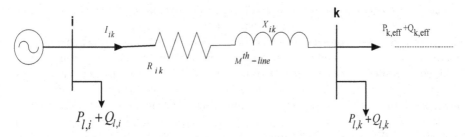

Fig. 3. Single line diagram for simple radial distribution system

Kirchhoff's current and voltage law (KCL and KVL respectively) are used to implement BFS. The real (P_{ik}) and reactive (Q_{ik}) power that flows through line 'M' from bus 'i' to bus 'k' can be calculated (i) Backward direction from the end node to first node and are given as [3],

$$P_{ik} = P_k' + R_{ik}\frac{(P_k'^2 + Q_k'^2)}{V_k^2} \tag{1}$$

$$Q_{ik} = Q_k' + X_{ik}\frac{(P_k'^2 + Q_k'^2)}{V_k^2} \tag{2}$$

Where, $P_k' = P_k + P_{l,k}$ and $Q_j' = Q_k + Q_{l,k}$

$P_{l,k}$ and $Q_{l,k}$ are loads connected at bus k. Pk, eff and Qk, eff are the effective real and reactive power flows out of bus "k".

The angle and voltage magnitude at each node are calculated (ii) Forward direction. Assume a voltage $V_i < \delta i$ at bus 'i' and $V_k < \delta_k$ at bus 'k', then the current flowing through the line 'M' having an impedance, $Z_{ik} = R_{ik} + X_{ik}$ between bus 'i' and 'k' can be obtained as,

$$I_{ik} = \frac{(V_i < \delta_i - V_k < \delta_k)}{R_{ik} + jX_{ik}} \tag{3}$$

and,

$$I_{ik} = \frac{(P_i - Q_k)}{V_i < -\delta_i} \tag{4}$$

The voltage at bus 'k' is obtained by evaluating Eqs. (3) and (4) as,

$$V_k = [V_i^2 - 2 * (P_iR_{ik}+jQ_iX_{ik})+(R_{ik}^2+X_{ik}^2) * (\frac{P_i^2+Q_i^2}{V_i^2})]^{0.5} \tag{5}$$

The power losses of the branch 'M' between nodes "i" and "k" can be found as,

$$P_{loss(ik)} = R_{ik}\frac{(P_{ik}^2 + Q_{ik}^2)}{V_i^2} \tag{6}$$

$$Q_{loss(ik)} = X_{ik}\frac{(P_{ik}^2 + Q_{ik}^2)}{V_i^2} \tag{7}$$

The total losses of the distribution system like active and reactive power can be obtained as,

$$f_1 = P_{Loss(ik)} = \sum_{k=1}^{N} P_{Loss(ik)} \tag{8}$$

$$f_2 = Q_{Loss(ik)} = \sum_{k=1}^{N} Q_{Loss(ik)} \tag{9}$$

Where, "N" is the number of branches, $N = nb - 1$, $i = 1: nb$, and "nb" is the number of buses.

B. Voltage deviation index: The deviation of voltage from the terminal value can be calculated as,

$$f_3 = VDI = \sum_{i=1}^{nb} (1 - V_i)^2 \tag{10}$$

Where, V_i is the voltage at bus i and nb is the number of buses.

C. Formulation of optimized function

The multi-objective function of this research is considered to minimize the real power loss, reactive power loss, and VDI.

$$\text{Minimize}(f) = \min(w_1 * f_1 + w_2 * f_2 + w_3 * f_3) \tag{11}$$

Where, $\sum_{k=1}^{3} w_k = 1$, w_k are weighting factors used to form the objective function and depend on the focus of the research.

The constraints to be satisfied when minimizing the objective function are:

• Power balance

$$\sum P_{DG} + P_{grid} = \sum P_{loss} + P_d \tag{12}$$

• Voltage limits

$$0.95 \leq V_i \leq 1.0 \tag{13}$$

• DG capacity limit

$$P_{DG}^{min} \leq P_{DG} \leq P_{DG}^{max} \tag{14}$$

D. Sensitivity factors analysis

The Voltage Sensitivity Factor (VSF) is obtained by the ratio of the base case voltage magnitudes at buses V(i) to the minimum limit of voltage (0.95 p.u). The buses with the smallest value of VSF (i.e. VSF < 1.0) are candidate buses for placement of DG. PSO uses VSF to identify the most critical bus to install DG and to size its proper capacity.

$$VSF = \frac{V_{(i)}}{0.95} \tag{15}$$

4 Particle Swarm Optimization Technique

Particle Swarm Optimization (PSO) proposed by Kennedy and Eberhart in 1995 which is one of the evolutionary algorithms [15]. The competition and cooperation among individuals through iterations helps to develop population of individuals in PSO. A potential solution to a problem is obtained from swarm of particles which is from individual particles. The position "Xi" and velocity "Vi" of the particle changes its movement and neighbors' movement experience, towards a better position for itself. The optimization problem of any engineering problem can be expressed as Minimize (f) (As fitness function). Changing and updating the position and velocity of the particle using Eqs. (17) and (16), respectively [3].

$$v_i^{1+t} = w * v_i^t + c_1 * r_1[pbest_i^t - x_i^t] + c_2 * r_2[gbest_i^t - x_i^t] \tag{16}$$

$$x_i^{1+t} = x_i^t + \Delta t * v_i^{t+1} \tag{17}$$

Where, c1 and c2 are acceleration constants, whereas r1 and r2 are two random values between 0 and 1.

5 Optimal Sizing and Siting of DG Using PSO and Voltage Sensitivity Factor

The procedures used to site and size DG using PSO and VSF is implemented in the following steps:

Step 1: Read load and line data of radial distribution system including base MVA and base KV.

Step 2: Run the power flow algorithm BFS to evaluate voltage profile, the real and reactive power loss including VSF to select the most critical buses for DG placement.

Step 3: Randomly initialize the PSO parameters like population of the swarm.

Step 4: Identify optimal location of DG based on VSF i.e. (VSF < 1), can be considered as candidate bus for DG placement.

Step 5: Update the particle position and velocity according to Eqs. (16, 17) by considering constraint limits in Eqs. (12–14).

Step 6: Run the load flow analysis method of BFS for each particle of PSO to acquire the data that are in step 1.

Step 7: Evaluate the objective function (f) in Eq. (11) for all condition.

Step 8: Do again from step 4 to step 7 until the constraints are satisfied and the objective function is minimized.

Step 9: Print results like voltage profile at each bus, DG location and size, real and reactive power loss of the system.

The flow chart below in Fig. 4 shows the procedure of how DG sizing and placement is done using particle swarm optimization in combination with load flow method of BFS.

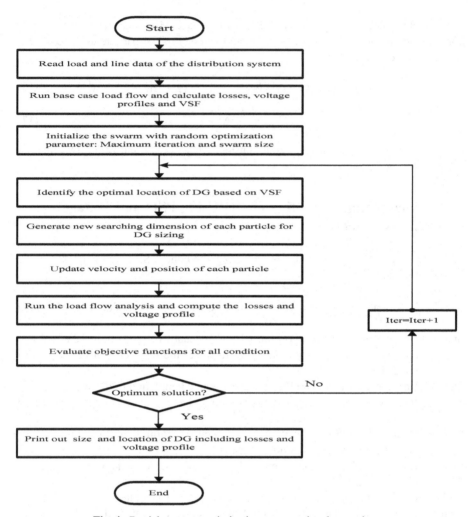

Fig. 4. Particle swarm optimization computational procedure

6 Reliability Analysis of the Radial Distribution System

Distribution system reliability indices are functions of repairs, restoration times and component failures which are unplanned in nature. The reliability assessment of distribution system needs the evaluation of system reliability and load point indices [4]. The load point indices used to determine system reliability indices are the average load point outage rate (r hr/failure), the average load point failure rate (λ failures/year), and the average annual load point outage time or average annual unavailability (U hr/year) [16]. The basic reliability indices which determine system reliability are SAIFI, SAIDI, and EENS.

System Average Interruption Frequency Index (SAIFI): It is the measure of a number of times a system customer faces failure over a period of time and can be calculated as,

$$SAIFI = \frac{\sum \lambda_i N_i}{N_T} \qquad (18)$$

Where, Ni is a total number of customer interruption at load point i, λ_i is the average failure rate of load point i. N_T is the total number of customers served for the area.

System Average Interruption Duration Index (SAIDI): It is the measurement of the total duration of an interruption in a system with a given time interval.

$$SAIDI = \frac{\sum U_{ai} N_i}{N_T} \qquad (19)$$

Electrical Energy Not Supplied (EENS): It is the total energy not supplied due to power outage.

$$EENS = \sum U_{ai} L_{ai} \qquad (20)$$

Where, Uai and ai are respectively the average annual outage time and the average connected load at load point i.

7 Discussions on Results

The proposed method is implemented on the 25-bus 15 kV Ethiopian power distribution at Bahir Dar city. Figure 5 shows the structure of the radial distribution system under study.

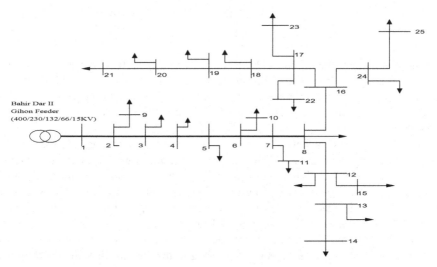

Fig. 5. The 25-bus radial distribution system

The total active and reactive loads of the 25-bus radial distribution system are 1.423 MW and 1.11 MVar respectively. The real power loss of the system is 87.0145 KW whereas its reactive power loss is 17.4197 KVar at the base case. Solar based DG is selected to improve voltage profile as well as to reduce the power loss because of the resource availability. The average solar irradiance of Bahir Dar city is from 4.0 to 5.5 kwh/m^2/day throughout the year which is a more abundant resource of energy as compared to wind resource of the city. Single DG unit is installed in the system to analyze the performance of the network. For PSO parameters, maximum number of iteration = 100, the size of the population = 100, c1 = c2 = 2, and w2 = 0.2, w1 = 0.6, w3 = 0.2. The system input data like base MVA = 100 and base KV = 15 which are used to change the base value in to per unit value.

The optimal location of solar based DG is bus 21 with the size of 0.710668 MW obtained by PSO. The voltage sensitivity factor of the candidate buses which have (VSF < 1.0) is shown in Table 2 below.

Table 2. Candidate bus for optimal allocation of DG based on VSF

Candidate buses	VSF	Candidate buses	VSF
13	0.9797	21	0.9744
14	0.9792	22	0.9770
15	0.9790	23	0.9768
16	0.9787	24	0.9781
17	0.9773	25	0.9780
18	0.9765	8	0.9867
19	0.9753	11	0.9925
20	0.9748	7	0.9927

The minimum voltage before DG installation was 0.9256 p.u whereas after DG installation all the voltage values are in the given limit between 0.95 and 1.0 p.u as shown in Fig. 6 below. The minimum voltage after DG integration is 0.955 p.u. The system voltage profile is improved when DG installed at bus 21 with a capacity of 710.668 kw.

From Table 3 shown below the real power loss decreases from 87.0145 kw to 14.0946 kw due to the installation of solar based DG at bus 21 with 710.668 kw capacity. This enables to save 72.9199 kw and it is 83.8% of the power loss. The reactive power loss also decreases from 17.4197 Kvar to 7.0785 Kvar which saves 10.3405 Kvar and this is 59.36% of the reactive power loss. The reduction of power loss helps to maintain the system voltage profile to be in the desired value.

For reliability analysis of the network, the failure rate of the distribution line is 1.49 f/yr.km whereas the repair time is 6 h according to the data obtained from Ethiopian Electric Power (EEP). The failure rate of transformers is 0.14 f/yr and its maintenance time is 6 h. Based on those data ETAP software is used to analyze the reliability indexes of

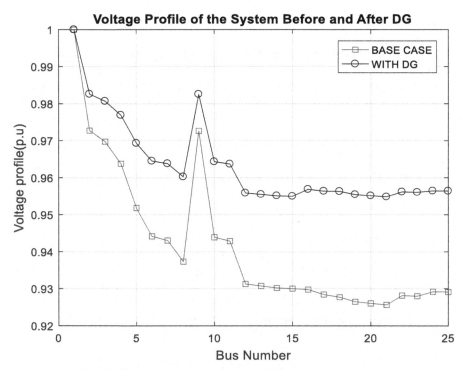

Fig. 6. The studied system voltage profile base case and with DG

Table 3. Comparing results of the system with and without DG

Parameters	Without DG	With DG
Power loss (KW), and loss reduction %	87.0145,0	14.0946,83.8
Reactive power loss (KVar) and loss reduction %	17.4197,0	7.0785,59.36
Minimum voltage (p.u), bus	0.9256,21	0.955,15
Optimal location and size of DG(KW)	–	21(710.668)
DGs power factor	–	0.85
SAIDI (hr/customer.yr)	286.7879	81.1748
SAIFI (f/customer.yr)	61.4003	18.1410
EENS (MWhr/yr)	407.3	110.232
Loss of energy due to power loss (MWhr/yr), and energy loss reduction %	762.247,0	123.468,83.8

the system. The reliability of the system improved by 70.45% due to the integration of DG at the optimal place with the desired size. The SAIDI decreases from 286.7879 h/cus.yr to 81.1748 h/cus.yr and enables to save the cost of energy losses due to power interruption. The SAIFI decreases from 61.4 f/customer.yr to 18.14 f/customer.yr and this determines the reliability of the system that gives continuous service for its end-users which is

70.46% reliability improvement. The reliability result of the system using ETAP software is shown in Figs. 7 and 8 below.

The EENS decreases from 407.3 MWhr/yr to 110.232 MWhr/yr this indicates that the objective of the utility achieved and the satisfaction of customers increase implies that the duration of power interruption and the frequency of power interruption also reduced. The lower value of SAIDI, SAIFI, EENS, and CAIDI indicates better reliability of the system.

Project:	Reliability analysis of radial distribution system	ETAP		Page:	1
Location:	Bahir Dar	16.0.0C		Date:	03-23-2019
Contract:				SN:	4359168
Engineer:	Elias M.		Study Case:　Gihon Feeder	Revision:	Base
Filename:	elias reliability			Config.:	Normal

SUMMARY

System Indexes

SAIDI	286.6281 hr / customer.yr
SAIFI	61.3957 f / customer.yr
ASAI	0.9673 pu
ASUI	0.03272 pu
CAIDI	4.669 hr / customer interruption
EENS	407.080 MW hr / yr

Fig. 7. Reliability index result of 25-bus Gihon feeder base case

Project:	Reliability of 25-bus after DG	ETAP		Page:	1
Location:		16.0.0C		Date:	04-14-2019
Contract:				SN:	4359168
Engineer:			Study Case:　Gihon feeder	Revision:	Base
Filename:	reliability with DG			Config.:	Normal

SUMMARY

System Indexes

SAIDI	81.1748 hr / customer.yr
SAIFI	18.1410 f / customer.yr
ASAI	0.9907 pu
ASUI	0.0093 pu
CAIDI	4. 4746 hr / customer interruption
EENS	110.232 MW hr / yr

Fig. 8. Reliability index result of Gihon feeder after DG Integration

Generally integrating solar based DG brings the better result in power loss reduction as well as reliability index minimization. Installation of DG increases the reliability of the system by supporting the system during normal operation and by acting as a backup power source for part of the load during failure of the utility. For modern distribution system installing DG is an effective and economically affordable method to mitigate the ever- increasing power demand.

8   Conclusion

Particle swarm optimization technique is used to locate and size solar based DG for minimizing the total power loss and the voltage deviation index of the system. Moreover, PSO based multi-objective function with voltage sensitivity factor is used for sizing and siting of DG in the distribution system using MATLAB software. Proper sizing and placement of DG bring the better result in performance improvements like the reduction of voltage deviation index and power loss of the system. The reliability of the proposed system is also studied using ETAP software and the result shows the reliability of the system increased after integration of DG. The abundance solar power resource of Ethiopia specifically Bahir Dar city indicates to shift the old energy resources to renewable which have a mutual benefit in the environment and economy. Distribution system companies use the proposed method to identify the optimum size and locations of solar based DG units to integrate with in their systems. Consequently, utilities can have a better understanding of the installation points and their impacts on system reliability and losses in the distribution network to mitigate the challenges of power demand.

Nomenclatures

ASAI	Average Service Availability Index
ASUI	Average Service Unavailability Index
BFS	Backward Forward Sweep
CAIDI	Customer Average Interruption Duration Index
DG	Distributed Generation
DSTATCOM	Distribution Static Compensator
EENS	Electrical Energy Not Supplied
EEP	Ethiopian Electric Power
ETAP	Electrical Transient Analysis Program
GA	Genetic Algorithm
GW	Giga Watt
HPSO	Hybrid Particle Swarm Optimization
IEEE	Institute of Electrical and Electronics Engineering
KCL	Kirchhoff Current Laws
KV	Kilo Volt
KVar	Kilo Var
KVL	Kirchhoff Voltage Laws
KW	Kilo Watt
KWh	Kilo Watt hour
m	Meter
MATLAB	Matrix Laboratory
mm	Millimeter
MVar	Mega Var
MW	Mega Watt
NPSO	New Particle Swarm Optimization
P	Active Power

Pd	Power Demand
P_{DG}	Power Injected by DG
P_{DG} $(^{max})$	Maximum Power Injected by DG
P_{DG} $(^{min})$	Minimum Power Injected by DG
Pgrid	Power Supplied by Grid
Ploss (ik)	Real Power Loss between Bus i and k
PSO	Particle Swarm Optimization
PV	Photovoltaic
Q	Reactive Power
Qloss (ik)	Reactive Power Loss between Bus i and k
Rik	Resistance of the line between Bus i and k
SAIDI	System Average Interruption Duration Index
SAIFI	System Average Interruption Frequency Index
VDI	Voltage Deviation Index
VSF	Voltage Sensitivity Factor
VSI	Voltage Sensitivity Index
Xik	Reactance of the line between Bus i and k

References

1. Ghatak, S.R., Acharjee, P.: Optimal allocation of DG using exponentential PSO with reduced search space. In: Proceedings of the 2016 2nd International Conference on Computational Intelligence & Communication Technology, CICT 2016, pp. 489–494 (2016)
2. Subramanya Sarma, S., Madhusudhan, V., Ganesh, V.: Evaluation and enhancement of reliability of electrical distribution system in the presence of dispersed generation. In: IEEE International Conference on Signal Processing, Communication, Power and Embedded System (SCOPES), pp. 357–362 (2016)
3. Tolba, M.A., Tulsky, V.N., Diab, A.A.Z.: Optimal sitting and sizing of renewable distributed generations in distribution networks using a hybrid PSOGSA optimization algorithm. In: 2017 IEEE International Conference on Environment and Electrical Engineering and 2017 1st IEEE Industrial and Commercial Power Systems Europe (EEEIC/I&CPS Europe), pp. 1606–1612 (2017)
4. Shaaban, M.F., El-Saadany, E.F.: Optimal allocation of renewable DG for reliability improvement and losses reduction. IEEE Power and Energy Society General Meeting, pp. 1–8 (2012)
5. Ethiopia - Energy_export: Ethiopia Energy Trade Development and Promotion (2018). https://www.export.gov/article?id=Ethiopia-Energy
6. Bahir Dar, Ethiopia - Sunrise, sunset, dawn and dusk times for the whole year - Gaisma (2018)
7. Sedighi, M., et al.: Sitting and sizing of DG in distribution network to improve of several parameters by PSO algorithm. In: IEEE 2010 International Conference on Mechanical and Electrical Technology (ICMET 2010), pp. 533–538 (2010)
8. Anwar, A., Pota, H.R.: Optimum allocation and sizing of DG unit for efficiency enhancement of distribution system. In: 2012 IEEE International Power Engineering and Optimization Conference, PEOCO 2012, pp. 165–170, June 2012
9. Musa, H., Adamu, S.S.: Enhanced PSO based multi-objective distributed generation placement and sizing for power loss reduction and voltage stability index improvement. In: 2013 IEEE Energytech, pp. 0–5 (2013)

10. Prasanna, H.A.M., Kumar, M.V.L., Ananthapadmanabha, T.: Genetic algorithm based optimal allocation of a distributed generator in a radial distribution feeder. In: IEEE 2014 International Conference on Circuits, Power and Computing Technologies, ICCPCT 2014, pp. 184–190 (2014)

11. Singh, S.: Optimal allocation and sizing of distributed for power losss reduction. In: IEEE International Conference & Workshop on Electronics & Telecommunication Engineering 2016, pp. 15–20 (2016)

12. Tiwari, D., Ghatak, S.R.: Performance enhancement of distribution system using optimal allocation of distributed generation & DSTATCOM. In: IEEE International Conference on Innovative Mechanisms for Industry Applications, ICIMIA 2017, pp. 533–538 (2017)

13. Mohan, V.J., Albert, T.A.D.: Optimal sizing and sitting of distributed generation using particle swarm optimization guided genetic algorithm. In: IEEE 2017 International Conference on Intelligent Computing and Control Technology, vol. 10, no. 5, pp. 709–720 (2017)

14. Abdel-Mawgoud, H., Kamel, S., Ebeed, M., Aly, M.M.: An efficient hybrid approach for optimal allocation of DG in radial distribution networks. In: IEEE Proceedings 2018 International Conference on Innovative Trends in Computer Engineering, ITCE 2018, vol. 2018, no. 1, pp. 311–316, March 2018

15. Kennedy, J., Eberhart, R.: Particle swarm optimization, pp. 1942–1948. IEEE (1995)

16. Yadav, A.C.: Reliability assessment of distribution system at presence of Distribution Generation, May 2015

Mobility Prediction in Wireless Networks Using Deep Learning Algorithm

Abebe Belay Adege[1](✉), Hsin-Piao Lin[2], Getaneh Berie Tarekegn[1], and Yirga Yayeh[1]

[1] Department of Electrical Engineering and Computer Science,
National Taipei University of Technology, Taipei, Taiwan
abbblybelay@gmail.com
[2] Department of Electronic Engineering,
National Taipei University of Technology, Taipei, Taiwan

Abstract. Recently, wireless-technologies and their users are rising due to productions of sensor-networks, mobile devices, and supporting applications. Location Based Services (LBS) such as mobility prediction is a key technology for the success of IoT. However, mobility prediction in wireless network is too challenging since the network becomes very condensed and it changes dynamically. In this paper, we propose a deep neural network based mobility prediction in wireless environment to provide an adaptive and accurate positioning system to mobile users. In the system development processes, firstly, we collect RSS values from three Unmanned Aerial Vehicle Base Stations (UAV-BSs). Secondly, we preprocess the collected data to get refine features and to avoid null records or cells. Thirdly, we exhaustively train the Long-short term memory (LSTM) network to find the optimum model for mobility prediction of the smartphone users. Finally, we test the designed model to evaluate system performances. The performance of the proposed system also compared with Multilayer Perceptron (MLP) algorithm to assess the soundness of mobility prediction model. The LSTM outperforms the MLP algorithm in different evaluating parameters.

Keywords: Long-short term memory · Location based services · Mobility prediction

1 Introduction

In Internet of things (IoT) era, where everything is connecting through internet to create smart home, smart city, smart world as well as smart society, Location Based Service (LBS) such as mobility prediction plays key roles for the success of IoT. However, developing the mobility prediction model in wireless environment is very challenging since the place and time are changed recklessly [1]. Moreover, the speed and directions of mobile users, and the dynamical oscillations of wireless network traffics are challenges in mobility prediction modeling. Mobility prediction in wireless network focuses on locating the movements of different objects, such as vehicles, animals, typhoons and tourists on a regional environments in different areas. It becomes hot issues in different

© ICST Institute for Computer Sciences, Social Informatics and Telecommunications Engineering 2020
Published by Springer Nature Switzerland AG 2020. All Rights Reserved
N. G. Habtu et al. (Eds.): ICAST 2019, LNICST 308, pp. 454–461, 2020.
https://doi.org/10.1007/978-3-030-43690-2_31

areas, such as computer science, geographical information science and visual analytics [2]. As discussed in [3], locating users in mobile technologies can be applicable ranging from location-based services to robotics and route findings to create ranges from smart home up to smart world and society. Mobility prediction can be exploited for improving resource reservation in mobile networks. It is also uses for efficient base station deployments, efficiently planning and managing risks, properly controlling resource consumptions, safe time in certain operations and activities specifically when there will be simultaneous operations, and for improving quality of decisions.

Mobility prediction, more particularly tracking, of the movable objects are commonly predicted using satellite-based positioning such as Global Positioning System (GPS), Global Navigation Satellite System (GLONASS) and Galileo [4, 5]. Nevertheless, satellite-based applications are not well appropriate for all types geolocation applications due to the lacks of Line of Sight (LoS) and its sensitivity to occlusion [6]. The shadowing and blocks in urban areas make the usages of satellite technology inadequate accuracy. The Wi-Fi signal was proposed as additional technology to alleviate global satellite fluctuations [7], while it still has much signal fluctuation problems for outdoor environments. Moreover, Wi-Fi has coverage constraints as the Wi-Fi access points enable to cover only fewer radius. Sensor networks are other means of tracking mobile users, nevertheless it is not cost effective to apply in wider coverage.

Mobility prediction (Tracking) in mobile technology has great importance when the prediction system is more accurate and robust. It uses to aware the current and future possible destination zones of mobile users. We can apply tracking system to locate mobile carriers or users using vision based or radio signal sources of data. The vision based mobility predictions can be computed through the aid of image and video data. This approaches cause unpredictable effect when the camera or the observed objects move or cross each other. It is quite difficult to find a reliable model that works well in the different regions of the image or video, and it has accuracy defects at blurry light [8]. It has also technical difficulties, lacks of adaptabilities in wider community, security issues and the operational complexity for LBS in urban and smart city environments. Thus, radio signal based mobility prediction becomes common for offering LBS in wireless environments as it can minimize the computational complexity, applied in wider areas and cost effective for fitting IoT business models. However, wireless based data sources have much signal fluctuations due to shadowing or different network traffics to provide accurate LBS, and the problem will be more serious when the located objects are in motion. Thus, we should apply more adaptive of the wireless environment, and flexible technology according to data natures to get accurate and cost effective tracking model.

In [9], clustering was applied for location prediction using Adaptive Resonance Theory (ART), and compare with k-Means algorithms. The work was evaluated through boundary level accuracy rather than specific path. This approach is difficult to evaluate system performances. In [3], the lookup table correlation technique was used. However, this type of approach is impractical when the data size is larger and complex. In [10], the trajectory prediction has been done in the indoor environment.

According to [11, 12], there are two widely classified mobility prediction approaches: network based and handset based methods. In network based technology, the network-based position determination equipment is required to position the mobile device.

The measurement can be done from BSs and Access Points (APs). This approach is highly depending on service providers. The common approaches under this method are Angle of Arrival (AoA), Time of Arrival (ToA) and Time Difference of Arrival (TDoA). In contrast, the handset based positioning technique determines the future location of the mobile device by putting its location by cell identification, and signal strengths of the home and neighboring cells. This type of approach is determined using client software installed on the handset or in server. This technique is easy and common. It is also cost effective because it doesn't require extra devices. Tracking in wireless and mobile network requires more adaptive algorithms since there is much signal fluctuations due to shadowing or network traffic effects [9].

In this work, we propose a Long-short term memory (LSTM) algorithm as it is very powerful in capturing spatial and temporal dependencies in input and output data sequences. LSTM has also a nonlinear transformations and hidden-state memory units, that uses to predict motions accurately. We use Unmanned Aerial Vehicle Base Stations (UAV-BSs) to collect data sources from 500 m by 300 m working area, which is located in Taiwan, National Taipei University of Technology (NTUT).

The rest of this paper is organized as follows. In Sect. 2, we discuss details of the proposed technique. The data collections, results and discussions are presented in Sect. 3. Finally, conclusions and recommendations are given in Sect. 4.

2 Proposed System

Figure 1 illustrates the general flow of system architectures in both training and testing phases. Once we collect relevant datasets from UAV-BSs, we apply preprocessing to filter and make structured data based on UAV height and the received power. The system has two phases: training and testing phases. After the LSTM is trained through adjusting various parameters, such as hidden layers, epochs, activation functions and optimizers, we were training the LSTM exhaustively until we get the optimum performances. In testing phase, we collect from unknown locations in the working path, during moving instances. The predicted values are compared with real values in graphical path and mathematical computations.

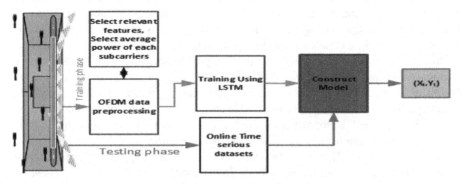

Fig. 1. Proposed algorithm pseudocode

In Fig. 2, the structure of LSTM algorithm with its gates is demonstrated. Cell A is the previous cell containing the previous stored memory C_{t-1} and previous hidden layers h_{t-1}. Each gate uses to predict the paths of the mobile users, which is determined based on the available OFDM signal. In general, LSTM network contains information or subparts such as current cell, current input unit X_t, current hidden state h_t, the current output gate O_t, the internal memory unit C_t, the input gate i_t, the forget gate f_t, and activation functions.

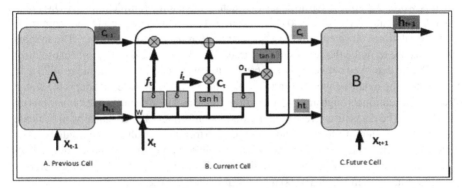

Fig. 2. The LST algorithm structural layouts

Where,

$$f_t = \delta(W_f.X_t + W_f.h_{t-1} + b_f) \tag{1}$$

$$i_t = \delta(W_i.X_t + W_i.h_{t-1} + b_i) \tag{2}$$

$$O_t = \delta(W_o.X_t + W_o.h_{t-1} + b_o) \tag{3}$$

$$C - in_t = tanh(W_c.X_t + W_c.h_{t-1} + b_{c-in}) \tag{4}$$

$$C_t = f_t.C_{t-1} + i_t.C - in_t \tag{5}$$

$$S_t = O_t.tanh(C_t) \tag{6}$$

The proposed system is evaluated by demonstrating the path direction as well as the moving object approaches. Moreover, we evaluate the system accuracy in each testing point relative to the actual places. The estimation errors are calculated by taking each estimated location in different time intervals. The errors of each mobile user at each different time intervals t $= \{1, 2, 3, \ldots.\}$ is evaluated, as shown in Eq. (7):

$$P_t^k = \sqrt{\left(X_{ol} - EL_{xt}^k\right)^2 + \left(Y_{ol} - EL_{xt}^k\right)^2} \tag{7}$$

where P_t^k is the error at time t from original location of (X_{ol}, Y_{ol}), l is the location where we measured in working environment, and EL_{xt} is the estimated locations of the user k in certain time instances. Moreover, the system performances are evaluated in mean square errors (MSE) and mean absolute errors (MAE) to show the bounded error of the system performances in each algorithm. The programing frameworks are done using Python 3.7 programming language with the Tensorflow framework.

3   Data Collection and Performance Evaluations

For this work, we collect Orthogonal Frequency Division Multiplexing (OFDM) data from defined path that covers 300 m by 500 m, NTUT. This data is collected from three UAV-BSs that are elevated on 40 m, 50 m and 60 m heights of buildings. The heights variations use to make the proposed system easily adapt the real scenario because most fixed BSs are deployed between 40 m to 60 m, while it can deployed in the range of 20 m to 80 m according to landscapes on outdoor environments [13]. Besides, it adapts the signal strength fluctuation through angle of elevations as the real world land scape has various up and downs. The datasets are recorded in three seconds interval, periodically, to evaluate the proposed system uniformly, and minimize performance evaluation biasedness. The collected data has the form of (I, H) ➔ (x, y), where I and H are scanned data or RSS values and the corresponding heights of the UAV-BSs, respectively. H has three different possible values: 40 m, 50 m and 60 m. In each record, we use one of the three H values. The sample signal distribution from two UAV-BSs at different heights is shown in Fig. 3.

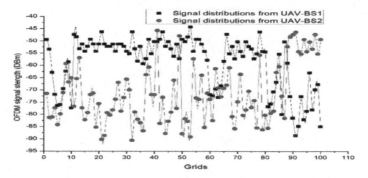

Fig. 3.   Sample signals distribution from two UAV-BSs

Table 1 shows some of the parameter setups in the UAV-BSs. We fix the bandwidth to be 15 kHz to make the proposed system can adaptive the wider signal fluctuations as the narrower bandwidth has much signal fluctuations. We use universal software radio peripheral (USRP) device and software defined radio (SDR) system to generate the real signal from Ubuntu computer. We used open SDR code with little modifications, where the SDR is originally written by GNU radio companion (GRC) in C language for Ubuntu platform. We used the power amplifier to increase the signal power from transmitter, Tx, since the power of USRP in the Tx side needs much power. Besides, we used dipole antenna in both Tx and receiver, Rx, and the output power of the USRP set 24.8 dBm. In Rx side, the computer reads and stores the OFDM signals that received from Tx in each reference point. We set carrier frequency to be 860 MHz as this frequency is free from Taiwan Telecommunication services while wireless media unable to be absolutely free from signal interferences.

Table 1. Simulation parameters.

Parameters	Values
Height of the buildings	40 m, 50 m, 60 m
Center frequency	860 MHz
Bandwidth	15 kHz
Signal type	OFDM
Transmission power (T_X)	33 dBm
Receive power (R_X)	24.8 dBm

Figure 4 shows the training and validation performances of the MLP and LSTM networks in loss functions and epoch sizes in model designs. The figure shows that the LSTM has lower loss values relative to MLP model whenever the epoch size increases from 40 onwards. The MLP has not visible progresses while the epoch is increased due to lower learning capacity. The LSTM network has better learning capacity due to integrative works of its gates such as input gate, output gate and forget gate, and its deeper learning capacity and learning principles. As a result, the LSTM can make performance differences in each larger epoch numbers over MLP algorithm. Figure 5 shows the performances of MLP and LSTM models compared to the real path of the mobile carriers. The black dotted line is the real path of the mobile user. The red color is the MLP based mobility predictions. The blue line shows the LSTM algorithm performances in the corresponding testing points. The MLP result shows more fluctuations and the results

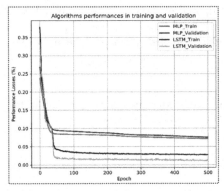

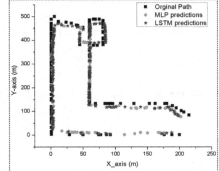

Fig. 4. The MLP and LSTM performances in mobility predictions

Fig. 5. Mobility prediction compared to actual path (Color figure online)

in each testing points are unstable relative to LSTM model. While there is bended paths in the working areas, the LSTM outperforms and nearly parallel as well as overlap with the actual paths.

The result implies that the MLP has lower adaptability while it has much possible hidden layers and other similar properties. However, this does not mean that MLP is useless. The higher performances behind LSTM algorithm are due to its gates and deeper learning capacity to the nonlinear datasets. Local maxima does not affect the LSTM model easily while this is a common trouble of MLP. The main implication of LSTM's outperformances is that the validation loss function is smaller than the training loss function, which is uncommon to most machine language models. The LSTM performance in Fig. 5 and Table 2 are the good implications.

In Table 2, the MSE and MAE are shown for both MLP and LSTM algorithms. In each evaluation parameters, the LSTM has better performances. Thus, the LSTM can provide motivated results in average as well as at distinct testing points, as shown in Table 2 and Fig. 5, respectively. Note that, in the models evaluations procedure, we used similar ranges of epoch, hidden layers, activation function and optimizers to avoid performance evaluation's biasedness.

Table 2. The MLP and LSTM performances in mobility predictions in m.

Algorithms	MSE	MAE
MLP	0.20	0.25
LSTM	0.0003	0.012

4   Conclusions and Future Works

In this paper, we evaluated the performance of LSTM algorithm for mobility prediction using cellular network data collected from UAV-BSs. The data is collected experimentally. The simulation results show that the proposed method can work well and it can cope the dynamical changes of environments. The proposed technique provides the state-of-the-art performances in distinct as well as bounded system performances. In the future work, we propose for mobility prediction of IoT devices through integration of IoT devices.

Acknowledgments. This work was partially supported by Ministry of Science and Technology (MOST) under Grant numbers 108-2634-F-009-006 and 107-2221-E-027-025.

References

1. Pathirana, P.N., Savkin, A.V., Jha, S.: Location estimation and trajectory prediction for cellular networks with mobile base stations. IEEE Trans. Veh. Technol. **53**(6), 1903–1913 (2004)

2. Versichele, M., Neutens, T., Delafontaine, M., Van de Weghe, N.: The use of Bluetooth for analyzing spatiotemporal dynamics of human movement at mass events. Appl. Geogr. **32**(2), 208–220 (2012)
3. Pan, J.J., Pan, S.J., Yin, J., Ni, L.M., Yang, Q.: Tracking mobile users in wireless networks via semi-supervised colocalization. IEEE Trans. Pattern Anal. Mach. Intell. **34**(3), 587–600 (2012)
4. Anisetti, M., Bellandi, V., Damiani, E., Reale, S.: Advanced localization of mobile terminal. In: ISCIT 2007 - 2007 International Symposium on Communications and Information Technologies, pp. 1071–1076, February 2007
5. Laoudias, C., Moreira, A., Kim, S., Lee, S., Wirola, L., Fischione, C.: A survey of enabling technologies for network localization, tracking, and navigation. IEEE Commun. Surv. Tutor. **20**, 3607–3644 (2018)
6. Adege, A.B., et al.: Applying deep neural network (DNN) for large-scale indoor localization using feed-forward neural network (FFNN) algorithm. In: Proceedings of the 4th IEEE International Conference on Applied System Invention, ICASI 2018, vol. 11, pp. 814–817 (2018)
7. Yuanfeng, D., Dongkai, Y., Huilin, Y., Chundi, X.: Flexible indoor localization and tracking system based on mobile phone. J. Netw. Comput. Appl. **69**, 107–116 (2016)
8. Zanella, A., et al.: Internet of things for smart cities. IEEE Internet Things J. **1**(1), 22–32 (2017)
9. Anagnostopoulos, T., Anagnostopoulos, C., Hadjiefthymiades, S.: An adaptive machine learning algorithm for location prediction. Int. J. Wirel. Inf. Netw. **18**(2), 88–99 (2011)
10. Oguejiofor, O.S., Okorogu, V.N., Abe, A., Osuesu, B.O.: Outdoor localization system using RSSI measurement of wireless sensor network outdoor localization system using RSSI measurement of wireless sensor network. Int. J. Innov. Technol. Explor. Eng. **2**(2), 1–7 (2015)
11. Sri, M.S.: Tracking and Positioning of Mobile in telecommunication 1, vol. 2, no. 1, pp. 1–47 (2015)
12. Samiei, M., Mehrjoo, M., Pirzade, B.: Advances of positioning methods in cellular networks. In: International Conference on Communications Engineering, pp. 174–178 (2010)
13. Lu, M., Liu, S., Liu, P.: The research of real-time UAV inspection system for photovoltaic power station based on 4G private network. J. Comput. **28**(2), 189–196 (2017)

Basic Facial Expressions Analysis on a 3D Model: Based on Action Units and the Nose Tip

Meareg A. Hailemariam^(✉)

Addis Ababa University, Addis Ababa, Ethiopia
meareg.abreha@aau.edu.et

Abstract. Facial expressions play a significant role in conveying emotions with a widespread use across diverse cultures and societies globally. In particular, the expressions anger, sadness, fear, disgust, surprise, happiness and also neutral are considered universal. 2D and 3D avatar models are used to simulate facial expressions and have different applications in many domains. In this work, we consider a 3D model with facial expressions as a platform to analyze the basic set of expressions. We considered direction weighted intensity values of the FACS Action Units (i.e., also referred here as shape keys) relative to the nose tip, serving as a reference point, to generate direction weighted score for each target expression. The scores also give numerical validations for the repeated correlations indicated between a specific set of expressions (i.e., anger vs. sadness, and fear vs. disgust) in other research works that focus on developing techniques for facial expressions recognition and classification. In addition, the normal distribution of these seven expressions was depicted and gave a close to bell-curve shape which is an indication of a common phenomenon in nature.

Keywords: 3D facial expressions · Facial expression analysis · FACS · Action Units · Blendshapes

1 Introduction

Facial expressions are important in conveying emotions effectively during communication. According to Mehrabian [1] up to 55% of the message during a face-to-face communication is transferred through facial expressions. Even though human facial expressions may vary across individuals, people or cultures there are seven universally accepted basic facial expressions. These are anger, sadness, fear, disgust, surprise, happiness and also the neutral expression [2]. The Facial Action Coding System (FACS) [3] provides description rule for all the visually detectable changes that can be demonstrated by contraction of the facial muscles; which are also widely known as Action Units (AUs). The FACS separates the facial expression into upper and lower expressions based on the set of Action Units evoked during performance.

© ICST Institute for Computer Sciences, Social Informatics and Telecommunications Engineering 2020
Published by Springer Nature Switzerland AG 2020. All Rights Reserved
N. G. Habtu et al. (Eds.): ICAST 2019, LNICST 308, pp. 462–471, 2020.
https://doi.org/10.1007/978-3-030-43690-2_32

In a daily interaction of human beings, the use of common correlation between facial expressions and emotions is a common approach to recognize emotions. However, other approaches, mainly in used in technical settings, such as the use of speech, electrocardiography (ECG), electromyography (EMG) and electroen-cephalography (EEG) [17–19] can be also be used to recognize emotions. Adolphs [5] gives the facial spatial points positions for the basic facial expressions and their commonly associated emotions. There is a great deal of interest in affect analysis. Ideally, facial expressions analysis consists of three steps [6]. The first is face detection; after localizing the facial expression image or tracking it in case of sequence of images correctly, then facial or face model features extraction follows. Finally, using the extracted features to come up with a categorization mechanism of facial expressions. A work by Sariyanidi et al. [7] surveys briefly the feature extraction techniques used for facial expression recognition. Among them include Principal Component Analysis (PCA), Discrete Cosine Transfor-mation (DCT) and supervised and unsupervised learning approaches.

The use of 3D avatars with realistic facial expressions has a wide application in domains such as entertainment, education, health and others. The advance-ment in facial expression research is applied when designing facial expressions of 3D avatars; such as the use of AU of the FACS as a basis to realistic facial ani-mation. But similarly, the advancement of 3D avatars based on facial animations can also contribute back to the facial emotion research, since the computer based tools provide a relatively easy and cheaper setting to perform computation and experiments which might be otherwise, if done with human subjects. The use Action Units (AU) of the FACS to perform facial expression analysis is not new. However, much of the literature focuses either on the recognition of AUs [22,23] or on determining the set of AUs useful for facial expression recognition [24,25] using learning algorithms or distance based approaches. On the other, in this study, we aim to extract a new understanding by analyzing the intensity value of actions units (i.e., here, interchangeably, we may refer to them as shape keys; a term associated with the 3D engine called blender which is used to model the 3D avatar we used in this study) of the seven basic facial expressions on a 3D facial animation model. The set of the basic 3D facial expressions used for our analysis were designed according to the AU rule of FACS for facial expressions and their textual description is similar to the description of the basic facial expressions detailed by Pandzic and Forchheimer [4]. Besides adding a new insight into the categorization and distribution of basic facial expression, this study shows the usefulness of 2D or 3D models in research of facial emotions.

2   Related Work

As facial expressions are basically combinations of movements of different set of facial action units, measuring these distances and intensities of action units is important in quantifying facial expressions. In particular, images of posed facial expressions have been instrumental in the research of facial expressions analysis. Bartlett et al. [8] explore three different techniques of image cues detection for classifying six facial actions that deal with the brows and the eye area. They used a database of over 1,100 sequences containing over 150 distinct actions or action combination images of facial actions. They applied feed-forward network based spatial analysis which also includes PCA generated coefficients as their input. The second is feature based measurement of facial wrinkles and eye openings which is a sum squared of differences of pixel intensities along the chosen segments. Then measurement results were fed to a neural network for target AU classification. Additionally, optic flow fields that estimate direction of motion gradient were also used for action unit classification based on template matching procedure. The three methods gave accuracy results of 88.6%, 57.1% and 84.5% respectively; while their hybrid improved the result to 90.9% which is close to the FAC human expert based classification accuracy of 91.8%.

Local features extraction, via Independent Component Analysis and also by measuring the ratio based geometrical relationship of different parts of the face during the basic facial expressions, was used for facial expression classification on image based dataset [11]. They give as input 9 geometrical ratio features which deal with various eye and mouth parts to a K-NN algorithm; while ANN used 5 local feature vectors of eye and mouth parts that are extracted by ICA. The hybrid of these techniques achieved an accuracy level above 90%.

Another work uses geometric positions and Gabor Wavelets coefficients extracted from facial expression image datasets at fiducial points for expression recognition [12]. Each image is represented by 68 vectors of geometric positions and 612 vectors as Gabor Wavelet coefficients and these extracted features are fed to Multi-layer Perceptron networks. The geometric based recognition gave 73%, the Gabor Wavelet 92.2% and their hybrid 92.3% level of accuracies.

Jaffar and Al Eisa [13] extracted features from facial image datasets using Discrete Cosine Transform (DCT), Haar wavelet transform and Gabor wavelets. The fusion of these features were trained on an SVM and gave a classification of accuracy of 76.11% on MMI, 77.40 on MUG and 95.69 on JAFFE facial expression datasets for the seven basic facial expressions.

A facial expression recognition system [14] based on six 3D distance-vectors that are calculated from 11 feature points located around the eyes, lips and close to ear areas of the face. A Neural Network was trained using the 3D distance vectors as inputs and gave an average accuracy 91.3% for the seven basic facial expressions.

3   Action Unit Intensities and Their Direction Based Analysis of Posed Facial Expressions

The Facial Action Coding System (FACS) is a widely used technique of quantifying facial movement which are the basis of facial expressions. Similarly, here, we rely on the use of Action Units of the FACS for analyzing target facial expressions but with a novel way of computation. Our goal is to get a new insight on understanding the distribution and correlations between the basic facial expressions. Basic facial expressions engage the most prominent AUs which cause detectable facial deformations allowing easy mapping to a subset of the 84 MPEG-4 feature point sets [10]. This relative advantage and their important role among of the list of expressions makes them a target of interest for analysis.

3.1 Dataset and Facial Feature Extraction

We used a 3D model [26] that has all the target 3D facial expressions. The Expressions (i.e., in this text it is also referred to as blendshapes, interchangeably) were encoded following the AU FACS rule for human facial expressions. In this work, since the target of analysis are the posed forms of the basic facial expressions, we captured the peak state (maximum level of intensity) for each target expression. The head pose information is not considered in our case; since we focus on frontal on peak level posed expressions. Each pose of an expression has 45 action units (i.e., which, interchangeably, in this text referred to as shape keys). Most of these shape keys deal with the brows, eyes and lips area of the face; and have the range of their intensity values set to between $[0, 1]$. The extracted intensity values of all the action units of each captured expression during its peak state are used as a feature vector for each target expression respectively. Obviously, intensity values of all the shape keys for the neutral expression are set to zeros.

3.2 Feature Analysis

Having gathered all the feature vectors, the next step would be the analysis. We consider the nose tip as the reference point on which we base our feature vector transformation. The main reason we chose the nose tip is, it is the part on the face which stays constant (without significant movement) for different set of expressions while other parts may change. It has also a special symmetrical property in respect to the whole face which makes it an important feature on the face [27]. Its symmetry makes it suitable for our direction based analysis of action units on the blendshapes of the basic expressions. In addition, the use of the nose tip in areas such as pose estimation, face alignment has given good results [15]. In our case, considering the nose tip as a reference point, we observe the intensities of shape keys causing facial muscles or bones to move either towards it or away from it. Therefore, we applied the 3D euclidean distance (on x, y, z dimensions) to determine and compare the distance between a target basic expression blendshape's particular shape key's position distance to the nose tip and a similar shape key's distance to the nose tip during the neutral expression. As shown below, we applied the euclidean distance based technique to decide the coefficient sign for a given shape key's intensity from a particular basic expression, to be applied when calculating the its direction weighted score later.

$$\left(dist\_neutral_{shapekey\_i}\right)^2 = \left(X_{neutral\_nose\_tip} - X_{neutral\_shapekey\_i}\right)^2$$
$$+ \left(Y_{neutral\_nose\_tip} - Y_{neutral\_shapekey\_i}\right)^2 + \left(Z_{neutral\_nose\_tip} - Z_{neutral\_shapekey\_i}\right)^2$$

$$(dist\_exp\_k_{shapekey_i})^2 = (X_{neutral\_nose\_tip} - X_{exp\_k\_shapekey\_i})^2$$
$$+ (Y_{neutral\_nose\_tip} - Y_{exp\_k\_shapekey\_i})^2 + (Z_{neutral\_nose\_tip} - Z_{exp\_k\_shapekey\_i})^2$$

We compare these two distances of a given shape key 'i' which were calculated from the neutral expression and the peak state in a target expression's respectively. If a shape key's distance w.r.t to the nose tip during neutral expression is bigger than the corresponding shape key's distance with w.r.t the nose tip during a target expression, then a negative coefficient unit (as it is direction weighted) will negate the intensity score value of that shape key for the target expression else intensity stays positive.

This whole process will be done for each action unit of each target basic expression. The list (represented by 'd') will contain the ± 1 s coefficient units vector for the corresponding shape keys' vector of the given basic expression as shown in Eq. 1.

In the cases, where the intensity of a given action unit during a target expression and neutral expression stays the same, the value of the corresponding 'd' will not matter; as equality of value with a neutral expression's shape key implies the zero (default) state.

Finally, we will have a set of feature vectors of intensity values of shape keys of each of the basic expression determined according to their movement direction w.r.t to the reference point. Then, we can further use these transformed features of each target expression to generate a single numeric value that can represent it on a linear line. Similar to techniques in image based difference calculated via difference which approximates derivatives, we apply direction based difference estimator in reference to the origin point.

Equation 1 calculates the weighted score of each target expression using the intensity values of its shape keys and their corresponding multiplier signs.

$$Expr_{weighted} = \frac{1}{N}\sum_{i=1}^{N} Shapekey_i Intensity * d \tag{1}$$

In Eq. 1, the intensity of each shapekey 'i' will be multiplied by its corresponding direction coefficient 'd' which can be either $+$ or -1. The total number of shape keys is represented by N, which in this case are 45. The final iterated summation of all the shape keys, averaged by the total number of shape keys will generate a single direction-weighted numeric score with a value between $[-1, 1]$ for each target expression,

Table 1 shows a list of the average direction weighted intensities of the target expressions calculated using Eq. 1. The expression anger scored the highest based on total average direction intensity value of its AUs heading towards the reference/origin point, while the expression fear on the other end scored highest for its direction weighted average intensity of its AUs' moving away from the origin point.

Table 1. List of average direction weighted intensities of action units of the basic expressions on the 3D model

Expression name	Average direction weighted expression value
Anger	−0.1026
Sadness	−0.0415
Neutral	0.0000
Happiness	0.0304
Surprise	0.0590
Disgust	0.0733
Fear	0.1212

Therefore, according to our results, the new sequence in reference to the origin point, starting from the expression with the highest direction weighted average heading towards the nose tip to the expression with the highest weighted average set of AUs moving away from it, would be anger, sadness, neutral, happiness, surprise, disgust and fear.

3.3   Probability Density Estimation of the Basic Facial Expressions

Measuring the normal probability density [20] of these basic set of expressions can be useful in understanding the distribution patten of the basic facial expressions and offer further insight on human facial expressions in general. Figure 1 depicts the probability density of the normal distribution for the basic facial expressions, including the neutral expression, based on the numeric value results from Table 1.

The low number of the total target expressions (which is seven) we considered literally make it impossible to make a proper comparison of the distribution result generated with the 68%–95%–99.7% rule of a perfectly normal distribution. However, from the result depicted, it is still possible evaluate the symmetry; and also quantitatively show that almost the overall probability mass falls within the 3 units of deviation only with anger's score lying beyond that range with an excess value around 0.02 which can be considered negligible. The mean value calculated is 0.011 with a deviation of 0.29.

The generated distribution is symmetric; it has a close to bell curve shape which indicates a distribution pattern for the basic set of facial expressions that is common in nature. This shows the significant role of the basic set of facial expressions in giving, potentially, a deeper insight into understanding the human emotions and their distribution patterns. The probability densities of the normal distributions for the six basic facial expressions based on the intensity distribution of their shape keys are shown in Figs. 2, 3 and 4 (except for the neutral expression; as all of its AU's intensity values stay at zero). These visualizations

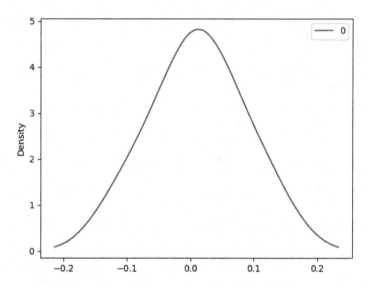

Fig. 1. Normal probability density visualization of the basic facial expressions.

depict the distributions of intensity values of all the shape keys for each of the basic expression. While, for the expressions angry and sad, it can be observed that there is a slight tendency for majority of the shape keys to be less than zero; it is on the contrary for the rest of the expressions, in particular, more visible for the disgust and fear expressions (Fig. 4).

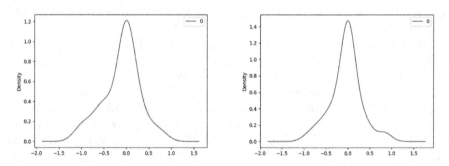

Fig. 2. Density distributions of shape key intensity values for angry and sad expressions depicted on the left and right side respectively.

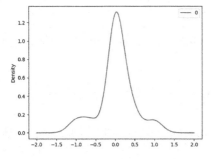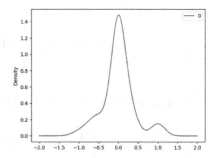

Fig. 3. Density distributions of shape key intensity values for happy and surprise expressions depicted on the left and right side respectively.

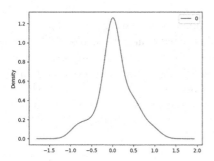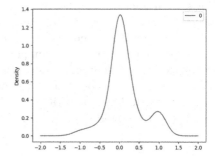

Fig. 4. Density distributions of shape key intensity values for disgust and fear expressions depicted on the left and right side respectively.

3.4   Result Discussion

Our analysis on shapes' intensity scores presents a new way to categorize the basic expressions using distance based scores. The result generated shows consistency with the pattern shown in other research work results; especially in terms of explaining the high confusion matrix error between a specific set of expressions. For instance, there is a high confusion error between the expressions anger and sadness [9,14,21]. Similarly, shown in Table 1, the distance based categorization puts both the expressions anger and sadness on the same side. They both have a weighted average intensities of AUs to the left side of zero. On the other hand expressions surprise, happiness, disgust and fear show a significant overlap in [18,21]. In Table 1, the direction weighted score puts the expressions surprise and happiness next to each other and also followed by disgust and fear in their order. In general, four of them are categorized on the right side from zero (all with positive numeric values).

According to [16] anger and fear are in the same dimension in terms of arousal/activity. Both are claimed to have a high activity level. Similarly in Table 1, magnitudes of the weighted numeric scores of anger and fear are found in the extreme ends. Having the highest results from the rest of the expressions can give a quantitative validation for the previous claim of a high activity group. In general, our analysis of the basic facial expressions generates a quantitative order and categorization along a plausible validation to the confusion error seen between a specific set of expressions.

4   Conclusion and Future Work

This research showed analysis of FACS AU (shape keys) in a 3D model generates a sensible way of categorization and quantification of distances between the basic human facial expressions. The results gained here confirms the usefulness of a 3D model platforms for analysis of facial expressions. Expanding this experiment to the other facial expressions on a 3D platform other than the basic ones, and also doing similar analysis on other different 3D models with FACS based AU, would be useful to further evaluate our method. Another interesting future task would be extracting the facial muscles' movement intensity measurements of the basic facial expression directly from human subjects or determining intensity values from images and then apply the same computation technique as done here. This would possibly help validate the insight gained here and also to show the co-relation between different settings; facial expressions analysis on virtual models and images or humans.

References

1. Mehrabian, A.: Communication without words. Psychol. Today **2**(4), 53–56 (1968)
2. Ekman, P., Friesen, W.: Pictures of Facial Affect. Consulting Psychologist, Palo Alto (1976)
3. Ekman, P., Friesen, W.: Facial Action Coding System: A Technique for the Measurement of Facial Movement. Consulting Psychologists Press, Palo Alto (1978)
4. Pandzic, I., Forchheimer, R. (eds.): MPEG-4 Facial Animation: the Standard, Implementationand Applications. Wiley, Hoboken (2002)
5. Adolphs, R.: Recognizing emotion from facial expressions: psychological and neurological mechanisms. Behav. Cognitive Neurosci. Rev. **1**(1), 21–62 (2002)
6. Pantic, M.: Automatic analysis of facial expressions: the state of the art. IEEE Trans. Pattern Anal. Mach. Intell. **22**(12), 1424–1445 (2000)
7. Sariyanidi, E., Gunes, H., Cavallaro, A.: Automatic analysis of facial affect: a survey of registration, representation, and recognition. IEEE Trans. Pattern Anal. Mach. Intell. **37**(62015), 1113–1133 (2015)
8. Bartlett, M.S., Hager, J.C., Ekman, P., Sejnowski, T.J.: Measuring facial expressions by computer image analysis. Psychophysiology **36**, 253–263 (1999)
9. Zhong, L., Liu, Q., Yang, P., Liu, B., Huang, J., Metaxas, D.N.: Learning active facial patches for expression analysis. In: CVPR (2012)
10. ISO/IEC JTC1/SC29/WG11 MPEG96/N1365: MPEG4 SNHC: Face and body definition and animation parameters (1996)
11. Hai, T.S., Thai, L.H., Thuy, N.T.: Facial expression classification using artificial neural network and k-nearest neighbor. Int. J. Inf. Technol. Comput. Sci. **7**, 27–32 (2015)

12. Zhang, Z., Lyons, M.J., Schuster, M., Akamatsu, S.: Comparison between geometry-based and gabor-wavelets-based facial expression recognition using multilayer perceptron. In: 3rd Automatic Face & Gesture Recognition. IEEE (1998)
13. Jaffar, M.A., Al Eisa, E.: Classification of facial expression using transformed features. Int. J. Inf. Electron. Eng. **4**(4), 269–273 (2014)
14. Soyel, H., Demire, H.: Facial expression recognition using 3D facial feature distances. In: Affective Computing, Focus on Emotion Expression, Synthesis and Recognition (2008)
15. de Bittencourt Zavan, F.H., Nascimento, A.C.P., e Silva, L.P., Bellon, O.R.P., Silva, L.: 3D face alignment in the wild: a landmark-free, nose-based approach. In: Hua, G., Jégou, H. (eds.) ECCV 2016. LNCS, vol. 9914, pp. 581–589. Springer, Cham (2016). https://doi.org/10.1007/978-3-319-48881-3_40
16. Scherer, K.R.: What are emotions? And how can they be measured? Soc. Sci. Inf. **44**(4), 695–729 (2005)
17. Takahashi, K.: Remarks on emotion recognition from bio-potential signals. In: Proceedings of the 2nd International Conference on Autonomous Robots and Agents. IEEE (2004)
18. Matlovic, T., Gaspar, P., Moro, R., Simko, J., Bielikova, M.: Emotions detection using facial expressions recognition and EEG. In: International Workshop on Semantic and Social Media Adaptation and Personalization. IEEE (2016)
19. Hamedi, M., Salleh, S.-H., Swee, T.T., Kamarulafizam: Surface electromyography-based facial expression recognition in bi-polar configuration. J. Comput. Sci. **7**(9), 1407–1415 (2011)
20. DasGupta, A.: Probability for Statistics and Machine Learning: Fundamentals and Advanced Topics. Texts in Statistics. Springer, New York (2011). https://doi.org/10.1007/978-1-4419-9634-3
21. Zhang, F., Zhang, T., Mao, Q., Xu, C.: Joint pose and expression modeling for facial expression recognition. In: CVPR (2018)
22. Ying, A.C.C., Ujir, H., Hipiny, I.: 3D facial expression intensity measurement analysis. In: Zulikha, J.N.H., Zakaria (eds.) Proceedings of the 6th International Conference of Computing and Informatics, pp. 43–48. School of Computing, Sintok (2017)
23. Pantic, M., Rothkrantz, L.: An expert system for recognition of facial actions and their intensity. American Association for Artificial Intelligence (2000)
24. Hussain, N., Ujir, H., Hipiny, I., Minoi, J.-L.: Facial action units recognition for emotional expression. Advanced Science Letters (ICCSE 2017), vol. 24 (2017)
25. Sun, Y., Reale, M., Yin, L.: Recognizing partial facial action units based on 3D dynamic range data for facial expression recognition. In: 8th IEEE International Conference on Automatic Face & Gesture Recognition, pp. 1–8 (2008)
26. https://github.com/hansonrobotics/HEAD/tree/master/src/blender_api. Accessed 11 Nov 2019
27. Mahmood, S.A., Ghani, R.F., Kerim, A.A.: Nose tip detection using shape index and energy effective for 3D face recognition. Int. J. Mod. Eng. Res. (IJMER) **3**(5), 3086–3090 (2013)

Pareto Optimal Solution for Multi-objective Optimization in Wireless Sensor Networks

Haimanot Bitew Alemayehu, Mekuanint Agegnehu Bitew[(✉)], and Birhanu Gardie Shiret

Computing Faculty, Bahir Dar Institute of Technology, Bahir Dar University, Bahir Dar, Ethiopia
haimanotmitku@gmail.com, memekuanint@gmail.com, birie16@gmail.com

Abstract. A wireless sensor network (WSN) consists of small sensors with limited sensing range, processing capability, and short communication range. The performance of WSNs is determined by multi-objective optimization. However, these objectives are contradictory and impossible to solve optimization problems with a single optimal decision. This paper presents multi-objective optimization approach to optimize the coverage area of sensor nodes, minimize the energy consumption, and maximize the network lifetime and maintaining connectivity between the current deployed sensor nodes. Pareto optimal based approach is used to address conflicting objectives and trade-offs with respect to non-dominance using non-dominating sorting genetic algorithm 2 (NSGA-2). The tools we have used for simulation are: NS2 simulator, tool command language script (TCL) and C language and Aho Weinberger keninghan script (AWK) are used. We have checked the coverage area, packet deliver ratio, and energy consumption of sensor nodes to evaluate the performance of proposed scheme. According to the simulation results, the packet delivery ration is 0.93 and the coverage ratio of sensor to region of interest is 0.65.

Keywords: Pareto optimal · Multi-objective · Energy consumption · Coverage · Wireless sensor networks

1 Introduction

WSN is an emerging and fast growing technological platform in many working environments. Nowadays, it has attracted a lot of research attention in many application areas. WSNs contain a collection of sensors that can be deployed rapidly and cheaply for various applications such as environment monitoring, object tracking, traffic and crime surveillance and ground water monitoring [10]. Deployment of sensors is a crucial issue in WSN design. Technologies have made the development of sensor to be small, low power, low-cost distributed devices, which can make local processing and wireless communication in reality. Sensor nodes failure may cause connectivity loss and in some cases network partitioning. This can cause serious damage in some environments that need critical monitoring [2]. WSN's quality is determined by optimizing multi objectives [1, 5, 7]. Since multi-objective optimization (MOOP) are contradictory and impossible to

© ICST Institute for Computer Sciences, Social Informatics and Telecommunications Engineering 2020
Published by Springer Nature Switzerland AG 2020. All Rights Reserved
N. G. Habtu et al. (Eds.): ICAST 2019, LNICST 308, pp. 472–479, 2020.
https://doi.org/10.1007/978-3-030-43690-2_33

solve optimization problems with a single optimal decision. Sensor nodes are equipped with non-rechargeable and irreplaceable batteries. In addition, sensors have limited sensing range, processing and communication range. Hence, Optimizing the basic network metrics such as network lifetime, energy consumption, sensing coverage at once while maintaining connectivity between each sensor node and sink leads conflicting objectives.

The aim of this paper is to find non-dominated Pareto-optimal points in multi-objectives optimization problems to design WSNs. It tries to minimize energy consumption, maximize coverage area, maintain active communication within sensor nodes, and get better fitness by finding the balance trade-off point. This paper solves MOOP by finding the Pareto solutions for the system to optimize conflicting objectives and quantifying trade-off.

2   Related Works

Recently, a number of research contributions have addressed diverse aspects of WSNs including routing, energy conservation and network lifetime [1]. The growing demand of usage of wireless sensor applications in different aspects makes the quality-of services to be one of paramount issue in wireless sensor applications. In [6] authors studied the sensing range of WSNs. On the paper, a large numbers of sensor nodes were deployed in the target area to mitigate node replacement problem and to effectively monitor the field. However, number of sensor nodes increased on the specific area and it needs more cost to deploy. The authors classified WSN area coverage into the three types: area coverage, point coverage and barrier coverage [3]. Characterization of the coverage varies depending both on the underlying models of each node's field of view and on the metric used for appraising the collective coverage. To achieve their objectives; they used several models for different application scenarios.

Network connectivity is another metric criterion for efficient functioning of WSNs which depends on the selected communication protocol [3]. Two sensor nodes are directly connected if the distance of the two nodes is smaller than the communication range. Connectivity requires the location of an active node to be within the communication range of one or more active nodes. So that all active nodes can form a connected communication.

3   Methodology

We assumed sensor nodes are deployed in a square region area and all sensor nodes can sense and communicate within the region. Every sensor nodes have direct or indirect link to the sink node and sensing range of node n is assumed to be circular with radius r. The paper focused to optimize the following performance metrics (parameters') of WSNs: coverage area, energy consumption and network lifetime. The performance metrics we considered are: coverage area, energy consumption, packet delivery ratio, and network lifetime. Coverage area: describes the region WSN sensing area ranges. Stationary sensor nodes are randomly deployed at the target area. Sensor S_i is deployed at point (x_i, y_i).

For any point p at (x, y), the Euclidean distance between Si and p can be calculated by the equation:

$$d(s_i, P) = \sqrt{(x_i - x)^2 + (y_i - y)^2} \qquad (1)$$

Each sensor has sensing range within the circular sensing radius r by using binary sensing model. Area A covered in a sensor networks [7]

$$A_{Cover} = \sum_{i=1} \frac{(d[(s_i, p)])^2}{total\_area} \qquad (2)$$

Among the sensing models, binary disk sensing model describes a node whether it senses the point on its sensing range or not. The sensing range of each node within the circular sensing radius r

$$C_{xy}(si) = \begin{Bmatrix} 1 \ if \ d(si, p) < r \\ 0 \quad otherwise \end{Bmatrix} \qquad (3)$$

Energy consumption: each sensor contains limited battery power, so sensor nodes need to increase the network lifetime. Energy consumed by a sensor i in time t is:-

$$E_i(si, ti, ri, I) = s(si) + t(ti) + r(ri) + I \qquad (4)$$

Where s(si) is the energy consumed at sensing, t(ti) is the energy consumed at transmitting, r(ri) is the energy consumed at receiving and i energy consumed at idle state in given time t. To maximize coverage area with connectivity: coverage Function.

$$F(X) = f1(x1), \ f2(x2) \ldots f(xn)$$

Maximize C_{area} Subject to:

$$C_{xy}(si) = \begin{Bmatrix} 1 \ if \ d(si, p) < r \\ o \quad otherwise \end{Bmatrix}$$

Connectivity must exist within area. To minimize energy consumption, the energy consumed by each sensor node need to be: energy consumption function

$$Minimize \ (Ei(Si, ti, ri, i))$$

The Total Energy consumption on sensing radius si of node ni with u factor is formulated as:

$$E(total[si]) = \sum_{i=1}^{n} *r$$

$$E(total[ti]) = \sum_{i=1}^{n} *r$$

$$E(total[ri]) = \sum_{i=1}^{n} *r$$

3.1 Non-dominated Sorting Genetic Algorithm-II (NSGA2)

It's computational intelligence which applies the principle of natural selection and survival of the fittest to find near optimal solution in the search space. There are many Multi-objective optimization algorithms among them:- Multi-Objective evolutionary algorithm (MOEA), Strength Pareto evolutionary algorithm (SPEA), Pareto envelop Strategy algorithm (PESA), and improved Non-dominated Sorting Algorithm (NSGA-II) [12].

In this paper, NSGA-II algorithm is used, because it has better performance than others. NSGA-II uses an elitist principle, diversity preserving mechanisms and emphasizes the non-dominated solutions. NSGA-II working based on genetic operators such as, crossover and mutation to MOOP.

To analysis non-dominance points and ranking population of sensor node deployment works in the following logic (Fig. 1 and Table 1).

- Item Take all sets of solutions of node population p
- Item any i^{th} solution (xi) which belongs to p
- Item Set of solutions which dominates (S) the solution xi and number of solutions (ni) which dominates xi.
- Item Any non-domination front (PK) at K^{th} level.

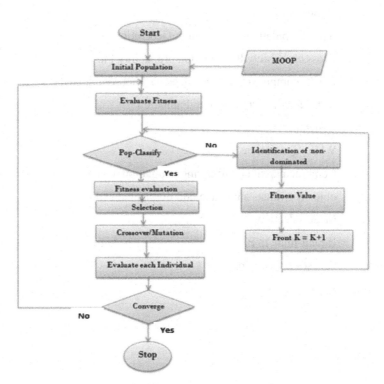

Fig. 1. Flow chart of NSGA-II

Table 1. NSGA-II parameter's list

Parameter	Value
Population size	20
Maximum generation	50
Mutation probability	0.1
Crossover probability	0.9

4   Simulation Setup and Results

We have installed NS2.35 simulator on 8 GB, RAM of Ubuntu Linux operating system. Initial population of stationary sensor nodes deploy randomly. The following simulation parameters used to find balanced trade-off between objective function. In the above section, the details of the proposed algorithm is described; A non-dominated sorting genetic algorithm II (NSGA-II) was first proposed in [4] as a biological heuristics algorithm which usually used to solve complex industrial optimization problems. This algorithm has been wide attention by authors due to its faster convergence, stronger robustness, and better draw near the true Pareto-optimal front.

Begin

Input: Population P; Maximum Generation *GMax*;

Cross probability Pc; mutation probability Pm

Initial: compute objective values, fast non-dominated

sort, selection, crossover and mutation.

Generation = 1;

While Generation$\leq$ *GMax* do

Combine parent and offspring population, compute

objective values and make non-dominated sort.

Made selection

If rand-num()$\leq$ Pc

Crossover operation;

End

If rand-num() ≤ Pm

Made mutation;

End

Generation = Generation + 1;

End

Output: best individuals

End

At the beginning, we made some assumptions: the nodes are deployed randomly, each one are static and knows its own location using some location systems [9]. The simulation region is a square area with the size of 401 m by 401 m in all the experiments, and 20 sensor nodes are deployed randomly in this two dimensional area.

The packet delivery ratio indicates how much the sensor networks are communicated with each other. According to the simulation result, we have achieved a packet delivery ratio of 92.89 which indicates the existence of better connectivity within the network system. Figure 3 shows the evaluation of energy consumption fitness function (Table 2).

Table 2. Definitions and values of simulation parameters

Parameter	Definition	Value
X	Maximum width of RoI	401 m
Y	Maximum length of RoI	401 m
Rc	Communication radius	10 m
Rs	Sensing radius	250 m
Ns	Number of sensors	20
IE	Initial energy	10 J
Si	Sensing energy for node i	0.6 mA
TEi	Transmission energy for node i	0.9 mA
REi	Reception energy	0.7 mA
I	Idle	0.1 mA

Figure 2 below shows the design layout of the 20 sensor nodes in 401 m by 401 m is plotted as shown below in NS2 working simulation environments.

The best Pareto optimal solutions are find by using [11] NSGA-II. In NSGA-II algorithm, its main operation consists of two components like; one part of genetic algorithm includes the operation, such as crossover, selection, and mutation. The other part refers to the unique non-dominated sorting operation in the multi-objective optimization algorithm. The selection operation can contain the better individuals with their fitness values. The mutation operation is designed according to the genetic mutation in the biology, in order to ensure that the algorithm has strong global convergence ability. And, the

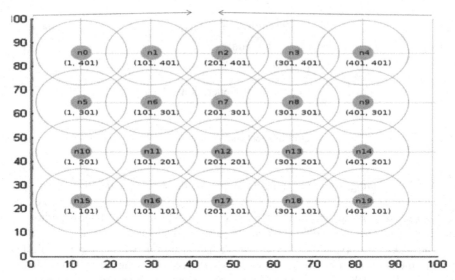

Fig. 2. Design of the deployed sensor nodes in the area

crossover operation is designed based on the principle that homologous chromosomes cross to generate new improve the algorithm search ability.

As the result shows the sensing coverage of each sensor nodes are varies depending on its location from the sink node; it's location is at the center of deployment area. The more near to sink node, the more energy dissipate to cover its sensing region. The coverage area of Fitness for every sensor has their own sensing capacity; for example node1 has 0.91, node2 has 0.93, node3 has 0.94 and node12 has 1.0 etc. According to [8], it's ratio of the number of packets sent by the source node and the number of packets received by the destination node. The packet delivery ratio within our deployed sensor nodes is quantified in the simulation from 591 sent packet, 549 is received packets.

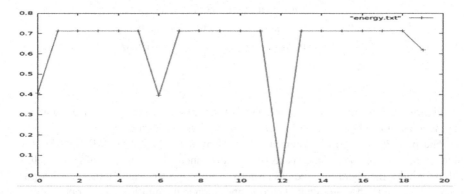

Fig. 3. Energy consumption of each sensor fitness function

5 Conclusions

In this Paper we have proposed Pareto optimal based approach to simultaneously optimize the basic performances metrics of WSNs: area of coverage, energy consumption and network lifetime. NS2 simulation tool is used to evaluate the performance of the proposed scheme. According to the simulation results; the packet delivery ratio is 0.93 and the coverage ratio of sensors to region of interest is 0.65.

References

1. Akyildiz, I.F., Su, W., Sankarasubramaniam, Y., Cayirci, E.: A survey on sensor networks. IEEE Commun. Mag. **40**(8), 102–114 (2002)
2. Carlos-Mancilla, M., López-Mellado, E., Siller, M.: Wireless sensor networks formation: approaches and techniques. J. Sens. **2016**, 1–18 (2016)
3. Shu, L., Zhu, C., Zheng, C., Han, G.: A survey on coverage and connectivity issues in wireless sensor networks. J. Netw. Comput. Appl. **35**(2), 619–632 (2012)
4. Deb, K., Pratap, A., Agarwal, S., Meyarivan, T.A.M.T.: A fast and elitist multiobjective genetic algorithm: NSGA-II. IEEE Trans. Evol. Comput. **6**(2), 182–197 (2002)
5. Fei, Z., Li, B., Yang, S., Xing, C., Chen, H., Hanzo, L.: A survey of multi-objective optimization in wireless sensor networks: metrics, algorithms, and open problems. IEEE Commun. Surv. Tutor. **19**(1), 550–586 (2016)
6. Jain, S., Gupta, N., Kumar, N.: Coverage problem in wireless sensor networks: a survey. In: International Conference on Signal Processing, Communication, Power and Embedded System (SCOPES) (2016)
7. Iqbal, M., Naeem, M., Anpalagan, A., Ahmed, A., Azam, M.: Wireless sensor network optimization: multi-objective paradigm. Sensors **15**(7), 17572–17620 (2015)
8. Khan, M.F., Felemban, E.A., Qaisar, S., Ali, S.: Performance analysis on packet delivery ratio and end-to-end delay of different network topologies in wireless sensor networks (WSNs). In: 2013 IEEE 9th International Conference on Mobile Ad-hoc and Sensor Networks, pp. 324–329. IEEE (2013)
9. Estri, D., Bulusu, N., Heidemann, J.: GPS-less low-cost outdoor localization for very small devices. IEEE Pers. Commun. **7**, 28–34 (2000)
10. Sohraby, K., Minoli, D., Znati, T.: Wireless Sensor Networks: Technology, Protocols, and Applications. Wiley, Hoboken (2007)
11. Wang, P., Xue, F., Li, H., Cui, Z., Chen, J.: A multi-objective DV-Hop localization algorithm based on NSGA-II in internet of things. Mathematics **7**(2), 184 (2019)
12. Zitzler, E., Thiele, L.: Multiobjective evolutionary algorithms: a comparative case study and the strength Pareto approach. IEEE Trans. Evol. Comput. **3**(4), 257–271 (1999)

E-Learning Readiness of Technology Institutes in Ethiopian Public Universities: From the Teachers' Perspective

Abinew Ali Ayele[✉] and Worku Kelemework Birhanie

Faculty of Computing, Bahir Dar Institute of Technology,
Bahir Dar University, Bahir Dar, Ethiopia
abinewaliayele@gmail.com, workukelem@gmail.com

Abstract. In this paper, we have presented an empirical study that aimed to investigate e-learning readiness of technology institutes in Ethiopia. Data was gathered from five technology institutes of Ethiopian universities. 400 teachers were sampled using simple random sampling method. An E-learning readiness level of those institutes has been assessed from the teachers' perspective. In terms of employee readiness, academic institutions have achieved the heist readiness index in general. This indicates that teachers are ready to go ahead for implementing e-learning. Particularly, employee readiness parameters like technical skill, awareness and attitudinal readiness were found to be above the expected level of readiness. Whereas, organizational readiness in general was found bellow the expected level that indicated academic institutions are not ready and needs some work to get ready. Particularly, all organizational readiness parameters like cultural, policy, top management and technological readiness were found to be below the expected level of readiness.

Keywords: E-learning readiness · E-learning implementation · Employee readiness · Organizational readiness · Academic institutions

1 Introduction

Academic institutions are integrating new information systems in their teaching, research and administrative works in order to utilize the benefits of those new technologies. The developments of Information and communication technologies (ICTs) have changed the world into an increasingly networked society in all sectors of the economy through creating vital opportunities. These days, the development of a nation is highly dependent on the strength of its information system and connectivity to the world [1]. It seems mandatory to use ICTs (like e-learning systems) in the day to day activities of academic institutions so as to successfully accomplish their objectives and compete with other similar institutions.

Hence, e-learning is becoming a useful tool for academic institutions. Measuring and assessing e-learning readiness of academic institutions must be the first priority

© ICST Institute for Computer Sciences, Social Informatics and Telecommunications Engineering 2020
Published by Springer Nature Switzerland AG 2020. All Rights Reserved
N. G. Habtu et al. (Eds.): ICAST 2019, LNICST 308, pp. 480–491, 2020.
https://doi.org/10.1007/978-3-030-43690-2_34

before implementing and investing on digital technologies. Moreover, identifying the main determinants of e-learning readiness is indispensable for the successful implementation of e-learning as a platform for learning environments. The greatest success of e-learning implementation in academic institutions can be achieved through assessing and understanding e-learning readiness levels [2]. Therefore, academic institutions should have clear and broad understanding about their e-learning readiness levels before implementation.

Implementing e-learning in any academic institution happens in one of the following three approaches. The first approach uses e-learning technologies to augment or supplement the traditional face-to-face course delivery systems. The second approach for implementing e-learning focuses on integrating online activities into a traditional course to improve the usual learning experience, while the third and the last approach emphasizes on a course that is delivered entirely online [3]. The choice of these implementation approaches that an institution may decide depends on the level of readiness in terms of infrastructure as well as human resources readiness in terms of experience, knowledge, skill, awareness and attitude [3].

More precisely, e-learning implementation highly requires the readiness of physical infrastructure, technical expertise, psychological motivation, policy and cultural transformation as well as management support and commitment. It is mandatory to have people with some level of psychological motives and technical skills in order to manage and administer e-learning platforms [4].

E-Learning implies learning conducted through electronic media, mainly on the Internet. [5], mentioning European Commission (2001), described that e-Learning entails the utilization Internet and state-of-the-art multimedia technologies in order to improve the quality of learning through creating easy access to services and facilities. It has been proved that e-learning can improve the collaborations among educators, administrators and, learners in academic institutions [5].

According to Webster's New College Dictionary, readiness has been defined as being "prepared mentally and or physically for some experience or action". Similarly, [6] defined that e-learning readiness is "the mental or physical preparedness of an institution for some e-learning experience or action". Therefore, the mental and physical preparedness of academic institutions for using e-learning must be evaluated before its implementation and deployment.

The objective of this investigation was to empirically assess and measure the e-learning readiness levels of academic institutions (mental or physical preparedness) of the technology institutes of Ethiopian Universities. The study has also tried to investigate the major determinant factors of e-learning implementation readiness specifically from the teachers' perspective.

2 Background and Literature Review

E-Learning can be upsetting and intrusive in learning environments if it is not implemented with prior and appropriate planning and management. The assessment of institutional readiness for up-to-date technological innovations can minimize the risk of its failure after implementation [7] as cited in Demiris et al. (2004). The well known scientist, Thomas Edison, stated that "success is 2% inspiration and 98% perspiration".

This is to mean that awareness and motivation only contributes 2% for success. Hence, the major determinant is perspiration which implies exerting a continuous effort on action and execute for successful implementation.

Readiness is an integral and preliminary step for successfully implementing new changes like adoption of new information systems. Therefore, evaluating e-learning readiness prior to its implementation saves money, time and energy by identifying the barriers that are going to limit and the communities that are not able to support the implementation process [8, 9].

Among the different studies conducted on e-learning readiness, a study conducted on measuring e-learning readiness had considered five factors namely motivation, self competence, financial, self-directed learning and usefulness [10]. Similarly, a study conducted in Malaysia considered students, lecturers, technology and the environment to be ready prior to e-learning implementation and had given special focus for technological readiness factor since it was the major determinant of e-learning implementation [11]. Another study conducted on the students' e-learning readiness and acceptance in Northeastern Thailand had also shown the situations and variables that impact the implementation of e-learning in the case of developing countries [12].

In addition, many other studies have showed that Organizational readiness and employee readiness are among the major e-learning readiness determinants that influence the implementation success [13]. Organizational readiness is the extent to which the organization is prepared for new technology implementations in terms of infrastructure, policy and culture [9]. This study has tried to measure the preparedness of academic institutions in terms of top management support and commitment, technology, infrastructure, policy and culture.

Employee readiness is the extent to which individual members of an organization are prepared psychologically, attitudinally, behaviorally and in terms of technical skill capabilities and basic awareness [9]. In this regard, the readiness of employees' technical skill, attitude and awareness are evaluated to use e-learning systems in technology institutes of Ethiopian Universities. The success of teachers in using e-learning systems depends on their prior technical competency, awareness and attitude to use new information and communication technologies [14, 15].

An empirical study conducted on e-Learning Readiness in Turkey has identified groups of e-learning readiness dimensions that can influence the implementation of e-learning. Among these, technical skill readiness, attitudinal readiness, cultural readiness and infrastructure readiness are the major once [1]. This study has also considered these factors as core determinants of e-learning readiness.

As defined by [1], these dimensions are described as follows:

- Technical skill readiness: refers to the observable as well as measurable technical competencies concerning users' abilities with computers and the Internet.
- Infrastructure readiness dimension: it is defined as the right infrastructure or equipment readiness, e-learning content delivery, provision of technical support and a learning management system adopted by the organizations.
- Attitude readiness: it refers to the users' attitude that involves confidence, motivation, enjoyment, importance and preference influencing the use of technology.

- Cultural readiness: It refers to the use of e-learning through the application of Internet and networked technologies to disseminate information enhance communication, interaction and teaching.

The role of top management readiness is also described as a core critical success factor for e-learning implementation. Top management readiness is the extent to which the top management is committed to support and encourage employees to use new technologies [16].

3   The E-Learning Readiness Assessment Framework

3.1   Readiness Assessment Framework

Measuring the extent of e-learning implementation readiness in higher education institutions needs clear understanding of the key e-learning platform environmental components and their interactions. The main e-learning implementation components that need to be examined are the people in the organization and the organization itself. Among the people component, the teachers are the once whose preparedness to accept and use e-learning should be measured. Moreover, the organization's infrastructure, technology, policy, culture and top management readiness to use e-learning systems should also be evaluated. The following framework shows the different levels of readiness cut points in an e-learning environment [17]. In this study, these cut points are used to differentiate the various levels of e-learning readiness in the selected technology institutes.

The model has been proved by different studies conducted in academic institutions [4, 14]. The readiness index level of 1–2.6 indicated that the institutions are not ready and needs a lot of work to get ready while the readiness index level of 2.6–3.4 showed that the institutions are not ready and needs some work to get ready. The readiness index cut point that ranges from 3.4–4.2 indicted that the institutions are ready but needs few improvements to implement e-learning. Whereas the readiness index cut point between 4.2 and 5.0 showed that the institutions are ready to go ahead in implementing e-learning. The model determines the expected level of readiness index reference cut point to be 3.4 [17]. Therefore, readiness index parameter values greater than 3.40 had achieved the readiness index cut point to implement e-learning.

Table 1. The readiness scales and indication of means

Readiness average scores	Readiness scale level
1.00–2.60	Not ready needs a lot of work
2.61–3.40	Not ready needs some work
3.41–4.20	Ready but needs a few improvements
4.21–5.00	Ready to go ahead

Each indicator has alternatives coded as $1 =$ strongly Disagree, $2 =$ Disagree, $3 =$ Undecided, $4 =$ Agree, and $5 =$ Strongly Agree in a five-point Likert scale type.

The alternatives were organized in a way that they provide easy coding and assessment. Aydin and Tasci [17] have designed a model by determining the different levels of e-learning readiness. These levels were obtained by identifying the critical level values (i.e. 4 intervals/5 categories = 0.80). Therefore the 3.41 mean average score was determined as an expected level of readiness. Based on the 0.80 distance critical level values, the actual levels of different readiness cut points were also identified as depicted in Fig. 1 and Table 1.

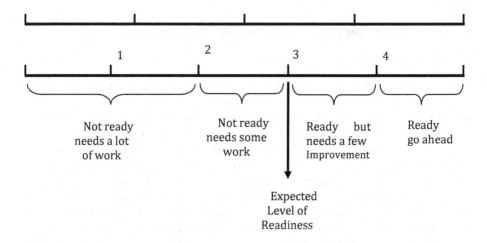

Fig. 1. E-learning readiness assessment model Adopted from [17]

3.2 Materials and Methods

Since the main objective of this study was to empirically investigate teachers' e-learning readiness in technology institutes of Ethiopian public universities. The study mainly used a quantitative research approach. Self administered questionnaires were used as data collection instrument. Simple random sampling technique has been used to select representatives from the target population. The research data were collected from the faculty members of 5 technology institutes in Ethiopia. The size of representative samples was determined using the following formula [18]. The formula is appropriate for determining sample size of finite populations.

$$no = \frac{(z\alpha/2)^2 * p(1-p)}{\delta^2}$$

Where: N = total population
n = required sample size
$\alpha = 0.05$ = level of significant (type-I error)
$\delta^2 = 0.05$ which is the margin of error

P = 0.5 for sample proportion of teachers

$$no = \frac{(1.96)^2 * 0.5(1-0.5)}{(0.05)^2}$$
$$no = \frac{(3.84) * 0.5 * 0.5}{0.0025} = 384.16 = 385$$
$$n = \frac{no}{1+\frac{no}{N}}$$
$$n = \frac{385}{1+\frac{385}{1385}} = \frac{385}{1.278} = 301.257 = 302$$

Based on the above calculation, the minimum sample size to study the target population was 302 teachers. However, this study has used random sample of 400 respondents which was more than the minimum sample size to insure that the samples are more representative of the target population. The target population of the study consisted of 1,385 faculty members from the five technology institutes of Ethiopian public Universities (Bahir Dar Institute of Technology-BiT = 460, Addis Ababa Institute of Technology-AAiT = 290, Ethiopia Institute of Textile & Fashion Technology-EiTex = 200, Jima Institute of Technology-JiT = 210 and Hawasa Institute of Technology-HiT = 225).

For the descriptive part of this study, Statistical package for social science (SPSS version 20) has been applied. Means, standard deviations and cross tabulations were computed for each indicator and construct in order to determine the expected level of e-learning readiness.

4 Results and Discussions

4.1 Socio-Demographic Characteristics

As this study is the continuation of our previous work [19], we have used same samples but different parameter. Moreover, some of the basic facts and figures might also overlap. Out of 400 questionnaires distributed, 372 were collected. This indicated that the response rate of 93% was achieved. From 372 questionnaires collected, 356 (89%) questionnaires were found usable. The remaining 16 questionnaires which constitute 4% were rejected since they were either not properly filled or incomplete. Therefore, the main survey has achieved 7% non-respondent rate. This indicated that response rates exceeding 50% are acceptable, 60% are good, 70% are very good and 85% are excellent for questionnaire surveys [20] citing Mangione (1995). Hence, the 93% response rate in this study is Excellent.

As shown in Table 2, the majority of respondents 156 (44%) are from BiT (Bahir Dar Institute of Technology). The rest of respondents were taken from Ethiopia Institute of Textile & Fashion, Addis Ababa, Hawasa and Jima Institutes of Technology in order of the sample sizes. As indicated in the data, out of 356 respondents, 283 (79.5%) and 73 (20.5%) were found male and female respectively.

Concerning academic qualification, 82 (23%), 230 (64.6%) and 44 (12.4%) of the study participants had BSc degree, MSc degree and PhD degree respectively. Out of 356 respondents, 179 (50.3%), 121(34%), 46 (12.9), 8 (2.2%) and 2 (0.6%) were 21–30 years, 31–40 years, 41–50 years, 51–60 years and above 60 years old respectively as depicted in Table 3. Theses clearly indicated that the majority of teachers participated in the survey (84.3%) were young adults' with age bellow 40 years old.

Table 2. Respondents institute & Gender distribution

Institute	Gender		Total
	Male	Female	
Addis Ababa Institute of Technology	42	13	55
Bahir Dar Institute of Technology	123	33	156
Ethio. Inst. of Textile & Fashion Techno.	54	16	70
Hawasa Institute of Technology	38	7	45
Jimma Institute of Technology	26	4	30
Total	**283(79.5%)**	**73(20.5%)**	**356**

In the study, it has been indicated that colleagues and friends were the main source of awareness about e-learning (46.6%). The available facilitating conditions (33.4%) and the management body of the institutions (28.4%) were the next sources of e-learning awareness respectively.

Table 3. Age & Educational qualifications distribution

Age	Educational qualifications			Total
	BSc	MSc	PhD	
21–30 years	77	101	1	179 (50.3%)
31–40 years	5	99	17	121(34%)
41–50 years	0	24	22	46 (12.9)
51–60 years	0	5	3	8 (2.2%)
Above 60 years	0	1	1	2 (0.6%)
Total	**82 (23%)**	**230 (64.6%)**	**44 (12.4%)**	**356**

As indicated in this study, about 40.5% of the teachers participated in the survey had bellow 5 years teaching experience. The next portion of respondents, i.e. 36.5% constitutes teachers with 6-10 years of teaching experience. The majority of study participants, i.e. 289 (81.2%) were informed about the presence of e-learning system platforms in their Institute. Regarding the level of awareness, 162 (45.5%) of respondents were well informed about the presence of e-learning system in their institute. Another 127 (35.7%) of respondents were somehow aware of e-learning systems. The remaining 67 (18.8%) of respondents were not informed at all about the presence and importance of e-learning systems in their Institute as shown Table 4.

Table 4. Experience * Awareness level cross-tabulation

Experience	Level of awareness			Total
	Awared	Awared to some extent	Not awared	
Bellow 5 Years	51	50	43	144 (40.5%)
6–10 Years	74	46	10	130 (36.5%)
11–15 Years	25	22	12	59 (16.6%)
16–20 Years	6	5	2	13 (3.7%)
Above 20 Years	6	4	0	10 (2.8%)
Total	**162 (45.5%)**	**127 (35.7%)**	**67 (18.8%)**	**356 (100%)**

4.2 E-Learning Readiness in the Technology Institutes of Ethiopian Universities

The readiness of respondents measured in a five point Likert scale has been presented for two major e-learning readiness constructs (employee readiness and organizational readiness). The employee readiness construct consisted of three parameters namely technical skill, awareness, & attitude readiness. Organization readiness construct had also other five parameters; infrastructural, top management, cultural, policy and technological readiness. The reliability of the 22 readiness questions on the survey has been measured on cronbach's alpha method of reliability statistics as depicted in Table 5.

Table 5. Reliability statistics of e-learning readiness items

Construct	Number of items	Cronbach's alpha coefficient
Employee readiness	6	0.744
Organizational readiness	16	0.894
Total	22	0.882

Therefore, reliability of 0.744 and 0.894 has been achieved for employee readiness and organizational readiness indicators respectively. In addition, the overall reliability of 0.882 for the 22 e-learning readiness items was found. These values had confirmed a strong consistency of the responses on the indicators of the study [21].

E-Learning Readiness Components and Indicators

A total of 22 indicators were used in this study. These 22 indicators were grouped in two core readiness components of employee readiness and organizational readiness. The employee readiness construct consisted of three parameters, namely technical skill, awareness and attitude. The organizational readiness construct embraces infrastructural, policy, cultural, technological and managerial readiness parameters. The means and standard deviations of all the indicators and constructs have been computed as shown in Table 6.

Table 6. Average e-learning readiness measures for each indicator

Employee readiness items		Mean			Std. deviation
Technical skill readiness	Basic knowledge & skills to use computers	4.70	4.45	4.20	0.594
	Basic skills to use the Internet	4.71			0.562
	Basic knowledge & skills to use e-learning systems	3.94			1.071
Awareness	Enough awareness about the importance of e-learning	4.13	4.13		1.065
Attitude	Prefer to use e-learning than the traditional methods	3.84	4.02		0.997
	I intend to use the e-learning systems in the future	4.19			0.736
Infrastructural readiness	Sufficient access to wireless and or wired Internet	3.53	3.17	2.77	1.206
	Sufficient internet speed to use e-learning	2.91			1.238
	Have the necessary resources to use e-learning	3.07			1.130
Cultural readiness	Institute has good culture of using new technologies	2.88	2.50		1.114
	Inclusion of e-learning usage plan in course outline	2.12			0.876
Policy readiness	Curricula designed properly to align with e-learning	2.36	2.35		0.934
	Institute has an e-learning implementation policy	2.33			0.911
Technology readiness	The e-learning system has all the necessary functionalities	3.20	3.20		1.088
Top management readiness	The top management involvement with e-learning function is strong	2.56	2.63		0.940
	The top management is interested in the e-learning function	2.74			0.962
	The top management understand the importance & opportunities of e-learning	2.88			.950
	The top management support & encourage me to use the e-learning system	2.65			0.966
	The top management consider e-learning as a strategic resource	2.72			0.957
	The top management puts pressure on departments to use e-learning	2.56			0.940
	The top management of my institute owns e-learning as a core task	2.43			0.954
	The top management has a strong commitment to implement e-learning	2.47			0.965

In order to measure the expected level of readiness, the average readiness level for each construct in general and for each indicator in particular were computed as shown in Table 6. The results were compared against the expected level of readiness standards [17].

As the model clearly depicted 3.41 to be the expected level of readiness, the 4.20 average score of employee readiness implies that teachers were ready to use the e-learning systems. This is because; the 4.20 employee readiness index was higher than the expected level of readiness (3.40). The readiness index was computed for the three parameters of employee readiness (employees' technical skill = 4.45, awareness = 4.13 and attitude = 4.02). The employees' technical skill readiness index, TR = 4.45, clearly showed that teachers had sufficient technical skill to use e-learning systems. In terms of (attitude = 4.02 and awareness = 4.13), teachers were ready to use e-learning systems, yet needs some support and improvements. Therefore, academic institutions have no problem related to employee readiness to implement e-learning systems.

The organizational readiness index (OR = 2.77) was found bellow the expected level of readiness. Readiness index for all organizational parameters (Infrastructural Readiness = 3.17, Cultural Readiness = 2.50, Policy Readiness = 2.35, management readiness = 2.63 and Technological Readiness = 3.20) had been computed. The average readiness scores for infrastructure, technology and management lay under the category "not ready that needs the academic institutions to do some work to get ready" since their scores are between 2.61 and 3.40 cut points. The policy and cultural readiness index values lay between 1.81 and 2.60 cut points that indicated the academic institutions are not ready to implement e-learning and need a lot of work to get ready. Therefore, the management body of those institutions should play important roles and responsibly in creating favorable e-learning implementation environments. All other parameters can be expressed as a function management support and commitment as the top management is responsible to expand the infrastructure, establish good culture, policy, awareness and attitude and adopt new technologies.

5 Conclusion

Measuring e-learning readiness of universities is very crucial to utilize the advantages of new technologies. The study has revealed that universities have achieved good level of readiness in terms of employee readiness parameters (technical skill, awareness and attitude). The highest readiness index has been achieved for technical skill parameter. However, the organizational readiness parameters (like cultural, policy, management and technological readiness) have shown low level of readiness index to implement and use e-learning systems in universities. The worst readiness index was registered in the policy and cultural readiness parameters. The support and commitment of the top management was also found far below the readiness cut point index. This showed that universities shall improve their institutional weaknesses to implement e-learning systems and encourage teachers to use the technology.

6 Recommendation

According to the findings achieved so far in this study, the following recommendations are suggested to improve the utilization of e-learning systems in technology institutes of Ethiopian Universities. Besides, recommendations for future works are also forwarded.

The first suggestions recommended for the management body of the institutes at different administration levels. In order to be successful in e-learning implementation, members of the top management in those institutions should:

- Improve the infrastructures like internet connectivity, speed and accessibility in their campuses to succeed in e-learning.
- Design and deploy an e-learning implementation policy.
- Encourage and support their staff to build a better culture of applying new technologies.
- Encourage and support teachers to integrate e-learning usage plan while preparing their course guide books.

The recommendation for further research is the second suggestion. In this study, only teachers of the five technology institution were considered. Therefore, considering student respondents is another area to extend the study. In addition, incorporating respondents from all disciplines in study can also be another topic to deal with.

References

1. Parlakkılıç, A.: E-learning readiness in medicine: Turkish family medicine (FM) physicians case. Turkish Online J. Educ. Technol. **14**(2), 59–62 (2015)
2. Rohayani, A.H.H., Kurniabudi, Sharipuddin: A literature review: readiness factors to measuring e-learning readiness in higher education. Procedia Comput. Sci. **59**(Iccsci), 230–234 (2015)
3. Rais, M., Karim, A., Hashim, Y.: The experience of the e-learning implementation at the Universiti Pendidikan Sultan Idris, Malaysia. Malaysian Online J. Instr. Technol. **1**(1), 50–59 (2004)
4. Borotis, S., Poulymenakou, A.: Critical Success Factors for e-Learning Adoption: Handbook of Research on Instructional Systems and Technology, pp. 131–134. IGI Global, Greece (2008)
5. Ouma, G.O., Awuor, F.M., Kyambo, B.: E-learning readiness in public secondary schools in Kenya. Eur. J. Open, Distance, E-Learn. **16**(2), 97–110 (2013)
6. Arkorful, V., Abaidoo, N.A.: The role of e-learning, advantages and disadvantages of its adoption in higher education. Int. J. Instr. Technol. Distance Learn. **12**(1), 29–43 (2015)
7. Li, J., Ray, P., Seale, H., MacIntyre, R.: An e-health readiness assessment framework for public health services–pandemic perspective. In: 2012 45th Hawaii International Conference on System Sciences, pp. 2800–2809 (2012)
8. Jennett, P., et al.: Preparing for success: readiness models for rural telehealth. J. Postgrad. Med. **51**(4), 279–285 (2005)
9. Weiner, B.J., Lee, S.D.: Conceptualization and measurement of organizational readiness for change: a review of the literature in health services research and other fields. Med. Care Res. Rev. **65**(4), 379–436 (2008)

10. Alem, F., Plaisent, M., Zuccaro, C., Bernard, P.: Measuring e-Learning readiness concept: scale development and validation using structural equation modeling. Int. J. e-Educ. e-Bus. e-Manag. e-Learn. **6**(4), 193–207 (2016)
11. Mosa, A.A., Naz'ri bin Mahrin, M., Ibrrahim, R.: Technological aspects of e-learning readiness in higher education: a review of the literature. Comput. Inf. Sci. **9**(1), 113 (2016)
12. Ngampornchai, A., Adams, J.: Students' acceptance and readiness for e-learning in Northeastern Thailand. Int. J. Educ. Technol. High. Educ. **13**(1), 34 (2016)
13. Schreurs, J., Ehlers, U.D., Sammour, G.: E-learning readiness analysis (ERA): an e-health case study of e-learning readiness. Int. J. Knowl. Learn. **4**(5), 496 (2008)
14. Ouma, G.O., Awuor, F.M., Kyambo, B.: Evaluation of e-learning readiness in secondary schools in Kenya. World Appl. Program. **310**, 493–503 (2013)
15. Darab, B., Montazer, G.A.: An eclectic model for assessing e-learning readiness in the Iranian universities. Comput. Educ. **56**(3), 900–910 (2011)
16. Al-mamary, Y.H., Shamsuddin, A., Aziati, A.H.N.: Key factors enhancing acceptance of management information systems in Yemeni companies. J. Bus. Manag. Res. **5**, 108–111 (2014)
17. Aydin, C.H., Tasci, D.: Measuring readiness for e-learning: reflections from an emerging country. Educ. Technol. Soc. **8**(4), 244–257 (2005)
18. Cochran, W.G.: Sampling techniques. Wiley, Hoboken (1977)
19. Ayele, A.A., Birhanie, W.K.: Acceptance and use of e-learning systems: the case of teachers in technology institutes of Ethiopian Universities. Appl. Inf. **5**(1), 1–11 (2018). https://doi.org/10.1186/s40535-018-0048-7
20. McColl, E., et al.: Design and use of questionnaires: a review of best practice applicable to surveys of health service staff and patients. Core Res. **5**(31), 101–174 (2001)
21. Chin, W.W.: The partial least squares approach to structural equation modeling. Modern Methods Bus. Res. **295**(2), 295–336 (1998)

Reconfigurable Integrated Cryptosystem for Secure Data Exchanges Between Fog Computing and Cloud Computing Platforms

Abiy Tadesse Abebe[1]([✉]), Yalemzewd Negash Shiferaw[1], and P. G. V. Suresh Kumar[2]

[1] Addis Ababa Institute of Technology, AAU, Addis Ababa, Ethiopia
abiytds@yahoo.com, yalemzewdn@yahoo.com
[2] Ambo University, Ambo, Ethiopia
pendemsuresh@gmail.com

Abstract. This study is aimed to propose a cryptosystem which integrates only two algorithms for secure data transmissions during fog nodes to cloud server communications. It provides a method of authenticated key distribution and authenticated encryption with robust and multiple crypto services. It is optimized for high throughput achievement based on FPGA to improve the efficiency of the existing hybrid cryptosystems and integrated encryption schemes which incorporated many independent algorithms for strong security. The separate keys which are needed for each component algorithm leading to extra key management and key storage requirements and the overall hardware complexity with increased computation cost are some of the limitations of the existing methods. The implementation outcomes show the efficiency, enhanced throughput, and reasonable resource utilization of the proposed method compared to the existing reported outcomes. It can be suitable for securing data exchanges among high performance computing environments including secure communications between fog computing layer and central cloud which require high speed cryptosystems with strong security and lower latency.

Keywords: AEGIS · Authenticated encryption · FPGA · Integrated cryptosystem · Key distribution · RSA

1 Introduction

For effective utilization of the advantages of the modern cryptographic mechanisms such as symmetric key and asymmetric key algorithms, hash functions, Message Authentication Code (MAC) generators, and digital signature algorithms [1], many researchers have proposed various methods. They have increased the capabilities of the existing algorithms in terms of performance and security. For instance, the authenticated encryption algorithms [2, 3] which can provide data confidentiality, data integrity, and data origin authentication services simultaneously using only one algorithm are improvements over symmetric key algorithms. Similarly, signcryption methods [4, 5] which can provide data confidentiality and digital signature crypto services simultaneously using only one

© ICST Institute for Computer Sciences, Social Informatics and Telecommunications Engineering 2020
Published by Springer Nature Switzerland AG 2020. All Rights Reserved
N. G. Habtu et al. (Eds.): ICAST 2019, LNICST 308, pp. 492–501, 2020.
https://doi.org/10.1007/978-3-030-43690-2_35

algorithm are improvements over the public key algorithms. Despite their advantages, the authenticated encryption and signcryption methods generally share the inherent limitations of symmetric and asymmetric key algorithms. Symmetric key algorithms are efficient, but are limited by the lack of key distribution capability requiring sharing of secret key before starting secret communications. The asymmetric key algorithms have circumvented the need of sharing of secret key by providing key pair, one for encryption and another for decryption. But, their performance is generally considered as slower because of the intensive mathematical operations needed for encryption and decryption processes.

To provide more crypto services for strong security, various researchers have proposed hybrid cryptosystems [6, 7] and integrated encryption schemes such as Diffie-Hellman Integrated Encryption Scheme (DHIES) [8] and Elliptic Curve Integrated Encryption Scheme (ECIES) [9] by integrating different crypto mechanisms. The main goal of these methods has been to effectively utilize the advantages of the different cryptographic mechanisms particularly the symmetric key and asymmetric key algorithms so that the combined cryptosystem could use the symmetric key algorithm for large amount of data encryption and decryption while using the asymmetric key algorithm for key distribution. As a result, cryptosystems as efficient as the symmetric key algorithms and as secured as asymmetric key algorithms have been developed in addition to the services of hashing, MAC generation, and digital signature.

Secure information exchanges between central cloud servers and the recently introduced intermediate layer called fog computing layer, which is sited between the cloud and the Internet of Things (IoT) devices for efficient communication, require high speed cryptosystems which can provide high throughput and low latency along with major cryptographic services for strong security, as the attack surface is wider [10]. Therefore, hardware based implementations of cryptosystems are useful to provide high speed performance as well as physical security. Depending on the application scenarios, FPGA based implementations are preferable as they can be reconfigured based on the contemporary attack risks and are also as flexible as software for implementations and as high speed as hardware in terms of performance [11]. In this work, our aim is to effectively utilize and optimize the existing crypto mechanisms and provide the major cryptographic security services along with better performance suitable for the intended application by integrating only few number of algorithms while saving extra costs of key management, key storage, and hardware complexity compared to existing similar FPGA based implementations.

The rest of the paper is organized as follows: Sect. 2 describes related works. Section 3 describes the background of the algorithms used in this work. Section 4 explains the proposed method. Implementation approaches are described in Sect. 5. Section 6 presents the implementation outcomes. Finally, Sect. 5 concludes the paper.

2   Related Works

Several researchers have proposed various techniques to increase the capabilities of the existing standard cryptographic algorithms in terms of performance and security. In addition to authenticated encryption algorithms [2, 3] and signcryption methods [4, 5], hybrid cryptosystems [6, 7] and integrated encryption schemes have been proposed to enhance the efficiencies of such schemes, and at the same time, to remove their inherent limitations. Integrated Encryption Schemes such as Diffie Hellman Integrated Encryption Scheme (DHIES) [8] and Elliptic Curve Integrated Encryption Scheme (ECIES) [9] are standardized methods integrating different cryptographic mechanisms such as hash function, message authentication code algorithm, Key Derivation Function (KDF), in addition to the encryption algorithm and key exchange protocol [8, 9]. Moreover, some hybrid cryptosystems have also included digital signature algorithm [7]. Since these cryptosystems combined four or more different algorithms to provide more cryptographic security services such as data confidentiality, data integrity, authentication, non-repudiation, etc., where each component algorithm requiring a separate key for security purpose [8, 9], the key management, key storage, and compatibility issues as well as the overall storage space requirement with significant hardware complexity of the system need critical considerations.

The FPGA based integrated cryptosystem proposed in this work incorporates a public key scheme and an authenticated encryption algorithm to provide authenticated key distribution and authenticated information exchange for secure communications between fog computing and the cloud using only two algorithms for improved performance, lower latency, and reduced hardware complexity.

3 Background

3.1 AEGIS-128 Algorithm

AEGIS-128 algorithm [12] is an Advanced Encryption Standard (AES) [13] based algorithm which uses the AES round functions such as Sub Bytes, Shift Rows, Mix Columns, and Add Round Key, excluding the last round. AEGIS-128 algorithm uses 128 bits key and 128 bits Initialization Vector (IV) to perform authenticated encryption and authenticated decryption processes. It can process less than 2^{64} lengths of plaintext and the associated data. The recommended length of the tag to be used for authentication is 128 bits, though lesser lengths of tags can also be used.

The algorithm uses the round functions to update the 640 bits (80 bytes) of state, S_i, with 128 bits (16 bytes) of data blocks, m_i, using its state update function such that: $S_{i+1} = StateUpdate128(S_i, m_i)$ as shown in Fig. 1. In Fig. 1, $\mathbf{R}$ indicates the AES encryption round function not being XORed with the round key. w is a temporary 16-byte word. The process can also be expressed step by step as follows:

$$S_{i+1,0} = AESRound(S_{i,4}, S_{i,0} \oplus m_i);$$

$$S_{i+1,1} = AESRound(S_{i,0}, S_{i,1});$$

$$S_{i+1,2} = AESRound(S_{i,1}, S_{i,2});$$

$$S_{i+1,3} = AESRound(S_{i,2}, S_{i,3});$$

$$S_{i+1,4} = AESRound(S_{i,3}, S_{i,4});$$

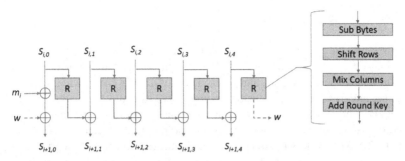

Fig. 1. The state update function of AEGIS-128

AEGIS-128 performs different execution steps including initialization, process of the authenticated data, encryption, and finalization. The decryption process follows the reverse order of the encryption, and requires the exact values of key size, *IV* size, and tag size for decryption and verification tasks. The details of AEGIS-128 algorithm can be found in [12]. It is designed for the security of high performance applications.

3.2 RSA Algorithm

The RSA algorithm is a public key crypto scheme which was proposed by Rivest, Shamir, and Adleman in 1978 [14]. Its security strength relies on the factorization of large integer numbers, and as the key size increases, the security strength of the RSA algorithm also increases [14].

RSA uses two keys, a public key and a private key, which are mathematically related, but are difficult to obtain one by knowing only the other. Generation of the RSA keys is done based on the following key steps:

- Selection of two large secret primes p and q.
- Calculation of a public modulus $n = p.q$.
- Computation of $\phi(n) = (p-1).(q-1)$, where, $\phi(n)$ is called Euler's totient function.
- Selecting the public exponent $e \in \{1, 2, \ldots, \phi(n) - 1\}$, such that e is relatively prime to $\phi(n)$, i.e., $GCD(e, \phi(n)) = 1$.
- Computation of the private key, d, such that $d.e \equiv 1 \bmod \phi(n)$, that means $d = e^{-1} \bmod \phi(n)$.

The public key generated is: $Pub_{key} = (e, n)$ and the private key is: $Priv_{key} = (d, n)$.

Encryption and Decryption processes are performed by applying modular exponentiation operation as shown by Eqs. (1) and (2), where, plaintext block M is encrypted to a ciphertext block C by Eq. (1) and the plaintext block M is obtained by Eq. (2) [14]:

$$C = M^e \bmod n \tag{1}$$

$$M = C^d \bmod n \tag{2}$$

4 The Proposed Method

For the security of the data exchanges during the communication between fog layer to the cloud server, we integrated AEGIS-128, a high speed authenticated encryption algorithm, and RSA, a public key algorithm. The AEGIS-128 can provide data confidentiality, data integrity, and authentication crypto services simultaneously, whereas RSA can provide encryption and digital signature security services simultaneously. Using only these two algorithms, the required major cryptographic security services can be obtained. The AEGIS-128 is intended for authenticated encryption/decryption of the actual large amount of data with high speed, and RSA is used for encryption/decryption of the secret key (the small amount of data) for key distribution with crypto services including digital signature, validation of data integrity, and verification of authenticity.

Figure 2 shows the structure of the proposed FPGA based integrated cryptosystem. Before any secure communication is started, it is assumed that the two communicating parties are agreed on the public parameters and have generated their independent key pair (a private key and a public key), and have exchanged the public keys through a trusted certificate authority or any other agreed secure method, but keeping their individual private keys secret. As shown in Fig. 2(a), at the sending end, a randomly generated symmetric key is used for encryption of the large amount data (plaintext) using AEGIS-128 algorithm. This same symmetric key is encrypted and signed by the public key of the recipient and the private key of the sender respectively, using the RSA algorithm. The ciphertext and MAC outputs of AEGIS-128 and the encrypted and signed key of RSA are then sent to the receiving end. At the receiving end, as shown in Fig. 2(b), RSA first verifies the signature using the public key of the sender. It performs decryption of the encrypted key using the private key of the recipient if and only if the signature is true; otherwise, it discards the received data. When the signature is valid and the symmetric key is recovered, then, RSA supplies the symmetric key to AEGIS-128. When the symmetric key is ready, the AEGIS starts the decryption process after validating the authenticity of the data origin and checking data integrity by comparing the received authentication tag T and the calculated authentication tag T' to ensure the validity of the received data. The plaintext will be obtained, accepted and further processed if and only if the two tags T and T' are equal; otherwise, error signal will be generated indicating invalid data reception, and then, the data will be immediately discarded before being utilized.

In this system, the RSA signature doesn't require hashing since it encrypts and signs a symmetric key which has only 128 bit key length (small data). The signature is used to ensure that the symmetric key is sent by a claimed sender. The ciphertext is not signed by the RSA since it is considered to be large amount data and effects the performance of the system. Instead, the AEGIS-128 performs encryption/decryption tasks of the large data and validates the authenticity of the data and checks the data integrity. Any modification which might be made by man-in-the-middle on the transported encrypted key or the ciphertext would be detected by RSA and AEGIS-128 respectively, since both schemes can validate authenticity and check data integrity; therefore, the data will be discarded if it is invalid.

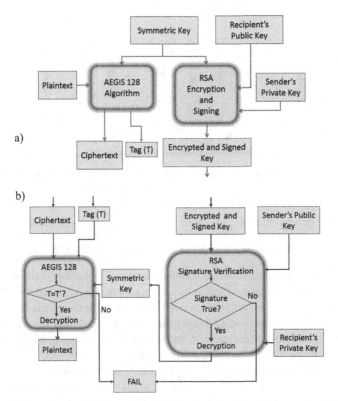

Fig. 2. Schematic structure of the proposed integrated cryptosystem: (a) Sending end (b) Receiving end

5 Implementation Approaches

The integrated cryptosystem composing AEGIS-128 authenticated encryption algorithm and, RSA public key scheme, has been implemented on Xilinx Virtex 5, Virtex 7, and Virtex II FPGA devices and synthesized using Xilinx ISE 14.5, Vivado Design Suite 2017.2, and Xilinx ISE 10.1, respectively. VHDL was used as a hardware description language.

As AEGIS-128 is an Advance Encryption Standard (AES) based authenticated encryption algorithm, for improving its throughput performance, we applied pipelined AES on the round operations for concurrent processing of the state in a clock cycle. In pipelining optimization technique [15], construction of the pipeline is performed by inserting registers at each round as shown in Fig. 3 [15]. The number of the pipeline steps, denoted by K, decides how many rounds should be executed in parallel to speed up the process. It is called a fully pipelined architecture if K is made to be equal to the total number of rounds in the algorithm. The required area and the target latency of the pipelining architecture are related to the applied number of K. By processing multiple blocks of date at the same time, the technique can increase the encryption and decryption

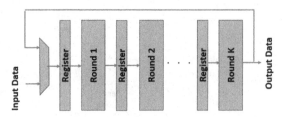

Fig. 3. Pipeline architecture

processes. In AEGIS-128 algorithm, five AES rounds are used. In this work, AEGIS-128 with 128 bits key and 128 bits blocks of data are implemented.

As the pipeline method processes encryption, decryption, or authentication in one clock cycle, the general throughput can be calculated as shown by Eq. (3):

$$Throughput\ (TP) = Max.Frequency\ x\ 128 \tag{3}$$

For RSA, as it involves modular exponentiation, Montgomery algorithm [16] is used to perform the modular multiplication. In this work, RSA is used only for encrypt and sign at the sending end, and then, verify and decrypt at the receiving end. This is performed as follows: let the sender wants to send an encrypted and signed message to a recipient. Let M denotes the message, d_s the sender's private key, and e_r the recipient's public key. Then, the sender encrypts the message M using the recipient's public key, e_r, as: $C = M^{e_r} \bmod n$, where, C is the ciphertext. The sender now signs a signature S by computing: $S = C^{d_s} \bmod n$. The sender then sends C and S to the receiving end. It is also possible to encrypt the signed result again by the public key of the recipient for more security (encrypt-sign-encrypt) as: $S_c = S^{e_r} \bmod n$. At the receiving end, verification of the signature and then decryption of the ciphertext will be performed as follows: let d_r be a private key of the recipient, and e_s, the public key of the sender. Verification of the signature is performed by computing: $S' = S^{e_s} \bmod n$, and if $C = S'$, the data is authentic, and then, decryption of the ciphertext will be performed to get the original data as: $M = C^{d_r} \bmod n$. Otherwise (if $C \neq S'$), all the received data will be discarded. When encrypt-sign-encrypt method is used, first, decryption of S_c is performed using private key of the recipient as: $S = S_c^{d_r} \bmod n$, keeping the other steps similar. For this work, RSA with 1024 bits modulus is used and integrated with AEGIS-128.

At the sending end, an '*Encrypt*' signal is asserted high so that both algorithms could read the symmetric key as input. A simple FSM control mechanism is used to synchronize the work of the two algorithms as an integrated system during decryption as shown in Fig. 4. A '*Start*' signal, which is in low state, setting the system in idle condition, will be asserted high when data is received. Then, RSA signature verification process will be started. When signature is true, the encrypted key will be decrypted. Then, the '*Sign*' signal will be high and the symmetric key will be supplied to AEGIS-128 decryption process making the AEGIS-128 '*Busy*' signal high. Otherwise, the key will be discarded and the system will return to the idle state again. When AEGIS-128 is busy with decryption process, the '*Busy*' signal is asserted high and waits until decryption process finishes. When the decryption process ends, the '*Busy*' signal becomes low and the system goes to idle state.

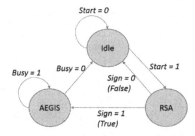

Fig. 4. A simple FSM control mechanism

6 Results

The implementation of the proposed integrated cryptosystem is performed on Xilinx Virtex 5, Virtex 7, and Virtex II FPGA devices for the purpose of comparison with the existing works. Tables 1, 2, and 3 show the performance comparisons of the proposed work with the existing reported outcomes. The FPGA resources consumed and the maximum frequency as well as the throughput achieved are presented in Table 1 compared to the results in [17]. In this case, the optimization method used by [17] is LUT based, whereas the present work used pipelining method. The implementation target of the present work is high throughput as mathematically expressed by Eq. (3). Therefore, for Virtex 5 device, our work achieved a throughput of 41.55 Gbps with area cost of 5478 slices and 4 BRAMs. For Virtex 7 device, this work achieved lesser area and better throughput compared to the work of [18] for the same pipelined optimization approach as shown in Table 2. Comparison of consumed FPGA resources on Virtex II device for the whole integrated cryptosystem of the present work with the ECIES implementation results reported by [19] is shown in Table 3. Smaller space utilization (slices and BRAMs) are shown in Table 3 for the present work compared to the reported outcomes of [19].

Table 1. Performance Comparison

Author	Target Device	Design	Slices	BRAM	Freq. (MHz)	Thrpt. (Gbps)
This work	Virtex 5	Pipelined	5478	4	324.6	41.55
[17]	Virtex 5	LUT based	1391	0	156.5	20.03

Contributions. The proposed method extends the capability of the authenticated encryption algorithm by integrating it with authenticated key distribution mechanism for strong security. It also increases the effectiveness of hybrid cryptosystems or integrated encryption schemes by reducing the extra key management and key storage requirements as well as hardware complexity. Integration of only two algorithms and providing

Table 2. Performance Comparison

Author	Target Device	Design	Slices	Thrpt. (Mbps)
This work	Virtex 7	Pipelined	9306	89354
[18]	Virtex 7	Pipelined	10610	88564

Table 3. Performance Comparison

Author	Target Device	Design	Slices	BRAM
This work	Virtex II	Hybrid of AEGIS + RSA	14572	4
	Virtex II	ECIES	21194	20

multiple crypto services for strong security as well as FPGA implementation and optimization of it for high throughput suitable for fog – cloud secure communications is another contribution of this study.

7   Conclusions and Future Work

An integrated cryptosystem using AEGIS-128 for authenticated encryption of actual data and RSA for authenticated key distribution by encrypting and signing of the symmetric key, has been implemented on different FPGA devices for fog-cloud security. The proposed cryptosystem has used only two algorithms providing multiple crypto services while saving extra key management and key storage requirements, as well as reducing computation costs. The implementation results show enhanced throughput achievement and reasonable FPGA resource utilization as compared to the existing reported outcomes of similar works. By applying additional optimization methods, we will further improve it to get smaller area and higher throughput.

References

1. Stinson, D.R., Paterson, M.B.: Cryptography Theory and Practice, 4th edn, pp. 1–9. CRC Press, Boca Raton (2019)
2. McGrew, D., Viega, J.: The Galois/Counter Mode of operation (GCM). Submission to NIST, May 2005
3. Koteshwara, S., Das, A.: Comparative study of authenticated encryption targeting lightweight IoT applications. IEEE Des. Test **34**(4), 26–33 (2017)

4. Pang, L., Kou, M., Wei, M., Li, H.: Efficient anonymous certificateless multi-receiver sign-cryption scheme without bilinear pairings. IEEE Access **6**, 78123–78135 (2018). https://doi.org/10.1109/access.2018.2884798

5. Zia, M., Ali, R.: Cryptanalysis and improvement of blind signcryption scheme based on elliptic curve. Electron. Lett. (2019). https://doi.org/10.1049/el.2019.0032

6. Gutub, A.A, Khan, F.A.: Hybrid crypto hardware utilizing symmetric-key & public-key cryptosystems. In: IEEE International Conference on Advanced Computer Science Applications and Technologies (ACSAT), pp. 116–121 (2013)

7. Alkady, Y., Habib, M.I., Rizk, R.Y.: A new security protocol using hybrid cryptography algorithms. In: IEEE International Computer Engineering Conference (ICENCO), pp. 109–115 (2013)

8. Abdalla, M., Bellare, M., Rogaway, P.: The oracle Diffie-Hellman assumptions and an analysis of DHIES. In: Naccache, D. (ed.) CT-RSA 2001. LNCS, vol. 2020, pp. 143–158. Springer, Heidelberg (2001). https://doi.org/10.1007/3-540-45353-9_12

9. Martínez, V.G., Encinas, L.H., Dios, A.Q.: Security and practical considerations when implementing the elliptic curve integrated encryption scheme. Cryptologia **39**(3), 244–269 (2015). https://doi.org/10.1080/01611194.2014.988363

10. Martin, et al.: OpenFog security requirements and approaches. In: IEEE Communications Society Invited Paper, November 2017

11. Rodríguez-Andina, J., Torre-Arnanz, E., Valdés-Peña, M.: FPGAs Fundamentals, Advanced Features, and Applications in Industrial Electronics. CRC Press, Boca Raton (2017)

12. Wu, H., Preneel, B.: AEGIS: a fast authenticated encryption algorithm. In: Lange, T., Lauter, K., Lisoněk, P. (eds.) SAC 2013. LNCS, vol. 8282, pp. 185–201. Springer, Heidelberg (2014). https://doi.org/10.1007/978-3-662-43414-7_10

13. FIPS Publication 197, the Advanced Encryption Standard (AES), U.S. DoC/NIST, November 2001

14. Rivest, R.L., Shamir, A., Adleman, L.: A method for obtaining digital signature and public-keycryptosystems. Commun. ACM **21**, 120–126 (1978)

15. Tadesse Abebe, A., Negash Shiferaw, Y., Gebeye Abera, W., Kumar, P.G.V.S.: Efficient FPGA implementation of an integrated bilateral key confirmation scheme for pair-wise key-establishment and authenticated encryption. In: Zimale, F.A., Enku Nigussie, T., Fanta, S.W. (eds.) ICAST 2018. LNICST, vol. 274, pp. 429–438. Springer, Cham (2019). https://doi.org/10.1007/978-3-030-15357-1_36

16. Montgomery, P.: Modular multiplication without trial division. Math. Comput. **44**, 519–521 (1985)

17. Abdellatif, K.M., Chotin-Avot, R., Mehrez, H.: AES-GCM and AEGIS: efficient and high speed hardware implementations. J. Signal Process. Syst. **88**(1), 1–12 (2016). https://doi.org/10.1007/s11265-016-1104-y

18. Katsaiti, M., Sklavos, N.: Implementation Efficiency and Alternations, on CAESAR Finalists: AEGIS Approach, pp. 661–665. https://doi.org/10.1109/dasc/picom/datacom/cyberscitec.2018.00117

19. Sandoval, M.M., Uribe, C.F.: A hardware architecture for elliptic curve cryptography and loss-less data compression. In: IEEE International Conference on Electronics, Communications and Computers, pp. 113–118 (2005)

Ethiopic Natural Scene Text Recognition Using Deep Learning Approaches

Direselign Addis$^{(\boxtimes)}$, Chuan-Ming Liu, and Van-Dai Ta

Department of Computer Science and Information Engineering,
National Taipei University of Technology, Taipei, Taiwan
{t106999405,cmliu,t104999002}@ntut.edu.tw

Abstract. The success of deep learning approaches for scene text recognition in English, Chinese and Arabic language inspired us to pose a benchmark scene text recognition for Ethiopic script. To transcribe the word images to the cross bonding text, we use a segmentation free end-to-end trainable Convolutional and Recurrent Neural Network (CRNN) hybrid architecture. In the network, robust representation features from cropped word images are extracted at convolutional layer and the extracted representations features are transcribed to a sequence of labels by the recurrent layer and transcription layer. The transcription is not bounded by lexicon or word length. Due to it is effective uses to transcribe sequence-to-sequence tasks, CTC loss is applied to train the network. In order to train the proposed model, we prepare synthetic word images from Unicode fonts of Ethiopic scripts, besides the model performance is evaluated on real scene text dataset collected from different sources. The experiment result of the proposed model, shows a promising result.

Keywords: Scene text recognition · Deep learning · Ethiopic script

1 Introduction

Extracting and analyzing scene text information found in the natural image, which carries high-level semantics has an extensive variety of uses including content-based image retrieval, tourist assistance, instant translation, assist visually impaired person, unmanned ground vehicle navigation, etc. Due to these, scene text recognition in computer vision and document analysis fields has recently received increasing attention. However, the diversity and variability of texts in natural images, such as written in different languages, available in different font colors, font styles, font sizes, text orientations, and shapes are the main challenges to develop a robust scene text detection method. Moreover, the complexity of unpredictable backgrounds and poor imaging conditions due to low resolution and severe distortions [1] are another challenges.

To ease the challenges of scene text recognition, several methods are proposed using traditional and deep learning techniques. The traditional algorithms were tested while the results were not satisfactory. Recently, the limitations of traditional algorithms in different areas are addressed using deep learning techniques and it shows a promising

© ICST Institute for Computer Sciences, Social Informatics and Telecommunications Engineering 2020
Published by Springer Nature Switzerland AG 2020. All Rights Reserved
N. G. Habtu et al. (Eds.): ICAST 2019, LNICST 308, pp. 502–511, 2020.
https://doi.org/10.1007/978-3-030-43690-2_36

result. In addition to its recognition performance, the deep learning techniques facilitate end-to-end trainable methods by freeing researchers from the exhaustive work of repeatedly designing and testing hand-crafted features.

The task of scene text recognition method in traditional approach possesses preprocessing, character segmentation and character recognition phases whereas in deep learning approach text detection and recognizing the detected text is the main tasks. In both traditional and deep learning approaches, several methods are proposed for scene text detection including Connected Components Analysis [2, 3], Sliding Window [4], MSER [5], EAST [6], SegLink [7], Corner localization [8], PixelLink [9] and TextSnake [10]. Using these scene text detection methods, several researchers proposed recognition methods such as RNN stacked with CNN [11], sequence prediction with attention-based models [17]. And they got promising scene text detection and recognition performance for Latin, Arabic, and Chinese scripts. However, there is no research for Ethiopic script as far as the researchers' knowledge is concerned.

Ethiopic script which is previously known as Ge'ez (ግዕዝ) is one of the oldest writing systems in the world [12]. It uses as a writing system for more than 43 languages including Amharic, Geez, Tigrigna, and others. The script has been largely used by Ge'ez and Amharic language, which are the liturgical and official languages of Ethiopia and some states of USA, respectively. The script is written down in a tabular format in which the first denotes the base character and the other columns are vowels derived from the base characters by slightly deforming or modifying the base characters. Ethiopic script has a total of 466 characters, out of these, twenty characters are digits, nine characters are punctuation marks, and the remaining 437 characters are alphabets. Developing a scene text recognition system for Ethiopic script is challenging, due to availability of similar characters especially between base characters and the derived vowels and there are number of many characters. Furthermore, unavailability of training and testing datasets are another limitation in the development of a model that can detect and recognize scene texts written in Ethiopic scripts.

In this paper, we use a modified version of CRNN [11] hybrid network that can train in an end-to-end manner. In addition, we prepare a synthetic and real dataset for training and testing the proposed model, respectively. In summary, the contributions of this paper are listed as follows:

- For training the proposed model, synthetic scene text datasets are prepared by changing the background textures and images, colors of text and other parameters.
- For testing the proposed model and to benchmark the recognition performance, hundreds of real scene text dataset was prepared.
- A segmentation free and end-to-end trainable CRNN model is employed.

The rest of the paper is presented as follows; previous related works are introduced in Sect. 2. In Sect. 3, we discuss about the proposed CRNN hybrid network. The experiment set-up, dataset and experiment results with discussions are conveyed in Sect. 4. To end, the conclusion and recommendations are drawn in Sect. 5.

2 Related Work

Scene text detection and recognition is currently the active area of research in computer vision and document analysis. In this section, we provide a short introduction to previous related works on methods of text detection and recognition.

2.1 Text Detection

Scene text detection is the sub process of text reading problem from natural images. Its main objective is to detect text areas from the given natural input image using different methods. Researchers uses different approaches to detect text areas from a natural image. Sliding window [4] and connected component [2, 3] methods are the most common conventional approaches for detecting scene text by considering the text as a composition of characters. Recently, deep learning techniques are applied to directly detect words from a natural image. As stated in [13], a vertical anchor mechanism was used to predict the fixed width sequential proposals and then connect them. Ma et al. [14] presents a novel rotation-based framework based on region proposal architecture for detecting arbitrary oriented texts from natural images. He et al. [7] presents deep direct regression methods for multi-oriented scene text detection. The model predicts words or text lines of arbitrary oriented and quadrilateral shapes in full images. In this paper, we focus on the recognition part of cropped scene images.

2.2 Text Recognition

In the text reading phases of natural images, text recognition is the second phase next to scene text detection. This method can be implemented independently or after scene text detection phases. In the scene text recognition phase, the cropped text regions are feed either from the scene text detection phase or from prepared input dataset and sequence of labels are decoded. Previous attempts were made by detecting individual characters and refine misclassified characters. Such a methods require training a strong character detector for accurately detecting and cropping each character out from the original word. These type of methods are more difficult for Ethiopic scripts due to its complexities. Despite to character level methods, word recognition [15], sequence to label [16], and sequence to sequence [17] methods are presented. Liu et al. [18] and Shi et al. [19] presents a spatial attention mechanism to transform a distorted text region from irregular input images into canonical pose suitable recognition. Shi et al. [11] presents a unique end-to-end trainable method by combining the robust convolutional features of CNN and transcription abilities of RNN. We use this design where the hybrid CNN-RNN network with a Connectionist Temporal Classification (CTC) loss is trained end-to-end.

3 CRNN Hybrid Architecture

The proposed CRNN hybrid network architecture has three fundamental components, including convolutional layers, recurrent layers, and transcription layers. The proposed CRNN hybrid network architecture is shown in Fig. 1. In the architecture, the image that contains scene texts are fed into the first convolutional layer then the sequences of features are extracted automatically using CNN network. Using the extracted sequence of features, the recurrent layer built prediction for each frame of the feature sequence. Finally, the transcription layer translates per-frame prediction into a label sequence by recurrent layers. The details of each layer are presented in the following subsections.

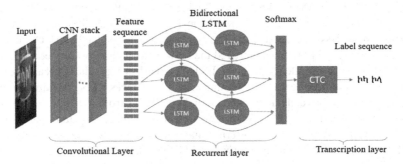

Fig. 1. The architecture of hybrid CRNN network

3.1 Convolutional Layer

The first layer of CRNN hybrid network architecture called convolutional layer is built based on the VGG [20] network architecture, with the exception of fully connected layers. The layer has a number of convolution and max-pooling layers. The convolution layer of CNN network extracts silent features of the input image such as edges, corners, and endpoints by applying convolution operation. From this operation, k-feature maps are extracted with the size of $(M - N + 1) \times (M - N + 1)$ from input images that have $M \times M$ square neuron nodes by using $N \times N$ convolutional kernel. The non-linearity decision function and the entire network is increased using the activation function in our case we use ReLU. Most commonly, the input images come in different sizes so that they have to be rescaled to the same size before being fed into the model. Max-pooling layer is another layer in CNN part of the model, which is periodically added between successive convolution layers and spatial invariance is achieved. In addition, the size of the representation feature maps, as well as the number of parameters and amount of computation in the network, are reduced, whereby overfitting is controlled. The extracted sequence of features from the input image uses as an input to the next recurrent layer.

3.2 Recurrent Layer

Next to convolutional layer, the recurrent layer is built using bidirectional RNN. The recurrent layer predicts a label y_t for each input frame x_t in the feature sequence $x_1, x_2, \ldots, x_T$. The advantages of using recurrent layer are can capture contextual information within a sequence, back propagate error differentials to its inputs, and able to work on a sequence of arbitrary lengths. Instead of treating each symbol independently, it is more stable and helpful to use contextual guide for image-based sequence recognition. In RNN, there are a number of self-connected hidden layers between input and output layers. As we discuss above the input for the recurrent layer is the output of the convolutional layer and after performing several recurrent operations, the recurrent layer predicts an output y_t. The predicted label y_t is based on the internal state h_t and also the value of hidden state h_t is determined based on the current input x_t, previous hidden state h_{t-1} and non-linear function. Mathematically described as $h_t = g(x_t, h_{t-1})$.

However, RNN have a limitation on learning long-term dependency. Because during training RNN with the gradient-based Backpropagation through time (BPTT) technique, it is difficult to build a precise model due to the vanishing and exploding gradient problems. To address this problem, LSTM networks was introduced by Hochreiter and Schmidhuber in 1997 [24], and improved the network structure by Gers et al. [25], to avoid the long-term dependency problem. LSTM network is a specific RNN architecture and state-of-the-art deep learning algorithm which introduces gates (i.e. input, output, and forget gate memory cells) to prevent gradient problems from vanishing and exploding. As the name indicates, the LSTM network can remember long-term values from several time steps as well as the short-term values. In this paper, we use two bidirectional LSTM designed by combining one forward and one backward LSTM.

3.3 Transcription Layer

Transcription layer is the last layer of the proposed CRNN network which takes the predictions from the recurrent layer and convert into label sequences by finding the highest probability. The transcription of label sequences can be performed either based on lexicon or lexicon free methods. In lexicon free methods, the prediction is made without lexicons whereas in lexicon based methods, highest probability label sequences are predicted from the collected lexicons. In this paper, we use a lexicon free transcription method to translate the predictions into label sequences for the target language.

4 Experiments and Results

4.1 Dataset Preparation

In any machine learning technique, dataset plays an important role to train and obtain a better machine learning model. Especially, deep learning methods are data hungry than traditional machine learning algorithms. However, preparing a large dataset was also a challenging task specifically for under resource languages. In [15], a deep learning based synthetic scene text dataset generation method was proposed. In this paper, we use a synthetically generated scene text dataset and real scene text dataset for training and testing the proposed model, respectively.

Synthetic Scene Text Dataset
As stated in [15], deep learning techniques are used to generate synthetic scene text datasets. The generated scene text images match similar to real scene images. This technique is very important to get more training data for those scripts that don't have prepared real scene text datasets. Using this technique, several synthetic scene text datasets are prepared to train and build a scene text recognition model, for instance,

Chinese, Arabic, Indian and Latin scripts. As far as the researchers' knowledge there is no prepared real scene text dataset for Ethiopic script. Therefore, using a similar approach, we prepare a synthetic scene text dataset for Ethiopic script.

To prepare the synthetic scene text dataset, 540,735 words (8, 250,800 characters) are collected from different social, political, and governmental websites written in Ethiopic script. Ethiopic script uses for more than 43 languages, even if we include all Ethiopic characters, the collected data is written in Amharic, Geez and Tigrigna languages. Using these collected words and freely available 72 Unicode fonts, words are rendered into the foreground layer of the image to form the synthetic scene images. To make more robust the generated synthetic scene images the font color, font size, rotation along horizontal line, skew and thickness parameters are tuned. In addition, we use different images as a background. Based on these, we generate 500K number of synthetic scene text word images. Sample images are shown in Fig. 2.

Fig. 2. Sample generated artificial scene text image

Real Scene Text Dataset
Besides to synthetic dataset, we prepare hundreds of real scene text benchmarking dataset collected from local markets, banners, navigation and traffic signs, billboards and image search using Google. After collecting the scene text images, equivalent texts of each image are annotated by bounding the text areas on the image. Based on this, we prepare around 2,500 scene text word images from hundreds of collected images. This dataset can also be used for the scene text detection task. In this paper, we only deal with the recognition of scene texts from the cropped word images. Sample real scene text images are shown in Fig. 3.

Fig. 3. Sample real scene text images before crop

4.2 Implementation Details

As discussed before, the hybrid CRNN network have convolution layer, recurrent layer, and transcription layer. The proposed CRNN network implementation detail is shown in Table 1. The convolution layer have a CNN network architecture which is designed based on the VGG architecture [20]. To get wider features from the input image and consecutive convolution layers, we use 1×2 pooling stride at the 3rd and 4th max-pooling layers instead of conventional 2×2 strides. To enable faster learning, the input images are converted into grayscale and rescaled into a fixed width and height (128×64) pixels. The training process for both CNN and RNN is very difficult in terms of computing power and time. To increase the training speed of the network, we add batch normalization [21] layers after 5th and 7th convolution layers. Even if batch normalization increases the training speed, the experiment shows that using at each convolution layer decreases the recognition performance.

After extracting features using convolution stacks, two BLSTM layers with 512 neurons are followed. The last BLSTM layer is fully connected with 467 number of label sequences, i.e. the number of characters in the script plus one additional extra label for blank. Finally, using the Softmax activation function on the outputs of the BLSTM layer, the CTC loss is calculated between the predicted probability and the actual value. Based on the variance between the predicted and the real values, the forward-backward [22] and backpropagation through time algorithm are applied to adjust the parameters of the network. The network parameters are optimized with AdaDelta optimization [23] while training the network using stochastic gradient descent (SGD).

The experiments are executed on Ubuntu machine containing Intel Core i7-7700 (3.60 GHz) CPU with 64 GB RAM and GeForce GTX 1080 Ti 11176 MiB GPU. For the implementation of the proposed system, we use Python 3.6 and library with TensorFlow backend.

Table 1. Configuration of the proposed network

Type	Configuration
Input	128×64 gray scale image
Conv2D	64, kernel 3×3, stride 1×1, padding 1×1
Max-pooling	Kernel 2×2, Stride 2×2
Conv2D	128, kernel 3×3, stride 1×1, padding 1×1
Max-Pooling	Kernel 2×2, Stride 2×2
Conv2D	256, kernel 3×3, stride 1×1, padding 1×1
Conv2D	256, kernel 3×3, stride 1×1, padding 1×1
Max-Pooling	Kernel 2×2, stride 1×2

(continued)

Table 1. (*continued*)

Type	Configuration
Conv2D	512, kernel 3 × 3, stride 1 × 1, padding 1 × 1, BN
Conv2D	512, kernel 3 × 3, stride 1 × 1, padding 1 × 1
Max-Pooling	Kernel 2 × 2, stride 1 × 2
Conv2D	512, kernel 3 × 3, stride 1 × 1, padding 1 × 1, BN
Map-to-sequence	–
BLSTM	#hidden 512
BLSTM	#hidden 512
Transcription	–

BN – stands for Batch normalization

4.3 Evaluation Metrics

The recognition performance of the hybrid CRNN network on the benchmarked real scene text dataset is evaluated at word level and character level using Word Recognition Rate (WRR) and Character Recognition Rate (CRR). CRR is the difference between total characters and the sum of Levenshtein distance between the Recognized Text (RT) and Ground Truth (GT) divided by the number of total characters.

$$CRR = \frac{C - \sum d(RT, GT)}{C} \tag{1}$$

where C is the number of total characters, d is the Levenshtein distance between RT and GT. Whereas WRR is computed by dividing the number of Correctly Recognized Text (CRT) by the number of Total Words (TW).

$$WRR = \frac{CRT}{TW} \tag{2}$$

4.4 Experiment Results and Discussion

The experiment is conducted to evaluate the recognition performance of the proposed hybrid CRNN network. Based on the network configurations stated above, the proposed model is trained using the prepared training dataset and its recognition performance is tested using testing datasets.

The recognition performance of the proposed model on the prepared real scene text dataset achieves 87.50% and 90.33%, WRR and CRR, respectively. In addition, to test the effects of using synthetic dataset, we test the proposed model using synthetic generated dataset and achieves a recognition performance of 94.35 and 97.23 for WRR and CRR, respectively. This shows that, using synthetic dataset has an important impact with some limitations because there is a big testing result difference between the real and synthetic testing dataset recognition results. This indicates that, using real scene text dataset for training the model will increase the current recognition performance of the proposed model. Sample recognition outputs are presented in Fig. 4.

Fig. 4. Sample predicted outputs

5   Conclusion

In this paper, we present a scene text recognition method which is written in Ethiopic scripts using CRNN hybrid network. The convolution layer of the network automatically extracts sequences of features from the input image and fed as an input to the next recurrent layer. The recurrent layer maps the sequence of extracted features into a sequence of labels. Finally, the CTC computes the loss between the predicted labeled sequences and the actual value. Using synthetically generated scene text dataset, the model is trained in an end-to-end fashion and its performance is evaluated using real scene text dataset collected from different sources. The experiment results show that the proposed model is promising. The introduction of new dataset and initial experiment results may introduce other researchers to pursue and improve scene text recognition which is written in Ethiopic script. In the future, we will increase the size of the real scene text dataset and incorporate a scene text detector rather than using cropped images. In addition, most commonly natural images contain more than one script, so we will conduct an end-to-end trainable multi script scene text detection, scene text recognition, and text spotting system.

References

1. Liang, J., Doermann, D., Li, H.: Camera-based analysis of text and documents: a survey. Int. J. Docu. Anal. Recogn. (IJDAR) **7**(2–3), 84–104 (2005)
2. Epshtein, B., Ofek, E., Wexler, Y.: Detecting text in natural scenes with stroke width transform. In: Proceedings of the 2010 IEEE Computer Society Conference on Computer Vision and Pattern Recognition, San Francisco, CA, USA, pp. 2963–2970. IEEE (2010)
3. Neumann, L., Matas, J.: A method for text localization and recognition in real-world images. In: Kimmel, R., Klette, R., Sugimoto, A. (eds.) ACCV 2010. LNCS, vol. 6494, pp. 770–783. Springer, Heidelberg (2011). https://doi.org/10.1007/978-3-642-19318-7_60
4. Neumann, L., Matas, J.: Scene text localization and recognition with oriented stroke detection. In: Proceedings of the IEEE International Conference on Computer Vision, pp. 97–104 (2013)
5. Donoser, M., Bischof, H.: Efficient maximally stable extremal region (MSER) tracking. In: Proceedings of the 2006 IEEE Computer Society Conference on Computer Vision and Pattern Recognition (CVPR 2006), New York, NY, USA, pp. 553–560. IEEE (2006)
6. Zhou, X., Yao, C., Wen, H., Wang, Y., Zhou, S., He, W.: EAST: an efficient and accurate scene text detector. In: Proceedings of the 2017 IEEE Conference on Computer Vision and Pattern Recognition (CVPR), Honolulu, HI, USA, pp. 5551–5560. IEEE (2017)
7. He, W., et al.: Deep direct regression for multi-oriented scene text detection. In: Proceedings of the IEEE International Conference on Computer Vision (2017)

8. Lyu, P., Yao, C., Wu, W., Yan, S., Bai, X.: Multi-oriented scene text detection via corner localization and region segmentation. In: Proceedings of the 2017 IEEE Conference on Computer Vision and Pattern Recognition (CVPR), Salt Lake City, UT, pp. 7553–7563. IEEE (2018)

9. Deng, D., Liu, H., Li, X., Cai, D.: PixelLink: detecting scene text via instance segmentation. In: Proceedings of the 2018 Thirty-Second AAAI Conference on Artificial Intelligence, New Orleans, Louisiana, USA, pp. 7553–7563. IEEE (2018)

10. Long, S., Ruan, J., Zhang, W., He, X., Wu, W., Yao, C.: TextSnake: a flexible representation for detecting text of arbitrary shapes. In: Ferrari, V., Hebert, M., Sminchisescu, C., Weiss, Y. (eds.) ECCV 2018. LNCS, vol. 11206, pp. 19–35. Springer, Cham (2018). https://doi.org/10.1007/978-3-030-01216-8_2

11. Shi, B., Bai, X., Yao, C.: An end-to-end trainable neural network for image-based sequence recognition and its application to scene text recognition. IEEE Trans. Pattern Anal. Mach. Intell. **39**(11), 2298–2304 (2017)

12. De Voogt, A.: The cultural transmission of script in Africa: the presence of syllabaries. Scripta **6**, 121–143 (2014)

13. Tian, Z., Huang, W., He, T., He, P., Qiao, Y.: Detecting text in natural image with connectionist text proposal network. In: Leibe, B., Matas, J., Sebe, N., Welling, M. (eds.) ECCV 2016. LNCS, vol. 9912, pp. 56–72. Springer, Cham (2016). https://doi.org/10.1007/978-3-319-46484-8_4

14. Ma, J., et al.: Arbitrary-oriented scene text detection via rotation proposals. IEEE Trans. Multimed. **20**(11), 3111–3122 (2017)

15. Jaderberg, M., Simonyan, K., Vedaldi, A., Zisserman, A.: Synthetic data and artificial neural networks for natural scene text recognition. arXiv preprint arXiv:1406.2227, 1–10 (2014)

16. Su, B., Lu, S.: Accurate scene text recognition based on recurrent neural network. In: Cremers, D., Reid, I., Saito, H., Yang, M.-H. (eds.) ACCV 2014. LNCS, vol. 9003, pp. 35–48. Springer, Cham (2015). https://doi.org/10.1007/978-3-319-16865-4_3

17. Lee, C.Y., Osindero, S.: Recursive recurrent nets with attention modeling for OCR in the wild. In: Proceedings of the 2016 IEEE Conference on Computer Vision and Pattern Recognition (CVPR), Las Vegas, NV, pp. 2231–2239 (2016)

18. Liu, W., Chen, C., Wong, K.Y.K., Su, Z., Han, J.: STAR-Net: a SpaTial attention residue network for scene text recognition. In: Wilson, R.C., Hancock, E.R., Smith, W.A.P. (eds.) Conference 2016, BMVC, York, UK, vol. 2, p. 7 (2016)

19. Shi, B., Wang, X., Lyu, P., Yao, C., Bai, X.: Robust scene text recognition with automatic rectification. In: Proceedings of the 2016 IEEE Conference on Computer Vision and Pattern Recognition (CVPR), Las Vegas, NV, pp. 4168–4176 (2016)

20. Simonyan, K., Zisserman, A.: Very deep convolutional networks for large-scale image recognition. arXiv preprint arXiv:1409.1556, 1–14 (2014)

21. Ioffe, S., Szegedy, C.: Batch normalization: accelerating deep network training by reducing internal covariate shift. arXiv:1502.03167v3, vol. abs/1502.03167, 1–11 (2015)

22. Graves, A., Fernández, S., Gomez, F., Schmidhuber, J.: Connectionist temporal classification: labelling unsegmented sequence data with recurrent neural networks. In: Proceedings of the 2006 ICML Conference on Machine Learning, Pittsburgh, Pennsylvania, USA, pp. 369–376 (2006)

23. Zeiler, M.D.: ADADELTA: an adaptive learning rate method. arXiv preprint arXiv:1212.5701 (2012)

24. Hochreiter, S., Schmidhuber, J.: Long short-term memory. Neural Comput. **8**(9), 1735–1780 (1997)

25. Gers, F.A., Schmidhuber, J., Cummins, F.: Learning to forget: continual prediction with LSTM. Neural Comput. **12**(10), 2451–2471 (2000)

Automatic Amharic Part of Speech Tagging (AAPOST): A Comparative Approach Using Bidirectional LSTM and Conditional Random Fields (CRF) Methods

Worku Kelemework Birhanie[1][(✉)] and Miriam Butt[2]

[1] Faculty of Computing, Bahir Dar Institute of Technology,
Bahir Dar University, Bahir Dar, Ethiopia
workukelem@gmail.com
[2] Department of Linguistics (Computational Linguistics),
University of Konstanz, Constance, Germany
miriam.butt@uni-konstanz.de

Abstract. Part of speech (POS) tagging is an initial task for many natural language applications. POS tagging for Amharic is in its infancy. This study contributes towards the improvement of Amharic POS tagging by experimenting using Deep Learning and Conditional Random Fields (CRF) approaches. Word embedding is integrated into the system to enhance performance. The model was applied to an Amharic news corpus tagged into 11 major part of speeches and achieved accuracies of 91.12% and 90% for the Bidirectional LSTM and CRF methods respectively. The result shows that the Bidirectional LSTM approach performance is better than the CRF method. More enhancement is expected in the future by increasing the size and diversity of Amharic corpus.

Keywords: Amharic · POS · BI-LSTM · CRF

1 Introduction

Amharic is the working language of Ethiopian Federal Government. There are also some states which use the language at a regional level. The language has 34 million speakers according to Meshesha and Jawahar (2008), which makes Amharic the second most spoken Semitic language in the world after Arabic (Gambäck et al. 2009; Gezmu et al. 2018). Amharic is written left to right unlike other Semitic languages such as Arabic and Hebrew. It uses the Ge'ez script as its orthography (Seid and Gambäck 2005; Gambäck et al. 2009). Amharic has thirty-three core letters. Each of the letters has six additional letter versions called orders (Bender et al. 1976).

This paper contributes towards the enrichment of Amharic with technological resources. The study explores automated Amharic POS tagging (AAPOST) using a deep learning approach and Conditional Random Fields (CRF). The POS tagging task is based on news text data, in which each token has been manually tagged as to its POS.

© ICST Institute for Computer Sciences, Social Informatics and Telecommunications Engineering 2020
Published by Springer Nature Switzerland AG 2020. All Rights Reserved
N. G. Habtu et al. (Eds.): ICAST 2019, LNICST 308, pp. 512–521, 2020.
https://doi.org/10.1007/978-3-030-43690-2_37

Amharic follows the Subject Object Verb (SOV) arrangement in a sentence structure; nouns often come at the start of a sentence and verbs tend to appear at the end of a sentence. Sometimes, objects and subjects may switch (Yimam 2017). We have used the sentence level as our input for tagging.

Amharic is a morphologically rich language like Arabic and other Semitic languages. The language is rich in inflectional and derivational morphology. This greatly affects POS tagging, as the POS of a word changes when the word form changes derivationally. Low performance is recorded in POS tagging when word forms are considered as an input in POS tagging (Tachbelie et al. 2011).

In previous Amharic POS studies, statistical approaches have been used for the POS classification of words/tokens. In this study, a comparison of an established statistical method and a new deep learning method has been made to explore a potentially better approach for the Amharic POS tagging task.

The paper first discusses related works on Amharic POS tagging in Sect. 2, and the tagset used in the study, preprocessing tasks done on the data used, methods used, results found and discussion based on the results in the next sections. The paper closes with conclusion and recommendations for the improvement of Amharic POS tagging.

2 Related Work

Studies done on Amharic part of speech tagging so far are: Getachew (2001), Adafre (2005), Demeke and Getachew (2006), Gambäck et al. (2009), Tachbelie and Menzel (2009), Kebede (2009), Gebre (2010), and Tachbelie et al. (2011).

According to Adafre (2005), the first study on Amharic automatic part of speech tagging was done by Getachew (2001). Getachew has identified 25 classes of POS and used the Hidden Markov Model (HMM) method for the task.

Adafre (2005) used 1,000 tokens extracted from 5 Amharic news articles. An accuracy of 74% was registered using the conditional random fields method. Ten tagsets have been used, these are: Noun, Verb, Auxiliary, Numeral, Adjective, Adverb, Adposition, Interjection, Punctuation, and Residual. The corpus size is limited, and the accuracy is not satisfactory.

Demeke and Getachew (2006) worked on manual part of speech tagging for Amharic. They developed an Amharic tagset at the Ethiopian Language Research Center (ELRC) under the project called "The Annotation of Amharic News Documents". The project aimed at filling the resource gap in Amharic. 1,065 Amharic news texts were collected from Walta Information Center (WIC), which is private broadcasting corporation. A total of 210,000 tokens were tagged with part of speech. This corpus has subsequently been used in most Amharic part of speech tagging studies and is also used in this study. Hereafter, this dataset is referred as "WIC dataset".

Gambäck et al. (2009) used three algorithms and three tagset types to experiment with Amharic part of speech tagging. The dataset used was the WIC dataset and the tagset types used were: ELRC, BASIC, and SISAY. ELRC is the tagset developed at Ethiopian Language Research Center by Demeke and Getachew (2006), which has 31 tags. BASIC tagset is the major tags in ELRC tagset, which includes 11 tags. SISAY tagset contains 10 tags recommended by Adafre (2005). The average accuracy results were 85.56%, 88.30% and 87.87% for the HMM, SVM and Maximum Entropy methods, respectively.

Tachbelie and Menzel (2009) presented "Amharic Part-of-Speech Tagger for Factored Language Modeling". They have used the WIC dataset; and the methods employed were Hidden Markov Model (HMM) and Support Vector Machine (SVM), which achieved 82.57% and 84.87% average accuracies respectively.

Kebede (2009) applied a decision tree algorithm for Amharic part of speech tagging and registered an accuracy of 84.9%. Here again, the WIC dataset was used, but only 800 sentences were selected as a sample.

Gebre (2010), used the WIC dataset for an Amharic part of speech experiment. As a methodology, he employed Conditional Random fields (CRF), Support Vector Machine (SVM), Brill tagger and Hidden Markov Model (HMM). The average accuracy results found were, 90.95%, 90.43%, 87.41% and 87.09% in order.

Tachbelie et al. (2011) also studied Amharic POS tagging based on the WIC data. The study applied POS tagging on segmented and unsegmented Amharic words. The average accuracies obtained are 86.30% and 93.5% for the unsegmented and segmented words, respectively. The segmented one removes the affixes and determines the tag of a given word. However, affixes are very important for the determination of POS of a word in Amharic. In this study, affixes are not removed from words and words are used as they appear in the corpus.

All of the studies used more or less similar tagsets with minor differences. Getachew come up with 25 tagsets for the first time. Adafre (2005) used a more compact form of the tagsets, which in turn are very similar to the major classes of the WIC dataset. Gambäck et al. (2009) tested three types of tagsets.

This study tries to enhance the performance by considering different factors. The sentence level is taken to be the most essential component for deciding the part of speech of a word as it provides important distributional information about the word. Word embedding has been incorporated for the betterment of the result since it is used to draw relationship between words.

3   Tagset

As already discussed, most Amharic part of speech tagging studies used the WIC dataset prepared by ELRC. The same dataset is utilized in this study. The dataset is tagged into 11 major parts of speech, these are: Noun (N), Pronoun (PRON), Verb (V), Adjective (ADJ), Preposition (PREP), Conjunction (CONJ), Adverb (ADV), Numeral (NUM), Interjection (INT), Punctuation (PUNC), and Unclassified (UNC).

4   Preprocessing

In the WIC dataset there is informative tagging related to the date of the news article, the file name, copyright information and tags that indicate the title and body of each of the news articles, etc. All this meta-information is not relevant for the task at hand. Hence, such embedded tags are excluded, and only relevant information is extracted for the task.

In the data, there are tokens which have not been given a POS tag. Such tokens are removed from the data. The other important preprocessing step is the identification of sentences. Sentence information is not included in the data. If·sentence structure is ignored, we cannot capture distributional information of words in the context of grammatical structure. Hence, further processing has been accomplished to identify sentences based on sentence punctuation markers in Amharic. Punctuation marks that signal the end of a sentence are: ጥያቄ ምልክት *Tyaqe mlkt* 'question mark' (?), ቃል አጋኖ *qalagano* 'exclamation mark' (!), and አራት ነጥብ *arat neTb* 'period' (።).

The format of the data in the WIC dataset is an Amharic word followed by its target tag, both in one file. Since the algorithms require separated input and output, the data is split into a list of words and their associated target tag.

The data is then converted in a way amenable to the algorithm used. Each token and tag have been integer encoded; additionally, the tags are converted into one hot vectors encoding. The vectorization is done to represent the text data and to feed it into the machine learning algorithms.

5 Methods

Two machine learning methods were applied in this study, Bidirectional Long Term Short Term Memory (BÏ-LSTM) and Conditional Random Fields (CRF). In both methods, different layers are used from the input to the output. In the layered model, Dropout has been used. Dropout helps to overcome the problem of overfitting by controlling the effect of noisy data in the training set (Srivastava et al. 2014).

A word embedding layer is also used in this study. Word embedding helps to produce linguistic relationships between words (Schnabel et al. 2015); which foster the model to produce good predictions. The word embedding layer used in this study is based on the word2vec algorithm developed by Mikolov et al. (2013). The underlying algorithms employed for the task part of speech tagging, BI-LSTM and CRF, are discussed below.

The deep learning method provides multiple layers to allow for more learning and to facilitate good data representation. This makes the overall result better (Chollet 2018). The great advantage of using Recurrent Neural Network (RNN) is the consideration of context information in a data, which is essential for modeling human language (Graves et al. 2005; Huang et al. 2015; Chollet 2018).

BI-LSTM combines the utility of Bidirectional RNN (BRNN) and LSTM. BRNN considers contexts by working both in a backward and forward manner over a sequence data. This is very helpful in a problem like POS tagging since the POS of a target word is affected by the POS of surrounding words. LSTM has the ability to consider long distance dependencies; as a result, it helps to solve problems of vanishing or decaying information exhibited by RNNs (Graves et al. 2005; Graves and Jaitly 2014; Huang et al. 2015).

Historical and future information can be considered in a BI-LSTM. The input layer in BI-LSTM is a sequence of vectors for the tokens of a sentence and the output layer is a sequence of hidden states for each token's vector. The final hidden state is determined by the combination of the forward and backward hidden layers' result (Lin et al. 2017).

A Time Distributed Dense layer and activation layer are parts of the model in this study. The Dense layer is a fully connected network used to output the part of speech of each Amharic token. The time distributed facility helps to create a one to one relationship between the input token and the output part of speech of a given Amharic token. The activation function helps to activate a neuron for the output layer. It calculates the probability of the 11 parts of speech, given a particular Amharic token.

CRFs are the other approach implemented in this study. They are based on probability estimation. CRF is defined as "Let G = (V, E) be a graph such that Y = (Yv)v ∈ V, so that Y is indexed by the vertices of G. Then (X, Y) is a conditional random field in case, when conditioned on X, the random variables Yv obey the Markov property with respect to the graph: p(Yv ∣ X, Yw, w ≠ v) = p(Yv ∣ X, Yw, w ∼ v), where w ∼ v means that w and v are neighbors in G" (Lafferty et al. 2001). In this study, X is Amharic sentences and Y is the range of POS tags given for tokens in those sentences.

The architecture of this study encompasses three major components: input, classifier, and output as illustrated in Fig. 1.

| Input | Classifier | Output |
| Amharic Sentence | BI-LSTM/CRF | POS |

Fig. 1. Model of AAPOST.

6 Result and Discussion

6.1 Data

8041 sentences have been identified for the experiment. Table 1 shows token statistics of the corpus for the 11 parts of speech used in the study after pre-processing.

Table 1. Token statistics.

No.	Part of speech	Number of tokens	Percentage (%)
1	Noun	116470	58.322
2	Pronoun	2696	1.35
3	Verb	37392	18.724
4	Adjective	11451	5.734
5	Preposition	5534	2.771
6	Conjunction	1364	0.683
7	Adverb	2294	1.149
8	Numeral	8629	4.321
9	Interjection	2	0.001
10	Punctuation	13700	6.86
11	Unclassified	170	0.085
Total		**199702**	**100**

The statistics indicates that nouns form the largest group and that the smallest group is represented by interjections. Interjections do not occur in large numbers because the document consists of very formal reporting of news articles.

The data has been split into two sets in the ratio of 95:5. The first set is composed of 7638 sentences, which is used for training and validation. The validation set is about 10% (764) of these sentences and the remaining 90% (6874) sentences are used for the training. The validation set is essential for controlling overfitting during learning. The other 5% (403) sentences are used for the purpose of evaluation. The model is evaluated using accuracy based on the test set.

6.2 Word Embedding

The model has been trained using an embedding layer, which utilizes pretrained word embedding developed via a combination of two corpora, the WIC (Getachew and Demeke 2006) and the Contemporary Amharic Corpus (Gezmu et al. 2018).

The embedding model from the combined corpus has a dimensionality of 100 and a window size of 5. The values are selected since they are default values in most applications (Elton et al. 2019).

The final vocabulary contains 744,269 tokens. The word embedding model is able to produce semantically related words given randomly selected Amharic words. Sample outputs for a word are depicted below. The algorithm has been told to show ten most likely related words for the word ሴት *sEt* 'female', and generate the output:

እናት *enat* 'mother', አንዲት *andit* 'one female', ሚስት *mist* 'wife', እህት *eht* 'sister', ወንድ *wend* 'male', ሴትና *sEtna* 'female and', እርጉዝ *erguz* 'pregnant', መበለት *mebelet* 'widow', ነፍስ *nefse* 'a word used in combination with other word to form a compound word, in this sense it can be used to form a compound word to refer to pregnancy', የደረሰች *yederesech* 'a female about to give birth'.

6.3 POS Experiment

Various epoch levels have been tried and a training over 15 epochs was found to be optimal. Figure 2 shows the trend in accuracy at various epochs. In the Figure, values on the vertical axis can be multiplied to determine the accuracy in terms of percentage. For example, 0.88 means 88% accuracy.

From Fig. 2 one can see that accuracy increases in the initial learning steps. After 15 epochs, the validation accuracy goes in a constant rate. Hence, epoch 15 was selected for the experiments.

The model is trained on two learning algorithms, and 91.12% and 90% accuracies are recorded for BI-LSTM and CRF methods respectively. The BI-LSTM learning method has showed an accuracy increase by 1.12% over the CRF method. Both methods consider contextual information, but BI-LSTM includes a long term memory that enables it to take into account longer distance relationships between parts of speech than what CRF allows. This may be the reason for the better performance by the BI-LSTM learning method. The highest accuracy in previous Amharic POS tagging studies was 90.95% using the unsegmented words, the detail is indicated in Sect. 2. In this study, the accuracy increased by 0.17%.

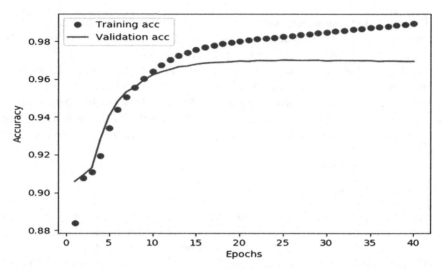

Fig. 2. Epoch vs accuracy.

The taggers Cohens Kappa results are 0.85 and 0.83 for the BI-LSTM and CRF classifiers in respectively. The Cohens Kappa result tells the quality of the classifiers (McHugh 2012; Gulzar et al. 2018). Based on McHugh (2012), if the Kappa result is above 0.9, it is almost perfect classifier and if the Kappa result lies between 0.8 and 0.9, it is a strong classifier. Hence, we can say that the models produced strong taggers. The BI-LSTM classifier is better than the CRF classifier by 0.02.

6.4 Error Analysis

Table 2 shows the confusion matrix for the BI-LSTM method. The result for CRF method has the same trend in the output except some variations.

Table 2. Amharic part of speech tagging confusion matrix.

Predicted / Actual	N	PRON	V	ADJ	PREP	CONJ	ADV	NUM	PUN	UNC
N	5584	4	90	51	19	0	16	12	0	0
PRON	25	96	3	3	2	0	0	1	0	0
V	349	0	1494	6	0	0	0	0	0	1
ADJ	130	5	21	388	1	0	2	8	0	0
PREP	13	1	2	0	272	1	1	0	0	0
CONJ	7	1	2	0	5	50	0	0	0	0
ADV	21	1	9	3	9	1	63	0	0	0
NUM	39	1	2	1	0	0	0	363	0	0
INT	0	0	0	0	1	0	0	0	0	0
PUN	3	0	0	0	0	0	0	0	685	0
UNC	1	0	3	0	0	0	0	0	0	2

From the total of 9874 tokens, 8997 (91.12%) tokens are correctly classified and 877 (8.88%) tokens are wrongly classified. The major misclassifications happened between verbs and nouns. 349 verbs are incorrectly tagged as noun and 90 nouns are misclassified as verbs. The second misclassification is between noun and adjective. 130 adjectives are incorrectly tagged as nouns and 51 nouns are wrongly classified as adjectives. This resulted in a misclassification of 620 (70.7%) tokens from a total of 877 misclassified tokens.

Most of the misclassifications in pronouns, numerals, prepositions, adverbs, and conjunctions part of speech were found to be in the noun tag. Two reasons may account for this. The first may be that nouns represent the most frequent POS in the data. Nouns constitute 58.32% of the total data in the corpus; as a result, tokens from less frequent POS may erroneously be tagged as the noun category. Secondly, nouns have a more variable distribution in Amharic sentences in comparison to the other Amharic POS. Nouns may occur at the very beginning of a sentence as a subject or may appear in the middle of a sentence as an object; hence, if there is an ambiguity in the classifier, it may incorrectly classify a token as a noun.

Adverbs classification performance is poor as compared to other part of speeches. There are 107 tokens classified as adverb. From these tokens, 63 (58.88%) are classified correctly and 44 (41.12%) are classified wrongly. Very few primary adverbs are available in Amharic. Most of the Adverbs are normally derived from other part of speeches, to clarify time, place, situation, etc. This may create confusion for the classifier and may assign a different part of speech for an adverb token.

In the CRF method, 8887 (90%) tokens are classified correctly and 987 (10%) tokens are misclassified into wrong POS out of 9874 tokens. The trend in the result is like the BI-LSTM output; similar kinds of misclassifications are recorded. The only difference here is a 1.12% decrease in accuracy.

7 Conclusion and Future Work

Part of speech tagging has been applied to a medium sized WIC corpus comprising news texts. The corpus was tagged on the basis of 11 major POS tags.

The plain text format of the corpus has been taken as an input for preprocessing. Preprocessing steps such as identifying words and tags from the corpus, finding sentence boundaries in the corpus and converting the data into one-hot vectors were accomplished.

The vector form of the data is feed into the learning algorithms, BI-LSTM and CRF. The algorithms have been further enhanced via a word embedding model. A dropout facility has also been incorporated into the model to overcome the negative impact of noise in the data. There are mistagged tokens in the corpus. The dropout helps to deal inconsistencies as a result of mistagging.

After training over 15 epochs, a 91.12% accuracy was registered for the BI-LSTM method and 90% accuracy for the CRF method. The result shows that BI-LSTM performs better than CRF and it also showed 1.12% accuracy increase as compared to previous highest Amharic POS tagger. This is likely due to the consideration of longer dependencies in the POS.

70.7% of the misclassification is between noun and verb, and noun and adjective tokens. Tokens in the other POS are misclassified to nouns in most cases. This is due to sparseness of some tag categories; that is, less frequent tokens are incorrectly tagged as the class of more frequent tokens by the model.

Error in the corpus contributed to the decrease in performance of the tagger. Hence, the corpus also needs some correction. The subsequent paragraphs discuss points to be considered for future research in the area.

Though the result produced is good, there are aspects that need improvement. The first is to increase the available Amharic corpus both in number and diversity. This study used texts from the news domain. Diverse sources and genres should be included to provide a more general training and test sets. This will also likely help to raise the representation of all parts of speech and help to minimize the misclassification problem.

The model has been tested only on the news domain. If used in a different context, it may not have similar performance. This remains to be tested. As another further step, it is desirable to scale up the domain under consideration.

The sparseness of the data contributed to the decrease in performance of the tagger. The situation is worse for adverb tokens. Hence, it is good to balance the dataset across various part of speeches.

Acknowledgement. We thank the research group of Computational Linguistics, University of Konstanz for the support and provision of required materials for the study. The appreciations is extended for Bahir Dar University, Bahir Dar Institute of Technology. We also thank Toqeer Ehsan for his constructive comments.

References

Adafre, S.: Part of Speech tagging for Amharic using conditional random fields. In: Proceedings of the ACL Workshop on Computational Approaches to Semitic Languages, pp. 47–54. ACL, Ann Arbor (2005)

Bender, L., Bowen, D., Cooper, R., Ferguson, C.: Language in Ethiopia. Oxford University Press, London (1976)

Chollet, F.: Deep Learning with Python. Manning Publications Co, Shelter Island, NY (2018)

Demeke, G., Getachew, M.: Manual annotation of Amharic news items with part of speech tags and its challenges. ELRC Working Pap. **2**(1), 1–16 (2006)

Elton, D., et al.: Using natural language processing techniques to extract information on the properties and functionalities of energetic materials from large text corpora. In: Proceedings of the 22nd International Seminar in New Trends in Research of Energetic Materials. arXiv e-prints (2019). https://arxiv.org/pdf/1903.00415.pdf

Gambäck, B., Olsson, F., Argaw, A., Asker, L.: Methods for Amharic part-of-speech tagging. In: Proceedings of the EACL Workshop on Language Technologies for African Languages – AfLaT, pp. 104–111. Association for Computational Linguistics, Athens (2009)

Gezmu, A., Seyoum, B., Gasser, M., Nürnberger, A.: Contemporary Amharic corpus: automatically morpho-syntactically tagged Amharic corpus. In: Proceedings of the First Workshop on Linguistic Resources for Natural Language Processing, pp. 65–70. Association for Computational Linguistics, Santa Fe (2018)

Gebre, B.: Part-of-Speech Tagging for Amharic. A Project submitted as part of a programme of study for the award of MA Natural Language Processing and Human Language Technology, Universite De Franche-Comt 'E Centre Lucien Tesniere' and The University of Wolverhampton School of Law, Social Sciences and Communications (2010)

Graves, A., Jaitly, N.: Towards end-to-end speech recognition with recurrent neural networks. In: Proceedings of the 31 International Conference on Machine Learning, Beijing, China, JMLR: W&CP, vol. 32 (2014)

Graves, A., Fernández, S., Schmidhuber, J.: Bidirectional LSTM networks for improved phoneme classification and recognition. In: Duch, W., Kacprzyk, J., Oja, E., Zadrożny, S. (eds.) ICANN 2005. LNCS, vol. 3697, pp. 799–804. Springer, Heidelberg (2005). https://doi.org/10.1007/11550907_126

Gulzar, M., Ali, A., Naqvi, B.: Performance evaluation and comparison of classification techniques for outcome estimation in strategic board games. Int. J. Comput. Sci. Netw. Secur. 18(7), 103–110 (2018)

Huang, Z., Xu, W., Yu, K.: Bidirectional LSTM-CRF Models for Sequence Tagging. arXiv e-prints (2015). https://arxiv.org/pdf/1508.01991.pdf

Kebede, G.: The application of Decision Tree for part of speech (POS) tagging for Amharic. A thesis submitted to school of graduate studies of Addis Ababa university in partial fulfillment of the requirements for the degree of Master of Science in information science (2009)

Lafferty, J., McCallum, A., Pereira, F.: Conditional random fields: probabilistic models for segmenting and labeling sequence data. In: Proceedings of the 18th International Conference on Machine Learning (ICML 2001), pp. 282–289. ACM (2001)

Lin, B., Xu, F., Luo, Z., Zhu, K.: Multi-channel BiLSTM-CRF model for emerging named entity recognition in social media. In: Proceedings of the 3rd Workshop on Noisy User-generated Text, pp. 160–165. Association for Computational Linguistics, Copenhagen (2017)

McHugh, M.: Interrater reliability: the kappa statistic. Biochem. Medica 22(3), 276–282 (2012)

Meshesha, M., Jawahar, C.: Indigenous scripts of African languages. Indilinga: Afr. J. Indigenous Knowl. Syst. 6(2), 132–142 (2008)

Mikolov, T., Chen, K., Corrado, G., Dean, J.: Efficient Estimation of Word Representations in Vector Space. arXiv e-prints (2013). https://arxiv.org/abs/1301.3781v3

Schnabel, T., Labutov, I., Mimno, D. Evaluation methods for unsupervised word embeddings. In: Proceedings of the Conference on Empirical Methods in Natural Language Processing, pp. 298–307. Association for Computational Linguistics, Lisbon (2015)

Seid, H., Gambäck, B.: Speaker independent continuous speech recognizer for Amharic. In: Interspeech, 9th European Conference on Speech Communication and Technology, Lisbon (2005)

Srivastava, N., Hinton, G., Krizhevsky, A., Sutskever, I., Salakhutdinov, R.: Dropout: a simple way to prevent neural networks from overfitting. J. Mach. Learn. Res. 15, 1929–1958 (2014)

Tachbelie, M., Menzel, W.: Amharic part-of-speech tagger for factored language modeling. In: International Conference RANLP, pp. 428–433. Association for Computational Linguistics, Borovets (2009)

Tachbelie, M., Abate, S., Besacier, L.: Part-of-speech tagging for under-resourced and morphologically rich languages – the case of Amharic. In: Conference on Human Language Technology for Development, pp. 50–55. Alexandria (2011)

Yimam, B.: Amharic Grammar, 3rd edn. Addis Ababa University B.E. Printing Press, Addis Ababa (2017). ባየ ይማም. የአማርኛ ሰዋሰው. ሶስተኛ እትም. አዲስ አበባ ዩኒቨርሲቲ ቢ.ኢ. ማተሚያ ቤት፦ አዲስ አበባ(2009)

Product Design, Manufacturing, and Systems Optimization

Effects of Shielded Metal Arc Welding Process Parameters on Mechanical Properties of S355JR Mild Steel

Kishor Purushottamrao Kolhe$^{(\boxtimes)}$ ⓘ, Fetene Teshome ⓘ, and Aragaw Mulu

Bahir Dar Institute of Technology, Bahir Dar University, Bahir Dar, Ethiopia
skishor75@gmail.com, fetenet2017@gmail.com

Abstract. In this work the effect of welding parameters on mechanical properties of S355JR structural mild Steel is studied using SMAW process and E6013 as filler electrode with Taguchi orthogonal array of L9. Welding parameters like, voltage, current and speed are used as independent variables and tensile strength, hardness of weld zone and hardness of HAZ are consider as the output response in this investigation. Signal to noise (S/N) ratio and ANOVA are performed to know the significant of the parameters and the optimal welding condition using MINITAB 18 software. The maximum mechanical properties of the welded sample are obtained for optimal welding conditions. The maximum tensile strength, hardness of weld zone and hardness of heat affected zone were obtained 494.47 Mpa, 269.77 and 255.06 respectively. From the investigation, the parameters of SMAW process like voltage, current and speed noted significant influence on the mechanical properties of the base metal.

Keywords: Shielded Metal Arc Welding · Welding parameters · Mechanical properties

1 Introduction

Shielded Metal Arc Welding (SMAW) is a type of arc welding process that uses a welding power supply to create an electric arc between an electrode and the base material to be melt at the welding point [1, 2]. SMAW is a manual arc welding process that uses a consumable flux coated electrode to lay the weld [3]. However; SMAW is having many applications in the various sectors like automobile, farm machinery and general-purpose fabrication work [4]. Moreover; in manufacturing engineering, SMAW is the basic manufacturing process to produce quality and low-cost weld product. Nevertheless; there are different welding variables that barriers from achieving quality and low-cost weld product. Those variables apply their influence on the metallurgical behavior, chemical composition and mechanical property of the overall welding structure and weldments. This leads to the failures of many fabricated structures like industrial construction; erection of buildings, bridges and pressure vessels. Also, the failures of these members and structures bring hazard on human beings. Mainly the present work emphasis on

© ICST Institute for Computer Sciences, Social Informatics and Telecommunications Engineering 2020
Published by Springer Nature Switzerland AG 2020. All Rights Reserved
N. G. Habtu et al. (Eds.): ICAST 2019, LNICST 308, pp. 525–536, 2020.
https://doi.org/10.1007/978-3-030-43690-2_38

analyzing the effect of welding parameters on hardness and tensile strength of S355JR structural mild steel joined by SMAW process. Furthermore, selection of proper welding parameters for the required job helps to get quality weld product, reduce welding defect, and save work material.

2 Experimental Procedures

The Shielded metal arc welding experimental setup is arranged at Bahir Dar Institute of Technology, Bahir Dar University, Ethiopia as shown in Fig. 1. Mainly S355JR structural mild steel as a base metal and the electrode E6013 of diameter of 3.2 mm is used in the present study for making a weld joint. The chemical compositions for both base metal and electrode are shown in Table 1. The welding specimens are prepared by the standard British Welding Standard (BWS) guidelines. The specimen of (200 × 100 × 5) mm length, width and thickness respectively. However, the work piece surface and edge are carefully clean and edge prepared for welding using grinding machine and wire brush. Also; during experimental work the proper work holding fixtures are used to hold and position the parts to be weld in proper orientation. Moreover, after completion of welding specimen, tensile strength test, hardness of weld zone and Heat Affected Zone (HAZ) are tested using Universal tensile testing machine and Brinell hardness testing respectively. The signal to noise ratio has been calculated using MINITAB18 software for each single number of experiments in the overall study.

Table 1. Chemical composition of electrode and BM

Matl	C	Si	Mn	P	S	Cu	Ti	Cr	Mo
BM	0.24	0.5	1.6	0.04	0.05	0.55	0.24	–	–
Electrode	0.5	1	3	–	–	1.5	1	6	1.6

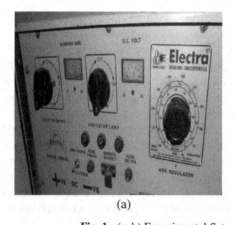 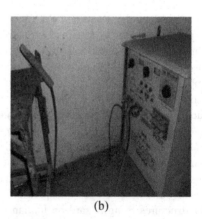

(a)   (b)

Fig. 1. (a, b) Experimental Set up of SMAW power sources.

Design of Experiment

The optimization of the mechanical properties for the selected material is carried out by using Taguchi method using nine levels of orthogonal arrays (L9) [5, 6]. The experimental design proposed by Taguchi involves using orthogonal arrays to organize the parameters affecting the process and the levels at which they should be varied [7]. However, optimization of welding parameters like; current (I), voltage (V) and travel speed (S) for forming each of them into three levels are presented in Table 2.

Table 2. SMAW Process Parameters and their level

S. N	Process parameters	Unit	Levels		
			1	2	3
1	Current (I)	A	90	110	130
2	Voltage (V)	V	30	35	40
3	Speed (S)	mm/s	2	3	4

Selection of Orthogonal Array

Orthogonal arrays (OA) is a standard design by which simultaneous and independent evaluation of two or more parameters for their ability to affect the variability of a process characteristics or output response in a minimum number of tests [8]. The optimum setting of process control parameters of orthogonal array is as shown in Table 3.

Table 3. Orthogonal arrays for number of experiments

Experiments	Experimental variables		
	I	V	S
1	90	30	2
2	90	35	3
3	90	40	4
4	110	30	3
5	110	35	4
6	110	40	2
7	130	30	4
8	130	35	2
9	130	4	3

The S/N ratio takes both the mean and the variability into account. The S/N ratio is the ratio of the mean (signal) to the standard deviation (noise) [10]. For example, to minimize defect. S/N $= -10\log(\text{MSD}_{SB})$ (1)., S/N $= 10\log(\text{MSD}_{NB})$ (2) Larger is better (LB): This type of signal to noise ratio is used when the research wants to maximize the value. S/N $= -10\log(\text{MSD}_{LB})$ (3).,

Where,

$$\text{MSD}_{LB} = \frac{1}{R}\sum_{j=1}^{R}\left(\frac{1}{Y_j^2}\right), \text{MSD}_{SB} = \frac{1}{R}\sum_{j=1}^{R}(Y_j^2), \text{MSD}_{NB} = \frac{1}{R}\sum_{j=1}^{R}\left(\frac{Y^2}{S^2}\right)$$

MSD $=$ mean square deviation, R $=$ number of repetitions, $Y_j =$ measured data, Y $=$ mean of measured data, S $=$ variance., S/N $=$ Signal/Noise $=$ Mean/Standard deviation (4).

Analysis of Variance (ANOVA)
ANOVA is used to explicate the input parameters, i.e. voltage, current and speed that mainly influence the hardness and tensile strength. This furnishes the information on weightage of each parameter on the hardness and tensile strength of the weld [9]. Taguchi recommended a logarithmic transformation of mean square deviation (S/N ratio) for the analysis of results. ANOVA separates the overall variation from the average S/N ratio into contribution by each of the parameters and the errors.

3 Results and Discussion

(1) Tensile Strength (TS)

The result of the tensile strength on different combination of parameters, recorded data and S/N ratio of each sample is presented in Table 4. Table 5 presents the response for tensile strength and average response characteristics (S/N ratio, means) for each level of variable.

Table 4. Test results of Tensile strength and S/N ratio

S. N	I	V	S	T.S (Mpa)	S/N
1	90	30	2	445	52.9672
2	90	35	3	462	53.2928
3	90	40	4	475	53.5339
4	110	30	3	462	53.2928
5	110	35	4	468	53.4049
6	110	40	2	485	53.7148
7	130	30	4	450	53.0643
8	130	35	2	459	53.2363
9	130	40	3	482	53.6609

Table 5. Response of S/N ratio for tensile strength

Level	V	I	S
1	53.26	53.11	53.31
2	53.47	53.31	53.42
3	53.32	53.64	53.33
Delta	0.21	0.53	0.11
Rank	2	1	3

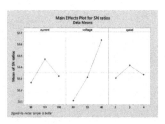

Fig. 2. Main effect plot for S/N ratio of tensile strength

Table 6. General linear model of Tensile strength verses current, voltage and speed for ANOVA

Source	DF	Seq SS	Contribution (%)	Adj SS	Adj MS	F-value	P-value	Significant
I	2	194.00	13.14	194.00	97.00	291	0.003	Less
V	2	1228.67	83.24	1228.67	614.33	184	0.001	Equal
S	2	52.67	3.57	52.67	26.333	79	0.012	Least
Error	2	0.67	0.05	0.67	0.333			
Total	8	1476.00	100					

Figure 2 depicts the voltage has a greater influence followed by current and welding speed on the signal to noise ratio. However; the level averages in the response shows that the S/N ratio and the mean are maximum, when the voltage is 40 V and the current and speed are as 110 A and 3 mm/s respectively. These values are observed for optimum welding variables on which maximum tensile strength is noted. Those are examined by using normal probability plot and plot of the residuals vs. predicted response as shown in Fig. 3. If the model is adequate, the residual points on the normal probability plot should form a straight line. On the other hand, the plot of residuals vs. predicted response should be structure less i.e. it should contain no obvious pattern. From the normal probability plot, it is found that the residuals fall on a straight line; it implies that the errors are distributed normally (Refer Fig. 4). The plot of residual vs. predicted/fitted surface roughness values reveals there is no obvious pattern and unusual structure. This implies that the proposed model is adequate and there is no reason to suspect any violation of the independence or constant variance assumption. From Table 6, it is observed that all the parameters have 'p' value less than 0.05%, which means each variable has their own influence on the tensile strength of the weld specimen using SMAW process, though their numerical value is different.

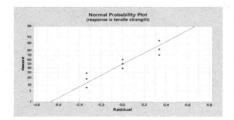

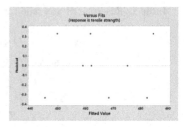

Fig. 3. Normal probability plot of residual for TS   **Fig. 4.** Plot of residual vs. fitted tensile strength values

Similarly, current has 0.003 'P' value and 291 'F' value, which has second contribution for the strength. Speed has 0.012 'P' value and 79 'F' value which has less contribution, when compared with voltage and current. However; percentage contribution is one way to know the influence of each parameter on the tensile strength. Moreover; the parameter with high percentage of contribution has high power to change the performance of the system. In this case voltage with 83.24%; current with 13.14% and speed with 3.57% have a rank of 1 to 3 respectively by their percentage of influence.

Hardness of Weld Zone (HWZ)

The hardness result for fusion (welded) zone can be obtained by combining different parameters at a time. The observed results for hardness and S/N ratio have been recorded in Table 7 below.

Table 7. Test results of Hardness of weld zone and S/N ratio

S. NO	I	V	S	HWZ (BHN)	S/N
1	90	30	2	208.68	46.3896
2	90	35	3	217.12	46.7340
3	90	40	4	221.25	46.8977
4	110	30	3	213.93	46.6054
5	110	35	4	229.49	47.2153
6	110	40	2	229.13	47.2016
7	130	30	4	222.13	46.9321
8	130	35	2	233.63	47.3706
9	130	40	3	236.69	47.4836

Table 8. Response of signal to noise ratio for HWZ

Level	Current	Voltage	Speed
1	46.67	46.64	46.99
2	47.01	47.11	46.94
3	47.26	47.19	47.02
Delta	0.59	0.55	0.07
Rank	1	2	3

The response observed in Table 8 presents average of each response characteristics (S/N ratio, means) for each level of every variable. The table contains the rank of each variable according to the delta statistics reading, which compares the relative magnitude of each variables effect. Figure 5 presents the main effect plot for S/N ratio of the welded zone hardness. This also indicates which level of each factor provides the best result by using the level averages in the response table. From the overall analysis the current has a greater influence followed by voltage and welding speed on the signal to noise ratio. The level averages in the response shows that the S/N ratio and the mean are maximum, when the current is 130A and the voltage and speed are 40 V and 4 mm/s respectively as shown in Fig. 5.

Table 9. General linear model of Hardness of weld zone verses current, voltage and speed

Source	DF	Seq SS	Contribution (%)	Adj SS	Adj MS	F-value	P-value	Significant
I	2	345.269	49.11	345.269	172.63	39.	0.025	Equal
V	2	344.303	48.98	344.303	172.15	39.	0.026	Equal
S	2	4.672	0.66	4.672	2.336	0.5	0.652	Least
Error	2	8.753	1.25	8.753	4.377			
Total	8	702.997	100	–				

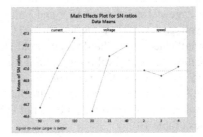

Fig. 5. Main effect plot for S/N of welded zone hardness

Therefore, this value of optimum welding variables for getting good hardness of weld zone. Figure 6 and presents the Plot of residual vs. fitted hardness and Normal probability plot of residual for hardness of WZ (Fig. 7).

Table 9 shows that the parameters like; current and voltage have 'P' value less than 0.05%, which means those variables have significant influence on the hardness of

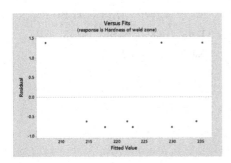

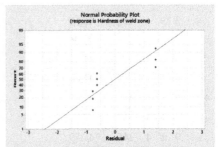

Fig. 6. Plot of residual vs. fitted hardness of WZ

Fig. 7. Normal probability plots of residual for hardness of WZ.

weld zone of the weld sample using SMAW process. However, after arranging their numerical value, current has a greater influence with 'P' and 'F' values of 0.025 and 39.45 respectively. Similarly, voltage has 0.026 'P' value and 39.34 'F' value; which has second contribution for the hardness of weld zone.

Analysis of Variance for Weld Zone
Speed has 0.652 'P' value and 0.53 'F' value, which has no contribution since its 'P' value is greater than 0.05. In this case current with 49.11%; voltage with 48.98% and speed with 0.66% have a rank of 1 to 3 respectively by their percentage of influence with total allowable error of 1.2%.

Hardness for Heat Affected Zone (HHAZ)
The response Table 11 shows that the average of each response characteristics (S/N ratio, means) for each level of every variable. However; the above table contains the rank of each variable according to the delta statistics reading which compares the relative magnitude of each variables effect. Figure 8 depicts the current has a greater influence followed by voltage and welding speed on the signal to noise ratio. However; the level averages in the response shows that the S/N ratio and the mean are maximum, when the current is 130 A and the voltage and speed are at 35 V and 3 mm/s respectively. Table 12 depicts that current and voltage have 'P' value less than 0.05%, which means those variables have significant influence on the hardness of weld HAZ of SMAW process. However; while arranging their numerical value current has a greater influence with 'P' and 'F' value of 0.006 and 163.94 respectively. Similarly, voltage has 0.021 'P' value and 46.79 'F' value which has second contribution for the hardness. Figures 9 and 10 presents Normal probability plot of residual for hardness of HAZ and Plot of residual vs. hardness of HAZ values (Table 10).

Table 10. Hardness of Heat affected zone reading and signal to noise ratio

S	I	V	HHA (BHN)	S/N
1	9	3	200	46.02
2	9	3	225	47.06
3	9	4	215	46.68
4	1	3	225	47.06
5	1	3	235	47.43
6	1	4	225	47.06
7	1	3	235	47.43
8	1	3	245	47.78
9	1	4	245	47.79

Table 11. Response Table for signal to noise ratio of the hardness of HAZ

Level	Current	Voltage	Speed
1	46.59	46.84	46.96
2	47.19	47.43	47.31
3	47.67	47.18	47.19
Delta	1.08	0.59	0.35
Rank	1	2	3

Table 12. General linear model of hardness of HAZ versus current, voltage and speed for ANOVA

Source	DF	Seq SS	Contribution (%)	Adj SS	Adj MS	F-value	P-value	Significant
I	2	1179.16	72.13	1179.16	589.58	163	0.006	Equal
V	2	336.55	2	336.55	168.27	46.	0.021	Less
S	2	111.95	6	111.95	55.975	15.	0.060	Least
Error	2	7.19	0	7.19	3.596			
Total	8	1634.85	1					

Fig. 8. S/N ratio for hardness of HAZ

Fig. 9. Normal probability plot of residual for hardness

Fig. 10. Plot of residual vs. hardness of HAZ values

Analysis of Variance for Hardness of HAZ

Speed has 0.060 'P' value and 15.56 'F' value which has no contribution, since its 'P' value is greater than 0.05. In this case current with 72.13%; voltage with 20.59% and speed with 6.85% have a rank of 1 to 3 respectively by their percentage of influence with total allowable error of 0.439%. Taguchi optimization formulas for confirmatory test is as, $P_{opt} = X + (I - X) + (V - X) + (S - X)$ (5)., Where:- P_{opt} = Optimal condition., X = is the overall mean of S/N data, I = mean of S/N data for welding current at optimal level. V = mean of S/N data for welding voltage at optimal level, S = mean of S/N data for welding travel speed at optimal level.

Taguchi Optimization Formula for Tensile Strength

From Table: 5, $P_{opt} = X + (I2-X) + (V3-X) + (S2-X)$., X = is the overall mean of S/N data = 53.35., I2 = mean of S/N data for welding current at level 2 = 53.47., V3 = mean of S/N data for welding voltage at level 3 = 53.64., S2 = mean of S/N data for welding travel speed at level 2 = 53.42., Then; $P_{opt} = 53.35 + (53.47-53.35) + (53.64-53.35) + (53.42-53.35)$ $P_{opt} = 53.83$., Predicted performance strength; Y^2 for larger is better., Y^2_{opt} optimal condition = $10(P_{opt}/10)$, $Y^2 = 10(53.83/10) = 10(5.383)$ = 241546.08344., $Y = \sqrt{241546.08344} = 491.47$., Therefore, the optimal value for tensile strength is 491.47.

Taguchi Optimization Formula for Hardness of Weld Zone

From Table: 8; $P_{opt} = X + (I3-X) + (V3-X) + (S3-X)$., X = is the overall mean of S/N data = 46.98., I3 = mean of S/N data for welding current at level3 = 47.26., V3 = mean of S/N data for welding voltage at level3 = 47.19., S3 = mean of S/N data for welding travel speed at level 3 = 47.02., Optimal condition for hardness of weld zone,

$$P_{opt} = X + (I3 - X) + (V3 - X) + (S3 - X)$$

$$P_{opt} = 46.98 + (47.26 - 46.98) + (47.19 - 46.98) + (47.02 - 46.98)$$

$P_{opt} = 47.51$. Predicted performance (hardness of weld zone); Y^2 for larger is better, Y^2_{opt} optimal condition $= 10^{(P_{opt}/10)}$, $Y^2 = 10^{(47.51/10)}$., $Y^2 = 10^{(4.751)} = 56363.765582$, $Y = \sqrt{56363.765582} = 237.41$., Therefore, the optimal value for hardness of weld zone becomes 237.41.

Taguchi Optimization Formula for Hardness of HAZ
From Table: 11, $P_{opt} = X + (I3-X) + (V2-X) + (S2-X)$, X = is the overall mean of S/N data = 47.15., I3 = mean of S/N data for welding current at level3 = 47.67., V2 = mean of S/N data for welding voltage at level2 = 47.43., S2 = mean of S/N data for welding travel speed at level2 = 47.31., Optimal condition for hardness of HAZ., P_{opt} = X + (I3-X) + (V2-X) + (S2-X)

$$P_{opt} = 47.15 + (47.67 - 47.15) + (47.43 - 47.15) + (47.31 - 47.15)$$

$$P_{opt} = 48.11., \text{Pedicted performance (hardness of HAZ); } Y^2$$

Y^2_{opt} optimal condition $= 10^{(P_{opt}/10)}$., $Y^2 = 10^{(48.11/10)}$, $Y^2 = 10(4.811) = 64714$. 2615748583, $Y = \sqrt{64714.2615748583} = 254.39$. Therefore, the optimal value for hardness of HAZ becomes 245.39. Hence; the optimal value for hardness of HAZ at parameters of current 130 A, voltage, 35 V and speed 3 mm/s is 245.39.

Confirmatory Tests
The last step of the Taguchi methodology is confirmation or verification experiment verify the optimum conditions. If the predicted and observed values are close to each other, then model consider adequate for describing the effect of Parameters on quality characteristics. And if there is a large difference in observed values and predicted values then the model is not adequate.

OPCTM:-**Optimum parametric condition obtained by Taguchi method.**, **MTSCT**:- Maximum tensile strength obtained by confirmatory test.

PPOTM: Prediction for parametric optimization by Taguchi method., **MHWZC**:- Maximum hardness of weld zone obtained by confirmatory test., **MHHZC**:- Maximum hardness of HAZ obtained by confirmatory test.

Table 13; depicts the comparison between the experimental and the theoretical values of the tensile strength, hardness of weld zone and heat affected zone of the welded specimens. The optimization is done by increasing the tensile strength, hardness of weld zone and hardness of HAZ. However; the tensile strength is increased from 491.97 Mpa to 494.47 Mpa with a minimum error of 0.508%. The hardness of weld zone has been increased from 254.39 to 269.77 and the hardness of HAZ increased from 237.41 to 255.06. The confirmatory test is done by taking the optimal parameters and the result into

Table 13. Comparison between actual (experimental value) and theoretical (expected value) of tensile strength, hardness of weld zone and hardness of HAZ

OPCTM		MTSCT	PPOTM	% Error
Current	110 A	494.47 Mpa	491.97Mpa	0.508%
Voltage	40 V			
Speed	3 mm/s			
OPCTM		**MHWZC**	**PPOTM**	
Current	130 A	269.77	254.39	6.04%
Voltage	40 V			
Speed	4 mm/s			
OPCTM		**MHHZC**	**PPOTM**	
Current	130 A	255.06	237.41	7.43%
Voltage	35 V			
speed	3 mm/s			

considerations to show that the improvement of the response variables is acceptable. The contribution of the parameters on the change of tensile strength, hardness of weld zone and hardness of heat affected zone are explained in terms of percentage. The parameter with higher percentage has a great contribution to the change and parameter with low percentage has low contribution on the performance change. Based on this principle; for tensile strength, voltage, current and speed have 83.24%, 13.14%, 3.57% percentage contribution respectively. Also for hardness of weld zone, current, voltage and speed have, 49.11%, 48.98%, 0.66% percentage contribution respectively. And for hardness of heat affected zone, current, voltage and speed have 72.13%, 20.59%, 6.85% percentage contribution for the change.

4   Conclusions

From this study following conclusions are made

1. For optimized parameter, the tensile strength is increased from 491.97 Mpa to 494.47 Mpa with a minimum error of 0.508%. Also, the hardness of weld zone has been increased from 254.39 to 269.77 and the hardness of HAZ increased from 237.41 to 255.06.
2. The parameter with higher percentage has a more contribution to the change and parameter with low percentage, has low contribution on the performance change. Based on this principle for tensile strength, voltage, current and speed have 83.24%, 13.14% 3.57% contribution respectively. For hardness of weld zone, current, voltage and speed have, 49.11%, 48.98%, 0.66% contribution respectively. And for hardness of heat affected zone, current, voltage and speed have 72.13%, 20.59%, 6.85% contribution for the change.

References

1. Kchaou, Y., Haddar, N., Hénaff, G., Pelosin, V., Elleuch, K.: Microstructural, compositional and mechanical investigation of shielded metal arc welding (smaw) welded superaustenitic uns n08028 (alloy 28) stainless steel. Mater. Des. **63**(3), 278–285 (2014)
2. Tong, L.G., Wang, L., Yin, S.W.: Influences of deposited metal material parameters on weld pool geometry during shield metal arc welding. Int. J. Heat Mass Transf. **90**(2), 968–978 (2015)
3. Kolhe, K.P.: Development and testing of tree climbing and harvesting device for mango and coconut trees. Indian Coconut J. **52**(3), 15–19 (2009). published by Ministry of Agriculture, CDB board Kochi Kerla
4. Kolhe, K.P.: Mechanized harvesting device A need of Coconut growers in India. Indian Coconut J. **73**(2), 15–19 (2010). published by Ministry of Agriculture, CDB board Kochi Kerla
5. Kolhe, K.P., Jadhav, B.B.: Testing and performance evaluation of tractor mounted hydraulic elevator for mango Orchard. Am. J. Eng. Appl. Sci. **4**(1), 179–186 (2011)
6. Kolhe, K.P., Powar, A.G., Dhakane, A.D., Mankar, S.H.: Stability and ergonomic design features of tractor mounted hydraulic elevator. Am. J. Eng. Appl. Sci. **4**(3), 380–389 (2011)
7. Kanakaraja, D., Reddy, A.K., Adinarayana, M., Vamsi, L., Reddy, K.: Optimization of CNC turning process parameters for prediction of surface roughness through Taguchi's parametric design approach. Int. J. Mech. Eng. Rob. Res. **3**(4), 708–714 (2014)
8. Jadhav, N.D., Patil, R.A.: Parametric optimization of spot welding metal by Taguchi approach. Weld. J. **3**(4), 857–860 (2015)
9. Thakur, P.P., Student, P.G.: Effect of GTAW-SMAW hybrid welding process parameters on hardness of weld. Weld. J. **10**(1), 782–786 (2017)
10. Kolhe, K.P., Datta, C.K.: Prediction of microstructure and mechanical properties of multipass SAW. J. Mater. Process. Technol. **197**(1–3), 241–249 (2007)

Development and Testing of Improved Double Skirt Rocket Stove for Reducing the Emission Level of Carbon Monoxide

Fetene Teshome$^{(\boxtimes)}$, Eyob Messele, and Kishor Purushottam Kolhe

Department of Mechanical and Industrial Engineering, Bahir Dar Institute of Technology,
Bahir Dar University, P.O.Box: 26, Bahir Dar, Ethiopia
`fetenet2017@gmail.com`

Abstract. Carbon monoxide is very poisonous and spreading rapidly in air, while using three stone open fire food cooking utmost in all parts of rural area. However, the carbon monoxide is very harmful to human being that resulted the severe diseases, like chronic obstructive pulmonary disease (COPD), lung cancer etc. By considering this fact a clean burning and fuel-efficient cooking stove, is designed and develop at Bahir Dar Institute of Technology (BiT), Bahir Dar, which uses mainly eucalyptus and other wood as a fuel. The present paper aims to reduce the requirement of firewood consumption and emission of carbon monoxide of the traditional three stone open fire stove (TSOFS) by replacing an improved double skirt rocket stove (IDSRS) at institutional cooking kitchen. Each part of the stove is designed based on Aprovecho research center design criteria. The emission of carbon monoxide and particulate matters are recorded by digital indoor air pollution (IAP) meter and results are presented. However; insulation material like Pumice; Loam soil; Synthetic asbestos are used for construction of double skirt rocket stove to reduce the value of firewood consumption and also to increase an efficiency of the rocket stove by 41% than the traditional three-stones cooking method and fabricating double skirt IRS to reduce the loss of heat makes the stove differ from previous single skirt stoves.

Keywords: Improved double skirt rocket stove · Insulation material · Carbon monoxide · Particulate matter

Nomenclature

IDSRS	Improved double skirt rocket stove
TSOFS	Three stone open fire stove
IAP	Indoor air pollution
CO	Carbon monoxide
PM	Particulate matters
WHO	World Health Organization
IRS	Institutional rocket stove

© ICST Institute for Computer Sciences, Social Informatics and Telecommunications Engineering 2020
Published by Springer Nature Switzerland AG 2020. All Rights Reserved
N. G. Habtu et al. (Eds.): ICAST 2019, LNICST 308, pp. 537–547, 2020.
https://doi.org/10.1007/978-3-030-43690-2_39

1 Introduction

Globally, more than one billion city dwellers suffer from poor quality air, mostly caused by particulates in the air. Air pollution is the fifth leading cause of death worldwide, responsible for more than 4 million premature deaths every year. There is a close, quantitative relationship between exposure to high concentrations of small particulates (PM10 and PM2.5) and increased mortality or morbidity, both daily and over time. Conversely, when concentrations of small and fine particulates are reduced, related mortality will also go down presuming other factors remain the same. In low- and middle-income countries, exposure to pollutants in and around homes from the household combustion of polluting fuels on open fires or traditional stoves for cooking, heating and lighting further increases the risk for air pollution related diseases, including acute lower respiratory infections, cardiovascular disease, chronic obstructive pulmonary disease and lung cancer. Carbon monoxide, unlike carbon dioxide, does not occur naturally in the atmosphere. The "incomplete" combustion of firewood char coal, natural gas, and oil is a known environmental source of carbon monoxide. Low levels of oxygen and low temperatures result in the formation of higher percentages of CO in the combustion chamber.

Fig. 1. Three stone open fire cooking method at BiT student's cafeteria

Around 2.5 billion peoples in the world, particularly belongs to rural areas, utilize biomass energy for a cooking fuel [1]. However; in Ethiopia, all households utilize a solid fuel like wood, open fire cooking methods for cooking their foods. Specially; in commercial and social, hotels, NGO's such as bakeries, restaurants, schools, detention centers, universities, and hospitals; used commonly wood as a cooking material for fuel. Also; as a result of the total amount of wood consumed for cooking, estimated about 62 million tons annually that makes up more than 80% of the total energy consumed in this country on biogas. This puts huge pressure on natural resource sustainability of the country [2]. Nevertheless; Bahir Dar Institute of Technology has a student cafeteria area that uses firewood to prepare food for more than 4000 students every day; uses an open fire or three stone traditional cooking stoves to prepare foods. Commonly, watt is cooked in three or more cooking pot which can hold 200 L every day. The purchasing price of one-meter cube wood is about 667.00 Birr. It means the annual expenditure of the institute for fuel wood will become about 8,731.64 USD, without considering transport and other related costs. The monthly consumption of wood fuel in the institute for this purpose is about 30-m cube. Mostly, the cooking custom in cooking kitchen includes more three stone open fire stove to finish their work in time, hence many women who engaged for cooking are highly exposed to particulate matters and carbon monoxide emission. The average 11.76% of moisture content is observed in a burning as a fuel for eucalyptus wood. The three stone Open fire cooking method at BiT student's cafeteria is as shown in Fig. 1. Samet *et al.* (2012) divided the major air pollutants by origin, they identified three major groups: (1) combustion sources, (2) biologic sources, and (3) other sources (e.g., radon and radon daughters, volatile and semi volatile organic compounds, and formaldehyde). Moreover; this review has central focus on indoor air pollution that emanates from combustion sources [4]. Smoke that emanates from wood stoves and fireplaces is a potential source of several indoor air pollutants. This is a much larger problem in lesser developed nations [5]. Approximately half of the world's population still relies on biomass fuels (wood, crop residues, and animal dung) for cooking and heating [6]. Wood burning, in addition to producing polycyclic aromatic hydrocarbons and increased respirable particles, is a significant source of indoor CO. The emphasis in this research is to develop Improved Double Skirt Rocket Stove as an alternative to save wood fuel and to reduce the effect of carbon emission. Furthermore; to minimize the dissipated energy, utilization of rocket stove is the best alternative solution. Rocket Stove (RS) is an efficient and hot burning portable stove using small diameter wood fuel. Moreover; the typical application areas of Improved Double Skirt rocket stoves are schools, hospitals, prisons and NGO's. The working condition of this stove is very simple, as fuel is burning in a simple combustion chamber and there is no heat dissipates to the surrounding atmosphere, because the combustion chamber is insulated by different types of heat-resistant materials, like pumice. In this stove, the complete combustion flames' directly reaching to the bottom surface of cooking pot to utilize maximum heat without any loss. Also, it minimizes the consumption of firewood by 41% of the traditional open fire stove. The main difference between a normal fireplace or woodstove and a rocket stove is that rocket combustion is close to complete. When wood is burned it releases volatile compounds that recognize as smoke or soot or creosote. As the fire starts, and the burn tunnel heats up, the rising hot air races up the heat riser, drawing lots of air behind it. This incoming air flows into the feed tube and across the burning wood creating the same effect as pointing a big air-blower at your fire. It gets really hot, the wood burns beautifully, and you hear the air roaring as it charges through the system.

1.1 Design Considerations for Improved Double Skirt Rocket Stove (IDSRS)

The design of Rocket stove is shown in Fig. 2; designed and develops by following engineering product development cycle [7–12]. Many influential characteristics affect the design of the part or, perhaps, the entire system of the stove. Usually, quite a number of such characteristics must be considered and prioritized in a given design situation. Therefore, the important design considerations to design the rocket stove are; High heat resistant, lightweight and portable insulation materials, Grate under fire, insulated heat flow paths, Proper gap. The casserole volume is calculated by using Volume = Area × total height, however the area and volume calculated are as 5,099.64 cm^2, and

224384 cm^3 or 224.38 L respectively Moreover; the design and manufacture of Double skirt rocket stove for a cylindrical diameter of 80.532 cm and height of 44 cm casserole. The space gap for A (height of pot seat from bottom), B (Gap between the insulation and the base of pot at inclined surface), C (Gap between corner of pot and base insulation), and D (Gap between the skirt wall and cooking pot) for air circulation is calculated as 5.5 cm, 4.32 cm, 1.91 cm and 1.93 cm respectively the details are shown in Fig. 2(a). The design of improved double skirt rocket stove is presented in Fig. 2 and it consists of mainly four parts as (1) Skirt (2) Combustion chamber and (3) wood fuel magazine and (4) Leg or Base part as shown in Fig. 2(a–c).

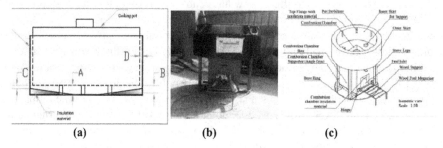

(a)   (b)   (c)

Fig. 2. (a–c) Design of Improved Double Skirt Rocket Stove

2   Materials and Method

The design of improved double skirt rocket stove is performed depending upon the parameter; like; water to be vaporized, heat loss, and environmental impact. This improved rocket stove is designed based on Aprovecho research center design parameters and the few refinement in the existing design for the better improvement. Also the local increadent in insulation composition is added for the less heat transfer of the combustion chamber of the rocket stove. The performance evaluation of the stove is determined by controlled cooking test (CCT) method. Based on this method of testing, the measurement for each cooking is recorded for three times by using Eucalyptus wood as a fuel. Moreover; The instruments used for the present study are, Analog Balance, Moisture meter, Infrared thermometer, Digital thermometer, IAP (indoor air pollution) meter, and Steel rule, 50 cm length respectively for the testing of both open fire stove and improved rocket stove as shown in Fig. 3(a–e).

However, the Indoor air pollution meter is used for recording the carbon monoxide, the recording of carbon monoxide for both methods, i.e. three stone and improved rocket stoves are carried out as per standard guidelines of Aprovecho research center [12, 13] (Figs. 4, 5).

The IAP meter is attached at a distance of 1.5 m × 1.5 m distance away and above from the cooking stove as shown in Fig. 6(a, b). The experiments are carried out under Controlled Cooking Test by following steps; (1) initially the local atmospheric conditions are recorded by using available scientific instruments using Digital thermometer. And

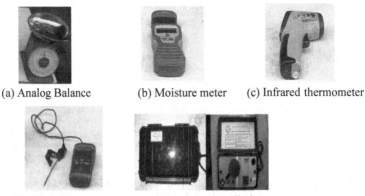

(a) Analog Balance   (b) Moisture meter   (c) Infrared thermometer

(d) Digital thermometer   (e) Indoor air pollution

Fig. 3. (a–e) Digital testing devices used for the measurement of weight, moisture, surface temperature, cooking temperature and carbon monoxide. Figure 6(a, b) presents the experimental set up of cooking methods for three stone method and improved rocket stove

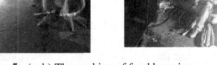

Fig. 4. Control panel of indoor air pollution.

Fig. 5. (a, b) The cooking of food by using traditional TSV and IDSKRS.

the moisture content of fuel wood is measured by digital moisture meter. (2) The weight of dry wood bundle of fuel is measured on digital Analog Balance for both the open fire stove and improved double skirt rocket stove precisely to avoid mistakes in weight. (3) The digital timer is started for time record during the cooking of food on open fire furnace and improved double skirt rocket stove. (4) While the cook performs the cooking task, the carbon monoxide emission is recorded by the Control panel of Indoor air pollution meter, and relevant observations are recorded during the cooking tenure by both methods. (5) After the completion of cooking, the stop watch is off, and the finished time is recorded. (6) Remove the pot(s) of food from the stove and weigh each pot with food on the digital weigh balance. The observations of the same are recorded. (7) Remove the unburned wood from the fire and extinguish it. Knock the charcoal from the ends of the unburned wood. Weigh the unburned wood from the stove with the remaining wood from the original bundle. Place all of the charcoal in the designated tray and weigh this too. Record both measurements on the Data sheet and Calculation form.

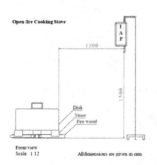
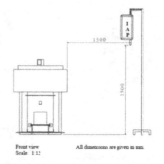

(a)   Traditional three stone method   **(b)** Improved Double skirt Rocket Stove.

Fig. 6.   (a, b) Experimental set up of IAP meter for recording carbon monoxide

3   Results and Discussion

3.1   Results

Based on the testing methodology, the measured results for the open fire stove and Modified double skirt rocket stove are presented in Figs. 7, 8, 9, 10, 11, 12.

Figure 7; depicts the results of Indoor air pollution meter for recording Carbon Monoxide and particulate matters for improved double skirt Rocket stove. However; it is observed from above figure that maximum intensity of carbon monoxide emission is 3.6 ppm recorded after 13 min; when cooking started in open shade; moreover, during these 13 min the fluctuations of Particulate matters from 0–152 ug/m^3 are observed. Furthermore the maximum flow of particulate materials in the atmosphere recorded is 191 ug/m^3 at 3.16 PM after a 19 min from the start of cooking food. Nevertheless; non-significant flow in fluctuations of Particulate matters and carbon monoxide are recorded upto the mid of cooking preparation; after that some significant changes in PM and CO are recorded for test 1 of Improved double skirt Rocket stove. Also; it is observed that the minimum and maximum intensity of carbon monoxide emission observed is as 0 and 3.6 ppm and the minimum and maximum intensity of particulate matters recorded is 0 and

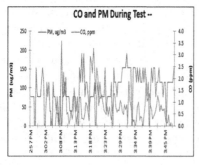
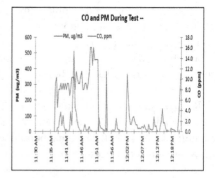

Fig. 7. CO and PM levels during IRS test-1   **Fig. 8.** CO and PM levels during IRS test 2

191 ug/m^3 respectively. Figure 8; depicts the second test results of Indoor air pollution meter for recording Carbon Monoxide and particulate matters for improved double skirt Rocket stove. However; it is observed from the above figure that maximum intensity of carbon monoxide emission is 15.4 ppm recorded after 13 min; when cooking started in open shade; moreover, during these 13 min the fluctuations of Particulate matters from 0–344 ug/m^3 are observed. Furthermore, the maximum flow of particulate materials in the atmosphere recorded is 536 ug/m^3 at 11.46 AM after 21 min from the start of cooking food. Nevertheless; non-significant flow in fluctuations of Particulate matters are recorded upto the mid of cooking preparation; after that zero value of PM recorded, however for carbon monoxide non-significant fluctuations are recorded from stat to end of testing. Also; it is observed that the minimum and maximum intensity of carbon monoxide emission observed is as 0 and 15.4 ppm and the minimum and maximum intensity of particulate.

Figure 9; depicts the third test results of Indoor air pollution meter for recording Carbon Monoxide and particulate matters for improved double skirt Rocket stove. However; it is observed from the above figure that maximum intensity of carbon monoxide emission is 13.2 ppm recorded after 18 min; when cooking started in open shade; moreover, during these 18 min the fluctuations of Particulate matters from 0–7903 ug/m^3 are observed. Furthermore, the maximum flow of particulate materials in the atmosphere recorded is 7,903 ug/m^3 at 04.07 PM after 4 min from the start of cooking food. Nevertheless; non-significant flow in fluctuations of Particulate matters and carbon monoxide are recorded for the complete test, also; it is observed that the minimum and maximum intensity of carbon monoxide emission observed is as 0 and 13.2 ppm and the minimum and maximum intensity of particulate matters recorded is 0 and 7,903 ug/m respectively.

Figure 10; depicts the first test results of Indoor air pollution meter for recording Carbon Monoxide and particulate matters for Three stone open fire stove. However; it is observed from the above figure that maximum intensity of carbon monoxide emission is 22.9 ppm recorded after 12 min; when cooking started in open shade; moreover, during these 12 min the fluctuations of Particulate matters from 0–96 ug/m^3 are observed. Furthermore, the maximum flow of particulate materials in the atmosphere recorded is 96 ug/m^3 from 2.56 PM to 3.17 PM. Nevertheless; significant flow in fluctuations of Particulate matters are recorded and non-significant fluctuations of carbon monoxide are recorded for the complete test, Also; it is observed that the minimum and maximum

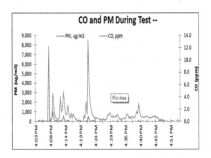

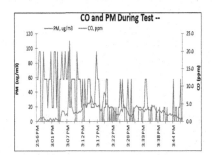

Fig. 9. CO and PM levels during IRS test 3.   **Fig. 10.** CO and PM levels during three stone open fire test 1

intensity of carbon monoxide emission observed is as 0 and 22.9 ppm and the minimum and maximum intensity of particulate matters recorded is 0 and 96 ug/m³ respectively. Figure 11; depicts the second test results of Indoor air pollution meter for recording Carbon Monoxide and particulate matters for Three stone open fire stove. However; it is observed from the above figure that maximum intensity of carbon monoxide emission is 8.6 ppm recorded after 30 min; when cooking started in open shade; moreover, during these 30 min the fluctuations of Particulate matters from 0–1,616 ug/m³ are observed. Furthermore, the maximum flow of particulate materials in the atmosphere recorded is 1616 ug/m³ after 8 min during cooking start. Nevertheless; non-significant flow in fluctuations of Particulate matters and carbon monoxide emission are recorded complete test, also; it is observed that the minimum and maximum intensity of carbon monoxide emission observed is as 0 and 8.6 ppm and the minimum and maximum intensity of particulate matters recorded is 0 and 1,646 ug/m³ respectively.

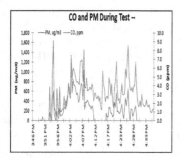

Fig. 11. CO and PM levels during three stone open fire test 2.

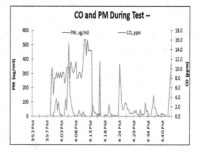

Fig. 12. CO and PM levels during three stone open fire test 3.

The comparative average test results of Indoor air pollution meter for recording Carbon Monoxide and particulate matters for Three stone open fire stove Double skirt rocket stove are presented in Table 1. Also Table 2 presents the Test results of Control cooling test for Three stone open fire stove and Double skirt IRS.

Table 1. Comparative results of average CO and PM levels for three stone open fire stove and double skirt IRS

Particular	Double Skirt IRS			Avg	WHO std	Three stone OFS			Ave
	1	2	3			1	2	3	
Avg CO, PPM	0.306	0.962	0.542	0.603	4	3.19	3.13	0.962	2.43
Avg PM kg/m	84.51	−93.59	38.68	9.870	25	7.1	−962.27	−93.591	−349.5

Table 2. Test results of CCT for three stone open fire stove and double skirt IRS

SN	Details of cooking	Unit	Test			Mean	Standard deviation	
1	Three stone stove		1	2	3			
	TWfc	g	57100	57100	57100	57100	–	–
	Wcr	g	2400	1750	1700	1950	391	391
	Edwc	g	28779	20985	40318	30027	9727	9727
	Sfc	g/kg	504	368	706	526	170	170
	Tct	min	57	59	58	58	1	1
2	Improved Double Skirt Rocket stove							
	Twfc	g	57100	57100	57100	57100	–	–
	Wcr	g	500	1250	1000	917		382
	Edwc	g	16,487	18136	18286	17636	998	998
	Sfc	g/kg	289	318	320	309	17	17
	Tct	min	87	102	97	95	8	8
3	Comparison TSOFS and IDSRS							
				% difference	T-Test	Sig @ 95%?		
	Sfc	g/kg		41%	−2.19			No
	Tct	min		−64%	−3.19			Yes

Twfc:- Total weight of food cooked, **Wcr:-** Weight of char remaining, **Edwc:-** Equivalent dry wood consum, **Sfc:-** Specific fuel consumption, **Tct:-** Total cooking time

3.2 Discussion

From Table 1; it is observed that the average of three experiments of 0.603 ppm value of carbon emission level is recorded for double skirt rocket stove. And for three stone open fire rocket stove average of three experiment carbon monoxide level recorded is 2.427 ppm. It means the that double skirt rocket stove is having 1.824 ppm carbon monoxide less as compared to three stone rocket stoves. However, the WHO recommends the safe value of carbon monoxide acceptable for human being is below 4.00 ppm in 24 h mean. However; the carbon emission level is safe in both cooking methods for using single stove. But for the commercial purpose there is a need to use a greater number of cooking stoves for cooking. Hence; if more than three stone open fire stoves used in a same cooking shade, the carbon emission level may exceed the value 4 ppm recommended by WHO guide line. While for double skirt IRS the value may not crossed the maximum value 4 ppm recommended by WHO in the same condition. Also, the average PM level for double skirt IRS observed in Table 1 is 9.87 ug/m^3 for three experiments. And for three stone the average of PM level for three experiments noted is −349.587 ug/m^3 means negligible. By following both methods, the value recorded is less than 25 ug/m^3 recommended by WHO. Hence; the double skirt rocket stove is safer and more suitable for cooking the food. CO and PM levels were significantly reduced with the improved double skirt stoves. CO levels over the 24 h period is much lower than the maximum allowable exposure level recommended by WHO. With the improved stoves, CO level is reduced by 24.85% compared to the three stone open fire stove conditions. From Table 2; it is observed that, while using three stone open fire stove, it needs to add much fuel wood once in three direction. After burning is started, much amount of heat is dissipated to the atmosphere. In addition, cookers are exposed to heat, Particulate matters and carbon monoxide during cooking. This stove can cook 57.1 kg W about in 1 h. The mean specific fuel consumption of the stove in three tests is about 526 g/Kg. However, for Double skirt IRS is 309 g/Kg. During testing institutional rocket stove (IRS), Limited burning fuel is adding in the specified burning chamber. After burning is started, less amount of heat is dissipated to the atmosphere. In addition, cookers are not exposed to heat, particulate matters and carbon monoxide during cooking. This stove can take about 1:30 h to cook 57.1 kg W. However, the cooking time is somehow longer in improved double skirt rocket stove, the fuel consumption is better than three stone open fire stove by 41%.

4 Conclusion

From this study the following conclusions are made;

(1) During the test, the average specific fuel consumption of improved double skirt rocket stove observed is lesser than by 41% over the three stone open fire stove.
(2) The improved double skirt rocket stove helps to reduce the emission of CO concentration levels in the kitchen by 24.85%. However, the average of three experimental results the emission of carbon monoxide is 0.603 ppm, and PM is 9.870 for the double skirt rocket stove.
(3) The improved double skirt rocket stoves help to keep the kitchen and nearer surrounding area clean and hygienic and free from carbon monoxide, and kept the atmosphere free from smoke and soot which can severely spoil the food and make running nose and watery eyes. The improved stove can store only 200-l sizes cooking pot in the assigned skirt.
(4) The double skirt rocket stove is constructed from structural steels, sheets, clay and insulation materials (pumice) that help it to reduce the heat loss during cooking.

The improved double skirt IRS stove is ergonomically safe less hazardous and preferred to work on cool, smokeless kitchen, and helped cookers to maintain their strength throughout the day.

References

1. Gaia Consulting Oy: Improved Cook Stoves Final Report GHG Mitigation and Sustainable Development Through the Promotion of Energy Efficient Cooking in Social Institutions in Ethiopia, p. 18 (2012)
2. Samet, J.M., Marbury, M.C., Spengler, J.D.: Health effects and sources of indoor air pollution (Part 1). Am. Rev. Respir. Dis. **136**, 1486–1508 (1987)

3. Gold, D.R.: Indoor air pollution. Clin. Chest Med. **13**, 215–229 (1992)
4. Cliff, J.: Indoor air pollution and acute respiratory infections in children. Lancet **339**, 396–398 (1992)
5. Koning, H.W., Smith, K.R., Last, J.M.: Biomass fuel consumption and health. Bull. World Health Organ. **63**, 11–26 (1985)
6. Kolhe, K.P.: Development and testing of tree climbing and harvesting device for mango and coconut trees. Indian Coconut J. **52**(3), 15–19 (2009). Published by Ministry of Agriculture, CDB board Kochi, Kerala
7. Kolhe, K.P.: Mechanized harvesting device a need of coconut growers in India. Indian Coconut J. **73**(2), 15–19 (2010). Published by Ministry of Agriculture, CDB Board Kochi, Kerala
8. Kolhe, K.P., Jadhav, B.B.: Testing and performance evaluation of tractor mounted hydraulic elevator for mango orchard. Am. J. Eng. Appl. Sci. **4**(1), 179–186 (2011)
9. Kolhe, K.P., Powar, A.G., Dhakane, A.D., Mankar, S.H.: Stability and ergonomic design features of tractor mounted hydraulic elevator. Am. J. Eng. Appl. Sci. **4**(3), 380–389 (2011)
10. Oluyamo, S.S., Bello, O.R.: Particle sizes and thermal insulation properties of some selected wood materials for solar device applications. IOSR J. Appl. Phys. **6**(2), 54–58 (2014)
11. Ghader, A.: Int. J. Adv. Appl. Sci. **1**(6), 31–36 (2014)
12. Celik, S., Family, R., Menguc, M.P.: Analysis of perlite and pumice based building insulation materials. J. Build. Eng. **6**, 105–111 (2016)
13. Bryden, M., et al.: Design Principles for Wood Burning Cook Stoves. Aprovecho Research Center, Cottage Grove (2002)

Shell and Tube Heat Exchanger, Empirical Modeling Using System Identification

Firew Dereje Olana[1]([✉]), Beza Nekatibeb Retta[2], Tadele Abera Abose[3],
and Samson Mekibib Atnaw[2]

[1] Faculty of Engineering and Technology, Mettu University, Mettu, Ethiopia
firew.dereje@gmail.com
[2] Addis Ababa Science and Technology University, Addis Ababa, Ethiopia
{beza.nekatibeb,samson.mekbib}@aastu.edu.et
[3] Addis Ababa Institute of Technology, Addis Ababa University, Addis Ababa, Ethiopia
tadenegn@gmail.com

Abstract. In many industrial process and operations, shell and tube heat exchangers are one of the most important thermal devices that sustained a wide range of operating temperature and pressure. However, the nonlinearity nature of the heat exchangers, and the exclusions of disturbances and uncertainties in linear models, makes the task of mathematical modeling of the system becomes challenging. Here, the solution followed for such problems is experimentally finding linear mathematical model that includes the effect of disturbances. To avoid problem of the system nonlinearities, the overall system is partitioned in to three operating ranges. Then, experimentally generated input-output data has been used in the MATLAB in order to identify the three partitioned system models. For each particular operating range, input-output data has been collected and analyzed using MATLAB environment. After iterative procedure, the plant models are obtained with satisfactory accuracy and residual analysis within range of limits. The results showed that the first test, the second test and the third test models have the best fit of 80.28%, 81.16% and 80.86% respectively. Finally, the overall model is approximated to single linear model that represent all operating ranges.

Keywords: Heat exchanger · System partitioning · System identification · Linear approximation

1 Introduction

In many engineering processes, such as nuclear plant, petrochemical, food processing, beverage and pharmaceutical industries heat exchangers are important thermal devices and they are usually characterized by high energy demands [1, 2, 6]. There are different types of heat exchangers that can be used in industries but the most commonly used ones are shell and tube heat exchangers. Most industrial processes require acceptable model for such devices. There are some methods of determining a model for a system, namely first principle and empirical models [3, 4]. First principle modeling involves accepted mathematical and scientific equations that describe the physics and principle of a given

© ICST Institute for Computer Sciences, Social Informatics and Telecommunications Engineering 2020
Published by Springer Nature Switzerland AG 2020. All Rights Reserved
N. G. Habtu et al. (Eds.): ICAST 2019, LNICST 308, pp. 548–556, 2020.
https://doi.org/10.1007/978-3-030-43690-2_40

process. The accuracy of this method increases with high level understanding of the physical system and the insertion of dynamic equation which affects the process, but practically it is difficult to take all dynamics into account. On the other hand, empirical modeling provides a way to handle unmolded dynamics and uncertainties [3, 5, 7].

Heat exchangers are nonlinear with changing process gains, time constants, and dead times. In spite of this fact, it has been traditionally modeled using linear techniques, which use constant gains, time constants and dead times. The heat exchangers have different gain, time constant and dead time at different range of flow rate, thus, the model of the system is time variant [5]. Many researchers have used linear time invariant model without inclusion of unmolded dynamics and uncertainty, this makes the system difficult to control [15–17]. In order to have the disturbance model of the system the experimental conduct has to be done between disturbance input to output controlled variable (Fig. 1).

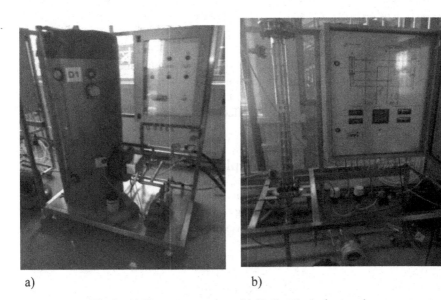

a)   b)

Fig. 1. (a) Hot water generator (b) Shell and tube heat exchange

2 Experimental Design and System Identification

The experiment is conducted using pilot plant of shell and tube heat exchanger. In the beginning, the partitioning strategy has been done, that is experimentally partitioning based on the flow rate [8]. This experiment takes 200 L/h of cold water or disturbance variable, hot water input as manipulated variable and cold water output as controlled variable. The Experiment is performed by varying the manipulated variable flow rate from 150 L/h up to 450 L/h. The range of the flow rate is determined by practical partitioning and capacity of the heat exchanger, for instance there is no significant model difference at 1 L/h to 150 L/h. Therefore, the remaining ranges also performed in the same way. In order to obtain the disturbance model, applying the input signal through disturbance input, and collect the data accordingly. The dimension of the heat exchanger is 1.5 × 0.7 × 2 m including its stand and measurement accessories. The input for the system is pseudo random signal with different amplitude. The experimental specifications are shown in Table 1. A separate data has been collected for model training and validation. The input-output signals for model training are shown in Fig. 2a, b and c and for model validation are shown in Fig. 3a, b, and c.

Table 1. System identification experimental specification

No of tests	Hot water flow rate (L/h)	Cold water flowrate (L/h)	Hot water temperature (°C)	Cold water temperature (°C)
Test one	150	200	42	28
Test two	300	200	48	28
Test three	450	200	40	28

For test one, the input data and validation data has been taken 315 with 1 s sample time. For test two, the input data and validation data has been taken 461 with 1 s sample time. For test three, the input data has been taken 462 with 1 s sample time and 460 validation data. In all the three cases the effect of the disturbance is included during experimenting.

3   Linear Approximation of Multiple Models

The idea of multiple modeling is to approximate a nonlinear system with a set of relatively simple local models valid in certain operating regions. In order to have one linear model that represents overall operating range the weighted sum of the individual models has to be calculated as following [9–14].

$$\mu_P = \frac{\frac{1}{\epsilon_p(t)}}{\sum_{j=1}^{m} \frac{1}{\epsilon_j(t)}} \tag{1}$$

$$X(k+1) = \sum_{P=1}^{m} \mu_P A_P X(k) + \sum_{P=1}^{m} \mu_P B_P U(k) \tag{2}$$

$$Y(k) = \sum_{P=1}^{m} \mu_P C_P X(k) \tag{3}$$

Where μ_P is the weighted function, $\epsilon_p(t)$ indicates the error between the system output value and the estimated output value of each linear model and, m is number of linear models.

4   Result and Discussion

The aim this paper is finding linear model for shell and tube heat exchanger using empirical modeling. The models obtained from the response for input signals are identified

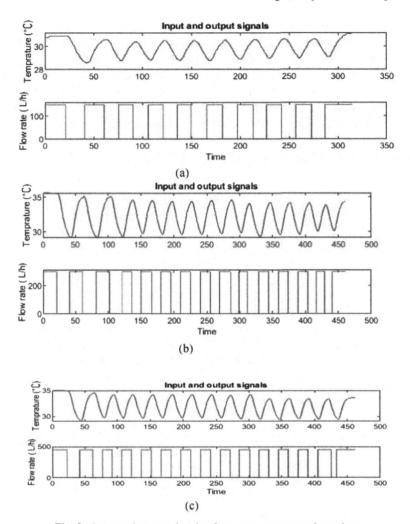

Fig. 2. Input and output signals of test one, test two and test three

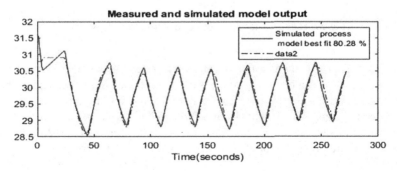

Fig. 3. The simulated and validation data output of test one

using process model (transfer function model). After reiterative procedure the model for the three tests are attained with different percentage of accuracy. Figures 3, 4, and 5 illustrated the output models using the validation data. Figures 6, 7, and 8 illustrate residual analysis test one, test two and test three respectively, the residual analyses are shown in 99% confidence interval. The residual analysis provides the information to accept the model. If the residual analysis exists between the limit line the model is acceptable. The variation in the simulated and validated data in the range of 0–50 s is because of the input and validation data has been collected in different days with different room temperature, this cause little variation in simulated and validation data (Tables 2 and 3).

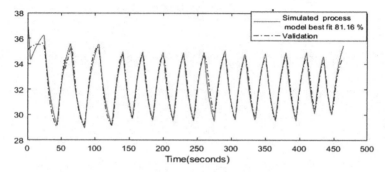

Fig. 4. The simulated and validation data output of test two

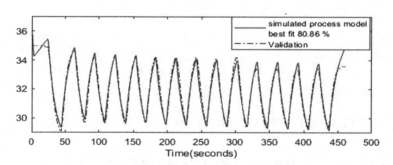

Fig. 5. The simulated and validation data output of test three

The linear approximation of the non-linearity system has to be calculated in the following equations. The overall system has been partitioned in to three regions based on manipulated variable of flow rate. In order to have one linear model that represents overall operating range the weighted sum of the individual models as following. The heat exchanger models are divided in to three regions with accuracy of 80.28%, 81.16%, and 80.86%. Therefore, the error of the three models are listed as follow:

$$\epsilon_1 = 0.1769, \ \epsilon_2 = 0.1381, \ \epsilon_3 = 0.1914$$

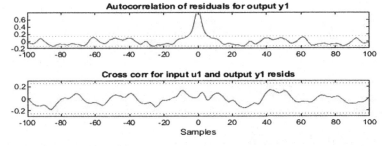

Fig. 6. Residual analysis of test one

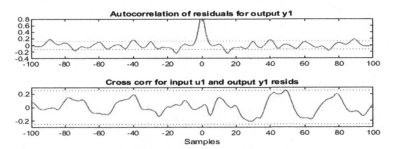

Fig. 7. Residual analysis of test two

$$\mu_P = \frac{\frac{1}{\epsilon_p(t)}}{\sum_{j=1}^{3} \frac{1}{\epsilon_j(t)}} \tag{4}$$

$$\sum_{p=1}^{m} \mu_p = 1 \tag{5}$$

$$\mu_1 = 0.31199, \ \mu_2 = 0.3996, \ and \ \mu_3 = 0.28835$$

$$X(k+1) = \sum_{P=1}^{m} \mu_P A_P X(k) + \sum_{P=1}^{m} \mu_P B_P U(k) \tag{6}$$

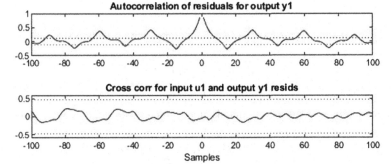

Fig. 8. Residual analysis of test three

Table 2. Transfer function model of shell and tube heat exchanger with different inputs

No	Plant model	Plant model best fit (%)	FPE	MSE
Test one	$G_1(s) =$ $\dfrac{0.40696(1+47.22\,S)e^{-3.5S}}{10168.7\,S^2+965.78\,S+1}$	80.28	0.0115	0.01439
Test two	$G2(s) =$ $\dfrac{0.21574(1+58.257\,S)e^{-3.15S}}{(1+475.55\,S)+(1+9.252\,S)}$	81.16	0.06881	0.06704
Test three	$G3(s) =$ $\dfrac{0.13938(1+46.941\,S)e^{-2.82S}}{(1+452.47\,S)+(1+8.2768\,S)}$	80.86	0.1075	0.1048

Table 3. Transfer function of disturbance model

No of models	Disturbance model
Test one	$G_{d1}(s) = \dfrac{0.31407(1-27.057*S)e^{-6S}}{6441\,S^2+831.3\,S+1}$
Test two	$G_{d2}(s) = \dfrac{0.31089(1-87.816*S)e^{-7.5S}}{11238\,S^2+1690.6\,S+1}$
Test three	$G_{d3}(s) = \dfrac{0.29977(1-69.871*S)e^{-2.3S}}{11804.8\,S^2+1663.7\,S+1}$

$$Y(k) = \sum_{P=1}^{3} \mu_P C_P X(k) \tag{7}$$

$$Y(k) = (\mu_1 C_1 X(k) + \mu_2 C_2 X(k) + \mu_3 C_3 X(k)) \tag{8}$$

The nonlinear system is approximated by the following global linear model.

$$X(k+1) = \begin{bmatrix} 0.9278 & -0.0271 & -0.0018 \\ 0.024 & 1 & 0 \\ 0 & 0.026 & 1 \end{bmatrix} X(k) + \begin{bmatrix} 0.0121 \\ 0 \\ 0 \end{bmatrix} U(k)$$

$$Y(k) = \begin{bmatrix} -0.0178 & 0.044 & 0.0351 \end{bmatrix} X(k) \tag{9}$$

The approximated linear model of shell and tube heat exchanger is shown as below equation.

$$G(s) = \frac{0.23601(1+49.8s)}{(1+9.625s)(1+567.9s)} e^{-3.252\,S} \tag{10}$$

The local linear disturbance models approximated to single global disturbance models.

$$G_d(s) = \frac{0.00013953\,(1+0.1772s)}{(1+0.1745s)(1+0.2342s)} \tag{11}$$

5 Conclusion

In this paper empirical model that represents the real system and handle unmolded disturbance and uncertainty is presented. Laboratory shell and tube heat exchanger has been used to conduct the experiment. Input-output data including the effect of disturbance was generated experimentally and fed to the MATLAB system identification toolbox as an input. To avoid system nonlinearities, the overall system is partitioned in to three operating range. For each particular operating range, input-output data has been collected and analyzed using MATLAB Software. Finally, after iterative procedure the partitioned plant models are obtained with satisfactory accuracy and residual values within range of limits. The results showed that the first test, the second test and the third test models have the best fit of 80.28% with MSE of 0.01439, 81.16% with MSE of 0.06704 and 80.86% with MSE of 0.1048 respectively. Finally, the overall model is approximated to single linear model that represent all operating ranges.

Acknowledgment. The Authors would like to acknowledge Department of Chemical Engineering of Addis Ababa Science and Technology University for their help during experimental setup.

References

1. Nithya, S., Gour, A.S., Sivakumaran, S., Radhakrishnan, T.K.: Predictive controller design for a shell and tube heat exchanger. In: IEEE International Conference on Intelligent and Advanced Systems, pp. 1075–1080 (2007)
2. Vasickaninova, A., Bakosova, M.: Robust controller design for a heat exchanger. In: IEEE International Conference on Process Control, pp. 113–118 (2016)
3. Tangirala, A.K.: Principles of System Identification Theory and Practice. CRC Press, New York (2015)
4. Vinaya, K.V., Ramkumar, K., Alagesan, V.: Control of heat exchangers using model predictive controller. In: IEEE International Conference Advance Engineering Science and Management, pp. 242–246 (2012)
5. Khan, S.: Modeling and Controlling Heat Exchanger Process. LAP Lambert Academic Publishing, Hamirpur (2017)
6. Thulukkanam, K.: Heat Exchanger Design Handbook. CRC Press, New York (2013)
7. Wayne, B.B.: Process Control Modeling, Design, and Simulation. Prentice Hall, Upper Saddle River (2002)
8. El Ferik, S., Ahmed, A.: Modeling and identification of nonlinear systems: a review of the multimodel approach—part 1. IEEE Trans. Syst. Man Cybern. Syst. **47**, 2168–2216 (2017)
9. Johansen, T., Bjarne, F.: Operating regime based process modeling and identification. In: Conference on Automatic Control, Trondheim, Norway, pp. 1–33 (1995)
10. Jingjing, D., Johansen, T.A.: Integrated multi-model control of nonlinear systems based on gap metric and stability margin. Ind. Eng. Chem. Res. **53**, 10206–10215 (2014)
11. El Ferik, S., Ahmed, A.: Modeling and identification of nonlinear systems: a review of the multi-model approach—part 2. IEEE Trans. Syst. Man Cybern. Syst. **47**, 2168–2216 (2017)
12. Palizban, H.A., Safavi, A.A., Romagnoli, J.A.: A nonlinear control design approach based on multi-linear models. In: Proceedings of the American Control Conference, New Mexico, pp. 3490–3494 (1997)

13. Nekoui, M.A., Sajadi, S.M.: Nonlinear system identification using locally linear model tree and particle swarm optimization. In: IEEE International Conference on Industrial Technology, Mumbai, pp. 1563–1568 (2006)
14. Imai, S., Yamamoto, T.: Design and experiment of a IMC-based PID controller using multiple local linear models. In: IEEE/ETFA International Conference on Emerging Technologies and Factory Automation, pp. 6505–6509 (2017)
15. Sivaram, A., Sainabha, M., Ramkumar, K.: Parameter identification and control of a shell and tube heat exchanger. Int. J. Eng. Technol. (IJET) 5(2), 1589–1593 (2013)
16. Abdulrahman, A.A., Emhemed, A.A., Hanafi, D.: Modelling and controller design for temperature control of power plant heat exchanger. Univ. J. Control Autom. 5(3), 49–53 (2017)
17. Mithun, P., Satheeshbabu, R., Thirunavukkarasu, I., George, V.I., Shreesha, C.: Non-linear controller design for shell and tube heat exchanger—an experimentation approach. In: Proceeding of 2nd The IRES International Conference, Berlin, pp. 31–35 (2015)

A Review on Design and Performance of Improved Biomass Cook Stoves

Atsede Tariku Woldesemayate$^{(\boxtimes)}$ and Samson Mekbib Atnaw

Department of Mechanical Engineering, College of Electrical and Mechanical Engineering,
Addis Ababa Science and Technology University, Addis Ababa, Ethiopia
Meng349dbu@gmail.com

Abstract. Nearly half of the world's population uses solid fuels for their domestic energy needs. Among those who use indoor cooking stoves, the poorest families living in rural areas most frequently use solid fuels. The use of indoor three stone fire cookers in rural areas of developing countries is known to be detrimental to the health of people. Hence, development of an improved biomass cook stove will be helpful for the betterment of people's lives especially women. This review presents results of studies carried out on improved biomass cook stoves. Traditional cook stove consumes high amount of resulting in higher health risks to people from higher carbon emissions. In order to avoid this health risk as well as reducing fuel consumption number of researchers in our countries could be design, develop and testing of a new improved cook stove. The discussion on the design of improved cook stoves was presented under different classifications with regarding to Air supply system, Fuel type, Operation, Number of pot and Construction material. In addition, results of experimental investigation done by various authors on the performance of cook stoves in terms of efficiency, burning rate, specific fuel consumption and power output is presented. Upon this parameter some of the researchers compare the traditional biomass cook stove with improved cook stove. From experimental test result the improved cook stoves are high performance than traditional stove.

Keywords: Biomass cook stove · Thermoelectric generator cook stove · Thermal efficiency

1 Introduction

Biomass cook stoves are commonly used for cooking and heating of food in rural households. A biomass cook stove is heated by burning wood, charcoal, animal dung or crop residue. So that nearly half of the world's population, approximately 3.5 billion people, uses biomass fuels for their domestic energy needs. Among those who use indoor cooking stoves, the poorest families living in rural areas most frequently use solid fuels, where it continues to be relied on by up to 90% of households [1]. In developing countries households consume significantly less energy than those in developed countries whereby over 50% of the energy is for food preparation purpose. The average rural family spends

© ICST Institute for Computer Sciences, Social Informatics and Telecommunications Engineering 2020
Published by Springer Nature Switzerland AG 2020. All Rights Reserved
N. G. Habtu et al. (Eds.): ICAST 2019, LNICST 308, pp. 557–565, 2020.
https://doi.org/10.1007/978-3-030-43690-2_41

20% or more of its income on purchasing of wood or charcoal for cooking. In urban area also frequently spend a significant portion of their income on the purchase of wood or charcoal. Deforestation and erosion often result from harvesting wood for cooking fuel [2].

Biomass cook stove technology is increasingly being used to address the performance goals of reduction of harmful emission due to incomplete combustion and increasing thermal efficiency, thus reducing fuel consumption. The three stone fire cook stove is the most basic, but still extremely common method for cooking with biomass fuel, and is often used as a benchmark for comparison. The three stone fire cook stove is simply an open fire cook stove, gaining its name from the stones used to hold the cook piece over the fire. Improved biomass cook stoves have been able to reduce Carbone mono oxide and particulate matter emissions by 50–75% and increase the fuel efficiency by 30–50% compared to the three stone fire cook stove configuration [3]. These reductions were accomplished largely by enclosing the fire in a combustion chamber. The primary benefits of chamber enclosure are airflow control (providing better mixing with reduced quenching) and reduced convective and radiative heat transfer losses. The combustion chamber also allows the stove designer to locate the cook piece for reduced emissions and increased heat transfer.

This review paper mainly focused on design and improvement of biomass cook stove. There are a number of researchers that developed biomass cook stone in rural areas as well as in developing countries. As we know in this area people mainly children's are preparing food in traditional mechanism. The traditional mechanism of cooking was on a three-stone cooking fire or on a mud stove. The three-stone fire is the cheapest stove to produce and requiring only three suitable stones of the same height on which a cooking pot can be balanced over a fire. However, this cooking method is known to have the following problems: Biomass fuel smoke is vented into the home, instead of outdoors and also it causing health problems, Fuel is wasted, as heat is allowed to escape into the open air this requires the user to gather more fuel and may result in increased deforestation for wood is used for fuel, during food preparation, people especially women's uses only one cooking pot at a time, the use of an open fire creates a risk of burns and scalds.

Therefore, in order to avoid the above problems a number of researchers tried to develop improved cook stoves. Improved cook stoves are more efficient, which means the stove users spending less time for gathering fuel wood or other fuels, suffer less emphysema and other lung diseases prevalent in smoke filed homes, while reducing deforestation and air pollution.

2   Working Principle and Design Improvement of Cook Stove

Improved cook stove consists of chimney, a grate ash scrapper, combustion chamber and air jacket for flow of air in primary and secondary streams. The combustion air is preheated through the hot surfaces of the stove before it is drawn in to the stove either by natural drafts or forced draft during the burning of the various solid fuels. Improvement of a biomass cook stove done by Nandish et al. [1], Ayo et al. [2], Pavan et al. [4] and Amiebenomo et al. [5] were by design of combustion chamber, proper provision of insulation around the combustion chamber and providing sufficient air for the combustion chamber. But their overall design structure and models were different from each other. Ayo et al. [2] and Amebomo et al. [5] constructed a proper pot sit and flu gas stack in order to reduce amount of Radiation heat loss and indoor air pollution with smoke emission.

According to their stove chimney construction Ayo et al. [2] constructed large chimney on the right side of the combustion chamber. Whereas Amebomo et al. [5] constructed the chimney at the top of the combustion chamber and its height was very short compared to Ayo et al. [2]. the construction of large chimney was important for reducing environmental pollution but it was not portable and bulky.

Nandish et al. [1] constructed the biomass cook stove without any flue gas stack (chimney) so during combustion process the carbon pollutes the environment. Srivastava et al. [3], Naher et al. [6] and Ezzati et al. [7] compared traditional Cook stove with improved cook stove, however the design improvement techniques they used were found to be widely different. Zongsha et al. [8] carried out experimental investigation in order to compare the thermal performance of improved cook stove with tradition cook stove and reported that the earlier is having a better performance than the latter. Srivastava et al. [3] compared the performance of improved three pot stove with traditional cook stove with his improved cook stove consisting of three pots (making cooking of three meals at once possible and saving cooking time as a result) while Zongsha et al. [8] presented results based on a single pot cook stove. A single pot cook stove was easy to construct, chip and portable compared to three pot cook stove and also its initial cost was cheap compared to three pot stove. The three-pot cook stove constructed in a fixed position and it could not be easily moving from one area to another. The improvement techniques reported in the work of [3, 9] was significant and easy to construct in developing countries.

Pavan et al. [4] claimed a significant heat saving and improved efficiency by incorporating smoke rings to seal the annulus between the pot and the pothole as well as by improving the design of the pot seat and the flue gas exit port position [4]. Amiebenomo et al. [5] also fabricate and evaluate the performance of an improved cook stove. In this study an increased heat transfer efficiency of the stove was claimed by providing a proper pot skirt around the combustion chamber and reducing heat loss [6]. Okafor et al. [9] presented a distinctive study by designing nozzle type improved cook stove whereby the shape of the stove seems like a nozzle. Mirt stoves are a good acceptance for Enjera baking so Dresen et al. [10] and Gizachew et al. [11] studied in detail about mirt stove on the carbon emission reduction as well as fuel wood saving and also, they discuss about the performance of improved cook stove in Ethiopia but Dresen et al. [10] studied in Afromontane forest of Ethiopia. In contrast Gizachew et al. [11] studied in bale eco region of Ethiopia. Risha et al. [12] and Champier et al. [13] studied about design, development and performance evaluation of thermoelectric generator integrated with forced draft cook stove. So, compared to other types of improved cook stove this type of cook stove were helpful for developing country as well as rural area. Because in rural area there is a shortage of electric power for charging mobile battery as well as lighting LED but thermoelectric generator cook stove technology avoid such problems and also it provides multi-functional purpose for rural areas. Inside the combustion chamber there was a high amount of heat, so by using TEG (Thermo electric generator) in order to recover the waste heat. The aim of this thermo electric generator is converted heat energy in to electrical energy.

3 Advances in Cook Stoves

3.1 Thermoelectric Power Generation

Risha et al. [12], Perumal et al. [14], and Champier et al. [13] studied about thermo electric generator incorporates in a multi-functional wood stove but their cook stove arrangement as well as methodology were differed from each other. Risha et al. [12] and Perumal et al. [14] by using water boiling test in order to evaluate the performance of thermo electric generator. Among these two researcher Risha et al. [12] able to boil 6.1 kg of water in 30 min according to this parameter they could get the power generation of TEG 3 to 5 W. Perumal et al. [14] from water boiling test they can get 4.5 W and also the temperature difference of 2400 c. In contrast Champier et al. [13] cook stove compared to the above two researchers stove they developed a permanently installed stove integrated with thermo electric generator. In addition to this, they install the permanent water tank inside the cook stove so this improved cook stove was multi-functional purpose. Experimental test was done by on thermo electric and heat transfer of the model. So, during experimental test compare the electrical power and temperature using thermo electric and heat transfer equation because the performance of generator depends up on heat transfer through the model. This type of stove compared to other type of cook stove in terms of its maintenance cost as well as the total cost, it was more expensive but in terms of functionality it has multi- functional than other types of cook stoves. Champier et al. [13] produced TEG up to 9.5 W.

4 Types of Cook Stove

The different types of cook stoves could broadly be classified according to their operation, air supply, exhaust flow, portability, construction materials, fuel types and stove functions. In addition, the stoves could also be categorized as single and multi- pot, based on the number of pots of the stoves. A number of researchers developed new cook stoves and the others were improved the existing one by providing proper insulation around the combustion chamber, by using a proper construction material and by installed thermo electric generator around the cook stove in order to generate electricity for multi-functional purpose. The performance of improved biomass cook stove and traditional three stone cook stove were tested by using water boiling test, controlled cooking test and kitchen performance test So most researchers [3–5, 15–18, 20–23, 25, 26], conducted the performance of cook stove by using water boiling test. Burning rate, specific fuel consumption rate, efficiency and power output were parameters that estimate the performance of cook stove. Most of the studies [8, 11, 13, 19, 21, 23, 24, 27–30], reported the performance of cook stove using controlled cooking test. Reduced carbon emission and minimized fuel consumption are the primary parameters during experimental test. Aashish et al. [31] checked the performance of the improved cook stove using CFD software and temperature distribution along the layer (Table 1).

Table 1. Types of biomass cook stoves

Types of cook stove	Author	Title	Air supply mechanism	Construction material	Thermal efficiency (%)
1.	Nandish et al. [1]	Performance enhancement of cook stove	Forced draft 12 V AC Fan	Combustion chamber ✓ refractory cement Outer body ✓ Galvanized iron sheet	23%
2.	Pavan et al. [4]	Energy efficient wood stove	Forced draft 10 V AC Fan	Combustion chamber ✓ clay outside of the combustion chamber ✓ lined by fiber glass Outer body ✓ milled steel	22.27%
3.	Dresen et al. [10]	Fuel wood saving and carbon emission reduced by the use of ICS in Afromontane forest, Ethiopia	Natural draft	The stove body made from cement and river sand	63%
4.	Rishia et al. [12]	Design, development and performance evaluation of TEG integrated forced draft biomass cook stove	TEG integrated forced draft	Combustion chamber ✓ Glass wool TEG-sandwiched between the aluminum plate	Thermo electric generator produced 3 to 5 W
5.	Champier et al. [13]	Study of TEG in corporate in a multifunctional wood stove	Forced draft	Combustion chamber ✓ ceramic The cooking pot and the fire does not directly contact	Thermo electric generator produced up to 9.5 W

(continued)

Table 1. (*continued*)

Types of cook stove	Author	Title	Air supply mechanism	Construction material	Thermal efficiency (%)
6.	Panwar et al. [16]	Design and performance evaluation of 5kw producer gas stove	Natural draft	Combustion chamber ✓ Refractory cement Outer body ✓ milled steel	26.5%
7.	Simone et al. [17]	Design and performance assessment of a rice husk fueled stove for house hold cooking in typical sub Saharan setting	Natural draft	The body of stove made from mud brick	18%
8.	Wilson et al. [18]	Avoided emission of fuel efficient BMCS dwarf embodied emission	Natural draft	Outer body of stove made from -Milled steel sheet Fire box made from stainless steel	35%
9.	Tanmay et al. [19]	Design of energy utilization test for a BMCS formulation of an optimum air flow recipe	Natural draft	Combustion chamber ✓ glass wool insulation Outer body ✓ milled steel	30%
10.	Mohammadreza et al. [21]	Comparative evaluation of the performance of an improved biomass cookstove and traditional stoves of Iran	Natural draft	Each part of the cook stove made from metal sheet and consists of -cylinder leg -inner cylinder -outer cylinder -outer and inner cylinder coupling	35%

NB. The above all cook stoves could have uses wood as a fuel

5   Conclusions

From the above discussion, it can be concluded that there is a need to replace the traditional and inefficient biomass cooking devices with efficient cooking devices such as the improved and advanced biomass cook stove. Because traditional three stone cook stove follows different health hazard for people especially women during preparation of food as well as it increases environmental pollution. For this reason, in order to reduce this problem a number of researchers to design, developed and investigating a new improved cook stove for rural area of developing countries. In this paper the researcher's improvement techniques can be assessed in two ways. First, in most of the studies to design developed and testing of an improved biomass cook stoves with locally available material and also using different air supply mechanisms. During these improvement techniques all these researchers cannot take in to account wastage of heat on the combustion chamber. However, the other researchers to design and investigate the most fantastic technology for rural area of developing country by designing and recovering the west heat on the combustion chamber using thermo electric generator through the hot surfaces of the stove before it is drawn in to the stove either by natural drafts or forced draft during the burning of the various solid fuels.

6   Recommendation

Almost all researchers to design, developed and testing of small size biomass cook stove. for this reason, still now in developing country especially in Ethiopia almost all institutions like hotels, universities, hospitals and other institutions to prepare food using traditional three stone fire biomass cook stove. So, in order to reduce fuel consumption as well as environmental pollution, anyone who are initiate and expert to this technology to design and developed large size cook stove using locally available material.

Acknowledgement. First and for most, I would like to thank to St. Merry and her son Jesus Christ, who saves me from any kinds of obstacles. Next, I would like to dedicate this work to everyone who helped me directly and indirectly during the course of my review paper. More importantly, I want to thank with utmost gratitude Mr. Tesfaye Wondatir, Mr. Gebre Fenta, Mr. Yibeltal Tilahun and Dr. Samson Mekbib for spending their time to provide me with all the guidance and support to complete my review.

References

1. Nandish, G.: Performance enhancement of cook stove. Int. J. Renew. Energy Environ. Eng. **3**, 95–98 (2015)
2. Samuel, A.A.: Design, construction and testing of an improved wood stove. AU J.T. **13**(1), 12–18 (2009)
3. Joshi, M., Srivastava, R.K.: Development and performance evaluation of an improved three pot cook stove for cooking in rural Uttarakhand, India. Int. J. Adv. Res. **1**, 596–602 (2013)
4. Pavan, H.: Energy efficient wood stove, aloysius Fernandez. Int. J. Eng. Innov. Res. **5**(4), 260–263 (2016)

5. Amiebenomo, S.O.: Fabrication and performance evaluation of an improved biomass cook stove. Int. J. Eng. Res. Technol. (IJERT) **2**(3), 1–9 (2013)
6. Brauer, M., Naeher, M., Lipsett, L.P., Zelikoff, J.T., Simpson, C.D., Koenig, J.Q.: Wood smoke health effects a review. Inhalation Toxicol. **19**, 67–106 (2007)
7. Lopez, A.D., Ezzati, M., Rodgers, A., Vander, H.S., Murray, C.J.: Selected major risk factors and global and regional burden of disease. Lancet **360**, 1347–1360 (2002)
8. Duanmu, L., Wang, Z., Yuan, P., Ning, M., Liu, Y.: Experimental study of thermal performance comparison based on the traditional and multifunctional biomass stoves in China. Procedia Eng. **121**, 845–853 (2015)
9. Okafor, I.F., Unachukwu, G.O.: Performance evaluation of nozzle type improved wood cook stove. Int. J. Sci. Eng. Res. **4**, 1195–1204 (2013)
10. Dresen, E.: Fuelwood savings and carbon emission reductions by the use of improved cooking stoves in an Afromontane Forest, Ethiopia. Land **3**, 1137–1157 (2014)
11. Tolera, M., Gizachew, B.: Adoption and kitchen performance test of improved cook stove in the Bale Eco-Region of Ethiopia. Energy. Sustain. Dev. **45**, 186–189 (2018)
12. Prasad, R., Mala, R., Vijayc, V.K., Vermad, A.R.: The design, development and performance evaluation of thermoelectric generator (TEG) integrated forced draft biomass cookstove. Procedia Comput. Sci. **52**, 723–729 (2015)
13. Champier, D.: Study of a TE (thermoelectric) generator incorporated in a multifunction wood stove. Energy **36**, 1518–1526 (2011)
14. Ram, N.K., Raman, P., Gupta, R.: Development, design and performance analysis of a forced draft clean combustion cookstove powered by a thermo electric generator with multi-utility options. Energy **69**, 813–825 (2014)
15. Rathod, A.P., Motghare, K.A.: Performance Evaluation and Heat transfer studies on Biomass Gasifier cook-stove. Int. J. Appl. Innov. Eng. Manag. (IJAIEM) **4**(5), 353–361 (2015)
16. Panwar, N.L., Rathore, N.S.: Design and performance evaluation of a 5kW producer gas stove. Biomass Bioenerg. **32**, 1349–1352 (2008)
17. Parmigiani, S.P., Vitali, F., Lezzi, A.M., Vaccari, M.: Design and performance assessment of a rice husk fueled stove for household cooking in a typical sub-Saharan setting. Energy. Sustain. Dev. **23**, 15–24 (2014)
18. Wilson, D.L.: Avoided emissions of a fuel-efficient biomass cookstove dwarf embodied emissions. Dev. Eng. **1**, 45–52 (2016)
19. Jain, Tanmay, Sheth, P.N.: Design of energy utilization test for a biomass cook stove: Formulation of an optimum air flow recipe. Energy **166**, 1097–1105 (2019)
20. Paulsen, A.D., Kunsa, T.A., Carpenter, A.L.: Gaseous and particulate emissions from a chimneyless biomass cookstove equipped with a potassium catalyst. Appl. Energy **235**, 369–378 (2019)
21. Amare, D., Endeblhatu, A., Muhabaw, A.: Enhancing biomass energy efficiency in rural households of Ethiopia. J. Energy Nat. Resour. **4**(2), 27–33 (2015)
22. Panwar, N.L., Mehetre, S.A., Sharma, D., Kumar, H.: Improved biomass cookstoves for sustainable development a review. Renew. Sustain. Energy Rev. **73**, 672–687 (2017)
23. Murali, J., Raman, P., Sakthivadivel, D., Vigneswaran, V.S.: Performance evaluation of three types of forced draft cook stoves using fuel wood and coconut shell. Biomass and Bio Energy **49**, 333–340 (2013)
24. Ochieng, C.A., Tonne, C., Vardoulakis, S.: A comparison of fuel use between a low cost, improved wood stove and traditional three-stone stove in rural Kenya. Biomass Bio Energy **58**, 258–266 (2013)
25. Ram, N.P., Kaushik, S.C., Jain, S.K.: Transient heat transfer for liquid boiling with a cookstove: a start of art. Chang Village **6**(6), 411–421 (1984)
26. Rowe, D.M., Nuwayhid, R.Y., Min, G.: Low cost stove-top thermoelectric generator for regions with unreliable electricity supply. Renewable Energy **28**, 205–222 (2003)

27. Vitali, F., Parmigiani, S.: Agricultural waste as household fuel: Techno-economic assessment of a new rice-husk cookstove for developing countries. Waste Manag. **33**, 2762–2770 (2013)
28. Still, D.K., et al.: Laboratory experiments regarding the use of filtration and retained heat to reduce particulate matter emissions from biomass cooking. Energy. Sustain. Dev. **42**, 129–135 (2018)
29. Singh, V.K., Suresh, R., Malik, J.K., Datta, A., Pal, R.C.: Evaluation of the performance of improved biomass cooking stoves with different solid biomass fuel types. Biomass Bioenergy **95**, 27–34 (2016)
30. Li, H., Huangfu, Y., Chen, X., Xue, C., Chen, C., Liu, G.: Effects of moisture content in fuel on thermal performance and emission of biomass semi- gasified cookstove. Energy. Sustain. Dev. **21**, 60–65 (2014)
31. Nagarhalli, M., Gandigudea, A.: Simulation of rocket cook-stove geometrical aspect for its performance improvement. Mater. Today **5**, 3903–3908 (2018)

Experimental Investigation of Augmented Horizontal Axis Wind Turbine

Abiyu Mersha Tefera[1][✉], Abdulkadir Aman[2], and Muluken Temesgen Tigabu[3]

[1] Faculty of Mechanical and Industrial Engineering,
Bahir Dar Institute of Technology, Bahir Dar University, P.O. BOX 26, Bahirdar, Ethiopia
abiyumu.16@gmail.com
[2] School of Mechanical and Industrial Engineering, Addis Ababa Institute of Technology
(AAiT), Addis Ababa University, Addis Ababa, Ethiopia
abdiaman2004@yahoo.com
[3] Faculty of Mechanical and Industrial Engineering, Bahirdar Energy Center, Bahir Dar Institute
of Technology, Bahir Dar University, P.O. BOX 26, Bahirdar, Ethiopia
mulhtemz@gmail.com

Abstract. An augmented wind turbine has been an interesting concept of wind energy conversion, due to the system capability to increase the performance of wind turbine relative to bare wind turbine with a similar size. Different capsulated wind energy systems have been studied to improve the performance of wind rotors by increasing the energy density of the wind. One of them is the nozzle-diffuser capsulated system. However, more studies concerned on the influence of the concentrator (nozzle) while little research has been done concerning on the diffuser influence and there is still a need to carry out experiment investigation. Therefore, this paper investigates the effect of the concentrator, diffuser and combined augmentation at different wind speed. In this paper, the main objective involves design and an experiment testing of the augmented wind turbine. Blade Element Momentum theory was used to design the blade. Glass fiber and thin sheet were used to manufacture non-twisted NACA 4412 blade and augmentation respectively. The tunnel wind speed was used in this experiment at 3 m/s, 4 m/s, 5 m/s, and 6 m/s. AC fan motor was used as a generator and direct measurement were performed for performance investigation. The result shows that all augmentation increases the power output. The average percentage of power variation between a bare wind turbine and augmented wind turbine was 33.8% for a diffuser, 88% for the nozzle and 81.6% for nozzle-diffuser combination. Also, augmentation is a capable of affecting the cut in speed.

Keywords: Diffuser · Nozzle · Nozzle-diffuser combined augmentation · Blade · Wind speed

© ICST Institute for Computer Sciences, Social Informatics and Telecommunications Engineering 2020
Published by Springer Nature Switzerland AG 2020. All Rights Reserved
N. G. Habtu et al. (Eds.): ICAST 2019, LNICST 308, pp. 566–575, 2020.
https://doi.org/10.1007/978-3-030-43690-2_42

1 Introduction

Wind turbine systems are among the most useful renewable energy resource in the world. To improve the aerodynamic efficiency of wind turbines under steady-state flow conditions both optimal design of wind turbine blade and integration with the electricity generation system are essential parameters [1]. There are two types of wind turbine system, horizontal axis wind turbines and vertical-axis wind turbines [2]. The criterion for maximum power extraction is called Betz criterion (Cp = 16/27). In practical operation, a commercial wind turbine may have a maximum power coefficient of about 0.4 [3]. Due to low density of air large system is require for conversion. Wind energy conversion can be improved by introducing non-rotating capsulation to rotating blade, like diffuser, nozzle, converging-diverging. A capsulated wind turbine has been an attractive concepts of wind energy conversion. Due to the system capability to increase the power performance relative to bare wind turbine with the similar size.

There is an extensive literature on augmented horizontal axis wind turbine system. Bontempo and Manna [4], analyze the performance of open and ducted wind turbines. The authors clearly conclude that with the same rotor size the capsulated wind turbine can produce a higher mass flow rate than the open wind turbine. Asl et al. [5] presents the effect of blade number and design for a ducted wind turbine. Khamlaj et al. [6] investigates the shape of the augmentation model and, although they did not carry out any experiment investigation. Rio et al. [7] studied what happen if the blade element momentum method applied to diffuser capsulated wind turbines. The results show that the power coefficient significantly influenced by the presence of the diffuser capsulation, this justify that the use of diffusers as a technology to improve performance of a wind energy system. More evidence, Vaz and Wood [8] performed a study on aerodynamic optimization of the blade of diffuser augmented horizontal wind turbines. This study was seeking a new approach to the aerodynamic optimization of a wind turbine with a diffuser. As a result, the diffuser speedup ratio was significantly influenced by an aerodynamic improvement of wind turbine geometry. In order to evaluate the proposed approach, a comparison with the classical Glauert optimization was performed for a flanged diffuser, which increased the efficiency by 35%. Pambudi et al. [9] investigated wind turbine using nozzle augmentation at lower wind speed situation. The Artificial of low wind speed have been used in this experiment at 2.4 m/s, 3.5 m/s and 4.5 m/s. This paper shows that the nozzle augmentation improves the performance of wind energy. The tip speed ratio of the turbine blade is directly proportional with nozzle diameter. The investigation shows difference number of blades, the three blades turbine consistently generates the highest power output compared to two blades and four blades turbines. The researchers, based on experimental evidence, conclude that the performance of wind energy can be improved by the combination of three blade and nozzle augmentation in areas where wind speed is low. Different capsulated wind energy system has been studied to improve the performance of wind rotor by increases the energy density of wind. One of them is nozzle-diffuser augmented wind energy system [10–12]. However, more studies concerned on the influence of nozzle augmentation and numerical investigation while little researchers have been done concerning on diffuser augmentation influence and the combination of bot. there is still a need to investigate in experiment. Therefore, this paper investigates the effect of the concentrator, diffuser and combined augmentation experimentally. Local fabrication turbine blade is also at early stage and this research has a particular ambition to analyze the aerodynamic performance of wind turbine blade that is fabricated by local available materials. To do this, the research focus on design analysis, modeling, fabrication and testing of the prototype model.

2   Materials and Methods

2.1   Design and Fabrication

The design procedures of a horizontal axis wind turbine start by determining forces in which lift forces on airfoils are the driving forces. The design of a wind rotor composed of two steps: first the choice of basic parameters such as the number of blades, the radius of the rotor, the type of airfoil shape and design tip speed ratio, and second the estimation of the blade twist angle and the chord distribution at a number of segments along with the blade. In order to produce optimum performance at a specific tip speed ratio by each segment of the blade. Calculation of blade chord and blade setting angles were done based on Blade Element Theory and by using Eqs. 1–3.

$$\phi = \frac{2}{3}\tan^{-1}(1/\lambda_r) \tag{1}$$

$$C = \frac{8\pi r}{N C_{ld}(1 - \cos\phi)} \tag{2}$$

$$C = 2.5(C_{0.9} - C_{0.5})\frac{r}{R} + 2.25C_{0.5} - 1.25C_{0.9} \tag{3}$$

Where;
ϕ is twist angle
λ_r is local tip speed ratio
C is chord
R is segment radius of rotor
N is number of blades
C_{ld} is design lift coefficient
$C_{0.9}$ is chord at 90% of radius
$C_{0.5}$ is chord at 50% of radius
R is radius of rotor

The blade was divided at equal segments based on medium density fiber wood which maximum thickness of (22 mm) and the chord values were calculated and presented in Fig. 1.

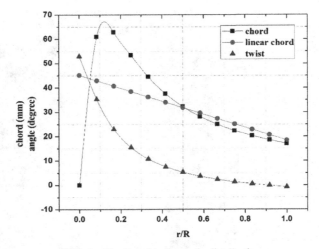

Fig. 1. Chord and twist angle distribution

The blade geometry profile of NACA 4412 taken as; root chord length 43 mm, tip chord length 15 mm, hub diameter 40 mm, length of blade 316 mm, and root cut-out 30 mm. The NACA 4412 is selected due to its suitability for power generation using three blades. As a result, the blade profile was formed by medium density fiber wood using the NACA 4412 airfoil shape. A medium density fiber wood was used because it is easy to form airfoils by using files mechanical tool. After the profile was done the mold formed by applying wax over the prepared profile. Then glass fiber was laminating over the mold with polyester resign. The polyester resign was mixed with 0.39 g hardener for hardening the fiber. After applied the resign the blade was allowed to dry for about 3 h. as show in the Figs. 2 and 3.

In order to increase the electrical power performance of the wind turbine, various augmentation system have been studied. One of them is converging diverging encapsulated wind turbine system. And step to construct the shape is presented as follow;

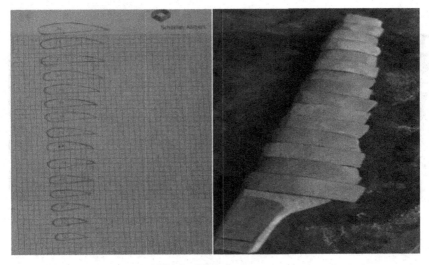

Fig. 2. Blade draft stage

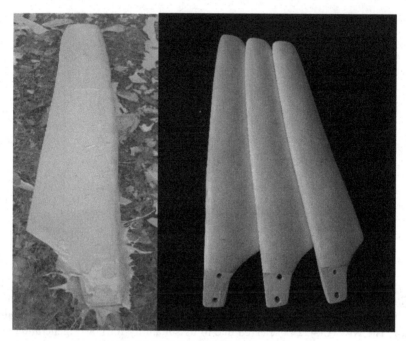

Fig. 3. Finished blade manufactured

- Draw the layout over sheet metal
- Cutting was performed in line with layout drawing
- Attaching the separate sheet metal by bending at the end of sheet metal with the dimension of 20 mm, the right and lift the end of sheet metal bent in reverse direction. Rivet bolt was used to strengthen the attachments
- Round 6 mm diameter metal was used to strengthen the augmentation and place at the right and lift end of all augmentation
- Finally, the painting was performed as shown in Figs. 4 and 5.

Fig. 4. First stage of augmentations manufacturing

Fig. 5. Final stage of augmentations manufacturing

2.2   Wind Tunnel Testing

The experiment was carried out in open wind tunnel with the capacity of 25 m/s wind speed. During the experimental work different measuring instruments, digital multimeter, digital tachometer, and digital cup anemometer were used. The experimental procedure was started with ensuring the uniformity of the up-coming freestream velocity at any point of the inlet of augmentation. Wind tunnel air velocity was measured directly by a digital cup anemometer, which was placed in front of the augmentation at different locations and velocity was measured directly. The aluminum paper was stick on at the back side of the generator shaft to measure the revolution per minute. A digital tachometer was used to measure the shaft revolution per minute at different operating condition. The hub and angle plate have been made to provide blade angle and permit to displaced (change) the blade angle. Hub was made from plastic and blade was made from fiber. The connection between hub and blade were by 6 mm bolt and nut as shown in Fig. 6. The assembled hub and blade mounted on the AC generator and the clamp was used to mount all this on the metal bar. Metal bar frame with 1.20×1.20 m was used to place the augmentation. The height of the frame was equal to the height of the tunnel in order to get the good free stream velocity. The frame and metal bar with all accessories placed in front of a wind tunnel. Digital Multimeter was used to measure current and voltage for each operating condition. The series connection was used for current measurement and a parallel connection was used for voltage measurement as well.

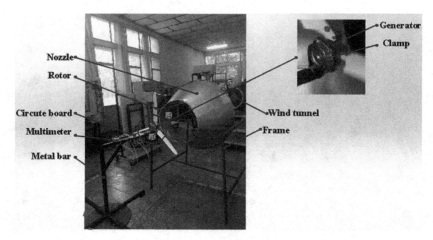

Fig. 6. Experimental set up

3   Results and Discussion

The experimental tests were conducted at wind tunnel on a diffuser, nozzle, nozzle-diffuser combination and bare at blade angle of 15. The wind speed was varying from 3–6 m/s. The wind speed limited 6 m/s because of experimental difficulties. It was not possible to measure the power for 7 m/s and above. The result obtained in this work were also compared with other data publish in literature obtained by Pambudi et al. [9], where the wind speed 2.5 m/s, 3.5 m/s and 4.5 m/s were made. To obtain the corresponding value of power with 3 m/s, 4 m/s, 5 m/s and 6 m/s we were use third order interpolation for better comparison as shown in Figs. 7 and 8. As can be seen from Figs. 7 and 8 a clear behavior of the power curve of this work and Pambudi et al. [9] power curve is presented. In our case the power curve is in the same behavior with those obtained on Pambudi et al. [9]. Due to design in different blade radius and nozzle diameter the value not expected to be agree.

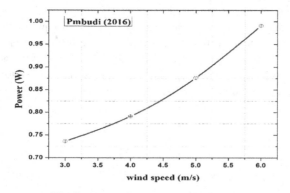

Fig. 7. Comparison used Pambudi result

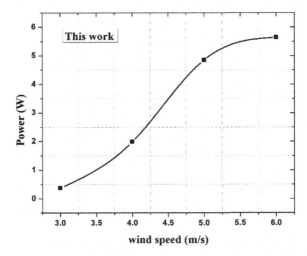

Fig. 8. Comparison of result this work result

The result from different augmentation and wind speed presented in the as shown in Fig. 12. There was no significant power difference between open and diffuser, but significant power recorded in nozzle and combined augmented wind turbine. Figures 9, 10, 11, and 12 gives the variation pf power between bare condition and augmented condition. Regarding to the variation relative to bare the maximum variation of approximately 68% was obtained with diffuser, 92% was obtained with nozzle and 88% was obtained with combined at 4 m/s wind speed. The average percentage of power variation between bare wind turbine and augmented wind turbine were 33.8% for diffuser, 88% for nozzle and 81.6% for nozzle-diffuser combination. The current study does not support previous research in this area. In fact, we found that the power curve increases gradually with increase of wind speed. Although, the curve shares the curve trained of existing wind power curve. Figure 12, is a plot of power versus wind speed for different capsulation. The cut in speed for nozzle and combination (converging and diverging) was 3 m/s. For diffuser and bare condition 4 m/s and almost 5 m/s were the cut in speeds respectively. As can be seen from the plot the diffuser and bare conditions do not show significant difference. The main objective of diffuser capsulation is to generate significant improvements in production output, as can be seen from Fig. 10, this goal was not achieved. In fact, diffuser capsulation can produce an enhancement in electric power, caused by the reducing the wake effect on the air ow that surrounding wind turbine. Nozzle and combined capsulation can effectively produce increments in air ow velocity resulting in a somewhat improved power output. Significant power variations were seen in the nozzle and combined capsulated condition.

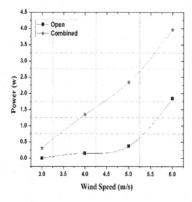

Fig. 9. Power curve of open vs combined

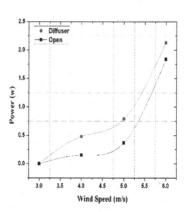

Fig. 10. Power curve of open vs diffuser

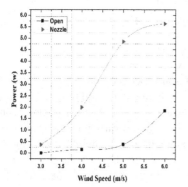

Fig. 11. Power curve of open vs nozzle

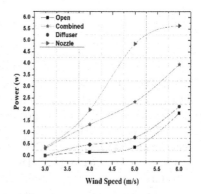

Fig. 12. Power curve of all conditions

4 Conclusions

In order to increase the performance of wind turbine different power augmentation systems have been studied and one of them is the ducted augmentation system. An augmented wind turbine has been an interesting concept of wind energy conversion, due to the system ability to increase the power generated relative to bare turbine with the similar size. We have found maximum power 5.64 W from nozzle augmented at 6 m/s wind speed. A resistor of 1000 Ω was used to determine electric power at different wind speed. A wind speed of 6 m/s gave the highest of 1.84 W with bare condition, 2.13 W with diffuser, 5.64 W nozzle and 3.96 W combined augmentation wind turbine. Although, the cut in speed for nozzle and converging and diverging augmented wind turbine was 3 m/s, while diffuser augmented and bare 4 m/s and almost 5 m/s were the cut in speed respectively.

References

1. Shonhiwa, C., Makaka, G.: Concentrator augmented wind turbines: a review. Renew. Sustain. Energy Rev. **59**, 1415–1418 (2016)
2. Tang, X., Huang, X., Peng, R., Liu, X.: A direct approach of design optimization for small horizontal axis wind turbine blades. Procedia CIRP **36**, 12–16 (2015)
3. Kosasih, B., Saleh Hudin, H.: Influence of inflow turbulence intensity on the performance of bare and diffuser-augmented micro wind turbine model. Renew. Energy **87**, 154–167 (2016)
4. Bontempo, R., Manna, M.: Performance analysis of open and ducted wind turbines. Appl. Energy **136**, 405–416 (2014)
5. Ahmadi Asl, H., Kamali Monfared, R., Rad, M.: Experimental investigation of blade number and design effects for a ducted wind turbine. Renew. Energy **105**, 334–343 (2017)
6. Khamlaj, T.A., Rumpfkeil, M.P.: Analysis and optimization of ducted wind turbines. Energy **162**, 1234–1252 (2018)
7. Tavares Dias Do Rio Vaz, D.A., Amarante Mesquita, A.L., Pinheiro Vaz, J.R., Cavalcante Blanco, C.J., Pinho, J.T.: An extension of the blade element momentum method applied to diffuser augmented wind turbines. Energy Convers. Manage. **87**, 1116–1123 (2014)
8. Vaz, J.R.P., Wood, D.H.: Aerodynamic optimization of the blades of diffuser-augmented wind turbines. Energy Convers. Manag. **123**, 35–45 (2016)
9. Pambudi, N.A., et al.: Experimental investigation of wind turbine using nozzle-lens at low wind speed condition. Energy Procedia **105**, 1063–1069 (2017)
10. Liu, Y., Yoshida, S.: An extension of the Generalized Actuator Disc Theory for aerodynamic analysis of the diffuser-augmented wind turbines. Energy **93**, 1852–1859 (2015)
11. Sorribes-Palmer, F., Sanz-Andres, A., Ayuso, L., Sant, R., Franchini, S.: Mixed CFD-1D wind turbine diffuser design optimization. Renew. Energy **105**, 386–399 (2017)
12. Uli, G.: Aerodynamic interaction of diffuser augmented wind turbines in multi-rotor systems. Renew. Energy **112**, 25–34 (2017)

Design and Simulation of Waste Heat Recovery System for Heavy Oil Preheating in Dashen Brewery Company

Addisu Yenesew Kebede[1(✉)] and Abdulkadir Aman Hassen[2]

[1] Faculty of Mechanical and Industrial Engineering, Bahir Dar Institute of Technology,
Bahir Dar University, Bahir Dar, Ethiopia
addiye2003@gmail.com
[2] School of Mechanical and Industrial Engineering, Addis Ababa Institute of Technology,
Addis Ababa University, Addis Ababa, Ethiopia
abdiaman2004@yahoo.com

Abstract. Industrial waste heat refers to energy that is generated in industrial processes without being put to practical use. In this paper an effort has made about waste heat recovery system design for Dashen Brewery Company. It is tried to identify source of waste heat and design a new plant layout for the purpose of waste heat recovery. In Dashen brewery company heat is basically lost at the boiler, process water heater pipe and Wort kettle chimney. The company uses heavy oil for boiler and this oil needs to be heated to convert in to light oil for better ignition. To heat this heavy oil the company still uses steam but this paper design a system to use exhaust steam at Wort kettle for heating of heavy oil instead of steam. Tasks performed in in this paper are direct temperature measurement on the waste heat source, heat loss calculation on the chimney and construct appropriate waste heat recovery routine. Head loss and other basic flow parameters had been considered. Furthermore from the analytical model it is possible to determine the amount of power needed to the boiler which is 56.947 MW from 6220 L/h of furnace oil and from exhaust steam 17.5 kW is gained which can burn 190 L/h of fuel; in terms of birr it is possible to save 456 L/day × 19.5 birr which is 8892 birr per day.

Keywords: Waste heat recovery · Head loss · Shell and tube heat exchange

1 Introduction

Industrial waste heat refers to energy that is generated in industrial processes without being put to practical use. Sources of waste heat include hot combustion gases discharged to the atmosphere, heated products exiting industrial processes, and heat transfer from hot equipment surfaces. The exact quantity of industrial waste heat is poorly quantified, but various studies have estimated that as much as 20 to 50% of industrial energy consumption is ultimately discharged as waste heat.

In Dashen Brewery Company there are three main sections; these are utility section or power house section, brew house and process flow section. Among these sections

N. G. Habtu et al. (Eds.): ICAST 2019, LNICST 308, pp. 576–586, 2020.
https://doi.org/10.1007/978-3-030-43690-2_43

the utility section is the back bone of the company because it is a source of steam, process water and purified carbon dioxide which have significant impact on production. In this paper an effort has made about waste heat recovery system design for brewery companies. It is try to identify source of waste heat and design a new plant layout for the purpose of waste heat recovery. Waste heat recovery power generation (WHRPG) started in the 1980s in Japan, within the cement industry. It grew mainly in Eastern Asia (China and Japan) from 2000, at a time when energy prices increased [1].

2 Literature Review

There were many works previously carried out on the Shell and tube heat exchangers. Some of them are listed here: Presented in this paper are how to design, construct and test the waste heat recovery pipe for air-preheating used for furnace in a hot brass forging process, Yodrak et al. [6]. Muhammad Zeeshan et al. [7] carried out a Waste Heat Recovery system for Electric Power Generation from Cement Industry. Those scholars is therefore try to recover waste heat from Fecto Cement Plant installing a 6 MW power in order to save energy, reduce heat consumption and production cost of waste heat recovery plant. Selvaraj and Varun [8] both scholars try to recover waste heat during metal casting. The waste heat source in this paper is the knocked out casting which has heat energy stored in it and is wasted into atmosphere as the casting cools down in the shop floor. Remeli et al. [9] is also investigating a system how to generate power using heat pipes and thermo-electric generators.

Saidawat et al. [11] carried out the research work on the power generation from the waste heat extracted through clinker production in the cement industry. This study includes the power generation calculation for a cement plant and the different methodologies used to generate power (Table 1).

3 Materials and Methods

For the three sample tests above there is some variation of surface temperatures due to room temperature variation or seasonal variations. Therefore consider the April temperature data, and temperature variation along the chimney is uniform, and then average surface temperature for April is 109 °C (Fig. 1).

Table 1. Three months average surface temperatures

Tests	Months	Chimney's average surface temperature T_S in °C
1	Feb	111
2	April	109
3	Jun	108

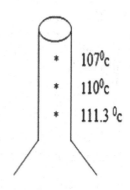

Fig. 1. Infrared temperature measurement taken on wort kettle

3.1 Energy Supplied for Wort Boiling

Wort input to the wort kettle = 345 hl, Cast Wort to the whirlpool = 315 hl, Exhaust wort in the form of steam = 30 hl. From the input and output data it is possible to know the amount of heat energy wasted in the form of waste gas through the chimney.

Amount of wort changed to steam (wasted through the chimney) = Amount of boiling wort in the kettle- amount of boiled wort out to whirlpool (storage tank for cast wort) = 345 hl – 315 hl = 30 hl. Then conventionally to boil 1 hl of cast wort about 14 kWh of energy is required. Therefore for 30 hl of steam 420 kWh energy is required. The wort in the wort kettle tanker is boiled for 1–2 h and the hot finished casting wort is produced. In Dashen brewery factory the time required for cast wort is 2 h. The energy used can be expressed in terms of Power. Therefore power is the given energy per total hours which is 210 kw [2].

3.2 Mathematical Modeling

For a hallow pipe exposed to convection environment on its outer and inner surfaces, the overall heat transfer would be expressed by

$$q = \frac{T_{1\infty} - T_{2\infty}}{\frac{1}{h_{1\infty} A_i} + \frac{\ln(r_0/r_i)}{2\pi k L} + \frac{1}{h_{2\infty} A_0}} = h_{1\infty} A (T_1 - T_{1\infty}) \qquad (1)$$

Where

$T_{1\infty}$ temperature of the steam in the chimney
$T_{2\infty}$ room temperature at the outer surface
ro   outer radius of the chimney
ri   inner radius of the chimney
L   height of the chimney

By direct measurements Outside Diameter of exhaust chimney D0 = 400 mm = 0.4 m, Inside diameter of exhaust chimney Di = 380 mm = 0.38 m, Thermal conductivity of stainless steel k = 16.2 W/m°C (Figs. 2 and 3).

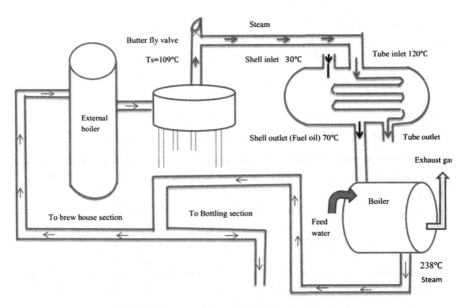

Fig. 2. Conceptual layout of the designed system

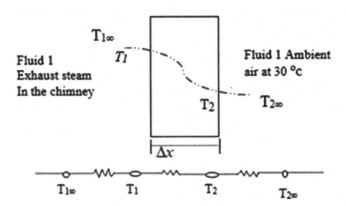

Fig. 3. Resistance circuit on the chimney

Fluid mean temperature on the chimney is:

$$T_f = \frac{T_s + T_\infty}{2} = \frac{109 + 30}{2} = 69.5\,°C$$

Properties of steam at mean temperature: Thermal conductivity k = 0.0296w/m.°C, Specific heat capacity Cp = 1.0075 kJ/kg, Density = 1.009 kg/m³, Kinematic, viscosity = 2.00 10 − 5 m²/s, Prandtl number Pr = 0.7, Reynolds number,

$$Re = \frac{u \times D}{v} \qquad (2)$$

Nusselt Number, $Nu = \frac{hD}{k}$

Volumetric flow rate, $\dot{V} = \frac{q}{c_p \rho dT} = 2.61 \, m^3/s$, where q = 210 kW

Velocity of the steam, $u = \frac{4\dot{v}}{\pi D^2} = 23 \, m/s$, $Re = \frac{u \times D}{v} = 438079$, (Turbulent)

Convective heat transfer coefficient h at the outer surface, $h_{2\infty} = \frac{Nu \times k}{D} = 47 \, W/m^2.k$.

From Fourier's law of heat conduction equation $q_{net} = \frac{k \times (T_{in} - T_{out})}{\Delta x}$

$$18.56 \, kW = \frac{16.2 \times (T_1 - 109)}{0.01}, T_1 = 120 \,°C$$

Assume inside surface temperature is equal to the fluid temperature, then $T_{1\infty} = 120\,°C$ inside convective heat transfer coefficient, $h_{1\infty} = \frac{q}{A_s(T_{1\infty} - T_{2\infty})} = 19 \, W/m^2.k$

3.3 Design of Waste Heat Recovery Route Equipment

Pipe line sizing: schedule 40 is most standard schedule and based on given pressure drop take Nominal Bore 10 in. (DN 250 mm), Outside Diameter 273.0 mm and thickness of the pipe t = 9.3 mm and internal diameter 254.4 mm (Fig. 4).

$$\text{Mass flow rate of steam } m = \frac{q_{net}}{h_{fg}} = 0.84 \, kg/s$$

$$\text{Average velocity of exhaust steam } u_a = \frac{4\dot{v}}{\pi D^2} = 4.24 \, m/s$$

$$Re = \frac{4.24 \times 0.254}{2 \times 10^{-5}} = 53874 \, (\text{turbulent})$$

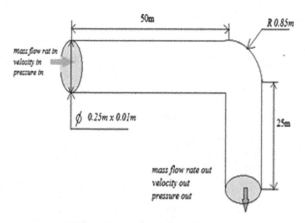

Fig. 4. Dimensions of pipeline route

3.4 Thermal Insulation

Insulation is defined as those materials or combinations of materials which retard the flow of heat energy by performing one or more of the following functions:

Conserve energy by reducing heat loss or gain, Control surface temperatures for personnel protection and comfort, Facilitate temperature control of a process, Prevent vapor flow and water condensation on cold surfaces (Fig. 5).

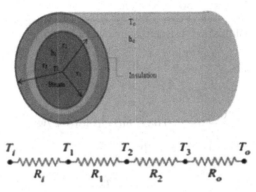

Fig. 5. Thermal insulation and circuit diagram

It should be realized that insulation does not eliminate heat transfer; it merely reduces it. The thicker the insulation, the lower the rate of heat transfers but also the higher the cost of insulation. Therefore, there should be an optimum thickness of insulation that corresponds to a minimum combined cost of insulation and heat lost. The determination of the optimum thickness of insulation is illustrated in Fig. 6.

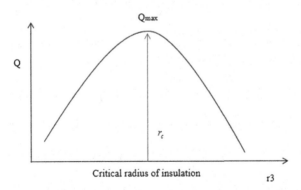

Fig. 6. Determination of the optimum thickness of insulation

Properties: Pipe internal temperature $T_i = 120\ °C$, thermal conductivity of stainless steel material $k = 16.2\ w/m°C$, Internal diameter $d_i = 0.254\ m$, Maximum allowable temperature of the outer surface insulation $T_0 = 30\ °C$.

Thermal conductivity of cellular glass insulation kinsulation $= 0.038$ w/m°C, Internal and external convective heat transfer coefficients ho $= 47$ w/m^2, hi $= 19$ w/m^2.

Letting r_3 represent the outer radius of the insulation, the areas of the surfaces exposed to convection for an $L = 50$ m long section of the pipe become

$$A_2 = \pi D0L = \pi \times 0.273 \times 50 = 42.88 \text{ m}^2 \quad A1 = \pi DinL$$

$$= \pi \times 0.254 \times 50 = 39.89 \text{ m}^2$$

$$A_3 = 2\pi \times r_3 \times 50 = 354r_3 \text{ m}^2$$

Then the individual thermal resistances are determined to be

$$R_i = R_{conv\,1} = \frac{1}{h_i A_1} = 1.32 \times 10^{-3}\,°\text{C/w} \quad R_1 = R_{pipe} = \frac{\ln(r_2/r_1)}{2\pi kL}$$

$$= 1.4 \times 10^{-5}\,°\text{C/w}$$

$$R_2 = R_{ins} = \frac{\ln(r_3/r_2)}{2\pi kL} = 0.0837 \ln(r_3/0.136)\,°\text{C/w}$$

$$R_0 = R_{conv\,2} = \frac{1}{h_0 A_3} = \frac{6 \times 10^{-5}}{r_3}\,°\text{C/w}$$

$$\dot{Q} = \frac{T_i - T_0}{R_{tot}} = \frac{T_I - T_0}{(\frac{1}{2\pi r_1 hL} + \frac{\ln(r_2/r_1)}{2\pi kL} + \frac{\ln(r_3/r_2)}{2\pi kL} + \frac{1}{2\pi r_3 hL}}$$

$$\dot{Q} = \frac{T_i - T_0}{R_{tot}} = \frac{120 - 30}{(133.4) \times 10^{-5} + 0.0837\ln\left(\frac{r_3}{0.136}\right) + \frac{6 \times 10^{-5}}{r_3}} \tag{3}$$

Hence the outer surface temperature of insulation is assumed to be 35 °C; the rate of heat loss over the routine can also be expressed as:

$$Q = \frac{T_3 - T_0}{R_0} = \frac{35 - 30}{\frac{6 \times 10^{-5}}{r_3}} = 37790.7\, r_3 \tag{4}$$

From Eq. (1) to find the value of thickness t for which Q maximum should be equated to zero or denominator should be minimum.

$$\frac{d}{dr_3}(Q) = ((\frac{1}{2\pi\, r_1 h\, L} + \frac{\ln(r_2/r_1)}{2\pi kL} + \frac{\ln(r_3/r_2)}{2\pi kL} + \frac{1}{2\pi\, r_3 h\, L}) = 0$$

Then by rearranging critical radius of insulation for cylinder becomes

$$r_3 = \frac{k}{h} = \frac{16.2}{47} = 0.344 \text{ m}$$

The rate of heat loss from Eq. (2) becomes $Q_{loss} = 37790.7r_3 = 13$ kW. Then the net heat transfer rate $Q_{net} = 18.56$ kW $- 13$ kW $= 5$ kW.

3.5 Major Loss, Minor Loss and Pressure Drop in Pipe Flow

Major loss across horizontal length, $h_f = 2 \times 0.0105\frac{50}{0.254}\left(\frac{4.24^2}{9.81}\right) = 7.57$ m

Similarly for major head loss h_f across vertical pipe length is

$$h_f = 2 \times 0.0105 \frac{25}{0.254} \left(\frac{4.24^2}{9.81} \right) = 3.78 \, \text{m}$$

Minor losses:

$$k_m = 0.015, \, h_m = 0.015 \frac{4.24^2}{2 \times 9.81} = 0.014 \, \text{m} \, \Delta P = \rho g \times loss$$

$$= 1.009 \times 9.81 \times 0.014 = 1.4 \, \text{pa}$$

Allowable Pressure drop: The pressure drop across the horizontal pipe can be calculated using the following equation:

The pressure drop $\Delta P = \rho g \times loss = \gamma h_f$, here, the specific weight $\gamma = \rho \times g$

$\Delta p = 2f \frac{L}{D} (\frac{\rho u^2}{g}) = \rho g h_f = 1.009 \times 9.81 \times 5.57 = 63 \, \text{Pa}$ Similarly for vertical length of pipe pressure drop $p = 38.4$ pa, Total pressure drop $p = 102.8$ pa (Fig. 7).

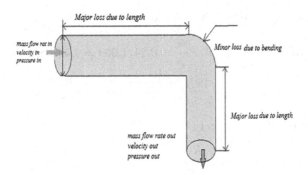

Fig. 7. Head losses

3.6 Shell and Tube Heat Exchanger Design for Preheating

Steam side properties

Inlet temperature of steam pipe line $T_{in} = 120 \, °C$, Inlet pressure of steam $P_{in} = P_{sat} = 198.5$ kPa, Specific heat capacity of steam $C_p = 1.075$ kJ/kg.k, Pressure drop p $= 102.4$ pa, Mass flow rate of steam $ms = 0.84$ kg/s, Fouling factor for heavy oil 0.0009 $(W/m^2 °C) - 1$, Fouling factor for steam 0.0001$(W/m^2 °C) - 1$

Shell side Furnace oil properties, Inlet temperature of furnace oil $tin = 30 \, °C$ Output temperature furnace $tout = 70 \, °C$, Density of furnace oil $= 800$ kg/m^3, Specific heat capacity of oil $= 2.3$ kJ/kg.k, Amount of fuel consumed $= 6220$ L/h, Mass Flow rate of fuel consumed $mf = 1.382$ kg/s, Specific heat capacity oil $= 2.3$ kJ/kg.k.

Heat exchanges between Steam-to-heavy fuel oil and overall heat transfer coefficient will be in the range 50–200 W/m^2°C so let's start with $U = 100$ W/m^2°C (Fig. 8).

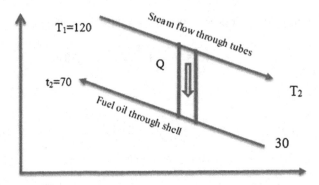

Fig. 8. Schematic diagram of counter flow heat exchanger

3.7 Heat Exchanger Type and Dimensions

The general tube layout is d0 = 20 mm, t = 2.0 mm, din = 16 mm, L = 2.44 m tubes on square pitch (Pt = 1.25d0) Area of one tube = 0.314 m^2

$$\text{Number of tubes } Nt = As/At = 2.99/0.314 = 9.5 \text{ say } 10$$

$$\text{Volume flow rate oil} = \frac{m}{\rho} = 0.84/1.009 = 0.00105 \text{ m}^3/s$$

$$\text{Tube side velocity } Ut = \frac{volume\ flow\ rate}{area\ per\ pass} = \frac{0.00105}{0.0001} = 10.5 \text{ m/s}$$

Overall heat transfer coefficient

$$\frac{1}{U_0} = \frac{1}{h_i} \times \frac{A_0}{A_i} + \frac{R_f, i}{A_i} + \frac{A_0 \ln(d_0/d_i)}{2\pi kL} + \frac{1}{h_s} + \frac{R_{f,o}}{A_0}$$

$$R_{f,i} = 0.0009 \text{ m}^2.°C/w \quad R_{f,0} = 0.0001 \text{ m}^2.°C/w$$

The need for calculating the overall heat transfer coefficient is to check whether the initial estimated value is safe or not, if it is safe proceed unless revise the estimation heat transfer coefficient.

4 Results and Discussion

From mathematical modeling of the waste heat recovery or exhaust steam it is possible to extract 17.5 kW power which can save 456 L/day of fuel. It increases the annual income of the company. But this result may partly affected due to measurement inaccuracy or improper material calibration because during testing of chimney temperature, the reading of thermocouple and infrared thermometer were having different reading values.

5   Conclusion

The main objective of this study was to design and simulate the waste heat recovery system for oil preheating system in Beverage Companies. Initially the study attempts to start the new designing process by constructing system design layout and proper material selection for each component. Designing of the system for exhaust steam were selected by comparing with exhaust flue gases at the boiler. At the beginning the validity of the study was checked by measuring the amount of temperature in the chimney. At the wort kettle chimney the amount of surface temperature was 109 °C which is enough to reheat heavy oil. Beside temperature measurement, amount of power wasted to the environment was determined. Wort input to the wort kettle = 345 hl, Cast Wort to the whirlpool = 315 hl, Exhaust wort in the form of steam = 30 hl. From the input and output data it is possible to know the amount of heat energy wasted in the form of waste gas through the chimney. Amount of wort changed to steam (wasted through the chimney) = Amount of boiling wort in the kettle- amount of boiled wort out to whirlpool (storage tank for cast wort) = 345 hl – 315 hl = 30 hl. According to company's manual to boil 30 hl exhaust wort with steam 210 kw power is required. The overall dimensions of the pipe line are 50 m horizontal length, 25 m vertical length, internal diameter 250 mm with thickness 10 mm and material insulation is needed with proper dimension. On the pipe line the main parameters determined first were head loss and pressure drop because these parameters are determinant factors for fluid flow through pipes. At the end of the pipe line the net amount of power was determined and made it ready for input of the preheater. Important assumptions were made during pipe flow, like steady state flow condition. At the preheater heat exchanging process between heavy oil and exhaust steam were taking place. Heavy oil has initial temperature 30 °C and reaches 70 °C. Quantity of Heavy fuel oil supplied to the preheater is 6220 L/h or 1.382 kg/s.

References

1. U.S. Department of energy: Waste Heat Recovery Technology and Opportunities in U.S. Industry, United States (2008)
2. Kunz, W.: Technology Brewing and Malting, 2nd edn. VLB, Berlin (1999)
3. Samantha, V.P.: Panorama of public policies supporting power generation from industrial waste heat (2012)
4. White, F.: Fluid Mechanics, 5th edn.
5. Boles, M.A., Cengel, Y.A.: Thermodynamics an Engineering Approach, 5th edn.
6. Rittidech, S., Yodrak, L.: Waste heat recovery by heat pipe air-preheater to energy thrift from the furnace in a hot forging process. Am. J. Appl. Sci. **7**, 675–681 (2010)
7. Mohammad, S., et al.: Waste Heat recovery, a special case research article
8. Selvaraj, J., Varun, V.: Waste heat recovery from metal casting and scrap preheating using recovered heat. Presented at the 12th global congress on manufacturing and management (2014)
9. Remeli, M.F., Kiatbodin, L., Singh, B.: Power generation from waste heat using heat pipe and thermoelectric generator, clean, efficient and affordable energy for a sustainable future. Presented at the 7th international conference on applied energy–ICAE 2015 (2015)
10. Sathiyamoorthy, M., Biglari, M.: Waste heat recovery and utilization for power generation in a cement plant (Phase-1). Int. J. Adv. Res. IT Eng. **5**(4), 1–26 (2016)

11. Saidawat, Y.: Power generation from waste heat extracted through clinker production in cement industry. Int. J. IT Eng. **03**, 23–33 (2015)
12. Parase, P.K., Raut, L.B.: Design of heat recovery system for dye effluent in textile industries. Int. J. Eng. Res. Technol. (IJERT) **3**, 1101–1105 (2014)
13. Zeeshan, M., Arbab, M.N.: Waste heat recovery and its utilization for electric power generation in cement industry. Int. J. Eng. Technol. IJET-IJENS **15**, 25–33 (2015)
14. American Society of Mechanical Engineers: Pipe Flanges and Flange Fittings NPS ½through NPS 24 Metric/Inch Standard, ASME B16-5-2013
15. Sinnott, R.K., Coulson, J.M., Richardson, J.F.: Chemical Engineering Design, vol. 6. Butterworth Heinemann, Boston (1999)
16. Int. J. Res. Aeronaut. Mech. Eng. **4**, 1–10 (2016)
17. Devi, K.M., Nagamani, M.G.V.: Design and thermal analysis of shell and tube heat exchanger by using fluent tool. Int. J. Mag. Eng.
18. Int. J. Res. Aeronaut. Mech. Eng. **4**, 1–23 (2016)
19. Devi, K.M., Nagamani, M.G.V.: Design and thermal analysis of shell and tube heat exchanger by using fluent tool. Int. J. Mag. Eng. **2** (2015)

Performance Evaluation of Motorized Maize Sheller

Solomon Tekeste[(✉)] and Yonas Mitiku Degu

Bahir Dar Institute of Technology, Bahir Dar University, Bahir Dar, Ethiopia
soltektata@gmail.com, yonasm@bdu.edu.et

Abstract. Maize is the major food crop, with highest yield and production in Ethiopia. At the same time, postharvest losses in maize production are very high. Maize shelling is one of the main stages of postharvest loss in maize production. The traditional method of maize shelling is tedious, time consuming and less productive. Hence, this research project focuses on modifying and evaluating the Bako maize sheller for better performance. In doing so, evaluation site and participant farmers were selected, and the performance tests were conducted according to FAO standard test procedures. The experiments were conducted with two commonly grown varieties of maize, BH661 and LIMU (P3812W), at two different moisture contents each. In addition, farmers' opinion about the evaluated sheller and the traditional method of shelling was assessed. The results show that the capacity of the modified sheller improved by 29% without compromising any other performance parameter of the original design. Moreover, higher shelling capacity has been recorded at lower moisture content for both maize varieties. As the moisture content decreased by 2.7% for BH661 and 3.5% for Limu, the shelling capacity increased by 326.2 kg/h and 543.333 kg/h, respectively. There is no significant variation in shelling efficiency, grain damage and cleaning efficiency for both varieties among treatments. Scattering losses are increased significantly as the moisture content of the maize kernel decreased.

Keywords: Maize sheller · Shelling performance · Shelling efficiency

1   Introduction

Maize is Ethiopia's leading cereal in production, with 7.8 million metric tons (t) produced in 2016 cropping season by 10.9 million households from 2.14 million hectares of land [1]. According to the report of Ethiopian central statistical agency (CSA), out of the total cultivated area in 2016, 81.27% was covered by cereals, from which teff, maize, sorghum, and wheat covered 24%, 16.98%, 14.97% and 13.49%, respectively. Cereals contributed 87.42% of the total grain production from which maize, teff, wheat and sorghum accounted for 27.02%, 17.27%, 15.63% and 16.36%, respectively. The national annual average production of maize, teff, wheat, and sorghum in the same season was 3.7, 1.7, 2.7 and 2.6 t/ha, respectively [1]. Compared to other cereals, maize has the highest potential yield per unit area. This shows that maize has become Ethiopia's major and strategic crop among cereals to improve farmers' livelihood.

© ICST Institute for Computer Sciences, Social Informatics and Telecommunications Engineering 2020
Published by Springer Nature Switzerland AG 2020. All Rights Reserved
N. G. Habtu et al. (Eds.): ICAST 2019, LNICST 308, pp. 587–596, 2020.
https://doi.org/10.1007/978-3-030-43690-2_44

Smallholder farmers mostly produce maize for subsistence, with 75% of the production being consumed by the farming household. According to International Food Policy Research Institute (IFPRI) 2010, maize is the cheapest source of calorie intake in Ethiopia, providing 20.6% of per capita calorie intake. Thus, it can be said that maize is an important crop for overall food security.

Maize is consumed as "Injera," Porridge, Bread and "Nefro." It is also consumed roasted or boiled as vegetables at green stage. The leaf and stalk are used for animal feed and dried stalk & cob are used for fuel. Moreover, it also supported the growing demand for industrial use [2].

In the Ethiopian context, the common methods of shelling maize under small-scale farmers' conditions are manual. This shelling activity can be done by stripping with fingers, rubbing two cobs against each other, rubbing cob on rough stone, and/or beating cobs or bagged cobs with sticks. All these traditional maize shelling methods are highly tedious, inefficient, require a lot of labor, and have outputs of a few kilograms an hour. Moreover, kernel damages in the form of bruises, cracks and/or breakage are inevitable with these shelling methods. Such kernel damage facilitates the infestation of pests during storage. Hence, maize shelling is one of the main problems encountered by the farmers in maize production and postharvest handling. To solve this problem, so many attempts have been made by governmental and non-governmental institutions to develop and introduce different types of maize shellers for smallholder farmers [3–5]. Even though attempts to introduce different types of maize shellers for farmers have been made, it has not been adopted until recent times. In some areas, adoption of motorized maize shellers is increasing, and maize producers are very keen to get shelling service through hiring [6].

Thus, there is a need to design, develop, and introduce appropriate maize shellers that reduce postharvest loss, increases labor and time productivity, and reduces drudgery. Hence, this research project focuses on modifying the Bako maize sheller to improve performance, and evaluating the sheller with farmers for further promotion and modification activities. This will facilitate the adoption of the technology by smallholder farmers.

2 Materials and Method

2.1 Participant Farmers' Selection

This participatory evaluation was conducted in North Western Ethiopia, at the Amhara region in Bure Woreda, Wadra Kebele, where most of the farmers grow maize as a major crop. To conduct the experiment with farmers' participation, one Farmers Research Group (FRG) was organized in collaboration with village level development agents. Gender, accessibility for demonstration sessions in the farm and willingness to use the maize sheller were considered as selection criteria from the FRG members. Ten farmer households were selected, from which four of them were female headed.

2.2 Description of the Maize Sheller

The sheller was initially made by Bako Rural Promotion Centre, for shelling maize. The average capacity of the maize sheller is 4,100 kg/h, with shelling efficiency of 98.3%. The average grain breakage and unshelled grain is 4.99% and 1.73%, respectively. The sheller uses 14 horse power (HP) diesel engine and the fuel consumption is 3.125 L/h [3, 4]. In order to improve the performance of the sheller, slight modification were made. The major modification was to increase the torque of the sheller drum by increasing the pulley size (both in diameter and weight). In the previous model the diameter of the pulley was 450 mm and in the modified model it was 500 mm.

The modified version of sheller also uses 14 horse power (HP) diesel engine. The main components of the sheller include: feeding hopper, shelling drum with perforated concave, blower, grain discharging auger, power transmission system and diesel engine. The sheller operates on the principle of axial flow movement of material. Shelling is done by the impact between a high-speed cylindrical drum and a perforated concave, equipped with three radial arranged bars at 120° along the axis mounted on its periphery. At the one end of the cylindrical drum the profile of the radial bars is changed to eject the shelled cob through the shelled cob outlet. The shelled grain and fine chaffs pass through the perforated concave and the air coming from the blower removes the chaff and other lighter materials. The clean grain falls to the lower chamber, and the grain discharging auger moves the grain through the outlet.

Sheller operation requires a total of 10 operators. Seven are required to feed the hopper with unshelled cobs, two work on the grain outlet, and one on the cob outlet side.

2.3 Assessing the Common Method of Maize Shelling in the Study Area

The common method of maize shelling in the study area was assessed through interview, observation and measurements of grain breakage. Average labor requirement and general demographic information (gender, age and role in the household) of each operator was recorded for this study.

2.4 Participatory Performance Evaluation of the Sheller

Performance evaluation tests were conducted for two common hybrid varieties of maize grown in the area: LIMU and BH661. The performance of the sheller was evaluated on shelling efficiency, cleaning efficiency, grain damage, unshelled grain, scattering loss and fuel consumption. FAO test procedure for evaluating maize shellers was used [7]. During evaluation, ease of handling, adjustment of working parts, and overall performance under farmers' opinion was recorded. Group and individual discussions were made with farmers.

Samples were taken according to [7] to determine grain parameters and sheller performance. Two digital balances, with measurement range of 0–40 kg $\pm$ 0.001 kg and 0–5 kg $\pm$ 0.0001 kg were used to measure grains and cob samples before and after shelling process. A digital optical tachometer with an accuracy of 0.04% $\pm$ 2 was used to measure the rotational shaft speeds of the sheller. Fuel consumption was measured by filling the engine fuel tank completely at the start and end of each time-recorded period and weighing the quantity of fuel added using graduated cylinder with an accuracy of $\pm$1 ml.

Maize grain parameters, variety, moisture content (MC), grain cob ratio (GCR), maize grain per cob (MGC), cob length (CL) and diameter (CD), were determined.

Oven dry method was used to determine the moisture content of maize in dry basis (DB). Vernier caliper with an accuracy of ±0.05 mm and steel measuring tape with an accuracy of ±1 mm were used to measure the cob diameter and length, respectively. Each test was conducted for two minutes and replicated three times for each variety, for two different moisture contents (Table 1).

Table 1. Crop parameters under experimentations.

Trial #	Variety	Mean MC (%)	Mean MGC	Mean GCR	Mean CL (mm)	Mean CD (mm)
1	LIMU	12.8 ± 1.0	0.84	4.7	180.5	48.0
2	LIMU	16.3 ± 0.7				
3	BH661	12.4 ± 0.9	0.84	5.3	201.8	46.3
4	BH661	15.1 ± 0.8				

The following measurements were also recorder: feed rate of cobs per unit time, weight of shelled grains at all outlets per unit time, weight of shelled grains at main outlet per unit time, weight of grain and residue mixture per unit time, weight of shelled damaged grains at all outlets per unit time, weight of shelled and unshelled grains at cob outlet per unit time, fuel consumed per unit time and rotational speed of the shelling drum and the input shaft with load and without load. Using mean values of the replications, shelling capacity (SC), shelling efficiency (SE), cleaning efficiency (CE), percent grain damage (GD) and percent scattering loss (SL) were estimated.

$$SC = \frac{Wa}{St} \tag{1}$$

$$SE(\%) = 100 - Ug(\%) \tag{2}$$

$$Ug(\%) = \frac{Wu}{TWK} * 100 \tag{3}$$

$$CE(\%) = \frac{Wm}{Wr} * 100 \tag{4}$$

$$Gd(\%) = \frac{Wd}{Wm} * 100 \tag{5}$$

$$SL = \frac{Wc}{TWK} * 100 \tag{6}$$

Where,

− St   - shelling time
− Wa   - weight of shelled grain per unit time at all outlet
− Ug   - percent unshelled grain

– Wu   - weight of unshelled kernel
– Wm   - weight of shelled grain per unit time at main outlet
– Wr   - weight of grain & residue mixture per unit time at main outlet
– Gd   - percent grain damage
– Wd   - weight of damaged grain
– Wc   - weight of grain collected at dust and cob outlet
– TWK   - total weight of kernel fed in to the hopper

2.5 Collecting Feedback from Participating Farmers

Farmers who participated during demonstration were encouraged to give their opinions about the maize sheller, based on observed performance, ease of handling and transportation, and their own selection parameters. Feedbacks were collected through semi-structured interviews and focus group discussions. Some of the issues discussed with the farmers during the discussions were:

- Quality of work in their observation, these include seed and cob breakage, shelling loss, cleaning efficiency in comparison to traditional shelling method and other mechanized sheller if they have previous acquaintance
- Threshing performance in comparison to traditional shelling method and other mechanized sheller if they have previous acquaintance
- Suggestions for future improvements of the demonstrated maize sheller
- Their willingness to use the technology

The figure below shows the event of on farm evaluation of the motorized maize sheller with participant farmers (Fig. 1).

Fig. 1. Motorized maize sheller during on farm evaluation

2.6 Data Analysis

Measurements were taken for crop and operating parameters. Multivariate analysis were performed on the experimental data collected using SPSS version 17 computer-based software. Mean difference between treatments were done using the LSD at 5% level of significance. Narrative summary and descriptive statistics were used.

3 Result and Discussion

3.1 Common Method of Maize Shelling in the Study Area

In the study area the common method of maize shelling is rubbing cob on rough stone and beating cobs with sticks. The majority of shelling activity was done by women and children. This method of maize shelling is tedious, time consuming and less productive. Moreover, higher grain damages, on average 7.1% for grain moisture content of 12.5% (DB), was observed. Farmers prefer to use the method of beating cobs with sticks when more than 1,500 kg of maize will be shelled. According to the response of the farmers, it requires 4 to 5 man-day to shell 1,600 to 2,000 kg of maize with average composition of 1–2 adult men, 2 children, 1–2 women.

Recently, mechanical shellers were introduced by service providers through custom hiring, with rate of 20ETB for 100 kg of shelled maize. As it has been expressed by farmers, using these threshers the grain damage and cob breakage is higher. They use the cob as a fuel for cooking food; hence, they prefer whole cob. As mentioned, by women farmers, as the grain damage increases, the processing quality of the grain is generally decreased.

Maize is mainly used to prepare a local beverage called 'tella'. The first step in this process is roasting the maize. The broken grain will roast faster, and the unbroken grain will roast slower. Hence, it becomes difficult to get optimum level of roasting. Even though, the introduced shellers have limitations, as expressed above, it was observed that farmers were interested to use these mechanized shellers, but the supply is limited, hence there was too much waiting.

3.2 Shelling Performance of the Evaluated Maize Sheller

Estimated marginal mean shelling performance parameters were analyzed under two different moisture contents for BH661 (Table 2) and Limu (Table 3).

Shelling Capacity. The previous model Bako maize sheller has a shelling capacity of 4,100 kg/h to 5,000 kg/h for different variety of maize at different moisture content [3, 4]. The current modified model has a shelling capacity of 5,800 kg/h to 7,000 kg/h. This shows that shelling capacity was improved by 29% without compromising any other performance parameters.

The results show that, higher shelling capacities were recorded at lower moisture contents for both varieties. As the moisture content decreased from 15.1% to 12.4% for BH661 variety, the shelling capacity increased by 326.2 kg/h. The results show that this mean difference is significant at 0.05 level of significance (Table 4). Similarly, for Limu (P3812W) maize variety, as the moisture content decreased from 16.3% to 12.8%, the shelling capacity increased by 543.333 kg/h, and this increment is significant at 0.05 level of significance (Table 5). Similar results have been reported previously [8, 9].

Table 2. Estimated marginal means shelling performance parameters for BH661

Dependent variable	Moisture content (%)	Mean	Std. error	95% confidence interval	
				Lower bound	Upper bound
Shelling capacity (kg/h)	12.4 ± 0.9	6343.23	77.87	6127.03	6559.43
	15.1 ± 0.8	6017.03	77.87	5800.83	6233.23
Shelling efficiency (%)	12.4 ± 0.9	99.83	0.03	99.74	99.93
	15.1 ± 0.8	99.67	0.03	99.57	99.76
Grain damage (%)	12.4 ± 0.9	2.30	0.07	2.09	2.51
	15.1 ± 0.8	2.07	0.07	1.86	2.27
Cleaning efficiency (%)	12.4 ± 0.9	98.93	0.14	98.55	99.32
	15.1 ± 0.8	98.77	0.14	98.38	99.15
Scattering loss (%)	12.4 ± 0.9	9.00	0.22	8.40	9.60
	15.1 ± 0.8	4.30	0.22	3.70	4.90
Fuel consumption (L/h)	12.4 ± 0.9	3.07	0.11	2.76	3.38
	15.1 ± 0.8	3.01	0.11	2.71	3.32

Table 3. Estimated marginal means shelling performance parameters for LIMU

Dependent variable	Moisture content (%)	Mean	Std. error	95% confidence interval	
				Lower bound	Upper bound
Shelling capacity (kg/h)	12.8 ± 1.0	6888.23	69.96	6693.99	7082.48
	16.3 ± 0.7	6344.90	69.96	6150.66	6539.14
Shelling efficiency (%)	12.8 ± 1.0	99.77	0.07	99.56	99.97
	16.3 ± 0.7	99.50	0.07	99.29	99.71
Grain damage (%)	12.8 ± 1.0	1.90	0.05	1.77	2.03
	16.3 ± 0.7	1.83	0.05	1.70	1.96
Cleaning efficiency (%)	12.8 ± 1.0	98.77	0.11	98.45	99.08
	16.3 ± 0.7	98.93	0.11	98.62	99.25
Scattering loss (%)	12.8 ± 1.0	9.03	0.25	8.33	9.74
	16.3 ± 0.7	6.27	0.25	5.56	6.97
Fuel consumption (L/h)	12.8 ± 1.0	3.00	0.11	2.69	3.30
	16.3 ± 0.7	3.05	0.11	2.75	3.36

Table 4. Mean difference between treatments for maize variety of BH661

Dependent variable	Mean difference (I-J)	Std. error	Sig.[a]	95% confidence interval for difference[a]	
				Lower bound	Upper bound
Shelling capacity (kg/h)	326.200[*]	110.124	0.041	20.447	631.953
Shelling efficiency (%)	0.167[*]	0.047	0.024	0.036	0.298
Grain damage (%)	0.233	0.105	0.091	−0.059	0.526
Cleaning efficiency (%)	0.167	0.197	0.446	−0.381	0.714
Scattering loss (%)	4.700[*]	0.306	0.000	3.852	5.548
Fuel consumption (L/h)	0.057	0.156	0.735	−0.376	0.490

*. The mean difference is significant at the 0.05 level.
a. Least significant difference (equivalent to no adjustments).

Table 5. Mean difference between treatments for maize variety of LIMU

Dependent variable	Mean difference (I-J)	Std. error	Sig.[a]	95% confidence interval for difference[a]	
				Lower bound	Upper bound
Shelling capacity (kg/h)	543.333[*]	98.940	0.005	268.633	818.034
Shelling efficiency (%)	0.267	0.105	0.065	−0.026	0.559
Grain damage (%)	0.067	0.067	0.374	−0.118	0.252
Cleaning efficiency (%)	−0.167	0.160	0.356	−0.611	0.277
Scattering loss (%)	2.767[*]	0.359	0.002	1.770	3.763
Fuel consumption (L/h)	−.057	0.156	0.735	−0.490	0.377

*. The mean difference is significant at the 0.05 level.
a. Least significant difference (equivalent to no adjustments).

Shelling Efficiency, Grain Damage and Cleaning Efficiency. The results show that, the mean difference between treatments on shelling efficiency, grain damage and cleaning efficiency have slight variations for both varieties. These variations are not statistically significant at 0.05 level of significance, except for shelling efficiency of BH661 variety (Tables 4 and 5).

Scattering Loss (%). The results show that, higher percentages of scattering losses have been recorded at lower moisture contents for both varieties. As the moisture content decreased from 15.1% to 12.4% for BH661 variety, scattering loss increased by 4.70%. Similarly, for Limu (P3812W) maize variety, as the moisture content decreased from 16.3% to 12.8%, the scattering loss percentage increased by 2.767%. These increments were significant at 0.05 level of significance (Tables 4 and 5). These losses were collected at dust and cob outlet. This is because as the moisture content decreases, the weight of the grain decreases, thus some grain will be blown with the dust.

Fuel Consumption. The results show that no significant difference was observed in fuel consumption for both trials among treatments. The average fuel consumption for BH661 and LIMU varieties were found to be 3.04 L/h (Table 4) and 3.03 L/h (Table 5), respectively. Moreover the average fuel consumption without load was found to be 1.14 L/h.

Engine and shelling drum rpm. The average rotational speed of the shelling drum with load and without load was 600.85 ± 4.58 and 619.42 ± 0.86 respectively. The average rotational speed of the engine with load and without load was 3193.08 ± 22.74 and 3211.69 ± 6.32 respectively.

Table 6. Mean fuel consumption, shelling drum and prime mover speed

Parameters	Units	Without load	With load
Average fuel consumption	L/h	1.14	3.04
Average drum speed	rpm	619.42 ± 0.86	600.85 ± 4.58
Average prime mover speed	rpm	3211.69 ± 6.32	3193.08 ± 22.74

3.3 Farmers' Opinion About the Evaluated Maize Sheller

Farmers who participated during the demonstration were encouraged to give their opinions about the maize sheller, based on observed performance, ease of handling and transportation, and their own selection parameters. According to their response, they are satisfied with the quality of work performed by the sheller. Excellent performance was observed by participant farmers regarding seed and cob breakage, shelling loss, cleaning efficiency. Nevertheless, farmers observed that the portability of the sheller has some limitations. It was observed that transporting the sheller from place to place is very difficult. Hence, farmers have suggested to incorporate a wheel and animal harnessing system to be pulled by draft animals to transport easily from place to place.

4 Conclusion

From this participatory evaluation research, the following conclusions can be made:

- The shelling capacity of the modified model is improved by 29% from the previous Bako model maize sheller without compromising any other performance parameters.
- Shelling capacity increased significantly, as the moisture content of the maize kernel decreased.
- Shelling efficiency, grain damage and cleaning efficiency has shown no significant difference as the moisture content of the maize varies from 12.4% to 16.3%
- Scattering losses increased significantly, as the moisture content of the maize kernel decreased.
- Traditional maize shelling is less productive, requires 4 to 5man-day to shell 1,600 kg to 2,000 kg of maize, and drudgeries. Hence, farmers have showed interest for mechanical threshers.
- For the farmers, the evaluated maize sheller has excellent performance in shelling maize regarding seed and cob breakage, shelling loss, cleaning efficiency, shelling capacity and efficiency. The sheller has some difficulties to transport from place to place. Hence farmers have suggested that to incorporate wheel and animal harnessing system to be pulled by draft animals.

Acknowledgement. The authors of this paper are very thankful to Appropriate-Scale Mechanization Consortium for Sustainable Intensification (ASMC-Ethiopia) project for their financial and measuring instruments support.

References

1. Central statistical agency, federal democratic republic of Ethiopia: Agricultural sample survey 2016/2017, vol. 1: Area and production of major crops, Addis Ababa, Ethiopia (2017)
2. Abate, T., et al.: Factors that transformed maize productivity in Ethiopia. Food Secur. 7(5), 965–981 (2015). https://doi.org/10.1007/s12571-015-0488-z
3. Amare, D., Endalew, W., Yayu, N.: Evaluation and demonstration of maize shellers for small-scale farmers. MOJ Appl. Bionics Biomech. 1(3), 93–98 (2017). https://doi.org/10.15406/mojabb.2017.01.00014
4. Dagninet, A., Fentahun, T., Abu, T.: On-farm evaluation and verification of maize-sorghum thresher. In: Proceedings of the 3rd Annual Regional Conference on Completed Research Activities on Soil and Water Management, Forestry and Agricultural mechanization, 1–4 September 2008, pp. 227–236. ARARI, Bahir Dar (2010)
5. Kelemu, F.: Agricultural mechanization in Ethiopian: experience, status and prospects. Ethiop. J. Agric. Sci. 25, 45–60 (2015)
6. Mohammed, A., Tadesse, A.: Review of major grains postharvest losses in Ethiopia and customization of a loss assessment methodology. USAID/Ethiopia Agriculture Knowledge, Learning, Documentation and Policy Project, Addis Ababa (2018)
7. Smith, D.W., Sims, B.G., O'Neill, D.H.: Testing and evaluation of agricultural machinery and equipment: Principles and practices. FAO agricultural series Bulletin No 110, Rome, Italy (1994)
8. Ajav, E.A., Igbeka, J.C.: Performance evaluation of a Nigerian maize sheller using an international test code. J. Eng. Int. Dev. 2(1), 1–8 (1995)
9. Naveenkumar, D.B., Rajshekarappa, K.S.: Performance evaluation of a power operated maize sheller. Int. J. Agric. Eng. 5(2), 172–177 (2012)

Computational Fluid Dynamic Modeling and Simulation of Red Chili Solar Cabinet Dryer

Eshetu Getahun[1,2(✉)], Maarten Vanierschot[3], Nigus Gabbiye[1], Mulugeta A. Delele[4], Solomon Workneh[1], and Mekonnen Gebreslasie[3]

[1] Faculty of Chemical and Food Engineering, Bahir Dar Technology Institute, Bahir Dar University, Bahir Dar, Ethiopia
eshetu201384@gmail.com
[2] Bahir Dar Energy Center, Bahir Dar Technology Institute, Bahir Dar University, Bahir Dar, Ethiopia
[3] Mechanical Engineering Technology Cluster TC, Campus Groep T, KU Leuven, A. Vesaliusstraat 13, 3000 Louvain, Belgium
[4] Department of Biosystems, MeBioS, KU Leuven, University of Leuven, De Croylaan 42, 3001 Louvain, Belgium

Abstract. Red chilies are important sources of nutrients for human diet. It is known that improper handling of the produces causes a significant loss. Drying is a primary and suitable preservation system of chili products before storage to minimize mold/mycotoxin development. This study investigates the potential of solar cabinet chili dryer through rigorous computational fluid dynamic modeling by considering red chili as porous media. The k-ε turbulence model was utilized to effectively predict the uniformity of drying air velocity, pressure and mass transfer. It was found that the CFD simulation gives accurate prediction of the drying air and velocity and pressure distribution in each tray at inlet air velocity of 1.5 m/s. The solar absorber temperature was reached up to 54 °C and the drying chamber temperature was in the range of 34–38 °C. The performance of the dryer was very promising to keep the quality of the dried red chili products.

Keywords: Solar cabinet dryer · Red chili · CFD modeling · Moisture transfer

1 Introduction

1.1 Background

Chili (Capsicum annum L.) is very significant condiment and cash crop throughout the world. Red chilies are important sources of digestible carbohydrates, minerals, antioxidants, fiber, and vitamins, particularly vitamin A, C and E which are balanced nutritious diet for human beings [1, 2]. Chili peppers are widely cultivated in Ethiopia for their utilization of stew preparation to be consumed with Ethiopian traditional stippled food (thin-layer bread, injira) made from cereal grain especially teff (Eragrostis tef). Moreover, it is an essential constituent of Ethiopian curry due to its good color and pungency.

© ICST Institute for Computer Sciences, Social Informatics and Telecommunications Engineering 2020
Published by Springer Nature Switzerland AG 2020. All Rights Reserved
N. G. Habtu et al. (Eds.): ICAST 2019, LNICST 308, pp. 597–609, 2020.
https://doi.org/10.1007/978-3-030-43690-2_45

It is indispensable in every household kitchen of Ethiopian societies throughout the year for everyday cooking and found in the form of green being consumed as salad and dried form called as *berbere* used for stew making and as flavoring agent. Chili peppers are also an important source of revenue in Ethiopia since its demand is very high in the international market.

According to the CSA, 453,608.8 ha of land is under vegetable in Ethiopia with annual production of 18,124,613.5 quintal and among these production, red chili accounts about 70.89% [3]. However the post-harvest loss of red chili is very high and it is about 48% in Ethiopia [2].

Drying is one of the preservation mechanism of red chili. Red chili is traditionally dried directly under the open sun in Ethiopia. Open sun drying requires a large open space and long drying times. Although this traditional method requires only a small investment, open sun drying is highly dependent on the availability of sunshine and is susceptible to contamination from foreign materials (dust and sand) as well as insect and fungal infestations, which thrive in moist conditions. Such contaminations result aflatoxin formation caused by Asprigulus flavus fungus species in which the quality of the products significantly reduced. Therefore, solar cabinet drying has become one of the most attractive and promising applications of solar energy systems as an alternative to open sun drying in small scale drying system. However, the uniform distribution of drying parameters such as drying air, velocity and pressure through the solar cabinet dryer have a great impact on the quality of dried products. Drying is characterized as a combined multiscale, multiphysics and multiphase problem which is a very complex process. To describe explicitly this complex drying process, advanced mathematical modelling techniques like CFD, multiscale, multiphysics, and modelling of product properties and the associated spread of product property variability must be considered [4]. The drying rate of any food product is highly depend on drying air properties, product characteristics, dryer design and operation procedure. However, it is very difficult, time taking and expensive to pinpoint the optimum drying parameters by using experimental measurements. Thus, to understand the dynamic and thermal behavior of the solar cabinet chili dryer, CFD modeling is very important. The CFD modeling implements influential computer and applied physics and mathematics to model the systems for the prediction of mass, heat and momentum transfer and to screen out the optimal design and operating conditions in chili drying process [5].

The aims of this study are to investigate the hydrodynamic and thermal performance of red chili solar cabinet dryer in terms of the uniform distribution of drying air velocity, temperature and pressure.

2   Materials and Methods

2.1   Materials

Chili pepper, fully maturated, Mereko Fana species, with moisture content of 80% (wb) was used for the modeling and simulation of solar cabinet dryer. Data logger and pyrometer were used to record the daily drying parameters.

2.2 Methods

CFD Modeling and Simulation of the Solar Cabinet Chili Dryer
Model set up: The solar cabinet dryer geometrical set up is shown in Fig. 1. The solar cabinet drying system consists of a double-pass solar collector (2 m × 4 m), a blower, and a flatbed drying chamber. The total area of the collector is 8 m². The drying chamber is 1.5 m in length, 1.0 m in width, and 1.94 m in height. There are eight trays with a distance of 0.1 m between each tray. The drying system is classified as a forced convection indirect type and angle of inclination of the collector was set to 22° and face to south. Blower is placed on the nozzle end to suck air. The red chili is considered as porous media which spread in each tray with 0.05 m thickness. The solar collector is a double pass and the upper channel depth is 0.09 m, and the lower depth is 0.09 m, in between a 0.02 m thick absorber is placed. The solar cabinet dryer was designed to hold 40 kg of red chili, which was divided and equally distributed on eight trays.

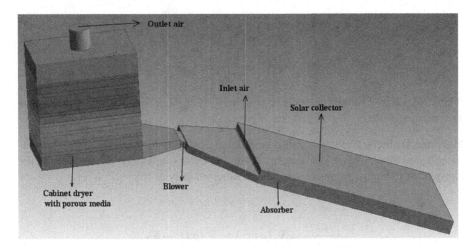

Fig. 1. Schematic sketch of the solar cabinet red chili dryer

Set Up the Governing Equations: The continuity, momentum and energy equations are determined as follow [6, 7]:
Continuity equation- The continuity equation is given by:

$$\frac{\partial \rho}{\partial t} + \nabla\left(\rho \vec{u}\right) = 0 \tag{1}$$

Where $\vec{u}$ and ρ are velocity and density of air respectively.
Navier-Stokes equation- The Navier Stokes equation is given by [7]:

$$\frac{\partial\left(\rho \vec{u}\right)}{\partial t} + \nabla.\left(\rho \vec{u}\vec{u}\right) = -\nabla P + \nabla\bar{\bar{\tau}} + \rho \vec{g} + S_m \tag{2}$$

Where $\bar{\tau}$ and S_m are Reynolds shear stress and momentum source term respectively.

Energy equation- The energy equation is given by:

$$\frac{\partial(\rho E)}{\partial t} + \nabla.\left(\vec{u}(\rho E + P)\right) = \nabla.\left(-\vec{q} + \bar{\bar{\tau}}.\vec{u}\right) + S_h \tag{3}$$

Where, $S_h, \vec{q}$ and E are heat source term, heat flux vector and total energy respectively. The total energy (E) is the sum of internal energy and kinetic energy which is given by

$$E = h - \frac{P}{\rho} + \frac{u^2}{2} \tag{4}$$

where, h is the sensible enthalpy of air.

Turbulent model- The K-ε turbulence model was used for this study and this model considered the conservation of turbulence kinetic energy, k and its corresponding dissipation rate, ε through the following expression [8]:

$$\frac{\partial(\rho k)}{\partial t} + \nabla.\left(\rho \vec{u} k\right) = \nabla.\left[\left(\mu + \frac{\mu_t}{\sigma_k}\right)\nabla k\right] + P_k - \rho\varepsilon \tag{5}$$

$$\frac{\partial(\rho \varepsilon)}{\partial t} + \nabla.\left(\rho \vec{u} \varepsilon\right) = \nabla.\left[\left(\mu + \frac{\mu_t}{\sigma_\varepsilon}\right)\nabla \varepsilon\right] + \frac{\varepsilon}{k}(C_{\varepsilon 1} P_k - C_{\varepsilon 2}\rho\varepsilon) \tag{6}$$

Where, $C_{\varepsilon 1}$, $C_{\varepsilon 2}$, σ_k and σ_ε constants given as 1.44, 1.92, 1.0 and 1.3 respectively for most computations.

Moisture Transport: Water vapor is considered as a scalar property that does not influence the solutions of continuity, momentum and energy equations. Consequently, the transport of the scalar property is solved in autonomously as [6]:

$$\frac{\partial(\rho w)}{\partial t} = \nabla.\left(\rho \vec{v} w\right) = \nabla.(\rho D) + S_W \tag{7}$$

where w is ratio of humidity (kg water vapor/kg dry air). D is the diffusion coefficient of water vapor and S_W is the source term. Moisture transfer from the surface of the product to the environment (moisture source term, S_W) is governed by the following equation.

$$M_w = h_m A_s(C_S - C_\infty) \tag{8}$$

Where,

$$C_S = \frac{P_{sat}}{RT} \tag{9}$$

$$C_\infty = P_{sat} * Rh \tag{10}$$

$$P_{Sat} = \exp\left(65.8\left(\frac{7066.3}{T}\right) - 5.98\ln T\right) \tag{11}$$

H_m is mass transfer coefficient and found from Nusselt number,

$$h_m = \frac{D_m}{d_p} Sch \tag{12}$$

D_m is molecular diffusion coefficient of vapor in the gas, d_p is chili diameter and Sch is the Sherwood number and Rh is relative humidity and As is specific surface area.

$$D_m = 104.91143 * 10^{-6} \frac{T^{1.774}}{P} \tag{13}$$

The heat source term is also given as [9]:

$$S_h = \rho \frac{\partial M}{\partial t} L_v \tag{14}$$

where L_v is the latent heat of vaporization of water from chili.

Moisture Content and Concentration: It is also clear that, in wet bases, moisture content is given by

$$X_C = \frac{m_W}{m_{chili}} = \frac{m_W}{\rho * V} \tag{15}$$

But, $m_w = nM$ and the parameter, n/V, is the concentration. Therefore, from Eq. 14, the concentration is determined as:

$$Conc = \frac{X_c * \rho_{chili}}{18 * 10^{-3}} \tag{16}$$

where, ρ_{chili} is bulk density of chili (500 kg/m^3) [10], M is molecular mass of water, m_w is sample mass of chili and n is mole of sample mass. Initial moisture content (Xc) of chili is about 80% and final allowable moisture content of chili is about 5–12%. The environmental conditions of Bahir Dar city have been taken for the simulation process. Radiation was modelled using Monte carlo radiation model.

Porous Media Modeling: The red chili is considered as porous media in the solar cabinet dryer. The porous media is modelled by the addition of a momentum source term to the standard fluid flow equations such as conservation of energy, momentum and moisture transport equation. In the momentum equation, the two losses such as inertial losses and viscous losses are found as source term and expressed as [6, 11]:

$$\frac{\partial P}{\partial z} = -\left(\frac{\mu}{\alpha}\right) u_z + C \frac{1}{2} \rho u_z^2 \tag{17}$$

where C is the inertial loss coefficient and $(1/\alpha)$ is the viscous loss coefficient. Ergun [12] developed an equation for packed beds which has been applied successfully for porous media.

$$\frac{\Delta P}{L} = \frac{150\mu \left(1 - \varepsilon^2\right)}{d_p^2 \varepsilon^3} u + \frac{1.75\rho(1 - \varepsilon)}{d_p(1 - \varepsilon)} u^2 \tag{18}$$

For this simulation study, the chili porosity was assumed to be constant at 0.4 and chili particle diameter (d_p) of 0.064 cm at 80% moisture content.

CFD Model Solution Procedures: The hydrodynamic solar cabinet chili dryer model was discretized with finite volume method and simulated using ANSYS- CFX software.

Initial and Boundary Conditions
Initial condition- The fluid in the solar tunnel chili dryer is initially assumed stagnant and at a uniform ambient temperature of 25 °C.
*Boundary Conditions-*Walls: A no slip wall condition was used.
Inlet- The optimum inlet drying air velocity was set at 1.5 m/s, and the turbulence intensity was set at 5%. The inlet temperature was varied throughout the drying time and expressed as:

$$T = -4e - 8 * t^2 + 0.0012 * t + 19.38 \tag{18}$$

The radiation intensity and relative humidity were also varied and the average daily solar intensity and relative humidity were 500 W/m^2 and 45% respectively.
Outlet- Gauge pressure $= 0$
For the solar collector Monte carlo radiation boundary was considered. The emissivity and diffuse fraction of the collector was 0.9 and 0.05 respectively.

3 Results and Discussions

3.1 Mesh Generation and Analysis

The mesh/grid of the model is shown in Fig. 2. The mesh was generated based on medium relevance center and has 15179 nods and 53053 elements. The grid was refined to confirm mesh independence. When the percentage different between the two successive meshes is negligible, it is possible to say there is mesh independency. To identify mesh independency, the simulation was proceeded from coarse to fine mesh and the variation of the desired simulation output was checked. It is also possible to have mesh independent solution by using a very fine uniform mesh. However, it would take days/months to end the simulation process and thus, the simulation of this study was conducted on medium mesh.

3.2 Drying Air Velocity Distribution

The velocity contour inside the drying chamber is shown in Fig. 3. As it can be seen in this figure, it was observed that a uniform velocity distribution throughout the drying chamber (at maximum velocity of 1.5 m/s) was prevailed. On the other hand, relatively high velocity was achieved at the inlet and outlet of the dryer. This may be due to small cross section in the specified area.

The velocity streamline is also presented in Fig. 4. From this figure, it was clearly seen that the solar cabinet dryer has good air distribution in solar collector and porous region which in turn will have huge positive impact on the product quality at the end.

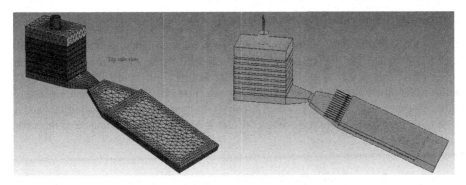

Fig. 2. The mesh/grid generation of the model

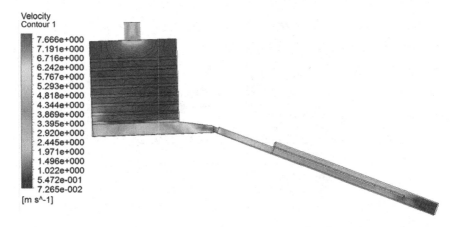

Fig. 3. Velocity contour of the drying chamber

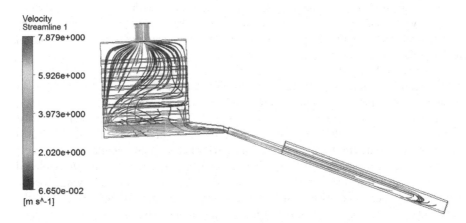

Fig. 4. Velocity streamline of the chili drying chamber

3.3 Drying Temperature Distribution

The double pass solar collector is very important to enhance temperature that required to heat the drying air. The temperature profile of solar absorber is shown in Fig. 5. As it can be seen from this figure, at the inlet of the absorber, the temperature was low, however, at the outlet of the absorber, high temperature was noticed. The maximum temperature of the absorber was about 54 °C which is enough to heat the prevailing drying air and it is an indication that double pass solar collector enhanced the performance of the solar cabinet chili dryer.

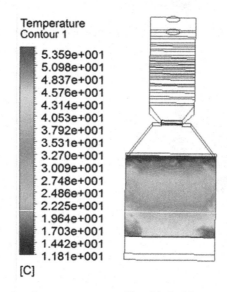

Fig. 5. Solar absorber temperature profile with double pass solar collector

This magnitude of temperature (54 °C) was utilized to heat the drying air throughout the drying chamber and hence the overall temperature profile of the solar cabinet drying system is presented in Fig. 6. It was observed that the temperature was reduced from 54 to 43 °C during chili drying process due to moisture removal.

The final utilized temperature in the porous media (chili) drying is very important. More specifically, the temperature profile of only porous media is shown in Fig. 7. As it can be seen in Fig. 7, the temperature profile of the porous media (red chili per tray) was in the range of 36–39.7 °C. Fudholi et al. [13] were studied experimentally, solar cabinet chili dryer and the temperature was in the range of 28–55 °C which indicated that there was some similarity of the thermal performance to this simulation study.

Inside the solar cabinet chili dryer chamber there are eight porous media/tray/placed at 0.1 m distance from the bottom to top of the dryer. At the beginning of drying process, the obtained energy serves only to evaporate water from the product. After that, the obtained energy serves, in the one hand, to evaporate the water of the product and, on the other hand, to increase the temperature of the media. The convective effect also increased the temperature in the first tray, thus due to these direct heating and convective heat transfer, evaporation of water was higher in the first, second and the third tray than the other trays. However, this is not the case for the next porous, where the obtained energy only serves to water evaporation and the convective heat transfer resulted saturation of the evaporated water due to accumulation of the evaporated water from the preceding layers. Similar study was conducted by Belhamri et al. [14].

High temperature was observed at the center of the dryer and to some extent low near to the corner of the dryer. Moreover, as it can be seen in Fig. 7, temperatures of the porous media were decreased starting from the third porous media to the last porous media due to moisture removal that reduced the next porous media temperature and it has been clearly identified through graphical representation as shown in Fig. 8.

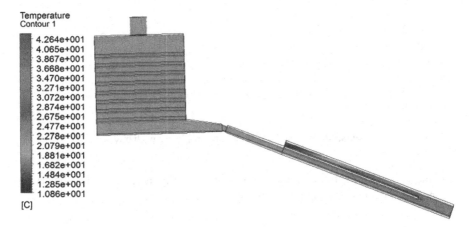

Fig. 6. Temperature profile of the solar cabinet chili drying system

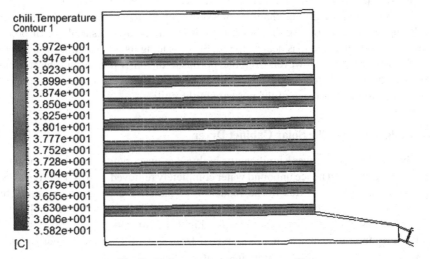

Fig. 7. Porous media temperature profile

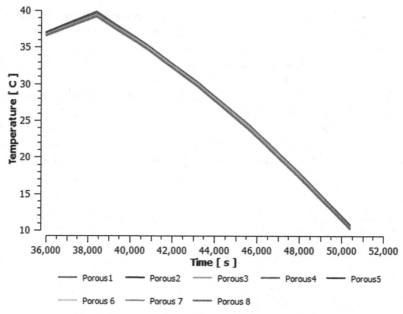

Fig. 8. Porous media temperature profile per each tray

In the start of drying time temperature was dramatically increased and as the drying time increased the temperature also decreased as shown in Fig. 8.

3.4 Pressure Drop Across the Porous Media

The pressure profile of solar cabinet red chili dryer is presented in Fig. 9. As it can be seen in this figure, the drying chamber pressure drop in general increased throughout the drying chamber as drying time increased. It is may be due to shrinkage of porous medium during experiment as heat supplied, thus reducing its permeability which is the cause of pressure drop. However, from one porous to the other porous (staring from the bottom to the top of dryer, porous 1–porous 8), at a fixed time, the pressure drops were reduced due to the resistance of the porosity of the chili.

3.5 Performance of the Solar Cabinet Dryer

Initially the drying rate was significantly high since evaporation took place near the surface of the chili and hence unbound water completely removed. As drying progressed, the drying rate decreased due to the reduction of moisture content. In this case, the moisture to be evaporated comes from internal cells within the structure (bound water) and must be transported to the surface in which highly resistive for mass and heat transfer.

The moisture content which was removed from the red chili by the heated air is shown in Fig. 10. As it can be seen in this figure, the inlet air has low water vapor inside it. Moreover, the air is found at high level of temperature and the water vapor content was increased at the first parts of the porous media (product) since most of the surface

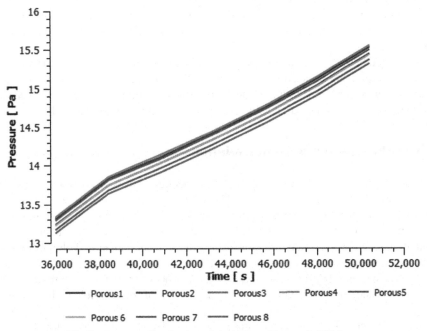

Fig. 9. Pressure distribution of the solar cabinet red chili dryer

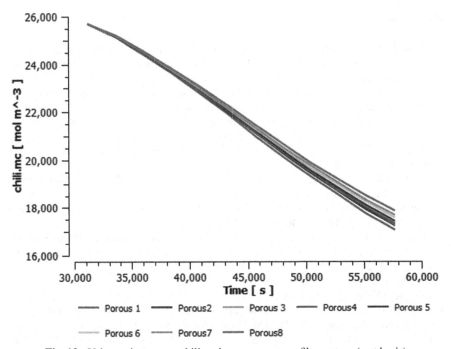

Fig. 10. Volumetric average chili moisture content profile per tray (wet basis)

water was removed and moved with the air. Water removal reduced from the first porous to the last porous media due to reduction in temperature along the vertical distance of the solar cabinet chili dryer.

Even though the moisture removal performance of the solar cabinet chili dryer was found in a promising trend, it was not sufficiently stabilized the removal of moisture content in the porous media due to the short simulation (drying) time. It reduced the moisture content form the initial value of 80% to 49% in wet bases within 16 h.

4   Conclusions and Recommendations

In this modeling and simulation, the drying temperature and velocity were found uniform throughout the solar cabinet dryer. The solar absorber temperature was 54 °C and the drying chamber temperature was found in the range of 36–39.7 °C. The moisture was reduced from 80% to 49% in wet bases within 16 h. Generally the modeling and simulation result showed that the performance of the solar cabinet red chili dryer was very promising one. Further optimization of drying temperature, velocity distribution is very essential through fully converged iteration process and it is under progress. The high performance computer will be also mandatory to analyze the whole drying process.

Acknowledgement. The research fund was granted from Bahir Dar Energy Center, Bahir Dar Institute of technology, Bahir Dar University, Ethiopia.

References

1. Demissie, T., Ali, A., Zerfu, D.: Availability and consumption of fruits and vegetables in nine regions of Ethiopia with special emphasis to vitamin A deficiency. Ethiop. J. Health Dev. **23**, 217–223 (2010)
2. Hailu, G., Derbew, B.: Extent, causes and reduction strategies of postharvest losses of fresh fruits and vegetables − a review. J. Biol. Agric. Healthc. **5**, 49–64 (2015)
3. C. S. A. (CSA) (2015/2016): Agricultural Sample Survey 2015/2016, vol. 1, Report on Area and Production of Major Crops, Addis Ababa (2016)
4. Defraeye, T.: Advanced computational modelling for drying processes - a review. Appl. Energy **131**, 323–344 (2014)
5. Xia, B., Sun, D.-W.: Applications of computational fluid dynamics (CFD) in the food industry: a review. Comput. Electron. Agric. **34**, 5–24 (2002)
6. Sanghi, A., Ambrose, R.P.K., Maier, D.: CFD simulation of corn drying in a natural convection solar dryer. Drying Technol. **36**(7), 859–870 (2018)
7. Demissie, P., Hayelom, M., Kassaye, A., Hailesilassie, A., Gebrehiwot, M., Vanierschot, M.: Design, development and CFD modeling of indirect solar food dryer. Energy Procedia **158**, 1128–1134 (2019)
8. Aukah, J., Muvengei, M.: Simulation of drying uniformity inside hybrid solar biomass dryer using ANSYS CFX. In: Sustainable Research, pp. 336–344 (2015)
9. Cârlescu, P.M., Arsenoaia, V., Roşca, R., Ţenu, I.: CFD simulation of heat and mass transfer during apricots drying. LWT - Food Sci. Technol. **85**, 479–486 (2017)
10. Charrondiere, U.R., Haytowitz, D., Stadlmayr, B.: FAO/ INFOODS Databases: Density Database Version 2.0, Database (2012)

11. Tegenaw, P.D., Gebrehiwot, M.G., Vanierschot, M.: On the comparison between computational fluid dynamics (CFD) and lumped capacitance modeling for the simulation of transient heat transfer in solar dryers. Sol. Energy **184**, 417–425 (2019)
12. Ergun, S.: Fluid flow through packed columns. Chem. Eng. Prog. **48**, 89–94 (1952)
13. Fudholi, A., Sopian, K., Yazdi, M.H., Ruslan, M.H., Gabbasa, M., Kazem, H.A.: Performance analysis of solar drying system for red chili. Sol. Energy **99**, 47–54 (2014)
14. Bennamoun, L., Belhamri, A.: Study of heat and mass transfer in porous media: application to packed-bed drying. FDMP **4**(4), 221–230 (2008)

Development and Performance Evaluation of a Solar Baking Oven

Bisrat Yilma Mekonnen$^{(\boxtimes)}$ and Addisu Yenesew Kebede

Faculty of Mechanical and Industrial Engineering,
Bahir Dar Institute of Technology, Bahir Dar University, Bahir Dar, Ethiopia
bisratyilma20@gmail.com, addiye2003@gmail.com

Abstract. The majorities of rural people in Ethiopia have low access to electricity and depend almost completely on biomass fuels traditionally. Traditional and inefficient burning of biomass fuels for cooking has an adverse effect on both human health and the global climate. Solar energy could be an alternative even though it cannot replace biomass completely. This work has focused on developing a solar baking oven and aimed to shorten the long cooking time in existing box type solar cookers by employing additional parabolic reflecting element under the box to gain additional heat input. The solar oven is designed for a baking purpose since most Ethiopian cultural foods require continuous whisking or stir during cooking which is not comfortable with solar cookers. The maximum absorber pipe temperature is found to be 121.1 °C and the first figure of merit (F_1) is calculated to be 0.1204. The baking test was done to evaluate the baker actual performance and the quality of the bread by placing row bread in the baking tray inside the absorber rectangular pipe. The performances of the baker demonstrated that these devices can play a role in combating domestic energy problem, mainly in rural areas.

Keywords: Solar baker · Box type solar cookers · Thermal performance · First figure of merit

1 Introduction

The majority of households in Ethiopia use traditional biomass for cooking due to the lack of alternative energy sources. The majority of the population cooks their food on an open fire inside or outside of their homes by burning different forms of biomass. A large amount of particulate matters and combustion products emitted from the traditional burning of each biomass fuels have an adverse effect on human health, global climate and local ecosystems in general. It is also highlighted by the World Health Organization that 1.6 million deaths per year are caused by unfavorable indoor air pollution [1]. Excessive dependence on biomass energy also minimizes agricultural productivity by diverting crop residues and animal wastes from farms for energy needs [2]. Similarly, wood scarcities have become more critical; to obtain wood fuel, rural households who depend on collective free wood have to travel further distances, this also causes loss of human availability

N. G. Habtu et al. (Eds.): ICAST 2019, LNICST 308, pp. 610–622, 2020.
https://doi.org/10.1007/978-3-030-43690-2_46

for productive work. Furthermore, wood fuel depletion leads to deforestation and degradation. Three-stone fire is free and quite easy to construct. Due to the simplicity and availability, three-stone fires have continued to be used for cooking in rural communities and wood fuel is being consumed at an unsustainable rate [3–5] (Fig. 1).

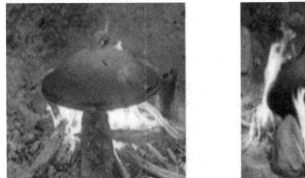
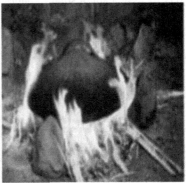

Fig. 1. Traditional three stone baking system in Ethiopia [18].

Solar energy could be an alternative even though it cannot replace biomass completely. Ethiopia is a country with all months of sunshine, and it can be converted into heat. A solar cooker is a device that cooks food using solar energy without consuming fuels and the early effort of using solar energy for cooking food was published in 1767, the effort has continued till today to improve the performance of different types of solar cookers [19]. There are different types of solar cookers. Box type solar cooker is quite simple to construct and cheap relative to concentrated type and indirect type solar cookers, but it requires longer cooking time compared to traditional cookers or concentrating type of solar cookers. Thus, researchers have been working to improve the performance

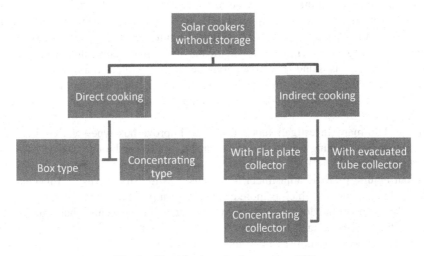

Fig. 2. Classification of solar cookers [17]

of box type cooker to achieve higher temperature and make them more suitable for different cooking traditions. In box type solar cooker the box is insulated at the side and glazed at the top to retain the heat. The booster mirrors or reflectors reflect the solar radiation into the box. Parabolic solar cooker is a concentrating type cooker and it can reach a much higher cooking temperature compared to box type cookers. Concentrating cookers focus a beam of solar radiation on the focus of the collector where the cooking pot is sited. Parabolic solar cookers require tracking of solar during the day in order to give the required cooking temperature [20] (Figs. 2 and 3).

Fig. 3. Conventional box type solar cooker [22, 23].

Many investigations have been conducted in order to improve the performance of the solar cooker and make them more suitable for users. Saitoh and El-Ghetany [6] investigated a solar water sterilization system theoretically and experimentally with thermally controlled flow. Amer [7] examined a novel design of solar cooker theoretically and experimentally in which the absorber is exposed to solar radiation from both the top and the bottom sides. El-Sebaii and Aboul-Enein [8] presented a work to determine the overall heat transfer coefficients between the components of a solar box cooker. Ozkaymak [9] modeled the performance of a box solar cooker. Asfafaw Haileselassie et al. [21] introduced new technology that enables Injera (the most popular food in Ethiopia) baking using a parabolic dish with an aperture area of 2.54 m². Adewole [25] evaluated a box solar cooker and he found the maximum plate temperature of 76 °C and first figure of merit is found to be 0.06. Sonali et al. [23] evaluated a box solar cooker with fins and he found the maximum plate temperature of 100 °C and first figure of merit is found to be 0.106. More authors investigated and evaluated different types of solar cookers [10–15].

Even if so many investigations conducted to improve box type solar cookers, the time required for cooking is quite long compared to traditional biomass stoves and concentrating solar cookers. Parabolic collector's cooking times are similar to a traditional stove but require periodic adjustment to refocus it as the sun moves or a mechanical solar tracking apparatus which is more expensive than panel and box cookers. A solar box cooker is cheap and doesn't require expensive tracking mechanism but a major limitation is the long cooking or baking time. The low efficiency and long cooking time in existing box type solar cooker can be improved by combining the principle of a solar box type cooker with a parabolic trough collector. The heating time for a solar box is shortened as the temperature is increased by applying additional parabolic reflection element employed under the box to gain additional heat input. A metal rectangular baking tray is positioned in its focal line. The need for alignment perpendicularly towards the sun is still there but does not require as frequent as it is with a classic parabolic solar cooker. By designing the cooker as a combination of the two, the limitation of a box cooker is dealt, and the work has focused on developing a solar baking oven for break baking purpose since most Ethiopian cultural foods require continuous whisking or stir during cooking which is not comfortable with solar cookers.

2 Methodology

2.1 Product Design Specification

In designing the solar oven, appropriate parameters should be considered, since it is highly considered as a consumer-specific device. The product design specification is based on the knowledge that was concluded in the field study, literature review and theoretical calculations to make sure the design meets the requirements of the users. If the oven is to be the source of income for a person, the output capacity must be large enough to make a sufficient profit. The number of times a person can bake is a variable to the function of bread/day. This number is calculated by dividing the total sun hours per day with the time that it takes to bake. The size of the bread that is to be baked is dependent on what type of bread it is. Even though it is possible to make smaller variants of a specific kind of bread it is important that the oven can bake a locally available size type of bread. To be able to bake good quality bread it is important to have the required temperature. The weight of the oven is considered because the user must be able to keep the oven perpendicular towards the sun as well as be able to transport. In order to be used by everyone, it is important that the oven is easy to use. Safety is also mandatory which describes specifications for stability, not causing burns and safety against theft. The solar baker is constructed from different materials and a number of criteria were considered for the selection of construction materials. Pugh's Method was used to evaluate and to quickly identify the best solution. Based on the decision matrix, Plywood is selected to construct the baker body, aluminum is selected for the parabolic reflector, and booster mirror is selected for the upper reflector.

2.2 Design Description

The solar baking oven is a concept that works by combining the principle of a solar parabolic trough cooker and a solar box cooker. Parabolic trough collector's heating time is shorter because it works by concentrating sunlight into a line which makes it effective but it needs accurate and expensive solar tracking mechanism. The solar box type cooker is less efficient and requires longer heating time but don't require expensive tracking mechanism; the need of alignment perpendicularly towards the sun is still there but does not require as frequent as it is with the typical parabolic solar cooker. The low efficiency and long cooking time in existing box type solar cooker can be aimed to improve by combining a solar box type cooker with a parabolic trough collector. The cooking time is shortened as the temperature is increased by replacing the box interior by parabolic reflection element to gain additional heat input. The baking is done in a focal line and the way of accessing the food is only through the sides where safety precautions have been taken (Figs. 4, 5, 6 and Table 1).

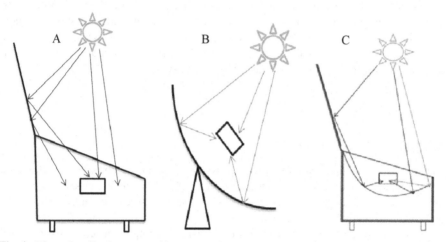

Fig. 4. View of realized concept of box type solar cooker (a), parabolic trough solar collector (b) and the combined solar baking oven (c).

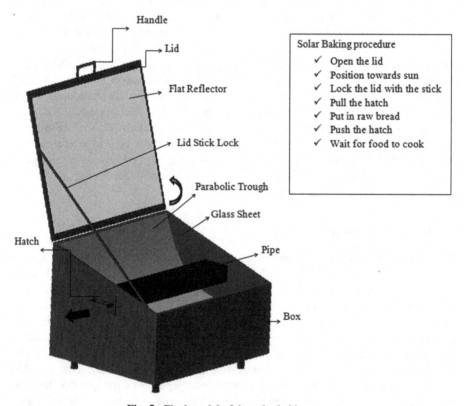

Solar Baking procedure
- ✓ Open the lid
- ✓ Position towards sun
- ✓ Lock the lid with the stick
- ✓ Pull the hatch
- ✓ Put in raw bread
- ✓ Push the hatch
- ✓ Wait for food to cook

Fig. 5. Final model of the solar baking oven

Fig. 6. Constructed Prototype of the solar baking oven (length is reduced for test only)

Table 1. Product specifications for the solar baking oven.

S/N	Design parameters	Specifications
A.	Capacity	
	1. Breads/day	60
	2. Use/day	4
	3. Number of breads/use	15
	4. Maximum bread size	$11 \times 10 \times 8$ cm
B.	Box dimension	
	1. Height (shorter, longer)	250 mm, 400 mm
	2. Width, Length, Thickness	500 mm, 1200 mm, 10 mm
	Box material	Plywood
C.	Glazing glass	
	1. Number	1
	2. Thickness	3 mm
	3. Transmittance	0.9 mm
D.	Reflector	
	Booster mirror	
	1. Number	1
	2. Material	Mirror
	3. Dimension	$1200 \times 470 \times 2$ mm
	Parabolic trough	

(*continued*)

Table 1. (*continued*)

S/N	Design parameters	Specifications
	1. Material	Aluminum (1 mm)
	2. Diameter	500 mm
	3. Depth	150 mm
	4. Focal length	104.17 mm
E.	Absorber pipe	
	1. Material	Aluminum (1 mm)
	2. Coating	Black glossy paint
	3. Absorbance	0.9
	4. Thermal conductivity	204 W/m. °C
	5. Dimension	130 × 90 × 1200 mm
F.	Baking tray	
	Material	Stainless steel

2.3 Experimental Methods

Type "k" thermocouples were attached to the absorber to measure the absorber pipe temperature rise sequentially at a given interval until the stagnation condition was found. The tracking of the cookers was done every thirty minutes. The solar radiation intensity was also measured and recorded at a regular interval using a digital solarimeter. Also, actual baking test was done by placing row bread in the baking tray inside the absorber rectangular pipe. The baking test was done to evaluate the baker actual performance and the quality of the bread. First figure of merit (F_1) was used as a performance criterion as per Indian Standard (IS 13429:2000) to evaluate the performance of the baker and to compare and validate the cooker with related cookers. The first figure of merit (F_1) is defined as the ratio of optical efficiency (η_0) and the overall heat loss coefficient (U_L). The desired higher figure of merit could be achieved when the optical efficiency is higher and the heat loss is lower.

$$F_1 = \frac{\eta_0}{U_L} \tag{1}$$

Experimentally,

$$F_1 = \frac{T_{PS} - T_{as}}{H_S} \tag{2}$$

Where T_{ps}, T_{as} and H_s are stagnation temperature, average ambient temperature and solar radiation intensity respectively.

Standard stagnation temperature is found from [16]:

$$SST = \left[\left(T_{stagnation} - T_{ambient} \right) \left(850 \, W/m^2 \right) \right] / G \tag{3}$$

3   Result and Discussion

Stagnation temperature and baking tests were performed under Bahir Dar weather conditions in January 2019. Bahir Dar is located in Ethiopia at 11°36′ N latitude and 37°23′ E longitude. The stagnation temperature test was intended to measure the standard stagnation temperature and to evaluate the first figure of merit (F_1) of the solar oven. The tests were started at around 11:00 AM and were stopped at 2:00 PM by placing the baker in the open sun (Fig. 7).

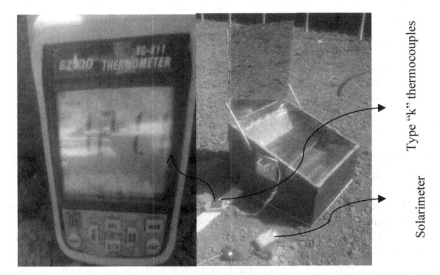

Fig. 7. Experimental set up on the solar oven

The maximum absorber pipe temperature is found to be 121.1 °C, which occurred at around 1:30 PM as shown in Fig. 8. The standard stagnation temperature is found to be 102.3 °C. F_1 is calculated to be 0.1204, and solar cooker with first figure of merit greater than 0.12 is marked as A-Grade solar cooker as per Indian Standard (IS 13429:2000) [15]. The first figure of merit can be improved by minimizing heat losses and leakages to the ambient (Table 2).

Table 2. The test result of ambient temperature, absorber temperature and solar insolation.

Time (hrs)	Ambient Temp. T_a (°C)	Absorber Temp. T_p (°C)	Insolation, I_s (W/m^2)
11:00	25	60	716
11:30	25	71	762
12:00	27	96	759
12:30	27	117	781
1:00	26	120	786
1:30	26	121.1	790
2:00	26	119	784

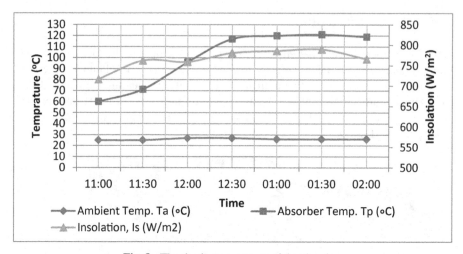

Fig. 8. The rise in temperature of the absorber

Figure 8 shows the temperature rise of the baker, ambient temperature and solar insolation versus time of the day. This experiment monitored the rise in temperature of the absorber plate when no baking has taken place to determine the peak temperature attainable at given solar insolation on a particular time. The pick is measured at noon when maximum insolation is recorded. The peak temperature of the absorber pipe (121.1 °C) is attained at 1:30 PM. The heat up time is shortened unlike most box type solar cookers because of the parabolic reflector inserted inside the box to attain additional heat input. The baking test was done to evaluate the baker actual performance and the quality of the bread by placing row bread in the baking tray inside the absorber rectangular pipe. The baking is done in a focal line and the way of accessing the food is only through the sides. It takes 50 min for the bread to be baked (Fig. 9 and Table 3).

Fig. 9. Bread baked by the constructed solar baker.

Table 3. Comparison of the constricted solar oven with related works.

Author	The type of the cooker	Performance criterion
Adewole [25]	See Fig. 10 **Fig. 10.** Reflector based solar box cooker [25]	$F_1 = 0.08$ $T_{stagnation} = 76\,°C$ Stagnation temperature reached after three hours and twenty minutes
Sonali et al. [23]	See Fig. 11 **Fig. 11.** Typical box type solar cooker [23].	$F_1 = 0.1061$ $T_{stagnation} = 100\,°C$ Stagnation temperature reached after four hours

(continued)

Table 3. (*continued*)

Author	The type of the cooker	Performance criterion
Saravanan and Janarathanan [26]	See Fig. 12 **Fig. 12.** Double exposure box-type solar cooker [26].	$F_1 = 0.1131$ $T_{stagnation} = 102\ °C$ Stagnation temperature reached after three hours
Bisrat and Addisu	See Fig. 13 **Fig. 13.** The constructed solar baking oven	$F_1 = 0.1204$ $T_{stagnation} = 121.1\ °C$ or stagnation temperature reached after two and half hour
Harmim et al. [19]	See Fig. 14 **Fig. 14.** Box type solar cooker with parabolic concentrator as booster-reflector [19].	$F_1 = 0.152$ $T_{stagnation} = 127.7\ °C$ (in cold season) $T_{stagnation} = 165\ °C$ (in hot season) Stagnation temperature reached after three hours

4   Conclusion

The performances of the baker demonstrated that the maximum absorber pipe temperature is found to be 121.1 °C and first figure of merit (F_1) is calculated to be 0.1204. It can be improved by minimizing heat losses and leakages to the surrounding. The heat up time is shortened compared to similar box type solar cookers because of the parabolic reflector employed inside the box to attain additional heat input. Generally, this kind of alternative device can play a major role in combating domestic energy problem especially in the rural areas for baking. Improvement on the baker to attain a higher temperature is recommended for further research work.

References

1. Rehfuess, E., World Health Organization: Fuel for life: household energy and health (2006)
2. Toonen, H.M.: Adapting to an innovation: Solar cooking in the urban households of Ouagadougou (Burkina Faso). Phys. Chem. Earth Parts A/B/C **34**(1-2), 65–71 (2009)
3. Sutar, K.B., et al.: Biomass cookstoves: a review of technical aspects. Renew. Sustain. Energy Rev. **41**, 1128–1166 (2015)
4. Kshirsagar, M.P., Kalamkar, V.R.: A comprehensive review on biomass cookstoves and a systematic approach for modern cookstove design. Renew. Sustain. Energy Rev. **30**, 580–603 (2014)
5. Still, D., et al.: Test Results of Cook Stove Performance, p. 126. Aprovecho Research Center, Shell Foundation, United States Environmental Protection Agency (2011)
6. Saitoh, T.S., El-Ghetany, H.H.: Solar water-sterilization system with thermally-controlled flow. Appl. Energy **64**(1-4), 387–399 (1999)
7. Amer, E.H.: Theoretical and experimental assessment of a double exposure solar cooker. Energy Convers. Manag. **44**(16), 2651–2663 (2003)
8. El-Sebaii, A.A., Aboul-Enein, S.: A box-type solar cooker with one-step outer reflector. Energy **22**(5), 515–524 (1997)
9. Özkaymak, M.: Theoretical and experimental investigation of a hot box-type solar cooker performance. Proc. Inst. Mech. Eng. Part A J. Power Energy **221**(1), 91–97 (2007)
10. Sethi, V.P., Pal, D.S., Sumathy, K.: Performance evaluation and solar radiation capture of optimally inclined box type solar cooker with parallelepiped cooking vessel design. Energy Convers. Manag. **81**, 231–241 (2014)
11. Cuce, E., Cuce, P.M.: A comprehensive review on solar cookers. Appl. Energy **102**, 1399–1421 (2013)
12. Rikoto, I.I., Garba, I.: Comparative analysis on solar cooking using box-type solar cooker with finned cooking pot. Int. J. Mod. Eng. Res. (IJMER) **3**(3), 1290–1294 (2013)
13. Mirdha, U.S., Dhariwal, S.R.: Design optimization of solar cooker. Renewable Energy **33**(3), 530–544 (2008)
14. Ayoola, M.A., et al.: Measurements of net all-wave radiation at a tropical location, Ile-Ife. Nigeria. Atmósfera **27**(3), 305–315 (2014)
15. Mullick, S.C., Kandpal, T.C., Kumar, S.: Testing of box-type solar cooker: second figure of merit F2 and its variation with load and number of pots. Sol. Energy **57**(5), 409–413 (1996)
16. Kahsay, M.B., et al.: Theoretical and experimental comparison of box solar cookers with and without internal reflector. Energy Procedia **57**, 1613–1622 (2014)
17. Muthusivagami, R.M., Velraj, R., Sethumadhavan, R.: Solar cookers with and without thermal storage—a review. Renew. Sustain. Energy Rev. **14**(2), 691–701 (2010)

18. Berrueta, V.M., Edwards, R.D., Masera, O.R.: Energy performance of wood-burning cookstoves in Michoacan, Mexico. Renewable Energy 33(5), 859–870 (2008)
19. Harmim, A., et al.: Design and experimental testing of an innovative building-integrated box type solar cooker. Sol. Energy 98, 422–433 (2013)
20. Tesfay, A.H.: Experimental Investigation of a Concentrating Solar Fryer with Heat Storage (2015)
21. Tesfay, A.H., Kahsay, M.B., Nydal, O.J.: Design and development of solar thermal Injera baking: steam based direct baking. Energy Procedia 57, 2946–2955 (2014)
22. Negi, B.S., Purohit, I.: Experimental investigation of a box type solar cooker employing a non-tracking concentrator. Energy Convers. Manag. 46(4), 577–604 (2005)
23. Kesarwani, S., Rai, A.K., Sachann, V.: An experimental study on box type solar cooker. Int. J. Adv. Res. Eng. Technol. 6(7), 1–6 (2015)
24. Folaranmi, J.: Performance evaluation of a double-glazed box-type solar oven with reflector. J. Renewable Energy 2013 (2013)
25. Adewole, B.Z., Popoola, O.T., Asere, A.A.: Thermal performance of a reflector based solar box cooker implemented in Ile-Ife, Nigeria. Int. J. Energy Eng. 5(5), 95–101 (2015)
26. Saravanan, K., Janarathanan, B.: Comparative study of single and double exposure Box-type solar cooker. Int. J. Sci. Eng. Res. 5(5), 620–624 (2014)

Design and Optimization of Continuous Type Rice Husk Gas Stove

Bimrew Tamrat[⊠], Bisrat Yilma, and Million Asfaw

Faculty of Mechanical and Industrial Engineering, Bahir Dar Institute of Technology, Bahir Dar University, Bahir Dar, Ethiopia
betselotbim@gmail.com, bisratyilma20@gmail.com, milliyardo@gmail.com

Abstract. Most of the people especially in rural areas of Ethiopia have been using charcoal, firewood and animal dung for many years. Due to these, women can be affected for different respiratory diseases. The country generates huge tonnes of rice husks at different locations. The main aim of this project was to design, manufacture and optimize the continues type rice husk gasifier which will be an efficient and convenient cooking device that produce gaseous flame using rice husk as a fuel Water Boiling Test (WBT) was performed to evaluate the performance of the gasifier stove. The indoor air quality was also tested using indoor air pollution meter. The power source specially to drive the fan was solar photovoltaic (PV). For different inlet air flow rates, WBT was checked. Air flow rate having 6.51 m^3/s delivers better performance of the gasifier. The newly designed model delivers the maximum particulate concentration of 229 $\mu g/m^3$ and the highest CO concentration of 3.8 ppm, and average PM concentration and CO concentrations are 63 $\mu g/m^3$ and 0.42 ppm, respectively. T he thermal efficiency of the gasifier for different in let air flow rates 8.94 m^3/s, 7.74 m^3/s and 6.51 m^3/s were checked and he result comes 36%, 30% and 45%, respectively. The specific fuel consumption for the above-mentioned inlet air flow rates in g/L were 153, 234 and 169, respectively.

Keywords: Gasifier · Air flow rate · Indoor air quality · PV power · Water boiling test

1 Introduction

Biomass fuels continue to play an essential role in domestic for cooking purpose in most of developing countries like Ethiopia an agriculturally based economy and fuel wood is often a major fraction of the total biomass use [1]. Biomass energy also plays a significant role for reduction of green house at the global level and keeping the eco-system clean when it is used in sustainable and efficient manner [2]. However, the majority of households in Ethiopia are using traditional biomass for cooking by traditional and inefficient stoves. Burning of these biomass fuels using inefficient stoves emits harmful

© ICST Institute for Computer Sciences, Social Informatics and Telecommunications Engineering 2020
Published by Springer Nature Switzerland AG 2020. All Rights Reserved
N. G. Habtu et al. (Eds.): ICAST 2019, LNICST 308, pp. 623–633, 2020.
https://doi.org/10.1007/978-3-030-43690-2_47

chemicals and large amounts of particulates. The most common method of cooking in the developing countries including Ethiopia, particularly in the rural areas is an open fire stove as shown in Fig. 1.

Fig. 1. Traditional three stone baking system [9].

Also there is an excessive dependency on only biomass energy due to lack of electric energy sources; this leads to an excessive deforestation and land degradation. Due to this reason, it is very important to search for effective technology for utilization of the biomass energy. The goals of the present project are: to ensure an efficient and user-friendly gasifier product for the users, to replace some of the total fuel wood consumption and thereby to decrease the deforestation and to create a good indoor air ventilation condition.

The highest total exposure too many air pollutants can occur in the rural homes of developing countries where biomass fuel forms the principal energy source for cooking and space heating [1]. Respiratory diseases are linked with poor air quality and lack of proper ventilation. According to a Federal Ministry of Health (FMoH) report it is found that the top ten causes of morbidity in cases of acute upper Respiratory Infections occurred during the 2003 E.C. (2010/11 G.C), which is linked with air pollution. A similar number of pneumonia cases (5%) were also reported during the same period, accounting for 7% of hospital admissions. Moreover, 2% of admissions were due to tuberculosis [6].

Evaluating the efficiency and emission performance is an upright way to compare one fuel stove with another [8]. Water boiling test is commonly utilized in laboratory emission measurement; the detailed procedure varies with various protocols [10].

Gasification is the process that converts carbon containing feedstock into carbon monoxide, hydrogen and carbon dioxide achieved by oxidation the material is kept at high temperature with controlled amount of oxygen. As it is seen from Fig. 2, rice husk can be an energy source in different forms. It can be used to generate fuel, heat, or electricity through thermal, chemical, or bioprocesses. It contains about 30–50% of organic carbon and has high heating value of 13–16 MJ/kg. It has a moisture content of 8 to 10% by weight.

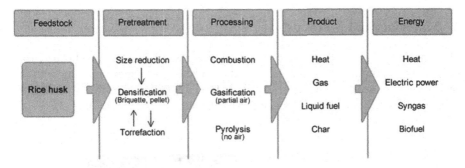

Fig. 2. The energy conversion processes of rice husk [11].

Compared to the traditional cooking stoves, the gasifier stoves are not only fuel efficient but also emission efficient. Owing to their low efficiency, the traditional cook stoves emit more than 10% of their carbon as products of incomplete combustion. In addition, even if, it varies by the type of wood, about 100–180 g of carbon monoxide and 7.8 g of particulate matter are also emitted per kg of used wood. Gases such as methane, total non-methane organic compounds and N_2O are added to this [13].

Nepal Academy of Science and Technology have developed a briquette gasifier stove by adopting the design done by Asian Institute of Technology, Thailand [14]. But this stove is bulky in size and high cost of fabrication for domestic cooking for low income people. The general objective of this paper is to design, develop and optimize to provide low income households an efficient and convenient cooking device that produced gaseous flame using rice husk as fuel.

Rice Husk Gasifier Working Principle
Gasification of rice husks is accomplished in an air sealed chamber which is the reactor. Restricted amount of air is introduced by a fan into the reactor to convert rice husks into high carbon contained char so that by a chemical reaction, it will produce carbon monoxide, hydrogen, and methane gases, which are combustible when ignition is occurred. The fan is driven by the power which is generated from solar photovoltaic power generation system.

Fundamentally, the gas produced during gasification is composed of: carbon monoxide, hydrogen, methane, carbon dioxide, and water vapor. The gasification and the reactions of gases during the process are illustrated below.

$$\text{Combustion} \quad C + O_2 = CO_2 \tag{1}$$

$$\text{Water gas} \quad C + H_2O = CO + H_2 \tag{2}$$

$$\text{Water shift reaction} \quad CO + H_2O = CO_2 + H_2 \tag{3}$$

$$\text{Bounded reaction } C + CO_2 = 2CO \tag{4}$$

$$\text{Methane reaction } C + 2H_2 = CH_4 \tag{5}$$

2   Materials and Methods

The constructed gasifier stove design specification is based on knowledge obtained from field study, literature review and theoretical calculations which are meeting with the needs or requirements of the user nearby Bahir Dar city. The gasifier stove is considered to meet the energy requirement for cooking of average size of 5 family (Fig. 3).

Fig. 3. Gasifier stove while construction.

Laboratory based tests were considered to construct gasifier stove which give an enhanced performance in a controlled environment. The water-boiling test is one of the tests performed under controlled conditions at stove testing room to measure performance metrics of the gasifier such as, time to boil water, thermal efficiency, Specific fuel consumption, and firepower. Water boiling test is a useful tool in the process of cook stove development and to compare different stoves.

A measured amount of same type rice husk of having 700 g was weighed out for each series of tests. The pot and lid weighed, and then a measured amount of water having 1000 g was poured to the pot and weighed again to determine the weight of the water. The weighed rice husk was set into the reactor/combustion chamber and a piece of fired paper is used for ignition. The pot was placed on the gasifier, and the time, the ambient temperature and the initial temperature of the water were recorded using temperature measuring thermocouple. The temperature of the water inside the pan was recorded at an intervals of 20 s until the water reaches the boiling point. The final weight of the remaining water, bio-char, and the final temperature of water were measured and recorded. Repeated tests were conducted in different times with same procedure with different air flow rate to the reactor by controlling the air flow using fan speed controller to know the air-fuel ration that can deliver better and an optimized result. Since air-fuel ratio is one of the major parameters which can affect the gasification process.

Variables that are Directly Measured
f_{hi} Weight of fuel before test (grams)
P_{hi} Weight of pot with water before test
T_{hi} Water temperature before test (°C)
t_{hi} Time at start of test (min)
C_h Weight of charcoal and container after test (grams)
p_{hf} Weight of pot with water after test (grams)
T_{hf} Water temperature after test (°C)
t_{hf} Time at end of test (min)

Variables that are Calculated [16]
Temperature adjusted time to boil the water

$$\Delta t_h^T = \left(t_{hf} - t_{hi}\right) \times \frac{75}{\left(T_{hf} - T_{hi}\right)} \tag{6}$$

Thermal efficiency of the system

$$h_h = \frac{4.186 \times (p_{hi} - p) \times \left(T_{hf} - T_{hi}\right) + 2260(w_{hv})}{f_{hd} \times LHV} \tag{7}$$

Burning rate (grams/min)

$$r_{hb} = \frac{f_{hd}}{t_{hi} - t_{hf}} \tag{8}$$

Specific fuel consumption (grams/grams water)

$$sc_h = \frac{f_{hd}}{p_{hf} - p} \tag{9}$$

Temperature corrected specific consumption

$$sc_h^T = \frac{f_{hd}}{p_{hf} - p} \times \frac{75}{\left(T_{hf} - T_{hi}\right)} \tag{10}$$

Firepower (W) can be calculated as:

$$FP_h = \frac{f_{hd} \times LHV}{60 \times \left(t_{hi} - t_{hf}\right)} \tag{11}$$

Where, LHV is net lower calorific value in MJ/kg, P is dry weight of empty pot (grams), w_{hv} Water vaporized (grams) during boiling test, f_{hd} is equivalent rice husk consumed in grams.

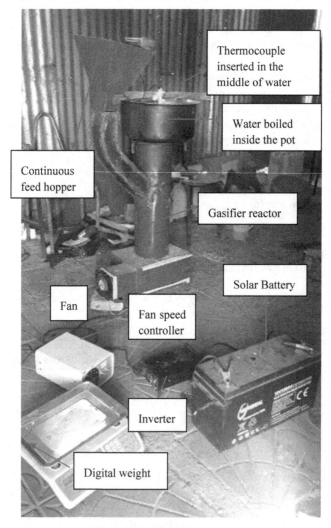

Fig. 4. Water boiling test set-up

The fan is powered by 100 W photovoltaic solar panel which absorbs sunlight as a source of energy since the majorities of rural communities in Ethiopia have low access to electrical energy (Fig. 4).

Beside the water boiling test, emission tests were also performed to measure the indoor air quality using a portable indoor air pollution meter (Figs. 5 and 6).

Fig. 5. A photovoltaic (PV) module.

Fig. 6. Indoor air pollution meter (b)

3 Result and Discussion

Figure (7) shows water boiling test results for different inlet air flow rate. It is observed from the figure, for different air flow rates, the rate of temperature rising varies. Up to 66 °C of water temperature rising, air flow rate having a value 7.74 m³/s gives better output than the other two inlet air flow rates. This might be due to high production of methane gas for this specific air flow rate. From 67 °C up to the boiling point of water (94.2 °C), 8.94 m³/s, 7.74 m³/s and 6.51 m³/s inlet air flow rates delivers better temperature rising of water with time on the order set in the above. After reaching boiling temperature of water, all the air flow rates gave constant temperature which is at phase change stage.

The moisture content and the freshness of rice husk have impact on the gasification process. The test show the gasification process for rice husk having a year old and moisture content of 10% of the total weight of the rice husk, it was not possible to get the gasification process simpler. When use fresh and a moisture content of about 6% from the total weight of the rice husk get much better gasification process.

Three different tests having the same amount of input energy that is 0.7 kg of rice husk, the same volume of water which is 1 L and the same initial ambient and water temperature 28.5 °C, and 26 °C were performed. The air flow rate which is important for partial burning (pyrolysis) was used. From Table 1 the efficiency of the stove is found 45% for the system operated with 6.51 m³/s of air flow rate. For this case the total temperature-corrected time taken to get the water boiled is 19 min and the burning rate is 8 g/min, specific fuel consumption 169 g/L. The fire power from this test is found 1788 W. The thermal efficiency of the constructed rice husk gasifier stove for 8.94 m³/s air flow rate is 36% is less than the efficiency of the system having 6.51 m³/s inlet air flow rate but greater than with the system having air flow rate of 7.74 m³/s (30%

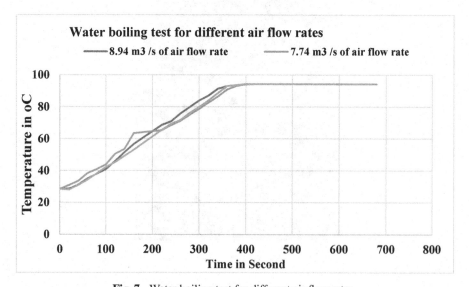

Fig. 7. Water boiling test for different air flow rates.

Table 1. Water boiling test results

High power test	Units	Test 1	Test 2	Test 3
Time to get the water boiled	Minutes	16	15	17
Temp-corrected time to boil	Minutes	18	16	19
Burning rate of the rice husk	g/Minutes	8	12	8
Thermal efficiency of the system	%	36%	30%	45%
Specific fuel consumption of the stove	g/liter	153	234	169
Temp-corrected specific consumption	g/liter	168	256	185
Temp-corrected specific energy cons.	kJ/liter	2,381	3,640	2,632
Firepower	Watts	1,900	2,895	1,788

Table 2. Water boiling test results

Average PM concentration	63	$\mu g/m^3$
Average CO concentration	0.42	ppm
Highest PM concentration	229	$\mu g/m^3$
Highest CO concentration	3.8	ppm

efficiency). The reason is sufficient oxygen is supplied to burn the fuel completely, rather than becoming partial burning of the fuel (pyrolysis), it becomes complete combustion and methane gas might not be generated. The constructed gasifier which is not gives flame for 4.78 m^3/s inlet air flow rate. The supplied air is not sufficient to achieve even partial burning of the fuel and found very dense smoke. From this investigation it is found that the optimum air flow rate to get better output to be given by the constructed rice husk gasifier stove.

Figure 8 show the emission that is the particulate matter (PM) and carbon monoxide (CO) concentration test results of water boiling test by using the designed rise husk gasifies stove for the three air flow amounts 8.94 m^3/s, 7.74 m^3/s and 6.51 m^3/s), mass of fuel of 0.7 kg. From Fig. 8 and Table 2, the maximum particulate matter concentration is 229 $\mu g/m^3$ and the highest CO concentration is 3.8 ppm. The average PM concentration and CO concentrations are 63 $\mu g/m^3$ and 0.42 ppm, respectively. From the existing literature, the indoor air quality which is the PM and CO of the three stone stove cooking system is 3300 $\mu g/m^3$ and 23.5 ppm [16, 17] and the improved modern stove emission test results show that the PM and CO concentration are 1520 $\mu g/m^3$ and 20.5 ppm, respectively. From the experimental emission test results, it is possible to give witness that using rice husk gasifier for cooking purpose gives better indoor air qualities than three stone stove and modern cooking stoves.

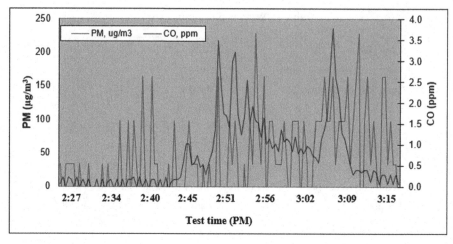

Fig. 8. Carbon monoxide and particulate matter concentration in the testing room.

4 Conclusion

Rice husks brought directly from rice mill or storage area has moisture content. When experiment on gasification is performed, the moisture content is better to reduce at least at the level of 6%. It is possible to reduce the moisture content by open sun drying mechanism or use oven. The freshness of the rice husk has also its own impact on the gasification process as well.

Parameters used to test the designed gasifier were 0.7 kg of rice husk, a litter of water, PV power source to drive the fan, water boiling pan. With the same parameters, input air flow rate of 6.513/s delvers better thermal efficiency (46%) than the other two input air flow rates (8.94 m^3/s and 7.74 m^3/s). The indoor air quality of the gasification is also tested and found much better than the three stone stove (particulate matter of 3300 $\mu g/m^3$ and CO concentration 23.5 ppm) and modern stove cooking mechanisms (particulate matter of 1520 $\mu g/m^3$ and CO concentration of 20.5 ppm). The maximum and the average PM obtained were 229 $\mu g/m^3$ and 63 $\mu g/m^3$ respectively. The maximum and average CO concentration of the test were 3.8 ppm and 0.42 ppm, respectively.

References

1. WHO Household air pollution and health.htm
2. Impact Assessment of Mirt Improved Biomass Injera Stoves Commercialization in Tigray, Amhara and Oromiya National Regional States. Prepared by: MEGEN POWER Ltd. Submitted to: The MoARD/GTZ SUN Energy Programme
3. Guta, D.D.: Assessment of biomass fuel resource potential and utilization in Ethiopia: sourcing strategies for renewable energies. Int. J. Renew. Energy Res. **2**(1), 134–136 (2012)
4. Hammed Suleiman, B.D., Asfaw, A.: Household fuel use and acute respiratory infections among younger children: an exposure assessment in Shebedino Wereda Southern Ethiopia. Afr. J. Health Sci. **18**(2), 32–33 (2011)

5. Njong, M., Johannes, T.A.: An analysis of domestic cooking energy choices in Cameroon. Eur. J. Soc. Sci. **20**(2), 25–36 (2011)
6. Energy Sector Management Assistance Program (ESMAP), Strategy to Alleviate the Pressure of Fuel Demand on National Wood fuel Resources, Haiti (2007)
7. KEY FINDINGS ON THE 2013 NATIONAL LABOUR FORCE SURVEY (CSA, 2013). file:///E:/KEY%20FINDINGS%20ON%20THE%202013%20NATIONAL%20LABOUR%20FORCE%20SURVEY.pdf
8. International year of rice (2004). http://www.fao.org/rice2004/en/rice-us.htm
9. Jetter, J., et al.: Pollutant emissions and energy efficiency under controlled conditions for household biomass cook stoves and implications for metrics useful in setting international test standards. Environ. Sci. Technol. **46**, 10827–10834 (2012)
10. https://energypedia.info/wiki/Firewood_Cookstoves
11. Arora, P., Das, P., Jain, S., Kishore, V.V.: A laboratory based comparative study of Indian biomass cookstove testing protocol and Water Boiling Test. Energy Sustain. Dev. **21**, 81–88 (2014)
12. http://www.knowledgebank.irri.org/step-by-step-production/postharvest/rice-by-products/rice-husk/using-rice-husk-for-energy-production. Accessed Feb 2019
13. Anderson, P.S.: TLUD Handbook. Mc-Graw Hill, New York (2010)
14. Grover, P.D.: Cost Estimates for a 'Dream Stove' for Asia (2003). http://www.ikweb.com/enuff/public_html/Dream/Paper-grover.htm
15. Singh, R.M., Shakya, G.R.: Study of the biomass briquetting system and cooking devices, a regional research and dissemination program phase II. Asian Institute of Technology (AIT), Bangkok, Thailand (2001)
16. Le, D.D., Do, D.T., Zwebe, D., Nguyen, M.H.: Rice husk gasifier stove performance testing report, August 2013
17. Singh, A., Tuladhar, B., Bajracharya, K., Pillarisetti, A.: Assessment of effectiveness of improved cook stoves in reducing indoor air pollution and improving health in Nepal. Energy. Sustain. Dev. **16**, 406–414 (2012). https://doi.org/10.1016/j.esd.2012.09.004
18. Hankey, S., et al.: Using objective measures of stove use and indoor air quality to evaluate a cookstove intervention in rural Uganda. Energy Sustain. Dev. **25**, 67–74 (2015). (particulate matter)

Material Science and Engineering (MSE)

Assessment of Quality of Sand Sources and the Effect on the Properties of Concrete (The Case of Bahir Dar and Its Vicinities)

Abel Fantahun[1]($\boxtimes$) and Kassahun Admassu[2]

[1] Faculty of Civil and Water Resource Engineering, Bahir Dar Institute of Technology, Bahir Dar University, P.O. Box 26, Bahir Dar, Ethiopia
abelfantahun10@gmail.com
[2] Ethiopia Institute of Architecture, Building Construction and City Development, Addis Ababa University, P.O. Box 518, Addis Ababa, Ethiopia
kassahun.admassu@eiabc.edu.et

Abstract. The main purpose of this study is to assess the quality of sand sources, the effect on workability, compressive strength and cost of concrete in and around Bahir Dar. Initially, questionnaires and interviews were made with stakeholders and suppliers. After that, different natural sand samples were collected from 13 sand supply locations. Then, their physical and chemical properties were tested in laboratory. Finally, mix design is prepared for a normal strength concrete. From the survey results, it was found that, about 87.5% of the stakeholders use Arno, Tana, Tis-Abay, Addis-Zemen, Andasa and Rib as the major sand sources out of the thirteen around Bahir Dar and its vicinities. And about 67.5% of the stakeholders use more than one source. Trial mix designs were prepared for concrete production focusing on six of the common sources. The results have shown that, for normal strength concrete, the blended sand from six common sand sources met workability of the fresh concrete and there is no significant difference in compressive strength of concrete with blended sand. Finally, the finding has indicated that, all the thirteen supply locations have quality problems; especially in gradation as well as, in silt and clay contents. Based on the research outcome blending Addis-Zemen sand with that of Ribb sand incurs the least cost, while at the same time fulfilling requirements of fresh and hardened concrete.

Keywords: Concrete · Sand · Sand quality · Chemical composition · Workability · Compressive strength · Cost

1 Introduction

1.1 Background and Objectives

Concrete is one of the major construction materials in the building construction industry and it is produced from three basic ingredients; namely: cement, aggregates and water. In addition, admixture is sometimes used to improve some of the properties of concrete; like,

© ICST Institute for Computer Sciences, Social Informatics and Telecommunications Engineering 2020
Published by Springer Nature Switzerland AG 2020. All Rights Reserved
N. G. Habtu et al. (Eds.): ICAST 2019, LNICST 308, pp. 637–650, 2020.
https://doi.org/10.1007/978-3-030-43690-2_48

workability and setting time [1–3]. The ingredients of concrete should be of good quality that satisfies the requirements of set standards. It means that, the process involved in the production of concrete requires due care and attention. The care starts from the selection and estimation of the amounts of constituents of the concrete. The materials used for concrete production should satisfy certain requirements in order to get the concrete of the desired workability, strength and durability within a reasonable economy [3]. Quality of constituent materials used in the preparation of concrete plays a paramount role in the development of both physical and mechanical properties of the resultant concrete. Water, cement, fine aggregate, coarse aggregate and any admixtures used should be free from harmful impurities that negatively impact the properties of hardened concrete [1, 3, 5]. Quality control is a means of checking those concrete ingredients and production processes are in compliance with the requirements stated in codes of practices. It must be done by the contractor who fully takes the responsibility to ensure that the quality of materials and workmanship are as per the contract document. The quality control work undertaken by the contractor should be assured by the quality assuring agent, which is the consulting engineer. Use of poor-quality construction materials (such as sand, coarse aggregates or water) results in poor quality structures and may cause structural failures leading to injuries, deaths and loss of investment for developers [3, 5].

Fine and coarse aggregates make about 70% by volume of concrete production. It goes without saying that, the quality of concrete is thus strongly influenced by aggregate's physical and mechanical properties as well as chemical composition of the parent aggregate making material [4]. In keeping the quality of concrete in line with acceptable standards, one should concentrate in the properties of the concrete making materials. As a result, since sand is among these, it is obvious that it plays a critical role as a concrete ingredient and thus it deserves a special attention. The demand of natural sand is quite high in developing countries to satisfy the rapid infrastructure growth and the extensive use of concrete; which is causing a very high global consumption of natural sand. The situation of developing countries, like, Ethiopia is challenged by a shortage of good quality natural sand. Now a days, in Bahir Dar and its surroundings many construction projects are being carried out to a very large extent. As a result, the City of Bahir Dar is growing very rapidly. The blooming of construction projects in Bahir Dar City and its surroundings indicates the necessity of conducting performance tests on concrete and its constituent ingredients in order to assure money worth and safe construction works. The multi-faceted projects being constructed in and around the City are; various types of buildings, water supply, irrigation, roads and bridges. Considering all the above, the ever-increasing development of construction projects is becoming a cause for cost increase of construction materials as well as the frequent occurrence of disparity between supply and demand.

Riverbeds and lakeshores are the main sources of fine aggregate (sand) in and around Bahir Dar. So far, there is no clear information about the qualities of natural sand among stakeholders. It is also impossible to get identical construction materials even from a single day supply from venders, with regard to; sand gradation, clay and silt content and organic impurities, which are the prime determinants of workability and compressive strength of acceptable grade and good quality concrete.

Furthermore, there is an adversarial standardization among suppliers of sand, contractors, clients and professionals a like, in the construction industry due to the ambiguous quality of sand sources. If the properties of sand sources are known, engineers and professionals can select the nearby sources with possible remedial measures; such as, blending, washing, and screening for the intended purpose.

Thus, this research will focus on assessing the quality of sand sources and the effect on the properties of concrete, within Bahir Dar and its vicinities by conducting a questionnaire survey, interviews and laboratory investigations.

The general objective of the study is to assess the quality of sand sources in Bahir Dar and its vicinities and investigate the effect on the properties of concrete to be followed by discussions and recommendations in accordance with the outcomes of the findings.

2 Methodology

2.1 Survey on Selected Active (Under Construction) Projects and Interviews

Initially, questionnaires were developed for contractors, consultants and sand suppliers. The aim of taking a survey questionnaire and interview was in order to know the common sand sources and the awareness of stakeholders regarding quality of sand sources. Questionnaires were distributed to contractors who are working on active projects and dealing with G + 5 and above buildings. The research also employs laboratory investigation methods and procedures. Different natural sand samples were collected from 13 sand supply locations. Sand was collected from thirteen main sand supply locations in Bahir Dar City and its environs. Mostly, the sand sources are found in between Gondar and Bahir Dar located about 30–180 km North West of the Bahir Dar City and also along the route of Tissisat within a distance of 30–90 km south of the City. By name they are: Arno, Tana (Delgi), Arbaye, Keha (Ibnat), Addis Zemen, Ribb, Gumera, Hamusit, Lalibela, Andasa (Tule), Tis-Abay, Mendel (Gug) and Zema. From each source, representative sand samples were taken from riverbeds and banks. Sampling is done according to ASTM D75-87 [6]. From each supply point, a minimum of 100 kg of sand is bought for grading and producing concrete cubes. Eventually, laboratory tests were conducted on each source sand samples and their physical and chemical properties were checked to understand their compliance with set standards. Finally, after selecting the common sand sources and knowing the level of the fine aggregate quality from the test results mix design was prepared for normal concrete strength. For a C-25 mix, fine aggregate the natural sand sources of Arno, Tana, Tis-Abay, Addis Zemen, Andasa and Ribb were taken; after washing and blending to fulfill the requirements of ASTM. A mix for normal strength (C-25) concrete, which has a slump of 25–50 mm and a nominal maximum aggregate size of 19 mm, was prepared per ACI 211.1 mix design procedure.

2.2 Laboratory Procedure

After selecting the common sand sources and knowing the level of the fine aggregate quality from the test results mix design was prepared for normal concrete strength.

This is done, by using the same type of cement or Ordinary Portland Cement (OPC) grade 42.5, coarse aggregate and clean potable water. The schematic flow chart of Fig. 1 shows the methodology used in this research work.

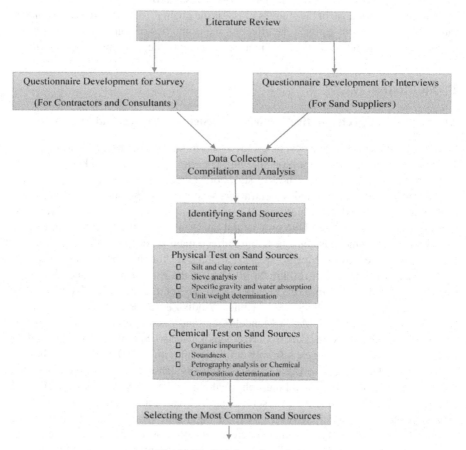

Fig. 1. Methodology flow chart

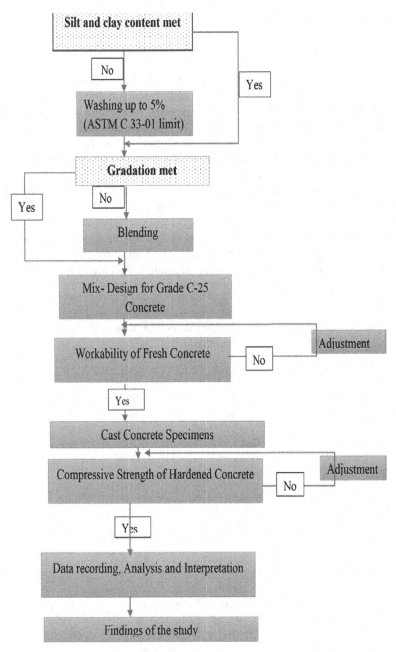

Fig. 1. (*continued*)

3 Results and Discussion

3.1 Acquisition of Data

Interviews were made with five sand suppliers working with different supply points mainly focusing on the major sources of fine aggregate for Bahir Dar City and its surroundings. According to suppliers, more than 13 sand sources are found in and around Bahir Dar. However, the sand that is supplied to customers do vary with seasonal variations, production methods, processes, and transportation cost. On the other hand, out of the 13 sand sources the most commonly purchased for concrete production are Arno, Addis Zemen, Ribb and Tana. Cost wise, those sands coming a far are expensive and are of good quality. The reason for this is transportation cost, in addition to their better quality and availability of sand. Of all the 13 sand sources those from Arbaye, Lalibela and Arno are costly.

The research appraised the major sources of fine aggregates for the construction industry of Bahir Dar and its environs. A total of 45 questionnaires were distributed to stakeholders out of whom 40 volunteers responded. This yields a response rate of

Table 1. Distribution of questionnaires and response rate

Respondent category	Questionnaires distributed (No.)	Questionnaires responded (No.)	Rate (%)	Valid responses (No.)	Valid responses (%)
Contractors	34	30	88.23	30	88.23
Site supervisors	11	10	90.91	10	90.91
Total	**45**	**40**	**88.88**	**40**	**88.88**

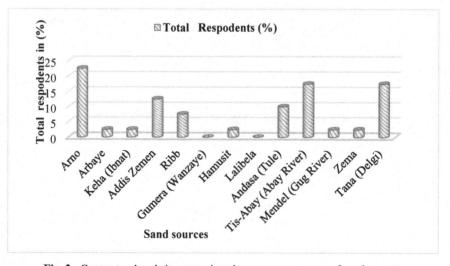

Fig. 2. Contractors' and site supervisors' responses on usage of sand sources

88.88%. Table 1 shows the number of questionnaires distributed to and collected from each respondent category.

Commonly used sand sources out of 13 are six and the cumulative of the six sand sources have 87.5% out of the total respondents as it is the shown in Fig. 2 above. Therefore, this shows that those six sand sources are significantly used by construction industry of Bahir Dar City and its environs. Sand used for concrete production is only from either one source or more than one for a single project. The assessment result shows, the 70% of the responded contractors use more than one sand source. In addition, among the responded site supervisors 60% of their supervising sites use more than one sand source. Totally 67.5% of the respondents replied that they use more than one sand source for concrete production. The result also shows, 90% of the responded contractors use natural sand for concrete production. The quality of the locally available fine aggregates is found to be unsatisfactory. Totally, 82.5% of the respondents replied that the quality of sand is not satisfactory. The result have shown that sieve analysis, silt and clay contents are the frequently conducted test for fine aggregate.

3.2 Laboratory Tests on Quality of Sand

The fine aggregate or sand samples were collected from 15th of October 2015 to 20th of December 2015. The test method used is ASTM C 136-01 [6, 7]. The fine aggregate gradation was within the limits of ASTM C33-01 or AASHTO M 6 and ES.C. D3.201 [4] is generally satisfactory for most concrete. A sieve analysis was conducted on samples collected from the 13 sand sources, the results of which were compared with those of applicable standards. From the results of the grain size analysis, it is observed that, all the common sand sources are more on the coarser side; except Ribb sand source. The gradation proportion for each blending batch was done with a minimum of ten trials (Table 2).

The results attained from this research have shown that 100% of the samples could not satisfy the set limits. As could be observed, 84.62% are more on the coarser side while 15.38% fall on to the finer sand. This has an implication that the fine aggregates supplied to the construction industry of Bahir Dar have problems as far as gradation requirements are concerned. The analysis of the sand sources have shown that, 53.85% of the samples have unacceptable fineness modulus value falling above the acceptable range and 46.5% complying with the Ethiopian Standard. Moreover, 76.93% of the sand sources have unacceptable fineness modulus value for mix design and 15.38% do comply with the requirements of ASTM C33-01. Regarding organic impurity, out of the 13 sand source samples tested, seven samples indicated lighter-straw and four colorless and two remained dark-straw than the standard solution in 24 h after mixing. This indicates that, 85% of the collected samples were within the organic content limit as set in AASHTO T 21-00, indicating a failure rate of 15%. Based on the 13 sand source samples tested, the maximum silt and clay content is 24.69% for TN (Tana) sample compared with the

Table 2. Summarized test results for the computation of sieve analysis of sand sources in percentage passing

Sieve size (mm)	AN (%)	TN (%)	TA (%)	AZ (%)	AD (%)	RB (%)	KH (%)	MD (%)	HM (%)	GM (%)	ZM (%)	AY (%)	LB (%)	AASHTO M6 (ES.C. D3.201) Limits (%)	
														Min	Max
9.5	92.8	98.3	91.3	88.3	90.2	98.7	94.8	97.8	94.3	99	93.7	94.6	99.5	100	100
4.75	73.0	92.6	77.1	75.4	80.8	96.4	87.4	92.7	84.3	97.3	86.1	90.5	97.4	95	100
2.36	48.2	76.7	61.7	65.3	64.7	94.1	73.2	82.1	67.0	95.1	78	83.2	91.1	80	100
1.18	31.1	58.9	49.0	56.2	48.1	91.9	54.6	65.8	48.8	92.7	68.7	70.5	78.8	50	85
0.6	13.9	21.7	21.3	33.2	23.2	85.3	22.8	24.9	17.2	67.7	41.0	33.4	40.9	25	60
0.3	4.3	1.1	1.7	7.5	6.4	16.8	5.5	2.8	2.5	7.4	6.6	9.4	7.2	10	30
0.15	1.0	0.2	0.1	1.1	1.4	1.7	0.9	0.3	0.4	0.9	0.7	2.3	0.8	2	10

minimum 4.83% for AY (Arbiya) sand sample by volume. In addition, 19.90% for HS (Hamusit) sample compared with the least of 1.70% of LB (Lalibela) sand sample by weight is quite large by any standard. ES.C. D3.201 recommends that, no more than a maximum of 6% by volume silt and clay content for fine aggregates be used in concrete production. Only one sand source out of the 13 met this limit, representing only 7.69%. An overwhelming percentage of 92.31 failed to meet the limit set in the Ethiopian Standard. Comparatively, this same Standard sets the allowable limit for silt and clay content in sand used for concrete production as 5% by weight. Only samples from three sources met this limit with a total of 33%, implying a failure rate of 77% of the tested sand samples per the quoted Ethiopian Standard. Surprisingly, only one source (AY), satisfied both by volume and by weight requirements for silt and clay content. The analysis of the samples shows 92.3% of the fine aggregates have loose unit weight whereas 76.9% have compacted unit weight values, which are not within the range stated in standard. Six major sand source samples were subjected to specific gravity test as detailed in ASTM C 128-01 for aggregates less than 10 mm diameter using the pycnometer glass vessel. Results have shown that, the bulk specific gravity in SSD lies between 2.44 and 2.66 while the water absorption is in the range of 1.66 to 2.92. As per the Ethiopian Standard requirement, the bulk specific gravity values lies between 2.4 and 3.0 for sand used in concrete production. This indicates that, the sand sources investigated are within the acceptable range for the production of structural concrete. Samples taken from the three sources and tested for soundness failed to satisfy the requirement. The values of the samples were too far above the maximum limit stated in standards. However, the good part of it is that, there is no ambient temperature variation and thermal energy difference in Bahir Dar City. The monthly maximum temperature difference is 16.2 °C and the annual variation of temperature ranges from 10.2 °C to 26.4 °C. That being the case, these aggregates might be used for concrete production.

The three sand sources (i.e. Arno, Tis-Abay and Tana) in and around Bahir Dar have a similar percentage of oxide composition. This implies that, the majorly sand sources have similar parent rock formation in their origin. On the other hand, they contain less SiO_2 concentration and have higher amount of Al_2O_3 and Fe_2O_3 as compared to sand from Dire Dawa sand, North Showa, Shoa Mugher sand, Tigray Adigrat sand and Tigray Sinkatta sand (Table 3).

Table 3. Comparison of three sand sources with different parent rock types in Ethiopia

Mineral oxide	SiO_2	Al_2O_3	Fe_2O_3	CaO	MgO	Na_2O	K_2O	MnO	P_2O5	TiO_2	H_2O	LOI
Sample TA	46.72	17.09	11.26	6.00	3.24	3.16	1.48	0.1	1.45	7.31	1.14	2.50
Sample TN	48.30	20.16	8.10	9.54	2.98	2.12	0.42	0.18	0.23	2.69	1.56	4.71
Sample AN	46.50	16.78	12.20	7.96	4.5	2.34	0.72	0.16	0.57	4.24	1.50	3.71
Dire Dawa sand	75.89	13.14	0.83	2.00	0.03	3.70	4.02	0.02	0.01	0.05	Nil	0.99
Sand from north showa jema river valley	99.09	0.34	0.01	0.04	0.01	0.01	0.01	0.02	0.01	0.05	Nil	0.48
Basalt (Tumura)	47.92	15.87	12.32	8.89	5.46	1.68	0.12	0.21	4.02	0.59	0.27	0.21
Shoa Mugher sand	96.1	1.91	0.32	0.1	0.1	0.1	0.1	Nil	Nil	Nil	Nil	0.49
Tigray Adigrat sand	99.5	0.27	0.04	<0.1	<0.1	<0.1	<0.1	<0.01	Nil	<0.02	–	0.24
Tigray Sinkatta	98.4–99.6	0.1–0.6	0.1–0.33	Nil	Nil	Nil	Nil	Nil	Nil	Nil	Nil	Nil
Akaki olivine Basalt	47.0	15.70	14.8	8.0	5.6	3.4	0.9	0.2	0.7	1.1	3.3	Nil
*CEN Standard sand	99.5	0.15–0.30	0.015–0.03	0.03	0.005	BDL	BDL	BDL	BDL	0.016–0.04	–	BDL

It can be concluded that three sand sources are of similar oxide composition indicating a basaltic rock origin. However, the sand sources have lower silicon dioxide relative to CEN (Committee for European Norms) as standard sand.

3.3 Mix Design

From the trial mix results shown in Fig. 3 for a water cement ratio of 0.491 a maximum slump of 30 mm is observed, which is considered as of a low workability.

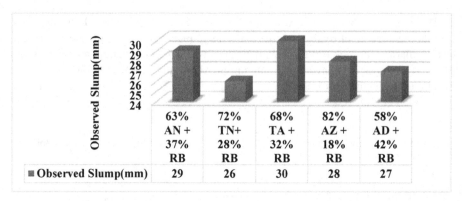

Fig. 3. Comparison of observed slump of the six blended sand sources

It is shown in Fig. 3 that, the observed slump of each blended sand from the different sources indicates no significant difference. This is due to similarity in their particle shape and surface texture. Even then, the observed slump of concrete mix with each blended sand proportions all fulfill the workability requirement of the mix, which is between 25- and 50-mm. Compressive strength of concrete specimens was determined by testing concrete cubes of 150 mm size. All specimens were weighed and measured to determine the density and the surface area of the cubes. The hardened properties of the concrete had been determined at the ages of 3, 7, 14 and 28 days. At each age, a minimum of three specimens were tested to ensure that the requirements of set standards are met.

It shown in Fig. 3 that, the different concrete mixes with five types of blended fine aggregates or sand proportions (i.e., 63%AN + 37%RB, 72%TN + 28%RB, 68%TA + 32%RB, 82%AZ + 18%RB and 58%AD + 42%RB) which impart a positive effect on the compressive strength of the produced concrete. The results are shown in Fig. 4 that, all the concrete mixes with different blending proportions have achieved the target mean strength, whereas, concrete mix proportions of 58%AD + 42% RB did not achieve the

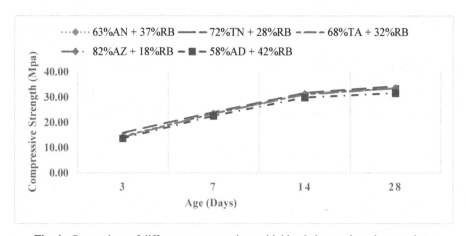

Fig. 4. Comparison of different concrete mixes with blended natural sand proportions

target: but has fulfilled the average compressive strength requirements. From this, we can conclude that using blended sand of the six available sources with specified proportions can improve the compressive strength of the produced concrete.

3.4 Cost Comparison of Concrete

The cost of concrete is assessed based on the material prices collected from most common coarse aggregate sources and cement suppliers within the City of Bahir Dar. Whereas, the price of sand is collected from six most common suppliers. These costs include both production and transportation as shown in Table 4.

Table 4. Cost of materials from different sources and suppliers

Ingredients	Cement (OPC 42.5 N) (Birr/Quintal)			Water (Birr/m^3)
Source	Messebo	Derba	Dangote	Tap water
Price	380	420	330	2.5
Average	377			2.5
Ingredients	Coarse aggregate (Birr/m^3)			
Source	Zenzelima	Bikolo	Kinbaba	
Price	575	555	525	
Average	552			
Ingredients	Natural sand (Birr/m^3)			
Source	Arno	Tana	Tis-Abay	Addis-Zemen	Andasa	Ribb
Price	556	450	510	480	470	490

Using the data of Table 4, a material cost for producing one cubic meter of concrete was calculated and the results are shown in Table 5 below.

Table 5 shows that, the cost of concrete differs from source to source with sand proportions. Moreover, from all the costs of concrete 82% Addis-Zemen with 18% Ribb natural sand proportion gives the lowest cost.

Table 5. Material and concrete cost per cubic meter of concrete for different proportions of blended natural sand

	Ingredients	Quantity (Kg/m^3)	Unit Price/kg	Price/m^3
63%AN + 37%RB	Cement	386.96	3.767	1457.5
	Natural sand Arno	486.93	0.311	151.3
	Natural sand Ribb	289.97	0.335	97.1
	Coarse Aggregate	1054.02	0.326	343.7
	Water	187.80	0.0025	0.5
	Total Price/m^3 of Concrete			2050.1
	Ingredients	Quantity (Kg/m^3)	Unit Price/kg	Price/m^3
72% TN + 28% RB	Cement	386.96	3.767	1457.5
	Natural sand Tana	534.08	0.294	157.3
	Natural sand Ribb	207.70	0.335	69.5
	Coarse Aggregate	1071.04	0.326	349.2
	Water	184.43	0.0025	0.5
	Total Price/m^3 of Concrete			2034.0
	Ingredients	Quantity (Kg/m^3)	Unit Price/kg	Price/m^3
68% TA + 32% RB	Cement	386.96	3.767	1457.5
	Natural sand Tis-Abay	523.04	0.284	148.5
	Natural Sand Ribb	246.13	0.335	82.4
	Coarse Aggregate	1064.19	0.326	347.0
	Water	187.46	0.0025	0.5
	Total Price/m^3 of Concrete			2035.9
	Ingredients	Quantity (Kg/m^3)	Unit Price/kg	Price/m^3
82% AZ + 18% RB	Cement	386.96	3.767	1457.5
	Natural sand Addis-Zemen	642.9	0.263	169.2
	Natural Sand Ribb	141.1	0.335	47.2
	Coarse Aggregate	1067.7	0.326	348.1
	Water	187.5	0.0025	0.5
	Total Price/m^3 of Concrete			2022.6
	Ingredients	Quantity (Kg/m^3)	Unit Price/kg	Price/m^3
58% AD + 42% RB	Cement	386.96	3.767	1457.5
	Natural sand Andasa	446.5	0.278	124.0
	Natural sand Ribb	323.3	0.335	108.2
	Coarse Aggregate	1059.1	0.326	345.3
	Water	187.0	0.0025	0.5
	Total Price/m^3 of Concrete			2035.6

4   Conclusion and Recommendation

From the survey results it was found that, the major source of natural fine aggregate are Arno, Tana, Tis Abay, Addis Zemen, Andasa and Ribb. Although there are several sand sources in the vicinity of Bahir Dar the contractors and consultants have no satisfaction on the availed quality of sand. As result of this, they use more than one source for concrete production. Though, stakeholders give little attention for sand quality tests, even then silt and clay contents and gradation tests relatively get a better attention. The sand test results have shown that, 100% of the sand sources could not satisfy the gradation requirements. 84.62% are more on coarser side and the rest on the finer side. However, the trail done on blending of the different sand sources have shown that gradation requirement can be achieved by blending the coarser sand with the finer one. The sand test result have shown that, sand directly taken from sources contain high silt and clay content and are not good in unit weight. In addition to this, the three top most common sand sources failed to satisfy the soundness requirements. However, 85% of the collected samples met the requirements of organic impurities, the six common sand sources samples met the specific gravity in SSD, and water absorption limits set in both AASHTO T 84 and Ethiopian standard. The three top most sand source have similar oxide compositions indicating a basaltic rock origin. However, they have lower silicon dioxide relative to standard sand. From this, it can be concluded that blending each source can have an advantages of; increasing the concentration of silica content which makes the sand to have more of sand stone properties rather than the basaltic one, reducing the amount of degraded sand and neglect of sand sources. This results in minimizing the environmental impact. As the cost analysis shows, using a blended sand in different proportions induces a variation in cost of concrete production. From all the produced concrete mixes, Addis Zemen with Ribb sand delivered the lowest cost of fresh concrete.

Based on the above conclusion the following recommendations are stipulated. Since stakeholders give little attention to sand quality, an awareness creation is of a prime importance. Sand users from the 13 sand sources are strongly advised to wash the sand before the production of concrete. Further investigation like, general evaluation on petrography of sand to assure quality against reactivity of aggregates is recommended. In order to get a concrete, which satisfies the fresh and hardened concrete requirements with least cost, it is better to use the blended sand from Addis Zemen and Ribb sources. Quarry sites should be checked periodically, by an independent body to enforce established quality assuring practices guided by set mandatory standards.

References

1. Kosmatka, S.H., Kerkhoff, B., Panarese, W.C.: Design and Control of Concrete Mixtures, 14th edn. Portland Cement Association, Skokie (2003)
2. Neville, A.M.: Properties of Concrete, 3rd edn. Longman Scientific & Technical, Harlow (1986)
3. Ngugi, H.N., Mutuku, R.N., Gariy, Z.A.: Effects of sand quality on compressive strength of concrete: a case of Nairobi county and its environs. Kenya. Open J. Civ. Eng. **4**, 255–273 (2014)
4. Dinku, A.: Construction Materials Laboratory Manual, vol. 1. Addis Ababa University Press, Addis Ababa (2002)

5. Dammo, M.N., Deborah, J.M., Aghidi, J., Isa, A., Falmata, A.K., Adams, K.: Effect of Ngala clay on the compressive strength of concrete. Int. J. Eng. Sci. Invention **3**(7), 07–10 (2014). ISSN (Online): 2319–6734, ISSN (Print): 2319–6726. www.ijesi.org
6. ACI 211.1-91, R.B.A.C. 211: Standard Practice for Selecting Proportions for Normal, Heavyweight, and Mass Concrete (1997)
7. ACI Education Bulletin E1-07: Aggregates for Concrete, Developed by ACI Committee E-701, Materials for Concrete Construction, August 2007

Fabrication and Characterization of Metakaolin Based Flat Sheet Membrane for Membrane Distillation

Tsegahun Mekonnen Zewdie[1,3]([✉]), Nigus Gabbiye Habtu[1], Abhishek Dutta[2], and Bart Van der Bruggen[3]

[1] Department of Chemical Engineering, Faculty of Chemical and Food Engineering, Bahir Dar University, Bahir Dar, Ethiopia
tsegmek@yahoo.com
[2] Faculty of Engineering Technology, KU Leuven, Campus Groep T Leuven, Technologiecluster Materialentechnologie, Andreas Vesaliusstraat 13, Leuven, Belgium
[3] Department of Chemical Engineering, Faculty of Engineering, KU Leuven, Celestijnenlaan 200F, 3001 Leuven, Belgium

Abstract. A low-cost flat sheet kaolin/metakaolin membrane was fabricated via a combined using phase inversion and sintering methods at different kaolin/metakaolin content and sintering temperature. The ceramic suspension with suitable viscosity was prepared by mixing the kaolin/metakaolin powder, Polyethersulfone(PESf) as a binder, N-methyl-2-pyrrolidone(NMP) as solvent and Polyvinylpyrrolidone(PVP) as a dispersant. The membrane precursor was then sintered in a controlled furnace to target temperature of 1200 °C, 1300 °C, 1400 °C and 1500 °C. Then, the surface of the kaolin/metakaolin membrane was modified by 1H,1H,2H,2H-perfluorooctyltriethoxysilane (PFAS). Finally, the ceramic membrane was characterized using a scanning electron microscope (SEM) and a contact angle analyzer. It was found that by varying the kaolin/metakaolin contents and sintering temperatures; different surface morphologies of flat sheet membranes were obtained. Moreover, the successful grafting with PFAS was evidenced by the increase in contact angle from nearly equal to 3.7° to 142°. Thus, it can be generally concluded that the metakaolin based flat sheet membrane has desirable characteristics for membrane distillation applications in terms of hydrophobic effect and chemical stability ($<1\%$ weight loss).

Keywords: Metakaolin · Ceramic membrane · Phase inversion · Sintering · Membrane distillation · Grafting

1 Introduction

Many countries around the world, especially in most parts of Africa and Asia, suffer from a shortage of clean drinking water. In order to satisfy the need and ensure an adequate supply of clean water, membrane-based technologies for water purification are necessary. The effort made in the literature is dedicated to developing less energy-intensive

© ICST Institute for Computer Sciences, Social Informatics and Telecommunications Engineering 2020
Published by Springer Nature Switzerland AG 2020. All Rights Reserved
N. G. Habtu et al. (Eds.): ICAST 2019, LNICST 308, pp. 651–661, 2020.
https://doi.org/10.1007/978-3-030-43690-2_49

and environmentally friendly water purification techniques. Membrane distillation is a membrane-based water purification technology in which the separation process takes place by a thermally driven distillation process combined with a microporous hydrophobic membrane separation process [1]. The driving force for membrane distillation is the vapor pressure gradient across the hydrophobic micro porous membrane due to the temperature difference between the feed, and permeate side of the hydrophobic micro porous membrane interface [1]. Membrane distillation appears to be a promising solution for the water purification and desalination whenever cheap, and abundant energy like low-grade waste heat or solar energy is available [2–5].

The most commonly used membrane materials for membrane distillation are porous hydrophobic membranes. These membranes can be fabricated from organic and inorganic materials. Organic membranes are made up of polymeric materials such as polypropylene (PP), polytetrafluoroethylene (PTFE), and polyvinylidene fluoride (PVDF). Polymeric membrane material commercially used for membrane distillation experiments in different membrane distillation configuration and membrane modules such as flat sheet, spiral wound, tubular, capillary, and hollow fiber [2, 6]. Inorganic membranes are made up of carbon, silica, zeolite, ceramic, various oxides (Alumina, Titania, Zirconia) and metals. Ceramic materials are the most commonly used materials for synthesis of inorganic membrane for the membrane distillation application. As compared to polymeric micro porous membranes, ceramic porous membranes can resist severe environments due to their high thermal stability, high chemical stability, excellent mechanical strength, biocompatibility, long lifetime, energy efficiency, availability and sustainability [7, 8]. These outstanding properties made inorganic micro porous membranes a primary candidate to be used for water purification and desalination applications. Many studies have been reported to explore ceramic micro porous membrane applications in membrane distillation [9–12]. In this study, kaolin was the primary raw material for ceramic membrane fabrication. It is locally available and from less expensive raw materials. An attempt has been made to fabricate kaolin based flat sheet membrane by combing phase inversion and sintering method. However, flat sheet ceramic membrane from kaolin was found to have very weak mechanical strength and difficult to handle during operation [10]. On the other hand, metakaolin based flat sheet ceramic membrane is expected to be hydrophilic due to the presence of hydroxyl groups (OH^-) on its surface. This hydrophilic property is not suitable for the membrane distillation process [13]. In order to improve the hydrophobic properties of ceramic membranes, it is necessary to modify the surface hydrophilic properties of metakaolin based ceramic membranes. According to Kayvani Fard et al. [14], there are three common methods in ceramic membrane hydrophobization, which are chemical modification, surface morphology modification and combination of chemical and morphology modifications [15]. Hydrophobic ceramic micro porous membranes are most commonly prepared by chemical surface modification. Among different modifying agents, grafting with perfluoroalkylsilanes (PFAS) is the most commonly applied, especially in membrane distillation applications [16–18].

Thus, the objective of the present study is to fabricate surface modified kaolin/metakaolin based flat sheet membrane by combining phase inversion and sintering techniques. The effect of kaolin/metakaolin loading and sintering temperature on the surface morphology of the kaolin/metakaolin based flat sheet membrane was investigated.

2   Materials and Methods

2.1   Raw Materials

A commercial kaolin powder (<1 μm, Sigma Aldrich., Belgium) was used as the precursor material and transformed kaolin to metakaolin by thermal treatment (calcination) in the range of 600–850 °C. Analytical grade Polyethersulfone (PESf, Radel 3100P, Solvay Advanced Polymer), Polyvinylpyrrolidone (PVP, VWR International, Belgium) and N-methyl-2-pyrrolidone (NMP, VWR International, Belgium) were purchased and used as a polymer binder, dispersant and solvent respectively. Deionized water was used as the non-solvent coagulation bath. 1H,1H,2H,2H-perfluorooctyltriethoxysilane (PFAS, 97%, VWR International, Belgium) was used as a grafting agent and ethanol (>99.8%, Sigma Aldrich, Belgium), acetone and alkaline solution. The composition of the ceramic suspensions is listed in Table 1.

Table 1. Composition of the ceramic suspensions

Membranes	1	2	3	4
Kaolin/metakaolin (wt. %)	35	40	45	47
NMP (wt. %)	59	45	49	47
PES (wt. %)	5	5	5	5
PVP (wt. %)	1	1	1	1

2.2   Fabrication of Kaolin/Metakaolin Based Flat Sheet Ceramic Membrane

Kaolin/metakaolin powder (<1 μm) and PES was dried to ensure that no moisture was trapped in the particle. Then, the required quantity of NMP was taken in a 100 ml glass bottle and PES was slowly added over a period of one hour to form the polymer solution. After the polymer solution was formed, PVP was then slowly added as dispersed in a polymer solution. The mixture was stirred by hot plate magnetic stirrer for 2 h at 60 °C and after the polymer solution was formed, kaolin/metakaolin powder was then added into a polymer solution slowly and then milled in a planetary ball mill for 48 h to ensure that the kaolin/metakaolin powder and polymer solution were mixed well. The resulting suspension was degassed for 30 min at room temperature to eliminate the air bubbles. The viscosity of the casting suspension was measured instantly prior to the casting process using a rheometer at room temperature. After measuring the viscosity, the casting suspension was cast on a casting machine and left for the evaporation process to occur for 30 s prior to the solvent exchange in the coagulation bath. The cast slurry was left in the water bath for 24 h to let the phase inversion process to be completed. Afterward, the membrane precursors were dried at room temperature for 24 h. Before the sintering process, the membrane precursor was cut in (50 mm × 50 mm square shape). The membrane precursor was then suspended in the furnace and fired in a controlled furnace to 600 °C at a rate of 2 °C min–1 for 2 h, then to target sintering temperature (1200–1500 °C) with an increment of 100 °C at a rate of 5 °C min–1 for 4 h. Lastly, the furnace was cooled down at a rate of 5 °C min–1 to room temperature.

2.3   Preparation of Hydrophobic Kaolin/Metakaolin Based Flat Sheet Membrane

Four equal sizes metakaolin flat sheet membrane prepared at various sintering temperatures mentioned above were used for this treatment. Prior to the chemical modification, the sintered flat sheet membranes were cut in a square form and cleaned by ethanol, acetone and distilled water for 10 min respectively. The flat sheet membrane was dried in an oven at 105 °C for approximately 12 h. After that, all the membranes have been treated by using alkaline solution (NaOH at pH 10) for 8 h. The flat sheet membranes were completely immersed and soaked into a 2 wt. % FAS (1H,1H,2H,2H-perfluorooctyltriethoxysilane) in ethanol solution for 8 h to allow the coupling reaction to occur. After grafting, the modified membranes were then washed in ethanol, acetone and distilled water successively and dried at 105 °C for 12 h in an oven.

2.4   Characterization of Kaolin/Metakaolin Powders and Membranes

The particle size of kaolin/metakaolin was examined by particle size analyzer using a diffraction light scattering (DLS, Model CGS-3 Goniometer) machine. Thermogravimetric analyses (TGA, Model Q600, TA Instruments) were used to analyze the thermal behavior of kaolin/metakaolin. The method of Wavelength dispersive X-ray fluorescence (WD-XRF, Philips PW 2400) spectrometer elemental analyses of clays has been continually showing the class of alumino-silicates to which the analyzed material corresponds. The elements determined in clays have been presented as a relative percentage of the elements expressed as oxides in the whole sample. X-ray diffraction (XRD, Seifert 3003 T/T) using Cu-Ka 1 radiation at a scanning rate of 2°/min. The membrane thickness was measured using a digital micrometer. Furthermore, the structure of kaolin/metakaolin based ceramic membrane prepared with different kaolin/metakaolin contents and treated at a different sintering temperature was examined using a scanning electron microscope (SEM, Philips XL40 LAB6). The kaolin/metakaolin based ceramic membrane samples were cut into 20 mm × 20 mm size and placed in a metal holder, which was then sputtered by platinum under vacuum before testing. The images of kaolin/metakaolin based ceramic membrane were captured to examine the overall view and porous structure of kaolin/metakaolin based flat sheet membrane at different kaolin/metakaolin contents; 35 wt. %; 40 wt. %; 45 wt. %; and 47 wt. %. Contact angle measurement has been performed on membranes to evaluate its surface hydrophobicity before and after grafting. The contact angle measurement of the sample was performed by a sessile drop method using a contact angle analyzer (Kruss DSA 10Mk2) at room temperature. All contact angle readings were taken 15 min after 0.5 ml water droplet was placed on the membrane surface. Chemical stability tests of the grafted membranes with analytical grade hexane were properly carried out at room temperature.

3 Results and Discussion

3.1 Characterization of Starting Materials

The particle size distribution of the precursor material is a critical factor in the fabrication of the ceramic membrane. It has affected the movement of the particles in ceramic suspension during phase inversion. Particles smaller than 1 μm do show a remarkable movement due to its lightweight and produced the macroporous structure. On the other hand, particles larger than 1 μm particles tend to move downward due to gravity effect and produced a dense structure [10]. Different sizes of kaolin and metakaolin particles relatively affect the morphological characteristic of kaolin/metakaolin based ceramic membrane [19]. Table 2 shows the particle size distribution of kaolin and metakaolin powder used in this study.

Table 2. Particle size distribution of kaolin and metakaolin powder

Component	Diameter(μm)	Particle size distribution (%)
Kaolin	<1	100
Metakaolin	<1	100

Table 3. Chemical and mineralogical composition (XRF) of kaolin and metakaolin sample

Sample chemical composition (Weight %)								
Component	SiO_2	Al_2O_3	K_2O	Fe_2O_3	CaO	MgO	P_2O_5	Lol
Kaolin	50.1	34.90	4.5	0.84	–	0.24	0.11	9.00
Metakaolin	55.53	38.30	4.27	0.79	–	0.26	0.10	0.75

The XRD diffractograms result revealed that kaolin is more crystalline than metakaolin which supposed to be amorphous in nature. This result supports the XRF result presented in Table 3. The crystallinity of kaolin was demonstrated by the XRD analysis shown in Fig. 1. The metakaolin was produced by the thermal treatment of kaolin clay. After thermal treatment kaolin clay at temperature 700 °C and heating time 3 h, characteristic peaks for kaolin (2 Theta 12.52,20.5,25.02,35.08,38.5°) was disappeared and SEM images (Fig. 2a and b) which shows a flake-like structure of kaolin and platy structure of metakaolin [20].

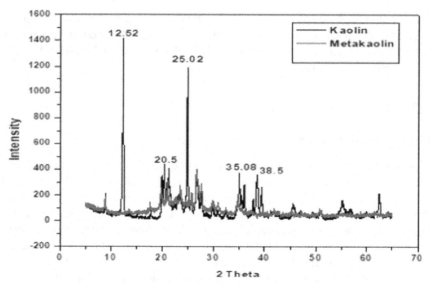

Fig. 1. XRD patterns of kaolin and metakaolin powder

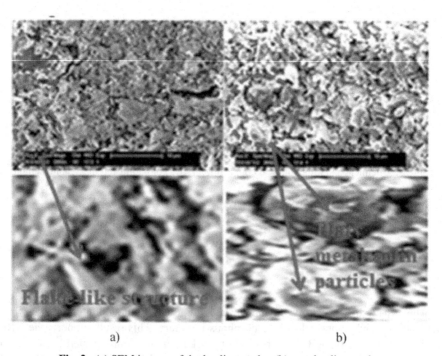

a)   b)

Fig. 2. (a) SEM images of the kaolin powder, (b) metakaolin powder

Figure 3 presents the TGA results of the kaolin and metakaolin. The TGA curve of kaolin shows a total weight loss of about 9%, which consists of two distinct regions. The first one between room temperature and 250 °C is due to the loss of physisorbed/bound water. The second one in the temperature range of 400 °C and 800 °C is mainly caused by the dehydroxylation of the kaolinite. In this region, phase transformation occurred (kaolin ($Al_2Si_2O_5$ (OH) $_4$) to metakaolin ($Al_2Si_2O_7$). The TGA curve of metakaolin shows no remarkable weight loss has occurred and stabilized at about 800 °C. Therefore, metakaolin is a preferred raw material for flat sheet ceramic membranes due to chemical composition and mineralogical qualities.

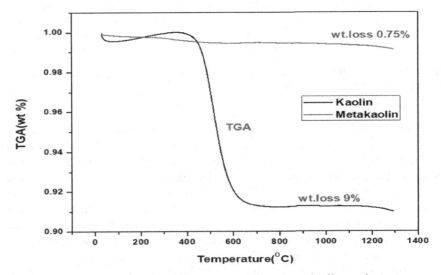

Fig. 3. Thermogravimetry analysis kaolin and metakaolin powder

3.2 Characterization of Kaolin/Metakaolin Flat Sheet Ceramic Membranes

3.2.1 Morphological Properties of Membranes

A significant shrinkage of the flat sheet precursor was observed during the phase inversion process. This is due to the rate of solvent (NMP) diffusion from the suspension is always faster than the rate of diffusion of water into the suspension. The dried flat sheet precursors were fired at various sintering temperatures mentioned above for sample kaolin and metakaolin in the controlled chamber (Nabertherm GmbH, Lilienthal, Germany). All the polymer binder components were expected to completely remove at 600 °C. The particle grain growth occurred at targeted sintering temperatures (1200 °C–1500 °C). Images of the precursor and membrane were recorded by using a digital camera. It can be clearly seen from the images (see Fig. 4), that the visualization of flat sheet membrane weight loss and shrinkage during sintering was higher as compared to the flat sheet precursor. A higher shrinkage of the flat sheet membrane was observed at elevated sintering temperatures. The increment in the shrinkage or densification of the flat sheet

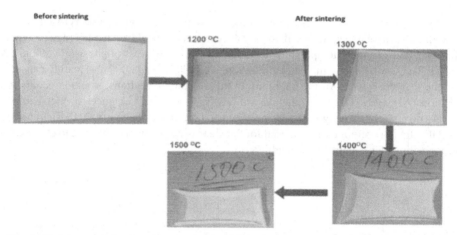

Fig. 4. Shrinkage of the flat sheet kaolin/metakaolin based ceramic membrane at a targeted sintering temperature (1200 °C–1500 °C).

membrane is due to the formation of sintering neck caused by the diffusion of the particles in the flat sheet membrane. Both types of membrane (kaolin and metakaolin based) got shrunk during phase inversion and sintering process. It is shown that the higher the shrinkage, the higher the internal stress generation. This results in more shape distortions and severe cracks or warps in the final sintered flat sheet membrane. It was found that the overall shrinkage of kaolin-based membrane was more than that of metakaolin based membrane due to completely removed organic substance from the ceramic precursor. The thickness of kaolin/metakaolin based membrane was measured and approximately 190 μm, indicating that the membrane is applicable for membrane distillation.

The prepared membranes were analyzed by SEM, and corresponding images are shown in Fig. 5. It can be concluded that the structure and surface morphology changed gradually with changing composition and sintering temperature.

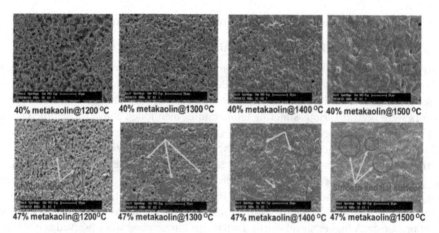

Fig. 5. SEM micrographs of the surface of the flat sheet metakaolin based ceramic membranes

Hydrophobic ceramic membranes are commonly prepared by chemical modification. The grafting process can be carried out by a reaction between OH-groups on the ceramic membrane surface and Si-O-alkyl groups of the silane [21]. As a matter of fact, the surface grafting process can be decreased the surface free energy and increased the contact angle of the membranes. During the sintering process at temperatures between 400 and 800 °C, the hydroxyl groups (OH$^-$) can be suppressed from the membrane surface. Therefore, alkaline pretreatment is required to restore hydroxyl groups (OH$^-$) on the membrane surface and allow more coupling reactions with PFAS. Water drops deposited on the flat sheet membrane forms a contact angle of 3.7° (super hydrophilic) (Fig. 6a). After surface modification, the contact angle becomes 142° (hydrophobic) (Fig. 6b), Confirming the transformation from hydrophilicity to the hydrophobicity of the membrane.

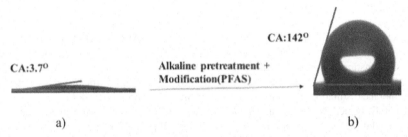

Fig. 6. The water contact angle of the membrane surface: (a) before grafting and (b) after grafting

Chemical stability tests of the grafted membranes with analytical grade hexane were properly carried out at room temperature. The test was repeated three times and the average value was reported. As the result is shown (Fig. 7) that, no membrane swelling, cracking, or breaking was observed. This is clear evidence that PFAS molecules were covalently bonded to the metakaolin based membrane and were stable in hexane.

under original conditions under grafted conditions after contact with hexane for 100 h

Fig. 7. Chemical stability tests of the grafted membranes (45% metakaolin @1200 °C)

4 Conclusion

The overall shrinkage of the kaolin-based membrane was more than that of the metakaolin based membrane due to the burning out of organic substance from the membrane. When the sintering temperature increased, the contact angle of the membrane increased, but the thickness of the membrane decreased. Based on the results discussed in the above sections, metakaolin based flat sheet membrane has desirable characteristics in terms of hydrophobic effect and chemical stability (<1% weight loss). Nevertheless, further research on the performance testing of the metakaolin based flat sheet membrane are required to effectively prepare the membrane for the intended applications.

Acknowledgments. The authors would like to thank and appreciate the Ethiopian government/Ministry of Higher Education and Germany government for its financial support and special thanks to the KU Leuven and the Bahir dar University, for providing necessary facilities for this research.

References

1. Al-Obaidani, S., Curcio, E., Macedonio, F., Di Profio, G., Al-Hinai, H., Drioli, E.: Potential of membrane distillation in seawater desalination: thermal efficiency, sensitivity study and cost estimation. J. Membr. Sci. **323**, 85–98 (2008)
2. El-Bourawia, M.S., Ding, Z., Ma, R., Khayet, M.: A framework for better understanding membrane distillation separation process. J. Membr. Sci. **285**, 4–29 (2006)
3. Banat, F., Jwaied, N.: Economic evaluation of desalination by small-scale autonomous solar-powered membrane distillation units. Desalination **220**, 566–573 (2008)
4. Galvez, J.B., Garcia-Rodriguez, L., Martin-Mateos, I.: Seawater desalination by an innovative solar-powered membrane distillation system: the MEDESOL project. Desalination **246**, 567–576 (2009)
5. Bouguecha, S.T., Aly, S.E., Al-Beirutty, M.H., Hamdi, M.M., Boubakri, A.: Solar driven DCMD: performance evaluation and thermal energy efficiency. Chem. Eng. Res. Des. **100**, 331–340 (2015)
6. Alklaibi, A.M., Lior, N.: Membrane-distillation desalination: status and potential. Desalination **171**, 111–131 (2004)
7. Gazagnes, L., Cerneaux, S., Persin, M., Prouzet, E., Larbot, A.: Desalination of sodium chloride solutions and seawater with hydrophobic ceramic membranes. Desalination **217**, 260–266 (2007)
8. Fang, H., Gao, J.F., Wang, H.T., Chen, C.S.: Hydrophobic porous alumina hollow fiber for water desalination via membrane distillation process. J. Membr. Sci. **403–404**, 41–46 (2012)
9. Khemakhem, S., Amar, R.B.: Modification of Tunisian clay membrane surface by silane grafting: application for desalination with Air Gap Membrane Distillation process. Colloids and Surf., A **387**(1–3), 79–85 (2011). 0927–7757
10. Hubadillah, S.K., Harun, Z., Othman, M.H.D., Ismail, A.F., Gani, P.: Effect of kaolin particle size and loading on the characteristics of kaolin ceramic support prepared via phase inversion technique. J. Asian Ceram. Soc. **4**(2), 164–177 (2016)
11. Wang, J.-W., Li, L., Zhang, J.-W., Xu, X., Chen, C.-S.: β-Sialon ceramic hollow fiber membranes with high strength and low thermal conductivity for membrane distillation. J. Eur. Ceram. Soc. **36**(1), 59–65 (2016). 0955–2219
12. Das, R., Sondhi, K., Majumdar, S., Sarkar, S.: Development of hydrophobic clay–alumina based capillary membrane for desalination of brine by membrane distillation. J. Asian Ceram. Soc. **4**(3), 243–251 (2016). 2187–0764
13. Gentleman, M.M., Ruud, J.A.: Role of hydroxyls in oxide wettability. Langmuir **26**, 1408–1411 (2010)

14. Kayvani Fard, A., et al.: Review: inorganic membranes preparation and application for water treatment and desalination. J. Mater. **11**, 74 (2018)
15. Wang, J.-W., et al.: Porous ß-Sialon planar membrane with a robust polymer derived hydrophobic ceramic surface. J. Membr. Sci. **535**, 63–69 (2017)
16. Picard, C., Larbot, A., Tronel-Peyroz, E., Berjoan, R.: Characterization of hydrophilic ceramic membranes modified by fluoroalkylsilanes into hydrophobic membranes. Solid State Sci. **6**, 605–612 (2004)
17. Hendren, Z.D., Brant, J., Wiesner, M.R.: Surface modification of nanostructured ceramic membranes for direct contact membrane distillation. J. Membr. Sci. **331**, 1–10 (2009)
18. Cerneaux, S., Strużyńska, I., Kujawski, W.M., Persin, M., Larbot, A.: Comparison of various membrane distillation methods for desalination using hydrophobic ceramic membranes. J. Membr. Sci. **337**(1–2), 55–60 (2009). 0376–7388
19. Lungu, A., Perrin, F.X., Belec, L., Sarbu, A., Teodorescu, M.: Kaolin/poly (acrylic acid) composites as precursors for porous kaolin ceramics. Appl. Clay Sci. **62**, 63–69 (2012)
20. Ismadji, S., Soetaredjo, F.E., Ayucitra, A.: Clay Materials for Environmental Remediation. SMS. Springer, Cham (2015). https://doi.org/10.1007/978-3-319-16712-1
21. Khemakhem, M., Khemakhem, S., Amar, R.B.: Surface modification of microfiltration ceramic membrane by fluoroalkylsilane. Desalin. Water Treat. **52**, 1786–1791 (2014)

The Effect of Mechanical Treatment and Calcination Temperature of Ethiopian Kaolin on Amorphous Metakaolin Product

Tadele Assefa Aragaw[✉]

Faculty of Chemical and Food Engineering, Bahir Dar Institute of Technology,
Bahir Dar University, Bahir Dar, Ethiopia
taaaad82@gmail.com

Abstract. Industrial practice of kaolin minerals reveals physicochemical and mineralogical characteristics which make them very useful in many different applications. Even kaolin is important for industrial applications, the presence of contamination can affect the properties of it. So, it is important to treat and characterize the kaolin for their appropriateness of industrial application. The effect of beneficiation and calcinations methods of treatment on the structure of kaolin was studied using XRD and FTIR for the determination of crystalline structure, functional group identification and the thermogravimetry properties of the kaolin. XRD analysis showed that the crystalline of raw kaolin were reduced via beneficiation and calcinations. The effect of beneficiation and calcinations results shows that improvement to a very high grade with physic-chemical characteristics of metakaolin close to that of ideal kaolin. The XRD results depicted that the characteristics reflection of kaolinite and quartz were as a major peak. The FTIR vibration indicates as the major kaolinite clay functional groups in the mineral. From this study, it can be conclude that the major properties for industrial grade specification significantly increased after a certain treatment process.

Keywords: Thermal treatment · Mechanical treatment · Kaolin · Characterization

1 Introduction

Kaolinite comes into view as stacked pseudo hexagonal platelets with a common brochure like shape. Each layer is assumed to have a strong dipole, where the siloxane surfaces have negative charges, while the aluminol surface exhibit positive charges. Consequently, the entity layers of kaolinite are strongly bonded by hydrogen and dipolar interactions. The boundaries of these layers enclose O atoms and OH groups [1]. Kaolin is a hydrated aluminum silicate. It has a wide variety of industrial applications, due to its sole physiochemical properties [2] Kaolin can be treated with mechanical, beneficiation, calcinations and chemical processes to prepare the material for use [3]. Kaolin originally exhibit white color with high kaolinite brightness, but it mainly contains various amounts

N. G. Habtu et al. (Eds.): ICAST 2019, LNICST 308, pp. 662–671, 2020.
https://doi.org/10.1007/978-3-030-43690-2_50

anatase (TiO_2), mica and iron oxides (Fe_2O_3), which provide low intensity and low quality [2]. The presence of such impurities is high-priced to the production of high-grade kaolin, so considerable reports have been dedicated to the problem of removing these contaminants with different treatment methods [4]. Separating the coarse particle like quartz and undesirable mineral such as mica is important steps. This is a simply process in case of a secondary deposit, but in contrast with the primary deposit as it is more difficult due to the presence of high proportion of the abrasive minerals that have survived the alteration process [5]. Industrial practice of kaolin minerals reveals physicochemical and mineralogical characteristics which make them very useful in many different applications [6, 7]. Typically, kaolin used in the paper industry where playing a dual role, as filler between the pulp fibers and as a surface coating for a white silky finish. To eliminate impurities, kaolin can be cleaned with a continuous high gradient magnetic separator to produce highly white material suitable for paper or porcelain [8]. The kaolin improvement is costly and in principle controlled by the composition. Therefore, the assortment different treatment techniques calcination temperature must be related to the physicochemical properties existing among the noticed mineral species [9, 10].

The major use of kaolin is in the paper industry (as filler and as a coating on the paper surface to enhance the printing) and the ceramics manufacture as additives [11]. Most of the industries required a great quality of the final products. Ethiopia imports kaolin abroad for industrial application even though the physicochemical and mineralogical properties of Ethiopian kaolin have been investigated which is good quality for industrial applications specifically which investigated for zeolite synthesis [12]. Ethiopian kaolin has impurity prior to iron oxides. This is the problem for not to use for different industrial application without treatment. So, the raw Ethiopian kaolin have undergone a certain treatment phase and was investigated the calcination temperature to obtain good quality metakaolin. As a result, the government should aware of Ethiopian kaolin can be used as industrial raw material with a basic treatment processes.

2 Methodology

2.1 Sample Collection

Kaolin used in this study was collected from south Gondar near debretabor city. Representative kaolin sample undergoes a mechanical size reduction, grinded and milled to passes less than 75 μm sieve. Size reduced kaolin was used for beneficiation, calcinations and characterization.

2.2 Beneficiation

To purify a certain impurities such as quartz, feldspar, mica, iron and titanium minerals and organic matter, wet processing is very important to produce industrial grade kaolin [13]. Mechanically treated kaolin was dispersed in water for stabilizing the kaolinite as a colloidal suspension and has been bunged so as to separate all agglomerate clay particles. The fine clay slurry has been dried at 60 °C for further analysis and characterization.

2.3 Calcinations

Wet treated kaolin was activated through calcination from 750 °C for 3 h to form reactive metakaolin. This is due to the calcinations temperature producing metkaolin is up to 850 °C as can be seen from the thermogravimetric analysis.

2.4 Characterizations of Kaolin

2.4.1 Thermal Analysis

TG-DSC curves of the air-dried sample were recorded using thermogravimeter (SDT Q600 V20.9 Build 20). Approximately 15.4 mg of sample was placed in a platinum crucible and was heated from ambient temperature, 20 °C, to 1000 °C. 100 mL/min supplied with nitrogen gas with a heating rate of 10 °C/min. Temperatures was calibrated by heating indium standards having a melting point of 156.6 °C at 10, 15 and 20 °C/min [14].

2.4.2 Mineralogy Study

Qualitative and quantitative characteristic of the phases, its crystallinity and the number of phases that is present in were determined by X-ray diffractometer MiniFlex 300/600 with Standard Sample Holder in a continuous scanning scan axis of 2theta/theta about a full scan of 36430 and scanning range from 10° to 70° anode material was used calcinations temperature having a K-Alpha1 wavelength and K-Alpha2 wavelength of 1.54059 and 1.54441 respectively.

2.4.3 Functional Group Determination with FTIR

Fourier Transformation Infrared, FTIR, spectrophotometer PerkinElmer (ILC38B6PD7) were used for qualitative characterization of surface functional groups of the kaolin. Infrared transparent pellets were made using KBr and transmittance was recorded within a scanning range of 400–4000 cm^{-1}.

2.5 Effect of Calcinations Temperature on Quality Metakaolin

pH value, surface area and brightness are the critical parameter which can affect the clay minerals (kaolin) to use for industrial application. This is dependent on the calcination's temperature. The effect of calcinations temperature on pH value and surface area were investigated.

2.5.1 pH Value

pH of the kaolin is important to use for industrial application. The pH solutions of raw and treated kaolin were measured as 1 g of kaolin powder in 100 ml of distilled water.

2.5.2 BET Surface Area Analysis

Surface area was measured with standard method by nitrogen adsorption and application of BET equation by means of Nova 4000e surface area and pore size analyzer. Measuring the number of N_2 molecules adsorbed at monolayer coverage, gives information needed for calculating the surface areas, which is calculated by the instrument. 0.5 g of the samples was weigh and loaded in to the BET glass sample tube, the weight of the tube before and after loading was recorded.

3 Results and Discussions

3.1 Thermogravimetry (TG-DSC) Analysis

Thermal analysis gives information on weight loss; crystallization/recrystallization, decomposition and phase transformation reveal the thermal behavior of the kaolinite structure [17]. The TG–DSC curves of the raw Ethiopian kaolin samples at 20–1000 °C are illustrated in Fig. 1. Up to 330 °C mass loss is ascribed both due to the surface moisture loss and the loss of the absorbed water molecules embedded in the kaolin and also the volatile organic matters that have been exhibited. Dehydroxylation continued up to 850 °C [18]. The DSC curve of kaolin showed a broad characteristic melting exothermic approximately 940 °C. This is due to the recrystallization and transformation of dehydrated substance to mullite, cristobalite, and quartz characteristic for metakaolin dissociation and formation of spinel [19].

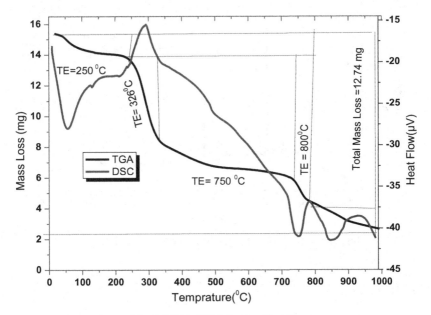

Fig. 1. TGA–DSC signals of kaolin.

3.2 Mineralogy with XRD

X-ray diffraction (XRD) result reveals structural defects in kaolin because of variability in the peak positions and modulation of their intensities in kaolin XRD patterns. XRD identification of order/disorder is challenging because of overlapping peaks and interferences in kaolin [20]. The degree of kaolinite XRD patterns exhibits sharp peaks between 2theta = 28 and 42 shown in Fig. 2 is a characteristic amorphous phase present metakaolin's [21]. The diffraction pattern shown in Fig. 2 is kaolin and quartz as the major minerals in metakaolin as well as raw kaolin. It was clear that the kaolin is mainly composed of kaolinite mineral as indicated from peaks existing from raw kaolin approximately at 2θ values are 28, 42 has been reported in previous studies [22]. This indicates that the kaolin used in this research is ideal kaolin with anorthic (triclinic) lattice structure. High proportion of quartz mineral was detected from peaks existing at 2θ values 28 metakaolin and small proportions 42 [23]. Figure 2 shows a small peak at 2θ = 20°, 24°, 35° and 42° from the calcined kaolin is an indication of deformed silica and alumina kaolinite materials [12]. As can be seen from the figure, calcined kaolin has shown low crystalline, amorphous, structure as compared with raw kaolin at the main kaolinite peaks 2θ = 28 and 42.

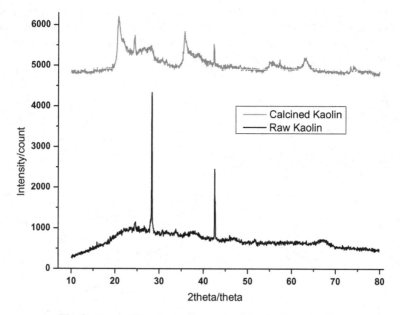

Fig. 2. X-ray diffraction patterns of calcined and raw kaolin

3.3 FTIR Analysis

FTIR spectral generally can be categorized into two regions as 4000–1300 cm^{-1} (functional group region) and 1300–400 cm^{-1} (finger-print region). The frequency assignment approach is adopted for the current investigation. As can be seen from the spectra Fig. 3, the bands placed between 3447 cm^{-1} regions corresponds to Si-OH stretching vibration both for raw and calcined kaolin and with the range of from 3625 to 3821 cm^{-1} small peak shows us to the inner layer OH (Al-O-H) stretching in the raw kaolin obtained by [20]. But no any peak at those of the calcined kaolin. From this it can be deduce that there is no hydroxyl group from the calcined kaolin. The absorption peak at 1114 cm^{-1} is assigned to Si-O in-plane stretching vibration. The bands placed at 1032 cm^{-1} region correspond to skeleton Si-O-Si in-plane stretching vibration. The FTIR spectra depict as predominance of kaolin mineral in the studied sample and did not show any peak for impurity such as smectite [24]. Si-O-Al bending vibration and Si-O bending vibration shows at 574 and 468 cm^{-1} respectively. The bending vibrations of water molecules adsorbed to kaolin surface (hygroscopic moisture) are responsible for the bands at 1635 cm^{-1} both in the raw and calcined kaolin. As can be seen from Fig. 3, the raw kaolin clearly shows sharp peak at those band but the calcined kaolin is insignificant exhibit due to the water molecule removed during thermal treatment. As can be seen, the percent transmittance of raw kaolin is much higher than the calcined kaolin. This is due to the decomposition of iron oxide during calcination responsible to the kaolin becomes red powder which will have less transparent than the raw (white powder) kaolin.

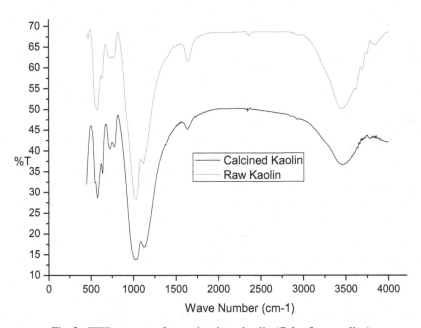

Fig. 3. FTIR- spectra of treated and raw kaolin (Color figure online)

3.4   Calcinations Temperature Effects on Active Kaolin

Surface Area (BET) Analysis
Figure 4 depicted as the surface area properties of raw, beneficiated, beneficiated with surfactant and reference kaolin with a thermal treatment from 550 °C and 1200 °C. Figure 4 shows as the calcination temperature increased there was a fast increase in the surface area up to 1050 °C, which can be accredited to the elimination of burnable impurities within the pores of the kaolin minerals, in the same way increase ease of access within the pores. From a calcination's temperature of 1050–1200 °C it can be seen that a dramatic decrease in the surface area of kaolin. This is the fact that as temperature increases the pore size increases with a subsequent Subside of the layer of the pores, leading to limited access within the material. That is the recrystallization which can formed structurally ordered spine kaolin.

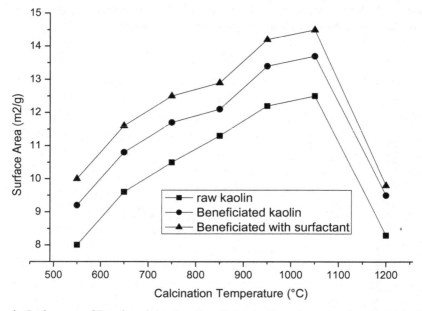

Fig. 4. Surface area of Raw, beneficiated and beneficiated with surfactant kaolin with calcination temperatures (550 °C–1200 °C)

Also, the surface area of beneficiated with surfactant treatment of Ethiopian kaolin is higher than the raw and beneficiated kaolin. This is due the surfactant can flock out the colloids materials as impurities. Even of beneficiated with surfactant and simple beneficiated kaolin have better surface area than the reference kaolin at 1050 °C which corresponds to the standard grade values for industrial application.

pH Value

Increasing the calcination temperature up to 750 °C, the pH values decrease and then increase to from 750–1200 °C as shown in Fig. 5. The decrease in pH in the metakaolin is possibly due to the kaolin rehydroxylation exploiting the OH functional groups shifted [25]. The pH values are different for the differently treated samples. As can be seen, the pH value of raw kaolin is acidic at the calcination temperature of 750 °C. But the pH value comes to neutral as go far to the calcination's temperature 850 °C and above. This is the fact that dissociated iron impurities at the most reactive (amorphous) kaolin having acidic medium. The pH value neutral far to the high calcination's temperature is due to iron recrystallizations to for spinel and mulite formations. Beneficiated with surfactant sample shows better (neutral) pH value than others even the reference kaolin initially and calcinations above 850 °C. As a result, beneficiation weather in simple or with chemical modifications is better treatment techniques for their neutral pH range values of kaolin.

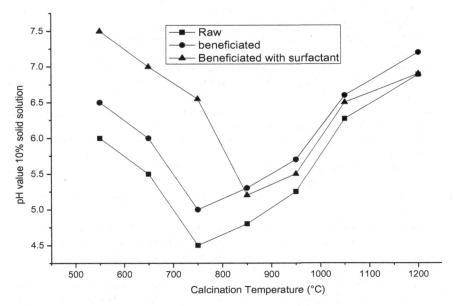

Fig. 5. Change in pH with calcination temperature

4   Conclusion

Quality of the kaolin was investigated with different treatment techniques. The calcination temperature has an effect on the surface characteristics and pH values the kaolin. Chemical modification can improve the surface area and pH values of the raw kaolin with indicate that the good grade industrial raw materials. From the thermal analysis, the calcinations temperature can be enough from 550 °C–900 °C for their good surface properties. The low weight loss up to 300 °C conforms as insignificant moisture and volatile organic matter which is suitable for industrial application. Impurities in raw kaolin are more as compared to treated kaolin which impacts the physicochemical properties. However, the treatment processes reduce the iron percentage to a lower level. From the FTIR and XRD spectra analysis, the main component exhibits the kaolinite material.

References

1. Chun-Hui, Z., John, K.: Clays and clay minerals: geology, properties and uses. Appl. Clay Sci. **74**, 58–65 (2013)
2. Asmatulu, R.: Removal of the discoloring contaminants of East Georgia kaolin clay and its dewatering. Turkish J. Eng. Environ. Sci. **26**, 447–453 (2002)
3. Mukherjee, S.: The Science of Clays: Applications in Industry, Engineering and Environment. Springer, Dordrecht (2013). https://doi.org/10.1007/978-94-007-6683-9
4. Du, F., Li, J., Li, X., Zhang, Z.: Improvement of iron removal from silica sand using ultrasound-assisted oxalic acid. Ultrason. Sonochem. **18**, 389–393 (2011)
5. Prasad, M.S., Reid, K.J., Murray, H.H.: Kaolin: processing, properties and applications. Appl. Clay Sci. **6**, 87–119 (1991)
6. Murray, H.H.: Applied Clay Mineralogy, 1st edn. Elsevier, Amsterdam (2007)
7. Chatterjee, K.K.: Uses of Industrial Minerals, Rocks and Freshwater. Nova Science Publishers Inc., New York (2009)
8. Yavuza, C.T., Prakash, A.B., Mayoa, J.T., Colvina, V.L.: Magnetic separations: from steel plants to biotechnology. Chem. Eng. Sci. **64**, 2510–2521 (2009)
9. Kogel, J.E., Trivedi, N.C., Barker, J.M.: Industrial Minerals and Rocks: Commodities, Markets and Uses, 7th edition. Society for Mining, Metallurgy, and Exploration, Inc., Littleton (2006)
10. Chandrasekhar, S., Ramaswamy, S.: Influence of mineral impurities on the properties of kaolin and its thermally treated products. Appl. Clay Mineral. Sci. **21**, 133–142 (2002)
11. Murray, H.H.: Major kaolin processing developments. Int. J. Miner. Process. **7**, 263–274 (1980)
12. Aragaw, T.A., Ayalew, A.A.: Removal of water hardness using zeolite synthesized from Ethiopian kaolin by hydrothermal method. Water Pract. Technol. **14**, 145–159 (2018)
13. Aroke, U.O., El-Nafaty, U.A., Osha, O.A.: Properties and characterization of kaolin clay from Alkaleri, NorthEastern Nigeria. Int. J. Emerg. Technol. Adv. Eng. **3**, 387–392 (2013)
14. Archer, J.D., Douglas, W.M., Brad, S.: The effects of instrument parameters and sample properties on thermal decomposition: interpreting thermal analysis data from Mars. Planet. Sci. **2**, 1–21 (2013). https://doi.org/10.1186/2191-2521-2-2
15. Twyman, R.M.: Wet Digestion. Elsevier Ltd., London (2005)
16. Potts, P.S.: A Handbook of Silicate Rock Analysis, pp. 47–58. Blackie and Sons Ltd., Glasgow (1992)
17. Hongfei, C., Qinfu, L., Jing, Y., Songjiang, M., Ray, L.F.: The thermal behavior of kaolinite intercalation complexes-a review. Thermochim. Acta **545**, 1–13 (2012)
18. Hongyan, W., Chunshan, L., Zhijian, P., Suojiang, Z.: Characterization and thermal behavior of kaolin. J. Therm. Anal. Calorim. **105**, 157–160 (2011). https://doi.org/10.1007/s10973-011-1385-0
19. Aragaw, T.A., Kuraz, F.: Physico-chemical characterizations of ethiopian kaolin for industrial applications: case study WDP propoxur formulations. In: Zimale, F.A., Enku Nigussie, T., Fanta, S.W. (eds.) ICAST 2018. LNICST, vol. 274, pp. 122–134. Springer, Cham (2019). https://doi.org/10.1007/978-3-030-15357-1_10

20. Peter, A.A., Yahaya, M.S., Wan, M.A.W.D.: Kaolinite properties and advances for solid acid and basic catalyst synthesis. RSC Adv. **5**, 101127–101147 (2015)
21. Kenne, D.B.B., Elimbi, A., Cyr, M., Dika, M.J., Tchakoute, H.K.: Effect of the rate of calcinations of kaolin on the properties of metakaolin-based geopolymers. J. Asian Ceram. Soc. **3**, 130–138 (2015)
22. Goulash, M., Buhl, J.-Ch.: Geochemical and mineralogical characterization of the Jabal Al-Harad Jordan for its possible utilization. Clay Miner. Mineral. Soc. **45**, 281–294 (2010)
23. Bundy, W.M., Murray, H.H.: The effect of aluminum on the surface properties of kaolinite. Clays Clay Miner. **21**, 295–302 (1973). https://doi.org/10.1346/CCMN.1973.0210505
24. https://www.indiamart.com/proddetail/olinpowder7107133755.html. Accessed June 2018
25. Burhan, D., Emin, C.: Investigation of central anatolian clays by FTIR spectroscopy. Int. J. Nat. Eng. Sci. **3**, 154–161 (2009)
26. Velho, J.A.L., Gomes, C.S.F.: Influence of calcination on physical and technological properties of kaolin's for paper filler applications. Geol. Carpath. Clays **45**, 21–26 (1994)

Analysis of Bending and Tensile Strength of Sisal/Bamboo/Polyester Hybrid Composite

Yesheneh Jejaw Mamo[✉]

Bahirdar Institute of Technology 2019, Bahirdar University, Bahir Dar, Ethiopia
yeshi.jeje@gmail.com

Abstract. Nowadays composite materials are promising material which can replace metals and they can be used in different applications so studying mechanical properties of composites is crucial. Hybridization of two different fibers improves properties of composites by compensating the weak properties of individual fibers. In this study sisal and bamboo fiber hybrid polyester composite are prepared to study the effect of hybridization on strength of composites. Tensile test Samples are prepared according to ASTM D3039 and bending test samples are prepared according D790. Mats are prepared from each fiber using manual mat making machine to reduce porosity, reduce effort aligning fibers to increase strength of the composite. Sisal/Bamboo/Polyester composites are prepared for tensile and bending test by varying the mixing weight ratio of fibers to matrix ratio. Samples prepared are (0%/30%/70%), (15%/15%/70%), (10%/20%/70%), (20%/10%/70%) and (30%/0%/70%), by wt% of Sisal/Bamboo/Polyester respectively for tensile and bending test to study how hybridization affect the strength of composite. Tensile and bending strength are tested using universal tensile tester machine and 5 samples are tested for each sample to reduce errors during testing. From the test result hybridizing fibers compensate the weak properties of one by another and increase the tensile and bending strength of individual fiber polyester composite. From tensile test of different weight ratio 10%/20%/70% by wt% of sisal/Bamboo/Polyester has better strength than other ratios. From bending test of Sisal/Bamboo/Polyester hybrid composite hybridizing the sisal and bamboo 10%/20%/70% wt% improve the yield strength of pure sisal polyester composite. Generally hybridizing fibers improves the tensile and bending yield stress of individual fiber polyester composites and compensates the weak properties one fiber by the other fiber.

Keywords: Bamboo · Sisal · Bending strength · Fiber · Hybrid

1 Introduction

Nowadays the world needs materials which are renewable, biodegradable, less cost, eco-friendly, and light in weight to save power loss. In Ethiopia, these natural fibres like sisal, bamboo and jute are abundantly available, but which are not having sufficient scientific evaluation proof for their strength. Natural fiber composites has a better strength but still their strength can be improved by different methods like hybridizing. This study

© ICST Institute for Computer Sciences, Social Informatics and Telecommunications Engineering 2020
Published by Springer Nature Switzerland AG 2020. All Rights Reserved
N. G. Habtu et al. (Eds.): ICAST 2019, LNICST 308, pp. 672–683, 2020.
https://doi.org/10.1007/978-3-030-43690-2_51

tries to know mechanical properties of Jute, Sisal and Bamboo fibers which are grown in Ethiopia and try get an optimized bending and tensile strength by hybridizing Sisal and Bamboo fibers.

The use of natural fibres for composites are increasing rather than artificial/synthetic fibres like Glass, Carbon and Kevlar. The main reason behind it is the ecological benefits, cheap cost, renewability and availability in abundance and also with good specific mechanical properties [1].

Natural fibred composites are widely used in different application areas such as automobiles, furniture, and sports equipment, due to the advantages of natural fibres compared to synthetic fibres, i.e. low cost, low density, less damage to processing equipment, renewability, and biodegradability and easily availability. Among several natural fibres like jute, sisal, bamboo etc. Bamboo fibre is the effective one for greater strength. Several bamboo species exist all around the world [2].

There are factors which affect the mechanical strength of composites, among those the ratio of fibers to matrix ratio is the one. Investigations has been made at different fiber to matrix ratio (20%/80%, 30%/70%, and 40/60% fiber to matrix ratio by weight percentage) to study effect fiber to matrix ratio on strength of composites. From the test result tensile strength composites decrease at 40 wt% of fiber and 60 wt% of matrix. On the basis of mechanical testing results it is found that 30 wt% of bamboo fibre to 70 wt% of matrix give optimum mechanical properties [3].

From the mechanical strength investigation kenaf and banana fiber with polyester composite. The bending strength of kenaf/banana hybrid fiber with polyester composite has better strength than individual kenaf and banana fiber polyester composite. From individual fiber composites kenaf fiber reinforced composite had a better bending strength than banana fiber, due to densified structure of kenaf fiber. Generally banana and kenaf fibers in the hybrid increases compressive and shear strength [4].

Many literatures show hybridizing has appositive effect on mechanical strength of composite. From bending strength test to study effect of fibers palm/jute fiber hybrid composites had better bending strength than pure palm fiber composite. In all hybrid composites bending strength on increasing weight ratio of jute fiber. The tensile strength of hybrid palm/jute composites also increases by 46% with increase of weight ratio of jute fiber (25% palm, 75% jute) as compared to pure palm fiber composites. Generally hybridization of fibers has a positive effect on bending and tensile strength of palm/jute hybrid composite [5].

From study of tensile, bending and impact properties of sisal/bamboo polyester hybrid composite hybridization shows a positive effect. The tensile, bending and impact strength increase as weight ratio bamboo fibers increase in the hybrid composite as compared to pure sisal polyester composite [6].

2 Methods and Materials

2.1 Materials

Sisal Fiber
Sisal fibre is one of the most widely used natural fibres and is very easily cultivated. Sisal fibre is a promising reinforcement for use in composites on account of its low cost, low

density, no health risk, easy availability and renewability. Sisal fibers traditionally used for making ropes, mats, carpets, fancy articles and others. In this research sisal plant is taken from highland of debrework wereda Amara Region, Ethiopia and extracted manually.

Bamboo Fibre
The bamboo fibre was prepared from species of Ethiopian hallow bamboo. Bamboo plants taken from Amhara Region around at Injibara (hollow bamboo). Bamboo were cut up to its culm then it just sliced in the longitudinal direction.

Matrix and Hardener
Polymer matrices can be either thermoplastic or thermoset. The most commonly used thermoset resins are epoxy, vinyl ester, polyester and phenolic. In general, the Polyester resins are being widely used for many advanced composites due to their many advantages such as Better adhesive properties, Superior mechanical properties (particularly strength and stiffness), Improved resistance to fatigue and micro cracking, Reduced degradation from water ingress (diminution of properties due to water penetration), Increased resistance to osmosis (surface degradation due to water permeability) and Good performance at elevated temperature etc. The resin used for this study is Polyester Resin with brand name of GPP (General Purpose Polyester) and catalyst used is methyl ethyl ketone peroxide with 5.8 g catalyst to 1 kg of polyester resin.

2.2   Methods

Fiber Extraction Methods for Bamboo Fiber
In this research two different methods of fiber extraction methods for bamboo fiber are used and the fiber strength are compared. Fibre are extracted according to ASTM D3379 (fiber length between 20–35 cm and diameter has a range of 0.09 mm to 0.25 mm [7] (Fig. 1).

Fig. 1. Extraction method of bamboo

Mechanical Extraction Method

- Initially bamboos of 2 years are cut and culms above 2 m from root are used in this research.
- Initially raw bamboo cut near to the culms and then cut and sliced in to four pieces.
- Those sliced pieces will be sliced again in to many very thin slices
- Dry the sliced for 5 days until it lost its moisture to facilitate easy fiber extraction.
- From those dry very thin slices of bamboo thin bamboo fibers extracted manually by hand.

Fiber Extraction of Sisal Fiber

Mechanical extraction

Fibers are extracted manually. Sisal plants are cut and fibers are extracted by eliminating resinous waste materials using knife by rasping until fiber strands are obtained (Fig. 2).

Fig. 2. Sisal plant and fibre

Mat Preparation

Preparing fibers in the form of mat has the following advantage (Figs. 3 and 4)

- It reduce time to prepare composite
- It reduce porosity of the composite so that we can make strong composite

Fig. 3. Mat preparing method

Fig. 4. Mats of sisal and bamboo fiber

Preparation of Polyester and Hardener

The matrix used to fabricate composite is general purpose polyester resin with methyl ethyl ketone per oxide catalyst. The mixing ratio is 6 g of methyl ethyl ketone per oxide for 1 kg of polyester resin.

Preparation of Composite Specimen

Composite samples are prepared with 30% fiber and 70% matrix ratio which is optimum ratio [3] by varying the weight ratio of two fibers by keeping other parameters constant from mats using hand- layup method. The mold used for preparing composites is made from rectangular wood according to ASTM D-790 and D-3039 for bending and tensile samples respectively. The sample size for bending test is length = 170 mm, width = 20 mm and thickness of 4 mm and for tensile test length 250 mm, width 25 mm and thickness-4 mm.

Tensile test samples of sisal/Bamboo/Polyester Composite

(A) Samples 1, 2, 3, 4, and 5, are made of Sisal/bamboo/polyester by differing weight ratio of fiber to matrix ratio constant according to ASTM 3039.

Sample 1 = 15%/15%/70% wt% (sisal/Bamboo/polyester Hybrid Composite)
Sample 2 = 20%/10%/70% wt% (Sisal/Bamboo/Polyester Hybrid Composite)
Sample 3 = 10%/20%/70% (Sisal/Bamboo/polyester Hybrid Composite)
Sample 4 = 30%/0%/70% (Sisal/Bamboo/polyester Hybrid Composite)
Sample 5 = 0%/30%/70% (Sisal/Bamboo/polyester Hybrid Composite)

Bending Test samples of Sisal/Bamboo/Polyester Composite

(B) Samples A, B, C, D, E and F, are made of Sisal/bamboo/polyester by differing weight ratio of fiber to matrix ratio constant according to ASTM D-790.

Sample A = 15%/15%/70% (Sisal/Bamboo/polyester Hybrid Composite)
Sample B = 10%/20%/70% (Sisal/Bamboo/polyester Hybrid Composite)
Sample C = 20%/10%/70% Sisal/Bamboo/polyester Hybrid Composite)
Sample D = 30%/0%/70% (Sisal/Bamboo/polyester Hybrid Composite)
Sample E = 0%/30%/70% (Sisal/Bamboo/polyester Hybrid Composite)
Sample F = 10%/10%/80% (Sisal/Bamboo/polyester Hybrid Composite) (Fig. 5)

Finally bending samples are cut for final test According to ASTM D-790 standard (Fig. 6).

Fig. 5. Samples for tensile test

Fig. 6. Samples for bending test according ASTM D-790

Universal Tensile Testing Machine

The universal tensile testing machine was the equipment where the tensile test and bending test has been done as shown in the Figure. It has a capacity of 100 KN, during test the machine has been set to 5 mm/min (Fig. 7).

Fig. 7. Universal Tensile Tester Machine

Flexural Test

Samples for flexural test are prepared with total length of 170 mm, span length of 128 mm, width of 20 mm and thickness of 4 mm according to ASTM D790. Five samples are tested to reduce errors.

Tensile Test

Tensile test samples are cut to size of length = 250 mm, width 20 mm and thickness = 4 mm according to ASTMD3039, and 5 samples were tested and the average result has been taken. During test the machine has been set to 5 mm/min.

3   Results and Discussion

3.1   Tensile Test Result of Composite

Comparison of Tensile Yield Strength (MPa), Yield Force (KN), Elongation (mm) and Density (Kg/m^3) of sisal/bamboo/polyester composite with different weight ratio, keeping other parameters constant (Figs. 8, 9 and 10).

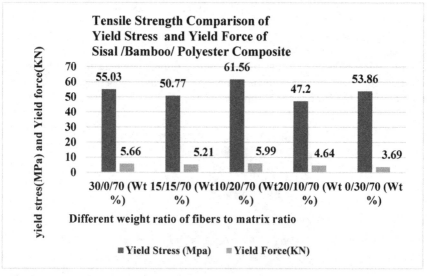

Fig. 8. Comparison of Yield Stress (MPa) and Yield Force (KN) of Sisal/Bamboo/Polyester Composite at different Weight ratio from tensile test.

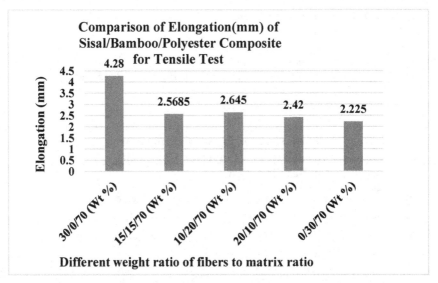

Fig. 9. Comparison Elongation (mm) of Sisal/Bamboo/Polyester Composite at different Weight ratio from tensile test.

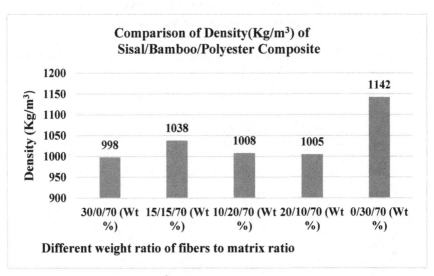

Fig. 10. Comparison Density (Kg/m^3) of Sisal/Bamboo/Polyester Composite at different Weight ratio tensile test.

3.2   Bending Test Result of Composite

Comparison of Flexural Yield Strength (MPa), Yield Force (KN), Elongation (mm) and Density (Kg/m^3) of sisal/bamboo/polyester composite with different weight ratio, keeping other parameters constant for bending test (Figs. 11, 12, 13 and 14).

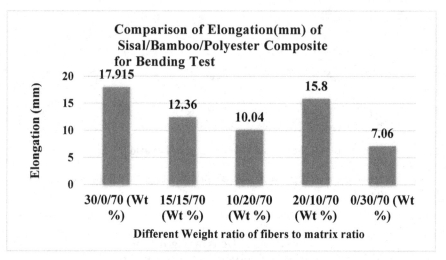

Fig. 11. Comparison Elongation (mm) of Sisal/Bamboo/Polyester Composite at different Weight ratio from bending test.

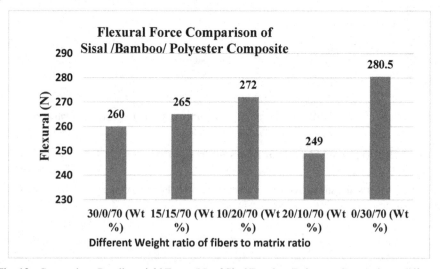

Fig. 12. Comparison Bending yield Force (N) of Sisal/Bamboo/Polyester Composite at different Weight ratio from bending test.

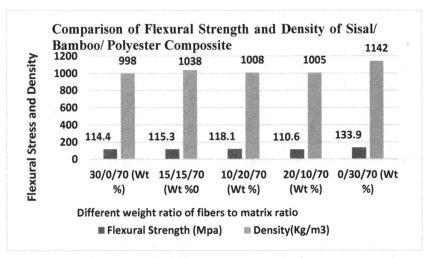

Fig. 13. Comparison Flexural Stress (MPa) and Density (Kg/m^3) of Sisal/Bamboo/Polyester Composite at different Weight ratio from bending test

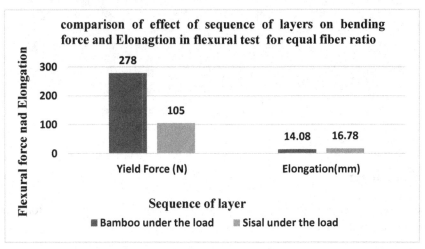

Fig. 14. Comparison Flexural yield force (N) and Elongation (mm) of Sisal/Bamboo/Polyester Composite with the same fiber Weight ratio from bending test.

3.3 Discussion

From tensile test of Sisal/Bamboo/Polyester hybrid composite 0/30/70 wt% 55.03 MPa, and 30/0/70 wt% has 53.86 MPa by hybridizing the sisal and bamboo 10/20/70 wt% improve the yield strength to 61.56 MPa.

From elongation result 30/0/70 wt% has large elongation of 4.28 mm whereas 0/30/70 wt% composite has small elongation of 2.225 mm and hybrid composite of 10/20/70 wt% has 2.645 mm.

From bending test of Sisal/Bamboo/Polyester hybrid composite 30/0/70 wt% has bending stress 114.4 MPa, and 0/30/70 wt% has bending stress of 133.9 MPa by hybridizing the sisal and bamboo 10/20/70 wt% has yield strength of 118.1 MPa. from bending elongation result 30/0/70 wt% has large elongation of 17.28 mm whereas 0/30/70 wt% composite has small elongation of 7.06 mm and hybrid composite of 10/20/70 wt% has 10.04 mm. comparing bending force of composites pure bamboo polyester composite has 260 N, and pure sisal composite has 280.5 N, hybrid composite of 10/20/70 by wt% has bending force of 272 N.

3.4   Failure Modes

Failed flexural and tensile specimens are shown in the figure below. Flexural specimens at the mid span of its length, due to matrix and fiber breakage (Fig. 15).

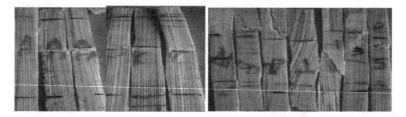

Fig. 15.   Bending and tensile samples after failure

4   Conclusion

From experimental test sisal/bamboo hybrid fiber polyester composite the following conclusions can be made.

- From tensile test of Sisal/Bamboo/Polyester hybrid composite hybridizing the sisal and bamboo to 10/20/70 wt% improve the yield strength to 61.56 MPa which is more than pure sisal and bamboo composites this is due to hybridization.
- From elongation result pure sisal composite has large elongation of 4.28 mm whereas pure bamboo composite has small elongation of 2.225 mm and hybrid composite of 10/20/70 wt% improve the elongation of pure bamboo composite.
- Comparing density of composites pure bamboo polyester composite has 1142 kg/m^3, and pure sisal composite has density of 998 kg/m^3, hybrid composite of 10/20/70 by wt% has a density of 1008 kg/m^3.
- From bending test of Sisal/Bamboo/Polyester hybrid composite hybridizing the sisal and bamboo 10/20/70 wt% improve the yield strength of pure Sisal composite.

- From bending elongation result hybrid composite of 10/20/70 wt% improves the elongation of pure bamboo composite due to hybridization compensates the weak property of bamboo fiber.
- From bending test to study the effect of sequence of layers bamboo layers under the load resist more load than when sisal layers are under the load but the elongation is better when sisal layers are under the load this is due to the loads are more shared by outer layers.
- Generally hybridizing natural fibers compensate the weak properties of one fiber by the other gives a better result in the bending and tensile test.

References

1. Nirmal, U., Hashim, J., Low, K.O.: Adhesive wear and frictional performance of bamboo fibres reinforced epoxy composite. Tribol. Int. **47**, 122–133 (2011). Faculty of Engineering and Technology, Multimedia University, Jalan Ayer Keroh Lama, 75450, Melaka, Malaysia10(2), 75–84
2. Baets, J., Wouters, K., Hendrickx, K., Van Vuure, A.W.: Compressive properties of natural fibre composites. Mater. Lett. **149**, 138–140 (2015). KU Leuven, Department of Materials Engineering, Kasteelpark Arenberg 44, 3001 Leuven, Belgium, 12(3), 68–74
3. Banga, H., Singh, V.K., Choudhary, S.K.: Fabrication and study of mechanical properties of bamboo fibre reinforced bio-composites. Innovative Syst. Des. Eng. **6**(1), 84–95 (2015)
4. Alavudeen, A., Rajini, N., Karthikeyan, S., Thiruchitrambalam, M., Venkateshwaren, N.: Mechanical properties of banana/kenaf fiber-reinforced hybrid polyester composites: effect of woven fabric and random orientation. Mater. Des. **66**, 246–257 (2014)
5. Shanmugam, D., Thiruchitrambalam, M.: Static and dynamic mechanical properties of alkali treated unidirectional continuous Palmyra Palm Leaf Stalk Fiber/jute fiber reinforced hybrid polyester composites. Mater. Des. **50**, 533–542 (2013)
6. Prasanna, V.R., Ramanathan, K., Srinivasa, R.V.: Tensile, flexual, impact and water absorption properties of natural fibre reinforced polyester hybrid composites. Fibres Text. Eastern Europe **24**, 90–94 (2015)
7. Trujillo, E., Moesenl, M., Osorio, L., van Vuurea, A.W., Ivens, J., Verpoest, I.: Weibull statistics of bamboo fibre bundles: methodology for tensile testing of natural fibres. In: European Conference on Composite Materials, pp. 24–28 (2012)

Dynamic Mechanical Properties of Kenaf, Thespesia Lampas and Okra Fiber Polyester Composites

Melak Misganew[1], D. K. Nageswara Rao[1(✉)], K. Raja Narender Reddy[2],
and Muralidhar Avvari[1]

[1] Mechanical and Industrial Engineering, Bahir Dar Institute of Technology, Bahir Dar, Ethiopia
melakmisganew33@gmail.com, dr.dknrao@gmail.com,
seemurali@gmail.com
[2] Mechanical Engineering Department, Kakatiya Institute of Technology & Science,
Warangal, India
krajanr@rediffmail.com

Abstract. Dynamic Mechanical Analysis is carried out on treated and untreated kenaf, thespesia lampas and okra fiber polyester composites. Results indicate that composites with fibers treated by sodium hydroxide have higher storage modulus, decreased loss modulus and damping factor Best properties are noted for treated okra fiber composite with highest storage modulus and glass transition temperature and lowest damping factor. The Scanning Electron Microscopy results indicate a superior interfacial bonding for treated kenaf fiber composite. Improved interfacial bonding upon treatment causing hindrance to the mobility of molecular chains can be seen clearly in the micrographs. The effect of chemical modification of the fibers in enhancing the dynamic mechanical properties is well demonstrated for kenaf, thespesia lampas and okra fiber composites in this paper.

Keywords: Chemical treatment · Dynamic mechanical analysis · Storage modulus · Loss modulus · Damping ratio · Glass transition temperature

1 Introduction

Dynamic Mechanical Analysis (DMA) is a sensitive technique that characterizes the mechanical response of materials by monitoring the property changes with respect to temperature, stress and frequency of loading. In this technique, a small sinusoidal time-varying oscillating force is applied on the specimen. This technique separates the dynamic response of the materials into two distinct parts: an elastic part and the viscous or damping component. The elastic process describes the ability of the material to store energy applied to it, known as the storage modulus (E'). The viscous component describes the material tendency to dissipate energy applied to it, usually termed as the loss modulus (E''). The polymer composites being viscoelastic material, they exhibit a combination of both elastic and viscous behavior. Damping is determined by the ratio

Published by Springer Nature Switzerland AG 2020. All Rights Reserved
N. G. Habtu et al. (Eds.): ICAST 2019, LNICST 308, pp. 684–694, 2020.
https://doi.org/10.1007/978-3-030-43690-2_52

between loss modulus and the storage modulus and is termed as *tan δ*. It is also known as the mechanical loss factor or the dynamic loss factor. This ratio depends on the degree of fiber and matrix adhesion. A weak fiber-matrix bonding will reflect in higher values of tan δ.

Ku and Wang [1] have noted that bleaching of hemp fibers has exhibited good results of enhancing interfacial bonding. Treatments like mercerization, permanganate, benzoylation, poly methyl methacrylate and admicellar polymerization on sisal fibers have improved the interfacial bonding and enhanced the tensile, flexural and impact strengths, dynamic mechanical behaviour, electrostatic charge, thermal stability, dielectric constant and ac conductivity properties of the sisal fiber polyester composites [2–5]. Storage modulus, loss modulus and damping factor have increased due to treatment and decreased with increase in fiber content. Akil et al. [6] have studied the dynamic mechanical properties of pultruded kenaf fiber composites under varying frequencies of oscillating load over a range of temperatures, Aziz and Ansell [7] have studied alkalized kenaf–polyester and hemp-polyester composites. Thermo gravimetric analysis (TGA), differential scanning calorimetry (DSC), and DMA have produced superior properties for composites with treated fibers. Mylsamy and Rajendran [8] have studied the dynamic and thermo mechanical behavior of agave americana fiber composites. Ornaghi Jr. et al. [9, 10] have studied the dynamic mechanical properties of glass/sisal fiber hybrid composites and found that adhesion has improved with glass fiber content. The glass transition temperature has increased with increase in frequency. Duc et al. [11] have studied the mechanical and damping properties of unidirectional, cross ply and 2 × 2 twill configurations with 40% flax fibers and 60% epoxy resin. The quality of impregnation, angle of twist of fibers, have improved matrix adhesion and enhanced the damping and stiffness properties of the composites significantly. Costa et al. [12] have presented a review on the recent publications on Dynamic Mechanical and Thermal Analysis (DMTA). Sezgin et al. [13] have studied the jute carbon polyester composites for different stacking sequence and found that for exterior carbon there is an increase in storage and loss modulus without significant effect on T_g. Monteiro et al. [14] have studied the viscoelastic and glass transition temperature behavior of fique natural fiber fabric composites that can replace Kevlar fiber composites for armor applications and noted that fiber content has increased these properties. Surya Nagendra et al. [15] have done DMA on glass/epoxy mixed with nano particles of banana fiber. 8% of banana particles by weight of resin have improved the properties by causing hindrance to mobility of molecular chains. Reduction in hysteresis and improvement in elastic properties is noted. Palanivel et al. [16] have studied treated and untreated hemp/epoxy composites filled with cellulose. Increase in cellulose filler loading and treatment by NaOH and Benzoylation have improved E' and decreased E'' and tan δ. Rashid et al. [17] have conducted DMA of phenolic sugar palm fiber powder composites. Increase in fiber content has improved the properties. NaOH treated fiber gave better results than by sea water treated fiber. A smooth semi-circular shaped Cole-Cole curves presented indicate a homogeneous mixture of fiber powder and matrix. Saba et al. [18] have presented a review of DMA on natural fiber and hybrid composites with thermoplastic, thermoset and biopolymer resins and also hybrid nano composites. They have presented clearly that E', E'', tan δ and T_g are influenced by the fiber content and treatment causing decreased mobility of molecular chains. They have also projected that DMA plays an important role on the application of composite materials used in aircraft and automobile components. Pothan et al. [19] have done DMA on banana polyester composites and stated that increased volume fraction of fibers causes more restraint at interfaces thus resulting in increased E', decreased E'' and tan δ and increase in T_g. Romanzini et al. [20] studied the properties of hybrid ramie/glass polyester composites by DMA for different ratios of ramie/glass fiber content. Higher activation energy was observed at 75% of glass fiber content. Jacob et al. [21] have reported the results of sisal/oil palm hybrid fiber natural rubber composites. The storage modulus has increased with fiber volume fraction and also up treatment. Abdullaha and Jamaludin [22] have studied the effect of aging of fibers on the properties of Arenga Pinnata fiber/epoxy composites by DMA. NaOH treated-accelerated aging process is adopted. The aged composites are reported to have better properties. Chaudhary et al. [23] have studied tribological properties and also by DMA for jute/hemp, hemp/flax and jute/hemp/flax combinations. Selvakumar et al. [24] have reported that higher mechanical and dynamic mechanical properties are noted for increasing human hair content in jute/human hair epoxy composites. Nimanpure et al. [25] have reported the dielectric properties and results of DMA on treated and untreated short fiber sisal/epoxy composites. 5% NaOH treated for 72 h have indicated higher values of E' for 35 g fiber with 65 g of resin with a lower value of E'' and tan δ. T_g also has increased for this fiber content.

This paper highlights the effect of NaOH treatment on the results of DMA for kenaf, thespesia lampas and okra treated and untreated fiber/polyester composites. These three plants belong to Malvaceae family. Similar cellulose fibers by other names like Nacha are available in Ethiopia. Fibers in the present work are available in India and other parts of Africa. The storage modulus, E', loss modulus, E'' and dynamic loss factor, tan δ and glass transition temperature, T_g are studied. The SEM also done to visualize the effect of treatment.

2   Methodology

2.1   Materials and Preparation of Composites

The fibers of kenaf, thespesia and okra are extracted from the stems of the plants and subjecting to water retting process for decomposition of the green substance. They are washed in running water and then dried in sun. These fibers are treated in 2% NaOH solution for 24 h at room temperature, thoroughly washed in distilled water and then dried. The treated and untreated fibers of kenaf, Thespesia lampas and Okra are shown in Fig. 1.

Unidirectional mats are prepared on an indigenous weaving set up and hand molded at room temperature. General purpose polyester resin, 2% catalyst, methyl ethyl ketone peroxide (MEKP) and 2% accelerator, cobalt naphthenate were used for the matrix. A fiber-matrix ratio of 1:6 by weight ratio has been arrived to give proper wetting of fibers and eliminating the entrapped air from the mix of resin-fiber and upper and lower glass plates. The two thick glass plates are coated with wax and poly vinyl alcohol (PVA) as releasing agents and a weight of 500 N is kept for 24 h.

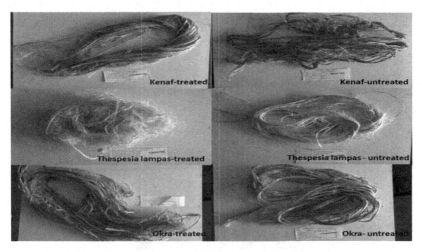

Fig. 1. Fibers used for making laminates

2.2 Dynamical Mechanical Analysis

The specimens for DMA are prepared as per ASTM D 4065. The dimensional details of each type of specimen are presented in Fig. 2.

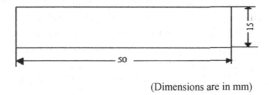

(Dimensions are in mm)

Fig. 2. DMA test specimen.

The specimens of kenaf fiber composite-untreated fiber (kfc-ut), thespesia lampas fiber composite (tfc-ut) and okra fiber composite (ofc-ut) are shown in Fig. 3. The Pyris Diamond DMA equipment by Perkin-Elmer Instruments is used for the testing. The specimen is placed in its holder and subjected to a small, time-varying sinusoidally oscillating force. The phase shift between the applied stress and the corresponding strain is measured.

2.3 Differential Scanning Calorimetry

Composites exhibit changes in material properties such as volume, enthalpy, heat capacity, thermal expansion and tensile modulus as the material is heated through glass transition temperature, T_g and it goes from glass to rubbery state. DSC is performed with the help of Mettler using Star SW 8.1 analyzer to measure T_g. The temperature is programmed in the range of 25°–300 °C with a heating rate of 10 °C/min in nitrogen atmosphere with a flow rate of 30 ml/min.

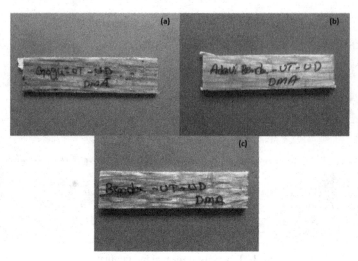

Fig. 3. Specimens for DMA(a) kfc (b) tfc (c) ofc.

2.4 Scanning Electron Microscopy

The morphology of the fractured surfaces of the composites is studied by Scanning Electron Microscopy (SEM) using EVOMA15 Smart SEM. SEM reveals the quality of fiber-matrix bond bonding that mainly affects the properties of the composite. A small electron beam spot (usually circa 1 μm) scans the fractured surfaces repeatedly. The importance of SEM is that it produces images that are similar to those of a large scale piece and even the irregularities on the surface of the material can be observed.

Before performing SEM, the surfaces of the fractured specimens are coated with platinum. They are placed on the stub and then inserted into the scanning barrel. The atmosphere in the scanning barrel is vacuumed to prevent interference effects on then scanned picture due to presence of air. Magnification, focus, contrast and brightness of the pictures are adjusted to produce the best micrographs.

3   Results and Discussion

3.1 Dynamic Mechanical Properties

The storage modulus is useful in assessing the molecular basis of the mechanical properties of the material. This property is very sensitive to the structural changes occurring at the fiber matrix interface due to variations in the degree of bonding. In order to analyze the DMA data, the storage modulus, loss modulus and tan δ are plotted against the temperature. Figure 4(a) shows the storage modulus of the untreated kfc, tfc and ofc. At room temperature, the initial storage modulus of kfc-ut, ofc-ut and tfc-ut are 7.85 GPa, 6.4 GPa and 6.3 GPa respectively. Nevertheless, it is important to emphasize the composite behavior at high temperatures. However, the storage modulus E′ gradually decreases with increase in temperature as the matrix softens and the drop is maximum in the temperature range between 50 °C–120 °C. At, the values of storage modulus are equal and are again matching from onwards for the three composites. The tfc (ut) has higher storage modulus between 50 °C–100 °C. The tfc fibers are basically stiffer than kenaf and okra fiber and could have resulted in the variation of the storage modulus. Onset of drop of modulus corresponds to the molecular mobility of the matrix.

The variation of storage modulus at different temperatures for treated kfc, tfc and ofc are presented in Fig. 4(b). At room temperature, the initial storage modulus of treated kfc, ofc and tfc are 8 GPa, 8.28 GPa and 4.9 GPa. The storage modulus and the thermal transition temperatures of the composites have shifted to higher values when the treated fibers are used. NaOH treatment has resulted in increase of storage modulus of the ofc-t and kfc-t by 31.63% and 2% compared to the ofc-ut and kfc-ut composites. It suggests that the surface treatment of fibers has increased the interfacial adhesion. In case of tfc, the treatment has resulted in 21.9% decrease of storage modulus. The loss modulus, E'' of the untreated kfc, tfc and ofc has reached a maximum value as the storage modulus, E' has decreased which can be seen in Fig. 4(c) and (d). This behavior is produced by the free movement of the polymeric chains at higher temperatures. The initial values of E'' for the composites studied are listed in Table 1. The change in slope of the loss modulus, E'' spectrum represents β-transition and it is clearly visible in loss modulus curves of the treated and untreated composites.

Unlike the curves shown in Fig. 4(e) for the kfc-ut, tfc-ut and ofc-ut, the loss modulus curves for the kfc-t, tfc-t and ofc-t shown in Fig. 4(f) are very much dispersed. It can be noted that the surface treatment of the fibers has increased the tan δ value for kfc-t from 0.22 at 76.2 °C to 0.24 at 81.6 °C, for tfc-t from 0.22 at 95.6 °C to 0.25 at 84.5 °C. But the tan δ has reduced for ofc-t from 0.21 at 81.7 °C to 0.19 at 104.5 °C upon surface treatment.

Increase in the value of T_g of kfc-t and ofc-t is taken as a measure of the increased interfacial interaction upon treatment. The presence of more fiber content in the composite reduces the magnitude of the peak value of tan δ. Decrease in tan δ for untreated tfc is probably due to the participation of more number of fibers in bending. The increase in width at the peak of the tan δ curve for the treated ofc is due to molecular relaxations that took place due to rise of temperature of the composite during loading process. The molecular motions generally contribute to the damping of the material apart from those of the constituents. Increase in peak height in kfc is due to the decrease in stress transfer from fiber to matrix because of fiber agglomeration and increase in fiber to fiber contact. Slight reduction in tan δ for the treated ofc composites compared to that of the untreated ofc. This indicates the restricted mobility of the molecules due to the stronger interfacial addition between fiber and the resin. Further, decrease in tan δ indicates an improvement of the fatigue property. The shift of the tan δ curves towards right into the higher temperature range is an indication of the presence of certain process that has restricted the mobility of the chains in the crystalline phase so that more energy is required for the transition. Therefore, it seems that natural fibers restricted the matrix polymer chains and increased the transition temperature.

Low values of tan δ associated with glass transition temperature of ofc-t reflects improved load bearing properties of the system. Reduction in tan δ represents an increase of storage modulus compared to loss modulus measured at the same temperature. An inherently high elasticity of the cellulose fibers might have contributed for the higher value of storage modulus and decrease in tan δ.

Cellulose content of Kenaf: 55%; Thespesia lampas: 60.6%; okra: 60–70% and tensile strength of Kenaf: 504.8 MPa; Thespesia lampas: 573 MPa; okra; 234–380 MPa; Young's modulus of Kenaf: 51.8 GPa; Thespesia lampas: 61.2 GPa; okra-5–13 GPa; It shows that okra fiber is a low strength fiber with high cellulose content among the three. High cellulose content has made it superior with high storage modulus compared to other two types of fibers.

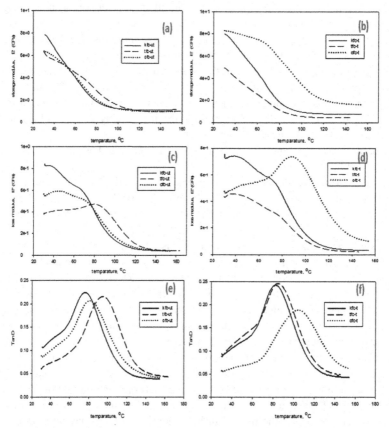

Fig. 4. (a) and (b). Storage modulus of untreated & treated fiber composites; (c) and (d): Loss modulus of untreated & treated fiber composites; (e) and (f): Dynamic Loss factor of untreated and treated fiber composites.

The storage modulus, loss modulus and the damping factor and the temperature at which test is conducted are given in Table 1. Generally, for hard plastics, the damping factor tan δ equal to 0.01–0.1 is considered as low damping, 0.1–1 as medium and >1 as high damping.

Table 1. Dynamic mechanical analysis data

Composite	Temp °C	E′ GPa	E″ GPa	Tan δ
kfc-ut	30.83	7.85	0.84	0.107
kfc-t	30.25	8.01	0.76	0.094
tfc-ut	30.09	7.31	0.39	0.061
tfc-t	30.06	4.93	0.44	0.088
ofc-ut	30.06	7.40	0.57	0.088
ofc-t	30.13	8.29	0.48	0.057

Table 2. Comparison of glass transition temperature.

Composite	T_g (°C) from			
	Tan δ peak	E′	E″	DSC
kfc-ut	77.2	66.4	67.2	72.8
kfc-t	81.9	61.5	71.9	71.7
tfc-ut	95.6	54.9	79.6	73.7
tfc-t	84.5	51.0	75.5	72.2
ofc-ut	81.7	49.3	70.8	74.4
ofc-t	104.6	67.2	88.5	73.9

3.2 Glass Transition Temperature

The transition of a polymeric material from glassy to rubbery state has been recognized as an important material property. From the curves of storage modulus, $E′$, loss modulus $E″$ and tan δ, the glass transition temperature, T_g can be found either from the first inflection point of the storage modulus curve or from the peak of loss modulus curve or from the peak of tan δ curve. ASTM D 4065 suggests that T_g to be taken as the peak of the loss modulus. The glass transition temperature of the material using DMA generally varies up to 25 °C due to the difference in methods adopted. The T_g from a DMA curve is slightly higher than the T_g measured using DSC as indicated in Table 2. Increase in glass transition temperature (T_g) of kfc-t and ofc-t is taken as a measure of the increased interfacial interaction upon treatment.

3.3 Scanning Electron Microscopy

The surface morphology of kfc-ut can be clearly seen in Fig. 5(a), wherein the individual fibers are protruding at the fracture surface. This indicates the poor wetting characteristic of the untreated Kenaf fiber (kfc-ut). The fracture surface of the kfc-t shown in Fig. 5(b) exhibits a relatively better bonding between fiber and the matrix. Contrary to the pull out of fibers in case of kfc-ut, there is a sharp breakage of fibers in case of kfc-t.

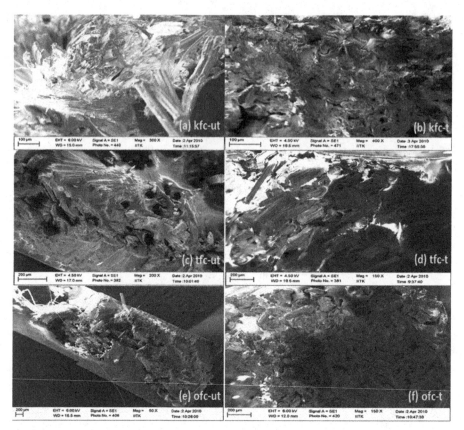

Fig. 5. SEM micrograph for fractured surface of (a) kfc-ut, (b) kfc-t. (c) tfc-ut, (d) tfc-t, (e) ofc-ut, (f) ofc-t.

The SEM image of the fractured tfc-ut shown in Fig. 5(c) the phenomenon of fiber pull out is clearly seen with many left out holes in the matrix. This indicates a week fiber-matrix interface due to poor interfacial bonding. The fibers are seen to be protruding from the fracture surface indicating considerable elongation of the fibers before fracture. This elongation of the fibers can be considered as the absence of brittleness in the untreated Thespesia lampas fibers.

In the fractograph shown in Fig. 5(d) for tfc-t, clearly indicates a better interfacial adhesion and good wetting demonstrating a strong bonding with a paucity of traces of fiber pull out in the matrix. In addition, a sharp breakage of the fibers without any trace of elongation is observed near the fractured surface of the composite. This can be understood as the phenomenon of increase in the stiffness of the fibers due to alkali treatment.

The fracture surface of the ofc-ut shown in Fig. 5(e) clearly indicates a poor compatibility of the matrix and the fiber depicting poor adhesion between matrix and the fibers. It also indicates a poor penetration of the matrix with the absence of matrix around the fibers. This is due to lack of proper wetting of the fibers in an ofc-ut. However, there is an improved bonding with less fiber pullout and better fiber dispersion of the matrix is observed in ofc-t composites as shown in Fig. 5(f). We can clearly see that no voids are visible between the matrix and the fiber as it is observed in case of the ofc-ut.

Thus the data obtained in DMA is highly indicative of the complex behavior of the material for the dynamic mechanical loading as well as temperature applications. Changes during the transition of a polymeric material from glassy to rubbery state can be observed by dynamic mechanical analysis. Similar to other properties, the dynamic mechanical properties depend on the type of fiber, length of fiber, fiber orientation, fiber dispersion and fiber-matrix adhesion.

4 Conclusions

- Higher storage modulus and glass transition temperature and lowest damping factor is noted for treated okra fiber composite (ofc-t). Good interfacial bonding as a result of NaOH treatment is observed in the SEM micrographs which has resulted in the superior properties.
- Loss modulus is highest for kfc-ut and hence the damping ratio is also high. Relatively low stiffness of kenaf fibers could have resulted in higher energy absorption.
- Highest glass transition temperature can be noted based on damping factor compared to other parameters. It is comparable with the value obtained by Differential scanning calorimetry.

References

1. Ku, H., Wang, H., Pattarachaiyakoop, N., Trada, M.: A review on the tensile properties of natural fiber reinforced polymer composites. Compos. B Eng. 42(4), 856–873 (2011)
2. Towo, A.N., Ansell, M.P.: Fatigue evaluation and dynamic mechanical thermal analysis of sisal fiber–thermosetting resin composites. Compos. Sci. Technol. 68(3–4), 925–932 (2008)
3. Sreekumar, P.A., et al.: Effect of chemical treatment on dynamic mechanical properties of sisal fiber-reinforced polyester composites fabricated by resin transfer molding. Compos. Interfaces 15(2–3), 263–279 (2008)
4. Sreekumar, P.A., et al.: Dynamic mechanical properties of sisal fiber reinforced polyester composites fabricated by resin transfer molding. Polym. Compos. 30(6), 768–775 (2009)
5. Oladele, I.O., Omotoyinbo, J.A., Adewara, J.O.T.: Investigating the effect of chemical treatment on the constituents and tensile properties of sisal fiber. J. Miner. Mater. Charact. Eng. 9(6), 569–582 (2010)
6. Akil, H.M., Mazuki, A.A.M., Safiee, S., Ishak, Z.A.M., Bakar, A.: A study on dynamic mechanical properties of pultruded kenaf fiber reinforced composites. In: The 7th Asian-Australian Conference on Composite Materials (ACCM), 15–18 November 2010, Taipei, Taiwan (2010)
7. Aziz, S.H., Ansell, M.P.: The effect of alkalization and fibre alignment on the mechanical and thermal properties of kenaf and hemp bast fibre composites: part 1 - polyester resin matrix. Compos. Sci. Technol. 64(9), 1219–1230 (2004)
8. Mylsamy, K., Rajendran, I.: Influence of alkali treatment and fiber length on mechanical properties of short Agave fiber reinforced epoxy composites. Mater. Des. 32(8–9), 4629–4640 (2011)

9. Ornaghi Jr., H.L., Bolner, A.S., Fiorio, R., Zattera, A.J., Amico, S.C.: Mechanical and dynamic mechanical analysis of hybrid composites molded by resin transfer molding. J. Appl. Polym. Sci. **118**, 887–896 (2010)

10. Ornaghi Jr., H.L., da Silva, H.S.P., Zattera, A.J., Amico, S.C.: Dynamic mechanical properties of curaua composites. J. Appl. Polym. Sci. **125**, E110–E116 (2012)

11. Duc, F., Bourban, P.-E., Manson, J.-A.E.: Dynamic mechanical properties of epoxy/flax fibre composites. J. Reinf. Plast. Compos. **33**(17), 1625–1633 (2014)

12. Costa, C.S.M.F., Fonseca, A.C., Serra, A.C., Coelho, J.F.J.: Dynamic mechanical thermal analysis of polymer composites reinforced with natural fibers. Polym. Rev. **56**(2), 362–383 (2016)

13. Sezgin, H., Berkalp, O.B., Mishra, R., Militky, J.: Investigation of dynamic mechanical properties of jute/carbon reinforced composites. World Acad. Sci. Eng. Technol. Int. J. Mater. Metall. Eng. **10**(12), 1492–1495 (2016)

14. Monteiro, S.N., et al.: A promising reinforcement for polymer composites. Polymers **10**(246), 1–10 (2018)

15. Surya Nagendra, P., Prasad, V.V.S., Ramji, K.: A study on dynamic mechanical analysis of natural nano banana particle filled polymer matrix composites. Mater. Today Proc. **4**, 9081–9086 (2017)

16. Palanivel, A., Veerabathiran, A., Duruvasalu, R., Iyyanar, S., Velumayil, R.: Dynamic mechanical analysis and crystalline analysis of hemp fiber reinforced cellulose filled epoxy composite. Polímeros **27**(4), 309–319 (2017)

17. Rashid, B., Leman, Z., Jawaid, M., Ghazali, M.J., Ishak, M.R.: Dynamic mechanical analysis of treated and untreated sugar palm fibre-based phenolic composites. BioResources **12**(2), 3448–3462 (2017)

18. Saba, N., Jawaid, M., Alothman, O.Y., Parida, M.T.: A review on dynamic mechanical properties of natural fibre reinforced polymer composites. Constr. Build. Mater. **106**, 149–159 (2016)

19. Pothan, L.A., Oommenb, Z., Thomas, S.: Dynamic mechanical analysis of banana fiber reinforced polyester composites. Compos. Sci. Technol. **63**, 283–293 (2003)

20. Romanzini, D., Ornaghi Jr., H.L., Amico, S.C., Zattera, A.J.: Influence of fiber hybridization on the dynamic mechanical properties of glass/ramie fiber-reinforced polyester composites. J. Reinf. Plast. Compos. **31**(23), 1652–1661 (2012)

21. Jacob, M., Francis, B., Thomas, S., Varughese, K.T.: Dynamical mechanical analysis of sisal/oil palm hybrid fiber-reinforced natural rubber composites. Polym. Compos. **27**(6), 671–680 (2006)

22. Abdullaha, A.H., Jamaludin, A.H.B.: Dynamic mechanical analysis of Arenga Pinnata fibre reinforced epoxy composites: effects of fibre aging. In: MATEC Web of Conferences, vol. 27, article no. 02001 (2015)

23. Chaudhary, V., Bajpai, P.K., Maheshwari, S.: An investigation on wear and dynamic mechanical behavior of jute/hemp/flax reinforced composites and its hybrids for tribological applications. Fibers Polym. **19**(2), 403–415 (2018)

24. Selvakumar, K., Meenakshisundaram, O.: Mechanical and dynamic mechanical analysis of jute and human hair-reinforced polymer composites. Polymer Compos., 1–10 (2018)

25. Nimanpure, S., Hashmi, S.A.R., Kumar, R., Nigrawal, A., Naik, A.: Electrical and dynamic mechanical analysis of sisal fibril reinforced epoxy composite. IEEE Trans. Dielectr. Electr. Insul. **25**(5), 2020–2028 (2018)

Synthesis and Characterization of β–Wollastonite from Limestone and Rice Husk as Reinforcement Filler for Clay Based Ceramic Tiles

Chirotaw Getem[1] and Nigus Gabbiye[2(✉)]

[1] School of Mechanical and Chemical Engineering, Kombolcha Institute of Technology, Wollo University, P.O. Box 208, Kombolcha, Ethiopia
chirotawgetem@gmail.com
[2] Faculty of Chemical and Food Engineering, Bahir Dar Institute of Technology, Bahir Dar University, P.O. Box 26, Bahir Dar, Ethiopia
nigushabtu@gmail.com

Abstract. This work focuses on the synthesis of β–Wollastonite and utilized as reinforcement filler for ceramic tile. β–Wollastonite was synthesized by taking the raw limestone as a lime precursor and rice husk as a source of silica. The lime and silica powders were mixed with 1:1 w/w ratio and then calcined at 900 °C for 4 h. The ceramic tiles were prepared by solid slip casting method for a wide range of β–wollastonite to clay ratio (5, 15 and 25%), particle size of 63, 75 and 125 μm at firing temperature of 950, 1000 and 1050 °C. The results show that a minimum linear shrinkage of 1.25% was recorded at 25% β–wollastonite-clay ratio with a particle size of 125 μm at a temperature of 950 °C. The ceramic tiles fabricated were exhibited minimum water absorption of 1.35% and maximum compressive strength of 38.35 MPa at 25% of β–wollastonite to clay ratio, particle size of 63 μm and 1050 °C firing temperature. Similarly, the maximum acid resistance of 99.985% was found on 75 and 125 μm particle sizes with a 25% ratio of β-Wollastonite and 950 °C firing temperature.

Keywords: Ceramic tile · Clay · β–wollastonite · Limestone · Rice husk

1 Introduction

Ceramic tiles are a thin slab, having a full cross-section, made from clays and/or other inorganic raw materials and an important construction material used in almost all construction sectors. The production of ceramic tiles starts from raw material, grinding and mixing and usually shaped at room temperature, then dried and subsequently fired at a temperature sufficient to develop the required properties [1]. The quality and cost of the final product of ceramic tiles depend on the composition of raw materials, firing cycle [2], mixing proportions [3] and particle size of the starting materials [4].

In developing countries, there is a great shortage of ceramic tile materials. For example, local materials are often used, like soil, stone, grass and palm leaves for roofs.

© ICST Institute for Computer Sciences, Social Informatics and Telecommunications Engineering 2020
Published by Springer Nature Switzerland AG 2020. All Rights Reserved
N. G. Habtu et al. (Eds.): ICAST 2019, LNICST 308, pp. 695–706, 2020.
https://doi.org/10.1007/978-3-030-43690-2_53

These roofs are characterized by their weak strength and have a low resistant to harsh environmental conditions such as rain. Currently, materials like corrugated iron sheets and asbestos cement sheets have replaced the traditional construction materials. The corrugated iron sheet roofs in tropical areas give a poor indoor climate and make a lot of noise when it rains and needs a lot of energy during their production. Asbestos cement sheets should not even be thought-about, due to health hazards [5].

Ceramic tiles are characterized by their weak plastic deformation properties, as a result, catastrophic failure takes place and also minor crack propagate quickly to critical sizes. Besides, ceramic tiles surfaces can allow water and contaminants to enter into and exit which often permeating into cavities behind the tiles, corroding the bonding agent, the substrate itself or perhaps the ceramic tile. It is very difficult to clean, over time they become dirty and have to be removed physically or mechanically; laborious and costly undertaking [6].

During the production of ceramic tile high amount of feldspars is added [7]. However, feldspar particles tend to stick to each other like socks with static cling from the dryer. Tiny bits of feldspar adhere to one another and resist being mixed into the clay body as individual particles. Therefore, replacing the existing material formulation of tiles and their properties by incorporating natural fibrous into its starting materials is a key step. Thus, in this research work the potential application of β–wollastonite as reinforcement filler for clay-based ceramic tile was investigated. β–wollastonite is composed of CaO and SiO_2 with the chemical formula of β–$CaSiO_3$ [8].

2 Materials and Methods

2.1 Materials and Chemicals

The primary raw materials were rice husk, limestone and clay. Rice husk was collected from local rice producers and millers located at Fogera Woreda, South Gonder, Ethiopia, where there is a high production of rice. Limestone and clay were collected from Abbay Gorge and Addis Zemen, Ethiopia, respectively. HCl (35.4%) was used for soaking of rice husk to remove soluble minerals. NaOH (97%) and H_2SO_4 (98%) were used for extraction of silica from rice husk ash and to extract silica gel from sodium silicate solution.

2.2 Methods

Extraction of Silica from Rice Husk (RH): Silica was extracted from RH by using alkaline extraction followed by acid precipitation [9]. RH was sieved and washed with water to removes dirties or impurities. Then, it was soaked in a solution of 1N HCl for 8 h to remove impurities attached on it and to make easy for calcination. After leached with HCl, it was washed again with distilled water until the pH became neutral. Then dried by sun light for about 48 h and calcined in an electric furnace at 700 °C for 6 h. 10 g of Rice Husk Ash (RHA) was dispersed in 60 ml, 2.5 M solution of NaOH for 2 h at 60 °C [10]. The silica content of the RHA leached out to the aqueous phase of the dispersion in the form of soluble sodium silicate according to Eq. 1 [11].

$$SiO_2(RHA) + 2NaOH \rightarrow Na_2SiO_3 + H_2O \tag{1}$$

The resulting sodium silicate solution was filtered using 110 mm filter paper in a vacuumed filtration condition. The filtrate was allowed to cool to room temperature and then acidified with 2N H_2SO_4, which precipitated the dissolved silicate in the form of white gelatinous solid with constant stirring to neutral pH. The precipitation using H_2SO_4 occurred according to Eq. 2 [12].

$$Na_2SiO_3 + H_2SO_4 \rightarrow SiO_2 + Na_2SO_4 + H_2O \tag{2}$$

Silica gels started to precipitate when the pH decreased to less than 10 followed by aging for 20 h. The gels were then dried at 80 °C for 12 h.

Experimental Procedure for Preparation of Lime (CaO): Limestone was soaked for three days in distilled water. Then, it was removed and washed again to avoid unwanted impurities that attached on the surface and dried at 105 °C in an oven for 24 h. The dried limestone was subjected to a disk mill for size reduction (0.1 mm). Then, it was washed using distilled water to remove the remain and water-soluble components and dried at 105 °C for 24 h. and calcined at 950 °C in an electric furnace for 5 h [13].

Synthesize of β–Wollastonite (β–CaSiO₃): β–wollastonite was synthesized by mixing of CaO and SiO_2 with 1:1 w/w ratio [14]. Distilled water was added to the mixtures under vigorous mixing at 500 rpm and temperature of 70 °C for 4 h. The resulting solution was kept at room temperature for 24 h and then decanted to obtain a precipitate. The precipitate was dried in an oven for 20 h at a temperature of 100 °C and then calcined in an electric furnace at a temperature of 900 °C for 4 h [15]. The prepared materials are kept in an inert atmosphere for subsequent characterization and manufacturing of the ceramic tile.

Manufacturing of Ceramic Tiles: Clay was separated manually from its impurities and soaked in water for three days and washed to remove unwanted matter. Then, it was dried for overnight in an oven at 105 °C and then introduced into disk mill followed by Ultra centrifugal mill. The powdered clay was then passed through a sieve with a nominal aperture of 75 μm whereas the β-wollastonite was sieved with the nominal aperture of 63, 75 and 125 μm. β-wollastonite was blended with clay at three different proportions (weight percentage) (5%, 15% and 25%). Then, water was poured into the mixture under vigorous mixing until the mixtures were easy to work by hand and allowed to stand for 16 h. The mixtures were cast into rectangular ($120 \times 65 \times 8$ mm^3) formwork (mold) and compacted by applied uniform force. The green tiles formed were then covered and kept in the cupboard for two days in an open air to slowly loss its moisture content. After this, the tiles were opened and then dried at 105 °C in an oven for 24 h. The dried tiles were loaded into the furnace and heated at 5 °C/min until 250 °C and hold at this temperature for 30 min. Then, the temperature was gradually increased to 950, 1000 and 1050 °C at a heating rate of 10 °C/min and allowed for 1 h to ensure complete firing. The tiles were then allowed to cool inside the furnace to room temperature and kept carefully for final characterization and testing.

2.3   Characterization and Material Testing

Fourier Transforms Infrared Spectroscopy (FTIR): FTIR spectroscopic tool is employed to identify the key functional groups of the extracted and synthesized products. Structural changes within the samples. A sample of 1 mg (<63 μm) was mixed with 100 mg of KBr and then pressed to prepare the pellets. The FTIR spectrum was recorded over a wavenumber range of 4000–400 cm^{-1} with a 4 cm^{-1} resolution and ordinate unit of transmittance (%).

Powder X-ray Diffraction (XRD): The crystalline structure of the synthesized material was characterized via XRD. The X-ray patterns were taken from radiation source Cu-Kα1 ($\lambda = 1.540593$ Å) by supplying 40 kV to X-ray generator. Spectra were observed from 0 to 60° at a step size of 0.02°.

Linear Shrinkage (LS) Test: The linear shrinkage test was determined for fired ceramic tile samples. The tiles length of the green body and the fired body was measured and determined using ASTM C356-03 method [16].

Water Absorption (WA) Test: The fired ceramic tiles were weighed, immersed in water and boiled for 2 h. Then, it was cooled to room temperature and stand for 12 h. The tiles then removed and the surface water wiped off and weighed. The absorption was determined using ASTM C373-88 method [17].

Acid Resistance Test (ART): To analyze the ceramic specimen's acid resistance test, the specimens were crushed and sieved in 2 mm sieve. Then, weigh a 10 g of crushed tile samples and immersed into 25 ml of acidic solution (0.5 M H_2SO_4) at 80 °C for 48 h. After this treatment, the specimens were successively washed with distilled water, dried at 80 °C for 24 h and weighed [18];

$$\text{Weight Loss (\%)} = \frac{\text{Intial weight} - \text{Final weight}}{\text{Intial weight}} \times 100 \qquad (3)$$

Compressive Strength (CS) Test: The compressive strength tests of the ceramic tiles were carried out using the compressive testing machine (Model: BN62223/2000). The compressive strength of the ceramic tiles determined using Eq. 4 [19];

$$\text{Compressive strength (CS)} = \frac{\text{Crushig load}}{\text{Effective surface area of tile}} \qquad (4)$$

3   Results and Discussions

3.1   Characterization of the Precursor Materials and β-Wollastonite

FTIR Spectra Analysis: The major functional groups present in silica powder were identified by the FTIR spectra as shown in Fig. 1(a). The broadband at 3440 cm^{-1} is due to silanol hydroxyl groups (responsible for the surface OH groups of –Si–OH). The absorption peak at 1638 cm^{-1} is attributed to the adsorbed water (HOH) bending vibration mode. The water has no substantial effect on the structure of the silica powder. The peak at 1103 and 620 cm^{-1} are associated with Si–O–Si asymmetrical and symmetrical stretch vibration mode, respectively. The peak at 486 cm^{-1} is attributed to the asymmetric bending vibration mode of a Si-O-Si bond [20, 21].

Figure 1(b) shows the FTIR spectra of lime. The broadband at 1426 cm^{-1} shown the vibrational stretching of Ca-O. The sharp peak at 874 cm^{-1} was assigned to the characteristic vibration bending of the Ca-O groups. [22]. The β-Wollastonite (Fig. 1(c)) exhibited characteristic absorption bands for the vibrational bending mode of Si-O-Si and O-Si-O at 567 cm^{-1}, the vibrational stretching mode of O-Si-O at 825 cm^{-1}, vibrational mode of Si-O-Ca appeared at 1026 cm^{-1} and the vibrational stretching modes of Si-O-Si at 1115 cm^{-1}. The peak at around 1456 cm^{-1} is due to the existence of Ca-O in the structure. The broadband at about 3440 cm^{-1} in the product can be assigned to stretching vibration of Si-OH group [23].

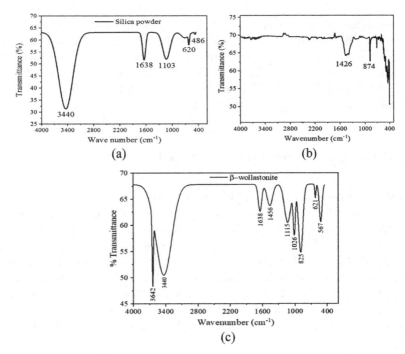

Fig. 1. FTIR spectra of (a) silica, (b) lime and (c) β–wollastonite

Powder X-ray Diffraction (XRD): The silica powder contained both the crystals (quartz) and an amorphous phase as shown in Fig. 2a. The sharper strong broad peaks were observed at $2\theta = 19.68°$, 20.18°, 20.92°, 21.4°, 27.7°, 29.38°, 31.34°, 33.1°, 33.98°, 36.68°, 37.78° and 40.86°. The major peaks of crystalline quartz occur at 2θ angles of 21.40° (d = 4.15 Å) which corresponds to a crystalline structure [24]. Figure 2b shows the powder X-Ray Diffraction pattern of lime. The lime was in the crystalline phase with one strong sharp peak and many low-intensity peaks. As can be seen in the figure, the peaks are observed at 2θ of 23.30°, 28.32°, 31.76°, 34.66°, 39.36°, 41.28°, 44.68°, 48.46°, 52.72°, 53.76° and 56.08°. The major peak was observed at 2θ equal to 34.66° (d = 2.59 Å).

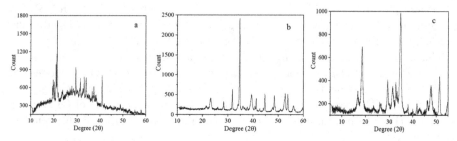

Fig. 2. X-Ray Diffraction of silica (a), lime (b) and β–wollastonite (c)

The phase formation behavior of β-wollastonite during calcination process was investigated using XRD as shown in Fig. 2c. It seems that almost all peaks were related to triclinic β-wollastonite of maximum relative intensity (98.8%) at a diffraction angle of 2θ equal to 34.5° (d = 2.6 Å), with the small amount of amorphous phase. The peaks obtained for β-wollastonite from XRD results at 2θ are 16.56°, 18.3°, 29.1°, 31.2°, 32.51°, 33.01°, 34.5°, 41.62°, 45.93°, 47.63° and 51.22°.

3.2 Effect of Operating Conditions on Ceramic Tile Properties

Effect of Operating Conditions on Linear Shrinkage
As it can be seen in Fig. 3a, the linear shrinkage of ceramic tile is increased with the firing temperature. The average values are 3.47%, 4.54% and 6.06% for firing temperature of 950 °C, 1000 °C and 1050 °C, respectively. A similar result have been reported elsewhere [25, 26] that the linear shrinkage of ceramic tiles is increased with the firing temperature. In contrast, linear shrinkage is decreased as the particle size increased (Fig. 3a) because coarse particle requires more energy and time to complete densification. Besides, a coarse particle has a small specific surface area which limit the densification process [27]. The average values are 5.32%, 4.77% and 3.98% for the particle size of 63, 75 and 125 μm, respectively.

The average linear shrinkage values are 6.53%, 4.68% and 2.87% for 5%, 15% and 25% of β-Wollastonite concentration, respectively (Fig. 3b). It seems that the ceramic tiles with high β-wollastonite concentration exhibited low linear shrinkage because of the low shrinkable tendency of β-wollastonite mineral [28, 29]. The linear shrinkage is decreased when the ratio of β–wollastonite to clay increased even at high firing temperature (1050 °C). Since, the formation of calcium aluminosilicates seems to involve a smaller amount of liquid phase during sintering, thereby resulting in a smaller firing shrinkage [30]. One of the methods for controlling firing shrinkage is the use of various calcium-containing materials [31].

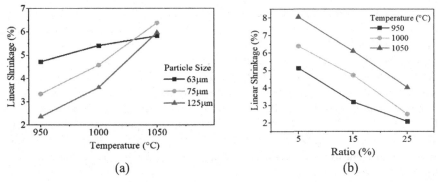

Fig. 3. Effect of firing temperature and particle sizes (a) and ratio of β–Wollastonite and firing temperature (b) on the linear shrinkage of ceramic tiles for different

Effect of Operating Conditions on Water Absorption

The result of water absorption of ceramic tiles is shown in Fig. 4(a) and (b). As it can be seen in Fig. 4(a), the water absorption of ceramic tiles decreased from 23.57% (15.47% to 11.82%) to 64.15% (11.82% to 4.24%), when the temperature increases from 950 °C to 1050 °C. The pore present in ceramic bodies during ceramic processing is filled due to the grain starts growing in the hole part of the ceramic body. The lower temperature used was insufficient to promote densification and consequently, promote substantial closing the porosity.

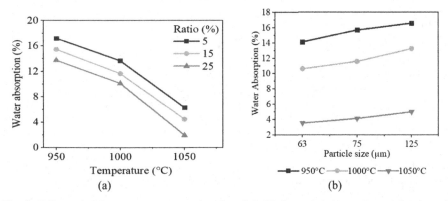

Fig. 4. Effect of firing temperature and ratio of β–Wollastonite (a) and particle size of β–wollastonite and firing temperature (b) on the water absorption of ceramic tiles

The water absorption of ceramic tiles is directly related to porosity and decreased when the firing temperature is increased [32]. Similarly, the water absorption is reduced by 30.6% (12.4, 10.53 and 8.6%) when the ratio of β-wollastonite increased from 5 to 25% (Fig. 4(a)). The presence of β–wollastonite in a high concentration increases the green body density during pressing and reduces the formation of pinholes in the firing stage, as a result, water absorption is decreased [33].

The average water absorption of ceramic tiles is 9.43%, 10.48% and 11.62% for particle size of 63, 75 and 125 μm, respectively (Fig. 4(b)). The water absorption increased with the particle size because of the coarse particle are less compacted and encourage the formation of voids in casting and pressing stages, as a result, it is easy to create pinholes at firing stage. Vieira and Monteiro were found that the water absorption of ceramic tiles is increased with the particle size of starting materials [34]. When the firing temperature raised from 950 to 1050 °C the water absorption of ceramic tiles is decreased from 14.12% to 3.55%, 15.69% to 4.15% and 16.59% to 5.02 for particle size 63 μm, 75 μm and 125 μm, respectively. During firing stage, fine particle accelerates the densification process, decreasing the open porosity as compared to ceramic tiles contained coarse particles of β–wollastonite.

Effect of Operating Conditions on Acid Resistance

Figure 5a shows the weight losses of ceramic tile samples are increased with firing temperature. The average weight losses of ceramic samples are 0.031%, 0.043% and 0.063% for firing temperature of 950 °C, 1000 °C and 1050 °C, respectively. The firing temperature raised from 950 to 1050 °C the internal structure of ceramic tiles was started deformation and phase change. As a result, the amorphous phase easily attacked by acid solution than the crystalline phase. The acid resistance of ceramic tiles is decreased when the firing temperature increased. This is due to the phase of the ceramic starting materials have a tendency to form the amorphous phase [18].

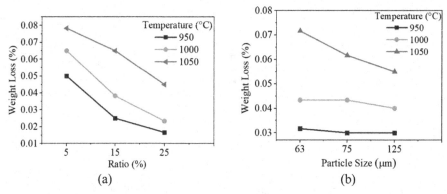

Fig. 5. Effect of firing temperature and ratio of β–wollastonite (a) and particle size of β–wollastonite and firing temperature (b) on the acid resistance of ceramic tiles

During acid etching, the alkaline metal (Ca^{2+}) ion replaced by H^+ ion and more silica-rich layer formation on the ceramic specimens. However, the concentration of β-wollastonite increased directly implies the Ca^{2+} ion concentration in the ceramic tile fabrication gives protection from the acidic condition. Because, if there is an excess alkaline metal ion present in the samples the H^+ ions are saturated and no more reaction takes place. The average weight losses of ceramic tile samples are 0.064%, 0.043% and 0.029% for 5, 15 and 25% concentration of β–wollastonite, respectively. The amount of β-wollastonite in the ceramic tile's compositions played a great role in both acid resistance and cleanability by alkaline detergent solutions [35].

Figure 5b shows the variation of the weight loss within the particle size of β-wollastonite. This test was conducted with the same particle size of ceramic tile samples (2 mm). However, the starting materials of ceramic tiles were in three different particle size of β-wollastonite (63, 75 and 125 μm). Therefore, this small variation in the acid resistance test result is due to the variation of the particle size of starting materials. The fine particles are easy to attack by acid solution compared to coarse particle since fine particle has a large specific surface area [36].

Effect of Operating Conditions on Compressive Strength
The average values are 17.21, 20.86 and 26.54 MPa for the firing temperature of 950, 1000 and 1050 °C, respectively (Fig. 6a). When the firing temperature increased the porosity of the specimens decreased for inorganic reinforcement fillers. The previous study confirms that the ceramic tiles which contain inorganic reinforcement filler, the compressive strength increased with firing temperature due to better densification [31].

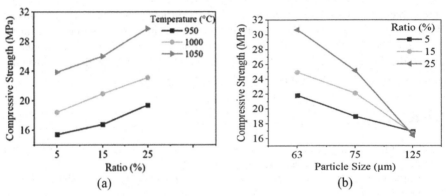

Fig. 6. Effect of firing temperature and ratio of β–Wollastonite (a) and particle size of β–Wollastonite and firing temperature (a) on the compressive strength of ceramic tiles

Moreover, there is no thermal transformation of clay to mullite below 1050 °C, mechanical strength decreases as a result of the presence of mullite [37]. On the other hand, anorthite forms from β–wollastonite and alumina at a temperature of 1025 °C. Anorthite ($CaAl_2Si_2O_8$) is considered the most effective mineral in increasing the mechanical strength of ceramic materials [38]. Consequently, the formation of anorthite is responsible for increasing the strength after adding 25% of β–Wollastonite. The average values of compressive strength for addition of 5, 15 and 25% ratio of β–Wollastonite is 19.24, 21.28 and 24.09 MPa, respectively (Fig. 6a). This implies that the compressive strength of ceramic tile is increased with the ratio of β–Wollastonite which densifies the microstructure of the ceramic tile matrix [39].

The compressive strength of ceramic tiles is decreased when the particle size of β–Wollastonite increased from 63 to 125 μm (Fig. 5b). The average values are 25.8, 22.08 and 16.73 MPa for 63, 75 and 125 μm particle size of β–Wollastonite, respectively. Many researchers agreed that the particle size and particle-size distribution directly influence the porosity which influences the compressive strength [40]. The similar finding also reported as the possibility of increasing the compressive strength (or decreasing porosity) by using a fine particle size or an optimized combination of different particle sizes is well known from other technical fields [41].

The fine particles under the influence of high temperature bonded by the particle-dissolving action and the grain grow between the particles and ultimately bond the particles together. As the boundaries between grains grow, porosity progressively decreases and pores close off.

4 Conclusion

In this study β–wollastonite was synthesized from lime and silica obtained from rice husk was tested as filler for ceramic tile production. It was found that silica as a precursor material for β–wollastonite was successfully extracted from rice husk by using alkaline extraction followed by acid precipitation with a yield of 91.34%. The synthesized β–wollastonite material with different proportion of clay was used to fabricate the ceramic tiles. Besides, the effect of particle size and firing temperature on the quality of final product was investigated. It was observed that percentage of β–wollastonite, firing temperature and particle size have an important effect on the quality of the fabricated ceramic tile. It was fond that the fabricated ceramic tiles reinforced with β–wollastonite have an acceptable material property for the intended application.

References

1. Wattanasiriwech, D., Saiton, A., Wattanasiriwech, S.: Paving blocks from ceramic tile production waste. J. Clean. Prod. **17**, 1663–1668 (2009)
2. Saleiro, G., Holanda, J.: Processing of red ceramic using a fast-firing cycle. Cerâmica **58**(347), 393–399 (2012)
3. El Ouahabi, M., et al.: Potentiality of clay raw materials from northern Morocco in ceramic industry: Tetouan and Meknes areas. J. Miner. Mater. Charact. Eng. **2**, 145–159 (2014)
4. Glymond, D., et al.: Production of ceramics from coal furnace bottom ash. Ceram. Int. **44**, 3009–3014 (2016)
5. Darsana, P., et al.: Development of coir-fibre cement composite roofing tiles. Procedia Technol. **24**, 169–178 (2016)
6. Lawrence, J., Li, L., Spencer, J.: A two-stage ceramic tile grout sealing process using a high power diode laser—II. Mechanical, chemical and physical properties. Opt. Laser Technol. **30**(3–4), 215–223 (1998)
7. Gennaro, R., et al.: Influence of zeolites on sintering and technological properties of porcelain stronware tiles. J. Eur. Ceram. Soc. **23**(13), 2237–2245 (2003)
8. Podporska, J., et al.: A novel ceramic material with medical application. Process. Appl. Ceram. **2**(1), 19–22 (2008)
9. Kamath, S.R., Proctor, A.: Silica gel from rice hull ash: preparation and characterization. Cereal Chem. **75**(75), 484–487 (1998)
10. Jembere, A.L., Fanta, S.W.: Studies on the synthesis of silica powder from rice husk ash as reinforcement filler in rubber tire tread part: replacement of commercial precipitated silica. Int. J. Mater. Sci. Appl. **6**(1), 37–44 (2017). https://doi.org/10.11648/j.ijmsa.20170601.16
11. Della, V.P., Kühn, I., Hotza, D.: Rice husk ash as an alternate source for active silica production. Mater. Lett. **57**(4), 818–821 (2002)

12. Todkar, B., Deorukhar, O., Deshmukh, S.: Extraction of silica from rice husk. Int. J. Eng. Res. Dev. **12**, 69–74 (2016)

13. Obeid, M.M.: Crystallization of synthetic wollastonite prepared from local raw materials. Int. J. Mater. Chem. **4**(4), 79–87 (2014)

14. Obradović, N., et al.: Influence of different pore-forming agents on wollastonite microstructures and adsorption capacities. Ceram. Int. **43**(10), 7461–7468 (2017)

15. Noor, A.H.M., et al.: Synthesis and characterization of wollastonite glass-ceramics from eggshell and waste glass. J. Solid St. Sci. Technol. Lett. **16**, 1–5 (2015)

16. ASTM C356-03: Standard Test Method for Linear Shrinkage of Preformed High-Temperature Thermal Insulation Subjected to Soaking Heat. Annual Book of ASTM Standards, **04**(06), ASTM, West Conshohocken, PA (2000)

17. ASTM C373-88: Standard Test Method for Water Absorption, Bulk Density, Apparent Porosity, and Apparent Specific Gravity of Fired Whiteware Products. Annual Book of ASTM Standards, **15**(02). ASTM, West Conshohocken, PA (2005)

18. Kim, B.-H., et al.: Chemical durability of β-wollastonite-reinforced glass-ceramics prepared from waste fluorescent glass and calcium carbonate. Mater. Sci. Pol. **22**(2), 83–91 (2004)

19. Odeyemi, S.O., et al.: compressive strength of manual and machine compacted sandcrete hollow blocks produced from brands of Nigerian cement. Am. J. Civ. Eng. **3**, 6–9 (2015)

20. Nariyal, R.K., Kothari, P., Bisht, B.: FTIR measurements of SiO2 glass prepared by sol-gel technique. Chem. Sci. Trans. **3**(3), 1064–1066 (2014)

21. Anjaneyulu, U., Sasikumar, S.: Bioactive nanocrystalline wollastonite synthesized by sol–gel combustion method by using eggshell waste as calcium source. Bull. Mater. Sci. **37**, 207–212 (2014)

22. Puntharod, R., et al.: Synthesis and characterization of wollastonite from egg shell and diatomite by the hydrothermal method. J. Ceram. Process. Res. **14**(2), 198–201 (2013)

23. Morsy, R., Abuelkhair, R., Elnimr, T.: Synthesis of microcrystalline wollastonite bioceramics and evolution of bioactivity. Silicon **9**, 489–493 (2017)

24. Liou, T.-H.: Preparation and characterization of nano-structured silica from rice husk. Mater. Sci. Eng. A **364**(1–2), 313–323 (2004)

25. Karaman, S., Ersahin, S., Gunal, H.: Firing temperature and firing time influence on mechanical and physical properties of clay bricks. J. Sci. Ind. Res. **65**, 153–159 (2006)

26. Klaytae, T., et al.: The effects of sintering temperature on the physical and electrical properties of SrTiO3 ceramics prepared via sol-gel combustion method. Ferroelectrics **491**(1), 79–86 (2016)

27. Bin, Z., et al.: The effect of particle size on the properties of alumina-based ceramic core. In: Zhouzhou, Y., Luo, Q. (eds.) Applied Mechanics and Materials. Trans Tech Publications, Zürich (2011)

28. Demidenko, N.I., et al.: Wollastonite as a new kind of natural material (a review). Sci. Ceram. Prod. **58**(9), 308–311 (2001)

29. Turkmen, O., Kucuk, A., Akpinar, S.: Effect of wollastonite addition on sintering of hard porcelain. Ceram. Int. **41**(4), 5505–5512 (2015)

30. Lira, C., et al.: Effect of carbonates on firing shrinkage and on moisture expansion of porous ceramic tiles. In: V World Congress on Ceramic Tile Quality-Qualicer (1998)

31. Das, S.K., et al.: Shrinkage and strength behaviour of quartzitic and kaolinitic clays in wall tile compositions. Appl. Clay Sci. **29**(2), 137–143 (2005)

32. Lin, K.-L., Lee, T.-C., Hwang, C.-L.: Effects of sintering temperature on the characteristics of solar panel waste glass in the production of ceramic tiles. J. Mater. Cycles Waste Manage. **17**(1), 194–200 (2015)

33. Tiggemann, H.M., et al.: Use of wollastonite in a thermoplastic elastomer composition. Polym. Test. **32**(8), 1373–1378 (2013)

34. Vieira, C.M.F., Monteiro, S.N.: Effect of the particle size of the grog on the properties and microstructure of bricks. In: Salgado, L., Filho, F.A. (eds.) Materials Science Forum. Trans Tech Publications, Zürich (2006)
35. Hupa, L., et al.: Chemical resistance and cleanability of glazed surfaces. Surf. Sci. **584**(1), 113–118 (2005)
36. Meddah, M.S., Zitouni, S., Belâabes, S.: Effect of content and particle size distribution of coarse aggregate on the compressive strength of concrete. Constr. Build. Mater. **24**(4), 505–512 (2010)
37. Junior, A.D.N., et al.: Influence of composition on mechanical behaviour of porcelain tile. Part II: mechanical properties and microscopic residual stress. Mater. Sci. Eng. A **527**(7–8), 1736–1743 (2010)
38. Kurama, S., Ozel, E.: The influence of different CaO source in the production of anorthite ceramics. Ceram. Int. **35**(2), 827–830 (2009)
39. Wahab, M.A., et al.: The use of Wollastonite to enhance the mechanical properties of mortar mixes. Constr. Build. Mater. **152**, 304–309 (2017)
40. Isabella, C., et al.: The effect of aggregate particle size on formation of geopolymeric gel (2003)
41. Spath, S., Drescher, P., Seitz, H.: Impact of particle size of ceramic granule blends on mechanical strength and porosity of 3D printed scaffolds. Materials **8**, 4720–4732 (2015)

Experimental Investigation of Bending Strength of Oxytenanthera Abyssinica and Yushania Alpina Bamboos

Fentahun Ayu Muche$^{(\boxtimes)}$ and Yonas Mitiku Degu

Faculty of Mechanical and Industrial Engineering, Bahir Dar Institute of Technology, Bahir Dar University, Bahir Dar, Ethiopia
fentahunayu30@gmail.com, yonasm@bdu.edu.et

Abstract. Bamboo has a long and well-established in many structure such as tradition building material, furniture and bicycle structure throughout the world. To use bamboo for industrial use and product fabrication, its bending strength is determinant mechanical property. The bending strength of these two species of bamboo was not studied sufficiently in Ethiopia. This research is mainly focused on the bending strength of two species of bamboo which is found abundantly in Ethiopian. Highland bamboos which are hollow and lowland bamboos are solid having scientific name of Yushania Alpine and Oxytenantheria Abyssinica respectively. Bending strength of bamboo for bending loading was experimentally tested and characterized with respect to its age and species typeSamples were prepared according to ISO standards and experiments were conducted on universal testing machine. The test results show that as the age of bamboo increased the bending strength of both Yushania alpine and Oxytenantheria abyssinica species bamboo were increased. Among the two species, Oxytenanthera abyssinica has a better bending strength compared to Yushania alpine. The bending strength of Oxytenanthera abyssinica were found 1.6, 2.9 and 2.0 times stronger than the Yushania alpine at year two, three and four respectively.

Keywords: Bending strength · Oxytenanthera abyssinica · Yushania alpina · Solid bamboo · Hollow bamboo · Highland bamboo · Lowland bamboo

1 Introduction

Bamboos are natural perennial grass-like composite and contain ligno-cellulosic-based natural fibers. Bamboos are abundantly found in tropical, subtropical and mild temperature regions. It has a fast growth rate and attains good mechanical property in short period of time. Ethiopia has got two bamboo species; both of them are native to the country, namely lowland bamboo (Oxythenanthera abyssinica) and highland bamboo (Yushania alpine). Although Ethiopia is well known in bamboo resources, the use of this resource is usually limited to traditional house construction, fences, and some rudimentary furniture and household utensils [1]. Bamboo is mainly characterized by two parts, the culm and rhizome which are steam above the ground under the ground respectively. The structure of bamboo is shown in Fig. 1 [2].

© ICST Institute for Computer Sciences, Social Informatics and Telecommunications Engineering 2020
Published by Springer Nature Switzerland AG 2020. All Rights Reserved
N. G. Habtu et al. (Eds.): ICAST 2019, LNICST 308, pp. 707–715, 2020.
https://doi.org/10.1007/978-3-030-43690-2_54

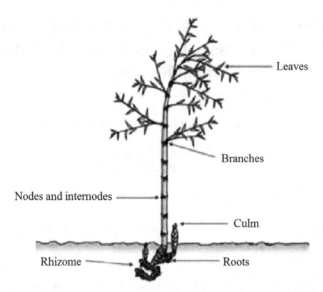

Fig. 1. Structure of bamboo plant [2]

The growth rate of bamboo is dependent on local soil and climatic conditions, as well as types of species [3].

Bamboo culms are a cylindrical shell divided by solid transversal diaphragms at nodes and have some exciting properties such as high strength in the direction parallel to the fibers, and low strength in a direction perpendicular to the fibers. Both physical and mechanical characteristics vary with respect to age, type, position along culm and moisture content in the bamboo [4, 5].

Any structure subjected to bending load has to withstand and provide the intended service for the designed life period. Hence it is critical to know the bending strength of a material before it comes to industrial or similar uses. Bending strength is the resistance of a material for bending load/lateral loading. Different researchers verified that the bending strength of various species of bamboo without node having higher bending strength than culms with nodes [6].

The bending test measures the magnitude of force required to bend specimen under three points/four point loading. In this study three point loading method was used for testing. The three point bending test induced maximum stress at the midpoint of the specimen span length. The main advantage of a three point bending test is an ease of the specimen preparation and testing [7]. Bending test is employed, in which a specimen having either a circular or rectangular cross section is bent until fracture or yielding.

So far, the bending strength of Oxytenanthera abyssinica and Yushania alpine is not studied sufficiently. The objective of the research is to test and characterize the bending strength of the two species of bamboo which are abundantly found in Ethiopia.

2 Methods and Materials

2.1 Methods

The experimental investigation was conducted following the following procedure:

The test method and specimen preparation, were done according to ISO/TR22157-2: 2004 (E) standard. This standard relates the sample length to its diameter as depicted in Fig. 2. It states that the length of the specimen should be equal to thirty times of its diameter plus half of the culm length [8].

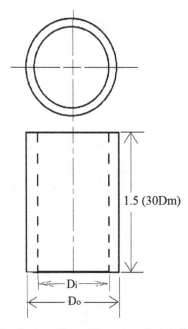

Fig. 2. Standard specimen dimensions for bending test [8]

When a beam with a straight longitudinal axis is loaded by lateral forces, the axis is deformed into a curve, called the deflection curve of the beam. The deflection (δ) at the center of the beam along the axis of the beam can be calculated using Eq. (1).

$$\delta = \frac{PL^3}{48EI} \tag{1}$$

Where:

P - Central load [N]
L - Length of the specimen [m]
E - Young's modulus, [N/m^2]
I - Second moment of area [m^4]

Second Moment of Area (I) of a hollow circular shape of the beam analyzed by using Eq. (2). For the solid bamboo consider the value of inner diameter zero.

$$I = \frac{\pi \left(Do^4 - Di^4 \right)}{64} \tag{2}$$

where:

D_o – average outer diameter of bamboo [m]
D_i – average inner diameter of bamboo [m]
D_m – Mean diameter i.e. 0.5 $(D_o + D_i)$

The bending stress induced can be analyzed analytically using Eq. (3)

$$\sigma_b = \frac{MC}{I} \tag{3}$$

$C = \frac{Do}{2}$ [m]
σ_b – bending stress [N/m^2]
M – maximum bending moment [Nm]

Figure 3 shows simply supported beam subjected to a point load at middle of the span length. And the induced stresses and deflection of a beam indicated.

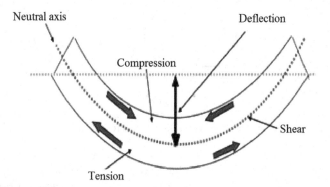

Fig. 3. Deflection and stress induced in a beam subjected to transverse load

2.2 Material

Solid bamboo and hollow bamboo were collected from Jawi and Injibara vicinity respectively for experimental investigation of the bending strength of. Specimens were prepared from the two species of Ethiopian bamboo from age two, three and four years.

A total of twenty four specimens were prepared from both species. Lowland bamboo (Oxytenantheria abyssinica/solid bamboo) and highland (Yushania alpin/hollow bamboo) bamboo found in Amhara Region around Jawi *Woreda* and at Injibara respectively.

Bamboo found around Injibara is hollow (Yushania alpine) and it has larger diameter compared to the solid (Oxytenantheria abyssinica) bamboo. Figure 4 shows the culm of both solid and hollow bamboo found in Ethiopia.

Fig. 4. Culms of hollow bamboo (left) and solid bamboo (right)

Lowland bamboos were found in Assosa is known as solid bamboo and it is distributed to Amhara region which is found at Awi *zone* around Jawi *Woreda* and around north Gonder at Kuara *Woreda*. The two species of bamboo are similar in their growth character. The lowland bamboo has a completely solid culm, with high bulk density and greater stability while the highland bamboo has a hollow culm, which is easier to process [1]. Figure 5 shows the cross section of a hollow bamboo and solid bamboo.

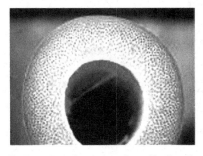 

Fig. 5. Transversal cross section of hollow bamboo (left) and solid bamboo (right) [1]

Universal testing machine (UTM), hand tools and measuring instruments were used for the specimen preparation and testing. Digital vernier caliper, steel rule and tape meter were used for measuring the dimension of the specimen during preparation and wood saw was used to cut bamboo to the required size.

Universal testing machine model type YF Zhejiang Tugong PN0206000031 WAW-1000B microcomputer controlled was used to test the three point bending strength of bamboo specimens. The capacity of the machine is 1000 kN with the load applying rating of 0.05 kN/s.

2.3 Experiment

From the bending test, deflection and bending stress of the beams subjected to lateral load can be measured but during the experiment the ultimate stress of the material were taken from the test.

The specimen preparation and test procedure followed the ISO standard. The steps followed during the sample preparation provided with seven steps.

1. Cut one meter from the bottom end of the bamboo, and measure a length of 30 times of its diameter and add half of it to get the final dimension of the specimen ().
2. Measure the diameter and thickness of the specimens at both ends and consider the average values for second moment of area and other analysis.
3. Mark the midpoint of the specimen along the span length.
4. Code the specimen for easy management of the data recording.
5. Fix the specimen on the test jig aligning the marked point of the test specimen to the load applicator (refer Fig. 6).
6. Applied steady load at the marked point until failure occurs.
7. Store results in the computer system for further analysis.

The test was conducted a three-point load method in which the load is applied at the center and two reaction loads are at the ends as shown in Fig. 6.

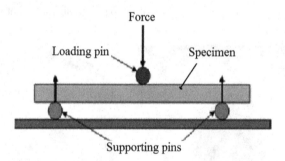

Fig. 6. Schematics for three point bending test set up

All specimens were coded based on species, position, and specimen number. Generally, the coding of both samples was given as follow:

SBYxy: SB stand for solid bamboo, Y: year, x: age in years and y: for specimen number.
HBYxy: HB stand for hollow bamboo, Y: year, x: age in years and y: for specimen number.

The two species of bamboo specimens were prepared for testing as shown in Fig. 7.

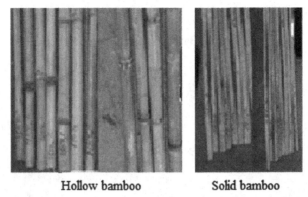

Hollow bamboo   Solid bamboo

Fig. 7. Bamboo specimens ready for bending test [Photo by the authors]

3 Results and Discussions

3.1 Results

Bending test was carried out in order to determine the maximum bending strength of bamboo due to load applied in the lateral direction. The bending test was carried out by considering age and species type as shown in Fig. 8. The ultimate strength data were recorded from the universal testing machine. The variation of bending strength with respect to age and types of species are given in Fig. 9.

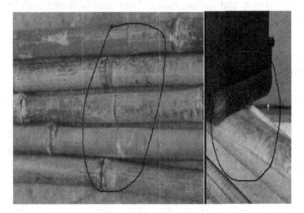

Fig. 8. Hollow bamboo specimen failure during bending test

3.2 Discussions

Bending Strength with Respect to Age: As depicted in Fig. 9, the bending strength of bamboo varies with the age increased. Lower bending strength was recorded at early age bamboos and the strength increases with the increase of age. These kinds of behavior

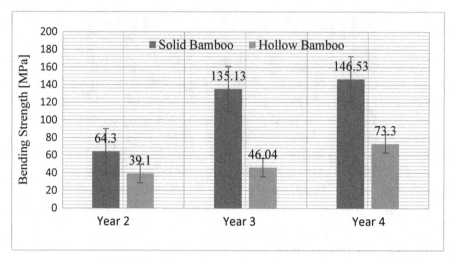

Fig. 9. Bending strength vs age and species bamboo

were observed for both solid bamboo and hollow bamboo. This is due to the fact that bamboo has higher moisture content at the early age and as the age increases fibers become interconnected with each other hence the bending strength will increase.

Bending Strength with Respect to Species: Solid bamboo is higher in bending strength than hollow bamboo. This is due to the fiber distribution of the plant. Solid bamboo is naturally dense and having more fibers than hollow bamboo which leads it to have a higher strength.

4 Conclusions

Bending strength of solid bamboo (Oxytenantheria abyssinica) for year two, three and four were 64.30 MPa, 135.13 MPa, and 146.53 MPa respectively and for hollow bamboo (Yushania alpine) of year two, three and four were 39.1 MPa, 46.04 MPa and 73.3 MPa respectively. The test result depict that for both species of bamboo higher bending strength were recorded at the age of four relative to year two and three for bending loading. This implies that both of species are recommended for higher load carrying application at year four. From the test results Oxytenantheria abyssinica has higher bending strength than the Yushania alpine species bamboo.

References

1. Bakala, F., Bekele, T., Woldeamanuel, T., Auch, E.: Value chain analysis of lowland bamboo products: the case of Homosha District, Northwestern Ethiopia. Ind. Eng. Lett. 6(10), 1–15 (2016)
2. Baldaniya Babulal, H., George, E., Patel, S.B.: Test of bamboo material for structural purpose. Indian J. Res. 2(4), 134–137 (2013). 2250-1991

3. Retrieved From Google, 20 January 2019. http://www.Dassoxtr.Com/Bamboo
4. Barmavath, S., et al.: Flexural strength of concrete by replacing bamboo in RCC beam. Int. J. Civ. Eng. Technol. (IJCIET) **8**(6), 10–18 (2017)
5. Singh, A., Kumar, S.K., Singh, A.K.: Experimental investigation on flexural strength of bamboo reinforced concrete beam. Int. J. Innov. Res. Sci. Eng. Technol. **5**(5) (2016)
6. Shao, Z.P., Zhou, L., Liu, Y.M., Wuand, Z.M., Arnaud, C.: Differences in structure and strength between internode and node sections of Moso bamboo. J. Trop. Forest. Sci. **22**(2), 133–138 (2010)
7. Baglietto, J., Kelly, C., Johnson, C.: Wood Bend Test Retrieved from Google (2013)
8. International Standard Organization/Technical report, 2.-2. Determination of physical and mechanical properties of bamboo part 2 laboratory manual (2004)

Plasma Polymer Deposition of Neutral Agent Carvacrol on a Metallic Surface by Using Dielectric Barrier Discharge Plasma in Ambient Air

Tsegaye Gashaw Getnet[1,2]([✉]) [ID], Nilson Cristino da Cruz[1], Milton Eiji Kayama[3], and Elidiane Cipriano Rangel[1]

[1] Technological Plasmas Laboratory, Paulista State University, Experimental Campus of Sorocaba, Sorocaba, SP, Brazil
tsegshchem2004@gmail.com,
{nilson.cruz,elidiane.rangel}@unesp.br, nilson@sorocaba.unesp.br
[2] Department of Chemistry, College of Science, Bahir Dar University, Bahir Dar, Ethiopia
[3] Laboratory of Plasma and Applications, Sao Paulo State University, Campus of Guaratinguetá, Guaratinguetá, SP, Brazil
milton.kayama@unesp.br

Abstract. This experiment was conducted by newly designed home-made planar type DBD plasma generator in ambient, with industrial argon as the primary plasma-forming and a carrier gas of monomer. Natural agent Carvacrol monomer was used as a precursor in order to deposit plasma polymeric thin film on the surface of metallic material. The discharge characteristics including, the plasma active power, the discharge voltage, and current were diagnosed. The applied voltage was measured by using a voltage divider and the current and the discharge-charge were measured by using the drop of voltage on a resistor and capacitor, respectively. The characteristics of the thin film deposited are presented by varying discharge conditions. The structures of the film, aging, and adhesion were characterized by infrared reflectance spectroscopy and its thicknesses and roughness by profilometry. The obtained thin film was exhibited smooth, dense, uniform, and having chemical similarity to carvacrol monomer. The obtained thin film also exhibited a high thermal resistivity, strong crosslink with good adhesion to the metallic surface. In general, the thin film can be used for practical application as the surface of a biomaterial.

Keywords: Plasma diagnostics · Dielectric barrier discharge · Plasma polymer

1 Introduction

Research in the field of low-pressure plasma has gained emphasis, mainly due to its versatility and the various results obtained in the modification of material physical-chemical properties [1]. However, the large-scale application of low-pressure plasma is mainly limited to the high cost of vacuum installations, and also on the restriction to

N. G. Habtu et al. (Eds.): ICAST 2019, LNICST 308, pp. 716–725, 2020.
https://doi.org/10.1007/978-3-030-43690-2_55

not be used in high vapor pressure materials such as living tissues [2, 3]. As a result, several alternative atmospheric or sub-atmospheric pressure plasma techniques, such as corona plasma, microwave, and micro hollow cathode discharge (MHCD), plasma torch and dielectric barrier discharge (DBD) [4, 5], are available nowadays to overcome these limitations since they do not require vacuum systems. Among those various types of plasma sources, DBD atmospheric plasma sources have drawn more attention due to their many advantages, such as low-cost and easy handling and operation [6]. In atmospheric pressure, DBD's can produce diffuse and relatively homogenous non-thermal plasma [7–9]. However, there is a need to improve the stability and repeatability of the discharge for practical and industrial application. In addition to this, as far as our knowledge, there is no study of the atmospheric dielectric discharge plasma of volatile natural agent to produce polymeric films. In this context, the present study was to investigate the use of carvacrol DBD plasma discharge to produce films on the stainless steel surface. This work also deals with the diagnosis of the argon discharge in the presence and absence of carvacrol. We choose stainless steel as a substrate due to its extensive use in many technological applications, consumer products, and biomedical applications.

2 Experimental Device and Operations

2.1 Plasma Diagnosis

In this present study, the dielectric barrier discharge (DBD) equipment was designed and built at the Laboratory of Technological Plasma (LaPTec) of Sao Paulo State University, Brazil. It consists of cylindrical brass with 2 cm in diameter and aluminum disk upper and lower electrodes, respectively. The electrodes were assembled axially with 3 mm gap and hold by circular polyacetal (Delrin) flanges (Fig. 1). The outer surface of the lower electrode was covered by a 0.1 mm thick polyester (Mylar) dielectric sheet. An atomizer with controlled temperature and gas flow rate was used to admixture the gas and the monomer, that was injected through an axial hole in the upper electrode. Argon gas was used because with ambient air in the gap it was not possible to produced filamentary discharge. The output of a neon lamp transformer with 15 kV peak-to-peak voltage with the primary controller by a variac, at 60 Hz frequency, was applied on the upper brass electrode, while the lower one was grounded. The voltage was measured with a voltage divider made with an array of $24 \times 330\,k\Omega$ resistors and $8.1\,k\Omega$ load resistor, all connected in series. The current $i(t)$ of the discharge was measured through the voltage drop on a resistor with resistance $R = 57\,\Omega$ connected between the lower electrode and the ground. The resistor was replaced by the capacitor $C = 10$ nF to measure the charge produced by the discharge. The signals were displayed and recorded using a 30 MHz and 500 MS/s resolution of two channel digital storage oscilloscope Tektronix TDS 1001C-30EDU to calculate the active power as follows:

$$P_R = \frac{1}{T} \int_t^{t+T} v_A i\, dt, \, v_A \gg v_R \tag{1}$$

$$P_C = \frac{1}{T} \int_0^Q v_A\, dq, \, v_A \gg v_C \tag{2}$$

where v_A is the applied voltage, v_R the voltage on the resistor, v_C the voltage on the capacitor, T the period, Q the charge in one period in the capacitor and q its instantaneous charge.

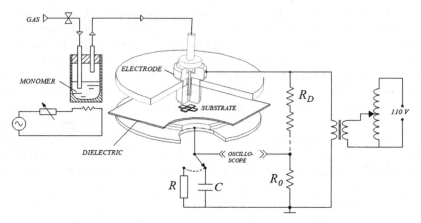

Fig. 1. Schematic representation of the experimental setup.

The chemical structure, aging, adhesion, and thermal resistivity of the films were evaluated by infrared reflectance absorbance spectroscopy (IRRAS), using a Jasco FTIR 410 spectrometer and co-adding 128 spectra with a resolution of 4 cm^{-1}. The thicknesses and roughness of the films were determined with a surface profilometer Veeco Dektak 150.

2.2 Numerical Program

The block diagrams for the numerical calculations of the Eqs. (1) and (2) are shown in the Fig. 2, codes named POWER-VI and LISSA, respectively. They were written to process the digitalized even with high signal to noise ratio. The calculation during one period is repeated as many time as possible on the recorded data. POWER-VI uses a smoothing algorithm for the applied voltage signals maintaining the original current signal. In LISSA, both signals, the applied voltage, and the capacitor voltage are smoothed by different methods. Power is calculated only on well-defined Lissajous figures. Noisy or ambiguous figures are disregarded.

3   Result and Discussion

3.1   Electrical Characteristics

Voltage and Current Waveforms
Figure 3a and b show a typical of the waveform of the current and applied voltage of the discharge of argon without and with carvacrol plasma, respectively. According to the current signal, the DBD plasma discharge worked in filamentary mode consisting

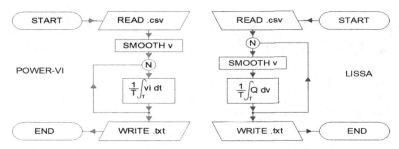

Fig. 2. Block diagrams of the numerical programs

of several micro-discharge channels with a very short time duration corresponding to the peaks on the signal [10]. This is in agreement with the photographic image of the discharge as shown in Fig. 4a and b. There is an augment on the light intensity when we add the monomer in the discharge. It is interesting to point out that the discharge regime of the argon DBD plasma was not altered by the addition of carvacrol monomer and works well for polymer deposition. However, the uniformity and intensity of the discharge are highly affected as we change the amplitude of the applied voltage, the gap of the electrodes and flow rate of the gas. That is when we increase the applied voltage keeping constant flow rate and gap distance, the intensity, and uniformity of the filamentary discharge increase in the gap between the upper electrode and dielectric, as consequence of the increase on the electric field. Similar phenomena were also observed for the increment of the flow rate of the gas. When we increase the gap, more powerful filamentary discharged was produced. On the other hand, when we place the metallic substrate in the gap, as we can see the image of the DBD plasma discharge in Fig. 4c, the discharge concentrates around the substrate. This is due to the distortion of electric field lines promoted by the sharp borders of the substrate.

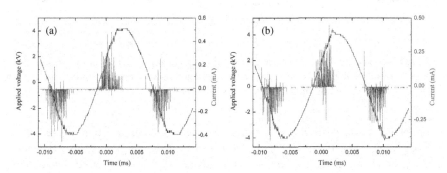

Fig. 3. Voltage and current waveforms of DBD plasma measured at 4.2 kV amplitude applied voltage with a gas flow rate of 5 L/min, (a) Ar only, (b), Ar with carvacrol.

Lissajous Figures

To further analysis of the electrical characteristics, the Q-V plots or the Lissajous figure was studied, as illustrated in Fig. 5. To generate the Lissajous figure, the x-axis is the

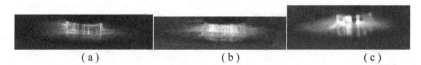

(a)   (b)   (c)

Fig. 4. Images of a DBD plasma discharge at 5.3 kV amplitude applied voltage with 5 L/min flow rate of gas (a), argon only, (b), admixture of argon and carvacrol (c), admixture of argon and carvacrol in the presence of stainless steel disk.

applied voltage in the DBD electrodes, and at the y-axis is the charge in the capacitor $q(t) = Cv_C(t)$. Regarding the shape of a Lissajous figure of the DBD filamentary discharge, it looks like a parallelogram as shown in Fig. 5a. In the Lissajous figure, the lines AB and CD represent the phase when no plasma is ignited, while lines DA and BC the phase when the plasma is formed in the gap. The slope of these lines can indicate approximately the total effective capacitance [11]. As we can see in the Lissajous figures, the area of the discharge with argon and carvacrol admixture increases when we place the metallic substrate in the gap, keeping the same remaining discharge condition. It indicates an increase of the plasma active power because of the distortion of electric field lines promoted by the sharp borders of the substrate.

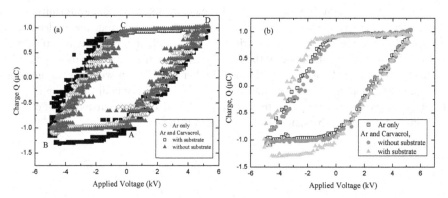

Fig. 5. A Lissajous figure of argon, an admixture of argon and carvacrol in the presence and absence of a substrate in the gap DBD plasma measured at 5.0 kV amplitude applied voltage with a gas flow rate of 5 L/min, (a), raw data, (b), smoothed data.

The active power of discharge in one cycle can be calculated from the area of the Lissajous figure [12]. But in our case, the raw data does not give the exact value of active discharge power, due to the noise in the signal (Fig. 5a). Therefore, a smoothing algorithm was used to obtain the Q-V plots. A typical result of the smoothing process is shown in the Fig. 5b. This reduced data was used to calculate the power according to Eq. 2. Figure 6a and b show the variation of the discharge power of argon only as a function of applied voltage and the gas flow rate, respectively. It is clear that the power increases from 0.4 to 1.4 W, with the applied voltage in the range 4.2–6.6 kV and flow rate of gas between 2 to 6 L/min. Figure 7a and b also shown the power as a function of applied voltage for the admixture of argon and carvacrol in the presence and absence of a substrate in the gap, respectively. The power calculated by the 57 Ω resistor is higher than the calculated by the capacitor with impedance 2.5×10^5 Ω due to the higher voltage on the discharge for the former.

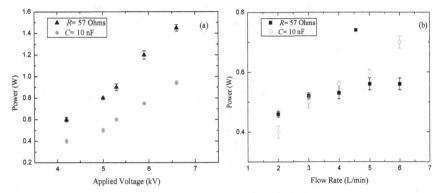

Fig. 6. The variation of the active power of argon DBD plasma at 5 L/min flow rate of gas (a) as a function of applied voltage, (b) as a function of flow rate at 5.3 kV amplitude applied voltage.

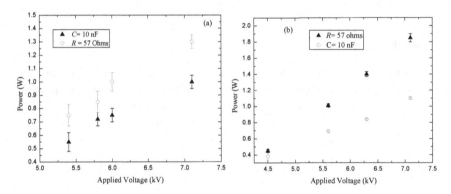

Fig. 7. Relationship between the applied voltage and the produced active power of DBD plasma discharge at 5 L/min flow rate of gas, (a) admixture of argon and carvacrol in presence of substrate (b) admixture of argon and carvacrol.

3.2   Thickness and Rate of Deposition

Polymer thin films were successfully fabricated from carvacrol monomer on both stainless steel and glass slides under different deposition time and applied voltage. Figure 8a and b show the variation of film thickness h with deposition time and applied voltage, respectively. The thickness of the film increases from 0.36 to 0.43 μm, with the applied voltage from 3.5 to 6.0 kV. After that, it declines to about 0.32 μm for further increases on the voltage up to 7.5 kV. This is due to the plasma ablation with the overvoltage.

Similarly, the thickness of the film increases with time until 30 min, and decline after this time as shown in Fig. 8b. This decrement of thickness with long disposition time may be attributed to competitive polymerization. The deposition rate also follows the same behaviour of thickness with increasing applied voltage, since the deposition time t is kept constant as shown in Fig. 7a. It is also obvious that the deposition rate increases with deposition time and decline down after a time t. In our case, similar behaviour was also observed as shown in Fig. 7b.

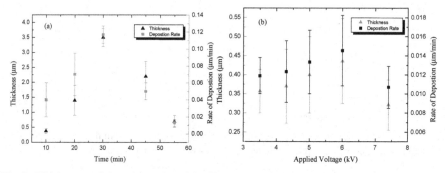

Fig. 8. Thickness and deposition rate of the film at 5 L/min flow rate of gas (a) as a function of time at 7.0 kV (b) as a function of applied voltage at 30 min deposition time.

3.3 Roughness

Figure 9 shows the roughness of the films as a function of active power on the discharge at 10 and 30 min deposition time. The roughness of the film increases with power. At 30 min it has a great deviation due to the creation of holes on the film by the filaments.

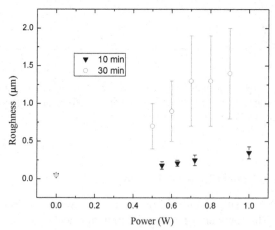

Fig. 9. The roughness of the film as a function of active power at 5 L/min gas flow rate for 10 and 30 min deposition times.

3.4 Chemical Structural Analysis

To complete the structure characterization, FTIR spectra analysis of the monomer (carvacrol) was also carried out in addition to the plasma polymerized carvacrol thin films as shown in Fig. 10a.

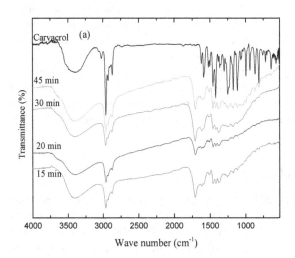

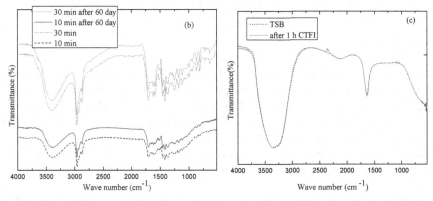

Fig. 10. IR spectra of carvacrol polymer thin film at 0.55 ± 0.06 W active power with 5 L/min flow rate of gas (a) by varying deposition time, (b) after 2 months expose in the air (c) IR spectra of TSB before and 1 h after the immersion of the film. CTFI is carvacrol thin film immersion.

Considering first the spectrum of monomer, a broad peak centered at 3412 cm^{-1} and strong peaks at 1058 and 1112 cm^{-1} shown the O-H and C-O stretching vibration of phenol, respectively. The shorter and strong signals which appeared in the region 3057–3017 cm^{-1} and 1519–1620 cm^{-1} showed the presence of aromatic C-H and C = C stretching vibration, respectively. The peaks at 991, 936 cm^{-1} and 1418 cm^{-1}, also indicated the symmetric and asymmetric in-plane bending of aromatic C-H group (overlapping with the OH bending vibration). Weak bands in the region 862–808 cm^{-1}

and 752–640 cm^{-1} was due to out of plane bending vibration of adjacent and isolated C-H of 1, 2, 4-substituted benzenoid compounds, respectively. On the other hands, strong absorbance peak in the region of 2959–2868 cm^{-1} indicate C-H stretch of branched isopropyl [13–16].

When we compare the FTIR spectra of the plasma polymer carvacrol films and of the monomer, the chemical structure was found to be notably similar without the reduction on the intensity of the transmittance peaks, particularly in the fingerprint region. This reduction in the intensity means that a small amount of monomer was polymerized and deposited. When we see the effect of deposition time keeping constant the flow rate, applied voltage and gap distance, the intensity of the peak increases with time. It is in agreement with film thickness referring back Fig. 8a. In general, the FTIR spectrum of all obtained thin films showed the presence of phenols, methyl and aromatic skeletal. It is clearly confirmed the preservation of the monomer functional group upon polymerization.

3.5 Aging and Adhesion of the Thin Film

The thin film aging was examined by using infrared spectroscopy after exposing the film in ambient air for 60 days. The film adhesion also tested by immersing the film in a clean tryptic soy broth (TSB) media for 1 h. As shown in Fig. 10b and c, the IR spectra of the film and TSB were not changed at all. This indicates that the obtained film is highly crosslinked with good adhesion on the surface of the substrate. Therefore, it cannot be easily degraded and removed even in harsh environment.

4   Conclusions

PolyCarvacrol thin film polymerization was successfully deposited by a filamentary dielectric barrier discharge on the metallic surface at different plasma discharge conditions. The surface property of the stainless steel disk was totally changed after treated with carvacrol plasma polymeric thin films. The obtained thin film is also thick, having good adhesion and cannot be aged when exposed to atmospheric air for a long period of time. Finally, the current result encouraging further investigation of carvacrol film coating for biomaterials and food package materials.

Acknowledgments. The authors thank TWAS and CNPq (190896/2015-9) and FAPESP (2012/14708-2) for financial support.

References

1. Alves, C.J., Guerra, C.N., Morais, G.H., Silva, C.F., Hajek, V.: Nitriding of titanium disks and industrial dental implants using hollow cathode discharge. Surf. Coat. Tech. **194**(2), 196–202 (2005). https://doi.org/10.1016/j.surfcoat.2004.10.009
2. Kanazawa, S., Kogoma, M., Okazaki, S., Moriwaki, T.: Glow plasma treatment at atmospheric pressure for surface modification and film deposition. Nucl. Instrum. Methods Phys. Res. Sect. B **37–38**, 842–845 (1989)

3. Yokoyama, T., Kogoma, M., Moriwaki, T., Okazaki, S.: The mechanism of the stabilization of glow plasma at atmospheric pressure. J. Phys. D App. Phys. **23**(8), 1125–1128 (1990)
4. Napartovich, A.P.: Overview of atmospheric pressure discharges producing no thermal plasma. Plasmas Polym. **6**(1), 1–14 (2001)
5. Kayama, M.E., Silva, L.J.S., Vadym, P., Kostov, K.G., Algatti, M.A.: Characteristics of needle-disk electrodes atmospheric pressure discharges applied to modify PET wettability. IEEE Trans. Plasma Sci. **45**(5), 843–847 (2017)
6. Laroussi, M., Lu, X., Keidar, M.: Perspective: the physics, diagnostics, and applications of atmospheric pressure low-temperature plasma sources used in plasma medicine. J. Appl. Phys. **122**(2), 020901 (2017)
7. Kanazawa, S., Kogoma, M., Moriwaki, T., Okazaki, S.: Stable glow plasma at atmospheric pressure. J. Phys. D Appl. Phys. **21**, 838 (1988)
8. Massines, F., Rabehi, A., Decomps, P., Gadri, R.B., Egur, P.S., Mayoux, C.: Experimental and theoretical study of a glow discharge at atmospheric pressure controlled by a dielectric barrier. J. Appl. Phys. **82**, 2950–2957 (1998)
9. Yokoyama, T., Kogoma, M., Moriwaki, T., Okazaki, S.: The mechanism of the stabilization of glow plasma at atmospheric pressure. J. Phys. D Appl. Phys. **23**, 1125 (1990)
10. Gherardi, N., Gouda, G., Gat, E., Ricard, A., Massines, F.: Transition from glow silent discharge to micro-discharges in nitrogen gas. Plasma Sources Sci. Technol. **9**, 340 (2000)
11. Liu, Y., Starostin, S.A., Peeters, F.J.J., Van De Sanden, M.C.M., De Vries, H.W.: Atmospheric-pressure diffuse dielectric barrier discharges in Ar/O2 gas mixture using 200 kHz/13.56 MHz dual frequency excitation. J. Phys. D Appl. Phys. **51**, 11 (2018)
12. Xu, X.: Gas Discharge Physics. Fudan University Press, Shanghai (1996)
13. Boughendjioua, H., Djeddi, S., Seridi, R.: A complementary analysis of thyme essential oil by Fourier transformed infrared spectroscopy. Int. J. Chem. Sci. **1**(1), 29–32 (2017)
14. Krepker, M., Prinz-Setter, O., Shemesh, R., Vaxman, A., Alperstein, D., Segal, E.: Antimicrobial carvacrol-containing polypropylene films: composition, structure, and function. Polymers **10**(1), 79 (2018)
15. Bizuneh, A.: GC-MS and FT-IR analysis of constituents of essential oil from Cinnamon bark growing in South-west of Ethiopia. Int. J. Herb. Med. **1**(6), 22–31 (2014)
16. Dias, R.F.: Organic Chemistry (CHEM311) Fall 2005, pp. 48–58 (2005)

Correction to: Dynamics of Eutrophication and Its Linkage to Water Hyacinth on Lake Tana, Upper Blue Nile, Ethiopia: Understanding Land-Lake Interaction and Process

Minychl G. Dersseh, Aron Ateka, Fasikaw A. Zimale,
Abeyou W. Worqlul, Mamaru A. Moges, Dessalegn C. Dagnew,
Seifu A. Tilahun, and Assefa M. Melesse

Correction to:
Chapter "Dynamics of Eutrophication and Its Linkage
to Water Hyacinth on Lake Tana, Upper Blue Nile, Ethiopia:
Understanding Land-Lake Interaction and Process"
in: N. G. Habtu et al. (Eds.): *Advances of Science
and Technology*, LNICST 308,
https://doi.org/10.1007/978-3-030-43690-2_15

In the version of this paper that was originally published, the author's affiliations were not correct. This has now been corrected.

The updated version of this chapter can be found at
https://doi.org/10.1007/978-3-030-43690-2_15

© ICST Institute for Computer Sciences, Social Informatics and Telecommunications Engineering 2020
Published by Springer Nature Switzerland AG 2020. All Rights Reserved
N. G. Habtu et al. (Eds.): ICAST 2019, LNICST 308, p. C1, 2020.
https://doi.org/10.1007/978-3-030-43690-2_56

Correction to: Dynamics of Eutrophication and Its Linkage to Water Hyacinth on Lake Tana, Upper Blue Nile, Ethiopia: Understanding Land-Lake Interaction and Process

Minychl G. Dersseh, Aron Ateka, Fasikaw A. Zimale,
Abeyou W. Worqlul, Mamaru A. Moges, Dessalegn C. Dagnew,
Seifu A. Tilahun, and Assefa M. Melesse

Correction to:
Chapter "Dynamics of Eutrophication and Its Linkage
to Water Hyacinth on Lake Tana, Upper Blue Nile, Ethiopia:
Understanding Land-Lake Interaction and Process"
in: N. G. Habtu et al. (Eds.): *Advances of Science
and Technology*, LNICST 308,
https://doi.org/10.1007/978-3-030-43690-2_15

In the version of this paper that was originally published, the author's affiliations were not correct. This has now been corrected.

The updated version of this chapter can be found at
https://doi.org/10.1007/978-3-030-43690-2_15

© ICST Institute for Computer Sciences, Social Informatics and Telecommunications Engineering 2020
Published by Springer Nature Switzerland AG 2020. All Rights Reserved
N. G. Habtu et al. (Eds.): ICAST 2019, LNICST 308, p. C1, 2020.
https://doi.org/10.1007/978-3-030-43690-2_56

Author Index

Abebe, Atikilt   258
Abose, Tadele Abera   415, 548
Abrha, Eyasu Berhanu   415
Addis, Direselign   502
Addisea, Meseret B.   268
Adege, Abebe Belay   454
Admassu, Kassahun   637
Alemayehu, Haimanot Bitew   472
Alemu, Agegnehu   315
Ali, Abdulkerim   366
Aman, Abdulkadir   566
Amare, Dessie   59
Anagnostou, Emmanouil   294
Annamalai, Pushparaghavan   337
Aragaw, Tadele Assefa   662
Aseres, Muluedel   126
Asese, Muludel   294
Asfaw, Million   623
Asres, Sisay   193
Assefa, Berhanu   82
Assefa, Eshetu   113
Assefa, Mekdim K.   71
Atalay, Enguday B.   148
Ateka, Aron   228
Atinkut, Haimanot   193
Atnaw, Samson Mekbib   557
Atnaw, Samson Mekibib   548
Avvari, Muralidhar   684
Awoke, Getnet K.   29
Ayele, Abinew Ali   480
Ayenew, Dereje M.   242

Babel, Mukand S.   113
Bantelay, Dessie Tarekegn   42
Banteyirga, Belachew   382
Bantiyrga, Belachew   436
Bantyirga, Belachew   395
Behailu, Beshah Mogesse   325
Bekele, Enguday   126, 193
Bekele, Engudye   294
Belachew, B.   366
Beyene, Abebech   193
Bihonegn, Bayu G.   169, 210
Birhanie, Worku Kelemework   480, 512

Bitew, Mekuanint Agegnehu   472
Bogale, Wondwossen   82
Butt, Miriam   512

da Cruz, Nilson Cristino   716
Dagnew, Dessalegn C.   228
Damtew, Alemayehu Ali   325
Darsema, Marsilas   382
Dedimas, Tsehaye   42
Degu, Yonas Mitiku   587, 707
Delele, Mulugeta A.   597
Demeke, Mequanint   3
Demessie, Berhanu A.   71
Demisse, Girma   98
Dersseh, Minychl G.   228
Dokou, Zoi   148, 294
Dutta, Abhishek   651

Emiru, Ayalew   59
Enku, Temesgen   268
Eshete, Daniel G.   148, 294

Fantahun, Abel   637

Gabbiye, Nigus   3, 98, 315, 597, 695
Gebreslasie, Mekonnen   597
Geletaw, Daniel   126
Geremew, Berhanu   126, 193
Getahun, Eshetu   597
Getem, Chirotaw   695
Getie, Wondale A.   148, 294
Getnet, Tsegaye Gashaw   716
Ghosh, S. K.   279

Habtu, Nigus Gabbiye   16, 651
Hailemariam, Meareg A.   462
Hassen, Abdulkadir Aman   576
Hertoga, Maarten   71

Jumber, Marshet B.   113

Kalsa, Karta Kaske   98
Kassaw, Amare   424

Kassaye, Gemechu 315
Kayama, Milton Eiji 716
Kebede, Addisu Yenesew 576, 610
Kebede, Tewelgn 424
Kelemu, Nigist 42
Ketema, Atikilt Abebe 325
Kindie, Agumase T. 294
Kolhe, Kishor Purushottam 537
Kolhe, Kishor Purushottamrao 525
Kumar, P. G. V. Suresh 492

Lin, Hsin-Piao 454
Liu, Chuan-Ming 502

Malmurugan, N. 337
Mamo, Yesheneh Jejaw 672
Mandefro, Elias 395, 436
Mekonnen, Bisrat Yilma 610
Mekonnen, Yanit 279
Melesse, Assefa M. 228
Messele, Eyob 537
Mihretu, Gashaw 337
Misganew, Melak 684
Moges, Mamaru A. 126, 148, 169, 210, 228,
    242, 294
Moges, Muluedel A. 148
Moges, Semu 294
Muche, Fentahun Ayu 707
Mulat, Asegdew G. 242
Mulu, Aragaw 525
Mulu, Endawoke 258
Mulu, Gerawork F. 169, 210
Musse, Dawit 82

Negash G., Tadele 59
Negash Shiferaw, Yalemzewd 492
Nicolai, Bart 71

Olana, Firew Dereje 548

Padma, K. 355
Petra, Schmitter 148

Rangel, Elidiane Cipriano 716
Rao, D. K. Nageswara 684
Rayes, Manuel R. 29
Reda, Mahlet 59

Reddy, K. Raja Narender 684
Retta, Beza Nekatibeb 548

Schmitter, Petra 16
Shiferaw, Yeshitela 355
Shimelis, E. A. 71
Shiret, Birhanu Gardie 472
Sinshaw, Berhanu G. 148, 210, 294
Sishu, Feleke K. 16
Steenhuis, Tammo S. 16, 268
Stenibrunn, Johannes 424
Subramanyam, Bhadriraju 98

Ta, Van-Dai 502
Tadesse Abebe, Abiy 492
Takele, Dagne Y. 148
Tamrat, Bimrew 623
Tarekegn, Getaneh Berie 454
Tariku Woldesemayate, Atsede 557
Tefera, Abiyu Mersha 566
Tegegne, Nigus H. 268
Tekeste, Solomon 587
Tena, Tilik 258
Teshome, Fetene 525, 537
Thegaye, Elsabeth K. 16
Tigabu, Muluken Temesgen 566
Tilahun, Seifu 126, 193
Tilahun, Seifu A. 16, 29, 113, 148, 228, 268,
    294

Van der Bruggen, Bart 651
Vanierschot, Maarten 597
Verboven, Pieter 71

Wagaw, Kefale 258
Wondie, Yihenew 424
Workneh, Solomon 98, 597
Worku, Admasu 98
Worku, Getachew Biru 415
Worqlul, Abeyou W. 228

Yayeh, Yirga 454
Ygzaw, Alganesh 382
Yilma, Bisrat 623
Yisaye, Nebiyu 395

Zewdie, Tsegahun Mekonnen 651
Zimale, Fasikaw A. 228, 242

Printed in the United States
By Bookmasters